Mathematical Models and Simulations

Mathematical Models and Simulations

Editor

Giovanni Nastasi

 Basel • Beijing • Wuhan • Barcelona • Belgrade • Novi Sad • Cluj • Manchester

Editor
Giovanni Nastasi
Department of Mathematics
and Computer Science
University of Catania
Catania
Italy

Editorial Office
MDPI
St. Alban-Anlage 66
4052 Basel, Switzerland

This is a reprint of articles from the Special Issue published online in the open access journal *Axioms* (ISSN 2075-1680) (available at: https://www.mdpi.com/journal/axioms/special_issues/5UGD44GX3T).

For citation purposes, cite each article independently as indicated on the article page online and as indicated below:

Lastname, A.A.; Lastname, B.B. Article Title. *Journal Name* **Year**, *Volume Number*, Page Range.

ISBN 978-3-7258-0509-9 (Hbk)
ISBN 978-3-7258-0510-5 (PDF)
doi.org/10.3390/books978-3-7258-0510-5

© 2024 by the authors. Articles in this book are Open Access and distributed under the Creative Commons Attribution (CC BY) license. The book as a whole is distributed by MDPI under the terms and conditions of the Creative Commons Attribution-NonCommercial-NoDerivs (CC BY-NC-ND) license.

Contents

Giovanni Nastasi
Mathematical Models and Simulations
Reprinted from: *Axioms* **2024**, *13*, 149, doi:10.3390/axioms13030149 1

Chunhua Feng
Oscillatory Behavior of the Solutions for a Parkinson's Disease Model with Discrete and
Distributed Delays
Reprinted from: *Axioms* **2024**, *13*, 75, doi:10.3390/axioms13020075 4

Juan Francisco Sánchez-Pérez, Joaquín Solano-Ramírez, Enrique Castro, Manuel Conesa, Fulgencio Marín-García and Gonzalo García-Ros
Analysis of the Burgers–Huxley Equation Using the Nondimensionalisation Technique:
Universal Solution for Dirichlet and Symmetry Boundary Conditions
Reprinted from: *Axioms* **2023**, *12*, 1113, doi:10.3390/axioms12121113 17

Yanbo Chong, Ankur Jyoti Kashyap, Shangming Chen and Fengde Chen
Dynamics Analysis of a Discrete-Time Commensalism Model with Additive Allee for the Host
Species
Reprinted from: *Axioms* **2023**, *12*, 1031, doi:10.3390/axioms12111031 31

Luis Sánchez, Germán Ibacache-Pulgar, Carolina Marchant and Marco Riquelme
Modeling Environmental Pollution Using Varying-Coefficients Quantile Regression Models
under Log-Symmetric Distributions
Reprinted from: *Axioms* **2023**, *12*, 976, doi:10.3390/axioms12100976 65

Valentyn Sobchuk, Oleg Barabash, Andrii Musienko, Iryna Tsyganivska and Oleksandr Kurylko
Mathematical Model of Cyber Risks Management Based on the Expansion of Piecewise
Continuous Analytical Approximation Functions of Cyber Attacks in the Fourier Series
Reprinted from: *Axioms* **2023**, *12*, 924, doi:10.3390/axioms12100924 85

Ayman Shehata, Ghazi S. Khammash and Carlo Cattani
Some Relations on the $_rR_s(P,Q,z)$ Matrix Function
Reprinted from: *Axioms* **2023**, *12*, 817, doi:10.3390/axioms12090817 100

Farah M. Al-Askar, Clemente Cesarano and Wael W. Mohammed
Effects of the Wiener Process and Beta Derivative on the Exact Solutions of the
Kadomtsev–Petviashvili Equation
Reprinted from: *Axioms* **2023**, *12*, 748, doi:10.3390/axioms12080748 123

Brajesh K. Singh, Haci Mehmet Baskonus, Neetu Singh, Mukesh Gupta and D. G. Prakasha
Study of Time-Fractional Nonlinear Model Governing Unsteady Flow of Polytropic Gas
Reprinted from: *Axioms* **2023**, *12*, 285, doi:10.3390/axioms12030285 134

Orazio Muscato
Electrothermal Monte Carlo Simulation of a GaAs Resonant Tunneling Diode
Reprinted from: *Axioms* **2023**, *12*, 216, doi:10.3390/axioms12020216 154

Ahmed M. Elaiw, Raghad S. Alsulami and Aatef D. Hobiny
Dynamic Behaviors of a COVID-19 and Influenza Co-Infection Model with TimeDelays and
Humoral Immunity
Reprinted from: *Axioms* **2023**, *12*, 151, doi:10.3390/axioms12020151 165

Susmit Bagchi
Analysis of Finite Solution Spaces of Second-Order ODE with Dirac Delta Periodic Forcing
Reprinted from: *Axioms* **2023**, *12*, 85, doi:10.3390/axioms12010085 205

Amar Benkerrouche, Mohammed Said Souid and Ivanka Stamova
Boundary-Value Problem for Nonlinear Fractional Differential Equations of Variable Order with Finite Delay via Kuratowski Measure of Noncompactness
Reprinted from: *Axioms* **2023**, *12*, 80, doi:10.3390/axioms12010080 225

E.R. El-Zahar and A. Ebaid
Analytical and Numerical Simulations of a Delay Model: The Pantograph Delay Equation
Reprinted from: *Axioms* **2022**, *11*, 741, doi:10.3390/axioms11120741 248

Editorial

Mathematical Models and Simulations

Giovanni Nastasi

Department of Mathematics and Computer Science, University of Catania, Viale Andrea Doria 6, 95125 Catania, Italy; giovanni.nastasi@unict.it

Citation: Nastasi, G. Mathematical Models and Simulations. *Axioms* **2024**, *13*, 149. https://doi.org/10.3390/axioms13030149

Received: 21 February 2024
Accepted: 23 February 2024
Published: 25 February 2024

Copyright: © 2024 by the author. Licensee MDPI, Basel, Switzerland. This article is an open access article distributed under the terms and conditions of the Creative Commons Attribution (CC BY) license (https://creativecommons.org/licenses/by/4.0/).

1. Introduction

In this editorial, we present the Special Issue of the scientific journal *Axioms* entitled "Mathematical Models and Simulations". Mathematical models constitute a fundamental tool for understanding physical phenomena, biological systems, and finance and engineering. In addition to theoretical aspects, simulations play a primary role in applications, because they allow for the prediction of the behavior of quantities of interest. We collected papers in the field of mathematical physics, where different categories of mathematical models are presented, both deterministic, i.e., based on ordinary or partial differential equations, and stochastic, i.e., defined by stochastic processes or based on stochastic differential equations. The study of mathematical aspects of the presented models has been tackled. To provide realistic applications, numerical simulations play an important role. Several numerical methods suited to the specific problem have been adopted. Moreover, in some cases, simulations have been performed by adopting real data for the parameters, and optimization procedures have been carried out.

2. Overview of the Published Papers

This Special Issue contains 13 papers that were accepted for publication after a rigorous review process.

In contribution 1, the authors E. El-Zahar and A. Ebaid study the pantograph delay differential equation. They determine the analytic solution of such an equation in a closed series form regarding exponential functions. The convergence of such a series is analyzed.

In contribution 2, B. Telli, M. Souid, and I Stamova present a paper devoted to boundary-value problems for Riemann–Liouville-type fractional differential equations of variable order involving finite delays. The existence of solutions is first studied using Darbo's fixed-point theorem and the Kuratowski measure of noncompactness. Second, the Ulam–Hyers stability criteria are examined.

In contribution 3, S. Bagchi proposes a generalized finite-dimensional algebraic analysis of the solution spaces of second-order ODEs equipped with periodic Dirac delta forcing. The proposed algebraic analysis establishes the conditions for the convergence of responses within the solution spaces without requiring the relative smoothness of the forcing functions. The analysis shows that smooth and locally finite responses can be admitted in an exponentially stable solution space.

In contribution 4, A. Elaiw, R. Alsulami, and A. Hobiny present a COVID-19 and Influenza Co-Infection Model with Time Delays and Humoral Immunity. The model considers the interactions among uninfected epithelial cells (ECs), SARS-CoV-2-infected ECs, IAV-infected ECs, SARS-CoV-2 particles, IAV particles, SARS-CoV-2 antibodies, and IAV antibodies. The model is constructed using a system of delayed ordinary differential equations (DODEs), which includes four time delays. They establish the non-negativity and boundedness of the solutions, examine the existence and stability of all equilibria, and perform numerical simulations to support the theoretical results.

In contribution 5, O. Muscato focuses on electron transport and heat generation in a Resonant Tunneling Diode semiconductor device. A new electrothermal Monte Carlo method is introduced. The method couples a Monte Carlo solver of the Boltzmann–Wigner transport equation with a steady-state solution of the heat diffusion equation. This methodology provides an accurate microscopic description of the spatial distribution of self-heating and its effect on the detailed nonequilibrium carrier dynamics.

In contribution 6, B. K. Singh, H. M. Baskonus, N. Singh, M. Gupta, and D. G. Prakasha analyze the dynamical behavior of two space-dimensional nonlinear time-fractional models governing the unsteady flow of polytropic gas that occurs in cosmology and astronomy. They adopt two efficient hybrid methods, the so-called optimal homotopy analysis J-transform method and the J-variational iteration transform method. The convergence of these methods is proven, and the numerical results demonstrate that both of the developed techniques perform better for the considered time-fractional model governing the unsteady flow of polytropic gas.

In contribution 7, F. M. Al-Askar, C. Cesarano, and W. W. Mohammed consider the stochastic Kadomtsev–Petviashvili equation with fractional beta-derivative. They find exact solutions employing the Riccati equation method and the Jacobi elliptic function method. The obtained solutions can also be used in practical applications, such as designing improved tsunami warning systems or optimizing wave energy converters. They investigate the effect of beta-derivatives and noise on the analytical solutions of the equation using graphs.

In contribution 8, A. Shehata, G. S. Khammash, and C. Cattani derive some classical and fractional properties of the rRs matrix function using the Hilfer fractional operator. The theory of special matrix functions is the theory of those matrices that correspond to special matrix functions such as the gamma, beta, and Gauss hypergeometric matrix functions. They also show the relationship with other generalized special matrix functions in the context of the Konhauser and Laguerre matrix polynomials.

In contribution 9, V. Sobchuk, O. Barabash, A. Musienko, I. Tsyganivska, and O. Kurylko propose a mathematical model of the process of cyber risk management in an enterprise, which is based on the distribution of piecewise continuous analytical approximating functions of cyberattacks in the Fourier series. This model makes it possible to move the system of the regulatory control of cyber threats of the enterprise from a discrete to a continuous automated process of regulatory control.

In contribution 10, L. Sánchez, G. Ibacache-Pulgar, C. Marchant, and M. Riquelme develop varying-coefficients quantile regression models based on the family of log-symmetric distributions. Moreover, they estimate the parameters of the model using the maximum penalized likelihood technique and a back-fitting algorithm. They incorporate the nonparametric structure through natural cubic smoothing splines and calculate local influence techniques for model diagnostics by assessing the normal curvatures under different perturbation scenarios. Further, they implement the obtained outcomes computationally within the R programming environment and apply these results to real data related to atmospheric pollutants in Padre Las Casas (Chile), recognized as one of the most contaminated cities in Latin America and the Caribbean.

In contribution 11, Y. Chong, A. J. Kashyap, S. Chen, and F. Chen study a class of discrete-time commensalism systems with additive Allee effects on the host species. First, the single species with additive Allee effects is analyzed for existence and stability; then, the existence of fixed points of discrete systems is given, and the local stability of fixed points is given by characteristic root analysis. Second, the bifurcation of a codimension of one of the systems at non-hyperbolic fixed points is examined. Furthermore, this work uses the hybrid chaos method to control the chaos that occurs in the flip bifurcation of the system. Finally, the analysis conclusions were verified by numerical simulations.

In contribution 12, J. F. Sánchez-Pérez, J. Solano-Ramírez, E. Castro, M. Conesa, F. Marín-García, and G. García-Ros apply the non-dimensionalization methodology to the Burgers–Huxley equation to obtain a universal solution to the problem posed. In this case, the symmetry condition is applied to one of the boundary conditions, and a constant value of the variable is applied to the other boundary condition (Dirichlet condition). Another objective is to study the weight of the variables in the problem. For the construction of the universal curves, the Network Simulation Method was used, which has demonstrated its effectiveness in solving this problem, as well as other engineering problems.

In contribution 13, C. Feng considers the oscillatory behavior of the solutions for a Parkinson's disease model with discrete and distributed delays. The distributed delay terms can be changed to new functions such that the original model is equivalent to a system in which it only has discrete delays. The stability analysis is performed employing the linearization technique. By analyzing the linearized system at the smallest delay, some sufficient conditions to guarantee the existence of oscillatory solutions for a delayed Parkinson's disease system can be obtained. It is found that under suitable conditions of the parameters, a time delay affects the stability of the system. Some numerical simulations are provided to illustrate the theoretical result.

Conflicts of Interest: The authors declare no conflict of interest.

List of Contributions:

1. El-Zahar, E.; Ebaid, A. Analytical and Numerical Simulations of a Delay Model: The Pantograph Delay Equation. *Axioms* **2022**, *11*, 741. https://doi.org/10.3390/axioms11120741.
2. Telli, B.; Souid, M.; Stamova, I. Boundary-Value Problem for Nonlinear Fractional Differential Equations of Variable Order with Finite Delay via Kuratowski Measure of Noncompactness. *Axioms* **2023**, *12*, 80. https://doi.org/10.3390/axioms12010080.
3. Bagchi, S. Analysis of Finite Solution Spaces of Second-Order ODE with Dirac Delta Periodic Forcing. *Axioms* **2023**, *12*, 85. https://doi.org/10.3390/axioms12010085.
4. Elaiw, A.; Alsulami, R.; Hobiny, A. Dynamic Behaviors of a COVID-19 and Influenza Co-Infection Model with Time Delays and Humoral Immunity. *Axioms* **2023**, *12*, 151. https://doi.org/10.3390/axioms12020151.
5. Muscato, O. Electrothermal Monte Carlo Simulation of a GaAs Resonant Tunneling Diode. *Axioms* **2023**, *12*, 216. https://doi.org/10.3390/axioms12020216.
6. Singh, B.; Baskonus, H.; Singh, N.; Gupta, M.; Prakasha, D. Study of Time-Fractional Nonlinear Model Governing Unsteady Flow of Polytropic Gas. *Axioms* **2023**, *12*, 285. https://doi.org/10.3390/axioms12030285.
7. Al-Askar, F.; Cesarano, C.; Mohammed, W. Effects of the Wiener Process and Beta Derivative on the Exact Solutions of the Kadomtsev–Petviashvili Equation. *Axioms* **2023**, *12*, 748. https://doi.org/10.3390/axioms12080748.
8. Shehata, A.; Khammash, G.; Cattani, C. Some Relations on the rRs(P,Q,z) Matrix Function. *Axioms* **2023**, *12*, 817. https://doi.org/10.3390/axioms12090817.
9. Sobchuk, V.; Barabash, O.; Musienko, A.; Tsyganivska, I.; Kurylko, O. Mathematical Model of Cyber Risks Management Based on the Expansion of Piecewise Continuous Analytical Approximation Functions of Cyber Attacks in the Fourier Series. *Axioms* **2023**, *12*, 924. https://doi.org/10.3390/axioms12100924.
10. Sánchez, L.; Ibacache-Pulgar, G.; Marchant, C.; Riquelme, M. Modeling Environmental Pollution Using Varying-Coefficients Quantile Regression Models under Log-Symmetric Distributions. *Axioms* **2023**, *12*, 976. https://doi.org/10.3390/axioms12100976.
11. Chong, Y.; Kashyap, A.; Chen, S.; Chen, F. Dynamics Analysis of a Discrete-Time Commensalism Model with Additive Allee for the Host Species. *Axioms* **2023**, *12*, 1031. https://doi.org/10.3390/axioms12111031.
12. Sánchez-Pérez, J.; Solano-Ramírez, J.; Castro, E.; Conesa, M.; Marín-García, F.; García-Ros, G. Analysis of the Burgers–Huxley Equation Using the Nondimensionalisation Technique: Universal Solution for Dirichlet and Symmetry Boundary Conditions. *Axioms* **2023**, *12*, 1113. https://doi.org/10.3390/axioms12121113.
13. Feng, C. Oscillatory Behavior of the Solutions for a Parkinson's Disease Model with Discrete and Distributed Delays. *Axioms* **2024**, *13*, 75. https://doi.org/10.3390/axioms13020075.

Disclaimer/Publisher's Note: The statements, opinions and data contained in all publications are solely those of the individual author(s) and contributor(s) and not of MDPI and/or the editor(s). MDPI and/or the editor(s) disclaim responsibility for any injury to people or property resulting from any ideas, methods, instructions or products referred to in the content.

Article

Oscillatory Behavior of the Solutions for a Parkinson's Disease Model with Discrete and Distributed Delays

Chunhua Feng

Department of Mathematics and Computer Science, Alabama State University, Montgomery, AL 36104, USA; cfeng@alasu.edu

Abstract: In this paper, the oscillatory behavior of the solutions for a Parkinson's disease model with discrete and distributed delays is discussed. The distributed delay terms can be changed to new functions such that the original model is equivalent to a system in which it only has discrete delays. Using Taylor's expansion, the system can be linearized at the equilibrium to obtain both the linearized part and the nonlinearized part. One can see that the nonlinearized part is a disturbed term of the system. Therefore, the instability of the linearized system implies the instability of the whole system. If a system is unstable for a small delay, then the instability of this system will be maintained as the delay increased. By analyzing the linearized system at the smallest delay, some sufficient conditions to guarantee the existence of oscillatory solutions for a delayed Parkinson's disease system can be obtained. It is found that under suitable conditions on the parameters, time delay affects the stability of the system. The present method does not need to consider a bifurcating equation. Some numerical simulations are provided to illustrate the theoretical result.

Keywords: Parkinson's disease model; delay; instability; oscillatory solution

MSC: 34K13

1. Introduction

It is known that Parkinson's disease (PD) is a common progressive neurodegenerative disease. Parkinson's disease is characterized by tremors and stiffness. Mathematical modeling can help understand such complex multifactorial neurological diseases and help diagnose and treat them. Many mathematical models have been established to discuss Parkinson's disease mathematically and biologically using the experimental method or analysis method. For example, Tuwairqi and Badrah provided the following model [1]:

$$\begin{cases} N'(t) = \sigma - \beta N(t)\alpha S(t) - a_1 N(t) - a_2 N(t) - \mu_1 N(t), \\ I'(t) = \beta N(t)\alpha S(t) - d_1 I(t) - a_1 T(t) - a_2 I(t), \\ \alpha S'(t) = e d_1 I(t) - a_1 \alpha S(t) - a_2 \alpha S(t) - \varepsilon_1 \widetilde{\alpha S}(t,\tau), \\ M'(t) = a_1 I(t) + a_1 \alpha S(t) - \varepsilon_2 \widetilde{M}(t,\tau) - \mu_2 M(t), \\ T'(t) = a_1 T(t) + (a_1 + a_2)\alpha S(t) - \varepsilon_3 \widetilde{T}(t,\tau) - \mu_3 T(t), \end{cases} \quad (1)$$

where $N(t)$, $I(t)$, and $\alpha S(t)$ represent the density of healthy neurons in the brain, the density of infected neurons in the brain, and the density of extracellular α-syn in the brain, respectively, $M(t)$ represents the density of activated microglia, and $T(t)$ presents the density of the activated T cell; a_1, a_2, ε_1, ε_2, ε_3, μ_1, μ_2, μ_3, σ, and β are parameters which belong to [0, 1]. The local stability of the free and endemic equilibrium points was established depending on the basic reproduction number. The authors pointed out that the administering time of immunotherapies plays a significant role in hindering the advancement of Parkinson's disease. Different from traditional viewpoints, Wang et al. provided a delayed model which contains a cortex inhibitory nucleus (INN), a direct

Citation: Feng, C. Oscillatory Behavior of the Solutions for a Parkinson's Disease Model with Discrete and Distributed Delays. *Axioms* **2024**, *13*, 75. https://doi.org/10.3390/axioms13020075

Academic Editor: Giovanni Nastasi

Received: 6 December 2023
Revised: 17 January 2024
Accepted: 18 January 2024
Published: 23 January 2024

Copyright: © 2024 by the author. Licensee MDPI, Basel, Switzerland. This article is an open access article distributed under the terms and conditions of the Creative Commons Attribution (CC BY) license (https://creativecommons.org/licenses/by/4.0/).

inhibitory projection from the subthalamic nucleus (STN), a cortex excitatory nucleus (EXN), and globus pallidus external (GPe). A simplified INN-EXN-STN-GPe resonance mathematical model is the following [2]:

$$\begin{cases} \tau_S S'(t) = F_S(-W_{GS} G(t-T_{GS}) + W_{CS} E(t-T_{CS})) - S(t), \\ \tau_G G'(t) = F_G(W_{SG} S(t-T_{SG}) - Str) - G(t), \\ \tau_E E'(t) = F_E(-W_{CC} I(t-T_{CC}) - W_{SC} S(t-T_{SC}) + C) - E(t), \\ \tau_I I'(t) = F_I(-W_{CC} E(t-T_{CC})) - I(t), \end{cases} \quad (2)$$

where $S(t)$ and $G(t)$ represent the subthalamic nucleus (STN) and the external segment of the globus pallidus (GPe), $E(t)$ represents the firing rate of cortical excitatory pyramidal neurons (EXN) and $I(t)$ represents the firing rate of inhibitory nuclei (INN). $T(t)$ and $W(t)$ represent the delay and connection weight in different projections. CIN is a constant excitatory input to the cortex, and Str represents the projection from the striatum. $F_Y(x) = \frac{M_Y}{1+\left(\frac{M_Y-B_Y}{B_Y}\right)\exp(-4x/M_Y)}$ $(Y = S, G, E, I)$ are activation functions.

It can be assumed that $\tau_S = \tau_G = \tau_E = \tau_I$, $T_{SG} = T_{GS} = T_{CC} = T_{SC} = T$, the Hopf bifurcation of system (2) is considered. A modified model of the system (2) is as follows:

$$\begin{cases} \tau_S S'(t) = F_S(-W_{GS} G(t-T_{GS}) + W_{CS} E(t-T_{CS})) - S(t), \\ \tau_G G'(t) = F_G(W_{SG} S(t-T_{SG}) - Str) - G(t), \\ \tau_E E'(t) = F_E(-W_{CC} I(t-T_{CC}) + W_{EE} E(t-T_{EE}) + C) - E(t), \\ \tau_I I'(t) = F_I(W_{CC} E(t-T_{CC}) - W_{II} E(t-T_{II})) - I(t). \end{cases} \quad (3)$$

Assume that

$$\tau_S = \tau_G = \tau_E = \tau_I = 10, \ T_{SG} = T_{GS} = T_1, \ T_{CC} = T_{II} = T_{CS} = T_2. \quad (4)$$

The Hopf bifurcation critical condition of the system (3) was provided in [3]. However, in models (1) to (3), the delays are discrete, and distributed delays are rarely introduced into neuron models with biological backgrounds. Recently, Kaslik et al. applied the bifurcation and stability theory of distributed delays to the interaction of the Wilson–Cowan model of excitatory and inhibitory mean–field interactions in neuronal populations [4]. Indeed, distributed delays can more truly describe the delay effects of signal transmissions between different neurons. Wang et al. also considered a Parkinson's model with distributed delays [5]:

$$\begin{cases} \tau_S S'(t) = F_S\left(-W_{GS} G(t-T_{GS}) + W_{CS} \int_{-\infty}^{t} K_1(t-s)E(s)ds\right) - S(t), \\ \tau_G G'(t) = F_G\left(W_{SG} S(t-T_{SG}) - W_{GG} \int_{-\infty}^{t} K_2(t-s)E(s)ds - Str\right) - G(t), \\ \tau_E E'(t) = F_E\left(-W_{SC} \int_{-\infty}^{t} K_3(t-s)S(s)ds - INN + C\right) - E(t), \end{cases} \quad (5)$$

where K_1, K_2, and K_3 represent the weak or strong gamma functions. The authors studied the stable, conditional stable, conditional oscillation, and absolute oscillation for model (5), which can explain different mechanisms of oscillation origin. Agiza et al. used the Taylor series transform to discuss two-delay differential equations for the Parkinson's disease models in [6]. The dynamic behavior of innate immune response to Parkinson's disease with a therapeutic approach was modeled in [7]. Some authors investigate Parkinson's disease models via electrical activity rhythms [8], activity patterns [9], the emergence of beta oscillations [10], the intra-operative characterization of subthalamic oscillations [11], the Bayesian adaptive dual control of deep brain stimulation [12]. Hu et al. investigated a bidirectional Hopf bifurcation of Parkinson's oscillation in a simplified basal ganglia model in [13]. Darcy et al. considered the spectral and spatial distribution of subthalamic beta peak activity [14]. Lang and Espay summarized the current approaches, challenges, and future considerations in Parkinson's disease in [15]. For other research results on Parkinson's disease, one can see [16–30].

In this paper, we extend the model (3) to the following system which includes not only discrete delays but also distributed delays:

$$\begin{cases} \tau_S S'(t) = F_S\left(-W_{GS}\, G(t-T_{GS}) + W_{CS}\int_{-\infty}^{t} K_1(t-s)E(s)ds\right) - S(t), \\ \tau_G G'(t) = F_G\left(W_{SG}\, S(t-T_{SG}) - W_{GG}\int_{-\infty}^{t} K_2(t-s)G(s)ds - Str\right) - G(t) \\ \tau_E E'(t) = F_E\left(-W_{SC}\, I(t-T_{ES}) + W_{EE}\int_{-\infty}^{t} K_3(t-s)S(s)ds - INN + C\right) - E(t). \\ \tau_I I'(t) = F_I\left(W_{CC}\, E(t-T_{CC}) - W_{II}\int_{-\infty}^{t} K_4(t-s)I(s)ds\right) - I(t). \end{cases} \quad (6)$$

According to the simulation result in [3], the parameters are $\tau_S = 12.80$ ms, $\tau_G = 20$ ms, $\tau_E = 10\text{--}20$ ms, and $\tau_I = 10\text{--}20$ ms. Therefore, the results in [3] are only for special parameters. Note that model (6) has four discrete delays. If the four delays are different real numbers, then the bifurcation method is hard to deal with in model (6) due to the complexity of the bifurcating equation. In this paper, using the method of mathematical analysis, the oscillatory behavior of the solutions for model (6) could be obtained. Our result indicated that the four discrete delays can be different real numbers, and condition (4) has been extended.

For convenience, we considered K_i ($i = 1, 2, 3, 4$) as the weak gamma functions, setting $K_i(t-s) = \alpha_i \exp(\alpha_i(t-s))$ ($\alpha_i > 0$, $i = 1, 2, 3, 4$), and let

$$Y_1(t) = \int_{-\infty}^{t} K_1(t-s)E(s)ds = \int_{-\infty}^{t} \alpha_1 \exp(\alpha_1(t-s))E(s)ds,$$

$$Y_2(t) = \int_{-\infty}^{t} K_2(t-s)G(s)ds = \int_{-\infty}^{t} \alpha_2 \exp(\alpha_2(t-s))G(s)ds,$$

$$Y_3(t) = \int_{-\infty}^{t} K_3(t-s)S(s)ds = \int_{-\infty}^{t} \alpha_3 \exp(\alpha_3(t-s))S(s)ds,$$

and $Y_4(t) = \int_{-\infty}^{t} K_4(t-s)I(s)ds = \int_{-\infty}^{t} \alpha_4 \exp(\alpha_4(t-s))I(s)ds.$

Then, using the fundamental theorem of calculus, we obtained

$$Y_1'(t) = -\alpha_1 \int_{-\infty}^{t} \alpha_1 \exp(\alpha_1(t-s))E(s)ds + \alpha_1 E(t) = -\alpha_1 Y_1(t) + \alpha_1 E(t),$$

$$Y_2'(t) = -\alpha_2 \int_{-\infty}^{t} \alpha_2 \exp(\alpha_2(t-s))G(s)ds + \alpha_2 G(t) = -\alpha_2 Y_2(t) + \alpha_2 G(t),$$

$$Y_3'(t) = -\alpha_3 \int_{-\infty}^{t} \alpha_3 \exp(\alpha_3(t-s))S(s)ds + \alpha_3 S(t) = -\alpha_3 Y_3(t) + \alpha_3 S(t),$$

$$Y_4'(t) = -\alpha_4 \int_{-\infty}^{t} \alpha_4 \exp(\alpha_4(t-s))I(s)ds + \alpha_4 I(t) = -\alpha_4 Y_4(t) + \alpha_4 I(t).$$

Thus, we can rewrite model (6) as the following equivalent system:

$$\begin{cases} S'(t) = -r_1 S(t) + r_1 F_S(-W_{GS}\, G(t-T_{GS}) + W_{CS}\, Y_1(t)), \\ G'(t) = -r_2 G(t) + r_2 F_G(W_{SG}\, S(t-T_{SG}) - W_{GG} Y_2(t) - Str), \\ E'(t) = -r_3 E(t) + r_3 F_E(-W_{SC}\, I(t-T_{ES}) + W_{EE}\, Y_3(t) - INN + C), \\ I'(t) = -r_4 I(t) + r_4 F_I(W_{CC}\, E(t-T_{CC}) - W_{II}\, Y_4(t)), \\ Y_1'(t) = -\alpha_1 Y_1(t) + \alpha_1 E(t), \\ Y_2'(t) = -\alpha_2 Y_2(t) + \alpha_2 G(t), \\ Y_3'(t) = -\alpha_3 Y_3(t) + \alpha_3 S(t), \\ Y_4'(t) = -\alpha_4 Y_4(t) + \alpha_4 I(t), \end{cases} \quad (7)$$

where $r_1 = \frac{1}{\tau_S}, r_2 = \frac{1}{\tau_G}, r_3 = \frac{1}{\tau_E}, r_4 = \frac{1}{\tau_I}$. From $F_Y(x) = \frac{M_Y}{1+\left(\frac{M_Y-B_Y}{B_Y}\right)\exp(-4x/M_Y)}$ $(Y = S, G, E, I)$
we know that $F_S < M_S$, $F_G < M_G$, $F_E < M_E$, and $F_I < M_I$, so we can obtain

$$\begin{cases} S'(t) < -r_1 S(t) + r_1 M_S, \\ G'(t) < -r_2 G(t) + r_2 M_G, \\ E'(t) < -r_3 E(t) + r_3 M_E, \\ I'(t) < -r_4 I(t) + r_4 M_I, \\ Y_1'(t) = -\alpha_1 Y_1(t) + \alpha_1 E(t), \\ Y_2'(t) = -\alpha_2 Y_2(t) + \alpha_2 G(t), \\ Y_3'(t) = -\alpha_3 Y_3(t) + \alpha_3 S(t), \\ Y_4'(t) = -\alpha_4 Y_4(t) + \alpha_4 I(t). \end{cases} \quad (8)$$

System (8) implies that $S(t) < \frac{r_1}{r_1} M_S = M_S$, $G(t) < \frac{r_2}{r_2} M_G = M_G$, $E(t) < \frac{r_3}{r_3} M_E = M_E$, $I(t) < \frac{r_4}{r_4} M_I = M_I$, $Y_1(t) < M_E$, $Y_2(t) < M_G$, $Y_3(t) < M_S$, and $Y_4(t) < M_I$. In other words, all of the solutions of system (7) are boundedness. According to the parameter values in [3]: $M_S = 300$ spk/s, $B_S = 17$ spk/s, $M_G = 400$ spk/s, $B_G = 75$ spk/s, $M_E = 71.77$ spk/s, $B_E = 3.62$ spk/s, $M_I = 276$ spk/s, $B_I = 7.18$ spk/s, we know that $F_Y(x)$ are monotone increasing functions for $Y = S, G, E$, and I. Therefore, system (6) has a unique equilibrium point $(S^*, G^*, E^*, I^*)^T$. Equivalently, system (7) has a unique equilibrium point $(S^*, G^*, E^*, I^*, Y_1^*, Y_2^*, Y_3^*, Y_4^*)^T$, where $Y_1^* = E^*$, $Y_2^* = G^*$, $Y_3^* = S^*$, and $Y_4^* = I^*$. If we make the change in variables $S(t) \to S(t) - S^*$, $G(t) \to G(t) - G^*$, $E(t) \to E(t) - E^*$, $I(t) \to I(t) - I^*$, $Y_i(t) \to Y_i(t) - Y_i^*$ ($i = 1, 2, 3, 4$), the Taylor expansion of system (7) at the equilibrium point is the following:

$$\begin{cases} S'(t) = -r_1 S(t) + a_{12} G(t - T_{GS}) + a_{15} Y_1(t) \\ \quad + \sum_{i+j \geq 2} \frac{[G(t-T_{GS})]^i}{i!} \frac{[Y_1(t)]^j}{j!} \cdot \left.\frac{\partial^{i+j} F_S}{\partial G^i \partial Y_1^j}\right|_{(G^*, Y_1^*)}, \\ G'(t) = -r_2 G(t) + a_{21} S(t - T_{SG}) + a_{26} Y_2(t) \\ \quad + \sum_{i+j \geq 2} \frac{[S(t-T_{SG})]^i}{i!} \frac{[Y_2(t)]^j}{j!} \cdot \left.\frac{\partial^{i+j} F_G}{\partial S^i \partial Y_2^j}\right|_{(S^*, Y_2^*)}, \\ E'(t) = -r_3 E(t) + a_{34} I(t - T_{ES}) + a_{37} Y_3(t) \\ \quad + \sum_{i+j \geq 2} \frac{[I(t-T_{CC})]^i}{i!} \frac{[Y_3(t)]^j}{j!} \cdot \left.\frac{\partial^{i+j} F_E}{\partial I^i \partial Y_3^j}\right|_{(I^*, Y_3^*)}, \\ I'(t) = -r_4 I(t) + a_{43} E(t - T_{CC}) + a_{48} Y_4(t) \\ \quad + \sum_{i+j \geq 2} \frac{[E(t-T_{CC})]^i}{i!} \frac{[Y_4(t)]^j}{j!} \cdot \left.\frac{\partial^{i+j} F_I}{\partial E^i \partial Y_4^j}\right|_{(E^*, Y_4^*)}, \\ Y_1'(t) = -\alpha_1 Y_1(t) + \alpha_1 E(t), \\ Y_2'(t) = -\alpha_2 Y_2(t) + \alpha_2 G(t), \\ Y_3'(t) = -\alpha_3 Y_3(t) + \alpha_3 S(t), \\ Y_4'(t) = -\alpha_4 Y_4(t) + \alpha_4 I(t), \end{cases} \quad (9)$$

where $a_{12} = r_1 \left.\frac{\partial F_S}{\partial G}\right|_{(G^*, Y_1^*)}$, $a_{15} = r_1 \left.\frac{\partial F_S}{\partial Y_1}\right|_{(G^*, Y_1^*)}$, $a_{21} = r_2 \left.\frac{\partial F_G}{\partial S}\right|_{(S^*, Y_2^*)}$, $a_{26} = r_2 \left.\frac{\partial F_S}{\partial Y_2}\right|_{(S^*, Y_2^*)}$, $a_{34} = r_3 \left.\frac{\partial F_E}{\partial I}\right|_{(I^*, Y_3^*)}$, $a_{37} = r_3 \left.\frac{\partial F_E}{\partial Y_3}\right|_{(I^*, Y_3^*)}$, $a_{43} = r_4 \left.\frac{\partial F_I}{\partial E}\right|_{(E^*, Y_4^*)}$, $a_{48} = r_4 \left.\frac{\partial F_I}{\partial Y_4}\right|_{(E^*, Y_4^*)}$. The linearized system of (9) is the following:

$$\begin{cases} S'(t) = -r_1 S(t) + a_{12} G(t - T_{GS}) + a_{15} Y_1(t), \\ G'(t) = -r_2 G(t) + a_{21} S(t - T_{SG}) + a_{26} Y_2(t), \\ E'(t) = -r_3 E(t) + a_{34} I(t - T_{ES}) + a_{37} Y_3(t), \\ I'(t) = -r_4 I(t) + a_{43} E(t - T_{CC}) + a_{48} Y_4(t), \\ Y_1'(t) = -\alpha_1 Y_1(t) + \alpha_1 E(t), \\ Y_2'(t) = -\alpha_2 Y_2(t) + \alpha_2 G(t), \\ Y_3'(t) = -\alpha_3 Y_3(t) + \alpha_3 S(t), \\ Y_4'(t) = -\alpha_4 Y_4(t) + \alpha_4 I(t). \end{cases} \quad (10)$$

Let $s = \min\{T_{GS}, T_{SG}, T_{ES}, T_{CC}\}$. We consider a special case of the system (10):

$$\begin{cases} S'(t) = -r_1 S(t) + a_{12} G(t-s) + a_{15} Y_1(t), \\ G'(t) = -r_2 G(t) + a_{21} S(t-s) + a_{26} Y_2(t), \\ E'(t) = -r_3 E(t) + a_{34} I(t-s) + a_{37} Y_3(t), \\ I'(t) = -r_4 I(t) + a_{43} E(t-s) + a_{48} Y_4(t), \\ Y_1'(t) = -\alpha_1 Y_1(t) + \alpha_1 E(t), \\ Y_2'(t) = -\alpha_2 Y_2(t) + \alpha_2 G(t), \\ Y_3'(t) = -\alpha_3 Y_3(t) + \alpha_3 S(t), \\ Y_4'(t) = -\alpha_4 Y_4(t) + \alpha_4 I(t). \end{cases} \qquad (11)$$

The matrix form of the system (11) is as follows:

$$u'(t) = Cu(t) + Au(t-s) \qquad (12)$$

where $u(t) = [S(t), G(t), E(t), I(t), Y_1(t), Y_2(t), Y_3(t), Y_4(t)]^T$, $u(t-s) = [S(t-s), G(t-s), E(t-s), I(t-s), 0, 0, 0, 0]^T$

$$A = (a_{ij})_{8\times 8} = \begin{pmatrix} 0 & a_{12} & 0 & 0 & 0 & 0 & 0 & 0 \\ a_{21} & 0 & 0 & 0 & 0 & 0 & 0 & 0 \\ 0 & 0 & 0 & a_{34} & 0 & 0 & 0 & 0 \\ 0 & 0 & a_{43} & 0 & 0 & 0 & 0 & 0 \\ 0 & 0 & 0 & 0 & 0 & 0 & 0 & 0 \\ 0 & 0 & 0 & 0 & 0 & 0 & 0 & 0 \\ 0 & 0 & 0 & 0 & 0 & 0 & 0 & 0 \\ 0 & 0 & 0 & 0 & 0 & 0 & 0 & 0 \end{pmatrix},$$

and

$$C = (c_{ij})_{8\times 8} = \begin{pmatrix} -r_1 & 0 & 0 & 0 & a_{15} & 0 & 0 & 0 \\ 0 & -r_2 & 0 & 0 & 0 & a_{26} & 0 & 0 \\ 0 & 0 & -r_3 & 0 & 0 & 0 & a_{37} & 0 \\ 0 & 0 & 0 & -r_4 & 0 & 0 & 0 & a_{48} \\ 0 & 0 & \alpha_1 & 0 & -\alpha_1 & 0 & 0 & 0 \\ 0 & \alpha_2 & 0 & 0 & 0 & -\alpha_2 & 0 & 0 \\ \alpha_3 & 0 & 0 & 0 & 0 & 0 & -\alpha_3 & 0 \\ 0 & 0 & 0 & \alpha_4 & 0 & 0 & 0 & -\alpha_4 \end{pmatrix}.$$

2. The Existence of Oscillatory Solutions

To discuss the existence of oscillatory solutions for system (7) including four-time delays, we first provide the following lemma.

Lemma 1. *Consider the following delayed differential equations:*

$$x'(t) = f(x(t-\tau_*)), \qquad (13)$$

$$x'(t) = f(x(t-\tau^*)), \qquad (14)$$

where $\tau^* > \tau_* > 0$, $x \in R^n$, $f = (f_1, f_2, \cdots, f_n)^T$, $f(0) = 0$. Assume that the trivial solution of system (13) is unstable, then the trivial solution of system (14) is also unstable.

Proof of Lemma 1. Since the trivial solution of system (13) is unstable, this means that for arbitrary $\varepsilon > 0$, there exists an infinite sequence $\{t_k\}$, where $\tau_* < t_1 < t_2 < t_3 < \cdots$, such that the trivial solution $x(t)$ of system (13) satisfies $|x(t_k - \tau_*)| > \varepsilon$. Noting that $\{t_k\}_{k=1}^{\infty}$ is an infinite sequence, one can select a subsequence $\{t_{k_i}\} \subset \{t_k\}$, such that $t_{k_i} = t_k + (\tau^* - \tau_*)$. Thus, for the trivial solution of system (14), we obtained the following:

$$|x(t_{k_i} - \tau^*)| = |x(t_k + (\tau^* - \tau_*) - \tau^*)| = |x(t_k - \tau_*)| > \varepsilon. \tag{15}$$

Inequivalent (15) indicates that the trivial solution of system (14) is also unstable. □

Since the system (10) is a linearized system of (9), we can see that system (9) is a disturbed system of (10). If the trivial solution of system (11) is unstable, then the trivial solution of system (10) is also unstable according to the Lemma 1. In what follows, we first consider the instability of the zero equilibrium point of the system (11) (or (12)). Therefore, we considered the following theorems.

Theorem 1. *Assume that the system (11) has a unique trivial solution and $\gamma_1, \gamma_2, \cdots, \gamma_8$ are characteristic values of matrix C. $\rho_1, \rho_2, \rho_3, \rho_4$, 0, 0, 0, 0, are characteristic values of matrix A. If there is a characteristic value, say γ_k, satisfying the following:*

(i) $Re(\gamma_k) = 0$, $Im(\gamma_k) \neq 0$, and $\gamma_k = \omega i$; or
(ii) $Re(\gamma_k) > 0$, and $Re(\gamma_k) > \max\{|\rho_1|, |\rho_2|, |\rho_3|, |\rho_4|\}$, or
(iii) $Im(\gamma_k) = 0$, $\gamma_k > 0$.

Then, the trivial solution of system (11) (thus system (9)) is unstable, implying that there exists a limit cycle in the system (7); namely, system (7) has a periodic solution.

Proof of Theorem 1. We show that the trivial solution of the system (11) is unstable. Since $\gamma_1, \gamma_2, \cdots, \gamma_8$ are characteristic values of matrix C and $\rho_1, \rho_2, \rho_3, \rho_4$, 0, 0, 0, 0 are characteristic values of matrix A, then the characteristic equation of (11) is the following:

$$\prod_{i=1}^{8} \lambda - \gamma_i - \rho_i e^{-\lambda s} = 0. \tag{16}$$

When there is a characteristic value γ_k such that $Re(\gamma_k) = 0$, $Im(\gamma_k) \neq 0$, and $\gamma_k = \omega i$, then

$$e^{i\omega t} = \cos \omega t + i \sin \omega t. \tag{17}$$

We know that $\cos \omega t$ is a periodic function; therefore, the trivial solution of system (11) is unstable. Noting that all characteristic values of matrix A are ρ_i or 0, there is a characteristic equation from the system (16) as follows:

$$\lambda - \gamma_k - \rho_k e^{-\lambda s} = 0. \tag{18}$$

or

$$\lambda - \gamma_k = 0. \tag{19}$$

If $Re(\gamma_k) > 0$ and $Re(\gamma_k) > \max\{|\rho_1|, |\rho_2|, |\rho_3|, |\rho_4|\}$, this means that Equation (18) has a positive real part characteristic value. If $Im(\gamma_k) = 0$, $\gamma_k > 0$, it suggests that there is a positive characteristic value from (19). Thus, the trivial solution of system (11) is unstable. Based on Lemma 1, the trivial solution of system (10) is unstable. This implies that the equilibrium point $(S^*, G^*, E^*, I^*, Y_1^*, Y_2^*, Y_3^*, Y_4^*)^T$ of system (9) is unstable.

Equivalently, the unique equilibrium point of the system (7) is unstable. This instability of the unique equilibrium point, together with the boundedness of the solutions, forces system (7) to generate a limit cycle, namely, a periodic solution according to the extended Chafee's criterion [31,32]. The proof is complete. □

Let $\sigma = \max\{\alpha_3 - r_1, \alpha_2 - r_2, \alpha_1 - r_3, \alpha_4 - r_4, |a_{15}| - \alpha_1, |a_{26}| - \alpha_2, |a_{37}| - \alpha_3, |a_{48}| - \alpha_4\}$, then we have Theorem 2.

Theorem 2. *Assume that system (11) has a unique trivial solution. If the following condition holds*

$$r + \sigma > 0, \quad (20)$$

where $r = \max\{|a_{12}|, |a_{21}|, |a_{34}|, |a_{43}|\}$. Then, the trivial solution of system (11) is unstable, implying that there exists a limit cycle of system (9); namely, system (7) has a periodic solution.

Proof of Theorem 2. To prove the instability of the trivial solution of the system (11), let $z(t) = S(t) + G(t) + E(t) + I(t) + \sum_{i=1}^{4} Y_i(t)$, then we have the following:

$$z(t) \leq \sigma z(t) + r z(t-s). \quad (21)$$

Specifically, consider the following scalar equation:

$$v(t) = \sigma v(t) + r v(t-s). \quad (22)$$

According to the comparison theory of the differential equation, we have $z(t) \leq v(t)$. We claim that the trivial solution of Equation (22) is unstable. Indeed, the characteristic Equation (22) is as follows:

$$\lambda = \sigma + r e^{-\lambda s}. \quad (23)$$

Consider a function $\phi(\lambda) = \lambda - \sigma - r e^{-\lambda s}$. Then, $\phi(\lambda)$ is a continuous function of λ. Noting that $\phi(0) = -\sigma - r = -(\sigma + r) < 0$. Clearly, there exists a real number $L > 0$ such that $\phi(L) = L - \sigma - r e^{-Ls} > 0$. Using the Intermediate Value Theorem, there exists $\lambda_0 \in (0, L)$ such that $\phi(\lambda_0) = 0$. In other words, there exists a positive characteristic root of Equation (22), which means that the trivial solution of Equation (22) is unstable, implying that the trivial solution of Equation (11) is unstable and that the trivial solution of system (11), thus (9), is unstable. Similar to Theorem 1, system (7) has a periodic solution. The proof is complete. □

3. Computer Simulation Result

This simulation is based on model (7). In model (7), according to the parameters in [3], we set $M_S = 300, B_S = 17, M_G = 400, B_G = 75, M_E = 71.77, B_E = 3.62, M_I = 276, B_I = 7.18, W_{GS} = 3, W_{SG} = 2.5, W_{SC} = 6, W_{CC} = 3, W_{EE} = W_{GG} = 1, W_{II} = 0.1, C = 277, Str = 40$. When we select $\alpha_1 = 0.8, \alpha_2 = 0.85, \alpha_3 = 0.5, \alpha_4 = 0.55$, time delay $T_{GS} = 15.5, T_{SG} = 18, T_{ES} = 16.5, T_{CC} = 17, \tau_S = 12.5, \tau_G = 20, \tau_E = 10, \tau_I = 15$, so $r_1 = 0.08, r_2 = 0.05, r_3 = 0.1, r_4 = 0.067$, then the unique positive equilibrium point $(S^*, G^*, E^*, I^*, Y_1^*, Y_2^*, Y_3^*, Y_4^*)^T = (98.4164, 163.4268, 44.8525, 60.5816, 44.8525, 163.4268, 98.4164, 60.5816)^T$. Thus,

$$a_{12} = r_1 \left.\frac{\partial F_S}{\partial G}\right|_{(G^*, Y_1^*)} = -0.2372, \quad a_{15} = r_1 \left.\frac{\partial F_S}{\partial Y_1}\right|_{(G^*, Y_1^*)} = 0.4744,$$

$$a_{21} = r_2 \left.\frac{\partial F_G}{\partial S}\right|_{(S^*, Y_2^*)} = 0.2256, \quad a_{26} = r_2 \left.\frac{\partial F_S}{\partial Y_2}\right|_{(S^*, Y_2^*)} = -0.0923,$$

$$a_{34} = r_3 \left.\frac{\partial F_E}{\partial I}\right|_{(I^*, Y_3^*)} = -0.0092, \quad a_{37} = r_3 \left.\frac{\partial F_E}{\partial Y_3}\right|_{(I^*, Y_3^*)} = 0.0031,$$

$$a_{43} = r_4 \left.\frac{\partial F_I}{\partial E}\right|_{(E^*, Y_4^*)} = 0.1496, \quad a_{48} = r_4 \left.\frac{\partial F_I}{\partial Y_4}\right|_{(E^*, Y_4^*)} = -0.0053.$$

The characteristic values of the matrix C are $0.0257, -0.0863, -0.5437, -0.5734, -0.2661 \pm 0.1496 i$, and $-0.2750 \pm 0.0994 i$. Since there exists a positive characteristic value of 0.0257, the conditions of Theorem 1 are satisfied. There exists a periodic oscillatory solution (see Figure 1). Figure 2 indicates a case for all parameters are the same as in Figure 1, but time delays are changed. When we select $\alpha_1 = 0.8, \alpha_2 = 0.85, \alpha_3 = 0.75, \alpha_4 = 0.78$, time delay is $T_{GS} = 12.5, T_{SG} = 14, T_{ES} = 13.5, T_{CC} = 13, \tau_S = 10, \tau_G = 20, \tau_E = 16, \tau_I = 12$, so $r_1 = 0.1, r_2 = 0.05, r_3 = 0.063, r_4 = 0.083$, then the unique positive equilibrium point $(S^*, G^*, E^*, I^*, Y_1^*, Y_2^*, Y_3^*, Y_4^*)^T = (75.4916, 127.1502, 55.3846, 64.9912, 55.3846, 127.1502, 75.4916, 64.9912)^T$. Thus,

$$a_{12} = r_1 \left.\frac{\partial F_S}{\partial G}\right|_{(G^*, Y_1^*)} = -0.0349, \ a_{15} = r_1 \left.\frac{\partial F_S}{\partial Y_1}\right|_{(G^*, Y_1^*)} = 0.0698,$$

$$a_{21} = r_2 \left.\frac{\partial F_G}{\partial S}\right|_{(S^*, Y_2^*)} = 0.1042, \ a_{26} = r_2 \left.\frac{\partial F_S}{\partial Y_2}\right|_{(S^*, Y_2^*)} = -0.0417,$$

$$a_{34} = r_3 \left.\frac{\partial F_E}{\partial I}\right|_{(I^*, Y_3^*)} = -0.0051, \ a_{37} = r_3 \left.\frac{\partial F_E}{\partial Y_3}\right|_{(I^*, Y_3^*)} = 0.0017,$$

$$a_{43} = r_4 \left.\frac{\partial F_I}{\partial E}\right|_{(E^*, Y_4^*)} = 0.2025, \ a_{48} = r_4 \left.\frac{\partial F_I}{\partial Y_4}\right|_{(E^*, Y_4^*)} = -0.0067.$$

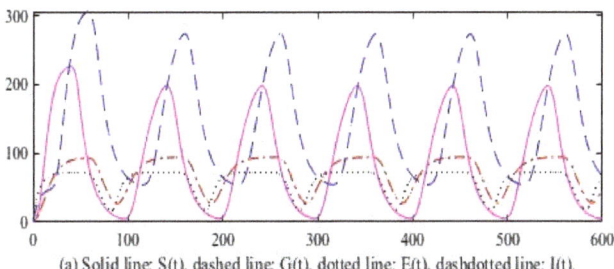

(a) Solid line: S(t), dashed line: G(t), dotted line: E(t), dashdotted line: I(t).

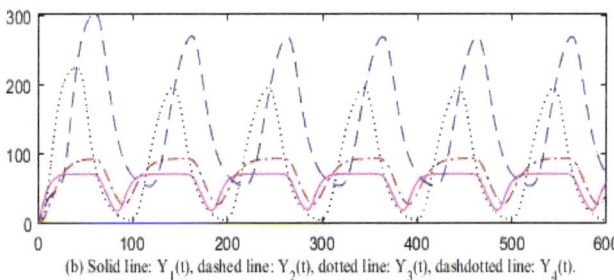

(b) Solid line: Y_1(t), dashed line: Y_2(t), dotted line: Y_3(t), dashdotted line: Y_4(t).

Figure 1. Oscillation of the solutions, $\tau_S = 12.5, \tau_G = 10, \tau_E = 10, \tau_I = 15$, and time delay $T_{GS} = 15.5, T_{SG} = 18, T_{ES} = 16.5, T_{CC} = 17, \alpha_1 = 0.4, \alpha_2 = 0.45, \alpha_3 = 0.5, \alpha_4 = 0.55$.

Thus, $\sigma = \max\{\alpha_3 - r_1, \alpha_2 - r_2, \alpha_1 - r_3, \alpha_4 - r_4, |a_{15}| - \alpha_1, |a_{26}| - \alpha_2, |a_{37}| - \alpha_3, |a_{48}| - \alpha_4\} = 0.8, r = \max\{|a_{12}|, |a_{21}|, |a_{34}|, |a_{43}|\} = 0.1042$, and $\sigma + r = 0.9042 > 0$. The condition of Theorem 2 is satisfied. The system (7) has an oscillatory solution (see Figure 3). In Figure 4, we changed the time delays and kept all parameters the same as in Figure 3. When we selected $\alpha_1 = 1.5, \alpha_2 = 1.6, \alpha_3 = 1.8, \alpha_4 = 1.75$, time delay is $T_{GS} = 18.5, T_{SG} = 17.5, T_{ES} = 18, T_{CC} = 17, \tau_S = 12.8, \tau_G = 16, \tau_E = 20, \tau_I = 14$, so $r_1 = 0.078, r_2 = 0.063, r_3 = 0.05, r_4 = 0.07$, then the unique positive equilibrium point $(S^*, G^*, E^*, I^*, Y_1^*, Y_2^*, Y_3^*, Y_4^*)^T = (98.5443, 151.1364, 52.1243, 63.4582, 52.1243, 151.1364, 98.5443, 63.4582)^T$.

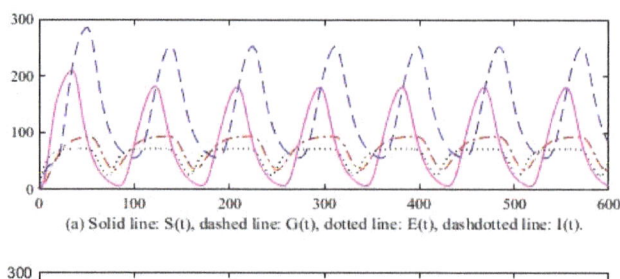
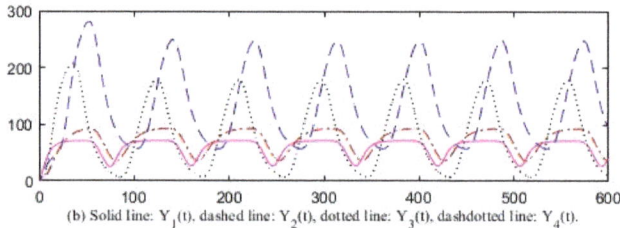

Figure 2. Oscillation of the solutions, $\tau_S = 12.5$, $\tau_G = 10$, $\tau_E = 10$, $\tau_I = 10$, and time delay $T_{GS} = 12.5$, $T_{SG} = 14$, $T_{ES} = 13.5$, $T_{CC} = 13$, $\alpha_1 = 0.4$, $\alpha_2 = 0.45$, $\alpha_3 = 0.5$, $\alpha_4 = 0.55$.

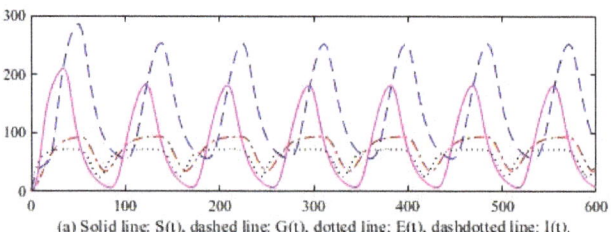
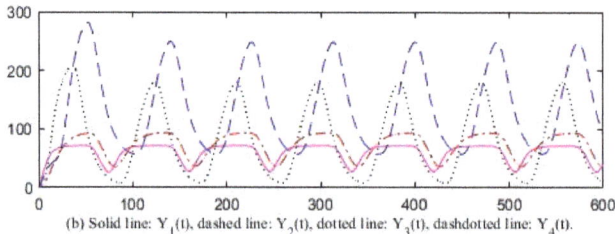

Figure 3. Oscillation of the solutions, $\tau_S = 10$, $\tau_G = 20$, $\tau_E = 16$, $\tau_I = 12$, and time delay $T_{GS} = 12.5$, $T_{SG} = 14$, $T_{ES} = 13.5$, $T_{CC} = 13$, $\alpha_1 = 0.8$, $\alpha_2 = 0.85$, $\alpha_3 = 0.75$, $\alpha_4 = 0.78$.

Therefore, we can obtain the following:

$$a_{12} = r_1 \left.\frac{\partial F_S}{\partial G}\right|_{(G^*, Y_1^*)} = -0.0108, \quad a_{15} = r_1 \left.\frac{\partial F_S}{\partial Y_1}\right|_{(G^*, Y_1^*)} = 0.0216,$$

$$a_{21} = r_2 \left.\frac{\partial F_G}{\partial S}\right|_{(S^*, Y_2^*)} = 0.1471, \quad a_{26} = r_2 \left.\frac{\partial F_S}{\partial Y_2}\right|_{(S^*, Y_2^*)} = -0.0588,$$

$$a_{34} = r_3 \left.\frac{\partial F_E}{\partial I}\right|_{(I^*, Y_3^*)} = -0.0062, \quad a_{37} = r_3 \left.\frac{\partial F_E}{\partial Y_3}\right|_{(I^*, Y_3^*)} = 0.0021,$$

$$a_{43} = r_4 \left.\frac{\partial F_I}{\partial E}\right|_{(E^*, Y_4^*)} = 0.1904, a_{48} = r_4 \left.\frac{\partial F_I}{\partial Y_4}\right|_{(E^*, Y_4^*)} = -0.0063.$$

It is easy to see that the condition of Theorem 2 holds. Therefore, system (7) has an oscillatory solution (see Figure 5). In Figure 6, we reduced the time delays. It can be seen that both the oscillatory frequency and amplitude were changed.

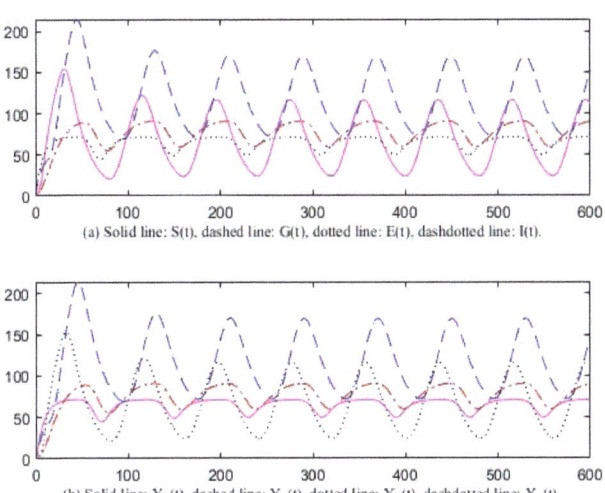

Figure 4. Oscillation of the solutions, $\tau_S = 12.8$, $\tau_G = 16$, $\tau_E = 20$, $\tau_I = 14$, and time delay $T_{GS} = 9.5$, $T_{SG} = 10$, $T_{ES} = 8.5$, $T_{CC} = 9$, $\alpha_1 = 0.8$, $\alpha_2 = 0.85$, $\alpha_3 = 0.75$, $\alpha_4 = 0.78$.

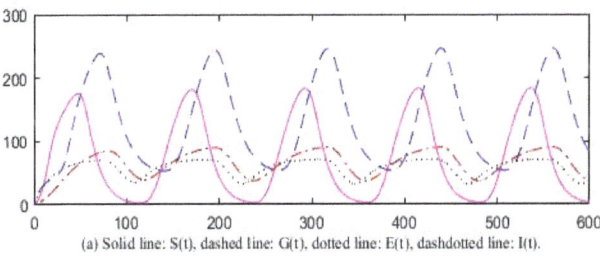

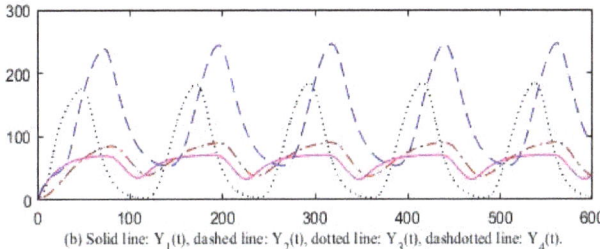

Figure 5. Oscillation of the solutions, $\tau_S = 12.8$, $\tau_G = 16$, $\tau_E = 20$, $\tau_I = 14$, and time delay $T_{GS} = 18.5$, $T_{SG} = 17.5$, $T_{ES} = 18$, $T_{CC} = 17$, $\alpha_1 = 1.5$, $\alpha_2 = 1.6$, $\alpha_3 = 1.8$, $\alpha_4 = 1.75$.

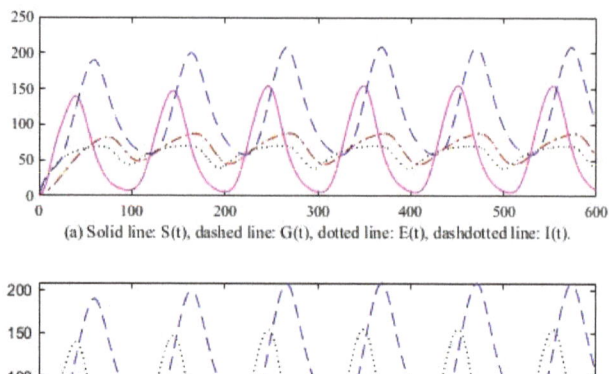

(a) Solid line: S(t), dashed line: G(t), dotted line: E(t), dashdotted line: I(t).

(b) Solid line: $Y_1(t)$, dashed line: $Y_2(t)$, dotted line: $Y_3(t)$, dashdotted line: $Y_4(t)$.

Figure 6. Oscillation of the solutions, $\tau_S = 12.8, \tau_G = 16, \tau_E = 20, \tau_I = 14$, and time delay $T_{GS} = 13.5, T_{SG} = 12.5, T_{ES} = 14, T_{CC} = 13, \alpha_1 = 1.5, \alpha_2 = 1.6, \alpha_3 = 1.8, \alpha_4 = 1.75$.

4. Discussion

Our result provides a criterion to determine whether or not there exists an oscillatory solution for model (6), which includes discrete and distributed delays. The oscillatory solution of the model (6) corresponds to the tremor of Parkinson's disease. Therefore, our main result is very significant. We also point out that the bifurcation method is hard to deal with in the present model. Because the bifurcation equation about model (10) is as follows:

$$\begin{aligned} & p_1(\lambda)\exp(-\lambda T_{GS}) + p_2(\lambda)\exp(-\lambda T_{SG}) \\ & + p_3(\lambda)\exp(-\lambda T_{ES}) + p_4(\lambda)\exp(-\lambda T_{CC}) + p_5(\lambda) = 0. \end{aligned} \quad (24)$$

It can be noted that if $T_{GS}, T_{SG}, T_{ES}, T_{CC}$ are different positive numbers, Equation (24) is a transcendental equation with four variables. Solving Equation (24) and finding the bifurcating points are hard work.

5. Conclusions

In this paper, we discussed the oscillatory behavior of the solutions for a Parkinson's disease model with discrete and distributed delays. Two theorems were provided to determine the existence of oscillatory solutions, which were easy to inspect to compare the method of bifurcation. We made the change in distributed delay terms as new functions such that the original system became only a discrete system. This method can be used to deal with all distributed systems. We point out that the present criteria are only sufficient conditions.

Funding: This research received no external funding.

Data Availability Statement: All data used are in [3].

Conflicts of Interest: The author declares no conflict of interest.

References

1. Tuwairqi, S.M.; Badrah, A.A. Modeling the dynamics of innate and adaptive immune response to Parkinson's disease with immunotherapy. *AIMS Math.* **2023**, *8*, 1800–1832. [CrossRef]
2. Wang, Z.; Hu, B.; Zhu, L.; Lin, J.; Xu, M.; Wang, D. The possible mechanism of direct feedback projections from basal ganglia to cortex in beta oscillations of Parkinson's disease: A theoretical evidence in the competing resonance model. *Commun. Nonlinear Sci. Numer. Simul.* **2023**, *120*, 107142. [CrossRef]
3. Wang, Z.; Hu, B.; Zhu, L.; Lin, J.; Xu, M.; Wang, D. Hopf bifurcation analysis for Parkinson oscillation with heterogeneous delays: A theoretical derivation and simulation analysis. *Commun. Nonlinear Sci. Numer. Simul.* **2022**, *114*, 106614. [CrossRef]
4. Kaslik, E.; Kokovics, E.A.; Radulescu, A. Stability and bifurcations in Wilson-Cowan systems with distributed delays, and an application to basal ganglia interactions. *Commun. Nonlinear Sci. Numer. Simul.* **2022**, *104*, 105984. [CrossRef]
5. Wang, Z.; Hu, B.; Zhou, W.; Xu, M.; Wang, D. Hopf bifurcation mechanism analysis in an improved cortex-basal ganlia network with distributed delays: An application to Parkinson's disease. *Chaos Solitons Fractals* **2023**, *166*, 113022. [CrossRef]
6. Agiza, H.A.; Sohaly, M.A.; Elfouly, M.A. Small two-delay differential equations for Parkinson's disease models using Taylor series transform. *Indian J. Phys.* **2023**, *97*, 39–46. [CrossRef]
7. Badrah, A.; Tuwairqi, S.A. Modeling the dynamics of innate immune response to Parkinson disease with therapeutic approach. *Phys. Biol.* **2022**, *19*, 056004. [CrossRef]
8. Mukhtar, R.; Chang, C.Y.; Raja, M.A.; Chaudhar, N.I. Design of intelligent neuro-supervised networks for brain electrical activity rhythms of Parkinson's disease model. *Biomimetics* **2023**, *8*, 322. [CrossRef]
9. Terman, D.; Rubin, J.E.; Yew, A.C.; Wilson, C.J. Activity patterns in a model for the subthalamopallidal network of the basal ganglia. *J. Neurosci.* **2020**, *22*, 2963–2976. [CrossRef]
10. Chen, Y.; Wang, J.; Kang, Y.; Ghori, M.B. Emergence of beta oscillations of a resonance model for Parkinson's disease. *Neural Plast.* **2020**, *2020*, 8824760. [CrossRef]
11. Geng, X.; Xu, X.; Horn, A.; Li, N.; Ling, Z.; Brown, P.; Wang, S. Intra-operative characterization of subthalamic oscillations in Parkinson's disease. *Clin. Neurophysiol.* **2018**, *129*, 1001–1010. [CrossRef] [PubMed]
12. Grado, L.L.; Johnson, M.D.; Netoff, T.I. Bayesian adaptive dual control of deep brain stimulation in a computational model of Parkinson's disease. *PLoS Comput. Biol.* **2018**, *14*, 1006606. [CrossRef] [PubMed]
13. Hu, B.; Xu, M.; Zhu, L.; Wang, Z.; Wang, D. A bidirectional Hopf bifurcation analysis of Parkinson's oscillation in a simplified basal ganglia model. *J. Theor. Biol.* **2022**, *536*, 110979. [CrossRef] [PubMed]
14. Darcy, N.; Lofredi, R.; Fatly, B.A.; Neumann, W.J.; Hubl, J.; Brucke, C.; Krause, P.; Schneider, G.; Kuhn, A. Spectral and spatial distribution of subthalamic beta peak activity in Parkinson's disease patients. *Exp. Neurol.* **2022**, *356*, 114150. [CrossRef] [PubMed]
15. Lang, A.E.; Espay, A.J. Disease modification in Parkinson's disease: Current approaches, challenges, and future considerations. *Mov. Disord.* **2018**, *33*, 660–677. [CrossRef]
16. Raza, C.; Anjum, R. Parkinson's disease: Mechanisms, translational models and management. *Strateg. Life Sci.* **2019**, *226*, 77–90. [CrossRef]
17. Burke, R.E.; Mally, K. Axon degeneration in Parkinson's disease. *Exp. Neurol.* **2013**, *246*, 71–83. [CrossRef]
18. Dovonou, A.; Bolduc, C.; Linan, V.S.; Gora, C.; Peralta, M.R.; Levesque, M. Animal models of Parkinson's disease: Bridging the gap between disease hallmarks and research questions. *Trans. Neurodegener.* **2023**, *12*, 36. [CrossRef]
19. He, B.; Luo, S. Joint modeling of multivariate longitudinal measurements and survival data with applications to Parkinson's disease. *Stat. Methods Med. Res.* **2016**, *25*, 1346–1358. [CrossRef]
20. Bushnell, D.; Martin, M. Quality of life and Parkinson's disease: Translation and validation of the US Parkinson's disease questionnaire (PDQ-39). *Qual. Life Res.* **1999**, *8*, 345–350. [CrossRef]
21. Bakshi, S.; Chelliah, V.; Chen, C.; Graaf, P.H. Mathematical biology models of Parkinson's disease. *CPT Pharmacomet. Syst. Pharmacol.* **2019**, *8*, 77–86. [CrossRef] [PubMed]
22. Buatois, S.; Retout, S.; Frey, N.; Ueckert, S. Item response theory as an efficient tool to describe a heterogeneous clinical rating scale in de novo idiopathic Parkinson's disease patients. *Pharm. Res.* **2017**, *34*, 2109–2118. [CrossRef] [PubMed]
23. Kuznetsov, I.A.; Kuznetsov, A.V. What can trigger the onset of Parkinson's disease—A modeling study based on a compartmental model of alpha-synuclein transport and aggregation in neurons. *Math. Biosci.* **2016**, *278*, 22–29. [CrossRef] [PubMed]
24. Braatz, E.M.; Coleman, R.A. A mathematical model of insulin resistance in Parkinson's disease. *Comput. Biol.Chem.* **2015**, *56*, 84–97. [CrossRef] [PubMed]
25. Cloutier, M.; Middleton, R.; Wellstead, P. Feedback motif for the pathogenesis of Parkinson's disease. *IET. Syst. Biol.* **2012**, *6*, 86–93. [CrossRef] [PubMed]
26. Poliquin, P.O.; Chen, J.; Cloutier, M.; Trudeau, L.E.; Jolicoeur, M. Metabolomics and in-silico analysis reveal critical energy deregulations in animal models of Parkinson's disease. *PLoS ONE* **2013**, *8*, e69146. [CrossRef] [PubMed]
27. Flagmeier, P.; Meisl, G.; Vendruscolo, M.; Galvagnion, C. Mutations associated with familial Parkinson's disease alter the initiation and amplification step of α-synuclein aggregation. *Proc. Natl. Acad. Sci. USA* **2016**, *113*, 10328–10333. [CrossRef] [PubMed]
28. Lotharius, J.; Brundin, P. Pathogenesis of Parkinson's disease: Dopamine, vesicles and α-synuclein. *Nat. Rev. Neurosci.* **2002**, *3*, 932–942. [CrossRef]
29. Plotegher, N.; Duchen, M.R. Crosstalk between lysosomes and mitochondria in Parkinson's disease. *Front. Cell Dev. Biol.* **2017**, *5*, 2011–2018. [CrossRef]

30. Gelders, G.; Baekelandt, V.; Perren, A. Linking neuroinflammation and neurodegeneration in Parkinson's disease. *J. Immunol. Res.* **2018**, *2018*, 4784268. [CrossRef]
31. Chafee, N. A bifurcation problem for a functional differential equation of finitely retarded type. *J. Math. Anal. Appl.* **1971**, *35*, 312–348. [CrossRef]
32. Feng, C.; Plamondon, R. An oscillatory criterion for a time delayed neural ring network model. *Neural Netw.* **2012**, *29*, 70–79. [CrossRef] [PubMed]

Disclaimer/Publisher's Note: The statements, opinions and data contained in all publications are solely those of the individual author(s) and contributor(s) and not of MDPI and/or the editor(s). MDPI and/or the editor(s) disclaim responsibility for any injury to people or property resulting from any ideas, methods, instructions or products referred to in the content.

Article

Analysis of the Burgers–Huxley Equation Using the Nondimensionalisation Technique: Universal Solution for Dirichlet and Symmetry Boundary Conditions

Juan Francisco Sánchez-Pérez [1,*], Joaquín Solano-Ramírez [2], Enrique Castro [1], Manuel Conesa [1], Fulgencio Marín-García [3] and Gonzalo García-Ros [4]

1. Department of Applied Physics and Naval Technology, Universidad Politécnica de Cartagena (UPCT), 30202 Cartagena, Spain; enrique.castro@upct.es (E.C.); manuel.conesa@upct.es (M.C.)
2. Department of Thermal Engineering and Fluids, Universidad Politécnica de Cartagena (UPCT), 30202 Cartagena, Spain; joaquin.solano@upct.es
3. Department of Automation Engineering, Electrical Engineering and Electronic Technology, Universidad Politécnica de Cartagena (UPCT), 30202 Cartagena, Spain; pentxo.marin@upct.es
4. Department of Mining and Civil Engineering, Universidad Politécnica de Cartagena (UPCT), 30202 Cartagena, Spain; gonzalo.garcia@upct.es
* Correspondence: juanf.sanchez@upct.es

Abstract: The Burgers–Huxley equation is important because it involves the phenomena of accumulation, drag, diffusion, and the generation or decay of species, which are common in various problems in science and engineering, such as heat transmission, the diffusion of atmospheric contaminants, etc. On the other hand, the mathematical technique of nondimensionalisation has proven to be very useful in the appropriate grouping of the variables involved in a physical–chemical phenomenon and in obtaining universal solutions to different complex engineering problems. Therefore, a deep analysis using this technique of the Burgers–Huxley equation and its possible boundary conditions can facilitate a common understanding of these problems through the appropriate grouping of variables and propose common universal solutions. Thus, in this case, the technique is applied to obtain a universal solution for Dirichlet and symmetric boundary conditions. The validation of the methodology is carried out by comparing different cases, where the coefficients or the value of the boundary condition are varied, with the results obtained through a numerical simulation. Furthermore, one of the cases presented presents a boundary condition that changes at a certain time. Finally, after applying the technique, it is studied which phenomenon is predominant, concluding that from a certain value diffusion predominates, with the rest being practically negligible.

Keywords: nondimensionalisation; universal solution; mathematical modelling; numerical simulation; engineering science; ordinary differential equations

MSC: 00A73; 00A69; 00A79

1. Introduction

Many engineering problems, such as heat transmission, fluid mechanics, contaminant emission, chloride diffusion in concrete, etc., involve the phenomena of diffusion, accumulation, generation, or the decay of species, and drag. In this sense, the Burgers–Huxley equation is a general equation that encompasses all these phenomena [1–28].

Thus, it is necessary, on the one hand, to obtain a universal solution that allows this equation to be easily solved, and on the other, to study the influence of the variables involved. In this way, the nondimensionalisation technique allows us to both obtain universal solutions and study the variables that have been grouped to form monomials [29–31].

The application of the nondimensionalisation technique to engineering problems formulated in ordinary differential equations is well known because it allows one to obtain dimensionless groups by grouping the variables, allowing us to know both the universal solution of the problem and the influence of each variable [31]. This procedure has recently been applied to different engineering problems, such as the diffusion of chlorides in concrete or soil consolidation, and the basis of the methodology has been explained in detail [29,31].

The objective of this study is to apply the nondimensionalisation methodology to the Burgers–Huxley equation to obtain, on the one hand, a universal solution to the problem posed. In this case, the symmetry condition will be applied to one of the boundary conditions, and to the other boundary condition, a constant value of the variable will be applied (Dirichlet condition). On the other hand, another objective is to study the weight of the variables in the problem. For the construction of the universal curves, the Network Simulation Method was used, which has demonstrated its effectiveness in solving this problem, as well as other engineering problems [32–35].

Thus, the Burgers–Huxley equation is an ordinary differential equation that is widely used in physics, biology, economics, etc., and includes terms such as drag, accumulation, generation or decay, and diffusion. This equation has the following form [2,3,32]:

$$\frac{du}{dt} + \alpha u^\delta \frac{du}{dx} - \zeta \frac{d^2 u}{dx^2} - \beta u \left(1 - u^\delta\right)\left(\varepsilon u^\delta - \gamma\right) = 0 \quad t \geq 0 \tag{1}$$

where u is the variable, such as concentration, temperature, etc.; x is the distance; t is the time; and, finally, α, β, γ, δ, ε, and ζ are coefficients. Thus, the first addend of the equation is associated with accumulation, the second with drag (coefficients α and δ), the third with diffusion phenomena (coefficient ζ), and, finally, the fourth with the generation or decay of species (coefficients β, γ, δ, and ε).

This article is structured as follows: the introduction and the Burgers–Huxley equation are presented in Section 1. In the next section, the procedure for the nondimensionalisation technique is detailed so that it can be applied to the Burgers–Huxley equation in the same section. The results used to validate the proposed methodology after the application of the nondimensionalisation technique are presented in Section 3. Finally, Section 4 presents the conclusions of this study.

2. Nondimensionalisation Technique and Its Application to the Burgers–Huxley Equation

The correct steps for applying the nondimensionalisation technique have been described in the literature, which have recently included those necessary to obtain universal solutions. Furthermore, several articles have focused on defining the behaviour of monomials based on the values obtained, establishing criteria in which some monomials can have little influence on the problem compared with others that govern it. Thus, as a summary, the following steps must be applied [30,31]:

(i) Choice of references

For the correct choice of references, a deep understanding of the problem is necessary because they may appear explicitly in the problem or may be hidden. Furthermore, the values selected for the references are related to each other through a physical interval (temporal or spatial) of the independent variable, limiting the dimensionless variables to the interval of values [0–1]. When the solution to the problem is asymptotic, references close to the limit are taken as the dependent variable, for example, 99% or 90% of the maximum value of the variable. Thus, there was no significant modification in the range [0–1] of the dimensionless variables.

(ii) Dimensionless variables and dimensionless governing equations

The divisions between the dimensional variables and their references are the dimensionless variables, e.g., $x' = \frac{x}{L}$, where x' is the dimensionless variable of the distance, x is the distance variable, and L is the reference, which in this case is the total length of the medium. Thus, these dimensionless variables are introduced into the governing equations of the problem and transform them into dimensionless equations. Each addend of these equations is formed by two factors: one that involves the grouping of boundary conditions, problem parameters, and/or references, and another with dimensionless variables and their changes, which can be assumed to be of the order of unity. Thus, based on this hypothesis, the first factor, known as the coefficient, must also be of the same order of magnitude.

(iii) Dimensionless groups

The dimensionless groups, or monomials, are the relation between the coefficients mentioned in the previous step, which will be at most as many addends as the dimensionless equation has minus one. Because some groups may be expressed as a combination of other groups with multiplications or divisions, or the same group may appear in more than one equation when the problem is a system of coupled equations, the final number of groups may be reduced. Additionally, the groups can be manipulated such that each unknown appears in a single group.

(iv) The existence of m groups with a different unknown each one (π_u) and n groups without unknowns (π_w)

The solution for each unknown is explicitly expressed as a function of groups that do not contain unknowns. That is, in the form

$$\pi_{u,i} = \Psi_i(\pi_{w,1}, \pi_{w,2}, \ldots, \pi_{w,n}) \text{ where } 1 \leq i \leq m \qquad (2)$$

where Ψ_i is an arbitrary function of the n π_w groups. When the groups are of unit order of magnitude, the arbitrary function will also be of this order of magnitude.

(v) Functionals

The Ψ_i functionals presented in the previous step were obtained by adjusting two monomials or dimensionless groups, keeping the rest at a constant value, as will be shown in the resolution of the problem posed in this article.

(vi) Universal solutions

The universal solution is obtained by representing the dimensionless variables defined above, which, as indicated by their own definition, are in the range of values [0–1].

The information provided above is very important because it allows us to both obtain universal solutions to the problem posed and know the influence of the variables on it. Thus, if we apply this methodology to the Burgers–Huxley equation, we can obtain its universal solution and study the influence of its variables.

The study problem must be defined before applying the nondimensionalisation methodology. In this case, we have a variable u that is found in a medium of length L and is subject to the accumulation, drag, generation or decay, and diffusion phenomena. Regarding the boundary conditions, on the left side, a Dirichlet condition is applied with a constant value of u, u_{ext}, and on the right side, there is a Neumann condition to apply with a symmetry condition [32]. Finally, the variable u can present initial values in the medium, u_{ini}, as shown in Figure 1.

Figure 1. Description of the study problem. Geometry, boundary, and initial conditions.

To apply the steps specified above for correct nondimensionalisation to Equation (1), the references must first be defined, and the dimensionless variables must be established (steps i and ii). Thus, dimensionless variables are the division of the variable with its reference.

$$u' = \frac{u - u_{ini}}{u_{ext} - u_{ini}} \quad x' = \frac{x}{L} \quad t' = \frac{t}{\tau} \tag{3}$$

The reference chosen for the dimensionless variable u' is the difference between the final value it can reach, that is, the value in the boundary condition, u_{ext}, and its initial value, u_{ini}. For the dimensionless variable x', the total length of the medium, L, was chosen. Finally, because the problem has an asymptotic tendency, for the dimensionless time variable t', the time at which 99% of the maximum value of u is reached, that is, 99% of u_{ext}, was chosen. The dimensionless variables were then introduced into the governing equation and the following dimensionless form was obtained:

$$\left[\frac{u_{ext}-u_{ini}}{\tau}\right]\frac{du'}{dt'} + \alpha((u_{ext}-u_{ini})u' + u_{ini})^{\delta}\frac{u_{ext}-u_{ini}}{L}\frac{du'}{dx'} - \left[\zeta\frac{u_{ext}-u_{ini}}{L^2}\right]\frac{d^2u'}{dx'^2} - \beta\varepsilon((u_{ext}-u_{ini})u' + u_{ini})^{\delta+1} + \beta\gamma((u_{ext}-u_{ini})u' + u_{ini}) + \beta\varepsilon((u_{ext}-u_{ini})u' + u_{ini})^{2\delta+1} - \beta\gamma((u_{ext}-u_{ini})u' + u_{ini})^{\delta+1} = 0. \tag{4}$$

The dimensionless equation gives us seven coefficients:

$$\frac{u_{ext}-u_{ini}}{\tau}, \frac{\alpha u_{ext}^{\delta}(u_{ext}-u_{ini})}{L}, \zeta\frac{u_{ext}-u_{ini}}{L^2}, \beta\varepsilon u_{ext}^{\delta+1}, \beta\gamma u_{ext}, \beta\varepsilon u_{ext}^{2\delta+1}, \beta\gamma u_{ext}^{\delta+1}.$$

As some coefficients of species generation or decay phenomena are contained in the others, there are finally five coefficients:

$$\frac{u_{ext}-u_{ini}}{\tau}, \frac{\alpha u_{ext}^{\delta}(u_{ext}-u_{ini})}{L}, \zeta\frac{u_{ext}-u_{ini}}{L^2}, \beta\varepsilon u_{ext}^{2\delta+1}, \beta\gamma u_{ext}^{\delta+1}.$$

These give rise to four dimensionless monomials:

$$\pi_1 = \frac{\zeta\tau}{L^2}, \quad \pi_2 = \frac{\zeta}{\alpha L u_{ext}^{\delta}}, \quad \pi_3 = \frac{\beta\gamma L u_{ext}}{\alpha(u_{ext}-u_{ini})}, \quad \pi_4 = \frac{\varepsilon}{\gamma}u_{ext}^{\delta}.$$

The first monomial, π_1, is typical of problems involving diffusion phenomena, relating time to the distance squared and the diffusion coefficient, in this case, coefficient ζ. This monomial is found in the literature on heat transmission problems, known as the Fourier number [9], chloride diffusion [29], etc. The second monomial, π_2, indicates the relationship between diffusion and drag phenomena. The third, π_3, relates to the drag phenomena and the generation or decay of species. Finally, π_4 relates the coefficients of generation and decay of the species. It should be noted that when β is zero, the monomial π_3 is zero, and the fourth monomial π_4 has no influence, since there would be no generation or decay of the species.

Applying the π theorem, $\pi_1 = \Psi(\pi_2, \pi_3, \pi_4)$, the same characteristic time can be expressed from each of the equations in the form

$$\tau = \frac{L^2}{\zeta}\Psi\left(\frac{\zeta}{\alpha L u_{ext}^{\delta}}, \frac{\beta\gamma L u_{ext}}{\alpha(u_{ext}-u_{ini})}, \frac{\varepsilon}{\gamma}u_{ext}^{\delta}\right). \tag{5}$$

where Ψ is an unknown function of the arguments.

If we apply step (v) of the nondimensionalisation technique, the value of the functional can be obtained. In this case, because we depend on three monomials, we adjust the monomials π_1 and π_2, keeping the rest, π_3 and π_4, with constant values. To perform the adjustment, the problem was simulated using the Network Simulation Method to determine the time necessary for the concentration at the right-hand end, $x = L$, to be

99% of the u_{ext} value, as defined above. Thus, Equations (6)–(10) show the fits for different values of π_3 and π_4.

$$\pi_3 = 0 \ \forall \ \pi_4 \ \pi_1 = 1.974 + 0.8186\pi_2^{-1.105} \ R^2 = 0.9987 \ \tau = \frac{L^2}{\zeta}\left(1.974 + 0.8186\left(\frac{\zeta}{\alpha L u_{ext}^\delta}\right)^{-1.105}\right) \quad (6)$$

$$\pi_3 = 1 \ \pi_4 = 1 \ \pi_1 = 1.974 + 0.6781\pi_2^{-1.13} \ R^2 = 0.9978 \ \tau = \frac{L^2}{\zeta}\left(1.974 + 0.6781\left(\frac{\zeta}{\alpha L u_{ext}^\delta}\right)^{-1.13}\right) \quad (7)$$

$$\pi_3 = 1 \ \pi_4 = 2 \ \pi_1 = 2.284 + 9708\pi_2^{-13.33} \ R^2 = 1.0000 \ \tau = \frac{L^2}{\zeta}\left(2.284 + 9708\left(\frac{\zeta}{\alpha L u_{ext}^\delta}\right)^{-13.33}\right) \quad (8)$$

$$\pi_3 = 2 \ \pi_4 = 1 \ \pi_1 = 1.978 + 0.562\pi_2^{-1.102} \ R^2 = 0.9990 \ \tau = \frac{L^2}{\zeta}\left(1.978 + 0.562\left(\frac{\zeta}{\alpha L u_{ext}^\delta}\right)^{-1.102}\right) \quad (9)$$

$$\pi_3 = 2 \ \pi_4 = 2 \ \pi_1 = 2.290 + 4674\pi_2^{-12.32} \ R^2 = 1.0000 \ \tau = \frac{L^2}{\zeta}\left(2.290 + 4674\left(\frac{\zeta}{\alpha L u_{ext}^\delta}\right)^{-12.32}\right) \quad (10)$$

As can be seen, in Equations (6)–(10), the R^2 fits are very close to unity. It should be noted that for Equation (6) β takes zero and, therefore, the monomial π_4 has no influence. Finally, Figure 2 shows the fit of Equations (6)–(10).

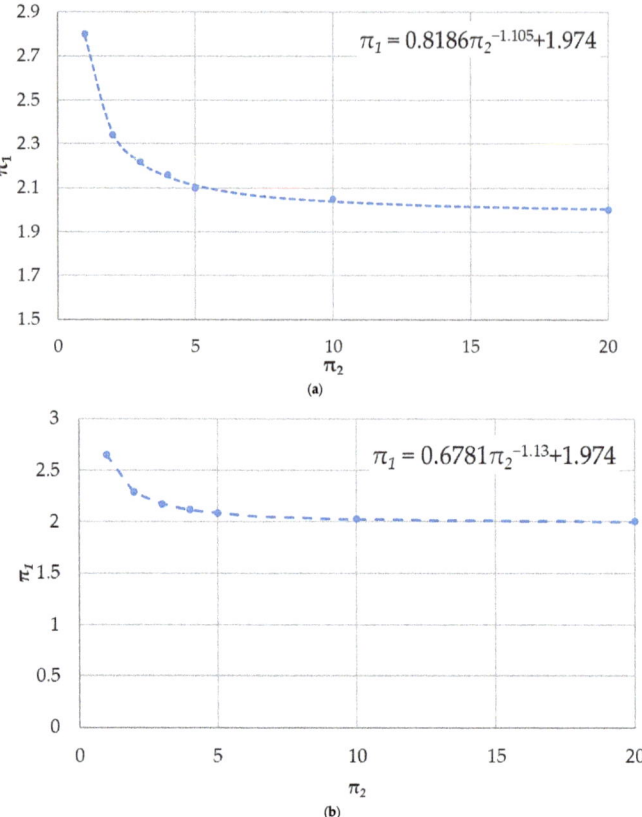

Figure 2. Cont.

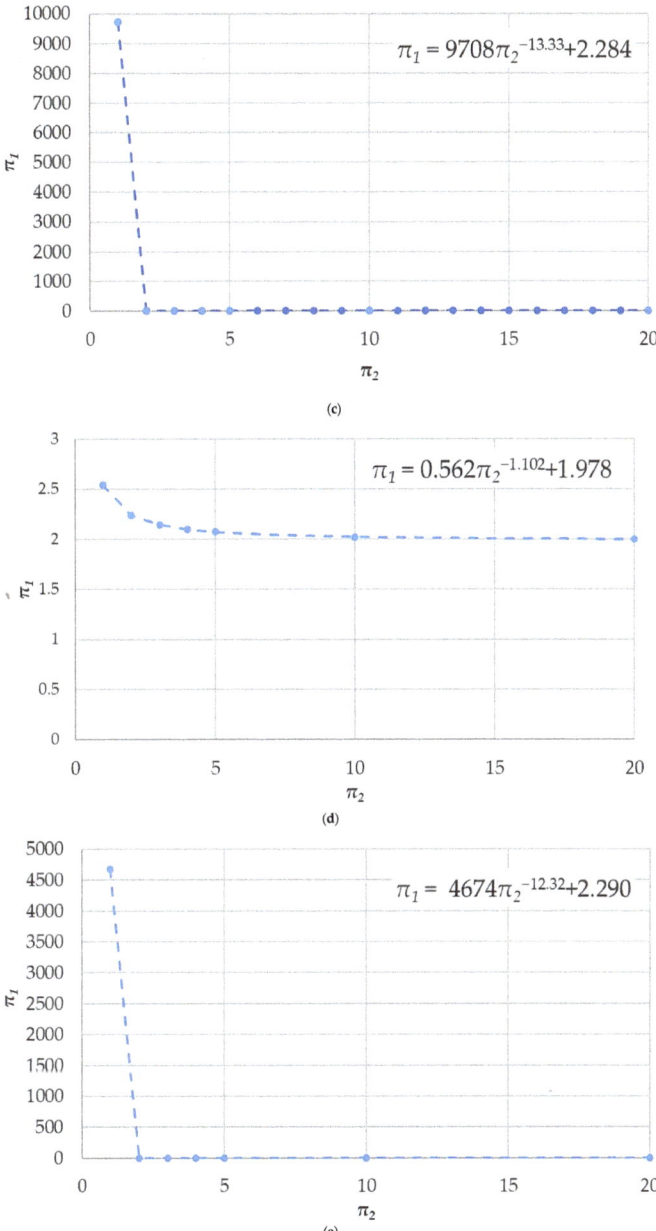

Figure 2. Representation of π_1 versus π_2 (**a**) with $\pi_3 = 0$ and independent of π_4, (**b**) with $\pi_3 = 1$ and $\pi_4 = 1$, (**c**) with $\pi_3 = 1$ and $\pi_4 = 2$, (**d**) with $\pi_3 = 2$ and $\pi_4 = 1$, and (**e**) with $\pi_3 = 2$ and $\pi_4 = 2$.

If the expressions obtained and Figure 2 are analysed, it can be seen that for very low values of π_2, very high values of π_1 are required, showing a tendency towards infinity. This indicates that the diffusion phenomenon is practically negligible, and with the drag phenomenon, it would be very difficult to reach a value of 99% of u_{ext}. This trend increased with increasing π_4, as shown in Figure 2. Owing to this tendency, the values provided by the fits for π_2 values lower than unity may have a higher error. On the other hand, for all the cases studied, from when π_2 takes a value between two and five, π_1 tends to be a value close to two, becoming practically independent of π_2, π_3, and π_4; therefore, the diffusion phenomenon governs the problem, as shown in Figure 2.

Finally, if step (vi) is applied by simulating the problem using the Network Simulation Method [32], and presenting u' versus x' for different values of t', the universal solution to the problem is obtained, as shown in Figure 3.

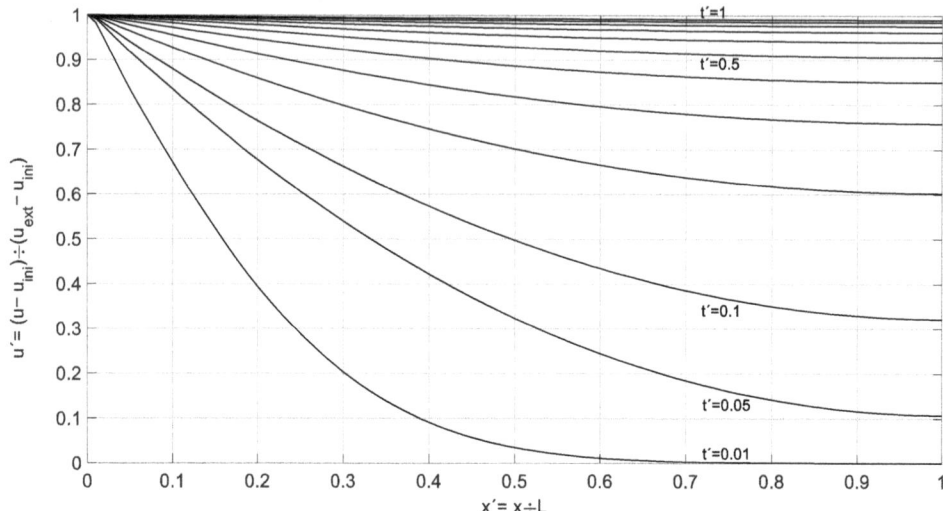

Figure 3. Universal curve for Burgers–Huxley equation with Dirichlet and symmetry (Neumann) boundary conditions.

The methodology for using the universal solution to obtain the value of u at a given position and time is as follows.

1. The values of position x and time t at which the u value is to be determined are known. In addition, the value of u at the boundary condition, u_{ext}, the initial value of u at position x, u_{ini}, and the length of the medium, L, are known. In addition, the coefficients α, β, γ, δ, ε, and ζ are known.
2. The monomials π_2, π_3, and π_4 are calculated.
3. The value of τ is determined using Equations (6)–(10). If the values of π_3 and π_4 are not those given in Equations (6)–(10), one can interpolate.
4. Calculate t' and x' with $t' = \frac{t}{\tau}$ and $x\prime = \frac{x}{L}$
5. The value of the curve t' is taken for position x' in Figure 3, and the value of u is obtained from the expression given for u', $u = u'(u_{ext} - u_{ini}) + u_{ini}$. If the value of t' lies between two curves, it is necessary to interpolate.

Similarly, the methodology can be used to obtain the time at which a given value of u is reached at a given position, the position at which a value of u is reached for a given time, etc.

3. Result and Validation

In the following, two types of studies are carried out to validate the methodology. In the first study, cases 1 to 3 (Table 1), we analyse different cases where the parameters of the problem change, and therefore the values of the monomials change. The results obtained using the universal solution were compared with those obtained by simulation using the Network Simulation Method [32]. In case 1, it is a problem where the variable

u is raised to one, since δ takes unit value. Moreover, the variable does not have initial values. In this case, all phenomena are present, that is, accumulation, drag, diffusion, and the generation and decay of species. If we compare the results obtained, following the methodology specified in the previous section, for the value of u at the 0.8 m position at a time of 0.458 s with those obtained by the simulation (Figure 4), we can see that the values obtained with both the universal solution and simulation are very similar. In the second case, where all the phenomena described above are involved again, the variable u is squared ($\delta = 2$), affecting the phenomenon of drag, generation, and the decay of species, and it also has initial values. Because these initial values influence the monomial π_3, it has a value of 0.667. Therefore, to obtain the value of τ, it is necessary to interpolate between Equations (5) and (6). Once again, the results obtained by the simulation (Figure 5) and those obtained with the universal solution have practically the same value; the difference is due to the carryover of errors in the application of the methodology. Finally, in case 3, where the phenomena of species generation and decay are not present, the variable u is raised to 0.5 ($\delta = 0.5$) for the drag phenomena. Furthermore, the variable does not have initial values. In this case, it is necessary to interpolate between the curves of the universal solution, Figure 3, because t' takes a value of 0.45. If we compare the results with those obtained through the simulation (Figure 6), again, they are practically the same.

Table 1. Comparison between simulated values and those calculated with the universal curve.

Case	α	β	γ	δ	ε	ζ	L (m)	u_{ext}	u_{ini}	x (m)	t (s)
1	0.5	0.5	0.5	1	0.5	6	2	2	0	0.8	0.458
2	2	1	1	2	0.25	16	1	2	0.5	0.3	0.0865
3	1	0	1	0.5	0	4	0.25	4	0	0.1	0.0145

								Universal Solution	Simulation
Case	π_3	π_4	π_2	π_1	τ	t'	x'	u	u
1	1	2	3	2.288	1.525	0.3	0.4	1.688	1.698
2	0.667	1	2	2.307	0.144	0.6	0.3	1.927	1.943
3	0	0	8	2.056	0.0321	0.45	0.4	3.673	3.667

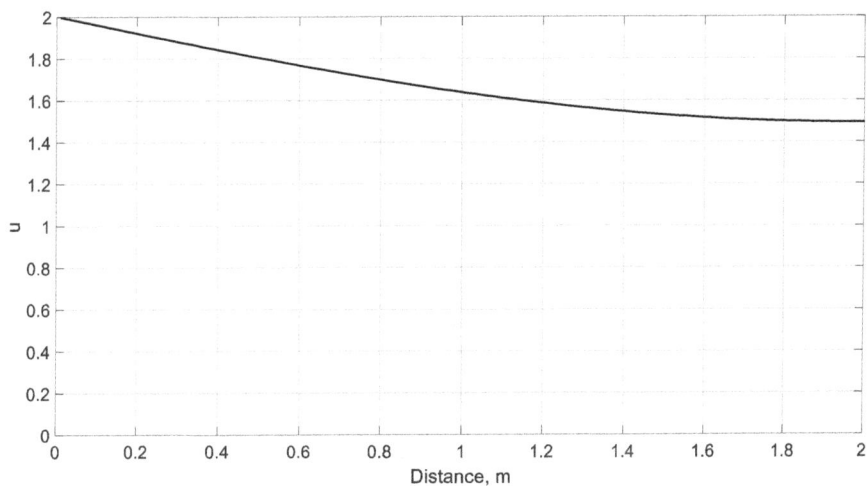

Figure 4. Simulation of case 1 for a time of 0.458 s.

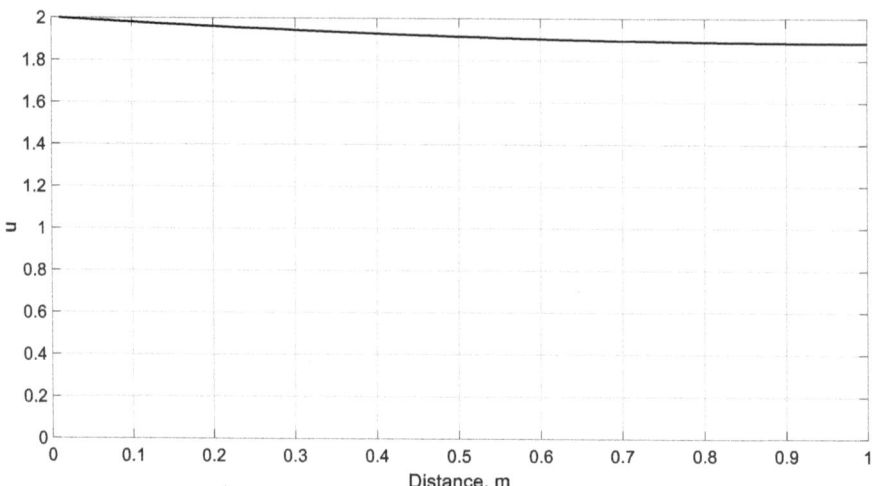

Figure 5. Simulation of case 2 for a time of 0.0865 s.

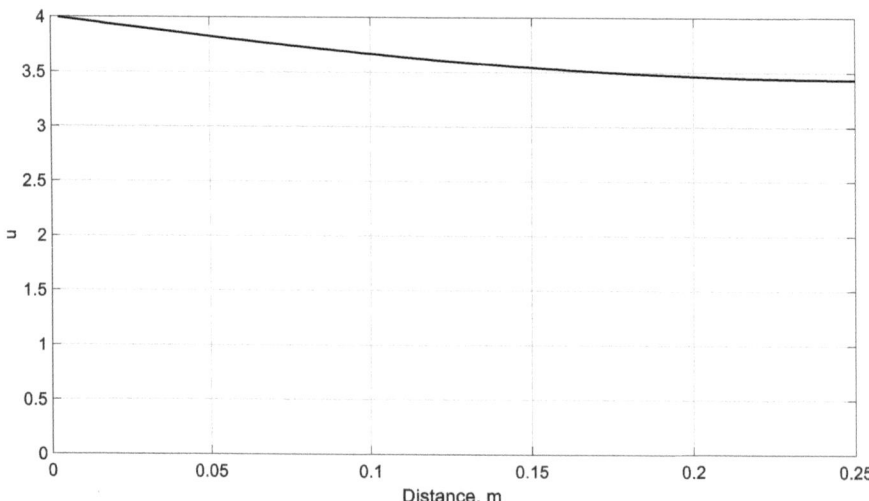

Figure 6. Simulation of case 3 for a time of 0.0145 s.

In the second study, the proposed methodology was applied to a case where the boundary condition changed value (case 4). Thus, for a time between 0 and 0.0269 s, the value of u_{ext} is unity, and then doubles for a time between 0.0269 and 0.3212 s, as shown in Table 2. To solve this case, it must be divided into two parts, cases 4a and 4b, by applying the indicated procedure twice. For case 4a, a time of 0.0269 s was used, and there were no initial values for the study variable. Once case 4a was solved, the procedure was applied, taking as initial values for case 4b the results obtained in case 4a. On the other hand, the time used for case 4b was 0.2943 s, the difference between 0.3212 s and 0.0269 s. For both cases 4a and 4b, three positions were taken, and their results were compared with those obtained by the simulation (Figure 7). As can be seen, for case 4a there are greater differences than in case 4b with respect to the values obtained by the simulation because the methodology is more sensitive to small times due to the possible accumulated errors when applying the procedure. However, for case 4b, the results were practically the same.

On the other hand, if we were in a case where the boundary condition will change more over time, we would have to apply the methodology explained in case 4 as many times as these changes occur.

Table 2. Comparison between simulated values and those calculated with the universal curve for a case with changing boundary conditions.

Case	α	β	γ	δ	ε	ζ	L (m)	u_{ext}	t (s)	Time Range (s)
4a	1	0	1	1	0	4	1	1	0.0269	0 ≤ t ≤ 0.0269
4b	1	0	1	1	0	4	1	2	0.2943	0.0269 ≤ t ≤ 0.3212

Case	x	u_{ini}	π_3	π_4	π_2	π_1	τ	t'	x'	Universal Solution u	Simulation u
	0.3	0							0.3	0.54	0.52
4a	0.6	0	0	0	4	2.151	0.5378	0.05	0.6	0.24	0.20
	0.9	0							0.9	0.11	0.07

Case	x	u_{ini}	π_3	π_4	π_2	π_1	τ	t'	x'	Universal Solution u	Simulation u
	0.3	0.54							0.3	1.92	1.91
4b	0.6	0.24	0	0	2	2.355	0.5888	0.5	0.6	1.85	1.85
	0.9	0.11							0.9	1.82	1.82

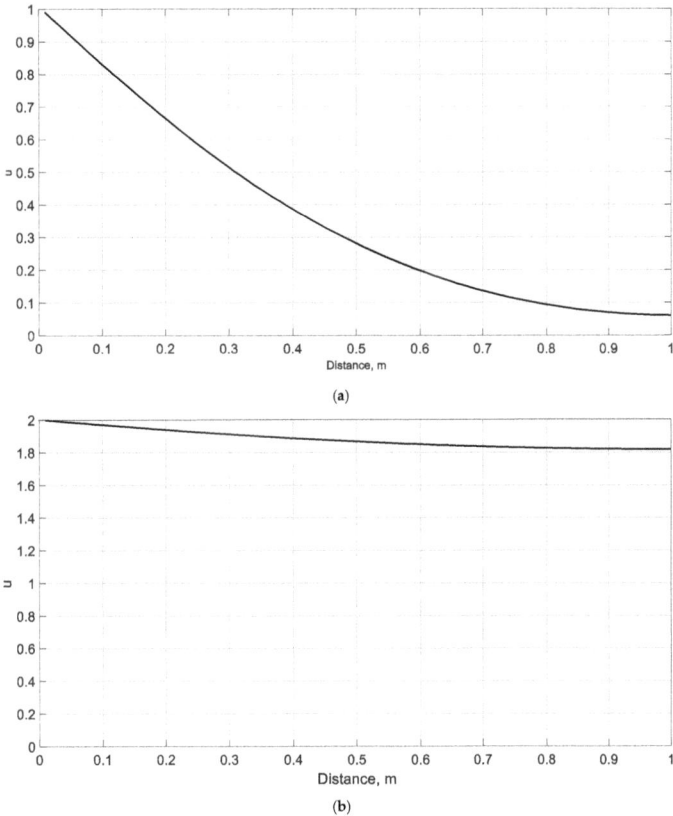

Figure 7. Simulation of case 4. (**a**) Case 4a: $t = 0.0269$ s and $u_{ext} = 1$, and (**b**) case 4b: $t = 0.3212$ s and $u_{ext} = 2$.

Finally, the proposed methodology allows us to obtain, by means of a relatively fast procedure, the same results as those obtained by means of a numerical simulation, which means a considerable saving of time, since, in some cases, depending on the discretisation of the problem used for the simulation and the time at which the solution is to be obtained, the calculation time can be large. On the other hand, the nondimensionalisation technique can be compared with other techniques used to obtain analytical solutions of linear and nonlinear differential equations such as the differential transformation method (DTM) [36]. This method is based on obtaining the analytical solution through the Taylor series expansion. One of the main differences between both methods is that when applying the DTM, the information provided by the nondimensionalisation technique is lost, since by grouping the variables into monomials with physical meaning, it is possible to determine the importance of each of the variables or to know which phenomenon predominates over the rest.

4. Conclusions

In this paper, the nondimensionalisation technique was applied to the problem of the Burgers–Huxley equation with Dirichlet and Neumann boundary conditions to obtain a universal solution and study the behaviour of the variables of the problem.

First, after applying the nondimensionalisation technique, it can be observed that for low values of the monomial π_2, the relationship between the diffusion and drag phenomena, very high values of π_1 are needed, the relationship between the time to reach a certain value in the medium and the diffusion phenomena. Thus, in this case, as the drag phenomenon predominates over the diffusion phenomenon, it becomes difficult to reach the required value in the medium because very large time values are required. This behaviour occurs for all the studied cases of π_3 and π_4, the relationship between the drag phenomenon and the generation or decay of species, and the relationship between the generation and decay coefficients of species, respectively. On the other hand, also for all cases of π_3 and π_4, from when π_2 takes a value between two and five, π_1 tends to take a value close to two; thus, from then on, the diffusion phenomenon predominates over the rest, which are practically negligible.

Regarding the validation of the proposed procedure for a universal solution to the proposed problem, several cases have been studied by comparing the results of this procedure with those obtained through simulation, observing that they are practically the same, and the difference may be due to errors in the application of the procedure. On the other hand, the methodology has been applied to a problem where the value of the boundary changes at a certain time, observing that the results are very similar.

Finally, as a strength of the work presented, it is worth highlighting that a simple methodology is presented that allows for universal solutions to various problems in science and engineering to be obtained. As a weakness, it is highlighted that for low values of the monomial π_2 the error in the proposed equations increases, because in these cases, the monomial π_1 tends to reach infinity.

Author Contributions: Conceptualisation, J.F.S.-P.; methodology, J.F.S.-P., F.M.-G., E.C., M.C., G.G.-R. and J.S.-R.; software, J.F.S.-P. and G.G.-R.; validation J.F.S.-P. and J.S.-R.; formal analysis, J.F.S.-P., F.M.-G., E.C., M.C., G.G.-R. and J.S.-R.; research, J.F.S.-P., F.M.-G., E.C., M.C., G.G.-R. and J.S.-R.; writing—original draft preparation, J.F.S.-P., F.M.-G., E.C., M.C., G.G.-R. and J.S.-R.; writing—review and editing, J.F.S.-P., F.M.-G., E.C., M.C., G.G.-R. and J.S.-R. All authors have read and agreed to the published version of the manuscript.

Funding: This research received no funding.

Data Availability Statement: Data are contained within the article.

Conflicts of Interest: The authors declare no conflict of interest.

References

1. Appadu, A.R.; Tijani, Y.O. 1D Generalised Burgers-Huxley: Proposed Solutions Revisited and Numerical Solution Using FTCS and NSFD Methods. *Front. Appl. Math. Stat.* **2022**, *7*, 1–14. [CrossRef]
2. Hashim, I.; Noorani, M.S.M.; Al-Hadidi, M.R.S. Solving the generalized Burgers-Huxley equation using the Adomian decomposition method. *Math Comput. Model* **2006**, *43*, 11–12. [CrossRef]
3. Wen, Y.; Chaolu, T. Study of Burgers–Huxley Equation Using Neural Network Method. *Axioms* **2023**, *12*, 429. [CrossRef]
4. Hemel, R.; Azam, M.T.; Alam, M.S. Numerical Method for Non-Linear Conservation Laws: Inviscid Burgers Equation. *J. Appl. Math. Phys.* **2021**, *9*, 1351–1363. [CrossRef]
5. Madrid, C.; Alhama, F. *Análisis Dimensional Discriminado en Mecánica de Fluidos y Transferencia de Calor*; Editorial Reverté: Barcelona, Spain, 2012.
6. Cengel, Y.A.; Cimbala, J.M. *Fluid Mechanics, Fundamentals and Applications*, 4th ed.; McGraw-Hill Education: New York, NY, USA, 2018; Volume 91, no. 5.
7. Bejan, A. *Convection Heat Transfer*; Wiley-Interscience: New York, NY, USA, 1984.
8. Bejan, A.; Kraus, A.D. *Heat Transfer Handbook*; John Wiley & Sons: Hoboken, NJ, USA, 2003; no. 3.
9. Kreith, F.; Manglik, R.M.; Bohn, M.S. *Principles of Heat Transfer*, 7th ed.; Cengage Learning: Boston, MA, USA, 1999; Volume 2.
10. Heinrich, B.; Hofmann, B.; Beck, J.V.; Blackwell, B.; St. Clair, C.R., Jr. Inverse Heat Conduction. Ill-Posed Problems. New York etc., J. Wiley & Sons 1985. XVII, 308 S., £ 46.00. ISBN 0-471-08319-4. ZAMM—*J. Appl. Math. Mech./Z. Angew. Math. Mech.* **1987**, *67*, 212–213. [CrossRef]
11. Fernández, C.F.G.; Alhama, F.; Sánchez, J.F.L.; Horno, J. Application of the network method to heat conduction processes with polynomial and potential-exponentially varying thermal properties. *Numeri. Heat Transf. A Appl.* **1998**, *33*, 549–559. [CrossRef]
12. Nigri, M.R.; Pedrosa-Filho, J.J.; Gama, R.M.S. An exact solution for the heat transfer process in infinite cylindrical fins with any temperature-dependent thermal conductivity. *Therm. Sci. Eng. Prog.* **2022**, *32*, 101333. [CrossRef]
13. Albani, R.A.S.; Duda, F.P.; Pimentel, L.C.G. On the modeling of atmospheric pollutant dispersion during a diurnal cycle: A finite element study. *Atmos. Environ.* **2015**, *118*, 19–27. [CrossRef]
14. Ku, J.Y.; Rao, S.T.; Rao, K.S. Numerical simulation of air pollution in urban areas: Model development. *Atmos. Environ.* **1987**, *21*, 201–212. [CrossRef]
15. Moradpour, M.; Afshin, H.; Farhanieh, B. A numerical investigation of reactive air pollutant dispersion in urban street canyons with tree planting. *Atmos. Pollut. Res.* **2017**, *8*, 253–266. [CrossRef]
16. Fenaux, M. Modelling of Chloride Transport in Non-Saturated Concrete: From Microscale to Macroscale. Ph.D. Thesis, E.T.S.I. Caminos, Canales y Puertos (UPM), Madrid, Spain, 2013.
17. Fenaux, M.M.C.; Reyes, E.; Moragues, A.; Gálvez, J.C. Modelling of chloride transport in non-saturated concrete. From microscale to macroscale. In Proceedings of the 8th International Conference on Fracture Mechanics of Concrete and Concrete Structures, FraMCoS 2013, Toledo, Spain, 10–14 March 2013.
18. Pradelle, S.; Thiéry, M.; Baroghel-Bouny, V. Comparison of existing chloride ingress models within concretes exposed to seawater. *Mater. Struct./Mater. Constr.* **2016**, *49*, 4497–4516. [CrossRef]
19. Guimarães, A.T.C.; Climent, M.A.; De Vera, G.; Vicente, F.J.; Rodrigues, F.T.; Andrade, C. Determination of chloride diffusivity through partially saturated Portland cement concrete by a simplified procedure. *Constr. Build. Mater.* **2011**, *25*, 785–790. [CrossRef]
20. Meijers, S.J.H.; Bijen, J.M.J.M.; De Borst, R.; Fraaij, A.L.A. Computational results of a model for chloride ingress in concrete including convection, drying-wetting cycles and carbonation. *Mater. Struct./Mater. Constr.* **2005**, *38*, 145–154. [CrossRef]
21. Nielsen, E.P.; Geiker, M.R. Chloride diffusion in partially saturated cementitious material. *Cem. Concr. Res.* **2003**, *33*, 133–138. [CrossRef]
22. Martín-Pérez, B.; Pantazopoulou, S.J.; Thomas, M.D.A. Numerical solution of mass transport equations in concrete structures. *Comput. Struct.* **2001**, *79*, 1251–1264. [CrossRef]
23. Fang, X.; Wen, J.; Bonello, B.; Yin, J.; Yu, D. Wave propagation in one-dimensional nonlinear acoustic metamaterials. *N. J. Phys.* **2017**, *19*, 053007. [CrossRef]
24. Sheng, P.; Fang, X.; Wen, J.; Yu, D. Vibration properties and optimized design of a nonlinear acoustic metamaterial beam. *J. Sound. Vib.* **2021**, *492*, 115739. [CrossRef]
25. Fu, L.; Li, J.; Yang, H.; Dong, H.; Han, X. Optical solitons in birefringent fibers with the generalized coupled space–time fractional non-linear Schrödinger equations. *Front. Phys.* **2023**, *11*, 1108505. [CrossRef]
26. Yasmin, H.; Aljahdaly, N.H.; Saeed, A.M.; Shah, R. Investigating Families of Soliton Solutions for the Complex Structured Coupled Fractional Biswas–Arshed Model in Birefringent Fibers Using a Novel Analytical Technique. *Fractal Fract.* **2023**, *7*, 491. [CrossRef]
27. Rodriguez, J.N.; Omel'yanov, G. General Degasperis-Procesi equation and its solitary wave solutions. *Chaos Solitons Fractals* **2019**, *118*, 41–46. [CrossRef]
28. Zhang, K.; Alshehry, A.S.; Aljahdaly, N.H.; Shah, R.; Shah, N.A.; Ali, M.R. Efficient computational approaches for fractional-order Degasperis-Procesi and Camassa–Holm equations. *Results Phys.* **2023**, *50*, 106549. [CrossRef]
29. Sánchez-Pérez, J.F.; Alhama, I. Universal curves for the solution of chlorides penetration in reinforced concrete, water-saturated structures with bound chloride. *Commun. Nonlinear Sci. Numer. Simul.* **2020**, *84*, 105201. [CrossRef]

30. Sánchez-Pérez, J.F.; García-Ros, G.; Conesa, M.; Castro, E.; Cánovas, M. Methodology to Obtain Universal Solutions for Systems of Coupled Ordinary Differential Equations. Examples of a Continuous Flow Chemical Reactor and a Coupled Oscillator. *Mathematics* **2023**, *11*, 2303. [CrossRef]
31. Conesa, M.; Sánchez-Pérez, J.F.; García-Ros, G.; Castro, E.; Valenzuela, J. Normalization Method as a Potent Tool for Grasping Linear and Nonlinear Systems in Physics and Soil Mechanics. *Mathematics* **2023**, *11*, 4321. [CrossRef]
32. Sánchez-Pérez, J.F.; Marín-García, F.; Castro, E.; García-Ros, G.; Conesa, M.; Solano-Ramírez, J. Methodology for Solving Engineering Problems of Burgers–Huxley Coupled with Symmetric Boundary Conditions by Means of the Network Simulation Method. *Symmetry* **2023**, *15*, 1740. [CrossRef]
33. Sánchez-Pérez, J.F.; Marín, F.; Morales, J.L.; Cánovas, M.; Alhama, F. Modeling and simulation of different and representative engineering problems using network simulation method. *PLoS ONE* **2018**, *13*, e0193828. [CrossRef]
34. Sánchez-Pérez, J.F.; Mascaraque-Ramírez, C.; Nicolás, J.A.M.; Castro, E.; Cánovas, M. Study of the application of PCM to thermal insulation of UUV hulls using Network Simulation Method. *Alex. Eng. J.* **2021**, *60*, 4627–4637. [CrossRef]
35. Sánchez-Pérez, J.F.; Alhama, F.; Moreno, J.A.; Cánovas, M. Study of main parameters affecting pitting corrosion in a basic medium using the network method. *Results Phys.* **2019**, *12*, 1015–1025. [CrossRef]
36. Hussin, C.H.C.; Mandangan, A.; Kilicman, A.; Daud, M.A.; Juhan, N. Differential transformation method for solving sixth-order boundary value problems of ordinary differential equations. *J. Teknol.* **2016**, *78*, 13–19. [CrossRef]

Disclaimer/Publisher's Note: The statements, opinions and data contained in all publications are solely those of the individual author(s) and contributor(s) and not of MDPI and/or the editor(s). MDPI and/or the editor(s) disclaim responsibility for any injury to people or property resulting from any ideas, methods, instructions or products referred to in the content.

Article

Dynamics Analysis of a Discrete-Time Commensalism Model with Additive Allee for the Host Species

Yanbo Chong [1], Ankur Jyoti Kashyap [2], Shangming Chen [1] and Fengde Chen [1,*]

[1] School of Mathematics and Statistics, Fuzhou University, Fuzhou 350108, China; 210320029@fzu.edu.cn (Y.C.); 210320019@fzu.edu.cn (S.C.)
[2] Department of Mathematics, Girijananda Chowdhury University, Guwahati 781017, Assam, India; ajkashyap.maths@gmail.com
* Correspondence: fdchen@fzu.edu.cn

Abstract: We propose and study a class of discrete-time commensalism systems with additive Allee effects on the host species. First, the single species with additive Allee effects is analyzed for existence and stability, then the existence of fixed points of discrete systems is given, and the local stability of fixed points is given by characteristic root analysis. Second, we used the center manifold theorem and bifurcation theory to study the bifurcation of a codimension of one of the system at non-hyperbolic fixed points, including flip, transcritical, pitchfork, and fold bifurcations. Furthermore, this paper used the hybrid chaos method to control the chaos that occurs in the flip bifurcation of the system. Finally, the analysis conclusions were verified by numerical simulations. Compared with the continuous system, the similarities are that both species' densities decrease with increasing Allee values under the weak Allee effect and that the host species hastens extinction under the strong Allee effect. Further, when the birth rate of the benefited species is low and the time is large enough, the benefited species will be locally asymptotically stabilized. Thus, our new finding is that both strong and weak Allee effects contribute to the stability of the benefited species under certain conditions.

Keywords: commensalism model; additive Allee; flip bifurcation; transcritical bifurcation; pitchfork bifurcation; fold bifurcation; chaos control

MSC: 92D25; 34D20

1. Introduction

Interactions between different species play a crucial role in shaping and maintaining balance within ecosystems. Interspecies interactions hold the potential to deliver mutual advantages, inflict harm, or yield no discernible impact on each of the participating species. These interactions are categorized by paired outcomes, symbolized as a positive, negative, or neutral result [1]. Commensal relationships, where one species gains a benefit while the other is unaffected, are often cited in the ecological literature, yet they receive surprisingly limited attention in research. In ecosystems, both commensalism and mutualism models involve positive interactions between populations. There is no harm in commensalism, in which one side is beneficial, while the other side is not beneficial and harmless.

A Belgian zoologist named Pierre-Joseph van Beneden was the pioneer in situating commensalism within a biological context. He contrasted commensalism with two other types of interactions: parasitism and mutualism [1]. In mutualism, species are interdependent and both benefit, while in commensalism, one species gains advantages without strong dependency or notable harm to the other. Despite its milder impact, commensalism adds complexity to ecological relationships and community organization. According to [2,3], depending on the population density, in some cases, the mutualism relationship shifts to a resemblance closer to commensalism, e.g., the relation among the carnivorous plant

Roridula dentata and hemipteran *Pameridae marlothii*. The larvae of midges and mosquitoes that live on pitcher plants exhibit a commensalism relationship. Midges, as upstream resource consumers, produce large quantities of bacteria and particles that contribute to the growth of mosquitoes. However, the experiments in [4] showed that mosquitoes do not affect midges. There is a symbiotic relationship between the two. Hari Prasad [5] pointed out that small green epiphytes that grow on other plants prepare themselves for survival by occupying the space of other plants to absorb the water and minerals that the roots obtain from the air. In turn, plants are unaffected. Squirrels burrow intooak trees for living space and food storage. Yet, the oak is neither beneficial nor harmful. To avoid it enemies, the clownfish will choose to hide in the tentacles of the sea anemone, and the tentacles are not affected by the clownfish, and so on.

From the standpoint of mathematical modeling, the investigation of the commensalism system was pioneered by Sun and Wei [6] in 2003. They were the first to explore this area using a two-species model. Over the past few years, an increasing number of researchers have directed their focus towards utilizing mathematical modeling methods to explore the commensalism model among populations (see [7–17] and the references therein). Afterwards, Han et al. [18] proposed a continuous time Lotka–Volterra-type commensalism system as follows:

$$\begin{cases} \dfrac{dx}{dt} = x(b_1 - a_{11}x) + a_{12}xy, \\ \dfrac{dy}{dt} = y(b_2 - a_{22}y), \end{cases} \quad (1)$$

where $x(0) > 0$, $y(0) > 0$ and $t \in [0, \infty)$. $x(t)$ and $y(t)$ denote the population densities of the commensal and host, respectively, at time t; b_1 and b_2 denote the intrinsic growth rates of the two species, respectively; a_{11} and a_{22} denote the intraspecific competition coefficient of the commensal and host; $a_{12} > 0$ denotes the coefficient of influence that the host produces in the commensal. We should notice that $b_1, a_{11}, a_{12}, b_2, a_{22}$ are positive constants. The authors' study showed that Model (1) has a globally stable coexistence fixed point. Next, feedback control is considered by adding control variables. The results showed that the position of the coexistence fixed point is altered without affecting its global steady-state properties.

After that, many scholars began to consider the effects of various factors based on the system (1) and analyze the dynamic behaviors of the corresponding systems, for example periodic solutions [19,20], harvesting [21–25], the Allee effect [26–28], and delay [29,30]. In [19], the authors investigated a modified commensal symbiosis model with Michaelis–Menten-type harvesting and observed positive periodic solutions. In [20], Chen et al. presented another discrete commensal symbiosis model with a Hassell–Varley-type functional response. Their study revealed a positive periodic solution of the system, which is both locally and globally stable. Considering a Lotka–Volterra-type commensal model subject to the Allee effect on the unaffected species, which occurs at a low population density, Xinyu Guan [27] observed that the Allee effect has no influence on the final densities of the unaffected species and the benefited species. The study involved numerical simulations that demonstrated a considerable elongation in the time required for the system subjected to an Allee effect to attain its stable steady-state solution, implying that the Allee effect has an unstable effect on the system. In [28], the authors explored a discrete-time commensal symbiosis model and observed period-doubling bifurcation phenomenon around the interior equilibrium state.

According to previous studies by W.C. Allee, population density has a positive impact on reproduction in a wide range of terrestrial and aquatic species. It could potentially contribute to the prolonged survival of the species in unfavorable environments and provide increased protection against harmful substances [31,32]. When the population density drops below a specific threshold or when the population is too diminutive, the task of finding a mate can become more challenging. Similarly, in species where group activities such as fending off predators or searching for sustenance are impeded due to low population densities, these activities become less proficient. This positive correlation between population size and individual fitness is termed the Allee effect. In the past few years, populations from various ecosystems have become low or even at risk of becoming endangered due to escalating human predation, heightened occurrences of natural disasters, and rising global temperatures. In such situations, the populations may have trouble mating, foraging, and fending off natural enemies. Previous mathematical studies have shown that Allees add more complexity to the system's dynamic behavior [33,34]. In 2022, He et al. [11] proposed the following continuous-time commensalism system incorporating an additive Allee to the host:

$$\begin{cases} \dfrac{dx}{dt} = x(r - bx) + cxy, \\ \dfrac{dy}{dt} = y\left(d - ey - \dfrac{m}{y+a}\right), \end{cases} \quad (2)$$

where all of the parameters are positive constants and initial values are $x(0) > 0, y(0) > 0$, and $t \in [0, \infty)$, the same as the previous definition in [11]. He et al. [11] gave the existence and local stability of equilibrium points, then proved that, under suitable conditions, $E_r(\frac{r}{b}, 0)$ and $E_1^*(x_1^*, y_1)$ are globally asymptotically stable, respectively. There are saddle-node bifurcation at $E_3^*(x_3^*, y_3)$, $E_3(0, y_3)$ and transcritical bifurcation at $E_0(0,0)$, $E_r(\frac{r}{b}, 0)$, respectively.

In recent years, discrete-time systems have also been one of the hotspots of scholars' research. The reason is that populations with non-overlapping generations are better described by difference equations, which are also easier to simulate numerically. Discrete-time systems also have more topological classifications and bifurcations at fixed points than corresponding continuous-time systems, with a codimension of one, such as flip, transcritical, pitchfork, fold, and Neimark–Sacker bifurcations, and a codimension of two, such as 1:1 and 1:2, and fold–flip bifurcations, e.g., [35–41]. To the best of the authors' knowledge, limited research has been conducted on discrete models incorporating additive Allee effects, highlighting an ongoing need for such investigations. In this work, we explored the qualitative behavior of the continuous-time commensal model (2) by converting it into a discrete-time model.

Transformation is the first step in reducing the parameters, and it uses $x = \frac{d}{b}\bar{x}$, $y = \frac{d}{e}\bar{y}$, $t = \frac{\tau}{d}$. Then, the bars are removed, and System (2) can be transformed as

$$\begin{cases} \dfrac{dx}{d\tau} = x(\alpha - x + \beta y), \\ \dfrac{dy}{d\tau} = y\left(1 - y - \dfrac{M}{y+A}\right), \end{cases} \quad (3)$$

where $\alpha = \frac{r}{d}$, $\beta = \frac{c}{e}$, $M = \frac{me}{d^2}$, and $A = \frac{ae}{d}$. The initial value is $x(0) > 0, y(0) > 0$ and $\tau \in [0, \infty)$. By using the piecewise constant parameter method [42] to discretize the system (3), we have

$$\begin{cases} \dfrac{1}{x(\tau)} \dfrac{dx}{d\tau} = \alpha - x([\tau]) + \beta y([\tau]), \\ \dfrac{1}{y(\tau)} \dfrac{dy}{d\tau} = 1 - y([\tau]) - \dfrac{M}{y([\tau]) + A'} \end{cases} \quad (4)$$

where $0 \leq n \leq \tau < n+1$ and $[\tau]$ is the round-down function. First, the simple rounding function operation can be used to determine that the right-hand side of the ordinary differential Equation (4) is a constant value, when other parameters are fixed. Secondly, the integral of the interval n to τ is performed on both sides of the equation at the same time, and when τ tends to $n+1$, the following is acquired:

$$\begin{cases} \ln \dfrac{x(n+1)}{x(n)} = \alpha - x(n) + \beta y(n), \\ \ln \dfrac{y(n+1)}{y(n)} = 1 - y(n) - \dfrac{M}{y(n)+A}, \end{cases}$$

for $n = \{0, 1, 2, ...\}$, so we obtain the following a discrete-time commensalism mode with the additive Allee effect for the host species:

$$\begin{cases} x_{n+1} = x_n \exp(\alpha - x_n + \beta y_n), \\ y_{n+1} = y_n \exp\left(1 - y_n - \dfrac{M}{y_n + A}\right), \end{cases}$$

where $x(n) := x_n$ and $y(n) := y_n$, $n = \{0, 1, 2, ...\}$.

The discrete-time commensalism system is now defined by mapping

$$F : \begin{pmatrix} x \\ y \end{pmatrix} \to \begin{pmatrix} x \exp(\alpha - x + \beta y) \\ y \exp\left(1 - y - \frac{M}{y+A}\right) \end{pmatrix}. \tag{5}$$

Then, the discrete-time single-species mode with the additive Allee is expressed as

$$f : y \to y \exp\left(1 - y - \dfrac{M}{y+A}\right), \tag{6}$$

where $\frac{M}{y+A}$ represents the additive Allee. The Allee effect in the map (5) and the map (6) is weak when $0 < M < A$. The Allee effect in the map (5) and the map (6) is strong when $M > A$.

In this paper, Section 2 provides the existence and local stability of the map (6) at fixed points. Then, Section 3 provides the existence and local stability of the map (5) at fixed points. Section 3.3 gives the bifurcation of different types of a codimension of one under certain conditionals including flip, fold, transcritical, and pitchfork bifurcations. Moreover, Section 3.4 provides a chaos-control system for the occurrence of chaos due to bifurcation. Finally, the correctness of the numerical simulations verifies the conclusions.

2. Dynamics Analysis of Map (6)

2.1. The Existence of Fixed Point

The fixed points of the map (6) satisfy the equations as follows:

$$y = y \exp\left(1 - y - \dfrac{M}{y+A}\right).$$

Obviously, 0 is a trivial fixed point of the map (6). Further, the positive fixed point of the map (6) needs to solve $1 - y - \frac{M}{y+A} = 0$, and we can obtain the following equation with the same solution through simplification:

$$G(y) = y^2 + (A-1)y + M - A = 0. \tag{7}$$

Let $\triangle(M)$ be the discriminant function of $G(y)$, then, according to the discriminant formula of the quadratic function, we have

$$\triangle(M) = (A-1)^2 - 4(M-A) = (A+1)^2 - 4M.$$

Let M^* be the zero point of $\triangle(M)$, then

$$M^* = \frac{(A+1)^2}{4} \geq A.$$

Thus, if $0 < M < M^*$, $\triangle(M) > 0$, then (7) has two roots of $y_1 = \frac{1-A-\sqrt{\triangle}}{2}$ and $y_2 = \frac{1-A+\sqrt{\triangle}}{2}$; if $M = M^*$, $\triangle(M) = 0$, then (7) has a double-root denoted by $y_3 = \frac{1-A}{2}$; when $M > M^*$, $\triangle(M) < 0$, then (7) has no root. Then, we obtain the following result.

Theorem 1. *The map always has a fixed point 0, regardless of how the parameters are altered in the map (6). The parameter requirements for the existence of positive fixed points are then stated:*

(1) (Case 1 : $0 < M < A$, i.e., weak Allee) Existence of a positive fixed point y_2 in the map (6).
(2) (Case 2 : $M = A$).

  (i) Map (6) has a positive fixed point y_2 if $0 < A < 1$.
  (ii) Map (6) has no other fixed point if $A \geq 1$.

(3) (Case 3 : $M > A$, i.e., strong Allee).

  (i) Map (6) has two positive fixed points y_1 and y_2 if and only if $0 < A < 1$ and $M < M^*$.
  (ii) Map (6) has a positive fixed point y_3 if and only if $0 < A < 1$ and $M = M^*$.
  (iii) Map (6) has no other fixed point if either ($0 < A < 1$ and $M > M^*$) or $A \geq 1$.

2.2. The Stability of Fixed Points $0, y_1, y_2,$ and y_3

Firstly, it is easy to see that the map (6) at a fixed point y satisfies

$$\frac{df}{dy} = \left(1 + y\left(-1 + \frac{M}{(y+A)^2}\right)\right)\exp\left(1 - y - \frac{M}{y+A}\right).$$

Then, by a simple computation, we have

$$\frac{df}{dy}(0) = \exp\left(1 - \frac{M}{A}\right),$$

$$\frac{df}{dy}(y_i) = 1 + y_i\left(-1 + \frac{M}{(y_i+A)^2}\right) \quad i = 1,2,3.$$

So, when $0 < M < A$, $\frac{df}{dy}(0) > 1$, the trivial fixed point 0 is a source; when $M > A$, $\frac{df}{dy}(0) \in (0,1)$, the trivial fixed point 0 is a sink that is locally asymptotically stable; when $M = A$, $\frac{df}{dy}(0) = 1$, the trivial fixed point 0 is non-hyperbolic.

Secondly, according to Theorem 1, if the positive fixed point $y_i, i = 1,2,3$ exists, we can obtain

$$\frac{df}{dy}(y_i) = 1 + y_i\left(-1 + \frac{M}{(y_i+A)^2}\right)$$

$$= 1 - \left(1 - \frac{M}{y_i+A}\right) + \frac{My_i}{(y_i+A)^2}$$

$$= \frac{M(A+2y_i)}{(y_i+A)^2},$$

and then,

$$\frac{d}{dy_i}\left(\frac{df}{dy}(y_i)\right) = -\frac{2My_i}{(y_i+A)^3} < 0.$$

Thus, it follows that y_i is a rigorously decreasing function of $\frac{df}{dy}(y_i)$. From Theorem 1, when $M = M^*$ and $A \in (0, 1)$, there is a positive fixed point y_3. By a direct computation, we have

$$\frac{df}{dy}(y_3) = \frac{M^*(A + 2y_3)}{(y_3 + A)^2} = 1.$$

Furthermore, it is possible to verify $y_1 < y_3 < y_2$. Namely, $\frac{df}{dy}(y_1) > 1 > \frac{df}{dy}(y_2)$. Hence, the positive fixed point y_1 is always the source; the positive fixed point y_3 is always non-hyperbolic.

Now, in order to compare $\frac{df}{dy}(y_2)$ to -1, we have

$$\frac{df}{dy}(y_2) - (-1) = 2 + y_2 \left(-1 + \frac{M}{(y_2 + A)^2}\right)$$

$$= \frac{M(A + 2y_2)}{(y_2 + A)^2} + 1 > 0.$$

So, by the above analysis, the positive fixed point y_2 is a sink. Thus, we have the following result.

Theorem 2. *When $M < A$, i.e., a weak Allee, or ($M = A$ and $0 < A < 1$), the map (6) has a unique positive fixed point y_2 that is globally asymptotically stable.*

Proof. From Theorem 1(1) and (2)(i), the map (6) has a unique positive fixed point y_2. Firstly, let $f(y) = y \exp\left(1 - y - \frac{M}{y+A}\right)$. Then, let us construct a Lyapunov function as

$$V(y) = \frac{1}{2}\left(y^2 - y_2^2\right) - y_2^2 \ln \frac{y}{y_2}.$$

Then, find the first derivative of $V(y)$. We can obtain

$$\frac{d(V(y))}{dy} = y - \frac{y_2^2}{y}$$

$$= \frac{(y + y_2)(y - y_2)}{y},$$

then, if $0 < y < y_2$, $\frac{d(V(y))}{dy} < 0$, then $V(y)$ is strictly monotonically decreasing with respect to y; if $y > y_2$, $\frac{d(V(y))}{dy} > 0$, then $V(y)$ is an increasing function with respect to y. Thus, $V(y)$ has a minimum value $V(y_2) = 0$. Obviously, $V(y)$ is positive definite for any $y > 0$ and for $y \neq y_2$.

$V(y)$ derives the solution of the map (6), and we have:

$$\Delta V(y) = V(f(y)) - V(y)$$

$$= \frac{1}{2}\left(f^2(y) - y_2^2\right) - y_2^2 \ln \frac{f(y)}{y_2} - \left[\frac{1}{2}\left(y^2 - y_2^2\right) - y_2^2 \ln \frac{y}{y_2}\right]$$

$$= \frac{1}{2}\left\{\left[y \exp\left(1 - y - \frac{M}{y+A}\right)\right]^2 - y_2^2\right\} - y_2^2 \ln \frac{y \exp\left(1 - y - \frac{M}{y+A}\right)}{y_2}$$

$$- \left[\frac{1}{2}\left(y^2 - y_2^2\right) - y_2^2 \ln \frac{y}{y_2}\right]$$

$$= \frac{1}{2}y^2\left\{\exp\left[2\left(1 - y - \frac{M}{A+y}\right)\right] - 1\right\} - y_2^2\left(1 - y - \frac{M}{A+y}\right).$$

To prove that the map (6) is globally stable is to prove that $\Delta V(y)$ is negative definite for all $y > 0$ and for $y \neq y_2$. To test this condition, we require that $\Delta V(y)$ has a unique global maximum at $y = y_2$, which is difficult to prove using pure analysis. For the specific parameter, this can often be performed computationally; first, we consider whether $y = y_2$ is the local maximum of $\Delta V(y)$, and we calculate:

$$\frac{d(\Delta V(y))}{dy} = y\left\{\exp\left[2\left(1 - y - \frac{M}{A+y}\right)\right] - 1\right\} - y_2^2\left(-1 + \frac{M}{(A+y)^2}\right)$$
$$+ y^2 \exp\left[2\left(1 - y - \frac{M}{A+y}\right)\right]\left(-1 + \frac{M}{(A+y)^2}\right)$$
$$= 0, \quad \text{if } y = y_2,$$

$$\frac{d^2(\Delta V(y))}{dy^2} = \exp\left[2\left(1 - y - \frac{M}{A+y}\right)\right] - 1 - \frac{2y^2 M}{(A+y)^3}\exp\left[2\left(1 - y - \frac{M}{A+y}\right)\right]$$
$$+ 2y^2 \exp\left[2\left(1 - y - \frac{M}{A+y}\right)\right]\left(-1 + \frac{M}{(A+y)^2}\right)^2$$
$$+ 4y \exp\left[2\left(1 - y - \frac{M}{A+y}\right)\right]\left(-1 + \frac{M}{(A+y)^2}\right) + \frac{2y_2^2 M}{(A+y)^3}$$
$$= 2y_2\left(-1 + \frac{M}{(A+y_2)^2}\right)\left[2 + y_2\left(-1 + \frac{M}{(A+y_2)^2}\right)\right] \quad \text{if } y = y_2,$$
$$= 2\left(\frac{df}{dy}(y_2) - 1\right)\left(\frac{df}{dy}(y_2) + 1\right) \quad \text{if } y = y_2,$$
$$< 0 \quad \text{if } y = y_2.$$

Hence, if $M < A$ or $M = A$ and $0 < A < 1$, there is a unique positive fixed point y_2, and $\Delta V(y)$ has global maximum at $y = y_2$. Then, Theorem 2 is proven. $\square$

Moreover, when $M = 1$, $A = 4$ and $y \in (0, 2.5)$, then V and $\Delta V(y)$ are drawn by calculation in Figure 1. Obviously, $\Delta V(y)$ is negative definite.

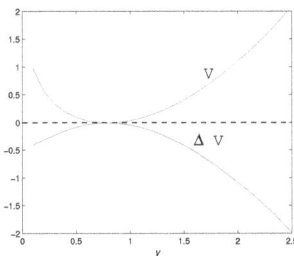

Figure 1. V and $\Delta V(y)$ function with $M = 1$, $A = 4$ and $y \in [0, 2.5]$.

Theorem 3. *(The case of a strong Allee, i.e., $M > A$) Let y be a solution of the map (6) and the initial value $y(0) > 0$. Then, we have:*

(1) *When $M < M^*$ and $0 < A < 1$, the map (6) has two positive fixed points y_1 and y_2:*
   (i) *If $0 < y(0) < y_1$, then $\lim\limits_{n \to \infty} y(n) = 0$.*
   (ii) *If $y_1 < y(0)$, then $\lim\limits_{n \to \infty} y(n) = y_2$.*

(2) *Moreover, when $M = M^*$ and $0 < A < 1$:*
   (i) *If $0 < y(0) < y_3$, then $\lim\limits_{n \to \infty} y(n) = 0$.*
   (ii) *If $y_3 < y(0)$, then $\lim\limits_{n \to \infty} y(n) = y_3$.*

(3) *When $M^* < M$ and $0 < A < 1$ or $A \geq 1$, then $\lim\limits_{n \to \infty} y(n) = 0$.*

Proof. Map (6) can be simplified as follows:

$$y \to y \exp\left(1 - y - \frac{M}{y+A}\right)$$
$$\to y \exp\left[\frac{1}{y+A}\left(-y^2 - (A-1)y + A - M\right)\right]$$
$$\to y \exp\left(\frac{Q(y)}{y+A}\right),$$

where $Q(y) := -y^2 - (A-1)y + A - M$. Further, when $A < M < M^*$ and $0 < A < 1$, if $y_2 > y(0) > y_1$, we have $Q(y) > 0$, then $y_2 > f(y) > y$ (in Figure 2b,d); if $y(0) > y_2$, i.e., $Q(y) < 0$, then $y > f(y) > y_2$ (in Figure 2a,b,d). Thus, if $y(0) > y_1$, the fixed point y_2 is globally asymptotically stable. In other cases, if $A < M < M^*$, $0 < A < 1$, and $0 < y(0) < y_1$, i.e., $Q(y) < 0$, then $0 < f(y) < y$ (in Figure 2c). When $M = M^*$ and $0 < A < 1$, i.e., $Q(y) \le 0$, then, if $0 < y(0) < y_3$, $0 < f(y) < y$ (in Figure 2f); if $y_3 < y(0)$, then $y_3 < f(y) < y$ (in Figure 2e). When $M > M^*$ and $0 < A < 1$ or $M > A$ and $A \ge 1$, i.e., $Q(y) < 0$, then $0 < f(y) < y$ (in Figure 2g,h). Then, the result follows. □

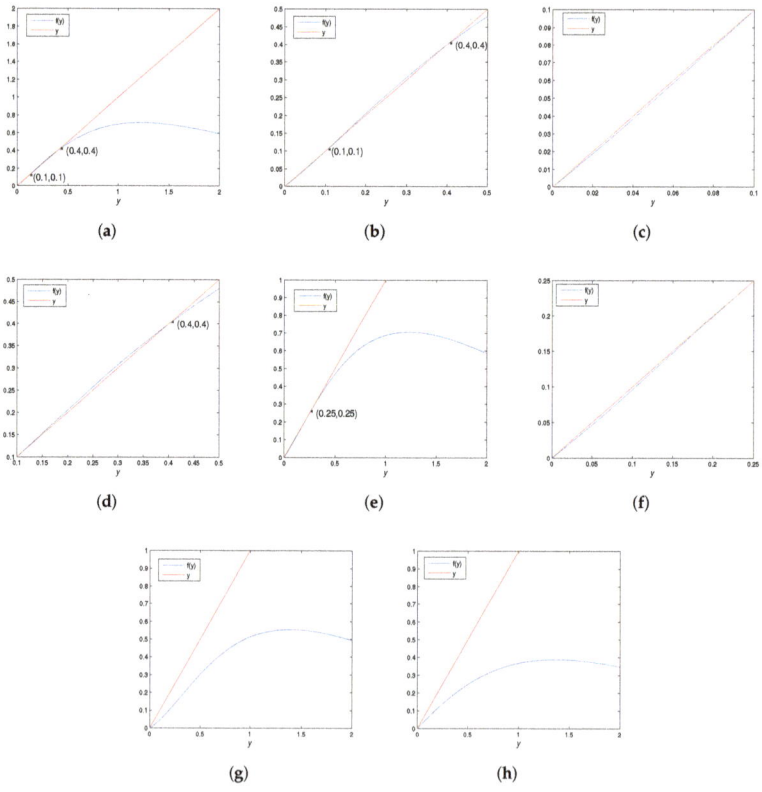

Figure 2. Positive fixed point existence diagram for map (6). (**a**) If $M = 0.54$, $A = 0.5$, the map (6) has two positive fixed points $y_1 = 0.1$, $y_2 = 0.4$. (**b**–**d**) Local diagrams with $y \in [0, 0.5]$, $y \in [0, 0.1]$ and $y \in [0.1, 0.5]$ corresponding to (**a**), respectively. (**e**) If $M = 0.5625$, $A = 0.5$, the map (6) has a unique positive fixed point $y_3 = 0.25$. (**f**) Local diagrams with $y \in [0, 0.25]$ corresponding to (**e**), respectively. (**g**) If $M = 1$, $A = 0.5$, the map (6) has no positive fixed point. (**h**) If $M = 3$, $A = 2$, the map (6) also has no positive fixed point.

Table 1 gives the above analysis.

Table 1. Fixed point of the map (6).

Parameter Conditions		Existence	Stability
$0 < M < A$		$0, y_2$	0 source, y_2 sink
$M = A$	$0 < A < 1$	$0, y_2$	0 non-hyperbolic, y_2 sink
	$A \geq 1$	0	0 non-hyperbolic
$A < M < M^*$	$0 < A < 1$	$0, y_1, y_2$	0 sink, y_1 source, y_2 sink
	$A \geq 1$	0	0 sink
$M = M^*$	$0 < A < 1$	y_3	0 sink, y_3 non-hyperbolic
	$A \geq 1$	0	0 sink
$M > M^*$		0	0 sink

3. Dynamics Analysis of Map (5)

3.1. Existence and Local Stability of Fixed Points

The fixed points of the map (5) satisfy the equations as follows:

$$\begin{cases} x = x \exp(\alpha - x + \beta y), \\ y = y \exp\left(1 - y - \frac{M}{y+A}\right). \end{cases}$$

Obviously, $E_0(0,0)$ and $E_1(\alpha, 0)$ are two boundary fixed points of the map (5). Further, the other fixed points of the map (5) are summed up in Table 2. Let $E_{2i}(0, y_i)$, $i = 1, 2, 3$ be the boundary fixed point of the extinction of the commensal species and $E^*_{3i}(x^*_i, y_i)$, $i = 1, 2, 3$ be the fixed points of the coexistence of the two populations, where $x^*_i = \alpha + \beta y_i$.

Table 2. Boundary and positive fixed point of the map (5)'s existence.

Parameter Conditions		Existence
$0 < M < A$		E_{22}, E^*_{32}
$M = A$	$0 < A < 1$	E_{22}, E^*_{32}
	$A \geq 1$	no other fixed points
$A < M < M^*$	$0 < A < 1$	$E_{21}, E_{22}, E^*_{31}, E^*_{32}$
	$A \geq 1$	no other fixed points
$M = M^*$	$0 < A < 1$	E_{23}, E^*_{33}
	$A \geq 1$	no other fixed points
$M > M^*$		no other fixed points

Remark 1. *To prepare for the prospect of bifurcations, we offer the following observations:*
(1) *If $M = M^*$ and $0 < A < 1$, then $y_1 = 0$, $y_2 = 1 - A > 0$;*
(2) *If $A = 1$ and $0 < M < M^* = A$, then $y_1 < 0$, $y_2 = \sqrt{1 - M} > 0$;*
(3) *If $A = 1$ and $M = M^* = A$, then $y_1 = y_2 = y_3 = 0$.*

At any fixed point $E(x, y)$, the Jacobian matrix of the map (5) is given as

$$J(E) = \begin{pmatrix} (1-x)\Gamma_1 & \beta x \Gamma_1 \\ 0 & \Gamma_2 \end{pmatrix},$$

where $\Gamma_1 = \exp(\alpha - x - \beta y)$, $\Gamma_2 = \left(1 + y\left(-1 + \frac{M}{(y+A)^2}\right)\right)\exp\left(1 - y - \frac{M}{y+A}\right)$. Let the eigenvalues of the matrix $J(E)$ be λ_1 and λ_2.

We classify fixed points topologically and examine their local stability by [43].

Definition 1. *A fixed point $E(x,y)$ of the map (5) is called:*

(1) *A sink if $|\lambda_1| < 1$ and $|\lambda_2| < 1$, and it is locally asymptotically stable;*
(2) *A source if $|\lambda_1| > 1$ and $|\lambda_2| > 1$, and it is unstable;*
(3) *A saddle if $|\lambda_1| > 1$ and $|\lambda_2| < 1$ (or $|\lambda_1| < 1$ and $|\lambda_2| > 1$);*
(4) *Non-hyperbolic if either $|\lambda_1| = 1$ or $|\lambda_2| = 1$.*

Now, using Definition 1, we topologically categorize fixed points and discuss their local stability.

Note that, when $M = 0$,

$$J(E_0) = \begin{pmatrix} e^\alpha & 0 \\ 0 & e \end{pmatrix}, \quad J(E_1) = \begin{pmatrix} 1 - \alpha & \alpha\beta \\ 0 & e \end{pmatrix},$$

and for the case $M > 0$,

$$J(E_0) = \begin{pmatrix} e^\alpha & 0 \\ 0 & e^{1-\frac{M}{A}} \end{pmatrix}, \quad J(E_1) = \begin{pmatrix} 1 - \alpha & \alpha\beta \\ 0 & e^{1-\frac{M}{A}} \end{pmatrix}.$$

Thus, the following conclusion can be drawn.

Theorem 4. *Assume that $M = 0$, and we have the following description:*

(1) *$E_0(0,0)$ is always a source since two eigenvalues are $e^\alpha > 1$ and $e > 1$.*
(2) *Two eigenvalues of $E_1(\alpha, 0)$ are $1 - \alpha < 1$ and $e > 1$. Then, $E_1(\alpha, 0)$ is:*
   (i) *A saddle when $0 < \alpha < 2$;*
   (ii) *A source when $\alpha > 2$;*
   (iii) *Non-hyperbolic when $\alpha = 2$.*

By Theorem 4(iii), the two eigenvalues of $J(E_1)$ are $\lambda_1 = -1, \lambda_2 = e$; hence, E_1 is non-hyperbolic. The conditions that satisfy Theorem 4(iii) for the set Ω_{E_f} are written as follows:

$$\Omega_{E_f} = \{(\alpha, \beta) \in \mathbb{R}^2 : \alpha = 2, \beta > 0\}.$$

Choose the bifurcation parameter α, and set it to $\alpha = 2 + \rho$. A suitably tiny perturbation term is ρ. According to a quick calculation, the center manifold of the map (5) in Ω_{E_f} is $y = 0$. In this instance, the map (5) may be expressed as $x \to -x - \rho x + \frac{1}{6}x^3 + \frac{1}{2}\rho x^2 + O((|x| + |\rho|)^3)$. As a result, at E_1, a flip bifurcation is formed.

Figure 3 depicts the bifurcation diagram of the numerical simulation for $\beta = 0$, $\alpha \in [0, 4]$, and $x \in [0, 20]$. Figure 3 shows that, when $0 < \alpha < 2$, the shape of the map (5) is stable; when $\alpha > 2$, the map (5) turns over due to instability and provides stable biperiodic solutions. A chaotic set is produced as α rises.

Theorem 5. *Assume that $M > 0$; in this case, the two eigenvalues of the map (5) at fixed point $E_0(0,0)$ are e^α and $e^{1-\frac{A}{M}}$, then $E_0(0,0)$ is:*

(1) *A source if $0 < M < A$;*
(2) *A saddle if $M > A$;*
(3) *Non-hyperbolic if $M = A$.*

Theorem 6. *The two eigenvalues of the map (5) at the fixed point $E_1(\alpha, 0)$ are $1 - \alpha$ and $e^{1-\frac{A}{M}}$; consequently, $E_1(\alpha, 0)$ is:*

(1) A sink if and only if $0 < \alpha < 2$ and $M > A$;
(2) A source if and only if $\alpha > 2$ and $0 < M < A$;
(3) A saddle if and only if $0 < \alpha < 2$ and $0 < M < A$ or $\alpha > 2$ and $M > A$;
(4) Non-hyperbolic if $M = A$ or $\alpha = 2$.

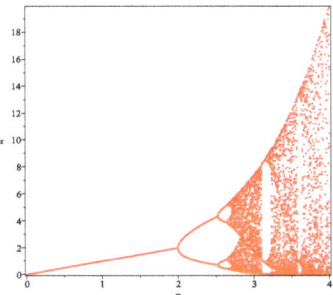

Figure 3. Flip bifurcation diagrams of commensal species at initial value $(x_0, y_0) = (0.5, 0.3)$ with $M = 0$ and $\alpha \in [0, 4]$.

Proof. At the boundary fixed point $E_1(\alpha, 0)$, whose eigenvalues are $1 - \alpha < 1$ and $e^{1-\frac{A}{M}} > 0$, it is simple to see that

$$1 - \alpha \begin{cases} > -1 & \text{if } 0 < \alpha < 2, \\ = -1 & \text{if } \alpha = 2, \\ < -1 & \text{if } \alpha > 2. \end{cases}$$

and

$$e^{1-\frac{A}{M}} \begin{cases} > 1 & \text{if } 0 < M < A, \\ = 1 & \text{if } M = A, \\ \in (0, 1) & \text{if } M > A. \end{cases}$$

Then, the result follows. □

Figure 4 displays the topological classification of the map (5) at boundary fixed point $E_1(\alpha, 0)$ when $\beta = 1$, $A = 1.5$, $\alpha \in [0, 4]$, and $M \in [0, 3]$.

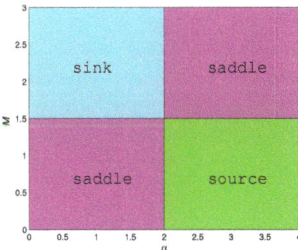

Figure 4. Topological classification at $E_1(\alpha, 0)$ with $\beta = 1$, $A = 1.5$, $\alpha \in [0, 4]$, and $M \in [0, 3]$.

Now, we give the Jacobian matrix of the map (5) at the boundary fixed points $E_{2i}(0, y_i)$ ($i = 1, 2, 3$) as follows:

$$J(E_{2i}) = \begin{pmatrix} e^{\alpha + \beta y_i} & 0 \\ 0 & J_i \end{pmatrix},$$

where $J_i = 1 + y_i\left(-1 + \frac{M}{(y_i + A)^2}\right)$. Clearly, the two eigenvalues of $J(E_{2i})$ are $e^{\alpha + \beta y_i} > 1$ and J_i. Note that J_i was analyzed in Section 2.2. Then, we have $J_1 > 1$, $J_2 \in (-1, 1)$ and $J_3 = 1$. Thus, we obtain the following conclusions:

Theorem 7. (1) When $A < M < M^*$ and $0 < A < 1$, the boundary fixed point E_{21} exists in the map (5), and the eigenvalues of $J(E_{21})$ are $e^{\alpha+\beta y_1} > 1$ and $J_1 > 1$. So, the fixed point E_{21} is always a source.
(2) When the boundary fixed point E_{22} exists, the eigenvalues of $J(E_{22})$ are $e^{\alpha+\beta y_2} > 1$ and $|J_2| < 1$. So, the fixed point E_{22} is always a saddle.
(3) When $M = M^*$ and $0 < A < 1$, the boundary fixed point E_{23} exists in the map (5), and the eigenvalues of $J(E_{23})$ are $e^{\alpha+\beta y_3} > 1$ and $J_3 = 1$. Consequently, E_{23} is always non-hyperbolic.

Next, the Jacobian matrix at positive points $E_{3i}^*(x_i^*, y_i)(i = 1, 2, 3)$ is obtained as

$$J(E_{3i}^*) = \begin{pmatrix} 1 - x_i^* & \beta x_i^* \\ 0 & J_i \end{pmatrix},$$

where $x_i^* = \alpha + \beta y_i$, whose eigenvalues are $1 - x_i^* < 1$, and J_i was analyzed above. Then, we obtain

$$1 - x_i^* \begin{cases} > -1 & \text{if } 0 < x_i^* < 2, \\ = -1 & \text{if } x_i^* = 2, \\ < -1 & \text{if } x_i^* > 2. \end{cases}$$

This is equivalent to the following two situations.
(1) If $0 < \alpha < 2$, we have

$$x_i^* \begin{cases} < 2 & \text{if } 0 < \beta < \beta_i^*, \\ = 2 & \text{if } \beta = \beta_i^*, \\ > 2 & \text{if } \beta > \beta_i^*. \end{cases}$$

where $\beta_i^* = \frac{2-\alpha}{y_i}, (i = 1, 2, 3)$.
(2) If $\alpha \geq 2$, we have $1 - x_i^* < -1$, which is equivalent to $x_i^* > 2$.

As a consequence of the above analysis, we have:

Theorem 8. (1) When $E_{31}^*(x_{31}^*, y_1)$ exists, it is:
(i) A saddle if and only if $0 < \alpha < 2$ and $0 < \beta < \beta_1^*$;
(ii) A source if and only if $0 < \alpha < 2$ and $\beta > \beta_1^*$ or $\alpha > 2$;
(iii) Non-hyperbolic if and only if $0 < \alpha < 2$ and $\beta = \beta_1^*$, where $\beta_1^* = \frac{2-\alpha}{y_1}$.

(2) When $E_{32}^*(x_{32}^*, y_2)$ exists, it is:
(i) A sink if and only if $0 < \alpha < 2$ and $0 < \beta < \beta_2^*$;
(ii) A saddle if and only if $0 < \alpha < 2$ and $\beta > \beta_2^*$ or $\alpha > 2$;
(iii) Non-hyperbolic if and only if $0 < \alpha < 2$ and $\beta = \beta_2^*$, where $\beta_2^* = \frac{2-\alpha}{y_2}$.

(3) When $E_{33}^*(x_{33}^*, y_3)$ exists and $0 < \alpha < 2$, it is always non-hyperbolic, where $\beta_3^* = \frac{2-\alpha}{y_3}$.

When $M = 0.52$, $A = 0.45$, $\alpha \in [0, 4]$ and $\beta_i^* \in [0, 10]$, Figure 5 shows the topological classification of the map (5) at positive fixed points $E_{3i}(x_i^*, y_i)(i = 1, 2)$.

3.2. Global Stability of Positive Fixed Point E_{32}^*

Firstly, we give two lemmas in [37].

Lemma 1. Suppose that the sequences $x(n)$ satisfy $x(n) > 0$ and

$$x(n+1) \leq x(n) \exp(a - bx(n)), n \in \mathbb{N},$$

where a and b are positive constants. Then,

$$\limsup_{n \to +\infty} x(n) \leq \frac{\exp(a - 1)}{b} := M.$$

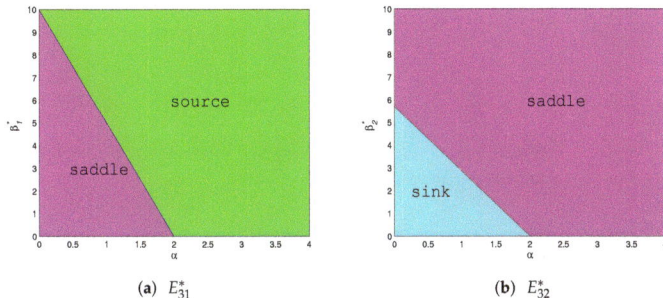

(a) E^*_{31} (b) E^*_{32}

Figure 5. Topological classification of the $\alpha - \beta^*_i$ plane at $E_{3i}(x^*_i, y_i)$ with $M = 0.52, A = 0.45$, $\alpha \in [0, 4]$, and $\beta^*_i \in [0, 10]$, $(i = 1, 2)$.

Lemma 2. *Suppose that the sequences $x(n)$ satisfy $x(n) > 0$ and*

$$x(n+1) \geq x(n) \exp(a - bx(n)), n \in \mathbb{N},$$

where a and b are positive constants. Then,

$$\liminf_{n \to +\infty} x(n) \geq \frac{a}{b} \exp(a - bM),$$

where M was given by Lemma 2.

Secondly, from Theorem 2, we obtain that, if $0 < M < A$ or $M = A, 0 < A < 1$ holds, $y(n)$ is any positive solution of the map (6), then

$$\lim_{n \to \infty} y(n) = y_2. \tag{8}$$

Now, we consider a system as follows:

$$x_1(n+1) = x_1(n) \exp(\alpha + \beta y_2 - x_1(n)), \tag{9}$$

where $x_1(n) = \alpha + \beta y_2$ is any positive solution of System (9). We obtain the following result.

Theorem 9. *If*

$$0 < M < A, \text{ or } (M = A, \ 0 < A < 1) \text{ and } 0 < \alpha + \beta y_2 < \ln 2 + 1 \tag{10}$$

holds, the positive fixed point $L^*_{32}(x^*_2, y_2)$ of the map (5) is globally attractive. In other words,

$$\lim_{n \to +\infty} [x(n) - x_1(n)] = 0,$$

where $x_1(n)$ is any positive solution of System (9).

Proof. From (8), for any sufficiently small $\varepsilon > 0$, there is an integer N_1 such that, if $n > N_1$, then

$$y_2 - \varepsilon < y_n < y_2 + \varepsilon. \tag{11}$$

In order to prove $\lim_{n \to +\infty} [x(n) - x_1(n)] = 0$, let

$$x(n) = x_1(n) \exp[k(n)].$$

43

Then, by using the differential mean value theorem, the first equation of (5) can be expressed as

$$\begin{aligned} k(n+1) &= \ln x(n) + \alpha - x(n) + \beta y(n) - \ln x_1(n+1) \\ &= k(n)(1 - x_1(n)\exp[\theta(n)k(n)]) + \beta(y_n - y_2), \end{aligned} \quad (12)$$

where $\theta(n) \in [0,1]$, and $x_1(n)\exp[\theta_1(n)k(n)]$ lies in the range of $x_1(n)$ to $x(n)$. Now, our primary purpose is to prove
$$\lim_{n \to +\infty} k_1(n) = 0.$$

because of $x(n)\exp[\alpha + \beta(y_2 - \varepsilon) - x(n)] \leq x(n+1) \leq x(n)\exp[\alpha + \beta(y_2 + \varepsilon) - x(n)]$, then with the help of Lemmas 1 and 2, we obtain

$$\limsup_{n \to +\infty} x(n) \leq \exp(\alpha + \beta(y_2 + \varepsilon) - 1) := U_1,$$

$$\liminf_{n \to +\infty} x(n) \geq (\alpha + \beta(y_2 + \varepsilon))\exp[\alpha + \beta(y_2 + \varepsilon) - U_1]$$
$$\geq (\alpha + \beta(y_2 - \varepsilon))\exp[\alpha + \beta(y_2 - \varepsilon) - U_1] := V_1.$$

In addition, from (9), Lemmas 1 and 2, we obtain

$$\limsup_{n \to +\infty} x_1(n) \leq \exp[\alpha + \beta y_2 - 1] := U_2 \leq U_1,$$

$$\liminf_{n \to +\infty} x_1(n) \geq (\alpha + \beta y_2)\exp[\alpha + \beta y_2 - U_2]$$
$$\geq (\alpha + \beta y_2)\exp[\alpha + \beta y_2 - U_1]$$
$$\geq (\alpha + \beta(y_2 - \varepsilon))\exp[\alpha + \beta(y_2 - \varepsilon) - U_1] := V_1.$$

Thus, for any sufficiently small $\varepsilon > 0$, there is an integer $N_2 > N_1$ such that, if $n \geq N_2$, then
$$V_1 - \varepsilon \leq x(n), \ x_1(n) \leq U_1 + \varepsilon, \ n \geq N_2. \quad (13)$$

Suppose that
$$\lambda = \max\{|1 - V_1|, |1 - U_1|\}.$$

Then, for any sufficiently small $\varepsilon > 0$, we suppose
$$\lambda_\varepsilon = \max\{|1 - (V_1 - \varepsilon)|, |1 - (U_1 + \varepsilon)|\}. \quad (14)$$

From (11)–(14), we obtain
$$|k(n+1)| \leq \max\{|1 - (V_1 - \varepsilon)|, |1 - (U_1 + \varepsilon)|\}|k(n)| + \beta\varepsilon$$
$$= \lambda_\varepsilon + \beta\varepsilon, \ n \geq N_2.$$

Then, we obtain the following inequality:
$$|k(n)| \leq \lambda_\varepsilon^{n-N_2}|k(N_2)| + \frac{1 - \lambda_\varepsilon^{n-N_2}}{1 - \lambda_\varepsilon}\beta\varepsilon, \ n \geq N_2. \quad (15)$$

Since $\lambda_\varepsilon < 1$ and ε is sufficiently small, we can have $\lim_{n \to +\infty} k(n) = 0$, i.e., $\lim_{n \to +\infty}[x(n) - x_1(n)] = 0$ holds when $\lambda_1 < 1$. Notice that
$$1 - U_1 < 1 - V_1 < 1,$$

then $\lambda_1 < 1$ is equivalent to
$$1 - U_1 > -1,$$

i.e.,
$$0 < \alpha + \beta(y_2 + \varepsilon) < 1 + \ln 2. \quad (16)$$

Since ε is sufficiently small when (10) holds, we obtain (16), so $\lim_{n \to +\infty} [x(n) - x_1(n)] = 0$. Thus, this completes the proof of Theorem 9. □

3.3. Bifurcation Analysis of a Codimension of One

According to the prior analysis of the map (5) at fixed points, in this section, the center manifold theorem is used to reduce dimensionality, and then, bifurcation theory is employed to investigate the bifurcations of a codimension of one at non-hyperbolic fixed points by [44,45].

3.3.1. Bifurcation at the Fixed Point $E_0(0,0)$

Theorem 10. *When parameters* $(\alpha, \beta, M, A) \in \Omega_{E0} = \{(\alpha, \beta, M, A) \in \mathbb{R}^4 : \alpha > 0, \beta > 0, M = A, A > 0\}$, E_0 *is a non-hyperbolic fixed point. Furthermore, we find that the map (5) will undergo:*

(1) *A transcritical bifurcation when parameters* $(\alpha, \beta, M, A) \in \Omega_{E0_{TR}} = \{(\alpha, \beta, M, A) \in \mathbb{R}^4 : \alpha > 0, \beta > 0, M = A, A \neq 1\}$ *hold;*
(2) *A pitchfork bifurcation when* $(\alpha, \beta, M, A) \in \Omega_{E0_{PF}} = \{(\alpha, \beta, M, A) \in \mathbb{R}^4 : \alpha > 0, \beta > 0, M = A = 1\}$ *holds.*

Proof. By Theorem 5, the two eigenvalues of $J(E_0)$ are $\lambda_1 = e^\alpha > 1, \lambda_2 = 1$, and the fixed point E_0 is called non-hyperbolic if $(\alpha, \beta, M, A) \in \Omega_{E0}$. We choose M as the bifurcation parameter, and ρ is the perturbation parameter near A, satisfying $M = A + \rho$. Then, through an iterative operation, we can easily calculate that the center manifold of the map (5) is given as $x = 0$ and that the constrained map (5) can be represented as $y \to y - \frac{(A-1)}{A}y^2 - \frac{1}{A}y\rho + \frac{(A^2-2A-1)}{2A^2}y^3 + \frac{1}{A}y^2\rho + \frac{1}{2A^2}y\rho^2 + O((|y|+|\rho|)^3)$. If $(\alpha, \beta, M, A) \in \Omega_{E0_{TR}} = \{(\alpha, \beta, M, A) \in \mathbb{R}^4 : \alpha > 0, \beta > 0, M = A, A \neq 1\}$ holds, thus the map (5) undergoes a transcritical bifurcation at $E_0(0,0)$; if $(\alpha, \beta, M, A) \in \Omega_{E0_{PF}} = \{(\alpha, \beta, M, A) \in \mathbb{R}^4 : \alpha > 0, \beta > 0, M = A = 1\}$, then the map (5) undergoes a pitchfork bifurcation at $E_0(0,0)$. □

3.3.2. Bifurcation around Boundary Fixed Point $E_1(\alpha, 0)$

Theorem 11. *The map (5) at* $E_1(\alpha, 0)$ *has:*

(i) *A transcritical bifurcation or a pitchfork bifurcation, whose boundary fixed point $E_1(\alpha, 0)$ is non-hyperbolic, if parameter* $(\alpha, \beta, M, A) \in \Omega_{E1_{TR}} = \{(\alpha, \beta, M, A) \in \mathbb{R}^4 : \alpha \neq 2, \beta > 0, M = A, A \neq 1\}$ *or* $\Omega_{E1_{PF}} = \{(\alpha, \beta, M, A) \in \mathbb{R}^4 : \alpha \neq 2, \beta > 0, M = A = 1\}$, *respectively;*
(ii) *A flip bifurcation if* $(\alpha, \beta, M, A) \in \Omega_{E1_{FB}} = \{(\alpha, \beta, M, A) \in \mathbb{R}^4 : \alpha = 2, \beta > 0, M \neq A, A > 0\}$.

Proof. (i) According to Theorem 6(4), when the parameters satisfy the conditions $(\alpha, \beta, M, A) \in \Omega_{E1_{TR}} = \{(\alpha, \beta, M, A) \in \mathbb{R}^4 : \alpha \neq 2, \beta > 0, M = A, A \neq 1\}$, one eigenvalue of the Jacobian matrix $J(E_1)$ is $1 - \alpha$ and the other is 1. First, we choose M as the bifurcation parameter. Set $\mu = M - A$, where $|\mu| \ll 1$, and it is a new variable. Next, we translate System (5) to the origin with $u = x - \alpha, v = y - 0$ and perform the Taylor expansion, leading to

$$\begin{pmatrix} u \\ v \end{pmatrix} \to \begin{pmatrix} 1-\alpha & \alpha\beta \\ 0 & 1 \end{pmatrix} \begin{pmatrix} u \\ v \end{pmatrix} + \begin{pmatrix} f_1(u,v,\mu) \\ f_2(u,v,\mu) \end{pmatrix}; \quad (17)$$

here,

$$f_1(u,v,\mu) = z_{11}uv + z_{20}u^2 + z_{02}v^2 + z_{21}u^2v + z_{12}uv^2 + z_{30}u^3$$
$$+ z_{03}v^3 + O((|u|+|v|+|\mu|)^3),$$
$$f_2(u,v,\mu) = b_{20}v^2 + b_{11}v\mu + b_{30}v^3 + b_{21}v^2\mu + b_{12}v\mu^2$$
$$+ O((|u|+|v|+|\mu|)^3),$$

and

$$z_{11} = -(\alpha-1)\beta, \quad z_{20} = \frac{(\alpha-2)}{2}, \quad z_{02} = \frac{\alpha\beta^2}{2},$$
$$z_{21} = \frac{(\alpha-2)\beta}{2}, \quad z_{12} = -\frac{(\alpha-1)\beta^2}{2}, \quad z_{30} = -\frac{(\alpha-3)}{6},$$
$$z_{03} = -\frac{\alpha\beta^3}{6}, \quad b_{20} = -\frac{(A-1)}{A}, \quad b_{11} = -\frac{1}{A},$$
$$b_{30} = \frac{(A^2-2A-1)}{2A^2}, \quad b_{21} = \frac{1}{A}, \quad b_{12} = \frac{1}{2A^2}.$$

The matrix of the linear part of the map (17) can be expressed as:

$$J(E_1) = \begin{pmatrix} 1-\alpha & \alpha\beta \\ 0 & 1 \end{pmatrix}.$$

Choose invertible matrix T:

$$T = \begin{pmatrix} 1 & \beta \\ 0 & 1 \end{pmatrix}.$$

Apply the following matrix transformation to the map (17):

$$\begin{pmatrix} u \\ v \end{pmatrix} = T \begin{pmatrix} U \\ V \end{pmatrix}. \tag{18}$$

Therefore, the map (17) becomes

$$\begin{pmatrix} U \\ V \end{pmatrix} \to \begin{pmatrix} 1-\alpha & 0 \\ 0 & 1 \end{pmatrix} \begin{pmatrix} U \\ V \end{pmatrix} + \begin{pmatrix} G_1(U,V,\mu) \\ G_2(U,V,\mu) \end{pmatrix}, \tag{19}$$

where

$$G_1(U,V,\mu) = z_{20}U^2 + (2\beta z_{20} + z_{11})UV + \left(z_{20}\beta^2 - b_{20}\beta + z_{11}\beta + z_{02}\right)V^2$$
$$- \beta b_{11}V\mu + (3\beta z_{30} + z_{21})U^2V + (3\beta^2 z_{30} + 2\beta z_{21} + z_{12})UV^2$$
$$+ z_{30}U^3 + \left(z_{30}\beta^3 + z_{21}\beta^2 - b_{30}\beta + z_{12}\beta + z_{03}\right)V^3 - b_{12}\beta V\mu^2$$
$$- b_{21}\beta V^2\mu + O\left((|U|+|V|+|\mu|)^3\right),$$
$$G_2(U,V,\mu) = b_{20}V^2 + b_{11}V\mu + b_{30}V^3 + b_{21}V^2\mu + b_{12}V\mu^2 + O\left((|U|+|V|+|\mu|)^3\right).$$

Then, to study the stability of $(U, V) = (0, 0)$ near $\mu = 0$, we can indirectly study a system of one-parameter equations limited to a center manifold. It can be defined as follows:

$$W^c(0,0,0) = \left\{ (U, V, \mu) \in \mathbb{R}^3 : U = g(V, \mu), g(0,0) = 0, Dg(0,0) = 0 \right\}$$

with V and μ small. Take

$$g(V, \mu) = g_1 \mu^2 + g_2 V \mu + g_3 V^2 + O((|V| + |\mu|)^3). \tag{20}$$

Then, we have

$$N(g(V, \mu)) = g(V + G_2(g(V, \mu), V, \mu), \mu) - (1 - \alpha) g(V, \mu) - G_1(g(V, \mu), V, \mu) = 0. \tag{21}$$

Substituting (20) into (21) and comparing the coefficients of μ^2, $V\mu$ and V^2 of (21), we obtain

$$g_1 = 0, \quad g_2 = \frac{\beta}{\alpha A}, \quad g_3 = \frac{\beta(A-1)}{A\alpha}.$$

Thus, the map restricted to the center manifold $W^c(0,0,0)$ is written as

$$F_1 : V \to V + b_{20}V^2 + b_{11}V\mu + b_{30}V^3 + b_{21}V^2\mu + b_{12}V\mu^2 + O((|V| + |\mu|)^3).$$

We can see that

$$F_1(0,0) = 0, \quad \frac{\partial F_1}{\partial V}(0,0) = 1, \quad \frac{\partial F_1}{\partial \mu}(0,0) = 0,$$

$$\frac{\partial^2 F_1}{\partial V \partial \mu}(0,0) = b_{11} = -\frac{1}{A} \neq 0, \quad \frac{\partial^2 F_1}{\partial V^2}(0,0) = 2b_{20} = -\frac{2(A-1)}{A}.$$

Hence, the map (5) undergoes a transcritical bifurcation at E_1 because of $\frac{\partial^2 F_1}{\partial V^2}(0,0) \neq 0$ if $(\alpha, \beta, M, A) \in \Omega_{E1_{TR}}$. Moreover, when $(\alpha, \beta, M, A) \in \Omega_{E1_{PF}} = \{(\alpha, \beta, M, A) \in \mathbb{R}^4 : \alpha \neq 2, \beta > 0, M = A = 1\}$, a direct calculation leads to $\frac{\partial^2 F_1}{\partial V^2}(0,0) = 0$ and $\frac{\partial^3 F_1}{\partial V^3}(0,0) = -6$; from [45] the map (5) will pass through a pitchfork bifurcation at E_1.

(ii) From Theorem 6(4), when $(\alpha, \beta, M, A) \in \Omega_{E1_{FB}} = \{(\alpha, \beta, M, A) \in \mathbb{R}^4 : \alpha = 2, \beta > 0, M \neq A, A > 0\}$ holds, it is evident that, for the non-hyperbolic $E_1(\alpha, 0)$, $\lambda_1 = -1$ and $\lambda_2 = \exp(1 - \frac{M}{A}) \neq 1$. Taking α as a bifurcation parameter and assuming ε that is a sufficiently small perturbation parameter, namely $\|\varepsilon\| \ll 1$, then, the perturbations corresponding to System (5) are mapped as follows:

$$\begin{pmatrix} x \\ y \end{pmatrix} \to \begin{pmatrix} xe^{2+\varepsilon-x+\beta y} \\ ye^{1-y-\frac{M}{y+A}} \end{pmatrix}. \tag{22}$$

Then, we shift E_1 in the map (12) to $(0,0)$ using a transformation $u = x - (2 + \varepsilon)$, $v = y - 0$, which leads to

$$\begin{pmatrix} u \\ v \end{pmatrix} \to \begin{pmatrix} -1 & 2\beta \\ 0 & \lambda_2 \end{pmatrix} \begin{pmatrix} u \\ v \end{pmatrix} + \begin{pmatrix} f_3(u,v,\varepsilon) \\ f_4(u,v,\varepsilon) \end{pmatrix}; \tag{23}$$

here,

$$f_3(u,v,\varepsilon) = \beta^2 v^2 - \beta uv + \beta v\varepsilon - u\varepsilon + \frac{1}{6}u^3 + \frac{1}{2}u^2\varepsilon - \beta uv\varepsilon - \frac{1}{2}\beta^2 uv^2$$

$$+ \frac{1}{3}\beta^3 v^3 + \frac{1}{2}\beta^2 v^2 \varepsilon + O\Big((|u|+|v|+|\varepsilon|)^3\Big),$$

$$f_4(u,v,\varepsilon) = -\frac{(A^2 - M)\lambda_2}{A^2}v^2 + \frac{(A^4 - 2MA^2 - 2MA + M^2)\lambda_2}{2A^4}v^3$$

$$+ O\Big((|u|+|v|+|\varepsilon|)^3\Big).$$

Taking the map (23) at origin $(0,0)$, the Jacobian matrix is

$$J(E_1) = \begin{pmatrix} -1 & 2\beta \\ 0 & \lambda_2 \end{pmatrix}.$$

Invertible matrices T are constructed as follows:

$$T = \begin{pmatrix} 1 & \frac{2\beta}{1+\lambda_2} \\ 0 & 1 \end{pmatrix}.$$

With the transformation

$$\begin{pmatrix} u \\ v \end{pmatrix} = T \begin{pmatrix} X \\ Y \end{pmatrix}, \tag{24}$$

the map (23) becomes

$$\begin{pmatrix} X \\ Y \end{pmatrix} \to \begin{pmatrix} -1 & 0 \\ 0 & \lambda_2 \end{pmatrix}\begin{pmatrix} X \\ Y \end{pmatrix} + \begin{pmatrix} G_3(X,Y,\varepsilon) \\ G_4(X,Y,\varepsilon) \end{pmatrix}, \tag{25}$$

where

$$G_3(X,Y,\varepsilon) = -\beta XY - X\varepsilon + \left(\beta^2 - \frac{2\beta^2}{1+\lambda_2} + \frac{2\beta\lambda_2(A^2-M)}{A^2(1+\lambda_2)}\right)Y^2 + \left(\beta - \frac{2\beta}{1+\lambda_2}\right)Y\varepsilon$$

$$+ \frac{1}{6}X^3 + \frac{\beta}{1+\lambda_2}X^2Y + \left(\frac{2\beta^2}{(1+\lambda_2)^2} - \frac{\beta^2}{2}\right)XY^2 + \left(\frac{2\beta}{1+\lambda_2} - \beta\right)XY\varepsilon$$

$$+ \left(\frac{4\beta^3}{3(1+\lambda_2)^3} - \frac{\beta^3}{1+\lambda_2} + \frac{\beta^3}{3} - \frac{\beta\lambda_2(A^4 - 2A^2M - 2AM + M^2)}{A^4(1+\lambda_2)}\right)Y^3$$

$$+ \frac{1}{2}X^2\varepsilon + \left(\frac{2\beta^2}{(1+\lambda_2)^2} - \frac{2\beta^2}{1+\lambda_2} + \frac{\beta^2}{2}\right)Y^2\varepsilon + O\Big((|X|+|Y|+|\varepsilon|)^3\Big),$$

$$G_4(X,Y,\varepsilon) = -\frac{(A^2-M)\lambda_2}{A^2}V^2 + \frac{(A^4 - 2A^2M - 2AM + M^2)\lambda_2}{2A^4}V^3$$

$$+ O\Big((|X|+|Y|+|\varepsilon|)^3\Big).$$

According to the center manifold theory, $(X,Y)=(0,0)$ is stable for $\varepsilon=0$ and can be determined as follows:

$$W^c(0,0,0) = \Big\{(X,Y,\varepsilon)\in\mathbb{R}^3 : Y = g(X,\varepsilon), g(0,0)=0, Dg(0,0)=0\Big\}$$

with small ε and X. Assuming that

$$g(X,\varepsilon) = g_1\varepsilon^2 + g_2 X\varepsilon + g_3 X^2 + O((|X|+|\varepsilon|)^3), \tag{26}$$

$g(X,\varepsilon)$ must satisfy the following relation:

$$N(g(X,\varepsilon)) = g(-X + G_3(X,g(X,\varepsilon),\varepsilon),\varepsilon) - \lambda_2 g(X,\varepsilon) - G_4(X,g(X,\varepsilon),\varepsilon) = 0. \tag{27}$$

Substituting (26) into (27) and comparing the coefficients of ε^2, $X\varepsilon$ and X^2 in (27), we obtain

$$g_1 = g_2 = g_3 = 0.$$

Consequently, the map restricted to the center manifold $W^c(0,0,0)$ is expressed as

$$F_2 : X \to -X - X\varepsilon + \frac{1}{6}X^3 + \frac{1}{2}X^2\varepsilon + O\Big((|X|+|\varepsilon|)^3\Big).$$

From [44], it can be seen that the conditions for flip bifurcation to occur are:

$$\alpha_1 = \left[\frac{\partial F_2}{\partial \varepsilon} + 2\frac{\partial^2 F_2}{\partial X \partial \varepsilon}\right](0,0) = -2 \neq 0,$$

$$\alpha_2 = \left[\frac{1}{2}\left(\frac{\partial^2 F_2}{\partial X^2}\right)^2 + \frac{1}{3}\left(\frac{\partial^3 F_2}{\partial X^3}\right)\right](0,0) = \frac{1}{3} \neq 0.$$

Thus, by [44], the system (5) undergoes a flip bifurcation if $(\alpha,\beta,M,A) \in \Omega_{E1_{FB}}$ holds at $E_1(\alpha,0)$. □

3.3.3. Bifurcation Analysis of Positive Fixed Point $E^*_{3j}(x^*_j,y_j)(j=2,3)$

Theorem 12. *If $E^*_{3j}(x^*_j,y_j)(j=2,3)$ exists, the map (5) has:*

(a) *A flip bifurcation for parameter $(\alpha,\beta,M,A) \in \Omega_{E32_{FB}} = \{(\alpha,\beta,M,A) \in \mathbb{R}^4 : 0 < \alpha < 2, \beta = \beta^*_2, M \neq M^*, 0 < A < 1\}$ at $E^*_{32}(x^*_2,y_2)$.*

(b) *A fold bifurcation for parameter $(\alpha,\beta,M,A) \in \Omega_{E33_{FOB}} = \{(\alpha,\beta,M,A) \in \mathbb{R}^4 : 0 < \alpha < 2, M = M^*, 0 < A < 1, \beta > 0 \text{ and } \beta \neq \beta^*_3\}$ at $E^*_{33}(x^*_3,y_3)$. In addition, with the increase of M, the number of positive fixed points of the map (5) has a 2-1-0 change. That is, when $M < M^*$, there are $E^*_{31}(x^*_1,y_1)$ and $E^*_{32}(x^*_2,y_2)$; when $M = M^*$, there is a unique positive fixed point $E^*_{33}(x^*_3,y_3)$, and when $M > M^*$ the positive fixed point disappears.*

Proof. (a) From Theorem 8 (2)(iii), we can easily obtain that, when $(\alpha,\beta,M,A) \in \Omega_{E32_{FB}} = \{(\alpha,\beta,M,A) \in \mathbb{R}^4 : 0 < \alpha < 2, \beta = \beta^*_2, 0 < A < 1, M \neq M^*\}$, $\lambda_1 = -1, |\lambda_2| = |1+y_2(-1+\frac{M}{(y_2+A)^2})| < 1$. Then, to obtain the flip bifurcation, we regard β as the bifurcation parameter and shift the fixed point $E^*_{32}(x^*_2,y_2)$ to $(0,0)$ through a transformation $u = x - x^*_2, v = y - y_2$ and $\delta = \beta - \beta^*_2$; here, $|\delta| \ll 1$ and is a sufficiently small new variable. We then have

$$\begin{pmatrix} u \\ v \end{pmatrix} \to \begin{pmatrix} a_{001} & a_{010} \\ 0 & b_{010} \end{pmatrix}\begin{pmatrix} u \\ v \end{pmatrix} + \begin{pmatrix} f_5(u,v,\delta) \\ f_6(u,v,\delta) \end{pmatrix}; \tag{28}$$

here,

$$f_5(u,v,\delta) = a_{210}u^2v + a_{201}u^2\delta + a_{120}uv^2 + a_{102}u\delta^2 + a_{021}v^2\delta + a_{012}v\delta^2 + a_{110}uv$$
$$+ a_{300}u^3 + a_{101}u\delta + a_{011}v\delta + a_{020}v^2 + a_{111}uv\delta + a_{200}u^2 + a_{003}\delta^3$$
$$+ a_{002}\delta^2 + a_{030}v^3 + O((|u|+|v|+|\delta|)^3)$$
$$f_6(u,v,\delta) = b_{020}v^2 + b_{030}v^3 + O((|u|+|v|+|\delta|)^3),$$

and

$$a_{100} = 1 - x_2^*, \quad a_{001} = x_2^* y_2, \quad a_{010} = x_2^* \beta_2^*,$$

$$a_{210} = \frac{\beta_2^*(x_2^* - 2)}{2}, \quad a_{201} = \frac{y_2(x_2^* - 2)}{2}, \quad a_{120} = -\frac{\beta_2^{*2}(x_2^* - 1)}{2},$$

$$a_{102} = -\frac{y_2^2(x_2^* - 1)}{2}, \quad a_{021} = \frac{x_2^* \beta_2^*(\beta_2^* y_2 + 2)}{2}, \quad a_{012} = \frac{x_2^* y_2(\beta_2^* y_2 + 2)}{2},$$

$$a_{110} = -\beta_2^*(x_2^* - 1), \quad a_{300} = -\frac{x_2^*}{6} + \frac{1}{2}, \quad a_{101} = -y_2(x_2^* - 1),$$

$$a_{011} = x_2^*(\beta_2^* y_2 + 1), \quad a_{020} = \frac{x_2^* \beta_2^{*2}}{2}, \quad a_{111} = (1 - x_2^*)(1 + \beta_2^* y_2),$$

$$a_{200} = \frac{x_2^*}{2} - 1, \quad a_{003} = \frac{x_2^* y_2^3}{6}, \quad a_{002} = \frac{x_2^* y_2^2}{2}, \quad a_{030} = \frac{x_2^{*3}}{6},$$

$$b_{010} = -\frac{1}{(A+y_2)^2}(A^2 y_2 + 2Ay_2^2 + y_2^3 - A^2 - 2Ay_2 - My_2 - y_2^2),$$

$$b_{020} = \frac{1}{2(A+y_2)^4}(A^4 y_2 + 4A^3 y_2^2 + 6A^2 y_2^3 + 4Ay_2^4 + y_2^5 - 2A^4$$
$$- 8A^3 y_2 - 2A^2 My_2 - 12A^2 y_2^2 - 4AMy_2^2 - 8Ay_2^3 - 2My_2^3$$
$$- 2y_2^4 + 2A^2 M + 2AMy_2 + M^2 y_2),$$

$$b_{030} = \frac{1}{6(A+y_2)^6}(A^6 y_2 + 6A^5 y_2^2 + 15A^4 y_2^3 + 20A^3 y_2^4 + 15A^2 y_2^5 + 6Ay_2^6$$
$$- 18A^5 y_2 - 3A^4 My_2 - 45A^4 y_2^2 - 12A^3 My_2^2 - 60A^3 y_2^3 - 18A^2 My_2^3$$
$$- 12AMy_2^4 - 18Ay_2^5 + y_2^7 - 3A^6 - 3My_2^5 - 3y_2^6 + 6A^4 M + 18A^3 My_2$$
$$+ 3A^2 M^2 y_2 + 18A^2 My_2^2 + 6AM^2 y_2^2 + 6AMy_2^3 + 3M^2 y_2^3 + 6A^3 M$$
$$- 45A^2 y_2^4 - 3A^2 M^2 + 12A^2 My_2 + 6AMy_2^2 - M^3 y_2 + 3M^2 y_2^2).$$

The linearization matrix for the map (28) is

$$J(E_{32}^*) = \begin{pmatrix} a_{100} & a_{010} \\ 0 & b_{010} \end{pmatrix}.$$

Find an invertible matrix T, for instance

$$T = \begin{pmatrix} a_{010} & a_{010} \\ -1 - a_{100} & \lambda_2 - a_{100} \end{pmatrix}$$

and make the transformation:
$$\begin{pmatrix} u \\ v \end{pmatrix} = T \begin{pmatrix} X \\ Y \end{pmatrix}, \tag{29}$$

the map (18) yields
$$\begin{pmatrix} X \\ Y \end{pmatrix} \to \begin{pmatrix} -1 & 0 \\ 0 & \lambda_2 \end{pmatrix} \begin{pmatrix} X \\ Y \end{pmatrix} + \begin{pmatrix} G_5(X,Y,\delta) \\ G_6(X,Y,\delta) \end{pmatrix}, \tag{30}$$

where
$$G_5(X,Y,\delta) = K_{300}X^3 + K_{210}X^2Y + K_{201}X^2\delta + K_{200}X^2 + K_{120}XY^2 + K_{111}XY\delta$$
$$+ K_{110}XY + K_{102}X\delta^2 + K_{101}X\delta + K_{030}Y^3 + K_{020}Y^2 + K_{021}Y^2\delta$$
$$+ K_{012}Y\delta^2 + K_{011}Y\delta + K_{003}\delta^3 + K_{002}\delta^2 + O((|X|+|Y|+|\delta|)^3),$$
$$G_6(X,Y,\delta) = C_{300}X^3 + C_{210}X^2Y + C_{200}X^2 + C_{120}XY^2 + C_{110}XY + C_3Y^3 + C_2Y^2$$
$$+ O((|X|+|Y|+|\delta|)^3),$$

where
$$K_{300} = a_{030}\Gamma^3 + a_{120}a_{010}\Gamma^2 + a_{210}a_{010}^2\Gamma + a_{300}a_{010}^3,$$
$$K_{210} = 3a_{030}\Theta\Gamma^2 + a_{120}a_{010}\Gamma^2 + 2a_{120}a_{010}\Gamma\Theta + 3a_{210}a_{010}^2\Gamma + 3a_{300}a_{010}^3,$$
$$K_{201} = a_{021}\Gamma^2 + a_{111}a_{010}\Gamma + a_{201}a_{010}^2,$$
$$K_{200} = a_{020}\Gamma^2 + a_{110}a_{010}\Gamma + a_{200}a_{010}^2,$$
$$K_{120} = 3a_{030}\Gamma\Theta^2 + 2a_{120}a_{010}\Gamma\Theta + a_{210}a_{010}^2\Gamma + a_{120}a_{010}\Theta^2 + 2a_{210}a_{010}^2\Theta + 3a_{300}a_{010}^3,$$
$$K_{111} = 2a_{021}\Theta\Gamma + a_{111}a_{010}\Gamma + a_{111}a_{010}\Theta + 2a_{201}a_{010}^2,$$
$$K_{110} = 2a_{020}\Theta\Gamma + a_{110}a_{010}\Gamma + a_{110}a_{010}\Theta + 2a_{200}a_{010}^2,$$
$$K_{102} = a_{012}\Gamma + a_{102}a_{010}, K_{101} = a_{011}\Gamma + a_{010}a_{101},$$
$$K_{030} = a_{030}\Theta^3 + a_{120}a_{010}\Theta^2 + a_{210}a_{010}^2\Theta + a_{300}a_{010}^3,$$
$$K_{021} = a_{021}\Theta^2 + a_{111}a_{010}\Theta + a_{201}a_{010}^2,$$
$$K_{020} = a_{020}\Theta + a_{110}a_{010}\Theta + a_{200}a_{010}^2,$$
$$K_{012} = \Theta a_{012} + a_{010}a_{102},$$
$$K_{011} = a_{011}\Theta + a_{010}a_{101}, K_{003} = a_{003},$$
$$K_{002} = a_{002}, \quad C_{300} = b_{030}\Gamma^3,$$
$$C_{210} = 3b_{030}\Theta\Gamma^2, \quad C_{200} = b_{020}\Gamma^2, \quad C_{120} = 3b_{030}\Theta^2\Gamma,$$
$$C_{110} = 2b_{020}\Theta\Gamma, \quad C_{003} = b_{030}\Theta^3, \quad C_{002} = b_{020}\Theta^2,$$
$$\Gamma = (-1 - a_{100}), \Theta = \lambda_2 - a_{100}.$$

According to the center manifold theory, a one-parameter simplified system of equations restricted to the manifold determines the stability of $(X, Y) = (0,0)$ in the neighborhood of $\delta = 0$, given by

$$W^c(0,0,0) = \{(X, Y, \delta) \in \mathbb{R}^3 : Y = g(X, \delta), g(0,0) = 0, Dg(0,0) = 0\}$$

with X and δ sufficiently small. Moreover, let

$$g(X, \delta) = g_1\delta + g_2 X^2 + g_3 X\delta + g_4\delta^2 + O((|X|+|\delta|)^3); \quad (31)$$

thus,

$$N(g(X,\delta)) = g(-X + G_5(X, g(X,\delta), \delta), \delta) - \lambda_2 g(X, \delta) - G_6(X, g(X, \delta), \delta) = 0. \quad (32)$$

From (31) and (32), we obtain

$$g_1 = 0, \quad g_2 = \frac{C_{200}}{1-\lambda_2}, \quad g_3 = \frac{C_{110}g_1}{1+\lambda_2}, \quad g_4 = \frac{C_{002}g_1^2}{1-\lambda_2}.$$

Hence, the map restricted to the center manifold becomes

$$F_3 : X \to -X + s_0\delta + s_1 X^2 + s_2 X\delta + s_3\delta^2 + s_4 X^2\delta + s_5 X\delta^2$$
$$+ s_6 X^3 + s_7 \delta^3 + O((|X|+|\delta|)^3).$$

where

$$s_0 = 0, \quad s_1 = K_{200}, \quad s_2 = K_{101}, \quad s_3 = K_{002}, \quad s_4 = K_{201} - \frac{C_{200}K_{011}}{\lambda_2 - 1},$$

$$s_5 = K_{102}, \quad s_6 = K_{300} - \frac{K_{110}C_{200}}{\lambda_2 - 1}, \quad s_7 = K_{003}.$$

We give the following two transversal conditions in [44]:

$$\alpha_1 = \left[\frac{\partial^2 F_3}{\partial X \partial \delta} + \frac{1}{2}\frac{\partial F_3}{\partial \delta}\frac{\partial^2 F_3}{\partial X^2}\right](0,0) = s_2 + s_0 s_1 \neq 0,$$

$$\alpha_2 = \left[\frac{1}{6}\left(\frac{\partial^3 F_3}{\partial X^3}\right) + \left(\frac{1}{2}\frac{\partial^2 F_3}{\partial X^2}\right)^2\right](0,0) = s_6 + s_1^2 \neq 0.$$

Therefore, a flip bifurcation occurs when $(\alpha, \beta, M, A) \in \Omega_{E32_{FB}}$ at the fixed point $E_{32}^*(x_2^*, y_2)$.

(b) From Theorem 8(3), it is easy to obtain that, when $(\alpha, \beta, M, A) \in \Omega_{E33_{FOB}} = \{(\alpha, \beta, M, A) \in \mathbb{R}^4 : 0 < \alpha < 2, M = M^*, 0 < A < 1, \beta > 0 \text{ and } \beta \neq \beta_3^*\}, |\lambda_1| = |1-x_3^*| \neq 1, \lambda_2 = 1$. Now, we select M as the bifurcation parameter. Take $\zeta = M - M^*$, $|\zeta| \ll 1$, and it is a new variable. We transform the fixed point $E_{33}^*(x_3^*, \frac{1-A}{2})$ of the map (5) to $(0,0)$ with $u = x - x_3^*, v = y - \frac{1-A}{2}$, and then, the map (5) becomes

$$\begin{pmatrix} u \\ \zeta \\ v \end{pmatrix} \to \begin{pmatrix} 1-x_3^* & 0 & \beta x_3^* \\ 0 & 1 & 0 \\ 0 & \frac{A-1}{1+A} & 1 \end{pmatrix}\begin{pmatrix} u \\ \zeta \\ v \end{pmatrix} + \begin{pmatrix} f_7(u,v,\zeta) \\ 0 \\ f_8(u,v,\zeta) \end{pmatrix}, \quad (33)$$

where

$$f_7(u,v,\zeta) = \left(\frac{x_3^*}{2} - 1\right)u^2 + \frac{\beta^2 x_3^*}{2}v^2 - \beta(x_3^* - 1)uv + \left(\frac{1}{2} - \frac{x_3^*}{6}\right)u^3 + \frac{\beta^3 x_3^*}{6}v^3$$
$$+ \frac{\beta(x_3^* - 2)}{2}u^2v - \frac{\beta^2(x_3^* - 1)}{2}uv^2 + O((|u| + |v| + |\zeta|)^3),$$

$$f_8(u,v,\zeta) = \frac{A-1}{1+A}v^2 - \frac{4A}{(1+A)^2}v\zeta - \frac{A-1}{(1+A)^2}\zeta^2 - \frac{4A}{(1+A)^2}v^3$$
$$- \frac{2(A^2 - 4A - 1)}{(1+A)^3}v^2\zeta + \frac{2(3A-1)}{(1+A)^3}v\zeta^2 + \frac{2(A-1)}{3(1+A)^3}\zeta^3$$
$$+ O((|u| + |v| + |\zeta|)^3).$$

The coefficient matrix is given by

$$J(E_{33}^*) = \begin{pmatrix} 1 - x_3^* & 0 & \beta x_3^* \\ 0 & 1 & 0 \\ 0 & \frac{A-1}{1+A} & 1 \end{pmatrix}.$$

Convert the matrix $J(E_{33}^*)$ in (33) into the normal form with matrix translation as follows:

$$\begin{pmatrix} u \\ \zeta \\ v \end{pmatrix} = T \begin{pmatrix} X \\ \eta \\ Y \end{pmatrix}, \tag{34}$$

where

$$T = \begin{pmatrix} \beta & -\frac{\beta}{x_3^*} & 1 \\ 0 & \frac{1+A}{A-1} & 0 \\ 1 & 0 & 0 \end{pmatrix}$$

is an invertible matrix. From (33) and (34), we have

$$\begin{pmatrix} X \\ \eta \\ Y \end{pmatrix} \to \begin{pmatrix} 1 & 1 & 0 \\ 0 & 1 & 0 \\ 0 & 0 & 1 - x_3^* \end{pmatrix} \begin{pmatrix} X \\ \eta \\ Y \end{pmatrix} + \begin{pmatrix} G_7(X,Y,\eta) \\ 0 \\ G_8(X,Y,\eta) \end{pmatrix}, \tag{35}$$

where

$$G_7(X,Y,\eta) = p_{101}X\eta + p_{200}X^2 + p_{102}X\eta^2 + p_{300}X^3 + p_{201}X^2\eta + p_{002}\eta^2$$
$$+ p_{003}\eta^3 + O((|X| + |Y| + |\eta|)^3),$$

$$G_8(X,Y,\eta) = m_{300}X^3 + m_{201}X^2\eta + m_{200}X^2 + m_{102}X\eta^2 + m_{101}X\eta$$
$$+ m_{020}Y^2 + m_{021}Y^2\eta + m_{011}Y\eta + m_{012}Y\eta^2 + m_{002}\eta^2$$
$$+ m_{111}XY\eta + m_{120}XY^2 + m_{003}\eta^3 + O((|X| + |Y| + |\eta|)^3),$$

and

$$p_{101} = -\frac{4A}{(1+A)(A-1)},$$
$$p_{200} = \frac{A-1}{1+A},$$
$$p_{102} = -\frac{2(-1+3A)}{(1+A)(A-1)^2},$$
$$p_{300} = -\frac{4A}{(1+A)^2},$$
$$p_{201} = -\frac{2(A^2-4A-1)}{(1+A)^2(A-1)},$$
$$p_{002} = \frac{1}{A-1},$$
$$p_{003} = \frac{2}{3(A-1)^2},$$
$$m_{300} = \frac{4\beta A}{(1+A)^2},$$
$$m_{201} = \frac{2\beta(A^2-4A-1)}{(1+A)^2(A-1)},$$
$$m_{200} = -\frac{\beta(A-1)}{1+A},$$
$$m_{102} = \left(\frac{\beta^3}{2x_3^{*2}} + \frac{(2-6A)\beta}{(1+A)(A-1)^2}\right),$$
$$m_{101} = \left(\frac{\beta^2}{x_3^*} + \frac{4\beta A}{(1+A)(A-1)}\right),$$
$$m_{020} = \left(\frac{(1-A)\beta}{4} + \frac{\alpha}{2} - 1\right),$$
$$m_{021} = \frac{\beta((A-1)\beta - 2\alpha + 6)}{(2A-2)\beta - 4\alpha},$$
$$m_{011} = -\frac{((A-1)\beta - 2\alpha + 4)\beta}{(A-1)\beta - 2\alpha},$$
$$m_{012} = \frac{\beta^2((A-1)\beta - 2\alpha + 6)}{((A-1)\beta - 2\alpha)^2},$$
$$m_{002} = -\frac{2((A-1)(\alpha+2)\beta - 2\alpha^2)\beta}{(A-1)((A-1)\beta - 2\alpha)^2},$$
$$m_{111} = -\left(\beta + \frac{\beta^2}{x_3^*}\right), m_{120} = \frac{\beta}{2},$$
$$m_{003} = \frac{8((\alpha+\frac{3}{2})(A-1)^2\beta^2 - 3\alpha^2(A-1)\beta + 2\alpha^3)\beta}{3(A-1)^2((A-1)\beta - 2\alpha)^3}.$$

By implementing the center manifold theorem, the stability of the map (35) at $(X,Y) = (0,0)$ in a neighborhood of $\eta = 0$ can be approximated as follows:

$$W^c(0,0,0) = \left\{(X,Y,\eta) \in \mathbb{R}^3 : Y = g(X,\eta), g(0,0) = 0, Dg(0,0) = 0\right\}$$

with X and η small. Then, assume

$$g(X,\eta) = g_1 X^2 + g_2 X\eta + g_3\eta^2 + O((|X|+|\eta|)^3), \tag{36}$$

and $g(X,\eta)$ have the following equation

$$N(g(X,\eta)) = g(X+\eta+G_7(X,g(X,\eta),\eta),\eta) - (1-x_3^*)g(X,\eta) - G_8(X,g(X,\eta),\eta) = 0. \tag{37}$$

Substituting (36) into (37) and comparing the coefficients of X^2, $X\eta$, and η^2 in (37), we obtain

$$g_1 = \frac{(1-A)\beta}{(A+1)x_3^*},$$
$$g_2 = \frac{((A-1)^2\beta - 4A\alpha)\beta}{(A^2-1)x_3^{*2}} + \frac{2g_1}{x_3^*},$$
$$g_3 = \frac{\beta((\alpha+2)(1-A)\beta + \alpha^2)}{2(A-1)x_3^{*3}} - \frac{g_1+g_2}{x_3^*}.$$

Thus, the restricted map to the center manifold $W^c(0,0,0)$ is given as

$$F_4 : X \to X + \eta + \frac{A-1}{1+A}X^2 - \frac{4A}{(1+A)(A-1)}X\eta - \frac{1}{A-1}\eta^2$$

$$- \frac{4A}{(1+A)^2}X^3 - \frac{2(A^2-4A-1)}{(1+A)^2(A-1)}X^2\eta + \frac{2}{3(A-1)^2}\eta^3$$

$$+ \frac{2(3A-1)}{(1+A)(A-1)^2}X\eta^2 + O((|X|+|\eta|)^3).$$

We can simply calculate

$$F_4(0,0) = 0, \qquad \frac{\partial F_4}{\partial X}(0,0) = 1, \qquad \frac{\partial F_4}{\partial \eta}(0,0) = 1,$$

$$\frac{\partial^2 F_4}{\partial X^2}(0,0) = \frac{2(A-1)}{1+A} \neq 0, \qquad \frac{\partial^2 F_4}{\partial X \partial \eta}(0,0) = -\frac{4A}{(1+A)(A-1)} \neq 0,$$

which leads to a fold bifurcation when $(\alpha, \beta, M, A) \in \Omega_{E33_{FOB}}$ at the $E_{33}^*(x_3^*, \frac{1-A}{2})$. □

3.4. Chaos Control

From Theorem 12(a), it can be seen that a flip bifurcation of the map (5) is shown at the coexistence fixed point $E_{32}^* = (x_2^*, y_2)$. This will cause chaos in the system, so we use a hybrid chaos-control method in [46], which is a combination of parameter perturbation and feedback control, to delay or get rid of chaos. First, the control system corresponding to the map (5) is given by

$$\begin{pmatrix} x \\ y \end{pmatrix} \to \begin{pmatrix} \rho x \exp(\alpha - x + \beta y) + (1-\rho)x \\ \rho y \exp(1 - y - \frac{M}{y+A}) + (1-\rho)y \end{pmatrix}. \tag{38}$$

where $0 < \rho < 1$ and ρ is an external control parameter. Moreover, the calculation shows that System (38) and the map (5) have the same fixed points. The linearized Jacobian matrix of the map (38) at fixed point $E_{32}^* = (x_2^*, y_2)$ is

$$J(E_{32}^*) = \begin{pmatrix} 1 - \rho x_2^* & \rho x_2^* \beta \\ 0 & 1 + \rho y_2\left(-1 + \frac{M}{(y_2+A)^2}\right) \end{pmatrix}.$$

Obviously, the two eigenvalues of the Jacobian matrix $J(E_{32}^*)$ are $\lambda_1 = 1 - \rho x_2^* < 1$ and $\lambda_2 = 1 + \rho y_2\left(-1 + \frac{M}{(y_2+A)^2}\right)$. According to the previous analysis, $J_2 < 1$, then $-1 + \frac{M}{(y_2+A)^2} < 0$. We have $\lambda_2 = 1 + \rho y_2\left(-1 + \frac{M}{(y_2+A)^2}\right) < 1$. Therefore, with the help of Definition 1(1), the controlled system (38) has the following statement.

Theorem 13. *If and only if*

$$\rho x_2^* < 2 \quad \text{and} \quad \rho y_2\left(1 - \frac{M}{(y_2+A)^2}\right) < 2$$

holds, the coexistence fixed point $E_{32}^*(x_2^*, y_2)$ of the map (38) is locally asymptotically stable.

4. Numerical Simulations

In this section, the analysis results obtained above are further studied through numerical simulations.

Case (1): Select different parameters of the map (6), in Table 3, to observe the solution curve in Figure 6.

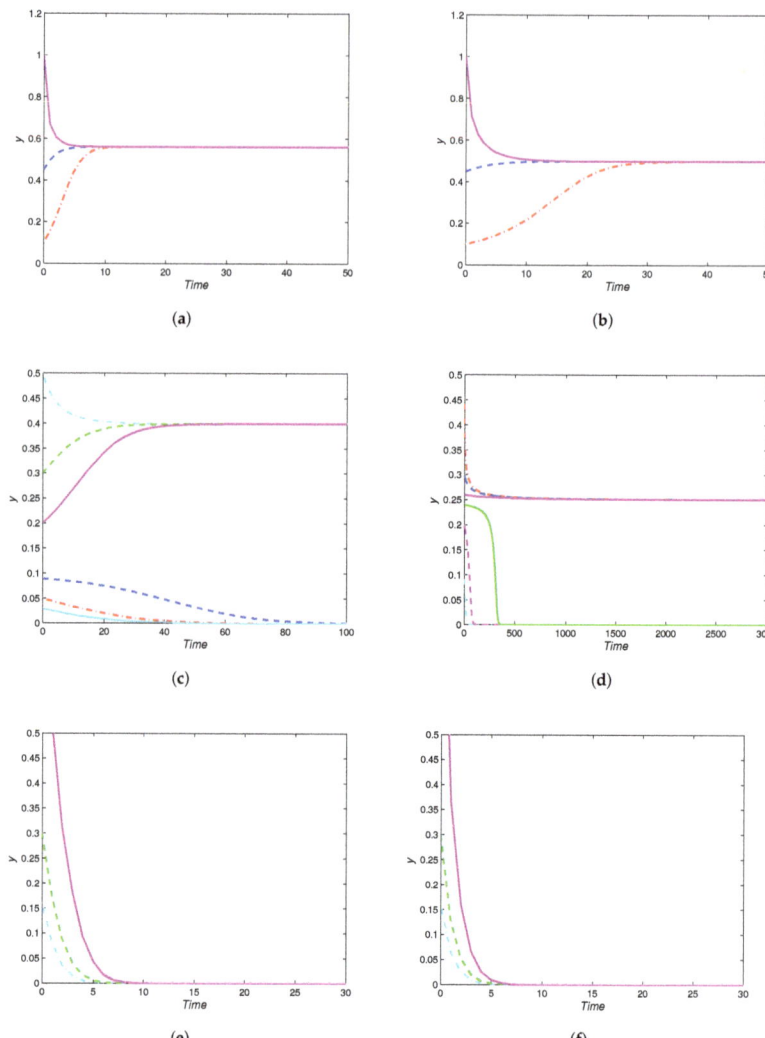

Figure 6. (a) With $M = 2$, $A = 4$, and the initial value as $y(0) = 0.1, 0.5, 1$, the map (6) has positive fixed points $y_2 = 0.5616$; (b) with $M = A = 0.5$ and the initial value as $y(0) = 0.1, 0.5, 1$, the map (6) has positive fixed points $y_2 = 0.5$; (c) with $M = 0.54$, $A = 0.5$, and the initial value as $y(0) = 0.09, 0.05, 0.02, 0.2, 0.3.0.5$, the map (6) has two positive fixed points $y_1 = 0.1$, $y_2 = 0.4$; (d) with $M = 0.5625$, $A = 0.5$, and the initial value as $y(0) = 0.09, 0.05, 0.02, 0.2, 0.3.0.5$, the map (6) has positive fixed points $y_3 = 0.25$; (e) with $M = 1$, $A = 0.5$, and the initial value as $y(0) = 0.15, 0.3, 1$, the map (6) has no positive fixed point; (f) with $M = 1$, $A = 1$, and the initial value as $y(0) = 0.15, 0.3, 1$, the map (6) has no positive fixed point.

Table 3. Parameter table.

Parameter	Positive Fixed Point	Initial Value
$M = 2, A = 4$	$y_2 = 0.5616$	$y(0) = 0.1, 0.5, 1$
$M = A = 0.5$	$y_2 = 0.5$	$y(0) = 0.1, 0.5, 1$
$M = 0.54, A = 0.5$	$y_1 = 0.1, y_2 = 0.4$	$y(0) = 0.09, 0.05, 0.02, 0.2, 0.3.0.5$
$M = 0.5625, A = 0.5$	$y_3 = 0.25$	$y(0) = 0.09, 0.2, 0.24, 0.26, 0.3.0.45$
$M = 1, A = 0.5$	no	$y(0) = 0.15, 0.3, 1$
$M = 2, A = 1$	no	$y(0) = 0.15, 0.3, 1$

Case (2): Set parameters $\alpha = \beta = 1, M = 2, A = 4$ and initial values as $(x(0), y(0)) = ((1.5, 0.3), (1.2, 0.6), (0.8, 0.2))$ in the map (5). There is a positive fixed point $E_{32}^*(1.5616, 0.5616)$ and global asymptotic stability by Theorem 9. Figure 7 shows the result.

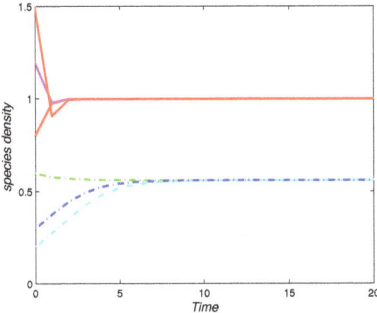

Figure 7. Stability of the fixed point E_{32}^* of the map (5) with $\alpha = \beta = 1, M = 2, A = 4$, and the initial values as $(x(0), y(0)) = ((1.5, 0.3), (1.2, 0.6), (0.8, 0.2))$.

Case (3): Set parameters $\alpha = 3, \beta = 1, A = 0.15$ in the map (5). We find that the two eigenvalues of the Jacobian matrix $J(E_1)$ at the boundary fixed point $E_1(3, 0)$ are $\lambda_1 = -2$, $\lambda_2 = 1$. Therefore, by Theorem 6, the fixed point $E_1(3, 0)$ is non-hyperbolic. According to Theorem 11(i) of the bifurcation analysis, the map (5) has transcritical bifurcation at E_1.

Figure 8 is a diagram of the transcritical bifurcation on the $M - y$ plane in the local range of the fixed point $E_1(3, 0)$ when $M \in [0, 0.331]$, and the other parameters are given in Case (3). From Figure 8, it can be found that, when $M < 0.15$, $E_1(3, 0)$ is unstable, but when $M > 0.15$, there is a stable fixed point $E_1(3, 0)$ and an unstable fixed point $E_{31}^*(3.425 - \frac{\sqrt{1.3225 - 4M}}{2}, 0.425 - \frac{\sqrt{1.3225 - 4M}}{2})$.

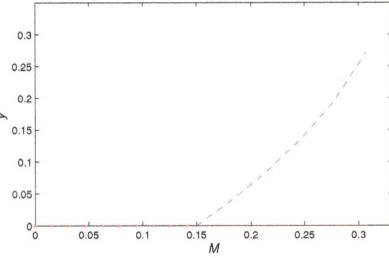

Figure 8. Transcritical bifurcation diagrams in the $M - y$ plane with $\alpha = 3, \beta = 1, A = 0.15$.

Case (4): Further, based on Case (3), we change the parameter A and let $A = 1$. At this time, by Theorem 11(ii), the map (5) generates a pitchfork bifurcation at $E_1(3,0)$. Namely, it is a pitchfork bifurcation point.

Figure 9 is a diagram of the pitchfork bifurcation on the $M - y$ plane in the local area of the fixed point E_1. Select the initial value of $x_0 = 0.5, y_0 = 0.3$, $M \in [0, 1.5]$, $\alpha = 3$, and $\beta = 1$. It can be seen from Figure 9 that the fixed point E_1 is unstable, when $M < 1$; the stable fixed point $E_1(3, 0)$ appears when $M > 1$. Additionally, there are two stable fixed points $E_{31}^* = (3 - \sqrt{1-M}, -\sqrt{1-M})$ and $E_{32}^* = (3 + \sqrt{1-M}, \sqrt{1-M})$ when $M < 1$; $E_{31}^* = (3 - \sqrt{1-M}, -\sqrt{1-M})$ and $E_{32}^* = (3 + \sqrt{1-M}, \sqrt{1-M})$ coincide to form the double-root $E_{33}^*(3, 0)$ when $M = 1$; E_{33}^* disappears when $M > 1$.

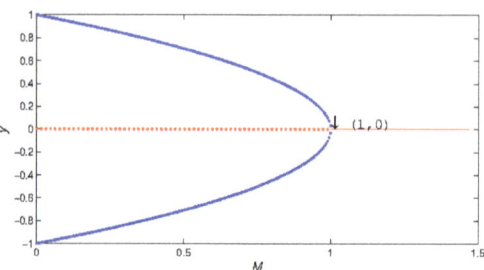

Figure 9. Pitchfork bifurcation diagrams in the $M - y$ plane with $\alpha = 3, \beta = 1, A = 1$.

Case (5): Set the parameters $\alpha = 1, M = 0.4, A = 0.3$ in the map (5). When $\beta = 2$, the corresponding eigenvalues of the matrix $J(E_{32}^*)$ are $\lambda_1 = -1, \lambda_2 = 0.8125$, respectively. From Theorem 8(2)(iii), $E_{32}^*(2, 0.5)$ is non-hyperbolic. Further, from Theorem 12(a), the map (5) has a flip bifurcation at E_{32}^*.

Figure 10a describes the diagram of the flip bifurcation on the $\beta - x$ plane at the initial value $x_0 = 0.5$, $y_0 = 0.3$, $\beta \in [0, 6]$, and the other parameters are shown in Case (5). From Figure 10a, the coexistence equilibria E_{32}^* are stable when $\beta < 2$, and when $\beta = 2$, the map (5) is unstable, resulting in a stable two-period solution; when $\beta > 3.065$, it will further generate four-dimensional solutions and constantly flip to generate chaotic sets.

Figure 10b shows the maximum Lyapunov exponents of Figure 10a, and β ranges in $[0, 6]$. When the exponent value is less than 0, this indicates that the map (5) is stable in the small field of $E_{32}^*(2, 0.5)$. In other words, when the exponent value is greater than 0, the map (5) is chaotic in the small field of $E_{32}^*(2, 0.5)$. From Figure 10b, when β varies in $[0, 2]$, the index is negative, except for $\beta = 2$, which is 0. When β belongs to $(2, 3.345]$, the index is only 0 at $\beta = 3.065$ and $\beta = 3.345$, and in other cases, the index is negative. When β is greater than 3.345, most of the indices are positive and very few are negative numbers, which indicates that the map (5) produces chaotic behavior near the fixed point $E_{32}^*(2, 0.5)$. We also give local bifurcation diagrams in Figure 11. Further, when we choose $\beta = 1, 2.5, 3.2, 3.345, 4.5, 5$, the phase diagrams are depicted in Figure 12. As β increases, it can be seen from Figure 12 that there will be one point, two points, four points, eight points, etc., gradually becoming chaotic.

Case (6): To study the impact of the Allee effect on the dynamic behavior of the map (5), we used the matlab 2017a drawing software to give the bifurcation diagram on the $M - x$ plane and $M - y$. We selected four sets of parameters. (a) Set the parameter $\alpha = 1.5, \beta = 1.5, A = 0.5, M \in [0, 1]$; (b) set the parameter $\alpha = 1.5, \beta = 1.5, A = 2$, $M \in [0, 2]$; (c) set the parameter $\alpha = 2.5, \beta = 1, A = 0.5, M \in [0, 1]$; (d) set the parameter $\alpha = 2.5, \beta = 1.5, A = 4, M \in [0, 6]$, taking the initial value $x_0 = 0.5$, $y_0 = 0.3$.

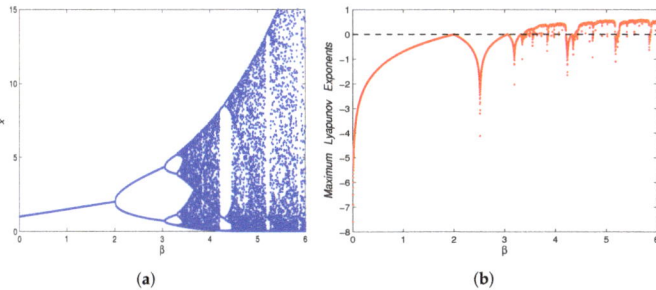

Figure 10. (a) Flip bifurcation diagrams on the $\beta - x$ plane with $\alpha = 1, M = 0.4, A = 0.3$; (b) maximum Lyapunov exponents corresponding to (a).

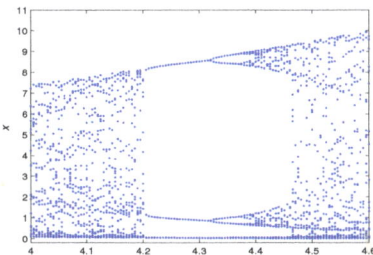

Figure 11. Local bifurcation diagrams corresponding to Figure 10a.

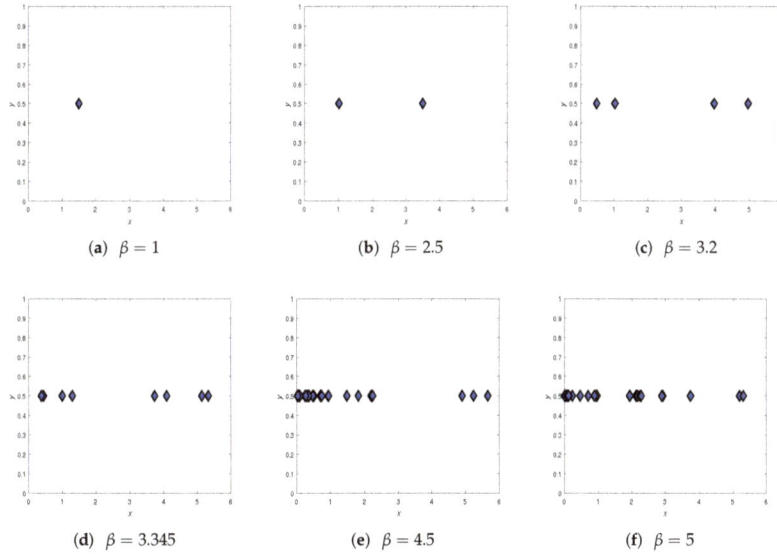

Figure 12. Phase diagrams corresponding to Figure 10a.

From Figure 13a,c, it is shown that, with the increase of M, it helps the stability of the commensal populations. Further, we also found that a strong Allee effect reduces the species density of the commensal. Figure 13b,d are graphs showing the impact of the Allee effect M on the population density of the host species. It can be seen from Figure 13b,d that, if M increases, the host population is accelerated to extinction. It can be seen from

Figure 13e,f that, as M increases, the map (5) moves from chaos to a two-period solution, but the map (5) is unstable.

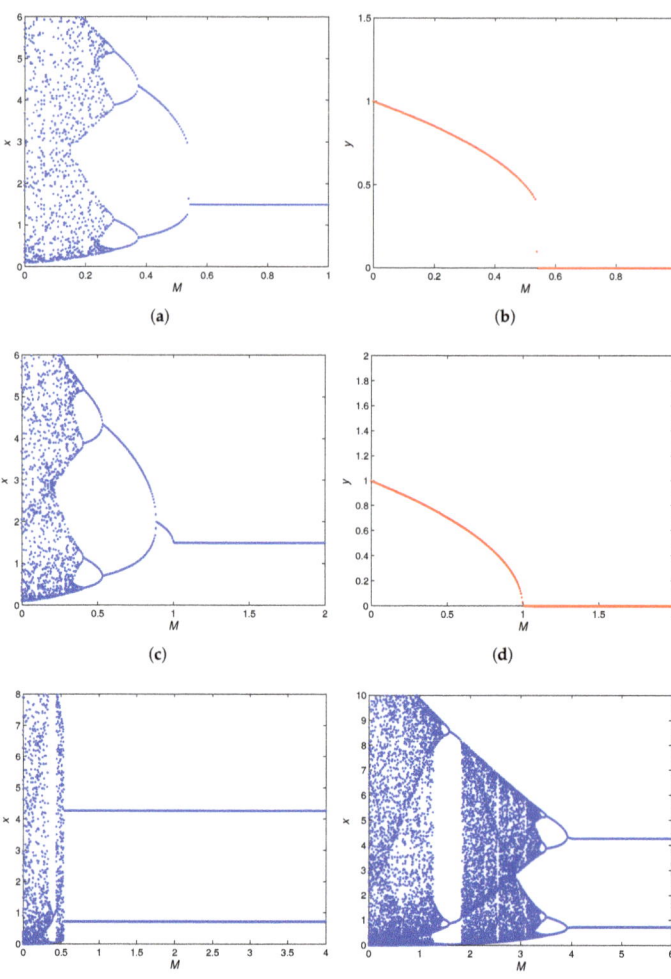

Figure 13. (a) Bifurcation diagrams in the $M - x$ plane with $\alpha = 1.5, \beta = 1.5, A = 0.5$; (b) bifurcation diagrams in the $M - y$ plane with $\alpha = 1.5, \beta = 1.5, A = 0.5$; (c) bifurcation diagrams in the $M - x$ plane with $\alpha = 1.5, \beta = 1.5, A = 2$; (d) bifurcation diagrams in the $M - y$ plane with $\alpha = 1.5, \beta = 1.5, A = 2$; (e) bifurcation diagrams in the $M - x$ plane with $\alpha = 2.5, \beta = 1.5, A = 0.5$; (f) bifurcation diagrams in the $M - x$ plane with $\alpha = 2.5, \beta = 1.5, A = 4$.

Case (7): Set parameters $\alpha = 1, \beta = 1, A = 0.5$ in the map (5). We can simply calculate $\beta_3^* = 4$. Then, the eigenvalues of the Jacobian matrix $J(E_{32}^*)$ of the map (5) are $\lambda_1 = -0.25, \lambda_2 = 1$, respectively. By Theorem 8(3), $E_{33}^*(1.25, 0.25)$ is non-hyperbolic. Through the bifurcation study of Theorem 12(b), a fold bifurcation occurs at coexistence equilibrium $E_{33}^*(1.25, 0.25)$, which is also called a fold point.

Figure 14 is a diagram of fold bifurcation on the $M - y$ plane within the local range of the fixed point $E_{33}^*(1.25, 0.25)$. Select the initial value $x_0 = 0.5$, $y_0 = 0.3$, $M \in (0, 1)$, and other parameters are given in Case (7). As M increases from 0 to 0.5625, the map (5) has an unstable fixed point $E_{31}^* = (1.25 - \sqrt{1-M}, 0.25 - \sqrt{1-M})$ (shown in red) and a stable fixed point $E_{32}^* = (1.25 + \sqrt{1-M}, 0.25 + \sqrt{1-M})$ (shown in blue). At $M = 0.5625$, System (5) undergoes a fold (also called saddle-node) bifurcation at $E_{33}^*(1.25, 0.25)$. Then, the fixed point $E_{33}^*(1.25, 0.25)$ vanishes for $M > 0.5625$.

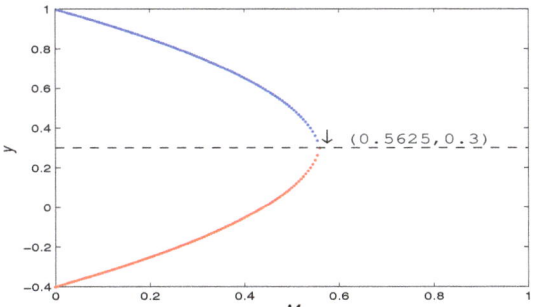

Figure 14. Fold bifurcation diagrams in the $M - y$ plane with $\alpha = 1, \beta = 1, A = 0.5$.

Case (8): Set the parameters $\alpha = 2.5, \beta = 1, M = 0.1, A = 4$, and the initial value $x_0 = 0.5, y_0 = 0.3$. We can simply calculate $y_2 \approx 0.96$, $x_2^* \approx 3.48$, and $\rho x_2^* < 2$ is equivalent to $\rho < 0.57$. Moreover, $\rho y_2(1 - \frac{M}{(y_2+A)^2}) < 2$ implies that $\rho < 2.04$. So, let us take a smaller ρ. From Theorem 13, when $0 < \rho < 0.57$, it is locally asymptotically stable. Figure 15 shows that when the external control parameters change in the range [0,0.57], the map (5) can be stabilized again. In addition, we set the parameter $\alpha = 2.5, \beta = 1, A = 4$, then the stability region diagram is given of the control system (28) in Figure 16.

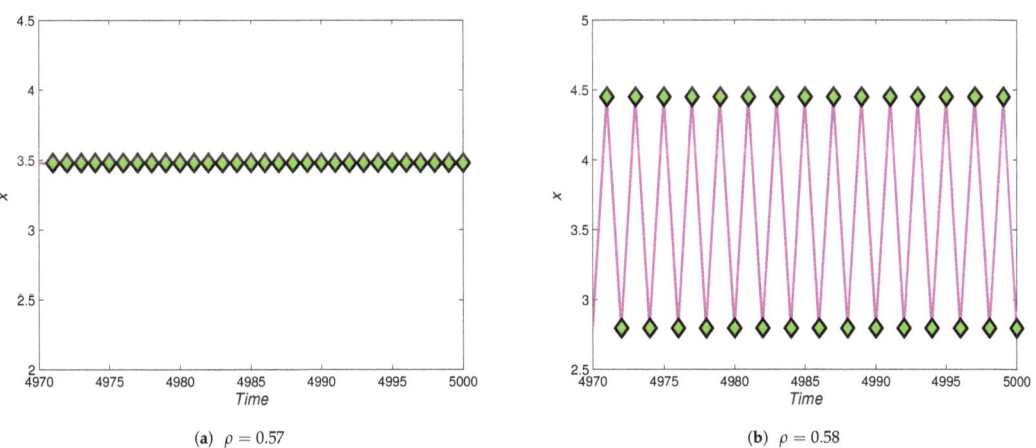

Figure 15. Time series of the commensal species for (28) with $\alpha = 0.5, \beta = 0.5, M = 0.2, A = 4$. (a) $\rho = 0.57$; (b) $\rho = 0.58$.

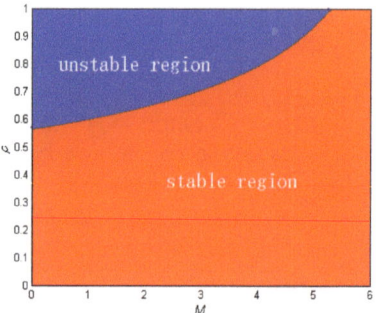

Figure 16. Stability region diagram in the $M - \rho$ plane with $\alpha = 2.5, \beta = 1, A = 4$.

5. Summary

This paper investigated a discrete-time commensalism mode with an additive Allee effect for the host species. First, we gave the existence and local stability of fixed points in the map (6), and we found that, under the weak Allee effect, the system has a unique positive fixed point of global attraction. Under the strong Allee effect, the stability of the system is related to the attraction domain, which has similar properties to the corresponding continuous system. Secondly, we studied the existence and stability of the solutions of the map (5), then gave the possible bifurcation of the map (5) by the center manifold theorem and bifurcation theory. We found that the map (5) has new bifurcation phenomena, such as flip and pitchfork bifurcations, which could not be found in the corresponding continuous-time system. Wei et al. [47] presented a commensal model with additive Allees in the first species and discussed the occurrence of saddle-node bifurcation and transcritical bifurcation. Examining a Lotka–Volterra commensal model featuring an Allee effect within the first species, Lin [48] revealed that heightened Allee effects lead to an escalation in the final population density of the species. In [13], Chen examined a comparable two-species commensal symbiosis model and noted that the Allee effect introduces instability to the system; nevertheless, this effect can be managed and controlled. From our investigation, it was revealed that the Allee increases the system complexity through multiple bifurcations. Recently, the studies by He et al. [11] revealed that, in the case of the weak Allee effect, the additive Allee effect negatively correlated with the final population density of both species. For a strong Allee effect, the additive Allee effect played a significant role in the extinction of the second species. Our study in this domain showed more-complex dynamics in comparison to the continuous-time model (2), which were presented through bifurcation analysis. Through numerical simulations of our proposed model, in the case where the first population had a lower birth rate, we observed that the Allee effect enhanced the stability of the commensal species, while hastening the extinction of the host species (see Figure 13a–d). These intricate and multifaceted dynamic behaviors mark our model as a truly novel contribution. Moreover, the map (5) may also have a fold–flip bifurcation of a codimension of two at fixed point $E^*_{33}(x^*_3, y_3)$, which is something we need to study in the future. When $M = 0$, the map (5) has at most four positive fixed points, and only flip bifurcation can occur. When $M \neq 0$, the system may have six positive fixed points, and they may undergo flip, fold, transcritical, pitchfork, and fold–flip bifurcations, which are left for future investigation.

Author Contributions: Y.C. was mainly responsible for the writing of the first draft of the article, and A.J.K. substantially rewrote the preface and conclusion sections, embellished the presentation of the full text, explored the flip bifurcation, and also, carefully and meticulously reviewed the the full text. S.C. was responsible for the numerical simulation part of the article drawings with the MATLAB software. F.C. was responsible for correcting the details and logic of the article. All authors have read and agreed to the published version of the manuscript.

Funding: This work was supported by the Natural Science Foundation of Fujian Province (2020J01499).

Data Availability Statement: Not applicable.

Conflicts of Interest: The authors declare no conflict of interest.

References

1. Mathis, K.A.; Bronstein, J.L. Our current understanding of commensalism. *Annu. Rev. Ecol. Evol. Syst.* **2020**, *51*, 167–189. [CrossRef]
2. Leung, T.L.; Poulin, R. Parasitism, commensalism, and mutualism: Exploring the many shades of symbioses. *Vie Milieu* **2008**, *58*, 107–115.
3. Anderson, B.; Midgley, J.J. Density-dependent outcomes in a digestive mutualism between carnivorous Roridula plants and their associated hemipterans. *Oecologia* **2007**, *152*, 115–120. [CrossRef]
4. Heard, S.B. Pitcher-plant midges and mosquitoes: A processing chain commensalism. *Ecology* **1994**, *75*, 1647–1660. [CrossRef]
5. Hari, P.B.; Pattabhi, R.N.C. Discrete model of commensalism between two species. *Int. J. Mod. Edu. Comput. Sci.* **2012**, *8*, 40–46.
6. Sun, G.C.; Wei, W.L. The qualitative analysis of commensal symbiosis model of two populations. *Math. Theory Appl.* **2003**, *23*, 65–68.
7. Chen, F.D.; Chong, Y.B.; Lin, S.J. Global stability of a commensal symbiosis model with Holling II functional response and feedback controls. *Wseas Trans. Syst. Contr.* **2022**, *17*, 279–286. [CrossRef]
8. Wu, R.X.; Li, L.; Lin, Q.F. A Holling type commensal symbiosis model involving Allee effect. *Commun. Math. Biol. Neurosci.* **2018**, *2018*, 6.
9. Chen, B.G. The influence of commensalism on a Lotka–Volterra commensal symbiosis model with Michaelis–Menten type harvesting. *Adv. Differ. Equ.* **2019**, *2019*, 43. [CrossRef]
10. Xu, L.L.; Lin, Q.F.; Lei, C.Q. Dynamic behavior of commensal symbiosis system with both feedback control and Allee effect. *J. Shanghai Norm. Univ.* **2022**, *51*, 391–396.
11. He, X.Q.; Zhu, Z.L.; Chen, J.L.; Chen, F. Dynamical analysis of a Lotka Volterra commensalism model with additive Allee effect. *Open Math.* **2022**, *20*, 646–665. [CrossRef]
12. Georgescu, P.; Maxin, D.; Zhang, H. Global stability results for models of commensalism. *Int. J. Biol.* **2017**, *10*, 1750037. [CrossRef]
13. Chen, B.G. Dynamic behaviors of a commensal symbiosis model involving Allee effect and one party can not survive independently. *Adv. Differ. Equ.* **2018**, *2018*, 212. [CrossRef]
14. Chen, J.H.; Wu, R.X. A commensal symbiosis model with non-monotonic functional response. *Math. Biol. Neurosci.* **2017**, *2017*, 5.
15. Lin, Q.F. Dynamic behaviors of a commensal symbiosis model with non-monotonic functional response and non-selective harvesting in a partial closure. *Commun. Math. Biol. Neurosci.* **2018**, *2018*, 4.
16. Li, T.T.; Lin, Q.X.; Chen, J.H. Positive periodic solution of a discrete commensal symbiosis model with Holling II functional response. *Commun. Math. Biol. Neurosci.* **2016**, *2016*, 22.
17. Xie, X.D.; Miao, Z.S.; Xue, Y.L. Positive periodic solution of a discrete Lotka–Volterra commensal symbiosis model. *Commun. Math. Biol. Neurosci.* **2015**, *2015*, 2.
18. Han, R.Y.; Chen, F.D. Global stability of a commensal symbiosis model with feedback controls. *Commun. Math. Biol. Neurosci.* **2015**, *2015*, 15.
19. Zhou, Q.M.; Lin, S.J.; Chen, F.D.; Wu, R. Positive periodic solution of a discrete Lotka–Volterra commensal symbiosis model with Michaelis–Menten type harvesting. *Wseas Trans. Math.* **2022**, *21*, 515–523. [CrossRef]
20. Chen, S.M.; Chong, Y.B.; Chen, F.D. Periodic solution of a discrete commensal symbiosis model with Hassell–Varley type functional response. *Nonauton. Dyn. Syst.* **2022**, *9*, 170–181. [CrossRef]
21. Xu, L.L.; Xue, Y.L.; Lin, Q.F.; Lei, C. Global attractivity of symbiotic model of commensalism in four populations with Michaelis–Menten type harvesting in the first commensal populations. *Axioms* **2022**, *11*, 337. [CrossRef]
22. Zhu, Z.L.; Wu, R.X.; Chen, F.D.; Li, Z. Dynamic behaviors of a Lotka–Volterra commensal symbiosis model with non-selective Michaelis–Menten type harvesting. *IAENG Int. J. Appl. Math.* **2020**, *50*, 1–9.
23. Liu, Y.; Guan, X.Y.; Xie, X.D.; Lin, Q. On the existence and stability of positive periodic solution of a nonautonomous commensal symbiosis model with Michaelis–Menten type harvesting. *Commun. Math. Biol. Neurosci.* **2019**, *2019*, 2.
24. Jawad, S. Study the dynamics of commensalism interaction with Michaels-Menten type prey harvesting. *Al-Nahrain J. Sci.* **2022**, *25*, 45–50. [CrossRef]
25. Chen, F.D.; Chen, Y.M.; Li, Z.; Chen, L. Note on the persistence and stability property of a commensalism model with Michaelis–Menten harvesting and Holling type II commensalistic benefit. *Appl. Math. Lett.* **2022**, *134*, 108381. [CrossRef]
26. Lei, C.Q. Dynamic behaviors of a Holling type commensal symbiosis model with the first species subject to Allee effect. *Commun. Math. Biol. Neurosci.* **2019**, *2019*, 3.
27. Guan, X.Y. Stability analysis of a Lotka–Volterra commensal symbiosis model involving Allee effect. *Ann. Appl. Math.* **2018**, *34*, 364–375.
28. Seval, I. Stability and period-doubling Bifurcation in a modified commensal symbiosis model with Allee effect. *Erzin. Univ. J. Sci. Technol.* **2022**, *15*, 310–324.

29. Li, T.Y.; Wang, Q.R. Bifurcation analysis for two-species commensalism (amensalism) systems with distributed delays. *Int. J. Bifurc. Chaos* **2022**, *32*, 2250133. [CrossRef]
30. Li, T.Y.; Wang, Q.R. Stability and Hopf bifurcation analysis for a two-species commensalism system with delay. *Qual. Theory Dyn. Syst.* **2021**, *20*, 83. [CrossRef]
31. Allee, W.C. *Animal Aggregations, a Study in General Sociology*; University of Chicago Press: Chicago, IL, USA, 1931.
32. Allee, W.C. *The Social Life of Animals*; William Heinemann: London, UK, 1938.
33. Gonzalez-Olivares, E.; Mena-Lorca, J.; Rojas-Palma, A.; Flores, J.D. Dynamical complexities in the Leslie-Gower predator-prey model as consequences of the Allee effect on prey. *Appl. Math. Model.* **2011**, *35*, 366–381. [CrossRef]
34. Sun, G.Q. Mathematical modeling of population dynamics with Allee effect. *Nonlinear Dyn.* **2016**, *85*, 1–12. [CrossRef]
35. Zhang, J.H.; Chen, X.Y. Dynamic behaviors of a discrete commensal symbiosis model with Holling type functional response. *IAENG Int. J. Appl. Math.* **2023**, *53*, 277–281.
36. Kundu, K.; Pal, S.; Samanta, S.; Sen, A.; Pal, N. Impact of fear effect in a discrete-time predator-prey system. *Bull. Calcutta Math. Soc.* **2018**, *110*, 245–264.
37. Zhou, Q.M.; Chen, F.D.; Lin, S.J. Complex dynamics analysis of a discrete amensalism system with a cover for the first species. *Axioms* **2022**, *11*, 365. [CrossRef]
38. Zhou, Q.M.; Chen, F.D. Dynamical analysis of a discrete amensalism system with the Beddington—DeAngelis functional response and Allee effect for the unaffected species. *Qual. Theory Dyn. Syst.* **2023**, *22*, 16. [CrossRef]
39. Garai, S.; Pati, N.C.; Pal, N.; Layek, G.C. Organized periodic structures and coexistence of triple attractors in a predator-prey model with fear and refuge. *Chaos Solitons Fractals* **2022**, *165*, 112833. [CrossRef]
40. Zhang, L.; Zhang, C.; He, Z. Codimension-one and codimension-two bifurcations of a discrete predator-prey system with strong Allee effect. *Math. Comput. Sim.* **2019**, *162*, 155–178. [CrossRef]
41. Chen, Q.L.; Teng, Z.D.; Wang, F. Fold–flip and strong resonance bifurcations of a discrete-time mosquito model. *Chaos Solitons Fractals* **2021**, *144*, 110704. [CrossRef]
42. Jiang, H.; Rogers, T.D. The discrete dynamics of symmetric competition in the plane. *J. Math. Bio.* **1987**, *25*, 573–596. [CrossRef]
43. Liu, X.L.; Xiao, D.M. Complex dynamic behaviors of a discrete-time predator-prey system. *Chaos Solitons Fractals* **2007**, *32*, 80–94. [CrossRef]
44. Kuznetsov, Y. *Elements of Applied Bifurcation Theory*; Springer: New York, NY, USA, 1998.
45. Winggins, S. *Introduction to Applied Nonlinear Dynamical Systems and Chaos*; Springer: New York, NY, USA, 2003.
46. Luo, X.S.; Chen, G.; Wang, B.H.; Fang, J.Q. Hybrid control of period-doubling bifurcation and chaos in discrete nonlinear dynamical systems. *Chaos Solitons Fractals* **2003**, *18*, 775–783. [CrossRef]
47. Wei, Z.; Xia, Y.H.; Zhang, T.H. Stability and bifurcation analysis of a commensal model with additive Allee effect and nonlinear growth rate. *Int. J. Bifurc. Chaos* **2021**, *31*, 2150204. [CrossRef]
48. Lin, Q.F. Allee effect increasing the final density of the species subject to the Allee effect in a Lotka–Volterra commensal symbiosis model. *Adv. Differ. Equ.* **2018**, *2018*, 196. [CrossRef]

Disclaimer/Publisher's Note: The statements, opinions and data contained in all publications are solely those of the individual author(s) and contributor(s) and not of MDPI and/or the editor(s). MDPI and/or the editor(s) disclaim responsibility for any injury to people or property resulting from any ideas, methods, instructions or products referred to in the content.

Article

Modeling Environmental Pollution Using Varying-Coefficients Quantile Regression Models under Log-Symmetric Distributions

Luis Sánchez [1], Germán Ibacache-Pulgar [2,3], Carolina Marchant [4,*] and Marco Riquelme [2]

1. Institute of Statistics, Universidad Austral de Chile, Valdivia 5110634, Chile; luis.sanchez@uach.cl
2. Institute of Statistics, Universidad de Valparaíso, Valparaíso 2360102, Chile; german.ibacache@uv.cl (G.I.-P.); marco.riquelme@uv.cl (M.R.)
3. Centro Interdisciplinario de Estudios Atmosféricos y Astroestadística, Universidad de Valparaíso, Valparaíso 2360102, Chile
4. Faculty of Basic Sciences, Universidad Católica del Maule, Talca 3480112, Chile
* Correspondence: cmarchant@ucm.cl

Abstract: Many phenomena can be described by random variables that follow asymmetrical distributions. In the context of regression, when the response variable Y follows such a distribution, it is preferable to estimate the response variable for predictor values using the conditional median. Quantile regression models can be employed for this purpose. However, traditional models do not incorporate a distributional assumption for the response variable. To introduce a distributional assumption while preserving model flexibility, we propose new varying-coefficients quantile regression models based on the family of log-symmetric distributions. We achieve this by reparametrizing the distribution of the response variable using quantiles. Parameter estimation is performed using a maximum likelihood penalized method, and a back-fitting algorithm is developed. Additionally, we propose diagnostic techniques to identify potentially influential local observations and leverage points. Finally, we apply and illustrate the methodology using real pollution data from Padre Las Casas city, one of the most polluted cities in Latin America and the Caribbean according to the World Air Quality Index Ranking.

Keywords: local influence techniques; log-symmetric distributions family; PM2.5 levels; quantile regression; semiparametric models

MSC: 62J20

1. Introduction

In the process of data modeling, it is common to utilize regression models that assume that the response variable follows a normal distribution, as this is well-established in theory. However, there are situations where using such models may not be appropriate, particularly when the response variable exhibits an asymmetric distribution and is restricted to the positive real line. Failing to account for this behavior can introduce bias in parameter estimates and the estimation of associated measures of variability; see [1]. To address the limitations associated with the assumption of normality, several authors have proposed alternative approaches that employ more flexible distributional assumptions. This allows for a better representation of the underlying data. Some examples of such approaches include the works of [2–7].

Vanegas and Paula [8] proposed a family of log-symmetric distributions, which are obtained by transforming symmetric distributed random variables whose probability density functions involve the exponential function. Some examples of log-symmetric distributions are the log-normal, log-power-exponential, log-Laplace, log-logistic, log-slash, where $J(\beta_k)$ corresponds to a penalty function on the function β_k that regulates the lack of smoothness of the estimated curve. Assuming that the design points t_k^0 belong to the compact set $[a_k, b_k]$ and that the functions β_k's belongs to the Sobolev function space [27]

$$W_{[a_k,b_k]} = \left\{ \beta_k : \beta_k \text{ and } \beta_k' \text{ are absolutely continuous on } [a_k, b_k], \text{ and } \int_{a_k}^{b_k} [\beta_k''(t_k)]^2 dt_k < \infty \right\},$$

Then one way to measure the roughness of the function β_k over the interval $[a_k, b_k]$ is by their squared norm given by $J(\beta_k) = \|\beta_k\|^2 = \int_{a_k}^{b_k} [\beta_k''(t_k)]^2 dt_k$. Green and Silverman [15] showed that $J(\beta_k) = \beta_k^\top K_k \beta_k$, where K_k is a $r_k \times r_k$ non-negative definite matrix. Please note that both β_k and K_k are evaluated at the values belonging to the set of knots $\{t_{k1}^0, t_{k2}^0, \ldots, t_{kr_k}^0\}$, for $k \in \{1, 2, \ldots, s\}$, and therefore have finite dimensions. Taking $\lambda_k^* = \lambda_k/2$, we can obtain the maximum penalized likelihood estimator (MPLE) of θ, denoted by $\hat{\theta}$, maximizing

$$\ell_p(\theta, \lambda) = \ell(\theta) - \sum_{k=1}^{s} \frac{\lambda_k}{2} \beta_k^\top K_k \beta_k, \qquad (3)$$

where $\lambda = (\lambda_1, \ldots, \lambda_s)^\top$ denotes an $s \times 1$ vector of smoothing parameters. Each $\lambda_k \geq 0$ measures the "rate of exchange" between goodness-of-fit and variability of the function β_k. In this scenario, the estimators of β_k's result in a cubic spline that is completely determined by the finite-dimensional set of knots $\{t_{k1}^0, t_{k2}^0, \ldots, t_{kr_k}^0\}$.

3. Parameter Estimation and Inference

In this section, we focus on estimating the parameters of the model described in Equation (1) and discuss aspects of statistical inference. We also provide a brief discussion on calculating the effective degrees of freedom and selecting smoothing parameters. To facilitate the parameter estimation process and associated inference, we have developed a routine in the R-project (https://www.r-project.org/; accessed on 15 May 2023).

3.1. Penalized Score Vector

First, we make the assumption that the function $\ell_p(\theta, \lambda)$ given in Equation (2) is regular, meaning that it has first and second partial derivatives with respect to the elements of the parameter vector θ. By performing partial derivative operations, we can express the score function for θ in matrix form as follows:

$$U_p^\top(\theta) = \frac{\partial \ell_p(\theta)}{\partial \theta} = \left(U_p^{\alpha\top}(\theta) \quad U_p^{\beta_1\top}(\theta) \quad \ldots \quad U_p^{\beta_s\top}(\theta) \quad U_p^{\phi\top}(\theta) \right)^\top,$$

where $U_p^\alpha(\theta) = W^\top D_a z$, $U_p^{\beta_k}(\theta) = \tilde{N}_k^\top D_a z - \lambda_k K_k \beta_k$, for $k \in \{1, \ldots, s\}$, and $U_p^\phi(\theta) = \text{tr}(D_b)$, with $D_a = \text{diag}\{a_1, \ldots, a_n\}$, $D_b = \text{diag}\{b_1, \ldots, b_n\}$, $z = (z_1, \ldots, z_n)^\top$, $z_i = v_i r(v_i)/Q_i \sqrt{\phi}$, $b_i = r(v_i) \phi^{-3/2} v_i [\log(y_i) - \log(Q_i)]/2 - 1/2\phi$ and $a_i = 1/h'(Q_i)$, being $r(v_i) = -2g'(v_i^2)/g(v_i^2)$. Please note that g' represents the derivative of the function g.

3.2. Penalized Hessian Matrix

To obtain the penalized Hessian matrix, we need to compute the second derivate of $\ell_p(\theta, \lambda)$ with respect to each element of θ, i.e., $\partial^2 \ell_p(\theta, \lambda)/\partial \theta_{j^*} \partial \theta_{l^*}$ for $j^*, l^* \in \{1, \ldots, p^*\}$ and $p^* = 2 + p + \sum_{k=1}^{s} r_k$. After performing some algebraic manipulations, we obtain the penalized Hessian matrix in the following form:

$$\ddot{L}_{\text{p}}(\boldsymbol{\theta}) = \frac{\partial^2 \ell_{\text{p}}(\boldsymbol{\theta},\boldsymbol{\lambda})}{\partial \boldsymbol{\theta} \partial \boldsymbol{\theta}^\top} = \begin{pmatrix} \ddot{L}_{\text{p}}^{\alpha\alpha} & \ddot{L}_{\text{p}}^{\alpha\beta_1} & \cdots & \ddot{L}_{\text{p}}^{\alpha\beta_s} & \ddot{L}_{\text{p}}^{\alpha\phi} \\ \ddot{L}_{\text{p}}^{\alpha\beta_1^\top} & \ddot{L}_{\text{p}}^{\beta_1\beta_1} & \cdots & \ddot{L}_{\text{p}}^{\beta_1\beta_s} & \ddot{L}_{\text{p}}^{\beta_1\phi} \\ \vdots & \vdots & \ddots & \vdots & \vdots \\ \ddot{L}_{\text{p}}^{\alpha\beta_s^\top} & \ddot{L}_{\text{p}}^{\beta_1\beta_s^\top} & \cdots & \ddot{L}_{\text{p}}^{\beta_s\beta_s} & \ddot{L}_{\text{p}}^{\beta_s\phi} \\ \ddot{L}_{\text{p}}^{\alpha\phi^\top} & \ddot{L}_{\text{p}}^{\beta_1\phi^\top} & \cdots & \ddot{L}_{\text{p}}^{\beta_s\phi^\top} & \ddot{L}_{\text{p}}^{\phi\phi} \end{pmatrix}, \quad (4)$$

with $\ddot{L}_{\text{p}}^{\alpha\alpha} = \boldsymbol{W}^\top \boldsymbol{D}_c \boldsymbol{W}$, $\ddot{L}_{\text{p}}^{\alpha\beta_k} = \boldsymbol{W}^\top \boldsymbol{D}_c \tilde{\boldsymbol{N}}_k$, $\ddot{L}_{\text{p}}^{\alpha\phi} = \boldsymbol{W}^\top \boldsymbol{D}_a \boldsymbol{m}$, $\ddot{L}_{\text{p}}^{\beta_k\phi} = \tilde{\boldsymbol{N}}_k^\top \boldsymbol{D}_a \boldsymbol{m}$, for $k \in \{1,\ldots,s\}$, $\ddot{L}_{\text{p}}^{\phi\phi} = \text{tr}(\boldsymbol{D}_d)$, and

$$\ddot{L}_{\text{p}}^{\beta_k\beta_{k'}^\top} = \begin{cases} \tilde{\boldsymbol{N}}_k^\top \boldsymbol{D}_c \tilde{\boldsymbol{N}}_k - \lambda_k \boldsymbol{K}_k, & k = k' \\ \tilde{\boldsymbol{N}}_k^\top \boldsymbol{D}_c \tilde{\boldsymbol{N}}_{k'}, & k \neq k' \end{cases}$$

where the matrices $\boldsymbol{D}_c = \text{diag}\{c_1,\ldots,c_n\}$, $\boldsymbol{D}_a = \text{diag}\{a_1,\ldots,a_n\}$ and vector $\boldsymbol{m} = (m_1,\ldots,m_n)^\top$, with c_i, a_i and m_i defined in Appendix A. The Hessian matrix presented in this section will be used in the construction of the normal curvature for the local influence method developed in Section 4.

3.3. Penalized Fisher Information Matrix

By taking the expectation of the matrix $-\ddot{L}_{\text{p}}(\boldsymbol{\theta})$ given in Equation (4), we derive the $p^* \times p^*$ penalized expected information matrix given by

$$J_{\text{p}}(\boldsymbol{\theta}) = \begin{pmatrix} J_{\text{p}}^{\alpha\alpha} & J_{\text{p}}^{\alpha\beta_1} & \cdots & J_{\text{p}}^{\alpha\beta_s} & J_{\text{p}}^{\alpha\phi} \\ J_{\text{p}}^{\alpha\beta_1^\top} & J_{\text{p}}^{\beta_1\beta_1} & \cdots & J_{\text{p}}^{\beta_1\beta_s} & J_{\text{p}}^{\beta_1\phi} \\ \vdots & \vdots & \ddots & \vdots & \vdots \\ J_{\text{p}}^{\alpha\beta_s^\top} & J_{\text{p}}^{\beta_1\beta_s^\top} & \cdots & J_{\text{p}}^{\beta_s\beta_s} & J_{\text{p}}^{\beta_s\phi} \\ J_{\text{p}}^{\alpha\phi^\top} & J_{\text{p}}^{\beta_1\phi^\top} & \cdots & J_{\text{p}}^{\beta_s\phi^\top} & J_{\text{p}}^{\phi\phi} \end{pmatrix}, \quad (5)$$

whose elements can be expressed as $J_{\text{p}}^{\alpha\alpha} = \boldsymbol{W}^\top \boldsymbol{D}_v \boldsymbol{W}$, $J_{\text{p}}^{\alpha\beta_k} = \boldsymbol{W}^\top \boldsymbol{D}_v \tilde{\boldsymbol{N}}_k$, $J_{\text{p}}^{\alpha\phi} = \boldsymbol{W}^\top \boldsymbol{D}_a \boldsymbol{s}$, $J_{\text{p}}^{\beta_k\phi} = \tilde{\boldsymbol{N}}_k^\top \boldsymbol{D}_a \boldsymbol{s}$, for $k \in \{1,\ldots,s\}$, $J_{\text{p}}^{\phi\phi} = \text{tr}(\boldsymbol{D}_u)$, and

$$J_{\text{p}}^{\beta_k\beta_{k'}^\top} = \begin{cases} \tilde{\boldsymbol{N}}_k^\top \boldsymbol{D}_v \tilde{\boldsymbol{N}}_k + \lambda_k \boldsymbol{K}_k, & k = k' \\ \tilde{\boldsymbol{N}}_k^\top \boldsymbol{D}_v \tilde{\boldsymbol{N}}_{k'}, & k \neq k', \end{cases}$$

where $\boldsymbol{D}_v = \text{diag}\{e_1,\ldots,e_n\}$, $\boldsymbol{D}_u = \text{diag}\{u_1,\ldots,u_n\}$ and $\boldsymbol{s} = (s_1,\ldots,s_n)^\top$, being $e_i = \mathbb{E}[-c_i]$, $s_i = \mathbb{E}[-m_i]$ and $u_i = \mathbb{E}[-d_i]$, with $\mathbb{E}[\cdot]$ denoting the expected value operator. This matrix will be utilized to approximate the variance-covariance matrix of $\hat{\boldsymbol{\theta}}$, as discussed in Section 3.5.

3.4. Iterative Process

The MPLE of $\boldsymbol{\theta}$ is obtained by maximizing the penalized log-likelihood function presented in Equation (3). Since the resulting estimation equation $\boldsymbol{U}_{\text{p}}(\boldsymbol{\theta}) = \boldsymbol{0}$ is nonlinear, an iterative process is necessary to solve it. In this regard, we propose to employ the Fisher scoring algorithm, which updates $\boldsymbol{\theta}$ using the matrix equation

$$J_{\text{p}}(\boldsymbol{\theta})\left[\boldsymbol{\theta}^{(m+1)} - \boldsymbol{\theta}^{(m)}\right] = \boldsymbol{U}_{\text{p}}(\boldsymbol{\theta})^{(m)}, \quad m = 0, 1, \ldots. \quad (6)$$

3.4.1. ϕ Unknown

After some algebraic operations, we obtain the following expressions for the iterative solutions for the case where ϕ unknown:

$$\begin{aligned}
\boldsymbol{\alpha}^{(m+1)} &= (\boldsymbol{W}^\top \boldsymbol{D}_v^{(m)} \boldsymbol{W})^{-1} \boldsymbol{W}^\top \boldsymbol{D}_v^{(m)} \left[\boldsymbol{\psi}_\alpha^{(m)} - \boldsymbol{D}_{v,a}^{(m)} \boldsymbol{s} \boldsymbol{\Phi}_\phi^{(m+1,m)} - \sum_{k=1}^s \tilde{\boldsymbol{N}}_k \boldsymbol{\Phi}_{\beta_k}^{(m+1,m)} \right], \\
\boldsymbol{\beta}_\ell^{(m+1)} &= (\tilde{\boldsymbol{N}}^\top \boldsymbol{D}_v^{(m)} \tilde{\boldsymbol{N}} + \lambda_k \boldsymbol{K})^{-1} \tilde{\boldsymbol{N}}^\top \boldsymbol{D}_v^{(m)} \left[\boldsymbol{\psi}_{\beta_\ell}^{(m)} - \boldsymbol{D}_{v,a}^{(m)} \boldsymbol{s} \boldsymbol{\Phi}_\phi^{(m+1,m)} - \boldsymbol{W} \boldsymbol{\Phi}_\alpha^{(m+1,m)} \right. \\
&\quad \left. - \sum_{k=1, k\neq \ell}^s \tilde{\boldsymbol{N}}_k \boldsymbol{\Phi}_{\beta_k}^{(m+1,m)} \right], \quad \ell \in \{1, \ldots, s\} \quad \text{and} \\
\phi^{(m+1)} &= \operatorname{tr}^{-1}(\boldsymbol{D}_u^{(m)}) \left[\operatorname{tr}(\boldsymbol{D}_b^{(m)}) + \operatorname{tr}(\boldsymbol{D}_u^{(m)}) \phi^{(m)} - \boldsymbol{s}^\top \boldsymbol{D}_a^{(m)} \boldsymbol{W} \boldsymbol{\Phi}_\alpha^{(m+1,m)} \right. \\
&\quad \left. - \boldsymbol{s}^\top \boldsymbol{D}_a^{(m)} \sum_{k=1}^s \tilde{\boldsymbol{N}}_k \boldsymbol{\Phi}_{\beta_k}^{(m+1,m)} \right],
\end{aligned}$$

where $\boldsymbol{\psi}_\alpha^{(m)} = \boldsymbol{D}_{v,a}^{(m)} \boldsymbol{z}^{(m)} + \boldsymbol{W} \boldsymbol{\alpha}^{(m)}$ and $\boldsymbol{\psi}_{\beta_\ell}^{(m)} = \boldsymbol{D}_{v,a}^{(m)} \boldsymbol{z}^{(m)} + \tilde{\boldsymbol{N}}_\ell \boldsymbol{\beta}_\ell^{(m)}$, with $\boldsymbol{D}_{v,a}^{(m)} = \boldsymbol{D}_v^{(m)-1} \boldsymbol{D}_a^{(m)}$.

3.4.2. ϕ Known

When ϕ is known, it is possible to obtain simplified expressions for the iterative solutions of $\boldsymbol{\alpha}^{(m+1)}$ and $\boldsymbol{\beta}_\ell^{(m+1)}$. In this case, we have that

$$\begin{aligned}
\boldsymbol{\alpha}^{(m+1)} &= (\boldsymbol{W}^\top \boldsymbol{D}_v^{(m)} \boldsymbol{W})^{-1} \boldsymbol{W}^\top \boldsymbol{D}_v^{(m)} \left[\boldsymbol{r}_{v,a}^{(m)} - \sum_{k=1}^s \tilde{\boldsymbol{N}}_k \boldsymbol{\beta}_k^{(m+1)} \right], \quad \text{and} \\
\boldsymbol{\beta}_\ell^{(m+1)} &= (\tilde{\boldsymbol{N}}^\top \boldsymbol{D}_v^{(m)} \tilde{\boldsymbol{N}} + \lambda_k \boldsymbol{K})^{-1} \tilde{\boldsymbol{N}}^\top \boldsymbol{D}_v^{(m)} \left[\boldsymbol{r}_{v,a}^{(m)} - \boldsymbol{W} \boldsymbol{\alpha}^{(m+1)} - \sum_{k=1, k\neq \ell}^s \tilde{\boldsymbol{N}}_k \boldsymbol{\beta}_k^{(m+1)} \right],
\end{aligned}$$

for $\ell \in \{1, \ldots, s\}$, where $\boldsymbol{r}_{v,a}^{(m)} = \boldsymbol{D}_{(v,a)}^{(m)} \boldsymbol{z}^{(m)} + \boldsymbol{\eta}^{(m)}$, with $\boldsymbol{\eta}^{(m)} = \boldsymbol{W} \boldsymbol{\alpha}^{(m)} + \sum_{k=1}^s \tilde{\boldsymbol{N}}_k \boldsymbol{\beta}_k^{(m)}$. It is possible to prove that these expressions correspond to the weighted back-fitting (Gauss-Seidel) iterations considering $\boldsymbol{r}_{v,a}^{(m)}$ as dependent modified variable and $\boldsymbol{D}_v$ as a matrix of weights that changes with each iteration of the process; see, for instance [28]. A general expression for these iterations is as follows:

$$\boldsymbol{\beta}_\ell^{(m+1)} = \boldsymbol{S}_\ell^{(m)} \left[\boldsymbol{r}_{v,a}^{(m)} - \sum_{k=0, k\neq \ell}^s \tilde{\boldsymbol{N}}_k \boldsymbol{\beta}_k^{(m+1)} \right], \quad \ell \in \{1, \ldots, s\}, \tag{7}$$

where $\boldsymbol{r}_{v,a}^{(m)} = \boldsymbol{D}_{v,a}^{(m)} \boldsymbol{z}^{(m)} + \boldsymbol{\eta}^{(m)}$, with $\boldsymbol{\eta}^{(m)} = \sum_{k=0}^s \tilde{\boldsymbol{N}}_k \boldsymbol{\beta}_k^{(m)}$, $\tilde{\boldsymbol{N}}_0 = \boldsymbol{W}$, $\boldsymbol{\beta}_0 = \boldsymbol{\alpha}$, $\boldsymbol{S}_0^{(m)} = (\tilde{\boldsymbol{N}}_0^\top \boldsymbol{D}_v^{(m)} \tilde{\boldsymbol{N}}_0)^{-1} \tilde{\boldsymbol{N}}_0^\top \boldsymbol{D}_v^{(m)}$ and $\boldsymbol{S}_k^{(m)} = (\tilde{\boldsymbol{N}}_k^\top \boldsymbol{D}_v^{(m)} \tilde{\boldsymbol{N}}_k + \lambda_k \boldsymbol{K}_k)^{-1} \tilde{\boldsymbol{N}}_k^\top \boldsymbol{D}_v^{(m)}$. A discussion about the consistency of the system of Equations (6) and the convergence of the back-fitting algorithm in (7) is given, for example, in [29].

3.5. Approximate Standard Errors

In this work, we propose to approximate the variance-covariance matrix of $\widehat{\boldsymbol{\theta}}$ using the inverse of the penalized Fisher information matrix defined in Equation (5). In effect, an estimation of the variance-covariance matrix of $\widehat{\boldsymbol{\theta}}$ is given by

$$\widehat{\operatorname{Cov}}(\widehat{\boldsymbol{\theta}}) \approx \boldsymbol{J}_\mathrm{p}(\widehat{\boldsymbol{\theta}})^{-1}. \tag{8}$$

Following [14], we can consider an approximate pointwise standard error band (SEB) for nonparametric functions β_k's to evaluate the accuracy of the estimators $\widehat{\beta}_k'$s for different locations within the range of interest. In our case, these approximate pointwise SEBs are provided by

$$\mathrm{SEB}_{\mathrm{approx}}\left(\beta_k\left(t_l^0\right)\right) = \widehat{\beta}_k\left(t_l^0\right) \pm 2\sqrt{\widehat{\operatorname{Var}}\left(\widehat{\beta}_k(t_l^0)\right)},$$

where $\text{Var}(\widehat{\beta}_k(t_l))$ is the l-th principal diagonal element of the matrix provided in Equation (8) for $l \in \{1, 2, \ldots, r_k\}$. Please note that t_l^0 corresponds to the knots associated with each variable with a nonparametric contribution to the model.

3.6. Effective Degrees of Freedom and λ_k's

The calculation of the degrees of freedom associated with the parametric and non-parametric contributions is based on the iterative process used in the parameters estimation of the proposed model. Assuming ϕ fixed, we have from the convergence of the iterative process that

$$\widehat{\beta}_\ell = (\widetilde{N}^\top \widehat{D}_v \widetilde{N} + \lambda_k K)^{-1} \widetilde{N}^\top \widehat{D}_v \widehat{r}^*_{v,a}, \quad \ell \in \{1, \ldots, s\},$$

where $\widehat{r}^*_{v,a} = \widehat{r}_{v,a} - \sum_{k=0, k \neq \ell}^{s} \widetilde{N}_k \widehat{\beta}_k$, $\widehat{r}_{v,a} = \widehat{D}_{(a,v)} \widehat{z} + \widehat{\eta}$, $\widehat{\eta} = W\widehat{\alpha} + \sum_{k=1}^{s} \widetilde{N}_k \widehat{\beta}_k$ and $\widehat{z} = (\widehat{z}_1, \ldots, \widehat{z}_n)^\top$, with z_i ($i \in \{1, 2, \ldots, n\}$) defined in Section 3.1. Note that $r^*_{v,a}$ can be interpreted as a modified variable and D_v a weight matrix that is updated at each stage of the iterative process. From this, we define the effective degrees of freedom (edf) associated with the smooth functions as (see, for instance [14])

$$\text{edf}(\lambda_k) = \text{tr}\{\widetilde{N}(\widetilde{N}^\top \widehat{D}_v \widetilde{N} + \lambda_k K)^{-1} \widetilde{N}^\top \widehat{D}_v\}, \quad \ell \in \{1, \ldots, s\}.$$

Following Ibacache-Pulgar and Reyes [23], we choose the optimal smoothing parameter for each smooth function by specifying an appropriate $\text{edf}(\lambda_k)$ value. Another way to select the λ_k's is to consider the Akaike Information Criterion (AIC). The idea is to minimize a function with respect to λ formulated as follows:

$$\text{AIC}(\lambda) = -2\ell_p(\widehat{\theta}, \lambda) + 2(2 + p + \text{edf}(\lambda)), \quad (9)$$

where $\ell_p(\widehat{\theta}, \lambda)$ denotes the penalized log-likelihood function evaluated at $\widehat{\theta}$ for a fixed λ and $\text{edf}(\lambda) = \sum_{k=1}^{s} \text{edf}(\lambda_k)$ denoting the number of effective parameters involved in the modeling of the smooth functions. A grid for different values of λ and its corresponding $\text{AIC}(\lambda)$ are helpful to choose the suitable smoothing parameters. The criteria defined in Equation (9) can also be used to select the best model within the class of varying coefficients quantile regression models based on the log-symmetric family.

4. Diagnostic Analysis

In this section, we extend the local influence method for the model given in Equation (1) and derive the generalized leverage matrix, which allows us to assess the influence of each observed value of the response variable y_i on its corresponding predicted value $\widehat{y}_i$.

4.1. Local Influence Analysis

Let $\omega = (\omega_1, \ldots, \omega_n)^\top$ be an $n \times 1$ vector of perturbations restricted to some open subset $\Omega \in \mathbb{R}^n$ and $\ell_p(\theta, \lambda \mid \omega)$ be the logarithm of the perturbed penalized likelihood function. It is assumed that exists $\omega_0 \in \Omega$, a vector of non-perturbation, such that $\ell_p(\theta, \lambda \mid \omega_0) = \ell_p(\theta, \lambda)$. To assess the influence of small perturbations on the MPL estimate $\widehat{\theta}$, we can consider the displacement of the penalized likelihood, which is given by $\text{LD}(\omega) = 2(\ell_p(\widehat{\theta}, \lambda) - \ell_p(\widehat{\theta}_\omega, \lambda))$, where $\widehat{\theta}_\omega$ is the MPL estimate under $\ell_p(\theta, \lambda \mid \omega)$. The measure $\text{LD}(\omega)$ is helpful for assessing the distance between $\widehat{\theta}$ and $\widehat{\theta}_\omega$. Cook [30] suggested studying the local behavior of $\text{LD}(\omega)$ around ω_0. The procedure involves selecting a unit direction $d \in \Omega$ with $|d| = 1$ and plotting $\text{LD}(\omega_0 + ad)$ against $a \in \mathbb{R}$. This plot, known as a lifted line, can be characterized by considering the normal curvature $C_d(\theta)$ around $a = 0$. To determine the direction $d = d_{\max}$ that corresponds to the largest curvature $Cd_{\max}(\theta)$, one can examine the index plot of $d_{\max}$. This plot helps identify cases that, under small perturbations, may have a significant potential influence on $\text{LD}(\omega)$. According to Cook [30], the normal curvature at the unit direction d can be expressed as

$$C_d(\theta) = -2(d^\top \Delta_p^\top \ddot{L}_p^{-1} \Delta_p d),$$

with $\ddot{L}_p(\theta) = \partial^2 \ell_p(\theta,\lambda)/\partial\theta\partial\theta^\top$ and $\Delta_p = \partial^2 \ell_p(\theta,\lambda\,|\,\omega)/\partial\theta\partial\omega^\top$ evaluated at $\theta = \hat{\theta}$ and $\omega = \omega_0$. Δ_p is called a penalized perturbation matrix. Observe that $C_d(\theta)$ denotes the local influence on the estimate $\hat{\theta}$ after perturbing the model or data. Escobar and Meeker [31] proposed to study the normal curvature at the direction $d = e_i$, where e_i is an $n \times 1$ vector with a one at the ith position and zeros at the remaining positions. Thus, the normal curvature, called the total local influence of the ith case, assumes the form $C_{e_i}(\theta) = 2|c_{ii}|$, for $i \in \{1,\ldots,n\}$, where c_{ii} is the ith principal diagonal element of the matrix $C = \Delta_p^\top \ddot{L}_p^{-1} \Delta_p$.

Next, we present the perturbed penalized log-likelihood function for four perturbation schemes, namely case weight, response variable, power parameter, and explanatory variable perturbation. The matrix Δ_p for each case is presented in Appendix B.

1. The case-weight perturbation scheme considers the perturbed penalized log-likelihood function as

$$\ell_p(\theta,\lambda\,|\,\omega) = \sum_{i=1}^n \omega_i \ell_i(Q_i,\phi;y_i) - \sum_{k=1}^s \frac{\lambda_k}{2}\beta_k^\top K_k \beta_k,$$

where $\omega = (\omega_1,\ldots,\omega_n)^\top$ is the vector of weights, with $0 \le \omega_i \le 1$ for $i \in \{1,\ldots,n\}$.

2. Regarding the response variable perturbation scheme, we consider an additive type of perturbation weighted by a scaling factor on the ith response variable, i.e., $y_i(\omega_i) = y_i + \omega_i s_{Y_i}$, where s_{Y_i} is a scale factor that can be the sample standard deviation of Y_i and $\omega_i \in \mathbb{R}$, for $i \in \{1,\ldots,n\}$. Then, the perturbed penalized log-likelihood function is written as

$$\ell_p(\theta,\lambda\,|\,\omega) = \sum_{i=1}^n \ell_i(Q_i,\phi;y_i(\omega_i)) - \sum_{k=1}^s \frac{\lambda_k}{2}\beta_k^\top K_k \beta_k.$$

3. Initially, the model given in Equation (1) assumes that the power parameter is constant across observations. However, we can introduce a perturbation in the power parameter such that it is not constant between the observations, i.e., $Y_i \sim \text{QLS}(Q_i,\phi_i,g)$, where $\phi_i = \phi/\omega_i$, with $\omega_i > 0$ for $i \in \{1,\ldots,n\}$. Under this perturbation scheme, the perturbed penalized log-likelihood function is constructed from the expression defined in Equation (3) with ϕ being replaced by ϕ_i.

4. The last perturbation scheme considered in this work consists of incorporating an additive type perturbation on one of the covariates $X_1,\ldots,X_s$, say X_l, given by $x_{li}(\omega_i) = x_{li} + \omega_i s_{x_l}$, where s_{x_l} is a scale factor that can be the sample standard deviation of X_l and $\omega_i \in \mathbb{R}$, for $i \in \{1,\ldots,n\}$. In this case, the perturbed penalized log-likelihood function can be expressed as

$$\ell_p(\theta,\lambda\,|\,\omega) = \sum_{i=1}^n \ell_i(Q_i(\omega_i),\phi;y_i) - \sum_{k=1}^s \frac{\lambda_k}{2}\beta_k^\top K_k \beta_k,$$

where $Q_i(\omega_i)$ is as given in Equation (1) replacing w_{li} for $w_{li}(\omega_i)$.

4.2. Generalized Leverage Matrix

The generalized leverage (GL) measures the influence of the observed value of the response variable y_i on its corresponding predicted value $\hat{y}_i$ based on the model given in Equation (1). Following the approach proposed by Wei et al. [32], the GL for $\hat{\theta}$ can be computed using the lemma they provided. The expression for the GL is given by $\partial \hat{y}/\partial y^\top = H_\theta(-\ddot{L}_p(\theta))^{-1}\ell_{\theta y}\big|_{\theta=\hat{\theta}}$, where $H_\theta = \partial\mu/\partial\theta^\top$, $\ddot{L}_p(\theta) = \partial^2\ell_p(\theta)/\partial\theta\partial\theta^\top$, $\ell_{\theta y} = \partial^2\ell_p(\theta)/\partial\theta\partial y^\top$, $y = (y_1,\ldots,y_n)^\top$ and $\mu = (\mu_1,\ldots,\mu_n)^\top$, with μ_i being the mean of the Y_i. Using the chain rule, we have

$$\frac{\partial \hat{y}}{\partial y^\top} = \frac{\partial \mu}{\partial Q^\top}\frac{\partial Q}{\partial \theta^\top}(-\ddot{L}_p(\theta))^{-1}\ell_{\theta y}\bigg|_{\theta=\hat{\theta}}.$$

Because of $\mu = \log(\lambda)$ and $Q = \lambda \exp(\sqrt{\phi} z_q)$, where z_q is the q-quantile of the distribution $S(0,1,g)$ [7], we have $\mu = \log(Q) - \sqrt{\phi} z_q$. Therefore, $\partial \mu / \partial Q^\top = \text{diag}\{1/Q_1, \ldots, 1/Q_n\}$. Also, we can obtain the $n \times p^*$ matrix

$$\frac{\partial Q}{\partial \theta^\top} = \left(\frac{\partial Q}{\partial \alpha^\top}, \frac{\partial Q}{\partial \beta_1^\top}, \ldots, \frac{\partial Q}{\partial \beta_s^\top}, \frac{\partial Q}{\partial \phi} \right) = \left(D_a W \ D_a \tilde{N}_1 \ \cdots \ D_a \tilde{N}_s \ \mathbf{0}_n \right),$$

where $\mathbf{0}_n$ is the $n \times 1$ null vector and $\ddot{\ell}_{\theta y} = \left(D_\psi D_a W \ D_\psi D_a \tilde{N}_1 \ \cdots \ D_\psi D_a \tilde{N}_s \ \tau \right)$ is a $n \times p^*$ matrix. Please note that the computation of the matrix $-\ddot{L}_p(\theta)$ relies on the availability of the penalized Hessian matrix given in Equation (4). By utilizing this penalized Hessian matrix, we have all the necessary elements to calculate the GL matrix $\partial \hat{y} / \partial y^\top$.

5. Real Data Analysis

In this section, we apply the model proposed in Section 2 to real pollution data from the Padre Las Casas Air Quality Monitoring Station (AQMS). The AQMS is situated in the commune of Padre Las Casas in the Araucanía region of southern Chile, approximately 695 km away from Santiago, the capital city of Chile. Padre Las Casas has gained notoriety for its elevated levels of pollution, particularly concerning PM2.5. It is recognized as one of the most heavily polluted cities in Latin America and the Caribbean, as indicated by the World Air Quality Index Ranking (https://bit.ly/3MXVP38; accessed on 20 August 2023). The average concentration of PM2.5 in Padre Las Casas exceeds the limits set by national and international regulations [22], highlighting the significance of analyzing this type of data and developing models that accurately capture its behavior.

By studying the pollution data from the Padre Las Casas AQMS, we aim to gain insights into the underlying patterns and factors contributing to pollution levels. The proposed model will help us to describe and understand the behavior of pollution in this area, providing valuable information for monitoring and management purposes.

5.1. Exploratory Data Analysis

The dataset used in this analysis consists of hourly (h) average values for the months of June and July 2020, acquired from the Chilean Ministry of Environment (MMA) website (http://sinca.mma.gob.cl; accessed on 11 January 2022). The dataset includes measurements of various variables related to air pollution and meteorological conditions in Padre Las Casas. The considered random variables in this dataset are: (i) Median of PM2.5 concentrations: this variable represents the median concentration of fine particulate matter with a diameter less than 2.5 micrometers in micrograms per normal cubic meter ($\mu g/Nm^3$). PM2.5 is a commonly monitored pollutant and is known to have detrimental effects on human health; (ii) Median of PM10 concentrations: this variable represents the median concentration of particulate matter with a diameter smaller than 10 micrometers (PM10) in $\mu g/Nm^3$. PM10 includes both fine and coarse particles and is also considered a significant air pollutant; (iii) Ambient temperature (TEMP): this variable represents the temperature at the monitoring station in degrees Celsius. Temperature is an important meteorological parameter that can influence air quality and pollutant levels; (iv) Wind speed (WIND): this variable represents the speed of wind at the monitoring station in meters per second. Wind speed plays a crucial role in the dispersion and transport of pollutants in the atmosphere; (v) Relative air humidity (HR): this variable represents the percentage of moisture in the air at the AQMS. Humidity can affect atmospheric stability and the formation of certain pollutants. By analyzing these variables, we can gain insights into the relationship between air pollution levels and meteorological conditions in Padre Las Casas during the specified period.

In the exploratory data analysis (EDA) of the median PM2.5 concentrations recorded by the Padre Las Casas AQMS during June–July 2020, Figure 1a shows a histogram with density kernel estimation. This plot provides an overview of the distribution of the data, and permits us to visualize the shape of the empirical distribution. From the histogram, it appears that the distribution of the PM2.5 concentrations has a positive skewness, indicating that most of the observations have lower values with a few extremely high values. Figure 1b presents a boxplot for the median PM2.5 concentrations. From the boxplot, we can see that there are some observations labeled as atypical data (#1, #3, #4, #14, #36, #45) that lie outside the whiskers. These observations deviate from the overall pattern of the data and may represent extreme or unusual values. This suggests that there may be some extreme pollution events or unusual conditions during the observed period. Based on the positive skewness of the empirical distribution and the presence of atypical data points, it is reasonable to consider using log-symmetrical distributions to model the PM2.5 concentrations. Log-symmetrical distributions can better capture the positive skewness and accommodate the potential presence of extreme values in the data.

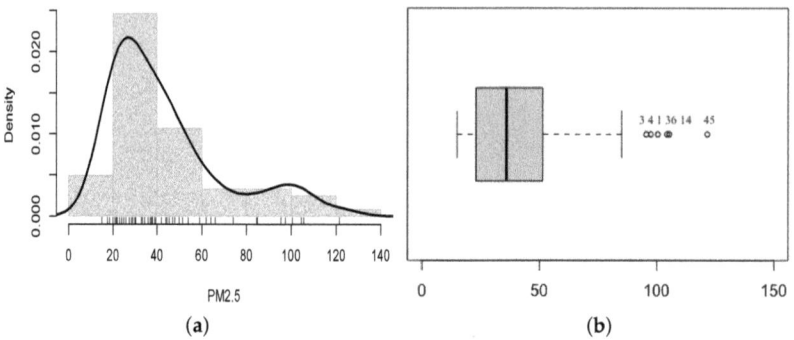

Figure 1. Histogram with density kernel estimation (solid black line) (**a**) and boxplot (**b**) for median PM2.5 concentrations recorded by Padre Las Casas AQMS during June–July 2020.

Table 1 provides descriptive statistics for the median PM2.5 concentrations recorded by the Padre Las Casas AQMS during June-July 2020. These statistics include measures of central tendency (mean, median), dispersion (range, standard deviation –SD–), as well as coefficients of skewness (CS) and kurtosis (CK). The descriptive statistics reveal that the median PM2.5 concentrations have a mean of 43.4 µg/Nm^3 and a median of 36.0 µg/Nm^3. The SD is relatively high, with a value of 26.0 µg/Nm^3, indicating substantial variability in the data. The CS is 1.3, indicating a positive skewness and confirming the observation from the histogram in Figure 1a. The positive skewness suggests that most of the observations have lower values, while a few extremely high values contribute to the right tail of the distribution. The CK is 0.8, which indicates a moderately peaked distribution compared to a normal distribution. Furthermore, as mentioned in the text, a significant quantity of levels that surpass the recommended Chilean thresholds for PM2.5, set at 50 µg/Nm^3. This suggests that the air pollution level in Padre Las Casas is dangerous from a toxicological perspective, posing potential health risks for the inhabitants of this commune in southern Chile. Overall, the descriptive statistics and Figure 1a,b provide evidence of the high pollution levels and the need for modeling approaches that can adequately capture the characteristics of the PM2.5 concentrations in this region.

Table 1. Descriptive statistics for median PM2.5 concentrations recorded by Padre Las Casas AQMS during June–July 2020.

Variable	n	Min	Max	Range	Mean	Median	SD	CS	CK
PM2.5	61	15	121.5	106.5	43.4	36.0	26.0	1.3	0.8

Figure 2 shows a correlation matrix for PM2.5, PM10, TEMP, WIND, and HR. From this figure, we detect: (i) a high positive association between PM2.5 and PM10 (Pearson coefficient of correlation equal to 0.99); (ii) medium negative association between PM2.5 and TEMP and WIND (Pearson coefficient of correlation equal to −0.70); (iii) low positive association between PM2.5 and HR (Pearson coefficient of correlation equal to 0.38). In

Figure 3, scatter plots depicting the explanatory variables, response variable, and potential interactions among the explanatory variables are presented. In Figure 3a, note that the relationship between PM2.5 and PM10 is linear, while in Figure 3b, the relationship between PM2.5 and WIND is not linear. Furthermore, Figure 3c,d imply that the explanatory variables TEMP and HR may be engaging with the WIND variable in a nonlinear manner.

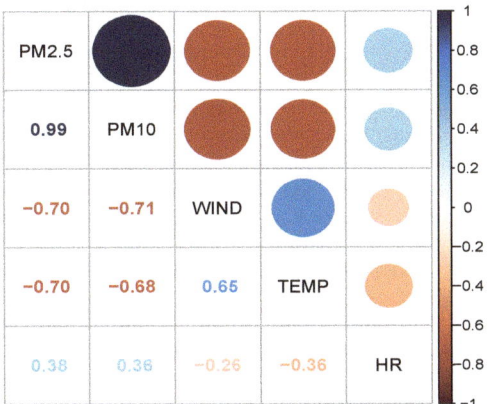

Figure 2. Correlation matrix displaying the respective Pearson correlation coefficient for the specified explanatory and response variables.

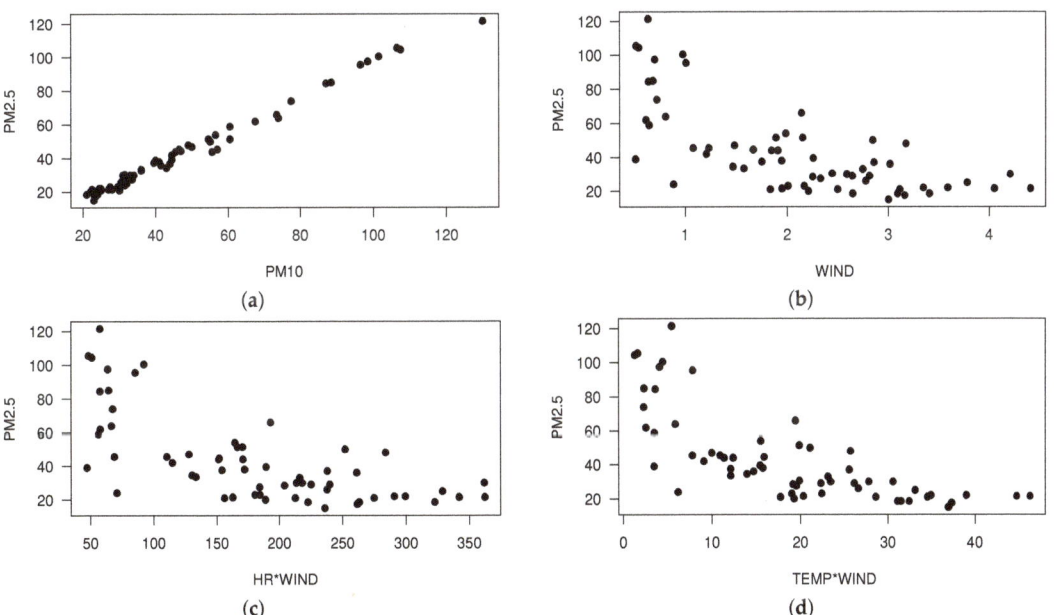

Figure 3. Scatter plots for median PM2.5 vs. PM10 concentrations (**a**); median PM2.5 vs. WIND (**b**); median PM2.5 vs. HR*WIND (**c**); and, median PM2.5 vs. TEMP*WIND (**d**) recorded by Padre Las Casas AQMS during June–July 2020.

5.2. Parameter Estimation

Based on the EDA and the observed relationships between the median PM2.5 concentration and the variables as PM10, WIND, TEMP, and HR, we suggest the following varying-coefficients quantile regression models to capture the trends:

$$\sqrt{Q_i} = \boldsymbol{w}_i^\top \boldsymbol{\alpha} + x_{1i}\beta_1(t_i) + x_{2i}\beta_2(t_i), \quad i \in \{1, 2, \ldots, 61\} \tag{10}$$

where $y_i \sim \text{QLS}(Q_i, \phi, g)$ with Student-t and normal PDF generator g, $\boldsymbol{\beta}$ represents the vector of regression coefficients, while $\boldsymbol{w}_i^\top = (1, w_{1i})^\top$ with w_{1i} denoting the values of the parametric covariate for the ith observation (PM10). The coefficients β_k (for $k \in \{1,2\}$) correspond to unknown, smooth, and arbitrary functions of the explanatory variable t_i (WIND), which are linked to the explanatory variables x_{1i} (TEMP) and x_{2i} (HR) from the ith case. These varying-coefficients quantile regression models allow for a more flexible and comprehensive characterization of the relationships between the median PM2.5 concentration and the other variables, considering potential variations across quantiles.

Table 2 presents the MPL estimates for the model parameters, their approximate standard errors (SEs), p-values obtained from a z-test, the AIC, selected smoothing parameters, and the degrees of freedom $\text{df}(\cdot)$ for the models defined by Equation (10). The best values of λ_1 and λ_2 were selected by considering a grid of values and choosing those that yielded a range of $\text{df}(\lambda_1)$ and $\text{df}(\lambda_2)$ within the range of $(4, 12)$, while minimizing the AIC value.

When comparing the results reported in Table 2, we observe that the estimates for α_0 and α_1 show similarity between both models, but the log-t model has smaller estimated standard errors (SEs) for these parameters compared to the log-normal model. Additionally, the estimated value of ϕ in the log-t model is smaller than that in the log-normal model. It is worth noting that based on the (AIC), the log-t model is preferred as it yields a lower AIC value.

Table 2. MPL estimates, SEs, p-values, AIC and selected smoothing parameters and $\text{df}(\cdot)$ of the indicated model.

Model	Parameter	Estimate	SE	p-Value	AIC
Log-normal	α_0	3.072	2.2×10^{-5}	<0.001	374.1
	α_1	0.068	1.1×10^{-3}	<0.001	
	ϕ	0.013	4.1×10^{-6}		
	λ_1	4034.3			
	λ_2	2.2×10^5			
	$\text{df}(\lambda_1)$	4.001			
	$\text{df}(\lambda_2)$	4.466			
Log-$t(\nu = 4)$	α_0	3.052	1.7×10^{-5}	<0.001	361.3
	α_1	0.070	8.3×10^{-4}	<0.001	
	ϕ	0.007	4.9×10^{-6}		
	λ_1	4034.3			
	λ_2	5.9×10^5			
	$\text{df}(\lambda_1)$	4.556			
	$\text{df}(\lambda_2)$	4.198			

To assess the distributional assumption made in the model, we examine the goodness-of-fit plots based on generalized Cox-Snell (GCS) residuals, as shown in Figure 4. Additionally, we provide the p-values associated with the Kolmogorov–Smirnov (KS) test, which are 0.73 for the log-normal model and 0.89 for the log-$t(\nu = 4)$ model. Based on the goodness-of-fit plots, the KS test, and the AIC, we can conclude that the log-$t(\nu = 4)$ model provides a better fit to the dataset. The log-t model captures the underlying distribution of the data more accurately compared to the log-normal model, as indicated by the higher p-value and better fit observed in the goodness-of-fit plots.

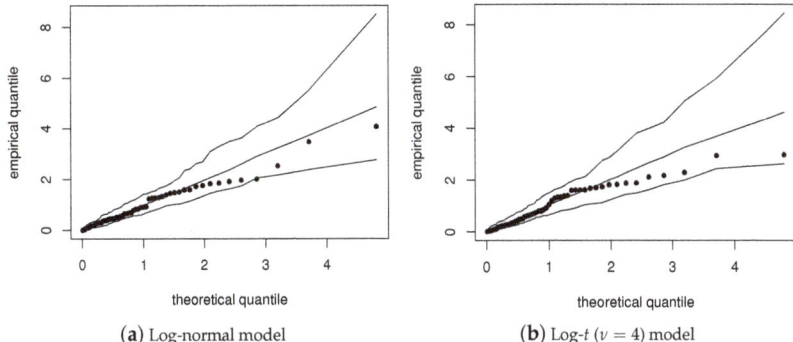

Figure 4. Goodness-of-fit plots with simulated envelope for GCS residual under the indicated model with the analyzed data set.

Figure 5 displays the plots of the partial residuals relative to the WIND covariate, with the superimposed estimated smooth functions β_1 (on the left) and β_2 (on the right). The behavior of the partial residuals (dots) in these plots appears reasonable, indicating that the fit of the log-$t(\nu = 4)$ varying-coefficients quantile regression model to the pollution dataset is adequate. The dots are closely aligned with the estimated curves, as expected, suggesting that the model captures the relationship between the WIND covariate and the partial residuals effectively. This agreement between the partial residuals and the estimated curves supports the appropriateness of the log-$t(\nu = 4)$ varying-coefficients quantile regression model for analyzing the pollution data.

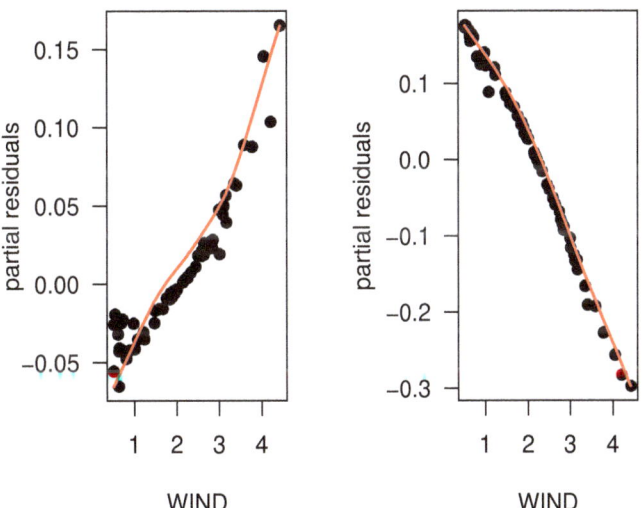

Figure 5. Plots of partial residuals in relation to the WIND covariate, with the estimated smooth functions β_1 (on the left) and β_2 (on the right) superimposed.

5.3. Diagnostic Analysis

In this section, we investigate the potential influence of individual observations using the local influence method for the selected varying-coefficients quantile regression model. We consider four perturbation schemes: case-weight perturbation, response variable perturbation, power parameter perturbation, and explanatory variable perturbation. Additionally, we examine the GL to assess the influence of each observed value on its own predicted value. These analyses allow us to identify potentially influential cases and understand their impact on the selected model. Details on the local influence method and the perturbation schemes can be found in Section 4.2.

In Figure 6, we present index plots illustrating $C_i(\theta)$ as defined in Section 4.2 for α, β_1, β_2 and ϕ under the case-weight perturbation (a,b,c,d), under response perturbation (e,f,g,h) and perturbation on the power parameter (i,j,k,l) schemes. Also, Figure 7 showcases the index plots of $C_i(\theta)$ when introducing perturbations in covariates X_1 (a, b, c, d) and X_2 (e, f, g, h). Despite different observations being detected as potentially influential, it is worth noting that there are four cases (#13, #18, #31, and #45) that consistently appear as potentially influential across multiple perturbation schemes. These cases exhibit characteristics that make them stand out and have a notable impact on the model results.

Figure 8 displays the GL plot, which assesses the influence of each observation on its own predicted value. From this plot, we observe that cases #45, #36, #14, #1, #3, #4 are potentially leverage points. These observations have response variable values that can exert a significant influence on their own predicted values. It is worth noting that these cases correspond to the outliers identified by the boxplot in Figure 1b. Their extreme values contribute to their influential nature within the model.

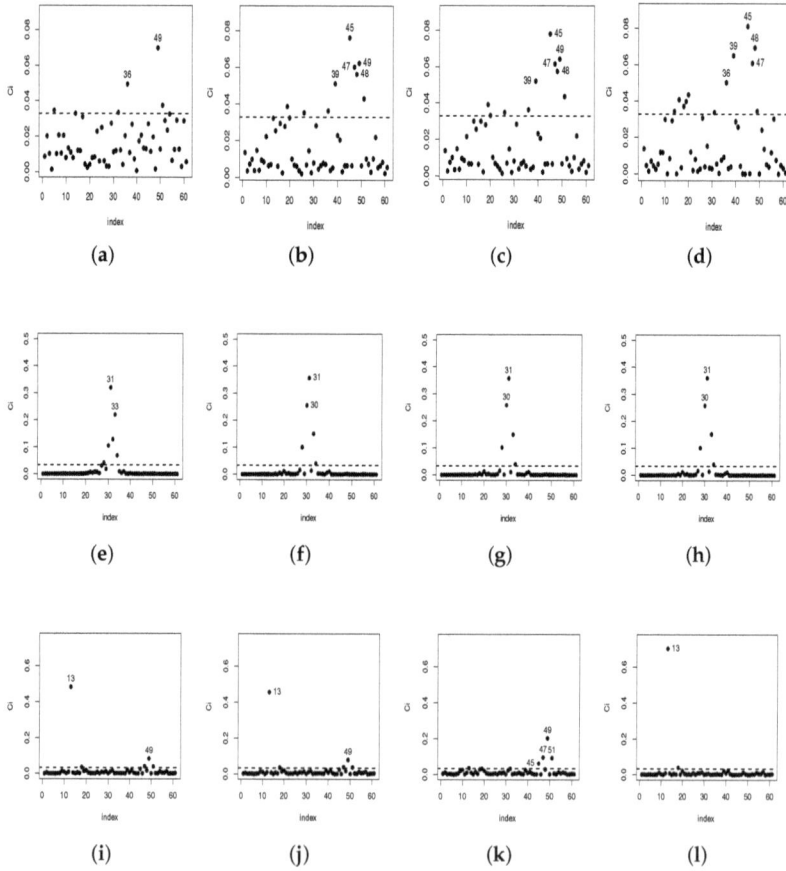

Figure 6. Case weight (a–d), response (e–h) and on the power parameter (i–l) perturbation for α, β_1, β_2 and ϕ.

It is interesting to observe that the cases identified as potentially influential in the parametric component may not necessarily be detected in the nonparametric component, and vice versa. This indicates that different aspects of the data and model may be driving their influence in different ways. Additionally, the local influence analysis technique has successfully detected some atypical cases that were previously identified as outliers in Figure 1b. This reinforces the effectiveness of the local influence method in identifying observations that have a considerable impact on the model.

In the sense of evaluating the impact of these observations in the selected model, the subsets of cases {#13}, {#18}, {#31}, {#45}, {#13, #18}, {#13, #31}, {#13, #45}, {#18, #31}, {#18, #45}, {#31, #45}, and {#13, #18, #31}, {#13, #18, #45}, {#18, #31, #45} and {#13, #18, #31, #45} are removed and the model parameters are re-estimated. To determine the variation in the estimates of model parameters, we use the value of the relative changes (RCs) for each parameter. The RCs for each estimated parameter are calculated using the formula: $RC_\theta = |(\hat{\theta}_j - \hat{\theta}_{j(i)})/\hat{\theta}_j| \times 100\%$, where $\hat{\theta}_j$ represents the MPLE of θ_j, and $\hat{\theta}_{j(i)}$ represents the MPLE of θ_j after removing the subset i of observations. Here, $j = 1, 2, 3$ with $\theta_1 = \alpha_0$, $\theta_2 = \alpha_1$, and $\theta_3 = \phi$.

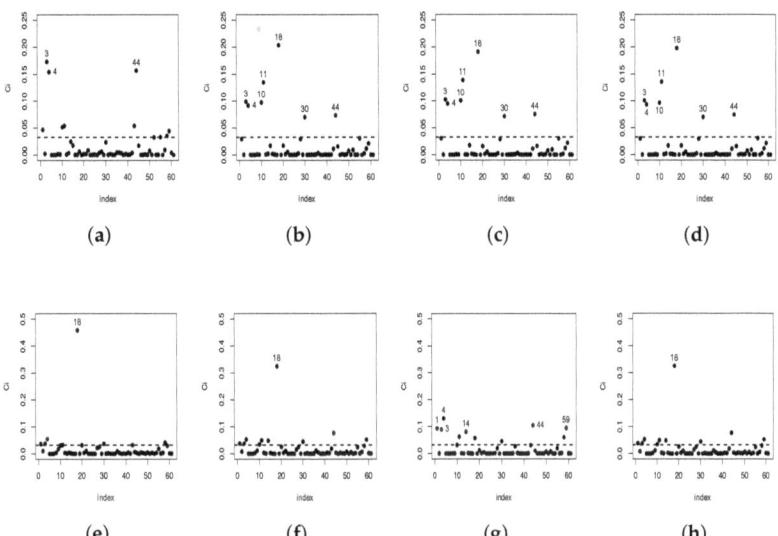

Figure 7. Perturbation in the covariate X_1 (a–d) and X_2 (e–h) scheme for α, β_1, β_2 and ϕ.

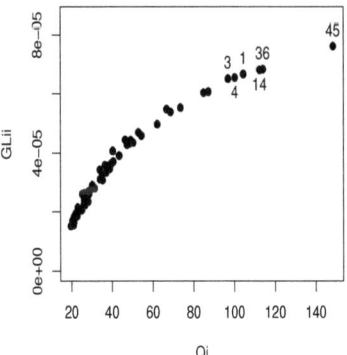

Figure 8. Generalized leverage.

Table 3 reports the values of RCs for the varying-coefficients quantile regression model after removing the indicated sets of cases. In this table, the individual elimination of cases #13 and #45 produces a RC in α_0 and α_1 of 5.1%, 4.7% and 5.3%, 5.6%, respectively, while the elimination of case #18 produces an RC in ϕ of 5.5%. In addition, note that set of cases {#13, #18} and {#13, #18, #31} produces the largest RCs in α_0, α_1 and ϕ.

During the analyzed period, it was observed that observation #45 had particularly high concentrations of PM2.5 and PM10 compared to other observations. On the other hand, observation purple #31 had a very low wind speed, close to the minimum recorded during the entire period. These observations exhibit extreme values in their respective covariates. When the sets of potentially influential cases {#13, #18, #31, #45} are excluded from the analysis, it is observed that their removal results in notable alterations solely in the estimation of ϕ, displaying a percentage change of 21.4%. This suggests that these observations have a notable influence on the estimation of the dispersion parameter ϕ in the model.

Table 3. RC (in %) on the MPL estimate of α_j and ϕ and respective p-values (in parenthesis) for varying-coefficients quantile regression model after removing the indicated sets of cases.

Removed Case	Parameters			Relative Changes		
	α_0	α_1	ϕ	RC_{α_0}	RC_{α_1}	RC_ϕ
none	3.052 (<0.001)	0.069 (<0.001)	0.007			
{#13}	3.213 (<0.001)	0.066 (<0.001)	0.007	5.1%	4.7%	4.0%
{#18}	2.961 (<0.001)	0.072 (<0.001)	0.006	3.0%	3.4%	5.5%
{#31}	3.095 (<0.001)	0.069 (<0.001)	0.007	1.4%	1.1%	3.9%
{#45}	2.891 (<0.001)	0.073 (<0.001)	0.006	5.3%	5.6%	4.0%
{#13, #18}	3.415 (<0.001)	0.065 (<0.001)	0.006	11.9%	6.7%	18.0%
{#13, #31}	3.223 (<0.001)	0.066 (<0.001)	0.006	5.6%	4.7%	9.4%
{#13, #45}	3.093 (<0.001)	0.069 (<0.001)	0.006	1.4%	0.4%	13.0%
{#18, #31}	3.011 (<0.001)	0.071 (<0.001)	0.006	1.3%	2.2%	9.5%
{#18, #45}	2.901 (<0.001)	0.073 (<0.001)	0.006	4.9%	5.4%	10.9%
{#13, #18, #31}	3.488 (<0.001)	0.064 (<0.001)	0.005	14.3%	7.8%	20.5%
{#13, #18, #45}	3.005 (<0.001)	0.071 (<0.001)	0.006	1.5%	2.8%	17.4%
{#18, #31, #45}	2.960 (<0.001)	0.072 (<0.001)	0.006	3.0%	4.0%	14.5%
{#13, #18, #31, #45}	3.046 (<0.001)	0.071 (<0.001)	0.005	0.2%	1.9%	21.4%

Finally, in Table 3, while certain RCs exhibit considerable values, there are no substantial alterations in inference, as evidenced by the diminutive p-values (less than 0.001) associated with the parameter estimates. It is important to note that when observations detected as influential in the diagnostic plots are eliminated, it can lead to significant changes in the parameter estimates. This indicates that the well-known robustness properties of maximum likelihood estimates from Student-t models may not necessarily apply to other perturbation schemes. Therefore, it is crucial to conduct diagnostic examinations specific to each case to properly assess the influence of observations and ensure the reliability of the model estimates.

6. Discussion, Conclusions and Future Research

In this work, we propose new varying-coefficients semiparametric quantile regression models based on the family of log-symmetric distributions, following the approach of [5–7]. By reparametrizing the family of log-symmetric distributions using a quantile, we introduce new quantile models that offer greater flexibility in modeling data compared to the model proposed by Saulo et al. [7], as a nonparametric component has been added (Section 2). We develop parameter estimation based on the penalized likelihood function and propose a back-fitting iterative algorithm implemented in the R language (Section 3). Additionally, we discuss diagnostic techniques for detecting potentially influential local observations and identifying leverage points (Section 4). Please note that the local influence analysis reinforces the need for diagnostic evaluation. It has been observed that parameter estimators in this class of models tend to be sensitive to the presence of atypical or influential data points. To the best of our knowledge, techniques for detecting leverage points have not been developed for semiparametric quantile regression models.

We illustrate the methodology developed in this work using data associated with PM2.5 pollution in Padre Las Casas city for predicting the daily median of 1-h average values. We propose and fit two models (log-normal and log-$t(\nu = 4)$) and evaluate them using CGS residuals and their AIC values. The plots of CGS residuals and partial residuals show a good fit of the selected model (log-$t(\nu = 4)$) to the data. We also apply our diagnostic techniques to detect potentially influential cases and leverage points (Section 4.2); however, no inferential changes are observed in the parameter estimates.

Thus, among the accomplishments of this work, we can highlight: (i) The development of novel quantile regression models suitable for modeling data following asymmetric distributions, which can be added into the existing toolkit for quantile modeling; (ii) The expansion of our model beyond the one presented in [7], incorporating nonlinear structures arising from interaction effects. (iii) The derivation of analytical tools for identifying potentially influential observations and leverage points.

One limitation of our study is that the proposed models may not be suitable for describing other types of data, such as temporally or spatially correlated data, as well as censored data. In such cases, the utilization of multivariate distributions for the response variable, reparametrized by quantiles of marginal distributions, may be necessary. Another area for future investigation is conducting a simulation study to evaluate the distributional behavior of the residuals used in this study and exploring alternative types of residuals appropriate for this type of regression. This aspect has received limited attention in the existing literature. Furthermore, we aim to establish inferences about the model parameters through asymptotic analysis of specific estimators. Lastly, we intend to compare our model with others, including models proposed by [7,12]. These are additional areas that remain unexplored, and we plan to address these open questions in our future research.

Author Contributions: Conceptualization, L.S. and G.I.-P.; methodology, L.S., G.I.-P. and C.M.; software, L.S. and C.M.; validation, L.S. and C.M.; formal analysis, L.S. and C.M.; investigation, L.S., G.I.-P. and C.M.; resources, C.M. and M.R.; data curation, L.S. and C.M.; writing—original draft preparation, L.S., G.I.-P. and C.M.; writing—review and editing, L.S., G.I.-P., C.M. and M.R.; visualization, L.S. and C.M. All authors have read and agreed to the published version of the manuscript.

Funding: The research was partially funded by FONDECYT, project grant number 11190636 (C.M.) from the National Agency for Research and Development (ANID) of the Chilean government under the Ministry of Science, Technology, Knowledge and Innovation.

Data Availability Statement: Data and computational codes are available upon request from the authors.

Conflicts of Interest: The authors declare no conflict of interest.

Appendix A

Here, we present the quantities c_i, m_i, and d_i, involved in the definition of the Penalized Hessian matrix presented in Section 3.2. In fact, we have

$$c_i = \frac{1}{\sqrt{\phi}} \left[-\frac{r(v_i)}{Q_i^2 \sqrt{\phi}} + \frac{v_i}{Q_i} \frac{\partial r(v_i)}{\partial Q_i} - \frac{v_i r(v_i)}{Q_i^2} \right] a_i^2 - z_i a_i \frac{h''(Q_i)}{(h'(Q_i))^2},$$

$$m_i = \frac{1}{Q_i} \left[\frac{\phi^{-2}}{2} (\log(Q_i) - \log(y_i)) r(v_i) + \frac{\partial r(v_i)}{\partial \phi} v_i \phi^{-1/2} - \frac{1}{2} v_i r(v_i) \phi^{-3/2} \right], \text{ and}$$

$$d_i = \frac{1}{2}[\log(y_i) - \log(Q_i)]\phi^{-3/2} \left[v_i \frac{\partial r(v_i)}{\partial \phi} - \frac{3}{2} v_i r(v_i) \phi^{-1} - \frac{1}{2} r(v_i)(\log(y_i) - \log(Q_i))\phi^{-3/2} \right] + \frac{1}{2\phi^2}.$$

In addition, the expression $\partial r(v_i)/\partial Q_i$ and $\partial r(v_i)/\partial \phi$ are, respectively,

$$\frac{\partial r(v_i)}{\partial Q_i} = 4 \left[\frac{g''(v_i^2) g(v_i^2) - (g'(v_i^2))^2}{(g(v_i^2))^2} \right] \frac{v_i}{Q_i \sqrt{\phi}}, \text{ and}$$

$$\frac{\partial r(v_i)}{\partial \phi} = 2 \left[\frac{g''(v_i^2) g(v_i^2) - (g'(v_i^2))^2}{(g(v_i^2))^2} \right] v_i \phi^{-3/2} [\log(y_i) - \log(Q_i)].$$

Appendix B

Here we present the matrix Δ_p for four perturbation schemes, namely case weight, response variable, power parameter, and explanatory variable perturbation. In general, this matrix is defined as

$$\Delta_p = \begin{pmatrix} \Delta_\alpha^\top & \Delta_{\beta_1}^\top & \cdots & \Delta_{\beta_s}^\top & \Delta_\phi^\top \end{pmatrix}^\top.$$

Appendix B.1. Case-Weight Perturbation

Here, the elements of the matrix Δ_p are given by

$$\Delta_\alpha = W^\top \widehat{D}_a \widehat{D}_z,$$
$$\Delta_{\beta_k} = \widetilde{N}_k^\top \widehat{D}_a \widehat{D}_z, \quad \text{for } k \in \{1,\ldots,s\},$$
$$\Delta_\phi = \widehat{b},$$

with $\widehat{D}_a$, $\widehat{D}_z$ and $\widehat{b}$ correspond to D_a, D_z and $b = (b_1,\ldots,b_n)^\top$ evaluated at $\theta = \widehat{\theta}$ and $\omega_0 = (1,\ldots,1)^\top$, respectively.

Appendix B.2. Response Variable Perturbation

Under this perturbation schemes, the elements of the matrix Δ_p are given by $\Delta_\alpha = W^\top \widehat{D}_a \widehat{D}_\psi \widehat{D}_\vartheta$, $\Delta_{\beta_k} = \widetilde{N}_k^\top \widehat{D}_a \widehat{D}_\psi \widehat{D}_\vartheta$, for $k \in \{1,\ldots,s\}$, $\Delta_\phi = \widehat{\tau}^\top \widehat{D}_\vartheta$, with $\widehat{D}_\vartheta = \text{diag}\{\widehat{\vartheta}_1,\ldots,\widehat{\vartheta}_n\}$, $\widehat{D}_\psi = \text{diag}\{\widehat{\psi}_1,\ldots,\widehat{\psi}_n\}$, and $\widehat{\tau} = (\widehat{\tau}_1,\ldots,\widehat{\tau}_n)^\top$, with

$$\widehat{\vartheta}_i = s_{Y_i},$$
$$\widehat{\psi}_i = \frac{1}{\widehat{\phi} \widehat{Q}_i y_i}[r(\widehat{v}_i) + \widehat{v}_i r'(\widehat{v}_i)],$$
$$\widehat{\tau}_i = -\frac{\widehat{\phi}^{-3/2}}{2} [v_i r'(\widehat{v}_i) + r(\widehat{v}_i)] \left[\frac{\log(y_i) - \log(\widehat{Q}_i)}{y_i \sqrt{\widehat{\phi}}} \right] + \frac{r(\widehat{v}_i)\widehat{v}_i}{y_i}, \quad i \in \{1,\ldots,n\},$$

and $r'(\widehat{v}_i) = dr(\widehat{v}_i)/d\widehat{v}_i$. In this case, $\widehat{v}_i$, $\widehat{Q}_i$ and $\widehat{\phi}$ are evaluated at $\theta = \widehat{\theta}$ and $\omega = (0,\ldots,0)^\top$.

Appendix B.3. Power Parameter Perturbation

Considering the power parameter perturbation, the elements of the matrix $\boldsymbol{\Delta}_p$ are given by $\boldsymbol{\Delta}_{\beta_k} = \tilde{\boldsymbol{N}}_k^\top \hat{\boldsymbol{D}}_a \hat{\boldsymbol{D}}_\varpi$, for $k \in \{1,\ldots,s\}$, $\boldsymbol{\Delta}_\phi = \hat{\boldsymbol{\varphi}}^\top$, where $\hat{\boldsymbol{D}}_\varpi = \text{diag}\{\hat{\omega}_1,\ldots,\hat{\omega}_n\}$ and $\boldsymbol{\varphi} = (\hat{\varphi}_1,\ldots,\hat{\varphi}_n)^\top$, with $\omega_i = -\hat{\phi}\hat{m}_i$ and $\hat{\varphi}_i = -\hat{\phi}\hat{d}_i$, for $i \in \{1,\ldots,n\}$. Here, $\hat{m}_i$ and $\hat{d}_i$ correspond to m_i and d_i evaluated at $\boldsymbol{\theta} = \hat{\boldsymbol{\theta}}$ and $\boldsymbol{\omega}_0 = (1,\ldots,1)^\top$, respectively.

Appendix B.4. Explanatory Variable Perturbation

In this case, the elements of the matrix $\boldsymbol{\Delta}_p$ can be expressed as follows:

(i) for $l = k$,

$$\boldsymbol{\Delta}_\alpha = \boldsymbol{W}^\top (\hat{\boldsymbol{D}}_{a'}\hat{\boldsymbol{D}}_z + \hat{\boldsymbol{D}}_a\hat{\boldsymbol{D}}_c) \hat{\boldsymbol{D}}_a s_{X_l} \hat{\boldsymbol{D}}_{\tilde{N}_l f_l},$$
$$\boldsymbol{\Delta}_{\beta_l} = \tilde{\boldsymbol{N}}_l \hat{\boldsymbol{D}}_a \hat{\boldsymbol{D}}_z s_{X_l} + \tilde{\boldsymbol{N}}_l^\top \hat{\boldsymbol{D}}_a \hat{\boldsymbol{D}}_{\tilde{N}_l f_l} s_{X_l} (\hat{\boldsymbol{D}}_{a'}\hat{\boldsymbol{D}}_z + \hat{\boldsymbol{D}}_c) - \lambda_l \boldsymbol{K}_l \hat{\boldsymbol{\beta}}_l, \text{ for } k \in \{1,\ldots,s\},$$
$$\boldsymbol{\Delta}_\phi = \hat{\boldsymbol{m}}^\top \hat{\boldsymbol{D}}_a \hat{\boldsymbol{D}}_{\tilde{N}_l f_l} s_{X_l};$$

(ii) for $l \neq k$,

$$\boldsymbol{\Delta}_\alpha = \boldsymbol{W}^\top (\hat{\boldsymbol{D}}_{a'}\hat{\boldsymbol{D}}_z + \hat{\boldsymbol{D}}_a\hat{\boldsymbol{D}}_c) \hat{\boldsymbol{D}}_a s_{X_l} \hat{\boldsymbol{D}}_{\tilde{N}_l \cdot f_l},$$
$$\boldsymbol{\Delta}_{\beta_l} = \tilde{\boldsymbol{N}}_1^\top \hat{\boldsymbol{D}}_a \hat{\boldsymbol{D}}_{\tilde{N}_l \beta_l} s_{X_l} (\hat{\boldsymbol{D}}_{a'}\hat{\boldsymbol{D}}_z + \hat{\boldsymbol{D}}_c) - \lambda_1 \boldsymbol{K}_1 \hat{\boldsymbol{\beta}}_1, \quad \text{for } k \in \{1,\ldots,s\},$$
$$\boldsymbol{\Delta}_\phi = \hat{\boldsymbol{m}}^\top \hat{\boldsymbol{D}}_a \hat{\boldsymbol{D}}_{\tilde{N}_l \beta_l} s_{X_l}.$$

where $\boldsymbol{D}_{a'} = \text{diag}\{a'_1,\ldots,a'_n\}$, with $a'_i = da_i/dQ_i$, and $\boldsymbol{D}_{\tilde{N}_l \beta_l}$ is the diagonalization of the vector $\tilde{\boldsymbol{N}}_l \boldsymbol{\beta}_l$. Here, $\boldsymbol{\omega}_0 = (0,\ldots,0)^\top$ corresponds to the vector of no perturbation.

References

1. Vanegas, L.; Paula, G. A semiparametric approach for joint modeling of median and skewness. *Test* **2015**, *24*, 110–135. [CrossRef]
2. Arellano-Valle, R.B.; Gómez, H.W.; Quintana, F.A. A New Class of Skew-Normal Distributions. *Commun. Stat. Theory Methods* **2004**, *33*, 1465–1480. [CrossRef]
3. Paula, G.A.; Leiva, V.; Barros, M.; Liu, S. Robust statistical modeling using the Birnbaum-Saunders-t distribution applied to insurance. *Appl. Stoch. Model. Bus. Ind.* **2012**, *28*, 16–34. [CrossRef]
4. Leiva, V.; Santos-Neto, M.; Cysneiros, F.J.A.; Barros, M. Birnbaum–Saunders statistical modelling: A new approach. *Stat. Model.* **2014**, *14*, 21–48. [CrossRef]
5. Sánchez, L.; Leiva, V.; Galea, M.; Saulo, H. Birnbaum-Saunders quantile regression and its diagnostics with application to economic data. *Appl. Stoch. Model. Bus. Ind.* **2021**, *37*, 53–73. [CrossRef]
6. Sánchez, L.; Leiva, V.; Marchant, C.; Saulo, H.; Sarabia, J.M. A new quantile regression model and its diagnostic analytics for a Weibull distributed response with applications. *Mathematics* **2021**, *9*, 2768. [CrossRef]
7. Saulo, H.; Dasilva, A.; Leiva, V.; Sanchez, L.; de la Fuente-Mella, H. Log-symmetric quantile regression models. *Stat. Neerl.* **2022**, *76*, 124–163. [CrossRef]
8. Vanegas, L.; Paula, G. Log-symmetric distributions: Statistical properties and parameter estimation. *Braz. J. Probab. Stat.* **2016**, *30*, 196–220. [CrossRef]
9. Vanegas, L.; Paula, G. An extension of log-symmetric regression models: R codes and applications. *J. Stat. Simul. Comput.* **2016**, *86*, 1709–1735. [CrossRef]
10. Ventura, M.; Saulo, H.; Leiva, V.; Monsueto, S.E. Log-symmetric regression models: Information criteria and application to movie business and industry data. *Appl. Stoch. Model. Bus. Ind.* **2019**, *35*, 963–977. [CrossRef]
11. Hao, L.; Naiman, D.Q. *Quantile Regression*; Sage Publications: London, UK, 2007.
12. Koenker, R.; Chernozhukov, V.; He, X.; Peng, L. *Handbook of Quantile Regression*; CRC Press: Boca Raton, FL, USA, 2018.
13. Noufaily, A.; Jones, M.C. Parametric quantile regression based on the generalized gamma distribution. *J. R. Stat. Soc. Ser.* **2013**, *62*, 723–740. [CrossRef]
14. Hastie, T.; Tibshirani, R. *Generalized Additive Models*; Chapman and Hall: New York, NY, USA, 1990.
15. Green, P.J.; Silverman, B.W. *Nonparametric Regression and Generalized Linear Models*; Chapman and Hall: Boca Raton, FL, USA, 1994.
16. Ibacache-Pulgar, G.; Paula, G.A.; Cysneiros, F.J.A. Semiparametric additive models under symmetric distributions. *Test* **2013**, *22*, 103–121. [CrossRef]
17. Ramires, T.; Ortega, E.; Hens, N.; Cordeiro, G.; Paula, G. A flexible semiparametric regression model for bimodal, asymmetric and censored data. *J. Appl. Stat.* **2018**, *45*, 1303–1324. [CrossRef]

18. Manghi, R.; Cysneiros, F.J.A.; Paula, G. Generalized additive partial linear models for analyzing correlated data. *Comput. Stat. Data Anal.* **2019**, *129*, 47–60. [CrossRef]
19. Oliveira, R.A.; Paula, G.A. Additive models with autoregressive symmetric errors based on penalized regression splines. *Comput. Stat.* **2021**, *36*, 2435–2466. [CrossRef]
20. Ferreira, C.; Montoril, M.; Paula, G. Partially linear models with p-order autoregressive skew-normal errors. *Braz. J. Probab. Stat.* **2022**, *36*, 792–806.
21. Cardozo, C.A.; Paula, G.A.; Vanegas, L.H. Generalized log-gamma additive partial linear models with P-spline smoothing. *Stat. Pap.* **2022**, *63*, 1953–1978. [CrossRef]
22. Cavieres, M.F.; Leiva, V.; Marchant, C.; Rojas, F. A methodology for data-driven decision making in the monitoring of particulate matter environmental contamination in Santiago of Chile. *Rev. Environ. Contam. Toxicol.* **2020**, *250*, 5–67.
23. Ibacache-Pulgar, G.; Reyes, S. Local influence for elliptical partially varying coefficient model. *Stat. Model.* **2018**, *18*, 149–174. [CrossRef]
24. Good, I.J.; Gaskins, R.A. Nonparametric roughness penalties for probability densities. *Biometrika* **1971**, *58*, 255–277. [CrossRef]
25. Silverman, B.W. Some aspects of the spline smoothing approach to non-parametric regression curve fitting. *J. R. Stat.* **1985**, *47*, 1–52. [CrossRef]
26. Green, P.J. Penalized likelihood for general semi-parametric regression models. *Int. Stat. Rev.* **1987**, *55*, 245–259. [CrossRef]
27. Adams, R.A.; Fournier, J. Sobolev Spaces. In *Pure and Applied Mathematics*; Academic Press: Boston, MA, USA, 2003.
28. Rigby, R.A.; Stasinopoulos, D.M. Generalized additive models for location, scale and shape. *J. R. Stat. Soc. Ser. (Appl. Stat.)* **2005**, *54*, 507–554. [CrossRef]
29. Berhane, K.; Tibshirani, J. Generalized additive models for longitudinal data. *Can. J. Stat.* **1998**, *26*, 517–535. [CrossRef]
30. Cook, R.D. Assessment of local influence (with discussion). *J. R. Stat. Soc.* **1986**, *48*, 133–169.
31. Escobar, L.; Meeker, W. Assessing influence in regression analysis with censored data. *Biometrics* **1992**, *48*, 507–528. [CrossRef]
32. Wei, B.C.; Hu, Y.Q.; Fung, W.K. Generalized leverage and its applications. *Scand. J. Stat.* **1998**, *25*, 25–37. [CrossRef]

Disclaimer/Publisher's Note: The statements, opinions and data contained in all publications are solely those of the individual author(s) and contributor(s) and not of MDPI and/or the editor(s). MDPI and/or the editor(s) disclaim responsibility for any injury to people or property resulting from any ideas, methods, instructions or products referred to in the content.

Article

Mathematical Model of Cyber Risks Management Based on the Expansion of Piecewise Continuous Analytical Approximation Functions of Cyber Attacks in the Fourier Series

Valentyn Sobchuk [1,†], Oleg Barabash [2,†], Andrii Musienko [2,†], Iryna Tsyganivska [1,†] and Oleksandr Kurylko [1,*,†]

[1] Faculty of Mechanics and Mathematics, Taras Shevchenko National University of Kyiv, 4E Academician Glushkov Avenue, 03127 Kyiv, Ukraine; sobchuk@knu.ua (V.S.); itsy8009@knu.ua (I.T.)
[2] Educational and Scientific Institute of Atomic Thermal Energy, National Technical University of Ukraine "Ihor Sikorsky Kyiv Polytechnic Institute", 6 Polytechnichna St., Building No. 5, 03056 Kyiv, Ukraine; bar64@ukr.net (O.B.); mysienkoandrey@gmail.com (A.M.)
* Correspondence: alexandr.kurylko@knu.ua
† These authors contributed equally to this work.

Abstract: The comprehensive system of information security of an enterprise includes both tactical aspects of information and strategic priorities, reflecting the information policy and information strategy of the enterprise. Ensuring a given level of cybersecurity requires the identification of threat actors, their purpose, intentions of attacks on the IT infrastructure, and weak points of the enterprise's information security. To achieve these goals, enterprises need new information security solutions. In this work, a mathematical model of the process of cyber risk management in the enterprise, which is based on the distribution of piecewise continuous analytical approximating functions of cyber attacks in the Fourier series, is obtained. A constant continuous monitoring and conduction of cyber regulatory control of the enterprise on time makes it possible to effectively ensure the cybersecurity of the enterprise in real time—predicting the emergence of cyber threats to some extent—which, in turn, determines the management of cyber risks arising in the field of information security of the enterprise. Such a Fourier series expansion of the piecewise continuous analytical approximating function of the intensity of cyber attacks on damage to standard software, obtained by approximating empirical–statistical slices of the intensity of cyber attacks on damage to standard software for each time period by analytical functions, opens up new mathematical possibilities of transition to systems of regulatory control of cyber threats of the enterprise from discrete to continuous automated process for such types of control.

Keywords: Fourier series; cyber threat; piecewise continuous function; mathematical model; information security of an enterprise

MSC: 42A16

1. Introduction

With the appearance of new IT technologies, the intensity of new cyber attacks on enterprise IT systems is increasing. It is also worth noting that traditional cybersecurity activities cannot fully prevent or contain these attacks due to the increasing speed and frequency of cyber attacks. The enterprise's comprehensive information security system includes both tactical aspects of information protection (express audit of the enterprise's information threats) and strategic priorities reflected in the enterprise's information policy and information strategy. Ensuring a given level of cybersecurity requires the identification of threat actors, their purpose, intentions of attacks on the IT infrastructure, and weak points of the enterprise's information security. To achieve these goals, enterprises need new information security solutions that not only meet the realities of today but also have significant development potential, taking into account current trends in the field of information security in general. At the same time, the issues of researching the intensity of cyber attacks, and their prediction and forecasting, are insufficiently researched in the scientific literature, which is related to the complexity of predicting cyber attacks as well as the availability of modern relevant methods for their forecasting.

The fight against the growing intensity of cyber threats requires the creation of a multifaceted information security strategy of the enterprise, which, in particular, includes the prediction of cyber attacks. In their scientific works, scientists Palash Goyal, Ashok Deb, and Nazgol Tavabi described computer programming methods based on neural networks and autoregressive time series models (AR, ARMA, ARIMA, ARIMAX) that use external signals from publicly available web sources to forecast cyber attacks. However, such models usually require a significant amount of data to implement computer programming in order to establish an accurate estimate of the model parameters. Most research efforts have focused on using network traffic to build predictive models. These studies are presented in the works of scientists such as E. Pontes, A. E. Guelfi, S. T. Kofuji, and A. A. Silva. Other researchers such as E. Gandotra, D. Bansal, and S. Sofat built cyber predictions using statistical modeling and algorithmic modeling. R. Douc, E. Moulines, and D. Stoffer were engaged in the use of ARCH and GARCH models, which are extensions of the classical autoregression model.

However, developing an accurate model of the dynamic behavior of time series is a difficult and important task. Therefore, there is a need for further research and development of a scientific and methodological apparatus for determining the relationship between the level of cyber risk and the frequency of audits, which makes it possible to ensure effective automation of enterprise cybersecurity processes. The general task of ensuring information security conditions the study of vulnerabilities of the IT infrastructure of the enterprise and relevant models of cyber attack prevention. In this regard, it is necessary to conduct a study of the relevant vulnerabilities and problems of all groups of cyber attacks on the enterprise.

As a result of the spread of freelance relations, as a modern type of business relation of an enterprise, there is a need to process and analyze statistical data of cyber attacks in the field of activity of an IT enterprise that involves a freelance resource. These studies should be designed to use temporal correlations between the number of cyber attacks over a period of time in order to predict the future intensity of cyber incidents, which will allow the creation of an effective forecasting system. Therefore, predicting the number of cyber attacks for a set rational time period is necessary to determine the effective frequency of the audit.

2. Literature Analysis

Fourier series are widely used in research in various fields of activity. Thus, particularly in [1–3], the speed of approximation of differentiable functions by generalized methods of summation of Fourier series was investigated. In [4,5], the conditions of convergence of Fourier transformations were investigated. Applied aspects of approximate properties of Fourier series were considered in [6–8], while the properties and application of isometric classes of functions based on their Fourier series were studied in [9,10].

In modern technical literature, the scientific problems of enterprise information security related, in particular, to the improvement of attack graphs for monitoring cybersecurity, handling of inaccuracies, cycle processing, display of incidents, and automatic selection of protective measures were investigated in the works of O.A. Lapteva [11–14], E.M. Galakhova [15], O.V. Kapustyan [16], S.P. Yevseiev, [17], and A.P. Musienko [18], respectively. The stability of the information system, in terms of functioning with the conditions of external and internal destabilizing factors, was studied in [19]. External and internal destabilizing factors include mean failures, failures of system modules, mechanical damage, thermal effects, and errors of service personnel. Ref. [20] investigated how, on the basis of the functional dependence of the probability of missing failures on a certain probability value, at different values of the probability of second-order control error, it is possible to determine the recommended interval of issuing the result, which will ensure, at a given intensity of readiness control, an acceptable probability of missing a failure. It was illustrated how, with a given intensity of issuing the result, it is possible to determine such an intensity of readiness control at which the probability of failure will not exceed the maximum permissible value. It was shown that it is possible to talk about a weak dependence of the probability of omission on the control error of the second kind, which means that the achievement of the specified reliability of the control is ensured on the basis of the intensity of the readiness control and depends less on the reliability of individual elementary checks. For the case when, in the intervals between the moments when the result is issued, the system checks the readiness of the modules randomly, the methodology for calculating the probability of failure was described. In [21], based on the use of a hierarchical concept of the organization of means of ensuring the functional stability of the company's information system, two algorithms were developed that form a two-level system for diagnosing hidden failures. Diagnosis begins with the execution of the first algorithm, the advantages of which compared with known algorithms are that it requires less system redundancy, only two rounds of message exchange between nodes of the information system, and provides diagnosis of the information system of the subtribe when almost half of its nodes fail. In the case of an ambiguous solution to the diagnosis problem, the algorithm generates a signal about its failure and the diagnosis of the information system continues according to the second algorithm, which uses the duration of the phases as a criterion.

In [22–24], for evolutionary nonlinear problems with control parameters, the problems of approximate minimax estimation and making optimal decisions were considered. The authors investigated the problems of the behavior of evolutionary systems, when the system is under the influence of impulse forces of an instantaneous nature. This is important, because even in the case of linear systems, the presence of impulse action makes the behavior of the system significantly nonlinear, and the control of solutions of such systems is extremely difficult. At the same time, cyber attacks have a similar nature when they try to destabilize the system through the influence of external forces. Prediction of the number of possible cyber attacks, statistical and analytical assessments of cyber attacks, timely identification, development of an action plan and preventive measures to eliminate identical cyber attacks, implementation of a control system, and the introduction of modernized approaches to regulatory control of cyber attacks in the enterprise were carried out in [25,26].

The purpose of this work is to develop a mathematical model of cyber risks management of the enterprise, which makes it possible to move the system of regulatory control of cyber threats of the enterprise from a discrete to a continuous automated process of regulatory control.

3. Main Part

Let us consider a mathematical model of the process of managing cyber risks of the enterprise, which makes it possible to move the system of regulatory control of cyber threats of the enterprise from a discrete to a continuous automated process of regulatory control. This model differs from the existing ones, based mainly on the statistical analysis of time series, in that piecewise continuous analytical approximating functions of cyber attacks are decomposed into a Fourier series.

The research interest of this model is to determine the recommended frequency for the cyber risk management process in the enterprise. The model focuses on the following key stages of research:

1. Retrospective statistical analysis of cyber risk identification time series.
    1.1. Determination of time intervals of regulatory control and approximation of statistical sections by analytical functions (Figures 1 and 2).
    1.2. Graphical visualization of the implemented statistical analysis of time series of cyber risk identification (Figure 1).

2. Analysis of the enterprise's existing cyber risks strategy based on the retrospective statistical analysis of cyber risk identification time series, conducted above, highlighting weaknesses of the existing strategy, possible cyber threats, identification of potential strengths, and opportunities for further modernization.
3. Development of a predictive and analytical model of regulatory control.
4. Introduction of modernized approaches into the existing system of regulatory control of the enterprise.

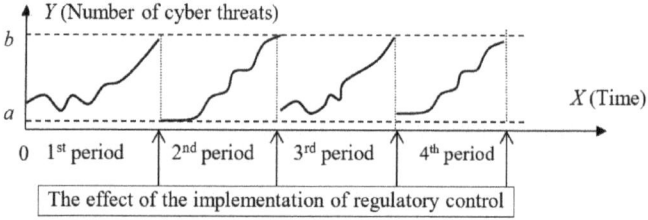

Figure 1. Dependence of the number of cyber threats on the frequency of regulatory control over 4 time intervals.

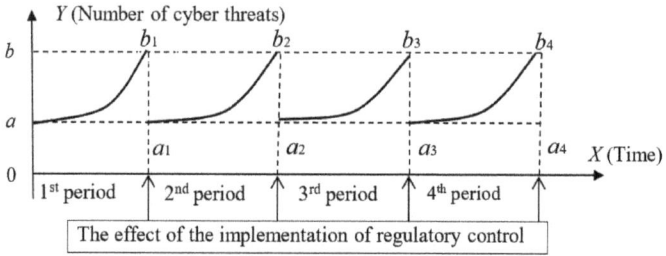

Figure 2. Approximation of statistical slices of cyber attacks on damage to network infrastructure by analytical functions.

Figure 1 shows 4 time periods of regulatory control within the framework of the proposed model. The implementation of consistent activities of regulatory control ensures the minimization of cyber threats in each time period, which is illustrated in Figure 1. Figure 1 illustrates similar effects from the implementation of regulatory control and almost the same behavior in the number of cyber threats between the conducted audits.

According to part 1.1 of the abovementioned key bases of model research, an approximation of the statistical slices of cyber attacks on damage to the network infrastructure was carried out by analytical functions in the period between 4 time periods of regulatory control within the framework of the proposed model (Table 1).

Table 1. Approximation of time series of cyber attacks on damage to network infrastructure by analytical functions.

Time Period	Nonlinear Equation of the Approximating Function on the Interval (0; 1)	Coefficient of Determination
1st period	$y = 1.0643 \times e^{0.064x}$	0.9032
2nd period	$y = 1.0534 \times e^{0.053x}$	0.9040
3rd period	$y = 1.0626 \times e^{0.065x}$	0.9012
4th period	$y = 1.0596 \times e^{0.059x}$	0.8933

Figure 2 presents a graphical interpretation of the approximation of the time series of cyber attacks on damage to the network infrastructure by analytical functions with averaged values for each time period in view of the almost identical equations of the approximating functions for different periods, which are presented in Table 1.

From Figure 2, we establish that the function is periodic with a period $T = 1$ ($2l = 1$, $l = 1/2$); then, we expand the given function into a Fourier series on the closed interval $[0, 2l] = [0, 1]$. Let us write down the equation of the given function presented in Figure 2 with unknown coefficients: $y = A \times e^{Bx}$. Let us determine the estimated coordinates of the points from the bundle of nonlinear curves approximating the statistical series, which are in the confidence interval with the smallest variances in the form $y = 1.0595 \times e^{0.060205x}$. Note that 0.52975 is the statistical average value of the cyber threat function at its points of jump discontinuity. Thus, we have

$$y = \begin{cases} 1.0595 \times e^{0.060205x} & k < x < k+1 \\ 0.52975 & x = k, k \in Z \end{cases} \quad (1)$$

For function (1), we find the coefficients of the Fourier series:

$$a_0 = \int_0^1 1.0595 \times e^{0.060205x} dx = \frac{1.0595}{0.060205} \times (e^{0.060205x})|_0^1 = 17.5982(e^{0.060205} - 1) = 1.09351. \quad (2)$$

Denoting the desired integral by I and applying the method of integration by parts twice, we obtain

$$a_n = \frac{1}{1/2} \int_0^1 1.0595 e^{0.060205x} \times \cos\left(\frac{\pi n x}{1/2}\right) dx = 2 \times 1.0595 \times I = 2.119 \times I$$

$$= \begin{vmatrix} e^{0.060205x} = U & 0.060205 e^{0.060205x} dx = dU \\ \cos(2\pi nx) dx = dV & V = \frac{1}{2\pi n} \sin(2\pi nx) \end{vmatrix}$$

$$= 2.119 \left[\left(e^{0.060205x} \times \frac{1}{2\pi n} \sin(2\pi nx) \right)|_0^1 - \frac{0.060205}{2\pi n} \int_0^1 e^{0.060205x} \sin(2\pi nx) dx \right] \quad (3)$$

$$= \begin{vmatrix} e^{0.060205x} = U & 0.060205 e^{0.060205x} dx = dU \\ \sin(2\pi nx) dx = dV & V = -\frac{1}{2\pi n} \cos(2\pi nx) \end{vmatrix}$$

$$= -2.119 \times \frac{0.060205}{2\pi n} \left[-\frac{e^{0.060205x}}{2\pi n} \cos(2\pi nx) \right]|_0^1 + \frac{0.060205}{2\pi n} \int_0^1 e^{0.060205x} \cos(2\pi nx) dx$$

$$= \frac{0.127574}{2\pi n} \left(-\frac{e^{0.060205} - 1}{2\pi n} + \frac{0.060205}{2\pi n} \right) \times I$$

To find the integral I, we solve the following equation:

$$2.119 \times I = \frac{0.127574}{2\pi n} \left(-\frac{e^{0.060205} - 1}{2\pi n} + \frac{0.060205}{2\pi n} \right) \times I \Rightarrow$$

$$\Rightarrow I \left(2.119 - \frac{0.127574}{2\pi n} \times \frac{0.060205}{2\pi n} \right) = -\frac{0.127574}{2\pi n} \times \frac{e^{0.060205} - 1}{2\pi n} \quad (4)$$

Thus, we have

$$I = \frac{0.127574(e^{0.060205} - 1)}{0.00678 - 2.119(2\pi n)^2}. \quad (5)$$

Then, the coefficients a_n are obtained in the form

$$a_n = \frac{1}{1/2} \int_0^1 1.06^{1-x} \times \cos\left(\frac{\pi n x}{1/2}\right) dx = 2.119 \times I$$

$$= \frac{2.119 \times 0.127574(e^{0.060205} - 1)}{0.00678 - 2.119(2\pi n)^2} = \frac{0.27033(e^{0.060205} - 1)}{0.00678 - 2.119(2\pi n)^2}. \quad (6)$$

Similarly, we find the coefficients b_n:

$$b_n = \frac{1}{1/2}\int_0^1 1.0595 e^{0.060205x}\sin\left(\frac{\pi n x}{1/2}\right)dx = 2\times 1.0595\times I = 2.119\times I$$

$$= 2.119\left[\left(-e^{0.060205x}\times\frac{1}{2\pi n}\sin(2\pi n x)\right)\Big|_0^1 + \frac{0.060205}{2\pi n}\int_0^1 e^{0.060205x}\cos(2\pi n x)dx\right]$$

$$\begin{vmatrix} e^{0.060205x} = U & 0.060205 e^{0.060205x}dx = dU \\ \sin(2\pi nx)dx = dV & V = -\frac{1}{2\pi n}\cos(2\pi nx) \end{vmatrix}$$

$$\begin{vmatrix} e^{0.060205x} = U & 0.060205 e^{0.060205x}dx = dU \\ \cos(2\pi nx)dx = dV & V = \frac{1}{2\pi n}\sin(2\pi nx) \end{vmatrix} \quad (7)$$

$$= 2.119\left[-\left(e^{0.060205}-1\right)\times\frac{1}{2\pi n}+\frac{0.060205}{2\pi n}\left[\frac{e^{0.060205x}}{2\pi n}\sin(2\pi nx)\Big|_0^1 - \frac{0.060205}{2\pi n}\int_0^1 e^{0.060205x}\sin(2\pi nx)dx\right]\right]$$

$$= \frac{2.119(1-e^{0.060205})}{2\pi n} - \frac{0.0076806}{(2\pi n)^2}\times I$$

To find the integral I, we solve the following equation:

$$2.119\times I = \frac{2.119(1-e^{0.060205})}{2\pi n} - \frac{0.0076806}{(2\pi n)^2}\times I \Rightarrow$$

$$\Rightarrow I\left[2.119+\frac{0.0076806}{(2\pi n)^2}\right] = \frac{2.119(1-e^{0.060205})}{2\pi n}. \quad (8)$$

Thus, we obtain

$$I = \frac{2.119(1-e^{0.060205})}{2\pi n\left(2.119+\frac{0.0076806}{(2\pi n)^2}\right)}. \quad (9)$$

Then, the coefficients b_n will have the following form:

$$b_n = \frac{4.49020(1-e^{0.060205})}{2\pi n\left(2.119+\frac{0.0076806}{(2\pi n)^2}\right)}. \quad (10)$$

Hence, let us write down the expansion of Function (1) in the Fourier series:

$$f(x) = 1.09351 + \sum_{n=1}^{\infty}\left[\frac{0.27033(e^{0.060205}-1)}{0.00678-2.119(2\pi n)^2}\times\cos(2\pi nx)+\frac{4.49020(1-e^{0.060205})}{2\pi n\left(2.119+\frac{0.0076806}{(2\pi n)^2}\right)}\times\sin(2\pi nx)\right] \quad (11)$$

Thus, Function (11) is a continuous function that models a piecewise continuous function with points of jump irremovable discontinuities. Such a mathematical model is based on the expansion of a piecewise continuous analytical approximating function into the Fourier series, which makes it possible to move the system of regulatory control of cyber threats of the enterprise from a discrete to a continuous automated process of regulatory control.

Therefore, the approximation of statistical slices of cyber attacks on damage to the network infrastructure by analytical functions in the period between 4 time periods of regulatory control within the framework of the proposed model provides an automated approach to minimizing cyber threats in each time period.

Let us consider the mathematical possibilities of transition from a discrete to continuous automated process of cyber regulatory control of the enterprise. The modern approach to the information security of an enterprise in the sphere of action of cyber attacks is determined by the following stages: forecasting the number of possible cyber attacks; carrying out empirical–statistical and analytical evaluation of cyber attacks; identification of cyber attacks on time; development of an action plan and preventive activities to eliminate similar cyber attacks; and, most importantly, the implementation of the control system and the introduction of innovative approaches to the timely regulatory control of cyber attacks in the enterprise.

Therefore, with the growth of cyber threats, the need for express audits and their implementation on time increases the effectiveness of the enterprise's comprehensive information security strategy.

Figure 3 schematically reflects the behavior of the intensity of cyber attacks on damage to standard software for 4 time periods between conducting the scheduled regulatory control. After the scheduled regulatory control before the first time period, activities were taken that ensured the minimization of cyber threats in the first 2 time periods after the scheduled regulatory control.

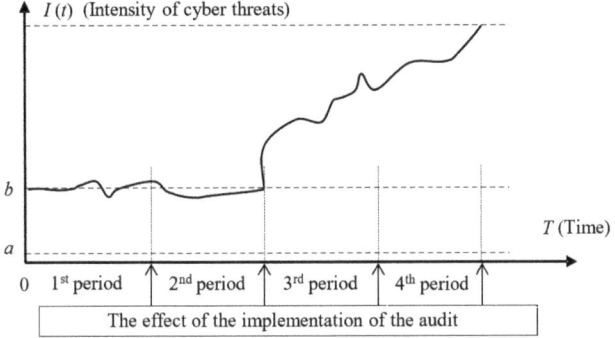

Figure 3. Dependence of the number of cyber attacks on the damage standard software from frequency of carrying out regulatory control for 4 time intervals.

Approximation of the statistical slices of cyber attacks on damage to standard software for each period by analytical functions was carried out (Table 2).

Table 2. Approximation of time series of cyber attacks on damage to standard software by analytical functions.

Time Period	An Equation of the Approximating Function on the Interval (0; 1)	Coefficient of Determination
1st period	$I(t) = 1.0364$	0.8731
2nd period	$I(t) = 1.0453$	0.8540
3rd period	$I(t) = 1.00076t$	0.8912
4th period	$I(t) = 1.0237t$	0.8721

Based on Table 2, given the almost identical equations of approximating functions for the 1st, 2nd and 3rd, and 4th periods, respectively, it is possible to represent analytically the function of the intensity of cyber attacks on damage to standard software, combining the 1st, 2nd and 3rd, and 4th periods. Then, analytically, the function of the intensity of cyber attacks can be represented as

$$I(t) = \begin{cases} 1, & 0 \leq t < 2 \\ t, & 2 \leq t \leq 4. \end{cases} \qquad (12)$$

Let us expand Function (12) into a Fourier series, which will make it possible to move the regulatory control system of cyber attacks on damage of the enterprise's standard software from a discrete to a continuous automated process of regulatory control.

Let us find the following coefficients:

$$a_n = \frac{1}{2}\int_0^4 f(t)\cos\frac{\pi nt}{2}dt = \frac{1}{2}\left(\int_0^2 \cos\frac{\pi nt}{2}dt + \int_2^4 t\cos\frac{\pi nt}{2}dt\right)$$

$$= \begin{vmatrix} t = U & dt = dU \\ \cos\frac{\pi nt}{2} = dV & V = \frac{2}{\pi n}\sin\frac{\pi nt}{2}\end{vmatrix} \quad (13)$$

$$= \frac{1}{2}\left(\frac{2}{\pi n}\sin\frac{\pi nt}{2}\Big|_0^2 + \left(\frac{2t}{\pi n}\sin\frac{\pi nt}{2} + \frac{4}{\pi^2 n^2}\cos\frac{\pi nt}{2}\right)\Big|_2^4\right)$$

$$= \frac{1}{2} \times \frac{4}{\pi^2 n^2}(\cos 2\pi n - \cos \pi n) = \frac{2}{\pi^2 n^2}(1 - \cos \pi n) = \frac{2}{\pi^2 n^2}(1 - (-1)^n);$$

$$a_0 = \frac{1}{2}\int_0^4 f(t)dt = \frac{1}{2}\left(\int_0^2 dt + \int_2^4 tdt\right) = \frac{1}{2}\left(2 + \frac{t^2}{2}\Big|_2^4\right) = \frac{1}{2}(2+6) = 4; \quad (14)$$

$$b_n = \frac{1}{2}\int_0^4 f(t)\sin\frac{\pi nt}{2}dt = \frac{1}{2}\left(\int_0^2 \sin\frac{\pi nt}{2}dt + \int_2^4 t\sin\frac{\pi nt}{2}dt\right)$$

$$= \begin{vmatrix} t = U & dt = dU \\ \sin\frac{\pi nt}{2} = dV & V = -\frac{2}{\pi n}\cos\frac{\pi nt}{2}\end{vmatrix}$$

$$= \frac{1}{2}\left(-\frac{2}{\pi n}\cos\frac{\pi nt}{2}\Big|_0^2 + \left(-\frac{2t}{\pi n}\cos\frac{\pi nt}{2} + \frac{4}{\pi^2 n^2}\sin\frac{\pi nt}{2}\right)\Big|_2^4\right) \quad (15)$$

$$= -\frac{1}{2} \times \frac{2}{\pi n}\left(\cos\frac{\pi nt}{2}\Big|_0^2 + t\cos\frac{\pi nt}{2}\Big|_2^4\right) = -\frac{1}{\pi n}(\cos \pi n - 1 + 4\cos 2\pi n - 2\cos \pi n)$$

$$= -\frac{1}{\pi n}(3 - \cos \pi n) = \frac{1}{\pi n}((-1)^n - 3).$$

The desired expansion looks like

$$I(t) = 2 + \sum_{n=1}^{\infty}\left[\frac{2}{\pi^2 n^2}(1 - (-1)^n)\cos\frac{\pi nt}{2} + \frac{1}{\pi n}((-1)^n - 3)\sin\frac{\pi nt}{2}\right]. \quad (16)$$

For all $t \in (0; 2)$, we have in the open interval $(0; 2)$ the sum of the series $s(t) = 1$, while in the open interval $(2; 4)$, we have the sum of the series $s(t) = t$. At the point of jump discontinuity $t = 2$,

$$s(t) = \frac{f(2-) + f(2+)}{2} = \frac{1+2}{2} = \frac{3}{2}. \quad (17)$$

At points $t = 0$ and $t = 4$, the sum $s(t)$ is equal to

$$s(t) = \frac{f(0) + f(4)}{2} = \frac{1+4}{2} = \frac{5}{2}. \quad (18)$$

Consider the first nine terms of the series (16)

$$I(t) = 2 + \sum_{n=1}^{8}\left[\frac{2}{\pi^2 n^2}(1-(-1)^n)\cos\frac{\pi n t}{2} + \frac{1}{\pi n}((-1)^n - 3)\sin\frac{\pi n t}{2}\right]$$

$$= 2 + \left(\frac{2}{\pi^2}(2)\cos\frac{\pi t}{2} + \frac{1}{\pi}(-4)\sin\frac{\pi t}{2}\right) + \left(\frac{1}{2\pi}(-2)\sin\pi t\right)$$

$$+ \left(\frac{2}{9\pi^2}(2)\cos\frac{3\pi t}{2} + \frac{1}{3\pi}(-4)\sin\frac{3\pi t}{2}\right) + \left(\frac{1}{4\pi}(-2)\sin 2\pi t\right) \quad (19)$$

$$+ \left(\frac{2}{25\pi^2}(2)\cos\frac{5\pi t}{2} + \frac{1}{5\pi}(-4)\sin\frac{5\pi t}{2}\right) + \left(\frac{1}{6\pi}(-2)\sin 3\pi t\right)$$

$$+ \left(\frac{2}{49\pi^2}(2)\cos\frac{7\pi t}{2} + \frac{1}{7\pi}(-4)\sin\frac{7\pi t}{2}\right) + \left(\frac{1}{8\pi}(-2)\sin 4\pi t\right).$$

Figure 4 presents the graphs of the expansion of $I(t)$ into the Fourier series, taking into account from 3 to 8 terms in (16), respectively.

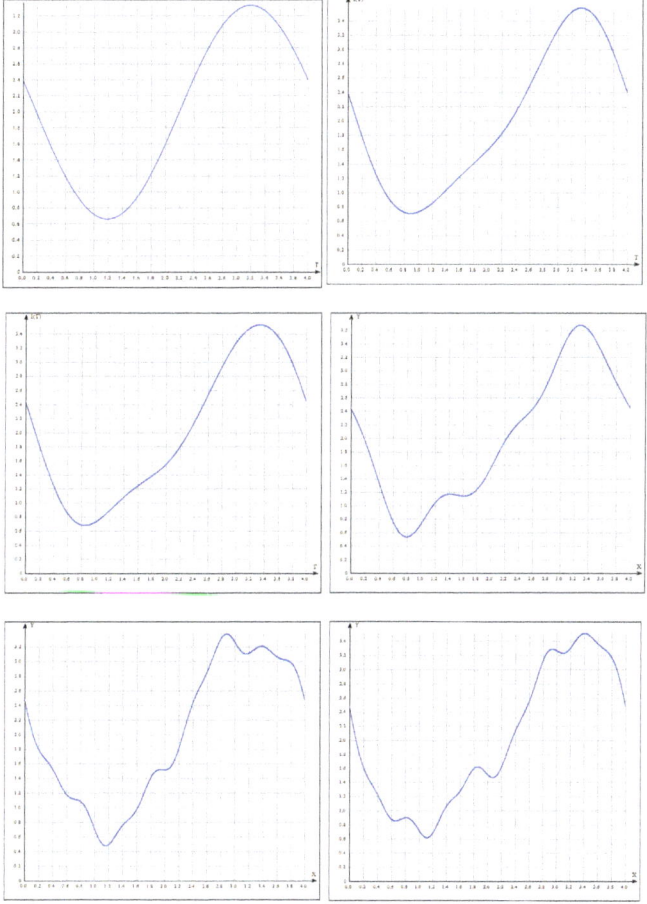

Figure 4. Visualization when increasing the terms of the Fourier series (from three members of the series to eight) as a function of the intensity of cyber attacks on damage to standard software.

Therefore, constant continuous monitoring and timely conduction of cyber regulatory control of the enterprise makes it possible to effectively ensure the cybersecurity of the enterprise in real time—predicting the emergence of cyber threats, to some extent—which, in turn, determines the management of cyber risks arising in the field of information security of the enterprise.

Such a Fourier series expansion of the piecewise continuous analytical approximating function of the intensity of cyber attacks on damage to standard software, obtained by approximating empirical–statistical slices of the intensity of cyber attacks on damage to standard software for each time period by analytical functions, opens up new mathematical possibilities of transition to systems of regulatory control of cyber threats of the enterprise from a discrete to a continuous automated process of regulatory control.

Figure 5 presents a graphical interpretation of the approximation of the time series of the intensity of cyber attacks on e-mail damage by analytical functions with averaged values for each time period.

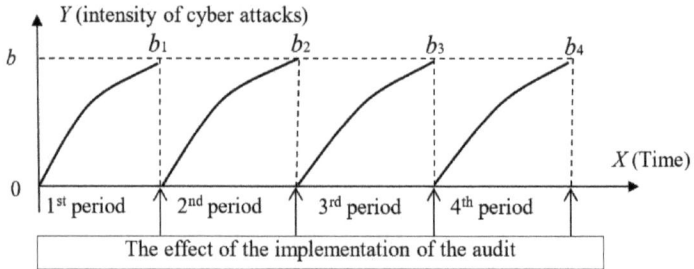

Figure 5. Dependence of the intensity of cyber attacks on e-mail damage on the frequency of regulatory control over 4 time intervals.

In view of the homogeneity of the behavior of the intensity of cyber attacks in each time period, the approximation of the statistical slices of the intensity of cyber attacks on e-mail damage for each period was carried out using analytical functions (Table 3).

Table 3. Approximation of time series of the intensity of cyber attacks on e-mail damage by analytical functions.

Time Period	An Equation of the Approximating Function on the Interval (0; 1)	Coefficient of Determination
1st period	$I(t) = -1.0754t^2 + 4.9954t$	0.7942
2nd period	$I(t) = -0.99164t^2 + 5.0127t$	0.8184
3rd period	$I(t) = -1.0032t^2 + 5.0073t$	0.8532
4th period	$I(t) = -1.0116t^2 + 5.0096t$	0.8258

Based on the data given in Table 3, it is possible to present analytically the function of the intensity of cyber attacks on e-mail damage, combining all periods in view of the standard cyclicality in each period. Then, analytically, the function of the intensity of cyber attacks can be represented as

$$I(t) = \begin{cases} -t^2 + 5t, & 0 \leq t < 1, \\ -(t-1)^2 + 5(t-1), & 1 \leq t < 2, \\ -(t-2)^2 + 5(t-2), & 2 \leq t < 3, \\ -(t-3)^2 + 5(t-3), & 3 \leq t \leq 4. \end{cases} \quad (20)$$

Let us write the Fourier series for Function (20) only on the first interval, the graph of which is shown in Figure 6, since periodicity is performed on the other intervals. This will make it possible to move the system of regulatory control of cyber attacks on damage to standard enterprise software from a discrete to a continuous automated process of regulatory control.

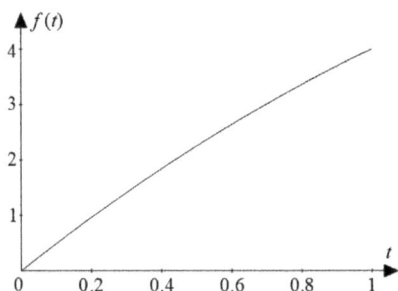

Figure 6. Analytical function of the intensity of cyber attacks on e-mail damage in the first time period.

Let us find the coefficients of the Fourier series for the function $f(t) = -t^2 + 5t$, $t \in [0; 1]$.

The Fourier series expansion on the interval $(-T; T)$ has the form

$$f(t) = \frac{a_0}{2} + \sum_{n=1}^{\infty}\left(a_n \cos\frac{\pi n t}{T} + b_n \sin\frac{\pi n t}{T}\right), \quad (21)$$

$$a_0 = \frac{1}{T}\int_{-T}^{T} f(t)dt, \quad (22)$$

$$a_n = \frac{1}{T}\int_{-T}^{T} f(t) \times \cos\frac{\pi n t}{T}dt, \quad (23)$$

$$b_n = \frac{1}{T}\int_{-T}^{T} f(t) \times \sin\frac{\pi n t}{T}dt. \quad (24)$$

In our case, $T = 1$; so,

$$a_0 = \int_0^1 (-t^2 + 5t)dt = \left(-\frac{t^3}{3} + \frac{5t^2}{2}\right)\Big|_0^1 = \frac{13}{6} - 0 = \frac{13}{6}, \quad (25)$$

$$a_n = \int_0^1 (-t^2 + 5t) \times (\cos \pi n t)dt$$

$$= \left[-t^2\frac{\sin(\pi n t)}{\pi n} + 5t\frac{\sin(\pi n t)}{\pi n} - 2t\frac{\cos(\pi n t)}{\pi^2 n^2} + 5\frac{\cos(\pi n t)}{\pi^2 n^2} + 2\frac{\sin(\pi n t)}{\pi^3 n^3}\right]\Big|_0^1 \quad (26)$$

$$= \left[4\frac{\sin(\pi n)}{\pi n} + 3\frac{\cos(\pi n)}{\pi^2 n^2} + 2\frac{\sin(\pi n)}{\pi n} - \frac{5}{\pi^2 n^2}\right] = \frac{3(-1)^n - 5}{\pi^2 n^2},$$

$$b_n = \int_0^1 (-t^2 + 5t) \times \sin(\pi n t)dt$$

$$= \left[-t^2\frac{\cos(\pi n t)}{\pi n} - 5t\frac{\cos(\pi n t)}{\pi n} - 2t\frac{\sin(\pi n t)}{\pi^2 n^2} + 5\frac{\sin(\pi n t)}{\pi^2 n^2} - 2\frac{\cos(\pi n t)}{\pi^3 n^3}\right]\Big|_0^1 \quad (27)$$

$$= \left[-4\frac{\cos(\pi n)}{\pi n} + 3\frac{\sin(\pi n)}{\pi^2 n^2} - 2\frac{\cos(\pi n)}{\pi^3 n^3} - \left(-\frac{2}{\pi^3 n^3}\right)\right]$$

$$= 2\frac{-2(-1)^n \pi^2 n^2 - (-1)^n + 1}{\pi^3 n^3}.$$

Hence, for even numbers n ($n = 2k$), we have $b_n = 0$, and for odd n ($n = 2k-1$),

$$b_k = \frac{4\pi^2(2k-1)^2 + 4}{\pi^3(2k-1)^3}. \tag{28}$$

Thus, we have

$$f(t) = \frac{13}{12} + \sum_{k=1}^{\infty}\left[\frac{3(-1)^k - 5}{\pi^2 k^2} \times \cos(\pi k t) + \frac{4\pi^2(2k-1)^2 + 4}{\pi^3(2k-1)^3} \times \sin(\pi(2k-1)t)\right]. \tag{29}$$

Figures 7–9 present graphs of the expansion of Function (20) on the interval (0;1) into the Fourier series, taking into account 3, 5, or 7 terms of the series, respectively.

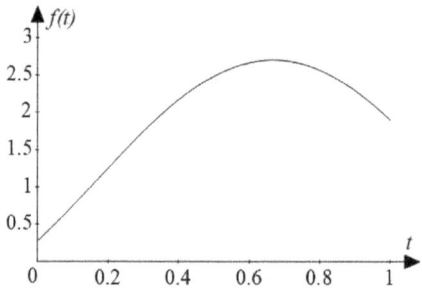

Figure 7. Expansion of the function of the intensity of e-mail cyber attacks in the Fourier series (29) for $k = 1$.

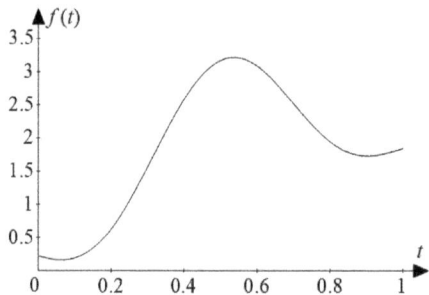

Figure 8. Expansion of the function of the intensity of e-mail cyber attacks in the Fourier series (29) for $k = 2$.

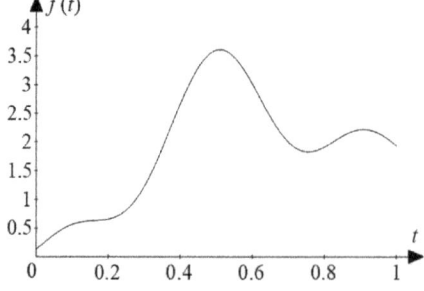

Figure 9. Expansion of the function of the intensity of e-mail cyber attacks in the Fourier series (29) for $k = 3$.

Figure 7 shows the graph of the function

$$f(t) = \frac{13}{12} - \frac{8\cos(\pi t)}{\pi^2} + \left(4 + 4\pi^2\right) \times \frac{\sin(\pi t)}{\pi^3}, \qquad (30)$$

which is obtained from (29) for $k = 1$ on the interval $(0,1)$.

Figure 8 shows the graph of the function

$$f(t) = \frac{13}{12} - \frac{8\cos(\pi t)}{\pi^2} + \left(4 + 4\pi^2\right) \times \frac{\sin(\pi t)}{\pi^3} - \frac{\cos(2\pi t)}{2\pi^2} + \left(4 + 36\pi^2\right) \times \frac{\sin(3\pi t)}{27\pi^3}, \qquad (31)$$

which is obtained from (29) for $k = 2$ on the interval $(0,1)$.

Figure 9 shows the graph of the function

$$f(t) = \frac{13}{12} - \frac{8\cos(\pi t)}{\pi^2} + \left(4 + 4\pi^2\right) \times \frac{\sin(\pi t)}{\pi^3} - \frac{\cos(2\pi t)}{2\pi^2}$$
$$+ \left(4 + 36\pi^2\right) \times \frac{\sin(3\pi t)}{27\pi^3} - \frac{8\cos(3\pi t)}{9\pi^2} + \left(4 + 100\pi^2\right) \times \frac{\sin(5\pi t)}{125\pi^3}, \qquad (32)$$

which is obtained from (29) for $k = 3$ on the interval $(0,1)$.

Therefore, with an increase in the number of terms of the Fourier series, the function will be continuous periodic in approximation to the piecewise continuous function, which enables constant continuous automated monitoring and timely conduction of cyber regulatory control of the enterprise in relation to e-mail attacks, which effectively ensures real-time cybersecurity of the enterprise.

This is due to the fact that information systems are widely implemented and used for processing, storing, and transmitting information, which, in turn, has led to the need to protect information systems, since information attacks can cause large financial and material losses. Auditing and monitoring serve to develop effective measures to ensure information security in enterprises, organizations, and institutions. With the help of an information security audit, the collection and analysis of information is carried out with regard to the information system being checked. It is conducted for the purpose of quantitative as well as qualitative assessment of the level of protection of the information system against possible attacks by intruders. The audit itself can provide an objective assessment of the security of any type of enterprise or institution, as well as prevent the realization of potential threats. The release of the company's products at the international level is not possible without the implementation of international and industry standards, such as ISO/IEC 27001:2013 "Information security management systems. Requirements", ITU-T X-1051 "Information security management systems. Requirements for telecommunications", as well as ISO/IEC 27035:2011 "Information technology. Security techniques. Information security incident management".

One of the most common types of audit is an active audit. It consists in studying the state of security of the information system from the point of view of an attacker (or an attacker with high IT skills). Active audits can be conditionally divided into two types—external and internal. Also, during an active audit, a study of system performance and stability, or stress test, is carried out. It is aimed at determining the critical load points at which the system, due to a denial-of-service attack or increased load, ceases to respond adequately to legitimate (defined by the security policy) user requests. The stress test will allow to identify "bottlenecks" in the process of formation and transmission of information and to determine the conditions under which normal operation of the system is impossible. Such testing involves simulating denial-of-service attacks as user requests to the system and conducting a general analysis of its performance. The result of an active audit is information about all vulnerabilities, degrees of their criticality and elimination methods, and information about publicly available information (information available to any potential violator) of the customer's network. Based on the results of an active audit, recommendations are provided for the modernization of the network protection system, which make it possible to eliminate dangerous vulnerabilities and, thus, increase the level of protection of the company's information system against the actions of an intruder with minimal costs for information security. It should be noted that the information security management system (ISMS) is a part of the overall management system, which is based on the assessment of business risks in order to create, implement, operate, constantly monitor, analyze, maintain, and improve the protection of information.

4. Conclusions

Constant continuous monitoring and regulatory control of enterprise's cyber threats provides management with key real-time information about the enterprise's cybersecurity efficiency, allowing not only to better understand problems when they occur but also to predict their occurrence, which improves the ability to manage risks and opportunities.

Note that the enterprise's comprehensive information security system should include both tactical aspects of information protection and strategic priorities, which are reflected in the information policy and information strategy of the enterprise.

Author Contributions: Conceptualization, V.S., O.B., A.M., I.T. and O.K.; methodology, V.S., O.B., A.M., I.T. and O.K.; formal analysis, V.S., O.B., A.M., I.T. and O.K.; investigation, V.S., O.B., A.M., I.T. and O.K.; writing—original draft preparation, V.S., O.B., A.M., I.T. and O.K.; writing—review and editing, V.S., O.B., A.M., I.T. and O.K. All authors have read and agreed to the published version of the manuscript.

Funding: This research received no external funding.

Data Availability Statement: Not available.

Acknowledgments: The authors express their sincere gratitude for the opportunity to publish the work in this journal on a free basis.

Conflicts of Interest: The authors declare no conflict of interest.

References

1. Kal'chuk, I.V.; Kharkevych, Y.I. Approximation Properties of the Generalized Abel-Poisson Integrals on the Weyl-Nagy Classes. *Axioms* **2022**, *11*, 161. [CrossRef]
2. Kal'chuk, I.V.; Kharkevych, Y.I. Approximation of the classes $W^r_{\beta,\infty}$ by generalized Abel-Poisson integrals. *Ukr. Math. J.* **2022**, *74*, 575–585. [CrossRef]
3. Zhyhallo, T.V.; Kharkevych, Y.I. On approximation of functions from the class $L^{\psi}_{\beta,1}$ by the Abel-Poisson integrals in the integral metric. *Carpathian Math. Publ.* **2022**, *14*, 223–229. [CrossRef]
4. Zhyhallo, T.V.; Kharkevych, Y.I. Fourier transform of the summatory Abel–Poisson function. *Cybern. Syst. Anal.* **2022**, *58*, 957–965. [CrossRef]
5. Kharkevych, Y.; Stepaniuk, T. Approximate Properties of Abel-Poisson Integrals on Classes of Differentiable Functions Defined by Moduli of Continuity. *Carpathian Math. Publ.* **2023**, *15*, 286–294. [CrossRef]
6. Kharkevych, Y.I. On some asymptotic properties of solutions to biharmonic equations. *Cybern. Syst. Anal.* **2022**, *58*, 251–258. [CrossRef]
7. Kharkevych, Y.I. Approximation Theory and Related Applications. *Axioms* **2022**, *12*, 736. [CrossRef]
8. Kharkevych, Y.I. Approximative properties of the generalized Poisson integrals on the classes of functions determined by a modulus of continuity. *J. Autom. Inf. Sci.* **2019**, *51*, 43–54. [CrossRef]
9. Bushev, D.; Abdullayev, F.; Kal'chuk, I.; Imashkyzy, M. The use of the isometry of function spaces with different numbers of variables in the theory of approximation of functions. *Carpathian Math. Publ.* **2021**, *13*, 805–817. [CrossRef]
10. Bushev, D.N.; Kharkevych, Y.I. Finding Solution Subspaces of the Laplace and Heat Equations Isometric to Spaces of Real Functions, and Some of Their Applications. *Math. Notes* **2018**, *103*, 869–880. [CrossRef]
11. Laptiev, O.; Shuklin, G.; Hohonianc, S.; Zidan, A.; Salanda, I. Dynamic model of ceber defence diagnostics of information systems with the use of Fozzy technologies. In Proceedings of the IEEE ATIT Conference, Kyiv, Ukraine, 18–20 December 2019; pp. 116–120. [CrossRef]
12. Laptiev, O.; Savchenko, V.; Kotenko, A.; Akhramovych, V.; Samosyuk, V.; Shuklin, G.; Biehun, A. Method of determining trust and protection of personal dat a in social networks. *Int. J. Commun. Netw. Inf. Secur.* **2021**, *13*, 15–21.
13. Laptiev, O.; Savchenko, V.; Pravdyvyi, A.; Ablazov, I.; Lisnevskyi, O.; Kolos, V.; Hudyma, V. Method of detecting radio signals using means of covert by obtaining information on the basis of random signals model. *Int. J. Commun. Netw. Inf. Secur.* **2021**, *13*, 48–54. [CrossRef]

14. Laptiev, O.; Tkachev, O.; Pravdyvyi, A.; Maystrov, O.; Krasikov, P.; Open'ko, P.; Khoroshko, V.; Parkhuts, L. The method of spectral analysis of the determination of random digital signals. *Int. J. Commun. Netw. Inf. Secur.* **2021**, *13*, 271–277. [CrossRef]
15. Halakhov, Y.M.; Barabash, O.V. Strategic priorities of the information security system of an enterprise that engages a freelance resource. Modern information protection. *DUT* **2019**, *3*, 30–35. (In Ukrainian)
16. Kapustian, O.A.; Kapustyan, O.V.; Ryzhov, A.; Sobchuk, V. Approximate Optimal Control for a Parabolic System with Perturbations in the Coefficients on the Half-Axis. *Axioms* **2022**, *11*, 175. [CrossRef]
17. Yevseiev, S.; Khokhlachova, Y.; Ostapov, S.; Laptiev, O.; Korol, O.; Milevskyi, S. *Models of Socio-Cyber-Physical Systems Security*; Monograph; PC Technology Center: Kharkiv, Ukraine, 2023; p. 184. [CrossRef]
18. Laptiev, V.; Musienko, A.; Nakonechnyi, A.; Sobchuk, V.; Gakhov, S.; Kopytko, S. Algorithm for Recognition of Network Traffic Anomalies Based on Artificial Intelligence. In Proceedings of the 5th International Congress on Human-Computer Interaction, Optimization and Robotic Applications (HORA), Istanbul, Turkiye, 8–10 June 2023; pp. 1–5. [CrossRef]
19. Sobchuk, V.; Olimpiyeva, Y.; Musienko, A.; Sobchuk, A. Ensuring the properties of functional stability of manufacturing processes based on the application of neural networks. *CEUR Workshop Proc.* **2021**, *2845*, 106–116.
20. Barabash, O.; Tverdenko, V.; Sobchuk, V.; Musienko, A.; Lukova-Chuiko, N. The Assessment of the Quality of Functional Stability of the Automated Control System with Hierarchic Structure. In Proceedings of the 2020 IEEE Second International Conference on System Analysis and Intelligent Computing (SAIC), Kyiv, Ukraine, 5–9 October 2020; Igor Sikorsky Kyiv Polytechnic Institute: Kyiv, Ukraine, 2020; pp. 1–4. [CrossRef]
21. Sobchuk, V.; Barabash, O.; Musienko, A.; Laptiev, V.; Kozlovskyi, V.; Shcheblanin, Y. Evaluation of Efficiency of Application of Functionally Sustainable Generalized Information System of the Enterprise. In Proceedings of the 2022 International Congress on Human-Computer Interaction, Optimization and Robotic Applications (HORA), Ankara, Turkey, 9–11 June 2022; pp. 1–7. [CrossRef]
22. Kapustyan, O.V.; Kapustyan, O.A.; Sukretna, A.V. Approximate stabilization for a nonlinear parabolic boundary-value problem. *Ukr. Math. J.* **2011**, *63*, 759–767. [CrossRef]
23. Nakonechny, A.G.; Kapustian, O.A.; Chikrii, A.A. Control of impulse systems in a conflict situation. *J. Autom. Inf. Sci.* **2019**, *51*, 1–11. [CrossRef]
24. Nosenko, T.V.; Stanzhyts'kyi, O.M. Averaging method in some problems of optimal control. *J. Nonlinear Oscil.* **2008**, *11*, 539–547. [CrossRef]
25. Zamrii, I.; Haidur, H.; Sobchuk, A.; Hryshanovych, T.; Zinchenko, K.; Polovinkin, I. The Method of Increasing the Efficiency of Signal Processing Due to the Use of Harmonic Operators. In Proceedings of the IEEE 4th International Conference on Advanced Trends in Information Theory (ATIT), Kyiv, Ukraine, 15–17 December 2022; pp. 138–141. [CrossRef]
26. Cheung, C.M.; Goyal, P.; Prasanna, V.K.; Tehrani, A.S. Oreonet: Deep convolutional network for oil reservoir optimization. In Proceedings of the IEEE International Conference on Big Data, Boston, MA, USA, 11–14 December 2017; pp. 1277–1282. [CrossRef]

Disclaimer/Publisher's Note: The statements, opinions and data contained in all publications are solely those of the individual author(s) and contributor(s) and not of MDPI and/or the editor(s). MDPI and/or the editor(s) disclaim responsibility for any injury to people or property resulting from any ideas, methods, instructions or products referred to in the content.

Article

Some Relations on the $_rR_s(P, Q, z)$ Matrix Function

Ayman Shehata [1], Ghazi S. Khammash [2] and Carlo Cattani [3,4,*]

[1] Department of Mathematics, Faculty of Science, Assiut University, Assiut 71516, Egypt; aymanshehata@science.aun.edu.eg
[2] Department of Mathematics, Al-Aqsa University-Gaza, Gaza Strip 79779, Palestine; ghazikhamash@yahoo.com
[3] Engineering School, DEIM, Largo dell'Universita, Tuscia University, 01100 Viterbo, Italy
[4] Department of Mathematics and Informatics, Azerbaijan University, Hajibeyli Str., Baku AZ1007, Azerbaijan
* Correspondence: cattani@unitus.it

Abstract: In this paper, we derive some classical and fractional properties of the $_rR_s$ matrix function by using the Hilfer fractional operator. The theory of special matrix functions is the theory of those matrices that correspond to special matrix functions such as the gamma, beta, and Gauss hypergeometric matrix functions. We will also show the relationship with other generalized special matrix functions in the context of the Konhauser and Laguerre matrix polynomials.

Keywords: $_rR_s(P, Q, z)$ matrix function; recurrence relation; integral representation; generalized (Wright) hypergeometric matrix functions; Mittag–Leffler matrix function; fractional integral; derivative operators

MSC: 26A33; 33E12; 47G10; 33C20; 33C60

Citation: Shehata, A.; Khammash, G.S.; Cattani, C. Some Relations on the $_rR_s(P,Q,z)$ Matrix Function. *Axioms* **2023**, *12*, 817. https://doi.org/10.3390/axioms12090817

Academic Editors: Giovanni Nastasi and Clemente Cesarano

Received: 29 May 2023
Revised: 8 August 2023
Accepted: 21 August 2023
Published: 25 August 2023

Copyright: © 2023 by the authors. Licensee MDPI, Basel, Switzerland. This article is an open access article distributed under the terms and conditions of the Creative Commons Attribution (CC BY) license (https://creativecommons.org/licenses/by/4.0/).

1. Introduction

Matrix functions are an important mathematical tool, not only in mathematics, but also in several fundamental disciplines like physics, engineering, and applied sciences. Special matrix functions are used in a variety of fields including statistics [1,2], but also in probability theory, physics, engineering [3,4], and Lie theory [2]. In particular, Jódar and Cortés [5,6], at the beginning of this century, initiated the investigation into the matrix analogs of the gamma, beta, and Gauss hypergeometric functions, thus giving the foundation of the theory of special matrix functions. Indeed, in [7], it is shown that the Gauss hypergeometric matrix function is the analytic solution of the hypergeometric matrix differential equation. Dwivedi and Sahai expanded their studies on one of the variable special matrix functions to include n variables [8,9]. In [10], this topic is discussed, in detail, in an extended work on the Appell matrix functions. The matrix analogs of the Appell functions and Lauricella functions of several variables were studied in [10,11].

Polynomials of one or more variables are introduced and investigated from a matrix perspective in [12–14]. Cetinkaya [15] introduced and studied the incomplete second Appell hypergeometric functions together with their properties.

Jódar and Cortés [6] defined the region of convergence and the integral representation of the Gauss hypergeometric matrix function by using the matrix parameters represented by $_2F_1(A; B; C; z)$. The generalized hypergeometric matrix function, abbreviated to $_pF_q$, is a natural generalization of the Gauss hypergeometric matrix function [16].

In particular, the hypergeometric matrix function plays a fundamental role in the solution of numerous problems in mathematical physics, engineering, and mathematical sciences [17,18].

The multidisciplinary applications of fractional order calculus have dominated recent advances in the subject. Without a doubt, fractional calculus has emerged as an exciting new mathematical approach to solving problems in engineering, mathematics, physics models, and many other fields of science (see, for example, [19–21]).

Because of their utility and applications in a variety of research fields, the fractional integrals associated with special matrix functions and orthogonal matrix polynomials have been recently receiving attention (see, for example, [22–28]).

The main goal of this paper is to investigate the analytical and fractional integral properties of the $_rR_s$ matrix function. This function is a combination of the generalized Mittag–Leffler function [29–31] and the generalized hypergeometric function; it is useful in many topics of mathematical analysis, fractional calculus, and statistics (see e.g., [32–36], as well as in the field of free-electron laser equations [19,37] and fractional kinetic equations [38].

In this paper, we will discuss the convergence of the matrix function $_rR_s$, as well as its analytic properties (type and order) that have certain integral representations and applications. The organization of this paper is as follows. Section 1 introduces the theory of matrix functions and includes some preliminary notes and definitions. In Section 2, we use the ratio test with perturbation lemma [39] to prove the convergence of the matrix function $_rR_s$. Section 3 presents a new Theorem 2 for obtaining the properties of the $_rR_s$ matrix function via Stirling's formula for the logarithm of the gamma function, including analytic properties (type and order). Section 4 discusses some contiguous relations, differential properties, matrix recurrence relations, and the matrix differential equation of the $_rR_s$ function that shows new theorems. Section 5 discusses some integral representations of the $_rR_s$ matrix function, as well as the generalized integral representation (see, Theorem 8), which involves some special cases that are related to integral representations, such as the Euler-type, Laplace transform, and the Riemann–Liouville fractional derivative operator of the $_rR_s$ matrix function. In the final section, we discuss the fundamental properties of the $_rR_s$ matrix function, as well as certain special cases, such as Laguerre and Konhauser matrix polynomials, the Mittag–Leffler matrix function, and the generalized Wright matrix function.

Preliminary Remarks

Throughout this paper, for a matrix A in $\mathbb{C}^{N \times N}$, its spectrum $\sigma(A)$ denotes the set of all eigenvalues of A. The two-norm will be denoted by $||A||_2$, and it is defined by (see [5,6])

$$||A||_2 = \sup_{x \neq 0} \frac{||Ax||_2}{||x||_2},$$

where for a vector x in $\mathbb{C}^N$, $||x||_2 = (x^T x)^{\frac{1}{2}}$ is the Euclidean norm of x. Let us denote the real numbers $M(A)$ and $m(A)$ as in the following

$$M(A) = \max\{Re(z) : z \in \sigma(A)\}; \quad m(A) = \min\{Re(z) : z \in \sigma(A)\}. \tag{1}$$

If $\mathbf{f}(z)$ and $\mathbf{g}(z)$ are holomorphic functions of the complex variable z, as defined in an open set Ω of the complex plane, and A and B are matrices in $\mathbb{C}^{N \times N}$ with $\sigma(A) \subset \Omega$ and $\sigma(B) \subset \Omega$, such that $AB = BA$, then it follows from the matrix functional calculus properties in [5,6] that

$$\mathbf{f}(A)\mathbf{g}(B) = \mathbf{g}(B)\mathbf{f}(A).$$

Throughout this study, a matrix polynomial of degree ℓ in x means an expression of the form

$$\mathbf{P}_\ell(x) = A_\ell x^\ell + A_{\ell-1} x^{\ell-1} + \ldots + A_1 x + A_0,$$

where x is a real variable or complex variable A_j for $0 < j < \ell$, and $A_\ell \neq 0$ are complex matrices in $\mathbb{C}^{N \times N}$, where $\mathbf{0}$ is the null matrix in $\mathbb{C}^{N \times N}$.

We recall that the reciprocal gamma function, denoted by $\Gamma^{-1}(z) = \frac{1}{\Gamma(z)}$, is an entire function of the complex variable z, and thus $\Gamma^{-1}(A)$ is a well defined matrix for any matrix A in $\mathbb{C}^{N \times N}$. In addition, if A is a matrix, then

$$A + \ell I \quad \text{is an invertible matrix for all integers } \ell \geq 0, \tag{2}$$

where I is the identity matrix in $\mathbb{C}^{N \times N}$. Then, from [5], it follows that

$$(A)_\ell = A(A+I)\ldots(A+(\ell-1)I) = \Gamma(A+\ell I)\Gamma^{-1}(A); \quad \ell \geq 1; \quad (A)_0 = I. \tag{3}$$

If ℓ is large enough so that for $\ell > \|B\|$, then we will mention the following relation, which exists in Jódar and Cortés [6,7], in the form

$$\|(B + \ell I)^{-1}\| \leq \frac{1}{\ell - \|B\|}; \quad \ell > \|B\|. \tag{4}$$

If $A(\ell, n)$ and $B(\ell, n)$ are matrices in $\mathbb{C}^{N \times N}$ for $n \geq 0$ and $\ell \geq 0$, then it follows, in a manner analogous to the proof of Lemma 11 [5], that

$$\sum_{n=0}^{\infty} \sum_{\ell=0}^{\infty} A(\ell, n) = \sum_{n=0}^{\infty} \sum_{\ell=0}^{[\frac{1}{2}n]} A(\ell, n - 2\ell),$$

$$\sum_{n=0}^{\infty} \sum_{\ell=0}^{\infty} B(\ell, n) = \sum_{n=0}^{\infty} \sum_{\ell=0}^{n} B(\ell, n - \ell). \tag{5}$$

According to (5), we can write

$$\sum_{n=0}^{\infty} \sum_{\ell=0}^{[\frac{1}{2}n]} A(\ell, n) = \sum_{n=0}^{\infty} \sum_{\ell=0}^{\infty} A(\ell, n + 2\ell),$$

$$\sum_{n=0}^{\infty} \sum_{\ell=0}^{n} B(\ell, n) = \sum_{n=0}^{\infty} \sum_{\ell=0}^{\infty} B(\ell, n + \ell). \tag{6}$$

Hypergeometric matrix function $_2F_1(A, B; C; z)$ is given in the following form:

$$_2F_1(A, B; C; z) = \sum_{\ell=0}^{\infty} \frac{(A)_\ell (B)_\ell [(C)_\ell]^{-1}}{\ell!} z^\ell, \tag{7}$$

for A, B, and C matrices in $\mathbb{C}^{N \times N}$m such that $C + \ell I$ is an invertible matrix for all integers $\ell \geq 0$ and for $|z| < 1$. Jódar and Cortés [6,7] observed that this series is absolutely convergent for $|z| = 1$ when

$$m(C) > M(A) + M(B),$$

where $m(Q)$ and $M(Q)$ in (1) are for any matrix Q in $\mathbb{C}^{N \times N}$.

Definition 1. As p and q are finite positive integers, the generalized hypergeometric matrix function is defined as (see [16])

$$
\begin{aligned}
{}_pF_q&(A_1, A_2, \ldots, A_p; B_1, B_2, \ldots, B_q; z) \\
&= \sum_{\ell=0}^{\infty} \frac{z^\ell}{\ell!} (A_1)_\ell (A_2)_\ell \ldots (A_p)_\ell [(B_1)_\ell]^{-1} [(B_2)_\ell]^{-1} \ldots [(B_q)_\ell]^{-1} \\
&= \sum_{\ell=0}^{\infty} \frac{z^\ell}{\ell!} \prod_{i=1}^{p} (A_i)_\ell \left[\prod_{j=1}^{q} (B_j)_\ell \right]^{-1},
\end{aligned}
\tag{8}
$$

where $A_i; 1 \leq i \leq p$ and $B_j; 1 \leq j \leq q$ are matrices in $\mathbb{C}^{N \times N}$ such that

$$B_j + \ell I \quad \text{are invertible matrices for all integers } \ell \geq 0. \tag{9}$$

1. If $p \leq q$, then the power series (8) converges for all finite z.
2. If $p > q + 1$, then the power series (8) diverges for all $z, z \neq 0$.
3. If $p = q + 1$, then the power series (8) is convergent for $|z| < 1$ and diverges for $|z| > 1$.
4. If $p = q + 1$, then the power series (8) is absolutely convergent for $|z| = 1$ when

$$\sum_{j=1}^{q} m(B_j) > \sum_{i=1}^{p} M(A_i). \tag{10}$$

5. If $p = q + 1$, then the power series (8) is conditionally convergent for $|z| = 1$ when

$$\sum_{i=0}^{p} M(A_i) - 1 < \sum_{j=0}^{q} m(B_j) \leq \sum_{i=0}^{p} M(A_i). \tag{11}$$

6. If $p = q + 1$, then the power series (8) diverges from $|z| = 1$ when

$$\sum_{j=0}^{q} m(B_j) \leq \sum_{i=0}^{p} M(A_i) - 1 \tag{12}$$

where $M(A_i)$ and $m(B_j)$ are as defined in (1).

2. Definition and Convergence Conditions for the ${}_rR_s(P, Q, z)$ Matrix Function

This section discusses the convergence properties of the ${}_rR_s$ matrix function.

Definition 2. Let us suppose that $P, Q, \mathrm{Re}(P) > 0, \mathrm{Re}(Q) > 0, A_i; \mathrm{Re}(A_i) > 0, 1 \leq i \leq r$ and $B_j; \mathrm{Re}(B_j) > 0, 1 \leq j \leq s$ are matrices in $\mathbb{C}^{N \times N}$ such that

$$B_j + \ell I \quad \text{are invertible matrices for all integers } \ell \geq 0, \tag{13}$$

where r and s are finite positive integers. The matrix function ${}_rR_s(P, Q, z)$ is then defined as

$$
\begin{aligned}
{}_rR_s&(A_1, A_2, \ldots, A_r; B_1, B_2, \ldots, B_s; P, Q; z) \\
&= \sum_{\ell=0}^{\infty} \frac{z^\ell}{\ell!} (A_1)_\ell (A_2)_\ell \ldots (A_r)_\ell [(B_1)_\ell]^{-1} [(B_2)_\ell]^{-1} \ldots [(B_s)_\ell]^{-1} \Gamma^{-1}(\ell P + Q) \\
&= \sum_{\ell=0}^{\infty} \frac{z^\ell}{\ell!} \prod_{i=1}^{r} (A_i)_\ell \left[\prod_{j=1}^{s} (B_j)_\ell \right]^{-1} \Gamma^{-1}(\ell P + Q) = \sum_{\ell=0}^{\infty} W_\ell,
\end{aligned}
\tag{14}
$$

where $W_\ell = \frac{z^\ell}{\ell!} \prod_{i=1}^{r}(A_i)_\ell \left[\prod_{j=1}^{s}(B_j)_\ell \right]^{-1} \Gamma^{-1}(\ell P + Q)$.

We will now investigate the convergence properties of the ${}_rR_s(P, Q, z)$, where one obtains

$$\frac{1}{R} = \limsup_{\ell \to \infty}(\|U_\ell\|)^{\frac{1}{\ell}} = \limsup_{\ell \to \infty}\left(\left\|\frac{\prod_{i=1}^{r}(A_i)_\ell[\prod_{j=1}^{s}(B_j)_\ell]^{-1}\Gamma^{-1}(\ell P+Q)}{\ell!}\right\|\right)^{\frac{1}{\ell}}$$

$$= \limsup_{\ell \to \infty}\left\|\prod_{i=1}^{r}\sqrt{2\pi}e^{-(A_i+\ell I)}(A_i+\ell I)^{A_i+\ell I-\frac{1}{2}I}\left(\prod_{j=1}^{s}\sqrt{2\pi}e^{-(B_j+\ell I)}(B_j+\ell I)^{B_j+\ell I-\frac{1}{2}I}\right)^{-1}\right.$$

$$\left.\left(\sqrt{2\pi}e^{-(\ell P+Q)}(\ell P+Q)^{\ell P+Q-\frac{1}{2}I}\right)^{-1}\frac{\prod_{i=1}^{r}\Gamma^{-1}(A_i)\prod_{j=1}^{s}\Gamma(B_j)}{\sqrt{2\pi}e^{-\ell-1}\ell^{\ell+\frac{1}{2}}}\right\|^{\frac{1}{\ell}}$$

$$= \limsup_{\ell \to \infty}\left\|\prod_{i=1}^{r}\sqrt{2\pi}e^{-(A_i+\ell I)}(A_i+\ell I)^{A_i+\ell I-\frac{1}{2}I}\left(\sqrt{2\pi}e^{-A_i}(A_i)^{A_i-\frac{1}{2}I}\right)^{-1}\right.$$

$$\prod_{j=1}^{s}\frac{1}{\sqrt{2\pi}}e^{(B_j+\ell I)}(B_j+\ell I)^{-B_j-\ell I+\frac{1}{2}I}\left(\frac{1}{\sqrt{2\pi}}e^{(B_j)}(B_j)^{-B_j+\frac{1}{2}I}\right)$$

$$\left.\frac{1}{\sqrt{2\pi}}e^{(\ell P+Q)}(\ell P+Q)^{-\ell P-Q+\frac{1}{2}I}\frac{1}{\sqrt{2\pi}e^{-\ell-1}\ell^{\ell+\frac{1}{2}}}\right\|^{\frac{1}{\ell}}$$

$$\approx \limsup_{\ell \to \infty}\left\|\prod_{i=1}^{r}\prod_{j=1}^{s}e^{B_j+\ell I+\ell P+Q-A_i-\ell I+\ell I-B_j+A_i}(A_i+\ell I)^{A_i+\ell I-\frac{1}{2}I}(B_j+\ell I)^{-B_j-\ell I+\frac{1}{2}I}\right.$$

$$\left.(\ell P+Q)^{-\ell P-Q+\frac{1}{2}I}\ell^{-\ell-\frac{1}{2}}\right\|^{\frac{1}{\ell}}$$

$$\approx \limsup_{\ell \to \infty}\left\|\prod_{i=1}^{r}\prod_{j=1}^{s}e^{\ell P+Q+\ell I}(A_i+\ell I)^{A_i+\ell I-\frac{1}{2}I}(B_j+\ell I)^{-B_j-\ell I+\frac{1}{2}I}(\ell P+Q)^{-\ell P-Q+\frac{1}{2}I}\ell^{-\ell-\frac{1}{2}}\right\|^{\frac{1}{\ell}}$$

$$\approx \|e^{P+I}\|\limsup_{\ell \to \infty}\left\|\prod_{i=1}^{r}\prod_{j=1}^{s}\frac{(A_i+\ell I)(B_j+\ell I)^{-1}(\ell P+Q)^{-P}}{\ell}\right\|$$

$$\left\|(A_i+\ell I)^{A_i-\frac{1}{2}I}(B_j+\ell I)^{-B_j+\frac{1}{2}I}(\ell P+Q)^{-Q+\frac{1}{2}I}\ell^{-\frac{1}{2}}\right\|^{\frac{1}{\ell}}.$$

The last limit shows that:

1. If $r \leq s+1$, then the power series in (14) converges for all finite z.
2. If $r = s+2$, then the power series in (14) converges for all $|z| < 1$ and diverges for all $|z| > 1$.
3. If $r > s+2$, then the power series in (14) diverges for $z \neq 0$.

The above definition of the $_rR_s(P,Q,z)$ matrix function can be referred to in reference to [40], whereby the different method is taken into consideration by being used in proving it is based on the perturbation lemma [39] and ratio test detailed in this paper.

As an analog to Theorem 3 in [6], we can state the following:

Theorem 1. *1. If $r = s+2$, then the power series in (14) is absolutely convergent on the circle $|z| = 1$ when*

$$\sum_{j=1}^{s}m(B_j) - \sum_{i=1}^{r}M(A_i) > 0. \tag{15}$$

2. If $r = s+2$, then the power series (14) is conditionally convergent for $|z| = 1$ when

$$\sum_{i=0}^{r}M(A_i) - 1 < \sum_{j=0}^{s}m(B_j) \leq \sum_{i=0}^{p}M(A_i). \tag{16}$$

3. If $r = s+2$, then the power series (14) diverges from $|z| = 1$ when

$$\sum_{j=0}^{s} m(B_j) \leq \sum_{i=0}^{r} M(A_i) - 1 \tag{17}$$

where $M(A_i); 1 \leq i \leq r$ and $m(B_j); 1 \leq j \leq s$ are defined in (1).

Thus, $_rR_s$ is an entire function of z when $\|P+I\| > 0$.

Remark 1. Let $A_i; 1 \leq i \leq r$ and $B_j; 1 \leq j \leq s$ be matrices in $\mathbb{C}^{N \times N}$ that satisfy (13), and where all matrices are commutative. As such, $P = Q = A_1 = I$ in (14) reduces to

$$_rR_s(I, A_2, \ldots, A_p; B_1, B_2, \ldots, B_s; I, I; z)$$
$$= \sum_{\ell=0}^{\infty} \frac{z^\ell}{k!} \prod_{i=2}^{p}(A_i)_\ell \left[\prod_{j=1}^{s}(B_j)_\ell\right]^{-1} \Gamma^{-1}(kP+Q) = \sum_{\ell=0}^{\infty} W_\ell \tag{18}$$
$$= {}_{r-1}F_s(A_2, \ldots, A_p; B_1, B_2, \ldots, B_s; z)$$

where $_{r-1}F_s$ is the generalized hypergeometric matrix function detailed in (8).

3. Order and Type of the $_rR_s(P, Q, z)$ Matrix Function

In this section, we obtain the properties of the $_rR_s$ matrix function, including its analytic properties (type and order).

Theorem 2. Let $A_i; 1 \leq i \leq r$, $B_j; 1 \leq j \leq s$, P and Q be matrices in $\mathbb{C}^{N \times N}$ that satisfy (13), and where all matrices are commutative. Then, the $_rR_s$ matrix function is an entire function of variable z of the order $\rho = \|(P+I)^{-1}\|$ and type $\tau = \|(P+I)P^{-P(P+I)^{-1}}\|$.

Proof. In applying Stirling's formula of the gamma matrix function, we obtain

$$\Gamma(A) \approx \sqrt{2\pi}e^{-A}A^{A-\frac{1}{2}I}, \tag{19}$$

which recovers Stirling's formula:

$$\ell! \approx \sqrt{2\pi\ell}\left(\frac{\ell}{e}\right)^\ell, \tag{20}$$

and which uses the asymptotic expansion

$$\ln\Gamma(A) \approx \ln\sqrt{2\pi}I - A + (A - \frac{1}{2}I)\ln(A)$$
$$\approx \frac{1}{2}\ln(2\pi)I - A + (A - \frac{1}{2}I)\ln(A) \tag{21}$$

To evaluate the order, we apply Stirling's asymptotic formula for a large ℓ, and the logarithm of the gamma function $\Gamma(\ell+1)$ is set at infinity as follows:

$$\rho(_rR_s) = \limsup_{\ell \to \infty} \left\|\frac{\ell \ln(\ell)}{\ln(\frac{1}{U_\ell})}\right\| = \limsup_{\ell \to \infty} \left\|\frac{\ell \ln(\ell)}{\ln(\ell! \prod_{j=1}^{s}(B_j)_\ell \Gamma(\ell P+Q)[\prod_{i=1}^{r}(A_i)_\ell]^{-1})}\right\|$$
$$= \limsup_{\ell \to \infty} \left\|\frac{\ell \ln(\ell)}{\ln(\ell! \prod_{j=1}^{s}\Gamma(B_j+\ell I)\Gamma^{-1}(B_j)\Gamma(\ell P+Q)\prod_{i=1}^{r}\Gamma^{-1}(A_i+\ell I)\Gamma(A_i))}\right\| \tag{22}$$
$$= \limsup_{\ell \to \infty} \left\|\frac{1}{\Psi}\right\| = \left\|(P+I)^{-1}\right\|,$$

where

$$\Psi = \prod_{i=1}^{r}\prod_{j=1}^{s} \frac{\ln\Gamma(\ell+1)I + \ln\Gamma(A_i) - \ln\Gamma(A_i+\ell I) + \ln\Gamma(B_j+\ell I) - \ln\Gamma(B_j) - \ln\Gamma(\ell P+Q)}{\ell\ln(\ell)}$$

$$= \prod_{i=1}^{r}\prod_{j=1}^{s} \frac{1}{2}\frac{\ln(2\pi\ell)}{\ell\ln(\ell)}I + \frac{\ell\ln(\ell)}{\ell\ln(\ell)}I - \frac{\ell\ln(e)}{\ell\ln(\ell)}I$$

$$+ \frac{1}{2}\frac{\ln(2\pi(B_j+\ell I))}{\ell\ln(\ell)} + \frac{(B_j+\ell I)\ln(B_j+\ell I)}{\ell\ln(\ell)} - \frac{(B_j+\ell I)\ln(e)}{\ell\ln(\ell)}$$

$$- \frac{1}{2}\frac{\ln(2\pi(B_j))}{\ell\ln(\ell)} - \frac{B_j\ln(B_j)}{\ell\ln(\ell)} + \frac{B_j\ln(e)}{\ell\ln(\ell)}$$

$$+ \frac{1}{2}\frac{\ln(2\pi(\ell P+Q))}{\ell\ln(\ell)} + \frac{(\ell P+Q)\ln(\ell P+Q)}{\ell\ln(\ell)} - \frac{(\ell P+Q)\ln(e)}{\ell\ln(\ell)}$$

$$+ \frac{1}{2}\frac{\ln(2\pi(A_i))}{\ell\ln(\ell)} + \frac{A_i\ln(A_i)}{\ell\ln(\ell)} - \frac{A_i\ln(e)}{\ell\ln(\ell)}$$

$$- \frac{1}{2}\frac{\ln(2\pi(A_i+\ell I))}{\ell\ln(\ell)} - \frac{(A_i+\ell I)\ln(A_i+\ell I)}{\ell\ln(\ell)} + \frac{(A_i+\ell I)\ln(e)}{\ell\ln(\ell)}.$$

Thus, we obtain the order $\rho = \left\|(P+I)^{-1}\right\|$.

We obtain the asymptotic estimate for $\Gamma(\ell P+Q)$ and $\Gamma(\ell+1)$ by repeatedly applying the asymptotic formula for the logarithm of the gamma function:

$$\tau = \tau(_rR_s) = \frac{1}{e\rho}\limsup_{\ell\to\infty}\left\|\ell\left(U_\ell\right)^{\ell}\right\|^{\frac{\rho}{\ell}} = \frac{1}{e\rho}\limsup_{\ell\to\infty}\left\|\ell\left(\frac{\prod_{i=1}^{r}(A_i)_\ell[\prod_{j=1}^{s}(B_j)_\ell]^{-1}\Gamma^{-1}(\ell P+Q)}{\ell!}\right)^{\frac{\rho}{\ell}}\right\|$$

$$= \frac{1}{e\rho}\limsup_{\ell\to\infty}\ell\left\|\prod_{i=1}^{r}\prod_{j=1}^{s}\sqrt{2\pi}e^{-(A_i+\ell I)}(A_i+\ell I)^{A_i+\ell I-\frac{1}{2}I}\left(\sqrt{2\pi}e^{-(B_j+\ell I)}(B_j+\ell I)^{B_j+\ell I-\frac{1}{2}I}\right)^{-1}\right.$$

$$\left.\left(\sqrt{2\pi}e^{-(\ell P+Q)}(\ell P+Q)^{\ell P+Q-\frac{1}{2}I}\right)^{-1}\frac{\Gamma^{-1}(A_i)\Gamma(B_j)}{\sqrt{2\pi}e^{-\ell}\ell^{\ell+\frac{1}{2}}}\right\|^{\frac{\rho}{\ell}}$$

$$\approx \frac{1}{e\rho}\limsup_{\ell\to\infty}\ell\left\|\prod_{i=1}^{r}\prod_{j=1}^{s}e^{B_j+\ell I+\ell P+Q-A_i-\ell I+\ell I}(A_i+\ell I)^{A_i+\ell I-\frac{1}{2}I}(B_j+\ell I)^{-B_j-\ell I+\frac{1}{2}I}\right.$$

$$\left.(\ell P+Q)^{-\ell P-Q-\frac{1}{2}I}\ell^{-\ell-\frac{1}{2}}\right\|^{\frac{\rho}{\ell}}$$

$$\approx \frac{1}{e\rho}\left\|e^{(P+I)\rho}\right\|\limsup_{\ell\to\infty}\ell\left\|\prod_{i=1}^{r}\prod_{j=1}^{s}(A_i+\ell I)^{A_i-\frac{1}{2}I}(A_i+\ell I)^{\ell}(B_j+\ell I)^{-B_j+\frac{1}{2}I}(B_j+\ell I)^{-\ell}\right.$$

$$\left.(\ell P+Q)^{-Q-\frac{1}{2}I}(\ell P+Q)^{-\ell P}\ell^{-\ell-\frac{1}{2}}\right\|^{\frac{\rho}{\ell}}$$

$$\approx \frac{1}{e\rho}\left\|e^{(P+I)\rho}P^{-P(P+I)^{-1}}\right\| = \left\|(P+I)P^{-P(P+I)^{-1}}\right\|.$$

Finally, we arrive at the type of function $\tau = \left\|(P+I)P^{-P(P+I)^{-1}}\right\|$. □

4. Contiguous Function Relations

The contiguous function relations and differential property of the $_rR_s$ matrix function are established in this section.

Assume that $A_i(i=1,2,\ldots,r)$ and $B_j(j=1,2,\ldots,s)$ have no integer eigenvalues for those matrices that commute with one another. The relation $A_i(A_i+I)_\ell = (A_i+kI)(A_i)_\ell$, when combined with the definitions of the matrix contiguous function relations, yields the following formulas:

$$_rR_s(A_1+) = \sum_{\ell=0}^{\infty} \frac{z^\ell}{n!}(A_1+I)_\ell (A_2)_\ell \ldots (A_r)_\ell [(B_1)_\ell]^{-1}[(B_2)_\ell]^{-1} \ldots [(B_s)_\ell]^{-1}\Gamma^{-1}(\ell P + Q) \quad (23)$$

$$= \sum_{\ell=0}^{\infty}(A_1+\ell I)\left(A_1\right)^{-1} W_\ell(z).$$

Similarly, we obtain

$$_rR_s(A_i+) = \left(A_i\right)^{-1} \sum_{\ell=0}^{\infty}(A_i+\ell I)W_\ell(z),$$

$$_rR_s(A_i-) = (A_i-I) \sum_{\ell=0}^{\infty}\left(A_i+(\ell-1)I\right)^{-1} W_\ell(z),$$

$$_rR_s(B_j+) = (B_j) \sum_{\ell=0}^{\infty}\left(B_j+\ell I\right)^{-1} W_\ell(z), \quad (24)$$

$$_rR_s(B_j-) = \left(B_j-I\right)^{-1} \sum_{\ell=0}^{\infty}(B_j+(k-1)I)W_\ell(z).$$

For all integers $n \geq 1$, we deduce that:

$$_rR_s(A_i+nI) = \prod_{k=1}^{n}\left(A_i+(k-1)I\right)^{-1} \sum_{\ell=0}^{\infty}\prod_{k=1}^{n}(A_i+(\ell+k-1)I)W_\ell(z),$$

$$_rR_s(A_i-nI) = \prod_{k=1}^{n}(A_i-kI) \sum_{\ell=0}^{\infty}\prod_{k=1}^{n}\left(A_i+(\ell-k)I\right)^{-1} W_\ell(z),$$

$$_rR_s(B_j+nI) = \prod_{k=1}^{n}(B_j+(k-1)I) \sum_{\ell=0}^{\infty}\prod_{k=1}^{n}\left(B_j+(\ell+k-1)I\right)^{-1} W_\ell(z), \quad (25)$$

$$_rR_s(B_j-nI) = \prod_{k=1}^{n}\left(B_j-kI\right)^{-1} \sum_{\ell=0}^{\infty}\prod_{k=1}^{n}(B_j+(\ell-k)I)W_\ell(z).$$

Remark 2. *If we apply the above results for (25), we obtain the contiguous relations for the generalized hypergeometric matrix function [16].*

Theorem 3. *Let A, B, P, and Q be commutative matrices in $\mathbb{C}^{N \times N}$ that satisfy the condition (13). Then, the following recursion formulas hold true for $_rR_s$*

$$_rR_s = \left(\theta P + Q\right) {}_rR_s(Q+I), \quad (26)$$

where $\theta = z\frac{d}{dz}$.

Proof. Starting with the right hand side, we have

$$Q \,_rR_s(Q+I) + zP\frac{d}{dz} \,_rR_s(Q+I)$$

$$= Q \,_rR_s(Q+I) + zP\left[\sum_{\ell=0}^{\infty} \frac{\ell z^{\ell-1}}{\ell!} \prod_{i=1}^{r}(A_i)_\ell \left[\prod_{j=1}^{s}(B_j)_\ell\right]^{-1} \Gamma^{-1}(\ell P + Q + I)\right]$$

$$= Q \,_rR_s(Q+I) + \sum_{\ell=0}^{\infty} \frac{(\ell P + Q)z^\ell}{\ell!} \prod_{i=1}^{r}(A_i)_\ell \left[\prod_{j=1}^{s}(B_j)_\ell\right]^{-1} \Gamma^{-1}(\ell P + Q)(\ell P + Q)^{-1}$$

$$- Q\sum_{\ell=0}^{\infty} \frac{z^\ell}{\ell!} \prod_{i=1}^{r}(A_i)_\ell \left[\prod_{j=1}^{s}(B_j)_\ell\right]^{-1} \Gamma^{-1}(\ell P + Q + I)$$

$$= \sum_{\ell=0}^{\infty} \frac{z^\ell}{\ell!} \prod_{i=1}^{r}(A_i)_\ell \left[\prod_{j=1}^{s}(B_j)_\ell\right]^{-1} \Gamma^{-1}(\ell P + Q) = \,_rR_s.$$

□

Remark 3. *For further specific values of the parameters in (26), we obtain the contiguous relations for the generalized hypergeometric matrix function [16].*

Theorem 4. *The $_rR_s$ matrix function has the following differential property:*

$$\left(\frac{d}{dz}\right)^\kappa \left[z^{Q-I} \,_rR_s(A_1, A_2, \ldots, A_r; B_1, B_2, \ldots, B_s; P, Q; cz^P)\right] \tag{27}$$
$$= z^{Q-(\kappa+1)I} \,_rR_s(A_1, A_2, \ldots, A_r; B_1, B_2, \ldots, B_s P, Q - \kappa I; cz^P).$$

Proof. By differentiating term by term under the sign of summation in (14), we obtain the result (27). □

Theorem 5. *Let A_i; $1 \leq i \leq r$ and B_j; $1 \leq j \leq s$, P, and Q be matrices in $\mathbb{C}^{N\times N}$ that satisfy (13), and where all matrices are commutative, then the following recurrence matrix relation for $_rR_s$ matrix function holds true:*

$$\theta \prod_{j=1}^{s}(\theta I + B_j - I) \,_rR_s - z\prod_{i=1}^{r}(\theta I + A_i) \,_rR_s(Q+P) = \mathbf{0}, \tag{28}$$

where $\mathbf{0}$ is the null matrix in $\mathbb{C}^{N\times N}$.

Proof. Consider the differential operator $\theta = z\frac{d}{dz}$, $D_z = \frac{d}{dz}$, $\theta z^\ell = \ell z^\ell$. For the matrices that commute with one another, we thus have

$$\theta \prod_{j=1}^{s}(\theta I + B_j - I) \,_rR_s = \sum_{\ell=1}^{\infty} \frac{\ell z^\ell}{\ell!} \prod_{j=1}^{s}(\ell I + B_j - I) \prod_{i=1}^{r}(A_i)_\ell \left[\prod_{j=1}^{s}(B_j)_\ell\right]^{-1} \Gamma^{-1}(\ell P + Q)$$

$$= \sum_{\ell=1}^{\infty} \frac{z^\ell}{(\ell-1)!} \prod_{i=1}^{r}(A_i)_\ell \left[\prod_{j=1}^{s}(B_j)_{\ell-1}\right]^{-1} \Gamma^{-1}(\ell P + Q).$$

When ℓ is replaced by $\ell + 1$, we have

$$\theta \prod_{j=1}^{s}(\theta I + B_j - I) \,_rR_s = \sum_{\ell=0}^{\infty} \frac{z^{\ell+1}}{\ell!} \prod_{i=1}^{r}(A_i)_{\ell+1} \left[\prod_{j=1}^{s}(B_j)_\ell\right]^{-1} \Gamma^{-1}(\ell P + Q + P)$$

$$= z\prod_{i=1}^{r}(\theta I + A_i) \,_rR_s(Q+P).$$

□

Theorem 6. Let A_i; $1 \leq i \leq r$ and B_j; $1 \leq j \leq s$, P, and Q be commutative matrices in $\mathbb{C}^{N \times N}$ that satisfy the condition (13), and where all matrices are commutative. Then, the ${}_rR_s$ matrix function satisfies the matrix differential equation

$$\begin{aligned}
{}_rR_s(P, Q+(\mu+1)I, z) - {}_rR_s(P, Q+(\mu+2)I, z) &= z^2 P^2 \frac{d^2}{dz^2} {}_rR_s(P, Q+(\mu+3)I, z) \\
&+ zP(P+2I+2(Q+\mu I))\frac{d}{dz} {}_rR_s(P, Q+(\mu+3)I, z) \\
&+ (Q+\nu I)(Q+(\mu+2)I) \, {}_rR_s(P, Q+(\mu+3)I, z).
\end{aligned} \quad (29)$$

Proof. In using the fundamental relation of the gamma matrix function $\Gamma(A+I) = A\Gamma(A)$ in (2), we have

$${}_rR_s(A_1, A_2, \ldots, A_p; B_1, B_2, \ldots, B_s; P, Q+(\mu+1)I; z)$$
$$= \sum_{\ell=0}^{\infty} \frac{z^\ell}{\ell!} \prod_{i=1}^{p}(A_i)_\ell \left[\prod_{j=1}^{s}(B_j)_\ell\right]^{-1} (\ell P + Q + \mu I)^{-1} \Gamma^{-1}(\ell P + Q + \mu I). \quad (30)$$

Similarly, we find

$${}_rR_s(A_1, A_2, \ldots, A_p; B_1, B_2, \ldots, B_s; P, Q+(\mu+2)I; z)$$
$$= \sum_{\ell=0}^{\infty} \left((\ell P + Q + \mu I)^{-1} - (\ell P + Q + (\mu+1)I)^{-1}\right) \frac{z^\ell}{\ell!} \prod_{i=1}^{p}(A_i)_\ell \left[\prod_{j=1}^{s}(B_j)_\ell\right]^{-1} \Gamma^{-1}(\ell P + Q + \mu I)$$
$$= {}_rR_s(A_1, A_2, \ldots, A_p; B_1, B_2, \ldots, B_s; P, Q+(\mu+1)I; z) \quad (31)$$
$$- \sum_{\ell=0}^{\infty}(\ell P + Q + (\mu+1)I)^{-1} \frac{z^\ell}{\ell!} \prod_{i=1}^{p}(A_i)_\ell \left[\prod_{j=1}^{s}(B_j)_\ell\right]^{-1} \Gamma^{-1}(\ell P + Q + \mu I).$$

Next, we denote the last term of (31) by L, which can be written as follows:

$$\begin{aligned}
L &= \sum_{\ell=0}^{\infty}(\ell P + Q + (\mu+1)I)^{-1} \frac{z^\ell}{\ell!} \prod_{i=1}^{p}(A_i)_\ell \left[\prod_{j=1}^{s}(B_j)_\ell\right]^{-1} \Gamma^{-1}(\ell P + Q + \mu I) \\
&= {}_rR_s(A_1, A_2, \ldots, A_p; B_1, B_2, \ldots, B_s; P, Q+(\mu+1)I; z) \\
&\quad - {}_rR_s(A_1, A_2, \ldots, A_p; B_1, B_2, \ldots, B_s; P, Q+(\mu+2)I; z).
\end{aligned} \quad (32)$$

The sum L can be expressed as

$$L = \sum_{\ell=0}^{\infty} \frac{z^\ell}{\ell!} \prod_{i=1}^{p}(A_i)_\ell \left[\prod_{j=1}^{s}(B_j)_\ell\right]^{-1} (\ell P + Q + \mu I)\Gamma^{-1}(\ell P + Q + (\mu+3)I)$$

$$+ \sum_{\ell=0}^{\infty} \frac{z^\ell}{\ell!} \prod_{i=1}^{p}(A_i)_\ell \left[\prod_{j=1}^{s}(B_j)_\ell\right]^{-1} (\ell P + Q + \mu I)(\ell P + Q + (\mu+1)I)\Gamma^{-1}(\ell P + Q + (\mu+3)I)$$

$$= P \sum_{\ell=0}^{\infty} \frac{\ell z^\ell}{\ell!} \prod_{i=1}^{p}(A_i)_\ell \left[\prod_{j=1}^{s}(B_j)_\ell\right]^{-1} \Gamma^{-1}(\ell P + Q + (\mu+3)I)$$

$$+ (Q + \mu I) \sum_{\ell=0}^{\infty} \frac{z^\ell}{\ell!} \prod_{i=1}^{p}(A_i)_\ell \left[\prod_{j=1}^{s}(B_j)_\ell\right]^{-1} \Gamma^{-1}(\ell P + Q + (\mu+3)I) \qquad (33)$$

$$+ P^2 \sum_{\ell=0}^{\infty} \frac{\ell^2 z^\ell}{\ell!} \prod_{i=1}^{p}(A_i)_\ell \left[\prod_{j=1}^{s}(B_j)_\ell\right]^{-1} \Gamma^{-1}(\ell P + Q + (\mu+3)I)$$

$$+ (2Q + (2\mu+1)I)P \sum_{\ell=0}^{\infty} \frac{\ell z^\ell}{\ell!} \prod_{i=1}^{p}(A_i)_\ell \left[\prod_{j=1}^{s}(B_j)_\ell\right]^{-1} \Gamma^{-1}(\ell P + Q + (\mu+3)I)$$

$$+ (Q + \mu I)(Q + (\mu+1)I) \sum_{\ell=0}^{\infty} \frac{z^\ell}{\ell!} \prod_{i=1}^{p}(A_i)_\ell \left[\prod_{j=1}^{s}(B_j)_\ell\right]^{-1} \Gamma^{-1}(\ell P + Q + (\mu+3)I).$$

On evaluating each term on the R.H.S. of Equation (33), we have

$$\frac{d^2}{dz^2}\left(z^2 \,_rR_s(A_1, A_2, \ldots, A_p; B_1, B_2, \ldots, B_s; P, Q + (\mu+3)I; z)\right)$$

$$= \sum_{\ell=0}^{\infty} \frac{(\ell+1)(\ell+2)z^\ell}{\ell!} \prod_{i=1}^{p}(A_i)_\ell \left[\prod_{j=1}^{s}(B_j)_\ell\right]^{-1} \Gamma^{-1}(\ell P + Q + (\mu+3)I)$$

or

$$z^2 \frac{d^2}{dz^2} \,_rR_s(A_1, A_2, \ldots, A_p; B_1, B_2, \ldots, B_s; P, Q + (\mu+3)I; z)$$

$$+ 4z \frac{d}{dz} \,_rR_s(A_1, A_2, \ldots, A_p; B_1, B_2, \ldots, B_s; P, Q + (\mu+3)I; z)$$

$$= \sum_{\ell=0}^{\infty} \frac{\ell^2 z^\ell}{\ell!} \prod_{i=1}^{p}(A_i)_\ell \left[\prod_{j=1}^{s}(B_j)_\ell\right]^{-1} \Gamma^{-1}(\ell P + Q + (\mu+3)I) \qquad (34)$$

$$+ 3 \sum_{\ell=0}^{\infty} \frac{\ell z^\ell}{\ell!} \prod_{i=1}^{p}(A_i)_\ell \left[\prod_{j=1}^{s}(B_j)_\ell\right]^{-1} \Gamma^{-1}(\ell P + Q + (\mu+3)I).$$

Similarly, we have

$$\frac{d}{dz}\left(z \,_rR_s(A_1, A_2, \ldots, A_p; B_1, B_2, \ldots, B_s; P, Q + (\mu+3)I; z)\right)$$

$$= \sum_{\ell=0}^{\infty} \frac{(\ell+1)z^\ell}{\ell!} \prod_{i=1}^{p}(A_i)_\ell \left[\prod_{j=1}^{s}(B_j)_\ell\right]^{-1} \Gamma^{-1}(\ell P + Q + (\mu+3)I)$$

or

$$z \frac{d}{dz} \,_rR_s(A_1, A_2, \ldots, A_p; B_1, B_2, \ldots, B_s; P, Q + (\mu+3)I; z)$$

$$+ \sum_{\ell=0}^{\infty} \frac{\ell z^\ell}{\ell!} \prod_{i=1}^{p}(A_i)_\ell \left[\prod_{j=1}^{s}(B_j)_\ell\right]^{-1} \Gamma^{-1}(\ell P + Q + (\mu+3)I). \qquad (35)$$

Therefore, from (34) and (35), we obtain

$$\sum_{\ell=0}^{\infty} \frac{\ell^2 z^\ell}{\ell!} \prod_{i=1}^{p}(A_i)_\ell \left[\prod_{j=1}^{s}(B_j)_\ell\right]^{-1} \Gamma^{-1}(\ell P + Q + (\mu+3)I)$$
$$= z^2 \frac{d^2}{dz^2} \, _rR_s(A_1, A_2, \ldots, A_p; B_1, B_2, \ldots, B_s; P, Q+(\mu+3)I; z) \qquad (36)$$
$$+ z \frac{d}{dz} \, _rR_s(A_1, A_2, \ldots, A_p; B_1, B_2, \ldots, B_s; P, Q+(\mu+3)I; z).$$

By taking into account (33), (34) and (36), we have

$$L = P^2 z^2 \frac{d^2}{dz^2} \, _rR_s(A_1, A_2, \ldots, A_p; B_1, B_2, \ldots, B_s; P, Q+(\mu+3)I; z)$$
$$+ z(P^2 + P + (2Q + (2\mu+1)I)P) \frac{d}{dz} \, _rR_s(A_1, A_2, \ldots, A_p; B_1, B_2, \ldots, B_s; P, Q+(\mu+3)I; z) \qquad (37)$$
$$+ (Q + \mu I + (Q + \mu I)(Q + (\mu+1)I)) \, _rR_s(A_1, A_2, \ldots, A_p; B_1, B_2, \ldots, B_s; P, Q+(\mu+3)I; z).$$

By substituting the equation in (37) and taking into account (37) and (32), we yield the desired proof. □

5. Integrals Involving the $_rR_s$ Matrix Function

Here, we establish the integral representations and differential property of the $_rR_s$ matrix function, whereby its integrals that involve relationships with other well-known fractional calculus and special functions are accounted for.

The integral representations of the $_rR_s$ matrix function in [6] can be extended to yield the following result:

Theorem 7. *Let A_i; $1 \leq i \leq r$ and B_j; $1 \leq j \leq s$ be matrices in $\mathbb{C}^{N \times N}$ such that $B_j + \ell I$ are invertible matrices for all integers $\ell \geq 0$. Suppose that A_i, B_j, and $B_j - A_i$ are positive stable matrices. If $r \leq s + 2$ for $|z| < 1$, then we have*

$$_rR_s(A_1, A_2, \ldots, A_r; B_1, B_2, \ldots, B_s; P, Q, z)$$
$$= \Gamma^{-1}(A_i) \Gamma^{-1}(B_j - A_i) \Gamma(B_j) \int_0^1 t^{A_i - I} (1-t)^{B_j - A_i - I} \qquad (38)$$
$$\times \, _{r-1}R_{s-1}\left(\begin{matrix} A_1, \ldots, A_{i-1}, A_{i+1} \ldots, A_r; \\ B_1, \ldots, B_{j-1}, B_{j+1} \ldots, B_s \end{matrix} ; P, Q, zt\right).$$

Proof. By definition of the pochammar matrix symbol (3) for $Re(B_1) > Re(A_1) > 0$, as well as by using the integral definition of the beta matrix function, we obtain

$$(A_i)_\ell [(B_j)_\ell]^{-1} = \Gamma^{-1}(A_i) \Gamma^{-1}(B_j - A_i) \Gamma(B_j) \int_0^1 t^{A_i + (\ell-1)I} (1-t)^{B_j - A_i - I} dt$$

where $A_i B_j = B_j A_i$. Also, we have

$$_rR_s\left(\begin{array}{c}A_1, A_2, \ldots, A_r;\\ B_1, B_2, \ldots, B_s;\end{array} z\right)$$

$$= \sum_{\ell=0}^{\infty} \frac{z^\ell}{k!}(A_1)_\ell \ldots (A_{i-1})_\ell (A_{i+1})_\ell \ldots (A_r)_\ell [(B_1)_\ell]^{-1} \ldots [(B_{j-1})_\ell]^{-1} [(B_{j+1})_\ell]^{-1}$$

$$\ldots [(B_s)_\ell]^{-1} \times \Gamma^{-1}(A_i)\Gamma^{-1}(B_j - A_i)\Gamma(B_j) \int_0^1 t^{A_i+(n-1)I}(1-t)^{B_j-A_i-I} dt$$

$$= \Gamma^{-1}(A_i)\Gamma^{-1}(B_j - A_i)\Gamma(B_j) \int_0^1 t^{A_i-I}(1-t)^{B_j-A_i-I}$$

$$\times \sum_{\ell=0}^{\infty} \frac{(zt)^\ell}{k!}(A_1)_\ell \ldots (A_{i-1})_\ell (A_{i+1})_\ell \ldots (A_r)_\ell$$

$$[(B_1)_\ell]^{-1} \ldots [(B_{j-1})_\ell]^{-1} [(B_{j+1})_\ell]^{-1} \ldots [(B_s)_\ell]^{-1} dt$$

$$= \Gamma^{-1}(A_i)\Gamma^{-1}(B_j - A_i)\Gamma(B_j) \int_0^1 t^{A_i-I}(1-t)^{B_j-A_i-I}$$

$$\times\ _{r-1}R_{s-1}\left(\begin{array}{c}A_1, \ldots, A_{i-1}, A_{i+1}, \ldots, A_r;\\ B_1, \ldots, B_{j-1}, B_{j+1}, \ldots, B_s;\end{array} zt\right) dt.$$

□

Remark 4. *If $A_1 = P = Q = I$ in (38), we obtain the results for the generalized hypergeometric matrix functions [16].*

Theorem 8. *The following integral representation holds true:*

$$\int_0^1 t^{Q+\mu I}\ _rR_s(A_1, A_2, \ldots, A_p; B_1, B_2, \ldots, B_s; P, Q + \nu I; t^P) dt$$
$$=\ _rR_s(A_1, A_2, \ldots, A_p; B_1, B_2, \ldots, B_s; P, Q + (\mu+1)I; 1) -\ _rR_s(A_1, A_2, \ldots, A_p; \quad (39)$$
$$B_1, B_2, \ldots, B_s; P, Q + (\mu+2)I; 1).$$

Proof. By putting $z = 1$ in (31), we obtain

$$_rR_s(A_1, A_2, \ldots, A_p; B_1, B_2, \ldots, B_s; P, Q + (\mu+2)I; 1)$$
$$=\ _rR_s(A_1, A_2, \ldots, A_p; B_1, B_2, \ldots, B_s; P, Q + (\mu+1)I; 1) \quad (40)$$
$$- \sum_{\ell=0}^{\infty} \frac{z^\ell}{\ell!} \prod_{i=1}^{p}(A_i)_\ell \left[\prod_{j=1}^{s}(B_j)_\ell\right]^{-1} (\ell P + Q + (\mu+1)I)^{-1} \Gamma^{-1}(\ell P + Q + \mu I).$$

One can observe that

$$z^{Q+\mu I}\ _rR_s(A_1, A_2, \ldots, A_p; B_1, B_2, \ldots, B_s; P, Q + \mu I; z^P)$$
$$= \sum_{\ell=0}^{\infty} \frac{z^{\ell P+Q+\mu I}}{\ell!} \prod_{i=1}^{p}(A_i)_\ell \left[\prod_{j=1}^{s}(B_j)_\ell\right]^{-1} \Gamma^{-1}(\ell P + Q + \mu I).$$

On integrating both sides with respect to z, this yields

$$\int_0^z t^{Q+\mu I}\ _rR_s(A_1, A_2, \ldots, A_p; B_1, B_2, \ldots, B_s; P, Q + \nu I; t^P) dt$$
$$= \sum_{\ell=0}^{\infty} \frac{1}{\ell!} \prod_{i=1}^{p}(A_i)_\ell \left[\prod_{j=1}^{s}(B_j)_\ell\right]^{-1} \Gamma^{-1}(\ell P + Q + \mu I) \int_0^z t^{\ell P+Q+\mu I} dt \quad (41)$$
$$= \sum_{\ell=0}^{\infty} \frac{1}{\ell!} \prod_{i=1}^{p}(A_i)_\ell \left[\prod_{j=1}^{s}(B_j)_\ell\right]^{-1} \Gamma^{-1}(\ell P + Q + \mu I)(\ell P + Q + (\mu+1)I)^{-1} z^{\ell P+Q+(\mu+1)I}.$$

By putting $z = 1$ in (41), we obtain

$$\int_0^1 t^{Q+\mu I} {}_rR_s(A_1, A_2, \ldots, A_p; B_1, B_2, \ldots, B_s; P, Q + \nu I; t^P) dt$$
$$= \sum_{\ell=0}^{\infty} \frac{1}{\ell!} \prod_{i=1}^p (A_i)_\ell \left[\prod_{j=1}^s (B_j)_\ell \right]^{-1} \Gamma^{-1}(\ell P + Q + \mu I)(\ell P + Q + (\mu+1)I)^{-1}. \tag{42}$$

Taking into account the work of (40) and (42), one can obtain the equation detailed in (39). □

Theorem 9. *The ${}_rR_s$ matrix function has the following integral representation*

$${}_rR_s(A_1, A_2, \ldots, A_r; B_1, B_2, \ldots, B_s; P, Q, z) = \Gamma^{-1}(A_1)$$
$$\int_0^\infty t^{A_1 - I} e^{-t} {}_{r-1}R_s(A_2, \ldots, A_r; B_1, B_2, \ldots, B_s; P, Q, zt) dt. \tag{43}$$

Proof. When using the definition of the gamma matrix function

$$\Gamma(A_1 + \ell I) = \int_0^\infty e^{-t} t^{A_1 + \ell I - I} dt,$$

we obtain (43). □

Theorem 10. *The ${}_rR_s$ matrix function satisfies the following representations*

$$\Gamma(\Phi) {}_{r+1}R_s(\Phi, A_1, A_2, \ldots, A_r; B_1, B_2, \ldots, B_s; z)$$
$$= \sqrt{2\pi} \mathfrak{F} \left[e^{\varphi u} \exp(-e^u) {}_rR_s(A_1, A_2, \ldots, A_r; B_1, B_2, \ldots, B_s; ze^u); \tau \right] \tag{44}$$

where $\Phi = \varphi + i\tau, \varphi > 0, r \leq s + 1$, *the $\mathfrak{F}(\Phi, \tau)$ is the Fourier transform of Φ ([41])*

$$\mathfrak{F}(\Phi, \tau) = \frac{1}{\sqrt{2\pi}} \int_{-\infty}^\infty e^{iu\tau} \Phi(u) du, \tau \in R > 0. \tag{45}$$

Proof. By substituting the $t = e^u$ in (43), we can easily acquire the Fourier transform representation of the ${}_rR_s$ matrix function. □

Theorem 11. *The Euler-type integral representation of the ${}_rR_s$ matrix function is determined as*

$${}_{r+\kappa}R_{s+\kappa}(A_1, A_2, \ldots, A_r, \Delta(P; \kappa); B_1, B_2, \ldots, B_s, \Delta(P+Q; \kappa); P, Q, cz^\kappa)$$
$$= z^{I-P-Q} \Gamma^{-1}(P) \Gamma(P+Q) \Gamma^{-1}(Q) \int_0^z t^{P-I}(z-t)^{Q-I} \tag{46}$$
$$\times {}_rR_s \left(\begin{array}{c} A_1, A_2, \ldots, A_r; \\ B_1, B_2, \ldots, B_s \end{array}; P, Q, ct^\kappa \right) dt.$$

where κ is a positive integer and $\Delta(P, r)$ is the array of parameters

$$\Delta(P, \kappa) = \frac{1}{\kappa} P, \frac{1}{\kappa}(P+I), \frac{1}{\kappa}(P+2I), \ldots, \frac{1}{\kappa}(P+(\kappa-1)I).$$

Proof. By putting $t = zu$ and $t = zdu$ into the equation, we obtain

$$\int_0^z t^{P+(\kappa\ell-1)I}(z-t)^{Q-I} dt = z^{P+Q+(\kappa\ell-1)I} \int_0^1 u^{P+(\kappa\ell-1)I}(1-u)^{Q-I} du$$
$$= z^{P+Q+(\kappa\ell-1)I} \Gamma(P) \Gamma(Q) \Gamma^{-1}(P+Q)(P)_{\kappa\ell}[(P+Q)_{\kappa\ell}]^{-1}. \tag{47}$$

□

Theorem 12. *The Euler-type integral representation of the $_rR_s$ matrix function is determined as*

$$_{r+\kappa+\iota}R_{s+\kappa+\iota}\left(A_1, A_2, \ldots, A_r, \Delta(P;\kappa), \Delta(Q;\iota); B_1, B_2, \ldots, B_s, \Delta(P+Q;\kappa+\iota); P, Q, \frac{c\kappa^\kappa \iota^\iota}{(\kappa+\iota)^{\kappa+\iota}}\right)$$

$$= \Gamma^{-1}(P)\Gamma(P+Q)\Gamma^{-1}(Q) \int_0^1 t^{P-I}(1-t)^{Q-I} \qquad (48)$$

$$\times {}_rR_s\left(\begin{matrix}A_1, A_2, \ldots, A_r; \\ B_1, B_2, \ldots, B_s\end{matrix}; P, Q, ct^\kappa(1-t)^\iota\right)dt.$$

Proof. When using the beta matrix function, we obtain

$$\int_0^1 t^{P+(\kappa\ell-1)I}(1-t)^{Q+(\iota\ell-1)I}du$$

$$= \Gamma(P)\Gamma(Q)\Gamma^{-1}(P+Q)(P)_{\kappa\ell}(Q)_{\iota\ell}[(P+Q)_{\kappa\ell+\iota\ell}]^{-1}. \qquad (49)$$

When using the above equation (49), we obtain (48) □

Theorem 13. *The Laplace transform of the $_rR_s$ matrix function is determined by*

$$\mathcal{L}\left[t^{Q-I}{}_rR_s(A_1, A_2, \ldots, A_r; B_1, B_2, \ldots, B_s; P, Q, zt^P); s\right]$$

$$= \int_0^\infty t^{Q-I} e^{-st}{}_rR_s(A_1, A_2, \ldots, A_r; B_1, B_2, \ldots, B_s; P, Q, zt^P)dt \qquad (50)$$

$$= s^{-Q}{}_rF_s(A_1, A_2, \ldots, A_r; B_1, B_2, \ldots, B_s; zs^{-P}),$$

where $\mathcal{L}[f(t); s]$ is the Laplace transform

$$\mathcal{L}[f(t); s] = \int_0^\infty e^{-st} f(t)dt = F(s), s \in \mathcal{C}.$$

Proof. When using Euler's integral, we have

$$\mathcal{L}[t^{\ell P+Q-I}; s] = \int_0^\infty e^{-st} t^{\ell P+Q-I} dt = \frac{\Gamma(\ell P+Q)}{s^{\ell P+Q}}, \qquad (51)$$

where $\min Re(\ell P + Q), Re(s) > 0$, $Re(s) = 0$, or $0 < Re(\ell P + Q) < 1$.
When using the above Equation (51), this yields the right-hand side of (50). □

Theorem 14. *As such, the following integral formula holds:*

$$\int_0^x (x-t)^{Q-I}{}_rR_s(A_1, A_2, \ldots, A_r; B_1, B_2, \ldots, B_s; P, Q, z(x-t)^P)$$
$$t^{Q'-I}{}_rR_s(A'_1, A'_2, \ldots, A'_r; B'_1, B'_2, \ldots, B'_s; P, Q', zt^P)dt \qquad (52)$$
$$= x^{Q+Q'-I}{}_rR_s(A_1+A'_1, A_2+A'_2, \ldots, A_r+A'_r; B_1+B'_1, B_2+B'_2, \ldots, B_s+B'_s; P, Q+Q'; zx^P).$$

Proof. On employing the convolution theorem of the Laplace transform, we obtain

$$\mathcal{L}\left[\int_0^x \Psi(x-\tau)\Omega(\tau)d\tau; s\right] = \mathcal{L}[\Psi(x); s]\mathcal{L}[\Omega(\tau); s]. \qquad (53)$$

When using (53), we obtain

$$\mathcal{L}[\int_0^x (x-t)^{Q-I} {}_rR_s(A_1, A_2, \ldots, A_r; B_1, B_2, \ldots, B_s; P, Q, z(x-t)^P)$$
$$t^{Q'-I} {}_rR_s(A'_1, A'_2, \ldots, A'_r; B'_1, B'_2, \ldots, B'_s; P, Q', zt^P)dt; s]$$
$$= \mathcal{L}[x^{Q-I} {}_rR_s(A_1, A_2, \ldots, A_r; B_1, B_2, \ldots, B_s; P, Q, zx^P); s]$$
$$\mathcal{L}[x^{Q'-I} {}_rR_s(A'_1, A'_2, \ldots, A'_r; B'_1, B'_2, \ldots, B'_s; P, Q', zx^P); s]$$
$$= \sum_{\ell=0}^{\infty} \sum_{j=0}^{\infty} \frac{z^\ell}{\ell!} \prod_{i=1}^{r}(A_i)_\ell \left[\prod_{j=1}^{s}(B_j)_\ell\right]^{-1} \frac{z^j}{j!} \prod_{i=1}^{r}(A'_i)_j \left[\prod_{j=1}^{s}(B'_j)_j\right]^{-1} s^{-(\ell+j)P-Q-Q'}$$
$$= \sum_{\ell=0}^{\infty} \sum_{j=0}^{\infty} \frac{z^{\ell+j}}{\ell!j!} \prod_{i=1}^{r}(A_i)_\ell \left[\prod_{j=1}^{s}(B_j)_\ell\right]^{-1} \prod_{i=1}^{r}(A'_i)_j \left[\prod_{j=1}^{s}(B'_j)_j\right]^{-1} s^{-(\ell+j)P-Q-Q'}$$
$$= \sum_{\ell=0}^{\infty} \sum_{j=0}^{\ell} \frac{z^\ell}{(\ell-j)!j!} \prod_{i=1}^{r}(A_i)_{\ell-j} \left[\prod_{j=1}^{s}(B_j)_{\ell-j}\right]^{-1} \prod_{i=1}^{r}(A'_i)_j \left[\prod_{j=1}^{s}(B'_j)_j\right]^{-1} s^{-\ell P-Q-Q'}$$
$$= \sum_{\ell=0}^{\infty} \sum_{j=0}^{\ell} \frac{z^\ell}{\ell!} \prod_{i=1}^{r}(A_i + A'_i)_\ell \left[\prod_{j=1}^{s}(B_j + B'_j)_\ell\right]^{-1} s^{-\ell P-Q-Q'}. \tag{54}$$

When using (51), we find that

$$\mathcal{L}^{-1}(s^{-\ell P-Q-Q'}) = x^{\ell P+Q+Q'-I} \Gamma^{-1}(\ell P+Q+Q'). \tag{55}$$

When we use the inverse Laplace transform, we obtain the right hand side of (54), and when we use (55), we obtain

$$x^{Q+Q'-I} {}_rR_s(A_1 + A'_1, A_2 + A'_2, \ldots, A_r + A'_r; B_1 + B'_1, B_2 + B'_2, \ldots, B_s + B'_s; P, Q+Q'; zx^P).$$
□

Theorem 15. *For $x > a$, the following relations hold true:*

$$\mathbb{I}_{a+}^{\alpha}\left[(z-a)^{Q-I} {}_rR_s(A_1, A_2, \ldots, A_r; B_1, B_2, \ldots, B_s; P, Q; c(z-a)^P)\right]$$
$$= (x-a)^{Q+(\alpha-1)I} {}_rR_s(A_1, A_2, \ldots, A_r; B_1, B_2, \ldots, B_s; P, Q+\alpha I; c(x-a)^P), \tag{56}$$

where $\mathbb{I}_{a+}^{\alpha}$ is the right-sided Riemann–Liouville (R–L) fractional integral operator ([42,43])

$$\left(\mathbb{I}_{a+}^{\alpha} f\right)(x) = \frac{1}{\Gamma(\alpha)} \int_a^x (x-t)^{\alpha-1} f(t) dt, x > a,$$

and

$$\mathbb{D}_{a+}^{\alpha}\left[(z-a)^{Q-I} {}_rR_s(A_1, A_2, \ldots, A_r; B_1, B_2, \ldots, B_s; P, Q; c(z-a)^P)\right]$$
$$= (x-a)^{Q-(\alpha+1)I} {}_rR_s(A_1, A_2, \ldots, A_r; B_1, B_2, \ldots, B_s; P, Q-\alpha I; c(x-a)^P), \tag{57}$$

where $\mathbb{D}_{a+}^{\alpha}$ is the right-hand-sided Riemann–Liouville (R–L) fractional derivative operator of order α

$$\left(\mathbb{D}_{a+}^{\alpha} f\right)(x) = \left(\frac{d}{dx}\right)^n \left(\mathbb{I}_{a+}^{n-\alpha} f\right)(x),$$

and

$$\mathbb{D}_{a+}^{\alpha,\beta}\left[(z-a)^{Q-I}\,_rR_s(A_1,A_2,\ldots,A_r;B_1,B_2,\ldots,B_s;P,Q;c(z-a)^P)\right] \tag{58}$$
$$= (x-a)^{Q-(\alpha+1)I}\,_rR_s(A_1,A_2,\ldots,A_r;B_1,B_2,\ldots,B_s;P,Q-\alpha I;c(x-a)^P),$$

where $\mathbb{D}_{a+}^{\alpha,\beta}$ is the right-hand-sided Riemann–Liouville (R–L) fractional derivative operator of order α,

$$\left(\mathbb{D}_{a+}^{\alpha,\beta}f\right)(x) = \left(\mathbb{I}_{a+}^{\beta(1-\alpha)}\frac{d}{dx}\left(\mathbb{I}_{a+}^{(1-\beta)(1-\alpha)}f\right)\right)(x), \alpha \in (0,1], \beta \in [0,1].$$

Proof. When using the relation, we obtain

$$\mathbb{I}_{a+}^{\alpha}\left[(z-a)^{\ell P+Q-I}\right] = \Gamma(\ell P+Q)\Gamma^{-1}(\ell P+Q+\alpha I)(x-a)^{\ell P+Q+(\alpha-1)I}, x > a, \tag{59}$$

this yields the right hand side of (56). Thus, we obtain

$$\mathbb{I}_{a+}^{\alpha}\left[(z-a)^{Q-I}\,_rR_s(A_1,A_2,\ldots,A_r;B_1,B_2,\ldots,B_s;P,Q;c(z-a)^P)\right]$$
$$= \sum_{\ell=0}^{\infty}\frac{z^\ell}{\ell!}\prod_{i=1}^{p}(A_i)_\ell\left[\prod_{j=1}^{s}(B_j)_\ell\right]^{-1}\Gamma^{-1}(\ell P+Q)\mathbb{I}_{a+}^{\alpha}(z-a)^{\ell P+Q-I}$$
$$= \sum_{\ell=0}^{\infty}\frac{z^\ell}{\ell!}\prod_{i=1}^{p}(A_i)_\ell\left[\prod_{j=1}^{s}(B_j)_\ell\right]^{-1}\Gamma^{-1}(\ell P+Q+\alpha I)(x-a)^{\ell P+Q+(\alpha-1)I}$$
$$= (x-a)^{Q+(\alpha-1)I}\,_rR_s(A_1,A_2,\ldots,A_r;B_1,B_2,\ldots,B_s;P,Q+\alpha I;c(x-a)^P).$$

When using the relation

$$\mathbb{I}_{a+}^{n-\alpha}\left[(z-a)^{\ell P+Q-I}\right] = \Gamma(\ell P+Q)\Gamma^{-1}(\ell P+Q+(n-\alpha)I)(x-a)^{\ell P+Q+(n-\alpha-1)I}, x > a, \tag{60}$$

and

$$\mathbb{D}^n\left[(z-a)^{\ell P+Q+(n-\alpha-1)I}\right] = \Gamma(\ell P+Q+(n-\alpha)I)\Gamma^{-1}(\ell P+Q-\alpha I)(x-a)^{\ell P+Q-(\alpha+1)I}, x > a \tag{61}$$

to prove assertion (57), we use (60) and (61), which gives

$$\mathbb{D}_{a+}^{\alpha}\left[(z-a)^{Q-I}\,_rR_s(A_1,A_2,\ldots,A_r;B_1,B_2,\ldots,B_s;P,Q;c(z-a)^P)\right]$$
$$= \left(\frac{d}{dx}\right)^n \mathbb{I}_{a+}^{n-\alpha}\left[(z-a)^{Q-I}\,_rR_s(A_1,A_2,\ldots,A_r;B_1,B_2,\ldots,B_s;P,Q;c(z-a)^P)\right]$$
$$= \left(\frac{d}{dx}\right)^n \left[(x-a)^{Q+(n-\alpha-1)I}\,_rR_s(A_1,A_2,\ldots,A_r;B_1,B_2,\ldots,B_s;P,Q+(n-\alpha)I;c(x-a)^P)\right]$$
$$= (x-a)^{Q-(\alpha+1)I}\,_rR_s(A_1,A_2,\ldots,A_r;B_1,B_2,\ldots,B_s;P,Q-\alpha I;c(x-a)^P).$$

By applying the $\mathbb{D}_{a+}^{\alpha,\beta}$ right-hand-sided Riemann–Liouville (R–L) fractional derivative operator of order α, we obtain

$$\mathbb{I}_{a+}^{(1-\beta)(1-\alpha)}\left[(z-a)^{\ell P+Q-I}\right] = \Gamma(\ell P+Q)\Gamma^{-1}(\ell P+Q+((1-\beta)(1-\alpha))I)(x-a)^{\ell P+Q+((1-\beta)(1-\alpha)-1)I}, \tag{62}$$

$$\mathbb{D}\left[(x-a)^{\ell P+Q+((1-\beta)(1-\alpha)-1)I}\right] = (\ell P+Q+((1-\beta)(1-\alpha)-1)I)(x-a)^{\ell P+Q+((1-\beta)(1-\alpha)-2)I}, \tag{63}$$

$$\mathbb{I}_{a^+}^{\beta(1-\alpha)}\left[(z-a)^{\ell P+Q+((1-\beta)(1-\alpha)-2)I}\right] = \Gamma(\ell P+Q+((1-\beta)(1-\alpha)-1)I) \tag{64}$$

$$\Gamma^{-1}(\ell P+Q+((1-\beta)(1-\alpha)-1)I+\beta(1-\alpha)I)(x-a)^{\ell P+Q+((1-\beta)(1-\alpha)-2)I+\beta(1-\alpha)I},$$

and

$$\left(\mathbb{D}_{a^+}^{\alpha,\beta}\left[(z-a)^{\ell P+Q-I}\right] = \Gamma(\ell P+Q)\Gamma^{-1}(\ell P+Q-\alpha I)(x-a)^{\ell P+Q-(\alpha+1)I}. \tag{65}$$

Thus, we obtain

$$\mathbb{D}_{a^+}^{\alpha,\beta}\left[(z-a)^{Q-I}{}_rR_s(A_1,A_2,\ldots,A_r;B_1,B_2,\ldots,B_s;P,Q;c(z-a)^P)\right]$$
$$= \mathbb{I}_{a^+}^{\beta(1-\alpha)}\frac{d}{dx}\mathbb{I}_{a^+}^{(1-\beta)(1-\alpha)}\left[(z-a)^{Q-I}{}_rR_s(A_1,A_2,\ldots,A_r;B_1,B_2,\ldots,B_s;P,Q;c(z-a)^P)\right]$$
$$= \mathbb{I}_{a^+}^{\beta(1-\alpha)}\frac{d}{dx}\left[(z-a)^{Q+(1-\beta)(1-\alpha)I}{}_rR_s(A_1,A_2,\ldots,A_r;B_1,B_2,\ldots,B_s;P,Q+(k-\alpha)I;c(z-a)^P)\right]$$
$$= (x-a)^{Q-(\alpha+1)I}{}_rR_s(A_1,A_2,\ldots,A_r;B_1,B_2,\ldots,B_s;P,Q-\alpha I;c(x-a)^P).$$
□

6. Some Special Cases and Applications

In this section, we develop an integral of the ${}_rR_s$ matrix function that involves a relation with some of the special cases related to the integral representations of the ${}_rR_s$ matrix function, which is also explained below.

Theorem 16. *As $|z|<1$, $Re(B)>Re(A)>0$ of the ${}_{r+1}R_r$ matrix function satisfies the following Euler-type integral representation, we obtain the following:*

$${}_{r+1}R_r(E,\Delta(A,r);\Delta(B,r);P,Q;z) = \Gamma(B)\Gamma^{-1}(A)\Gamma^{-1}(B-A)\int_0^1 t^{A-I}(1-t)^{B-A-I}\mathbf{E}_{P,Q,E}(zt^r)dt \tag{66}$$

where $\mathbf{E}_{P,Q,E}(z)$ is a three-parametric Mittag–Leffler matrix function [40].

Proof. For convenience, let ${}_{r+1}R_r$ be the left hand side of (66), then

$${}_{r+1}R_r(E,\Delta(A,r);\Delta(B,r);P,Q;z) = \sum_{\ell=0}^{\infty}\frac{z^\ell}{\ell!}(E)_\ell(\frac{1}{r}A)_\ell(\frac{1}{r}(A+I))_\ell\cdots\frac{1}{r}(A+(r-1)I)$$
$$\times [(\frac{1}{r}B)_\ell]^{-1}[(\frac{1}{r}(B+I))_\ell]^{-1}\cdots[\frac{1}{r}(B+(r-1)I)]^{-1}\Gamma^{-1}(\ell P+Q). \tag{67}$$

When using the relation [16], we obtain

$$(A)_{\ell r} = r^{\ell r}\prod_{i=1}^{r}\left(\frac{A+(i-1)I}{r}\right)_\ell, \ell=0,1,2,\ldots, \tag{68}$$

where r is a positive integer.
Thus, (67) becomes

$${}_{r+1}R_r(E,\Delta(A,r);\Delta(B,r);P,Q;z) = \sum_{\ell=0}^{\infty}\frac{z^\ell}{\ell!}(E)_\ell(A)_{r\ell}[(B)_{r\ell}]^{-1}\Gamma^{-1}(\ell P+Q), \tag{69}$$

and we find

$$(A)_{r\ell}[(B)_{r\ell}]^{-1} = \Gamma(B)\Gamma^{-1}(A)\Gamma^{-1}(B-A)\mathbf{B}(A+r\ell,B-A). \tag{70}$$

When using (69) and (70), we arrive at

$$_{r+1}R_r(E, \Delta(A,r); \Delta(B,r); P, Q; z)$$

$$= \sum_{\ell=0}^{\infty} \frac{z^\ell}{\ell!} (E)_\ell (A)_{r\ell} [(B)_{r\ell}]^{-1} \Gamma^{-1}(\ell P + Q)$$

$$= \Gamma(B)\Gamma^{-1}(A)\Gamma^{-1}(B-A) \sum_{\ell=0}^{\infty} \frac{z^\ell}{\ell!} (E)_\ell \Gamma^{-1}(\ell P + Q) \int_0^1 t^{A+(r\ell-1)I}(1-t)^{B-A-I} dt$$

$$= \Gamma(B)\Gamma^{-1}(A)\Gamma^{-1}(B-A) \int_0^1 t^{A-I}(1-t)^{B-A-I} E_{P,Q,E}(zt^r) dt.$$

□

Theorem 17. *For any matrix E in $\mathbb{C}^{N \times N}$, the following assertion integral holds true:*

$$_{r+1}R_r(E, \Delta(A,r); \Delta(B,r); I, Q; z)$$
$$= \Gamma(B)\Gamma^{-1}(A)\Gamma^{-1}(B-A)\Gamma^{-1}(Q) \int_0^1 t^{A-I}(1-t)^{B-A-I}\, {}_1\mathbf{F}_1(E; Q; zt^r) dt. \quad (71)$$

Proof. For $P = I$ in (66), the three-parameter Mittag–Leffler matrix function $E_{A,P,Q}(xt^2)$ coincides with the confluent hypergeometric matrix function. Thus, we obtain (71). □

Theorem 18. *For the $_{r+1}R_r$ matrix function, we find that it satisfies the following Euler-type integral representation:*

$$_{r+1}R_r(-nI, \Delta(A,r); \Delta(B,r); kI, Q; z) = \Gamma(B)\Gamma^{-1}(A)\Gamma^{-1}(B-A)$$
$$\times \Gamma(n+1)\Gamma^{-1}(nkI + Q) \int_0^1 t^{A-I}(1-t)^{B--A-I} \mathbf{Z}_n^{Q-I}(zt^r; k) dt \quad (72)$$

where $n, k \in \mathbb{N}$ and $\mathbf{Z}_n^{Q-I}(z; k)$ are the Konhauser matrix polynomials [16,44–48] of degree n in z^k.

Proof. By performing $E = -nI$ and $P = kI$, we find that (66) reduces to

$$_{r+1}R_r(-nI, \Delta(A,r); \Delta(B,r); kI, Q; z)$$
$$= \Gamma(B)\Gamma^{-1}(A)\Gamma^{-1}(B-A) \int_0^1 t^{A-I}(1-t)^{B-A-I} E_{kI,Q;-nI}(zt^r) dt$$

When using the result defined in [16,45], this leads to the right-hand side of (72). □

Yet another such integral representation is obtained in a straight forward manner as follows.

Theorem 19. *For $n \in \mathbb{N}$, the following integral representation reduces to*

$$_{r+1}R_r(-nI, \Delta(A,r); \Delta(B,r); 1I, Q; z) = \Gamma(B)\Gamma^{-1}(A)\Gamma^{-1}(B-A)$$
$$\times \Gamma(n+1)\Gamma^{-1}(Q+nI) \int_0^1 t^{A-I}(1-t)^{B-A-I} \mathbf{L}_n^{Q-I}(zt^r) dt, \quad (73)$$

where $\mathbf{L}_n^{Q-I}(z)$ is a Laguerre matrix polynomial [14].

Theorem 20. *The $_{r+1}R_r$ matrix function satisfies the following result:*

$$_{r+1}R_r(E, \Delta(A,r); \Delta(B,r); P, Q; z) = \Gamma(B)\Gamma^{-1}(A) \sum_{\ell=0}^{\infty} \frac{z^\ell}{\ell!} \Gamma^{-1}(B-A-\ell I)(A+\ell I)^{-1}$$
$$\times {}_{r+1}R_r(E, \Delta(A+\ell I, r); \Delta(A+(\ell+1)I, r); P, Q; z) \quad (74)$$

Proof. From the equation in (66) and when letting $_{r+1}R_r$ be the left-hand side of (74), we obtain

$_{r+1}R_r(E, \Delta(A,r); \Delta(B,r); P, Q; z)$

$= \Gamma(B)\Gamma^{-1}(A)\Gamma^{-1}(B-A) \int_0^1 t^{A-I}(1-t)^{B-A-I} \mathbf{E}_{P,Q;E}(zt^r)dt$

$= \Gamma(B)\Gamma^{-1}(A) \sum_{\ell=0}^{\infty} \frac{(-1)^\ell}{\ell!} \Gamma^{-1}(B-A-\ell I) \sum_{k=0}^{\infty} \frac{1}{k!}(E)_k z^k \Gamma^{-1}(kP+Q) \int_0^1 t^{A+(\ell+rk-1)I} dt$

$= \Gamma(B)\Gamma^{-1}(A) \sum_{\ell=0}^{\infty} \frac{(-1)^\ell}{\ell!} \Gamma^{-1}(B-A-\ell I) \sum_{k=0}^{\infty} \frac{1}{k!}(E)_k z^k \Gamma^{-1}(kP+Q)(A+(\ell+rk)I)^{-1}$

$= \Gamma(B)\Gamma^{-1}(A) \sum_{\ell=0}^{\infty} \frac{(-1)^\ell}{\ell!} (A+\ell I)^{-1} \Gamma^{-1}(B-A-\ell I) \sum_{k=0}^{\infty} \frac{1}{k!}(E)_k (A+\ell I)_{rk}$

$\times [(A+(\ell+1)I)_{rk}]^{-1} \Gamma^{-1}(kP+Q) z^k$

$= \Gamma(B)\Gamma^{-1}(A) \sum_{\ell=0}^{\infty} \frac{(-1)^\ell}{\ell!} (A+\ell I)^{-1} \Gamma^{-1}(B-A-\ell I)$

$\times {}_{r+1}R_r(E, \Delta(A+\ell I, r); \Delta(A+(\ell+1)I, r); P, Q; z).$

□

Corollary 1. *For $|z| < 1$, the ${}_2R_1$ matrix function is given by*

$${}_2R_1(A, I; B; P, I; z) = \Gamma(B)\Gamma^{-1}(A) \, {}_2\Psi_2(A, I; B, P; z). \tag{75}$$

Proof. From (38), we obtain

${}_2R_1(A, I; B; P, I, z) = \Gamma^{-1}(A)\Gamma^{-1}(B-A)\Gamma(B) \int_0^1 t^{A-I}(1-t)^{B-A-I} \, {}_1R_0(I; -; P, I, zt) dt$

$= \Gamma^{-1}(A)\Gamma^{-1}(B-A)\Gamma(B) \int_0^1 t^{A-I}(1-t)^{B-A-I} \sum_{\ell=0}^{\infty} \Gamma^{-1}(\ell P+I)(zt)^\ell dt$

$= \Gamma^{-1}(A)\Gamma^{-1}(B-A)\Gamma(B) \int_0^1 t^{A-I}(1-t)^{B-A-I} E_P(zt) dt,$

where $E_P(zt)$ is a Mittag–Leffler matrix function.

By using the relation between the Mittag–Leffler matrix function $E_P(zt)$ and the generalized Wright matrix function ${}_2\Psi_2$ [45], we find

$$\int_0^1 t^{A-I}(1-t)^{B-A-I} E_P(zt) dt = \Gamma(B-A) \, {}_2\Psi_2(A, I; B, P; z) \tag{76}$$

where ${}_2\Psi_2$ is a special case of the generalized Wright matrix function ${}_r\Psi_s$ in [22]. This completes the proof □

7. Conclusions or Concluding Remarks

We were motivated in this paper to obtain a recurrence relation and to then use this result to obtain an integral representation of the ${}_rR_s$ matrix function. The results presented in this paper appear to be novel in the literature. The convergence properties of the ${}_rR_s$ matrix function with some of its properties—including its analytic properties (type and order), as well as the contiguous function relations and differential property of the ${}_rR_s$ matrix function—were established. The contiguous relations for the generalized hypergeometric matrix function; the extended integral representations and the differential property of the ${}_rR_s$ matrix function with its integrals involving relationships with some other well-known fractional calculus equations with special functions; the transform method with an application to the Mittag–Leffler matrix function; Euler-type integral representation; and some special cases related to the integral representations of the $_rR_s$ matrix functions, are also explained in this paper. Since several of the results that involve the generalizations and extensions of the hypergeometric matrix functions have the potential to play important roles in the theory of the special matrix functions of mathematical physics, applied mathematics, engineering, probability theory, and statistical sciences, it would be interesting, and possible, to develop its study in the future. As a result, in this context, some particular cases, as well as our main results, can be applied theoretically, practically, and in some numerical, algorithmical points of view. With the assistance of this article, a variety of fields and their applications can be accessed, such as the representation of the matrix R-function via Fourier transformation, the distributional representation of the $_rR_s$ matrix function, and the Euler-type integral matrix representations of the generalized $_rR_s$ matrix function (which were developed in some special cases from the perspectives of the Konhauser and Laguerre matrix polynomials). We can also now study some applications in the areas of probability theory and groundwater pumping modeling via the pathway integral representation of the $_rR_s$ matrix function and the pathway transformation of the $_rR_s$ matrix function in terms of, as well as, the solution of the fractional matrix differential equations that involve the Hilfer derivative operator (which involves the composition of the Riemann–Liouville fractional integral and derivative). The conclusions of this work are thus diverse and important; therefore, it will be intriguing, and possible, to expand the study of these conclusions in the future.

Author Contributions: Writing—original draft, A.S., G.S.K. and C.C.; Writing—review & editing, A.S., G.S.K. and C.C. All authors have read and agreed to the published version of the manuscript.

Funding: This research received no external funding.

Data Availability Statement: The data that support the findings of this paper are available, as they are requested.

Conflicts of Interest: The authors declares no conflict of interest.

References

1. Constantine, A.G.; Muirhead, R.J. Partial differential equations for hypergeometric functions of two argument matrices. *J. Multivar. Anal.* **1972**, *3*, 332–338. [CrossRef]
2. James, A.T. *Special Functions of Matrix and Single Argument in Statistics in Theory and Application of Special Functions*; Academic Press: New York, NY, USA, 1975.
3. Mathai, A.M. *A Handbook of Generalized Special Functions for Statistical and Physical Sciences*; Oxford University Press: Oxford, UK, 1993.
4. Mathai, A.M.; Haubold, H.J. *An Introduction to Fractional Calculus*; Nova Science Publishers: New York, NY, USA, 2017.
5. Jódar, L.; Cortés, J.C. Some properties of Gamma and Beta matrix functions. *Appl. Math. Lett.* **1998**, *11*, 89–93. [CrossRef]
6. Jódar, L.; Cortés, J.C. On the hypergeometric matrix function. *J. Comput. Appl. Math.* **1998**, *99*, 205–217. [CrossRef]
7. Jódar, L.; Cortés, J.C. Closed form general solution of the hypergeometric matrix differential equation. *Math. Comput. Model.* **2000**, *32*, 1017–1028. [CrossRef]
8. Dwivedi, R.; Sahai, V. On the hypergeometric matrix functions of two variables. *Linear Multilinear Algebra* **2018**, *66*, 1819–1837. [CrossRef]
9. Dwivedi, R.; Sahai, V. A note on the Appell matrix functions. *Quaest. Math.* **2020**, *43*, 321–334. [CrossRef]
10. Abdullah, A.; Bayram, C.; Sahin, R. On the matrix versions of Appell hypergeometric functions. *Quaest. Math.* **2014**, *37*, 31–38.
11. Liu, H. Some generating relations for extended Appell's and Lauricella's hypergeometric functions. *Rocky Mt. J. Math.* **2014**, *44*, 1987–2007. [CrossRef]
12. Bayram, C.; Rabia, A. Multivariable matrix generalization of Gould-Hopper polynomials. *Miskolc Math. Notes* **2015**, *16*, 79–89.
13. Defez, E.; Jódar, L.; Law, A. Jacobi matrix differential equation, polynomial solutions, and their properties. *Comput. Math. Appl.* **2004**, *48*, 789–803. [CrossRef]
14. Jódar, L.; Sastre, J. On Laguerre matrix polynomials. *Util. Math.* **1998**, *53*, 37–48.
15. Cetinkaya, A. The incomplete second Appell hypergeometric functions. *Appl. Math. Comput.* **2013**, *219*, 8332–8337. [CrossRef]
16. Shehata, A. Some relations on Konhauser matrix polynomials. *Miskolc Math. Notes* **2016**, *17*, 605–633. [CrossRef]
17. Duran, A.J.; Van Assche, W. Orthogonal matrix polynomials and higher order recurrence relations. *Linear Algebra Appl.* **1995**, *219*, 261–280. [CrossRef]

18. Geronimo, J.S. Scattering theory and matrix orthogonal polynomials on the real line. *Circ. Syst. Signal Process.* **1982**, *1*, 471–495. [CrossRef]
19. Abbas, M.I. Nonlinear Alangana-Baleanu fractional differential equations involving the Mittag–Leffler integral operator. *Mem. Differ. Equ. Math. Phys.* **2021**, *82*, 1–13
20. Shiri, B.; Baleanu, D. System of fractional differential algebraic equations with applications. *Chaos Solitons Fractals* **2019**, *120*, 203–212. [CrossRef]
21. Zhang, X. The non-uniqueness of solution for initial value problem of impulsive differential equations involving higher order Katugampola fractional derivative. *Adv. Differ. Equ.* **2020**, *2020*, 85. [CrossRef]
22. Bakhet, A.; Jiao, Y.; He, F. On the Wright hypergeometric matrix functions and their fractional calculus. *Integral Transform. Spec. Funct.* **2019**, *30*, 138–156.
23. Duan, J.; Chen, L. Solution of fractional differential equation systems and computation of matrix Mittag—Leffler functions. *Symmetry* **2018**, *10*, 503. [CrossRef]
24. Eltayeb, H.; Kılıçman, A.; Agarwal, R.P. On integral transforms and matrix functions. *Abstr. Appl. Anal.* **2011**, *2011*, 207930. [CrossRef]
25. Kargin, L.; Kurt, V. Chebyshev-type matrix polynomials and integral transforms. *Hacet. J. Math. Stat.* **2015**, *44*, 341–350. [CrossRef]
26. Khammash, G.S.; Agarwal, P.; Choi, J. Extended k-Gamma and k-Beta functions of matrix arguments. *Mathematics* **2020**, *8*, 1715. [CrossRef]
27. Shehata, A. On Lommel Matrix Polynomials. *Symmetry* **2021**, *13*, 2335. [CrossRef]
28. Shehata, A.; Subuhi, K. On Bessel-Maitland matrix function. *Mathematica* **2015**, *57*, 90–103.
29. Salim, T.O. Some properties relating to the generalized Mittag–Leffler function. *Adv. Appl. Math. Anal.* **2009**, *4*, 21–30.
30. Sharma, K. Application of fractional calculus operators to related areas. *Gen. Math. Notes* **2011**, *7*, 33–40.
31. Shukla, A.K.; Prajapati, J.C. On a generalization of Mittag-Leffler function and its properties. *J. Math. Anal. Appl.* **2007**, *336*, 797–811. [CrossRef]
32. Bose, R.C. Early History of Multivariate Statistical Analysis. In *Analysis IV*; Krishnaiah, P.R., Ed.; North-Holland: Amsterdam, The Netherlands, 1977; pp. 3–22.
33. Jain, S.; Cattani, C.; Agarwal, P. Fractional Hypergeometric Functions. *Symmetry* **2022**, *14*, 714. [CrossRef]
34. Pham-Gia, T.; Thanh, D. Hypergeometric Functions: From One Scalar Variable to Several Matrix Arguments, in Statistics and Beyond. *Open J. Stat.* **2016**, *6*, 951–994. [CrossRef]
35. Saigo, M. On generalized fractional calculus operators. In Proceedings of the Recent Advances in Applied Mathematics, Kuwait City, Kuwait, 4–7 May 1996; Kuwait University Press: Kuwait City, Kuwait, 1996; pp. 441–450.
36. Srivastava, H.M.; Agarwal, P. Certain Fractional Integral Operators and the Generalized Incomplete Hypergeometric Functions. *Appl. Appl. Math.* **2013**, *8*, 333–345.
37. Boyadjiev, L.; Dobner, H.J. Fractional free electron laser equations. *Integral Transform. Spec. Funct.* **2001**, *11*, 113–136. [CrossRef]
38. Tassaddiq, A.; Srivastava, R. New results involving the generalized Krätzel function with application to the fractional kinetic equations. *Mathematics* **2023**, *11*, 1060. [CrossRef]
39. Dunford, N.; Schwartz, J. *Linear Operators, Part I*; Interscience: New York, NY, USA, 1957.
40. Sanjhira, R.; Dwivedi, R. On the matrix function $_pR_q(A, B; z)$ and its fractional calculus properties. *Commun. Math.* **2023**, *31*, 43–56.
41. Folland, G.B. *Fourier Analysis and Its Applications*; The Wadsworth and Brooks/Cole Mathematics Series; Thomson Brooks/Cole: Belmont, CA, USA, 1992.
42. Kilbas, A.A.; Srivastava, H.M.; Trujillo, J.J. *Theory and Applications of Fractional Differential Equations*; North-Holland Mathematics Studies Elsevier Science B.V.: Amsterdam, The Netherlands, 2006; Volume 204.
43. Samko, S.G.; Kilbas, A.A.; Marıchev, O.I. *Fractional Integrals and Derivatives*; Gordon and Breach Science Publishers: Yverdon, Switzerland, 1993.
44. Erkus-Duman, E.; Cekim, B. New generating functions for the Konhauser matrix polynomials. *Commun. Fac. Sci. Univ. Ank. Ser. A1 Math. Stat.* **2014**, *63*, 35–41. [CrossRef]
45. Sanjhira, R.; Nathwani, B.V.; Dave, B.I. Generalized Mittag-Leffer matrix function and associated matrix polynomials. *J. Indian Math. Soc.* **2019**, *86*, 161–178.
46. Sanjhira, R.; Dave, B.I. Generalized Konhauser matrix polynomial and its properties. *Math. Stud.* **2018**, *87*, 109–120.

47. Shehata, A. A note on Konhauser matrix polynomials. *Palestine J. Math.* **2020**, *9*, 549–556.
48. Varma, S.; Cekim, B.; Tasdelen, F. On Konhauser matrix polynomials. *Ars Comb.* **2011**, *100*, 193–204.

Disclaimer/Publisher's Note: The statements, opinions and data contained in all publications are solely those of the individual author(s) and contributor(s) and not of MDPI and/or the editor(s). MDPI and/or the editor(s) disclaim responsibility for any injury to people or property resulting from any ideas, methods, instructions or products referred to in the content.

Article

Effects of the Wiener Process and Beta Derivative on the Exact Solutions of the Kadomtsev–Petviashvili Equation

Farah M. Al-Askar [1], Clemente Cesarano [2] and Wael W. Mohammed [3,4,*]

[1] Department of Mathematical Science, College of Science, Princess Nourah bint Abdulrahman University, P.O. Box 84428, Riyadh 11671, Saudi Arabia; famalaskar@pnu.edu.sa
[2] Section of Mathematics, International Telematic University Uninettuno, Corso Vittorio Emanuele II 39, 00186 Rome, Italy; c.cesarano@uninettuno.it
[3] Department of Mathematics, College of Science, University of Ha'il, Ha'il 2440, Saudi Arabia
[4] Department of Mathematics, Faculty of Science, Mansoura University, Mansoura 35516, Egypt
* Correspondence: wael.mohammed@mans.edu.eg

Abstract: We take into account the (2 + 1)-dimensional stochastic Kadomtsev–Petviashvili equation with beta-derivative (SKPE-BD) in this paper. To develop new hyperbolic, trigonometric, elliptic, and rational solutions, the Riccati equation and Jacobi elliptic function methods are employed. Because the KP equation is required for explaining the development of quasi-one-dimensional shallow-water waves, the solutions obtained can be used to interpret various attractive physical phenomena. To display how the multiplicative white noise and beta-derivative impact the exact solutions of the SKPE-BD, we plot a few graphs in MATLAB and display different 3D and 2D figures. We deduce how multiplicative noise stabilizes the solutions of SKPE-BD at zero.

Keywords: stochastic KP; fractional KP; stability by noise; exact solution; beta derivative

MSC: 60H15; 83C15; 60H10; 35Q51; 35A20

1. Introduction

Fractional differential equations (FDEs) are often used in relation to optical fibers, chemical kinematics, solid-state physics, electrical circuits, nuclear-physics, fluid mechanics, elastic media, quantum field theory, plasma physics, neural physics, mathematical biology, and other domains [1–7]. Also, many physical phenomena, such as fluid dynamics, elasticity, heat, electrodynamics, gravity, sound electrostatics, quantum mechanics, and diffusion, are described by fractional-order derivatives. Consequently, it is essential in mathematical physics to seek exact solutions for FDEs. In recent years, multiple approaches for dealing with FDEs have been devised, such as the (G'/G)-expansion method [8,9], Kudryashov method [10], first-integral method [11], sine–cosine method [12,13], $exp(-\phi(\varsigma))$-expansion [14], direct algebraic method [15], perturbation method [16,17], tanh-sech [18,19], sine-Gordon expansion [20], Jacobi elliptic function [21], etc.

Recently, beta-derivative (BD), a new conformable fractional derivative, was proposed by Atangana et al. in [22]. From here, the BD for $\mathcal{Y} : (0, \infty) \to \mathbb{R}$ of order $\beta \in (0,1]$ is defined as follows:

$$\mathbb{D}_x^\beta \mathcal{Y}(x) = \lim_{\epsilon \to 0} \frac{\mathcal{Y}(x + \epsilon(x + \frac{1}{\Gamma(\beta)})^{1-\beta}) - \mathcal{Y}(x)}{\epsilon}.$$

The beta-derivative satisfies the next features for any constant a and b:

(1) $\mathbb{D}_x^\beta[a] = 0,$
(2) $\mathbb{D}_x^\beta[a\mathcal{R}(x) + b\mathcal{Y}(x)] = a\mathbb{D}_x^\beta \mathcal{R}(x) + b\mathbb{D}_x^\beta \mathcal{Y}(x),$
(3) $\mathbb{D}_x^\beta \mathcal{Y}(\theta) = (x + \frac{1}{\Gamma(\beta)})^{1-\beta}\frac{d\mathcal{Y}}{dx},$ (4) If $\theta = \frac{a}{\beta}(x + \frac{1}{\Gamma(\beta)})^\beta$, then $\mathbb{D}_x^\beta \mathcal{Y}(\theta) = a\frac{d\mathcal{Y}}{d\theta}.$

On the contrary, it is now well known that randomness or fluctuations play an essential role in a wide range of phenomena. Consequently, random impacts have assumed a greater role in demonstrating numerous physical processes that take place in disciplines such as telecommunications, cryptography, computer science, ecology, biology, information theory, signal processing, neuroscience, chemistry, image processing, physics, and finance, among others [23–25]. Partial differential equations are appropriate mathematical equations for modeling complex systems in the presence of noise or random effects.

It is essential to consider FDEs with a stochastic term. Therefore, we look at the following (2 + 1)-dimensional stochastic Kadomtsev–Petviashvili equation with beta-derivative (SKPE-BD):

$$\mathbb{D}_x^\beta [\mathcal{R}_t + 6\mathcal{R}\mathbb{D}_x^\beta \mathcal{R} + \mathbb{D}_{xxx}^\beta \mathcal{R} + \gamma \mathcal{R} \mathcal{W}_t] + \rho \mathbb{D}_{yy}^\beta \mathcal{R} = 0, \qquad (1)$$

where $\mathcal{R}$ denotes the rescaled velocities and the rescaled wave amplitude in surface shallow-water waves, $\rho = \pm 1$, γ is the noise strength and it is a real number, $\mathcal{W}_t(t) = \frac{\partial \mathcal{W}(t)}{\partial t}$ is the derivative of the Wiener process $\mathcal{W}(t)$, and $\mathcal{R}\mathcal{W}_t$ is an Itô multiplicative noise.

When $\gamma = 0$ and $\beta = 1$, we attain the Kadomtsev–Petviashvili (KP) equation [26,27] that can be used to characterize the development of quasi-one-dimensional shallow-water waves whenever the impacts of viscosity and surface tension are negligible:

$$\frac{\partial}{\partial x}[\frac{\partial \mathcal{R}}{\partial t} + 6\mathcal{R}\frac{\partial \mathcal{R}}{\partial x} + \frac{\partial^3 \mathcal{R}}{\partial x^3}] + \rho \frac{\partial^2 \mathcal{R}}{\partial y^2} = 0. \qquad (2)$$

The KP equation (2) has numerous applications in fluid dynamics and plasma physics. The equation is widely used to study various physical phenomena, such as the propagation of waves and solitons in different media. As such, the KP equation has been crucial in advancing our understanding of complex nonlinear systems. Its importance lies in its ability to accurately model and predict the behavior of waves and solitons, which has applications in a wide range of fields including oceanography, optics, and plasma physics. As a result, several approaches to acquiring the exact solutions of KP Equation (2) have been suggested, such as sine–cosine [28], Hirota's bilinear method [29], Hirota's method [30], trial equation method [31], novel generalized (G'/G)-expansion [32], extended mapping method [33], F-expansion method [34], etc.

Our contribution here is to find the exact solutions for SKPE-BD (1). To obtain these solutions, we utilize the Riccati equation method (RE-Method) and Jacobi elliptic function method (JEF-Method). Because Equation (1) is used in describing the propagation of waves on the surface of shallow water, the acquired solutions of the SKPE-BD (1) will help researchers to gain a deeper understanding of these phenomena and make predictions about their behavior. Additionally, the obtained solutions can also be used in practical applications, such as designing improved tsunami warning systems or optimizing wave energy converters. Furthermore, we investigate the effect of BD and noise on the analytical solutions of the SKPE-BD (1) by providing some graphs via the MATLAB program 2022b.

Following is the structure of the paper: In Section 2, the wave equation of SKPE-BD (1) is derived. In Section 3, the RE-Method and JEF-Method are utilized to obtain the exact solution of the SKPE-BD (1). In Section 4, we can examine the effect of the Wiener process and the beta-derivative on the achieved solutions of the SKPE-BD. In Section 5, we discuss the physical meaning of the obtained results. Finally, the conclusions of the paper are offered in Section 6.

2. Traveling Wave Equation for SKPE-BD

The wave equation for SKPE-BD (1) is found by using

$$\mathcal{R}(x,y,t) = \mathcal{Y}(\xi) e^{[-\gamma \mathcal{W}(t) - \frac{1}{2}\gamma^2 t]}, \quad \xi = [\frac{1}{\beta}(x + \frac{1}{\Gamma(\beta)})^\beta + \frac{1}{\beta}(y + \frac{1}{\Gamma(\beta)})^\beta - \lambda t], \qquad (3)$$

where $\mathcal{Y}$ is a deterministic and real function. It is worth noting that

$$\frac{\partial \mathcal{R}}{\partial t} = [-\lambda \mathcal{Y}' - \gamma \mathcal{Y} \frac{\partial \mathcal{W}}{\partial t}] e^{[-\gamma \mathcal{W}(t) - \frac{1}{2}\gamma^2 t]}, \quad (4)$$

and

$$\mathbb{D}_x^\beta \mathcal{R} = \mathcal{Y}' e^{[-\gamma \mathcal{W}(t) - \frac{1}{2}\gamma^2 t]}, \ \mathbb{D}_{xxx}^\beta \mathcal{R} = \mathcal{Y}''' e^{[-\gamma \mathcal{W}(t) - \frac{1}{2}\gamma^2 t]}, \ \mathbb{D}_{yy}^\beta \mathcal{R} = \mathcal{Y}'' e^{[-\gamma \mathcal{W}(t) - \frac{1}{2}\gamma^2 t]}. \quad (5)$$

Inserting Equation (3) into Equation (1) and using (4) and (5), we obtain

$$\mathcal{Y}'''' + (\rho - \lambda)\mathcal{Y}'' + 6[\mathcal{Y}\mathcal{Y}'' + (\mathcal{Y}')^2] e^{[-\gamma \mathcal{W}(t) - \frac{1}{2}\gamma^2 t]} = 0.$$

Taking into account the expectations of both sides, we achieve

$$\mathcal{Y}'''' + (\rho - \lambda)\mathcal{Y}'' + 6[\mathcal{Y}\mathcal{Y}'' + (\mathcal{Y}')^2] e^{-\frac{1}{2}\gamma^2 t} \mathbb{E} e^{[-\gamma \mathcal{W}(t)]} = 0. \quad (6)$$

Since $\mathcal{W}(t)$ is normal process, hence $\mathbb{E}(e^{-\gamma \mathcal{W}(t)}) = e^{\frac{1}{2}\gamma^2 t}$ for any real number γ. Therefore, Equation (6) becomes

$$\mathcal{Y}'''' + (\rho - \lambda)\mathcal{Y}'' + 6(\mathcal{Y}\mathcal{Y}')' = 0, \quad (7)$$

where we replaced $\mathcal{Y}\mathcal{Y}'' + (\mathcal{Y}')^2$ by $(\mathcal{Y}\mathcal{Y}')'$. Integrating Equation (7) twice and ignoring the integration constant, we have

$$\mathcal{Y}'' - (\lambda - \rho)\mathcal{Y} + 3\mathcal{Y}^2 = 0. \quad (8)$$

3. Exact Solutions of SKPE-BD

To obtain exact solutions for SKPE-BD (1), we employ two alternative methods: the RE-Method [35] and JEF-Method [36].

3.1. RE-Method

Let us assume the solution $\mathcal{Y}$ of Equation (8) is

$$\mathcal{Y}(\xi) = \sum_{j=0}^{K} a_j \mathcal{Z}^j, \quad (9)$$

where $\mathcal{R}$ solves the Riccati equation

$$\mathcal{Z}' = \mathcal{Z}^2 + b, \quad (10)$$

with b is a unknown constant. Equation (10) has the following solutions:

$$\mathcal{Z} = \frac{-1}{\xi}, \quad (11)$$

if $b = 0$, or

$$\mathcal{Z} = \sqrt{b} \tan(\sqrt{b}\xi) \text{ or } \mathcal{Z} = -\sqrt{b} \cot(\sqrt{b}\xi), \quad (12)$$

if $b > 0$, or

$$\mathcal{Z} = -\sqrt{-b} \tanh(\sqrt{-b}\xi) \text{ or } \mathcal{Z} = -\sqrt{-b} \coth(\sqrt{-b}\xi), \quad (13)$$

if $b < 0$.

In order to compute the parameter K in Equation (9), we balance $\mathcal{Y}^2$ with $\mathcal{Y}''$ in Equation (8) to obtain

$$2K = K + 2,$$

then

$$K = 2. \quad (14)$$

Rewriting Equation (9), with $K = 2$, as

$$\mathcal{Y}(\xi) = a_0 + a_1 Z + a_2 Z^2. \quad (15)$$

Substituting Equation (15) into Equation (8) we obtain

$$(6a_2 + 3a_2^2)Z^4 + (2a_1 + 3a_1 a_2)Z^3$$
$$+ (8ba_2 - (\lambda - \rho)a_2 + 3a_1^2 + 6a_0 a_2)Z^2$$
$$+ (2a_1 b - (\lambda - \rho)a_1 + 6a_0 a_1)Z$$
$$+ (2b^2 a_2 - (\lambda - \rho)a_0 + 3a_0^2) = 0.$$

We derive by setting each coefficient of Z^j to zero

$$6a_2 + 3a_2^2 = 0,$$

$$2a_1 + 3a_1 a_2 = 0,$$

$$8ba_2 - (\lambda - \rho)a_2 + 3a_1^2 + 6a_0 a_2 = 0,$$

$$2a_1 b - (\lambda - \rho)a_1 + 6a_0 a_1 = 0,$$

and

$$2b^2 a_2 - (\lambda - \rho)a_0 + 3a_0^2 = 0.$$

The next two families are obtained by solving these equations:
First family:

$$a_0 = \frac{-2}{3}b, \ a_1 = 0, \ a_2 = -2, \ \lambda = \rho + 4b. \quad (16)$$

Second family:

$$a_0 = -2b, \ a_1 = 0, \ a_2 = -2, \ \lambda = \rho - 4b. \quad (17)$$

First family: There are three cases relying on b.
Case 1: If $b = 0$, then the solution of (8), by using (11) and (15), is

$$\mathcal{Y}(\xi) = \frac{-2}{\xi^2}.$$

Consequently, the solution of SKPE-BD (1) is

$$\mathcal{R}(x,y,t) = -2[\frac{1}{\beta}(x + \frac{1}{\Gamma(\beta)})^\beta + \frac{1}{\beta}(y + \frac{1}{\Gamma(\beta)})^\beta - \rho t]^{-2} e^{[-\gamma \mathcal{W}(t) - \frac{1}{2}\gamma^2 t]}. \quad (18)$$

Case 2: If $b > 0$, then the solutions of (8), using (12) and (15), are

$$\mathcal{Y}(\xi) = \frac{-2}{3}b - 2b\tan^2(\sqrt{b}\xi),$$

or

$$\mathcal{Y}(\xi) = \frac{-2}{3}b - 2b\cot^2(\sqrt{b}\xi).$$

As a result, the solutions of SKPE-BD (1) are

$$\mathcal{R}(x,y,t) = [\frac{-2}{3}b - 2b\tan^2(\sqrt{b}\xi)]e^{[-\gamma \mathcal{W}(t) - \frac{1}{2}\gamma^2 t]}, \quad (19)$$

or

$$\mathcal{R}(x,y,t) = [\frac{-2}{3}b - 2b\cot^2(\sqrt{b}\xi)]e^{[-\gamma \mathcal{W}(t) - \frac{1}{2}\gamma^2 t]}. \quad (20)$$

Case 3: If $b < 0$, then the solutions of (8), by using (13) and (15), are

$$\mathcal{Y}(\xi) = \frac{-2}{3}b + 2b\tanh^2(\sqrt{-b}\xi),$$

or

$$\mathcal{Y}(\xi) = \frac{-2}{3}b + 2b\coth^2(\sqrt{-b}\xi).$$

Thence, the solutions of SKPE-BD (1) are

$$\mathcal{R}(x,y,t) = [\frac{-2}{3}b + 2b\tanh^2(\sqrt{-b}\xi)]e^{[-\gamma\mathcal{W}(t)-\frac{1}{2}\gamma^2 t]}, \tag{21}$$

or

$$\mathcal{R}(x,y,t) = [\frac{-2}{3}b + 2b\coth^2(\sqrt{-b}\xi)]e^{[-\gamma\mathcal{W}(t)-\frac{1}{2}\gamma^2 t]}. \tag{22}$$

where $\xi = \frac{1}{\beta}(x + \frac{1}{\Gamma(\beta)})^\beta + \frac{1}{\beta}(y + \frac{1}{\Gamma(\beta)})^\beta - (\rho + 4b)t$.

Second family: There are three cases also relying on b.

Case 1: If $b = 0$, then we have the same solution as announced before in the first set.

Case 2: If $b > 0$, then the solutions of (8), using (12) and (15), are

$$\mathcal{Y}(\xi) = -2b - 2b\tan^2(\sqrt{b}\xi),$$

or

$$\mathcal{Y}(\xi) = -2b - 2b\cot^2(\sqrt{b}\xi).$$

Thence, the solutions of SKPE-BD (1) are

$$\mathcal{R}(x,y,t) = [-2b - 2b\tan^2(\sqrt{b}\xi)]e^{[-\gamma\mathcal{W}(t)-\frac{1}{2}\gamma^2 t]}, \tag{23}$$

or

$$\mathcal{R}(x,y,t) = [-2b - 2b\cot^2(\sqrt{b}\xi)]e^{[-\gamma\mathcal{W}(t)-\frac{1}{2}\gamma^2 t]}. \tag{24}$$

Case 3: If $b < 0$, then the solution of (8), using (13) and (15), are

$$\mathcal{Y}(\xi) = -2b + 2b\tanh^2(\sqrt{-b}\xi) = -2b\operatorname{sech}^2(\sqrt{-b}\xi),$$

or

$$\mathcal{Y}(\xi) = -2b + 2b\coth^2(\sqrt{-b}\xi) = 2b\operatorname{csch}^2(\sqrt{-b}\xi).$$

As a result, the solutions of SKPE-BD (1) are

$$\mathcal{R}(x,y,t) = -2b\operatorname{sech}^2(\sqrt{-b}\xi)e^{[-\gamma\mathcal{W}(t)-\frac{1}{2}\gamma^2 t]}, \tag{25}$$

or

$$\mathcal{R}(x,y,t) = 2b\operatorname{csch}^2(\sqrt{-b}\xi)e^{[-\gamma\mathcal{W}(t)-\frac{1}{2}\gamma^2 t]}. \tag{26}$$

where $\xi = \frac{1}{\beta}(x + \frac{1}{\Gamma(\beta)})^\beta + \frac{1}{\beta}(y + \frac{1}{\Gamma(\beta)})^\beta - (\rho - 4b)t$.

Remark 1. *If we put $\beta = 1$ and $\gamma = 0$ in Equation (25), then we obtain the solution (2), reported in [37].*

3.2. JEF-Method

In this subsection, we use the JEF-method [36]. Assuming the solutions to Equation (8) has the form (with $K = 2$):

$$\mathcal{Y}(\xi) = \hbar_0 + \hbar_1 Z(\xi) + \hbar_2 Z^2(\xi), \tag{27}$$

where $\hbar_0$, $\hbar_1$, and $\hbar_2$ are undefined constants and $Z(\xi) = sn(\xi,\kappa)$ is the Jacobi elliptic sine function for $0 < \kappa < 1$. Differentiating Equation (27) twice,

$$\mathcal{Y}''(\xi) = 2\hbar_2 - \hbar_1(\kappa^2+1)Z - 4\hbar_2(\kappa^2+1)Z^2 + 2\hbar_1\kappa^2 Z^3 + 6\hbar_2\kappa^2 Z^4. \tag{28}$$

Plugging Equations (27) and (28) into Equation (8), we have

$$(2\kappa^2\hbar_2 + 3\hbar_2^2)Z^4 + (2\kappa^2\hbar_1 + 6\hbar_1\hbar_2)Z^3$$

$$+[6\hbar_0\hbar_2 - 4\hbar_2(\kappa^2+1) - \hbar_2(\lambda-\rho) + 3\hbar_1^2]Z^2$$

$$-[(\kappa^2+1)\hbar_1 + \hbar_1(\lambda-\rho) - 6\hbar_0\hbar_1]Z + (2\hbar_2 - \hbar_0(\lambda-\rho) + 3\hbar_0^2) = 0.$$

Equating coefficient of Z^n to zero for $n = 4, 3, 2, 1, 0$:

$$2\kappa^2\hbar_2 + 3\hbar_2^2 = 0,$$

$$2\kappa^2\hbar_1 + 6\hbar_1\hbar_2 = 0,$$

$$6\hbar_0\hbar_2 - 4\hbar_2(\kappa^2+1) - \hbar_2(\lambda-\rho) + 3\hbar_1^2 = 0,$$

$$(\kappa^2+1)\hbar_1 + \hbar_1(\lambda-\rho) - 6\hbar_0\hbar_1 = 0,$$

and

$$2\hbar_2 - \hbar_0(\lambda-\rho) + 3\hbar_0^2 = 0.$$

When these equations are solved, we derive

$$\hbar_0 = \frac{2(\kappa^2+1) + 2\sqrt{\kappa^4-\kappa^2+1}}{3}, \quad \hbar_1 = 0, \quad \hbar_2 = -2\kappa^2, \quad \lambda = \rho + 4\sqrt{\kappa^4-\kappa^2+1},$$

or

$$\hbar_0 = \frac{2(\kappa^2+1) - 2\sqrt{\kappa^4-\kappa^2+1}}{3}, \quad \hbar_1 = 0, \quad \hbar_2 = -2\kappa^2, \quad \lambda = \rho - 4\sqrt{\kappa^4-\kappa^2+1},$$

Thus, Equation (8), by using (27), has the solution

$$\mathcal{Y}(\xi) = \frac{2(\kappa^2+1) + 2\sqrt{\kappa^4-\kappa^2+1}}{3} - 2\kappa^2 sn^2(\xi,\kappa),$$

or

$$\mathcal{Y}(\xi) = \frac{2(\kappa^2+1) - 2\sqrt{\kappa^4-\kappa^2+1}}{3} - 2\kappa^2 sn^2(\xi,\kappa).$$

Hence, the solutions of SKPE-BD (1) is

$$\mathcal{R}(x,y,t) = [\frac{2(\kappa^2+1) + 2\sqrt{\kappa^4-\kappa^2+1}}{3} - 2\kappa^2 sn^2(\xi,\kappa)]e^{[-\gamma W(t) - \frac{1}{2}\gamma^2 t]}, \tag{29}$$

where $\xi = \frac{1}{\beta}(x + \frac{1}{\Gamma(\beta)})^\beta + \frac{1}{\beta}(y + \frac{1}{\Gamma(\beta)})^\beta - (\rho + 4\sqrt{\kappa^4-\kappa^2+1})t$, or

$$\mathcal{R}(x,y,t) = [\frac{2(\kappa^2+1) - 2\sqrt{\kappa^4-\kappa^2+1}}{3} - 2\kappa^2 sn^2(\xi,\kappa)]e^{[-\gamma W(t) - \frac{1}{2}\gamma^2 t]}, \tag{30}$$

where $\xi = \frac{1}{\beta}(x + \frac{1}{\Gamma(\beta)})^\beta + \frac{1}{\beta}(y + \frac{1}{\Gamma(\beta)})^\beta - (\rho - 4\sqrt{\kappa^4-\kappa^2+1})t$. If $\kappa \to 1$, then Equation (29) changes to

$$\mathcal{R}(x,y,t) = 2\text{sech}^2(\xi)e^{[-\gamma W(t) - \frac{1}{2}\gamma^2 t]}, \tag{31}$$

or

$$\mathcal{R}(x,y,t) = [\frac{2}{3} - 2\tanh^2(\xi)]e^{[-\gamma W(t) - \frac{1}{2}\gamma^2 t]}. \tag{32}$$

In a similar way, we can replace sn in (27) by cn to obtain the solutions of Equation (8) as follows:

$$\mathcal{Y}(\zeta) = [\frac{2\sqrt{\kappa^4 - \kappa^2 + 1} - 2(2\kappa^2 - 1)}{3} + 2\kappa^2 cn^2(\zeta, \kappa)].$$

Therefore, the solutions of the SKPE-BD (1) is

$$\mathcal{R}(x,y,t) = [\frac{2\sqrt{\kappa^4 - \kappa^2 + 1} - 2(2\kappa^2 - 1)}{3} + 2\kappa^2 cn^2(\zeta, \kappa)]e^{[-\gamma \mathcal{W}(t) - \frac{1}{2}\gamma^2 t]}. \quad (33)$$

where $\zeta = \frac{1}{\beta}(x + \frac{1}{\Gamma(\beta)})^\beta + \frac{1}{\beta}(y + \frac{1}{\Gamma(\beta)})^\beta - (\rho + 4\sqrt{\kappa^4 - \kappa^2 + 1})t$. If $\kappa \to 1$, then the solutions (33) takes the form

$$\mathcal{R}(x,y,t) = [2\text{sech}^2(\zeta)]e^{[-\gamma \mathcal{W}(t) - \frac{1}{2}\gamma^2 t]}. \quad (34)$$

4. The Effect of the Wiener Process and Beta Derivative

Here, the impact of SWP and BD on the analytical solutions of the SKPE-BD (1) is discussed. We illustrate the behavior of these solutions through a number of graphs. For different γ (noise strength), we generate certain figures for some found solutions including Equations (29) and (31). First, let us define the parameters $\rho = 1$ and $\kappa = 0.5$. Also, let $t \in [0,2]$ and $x \in [0,4]$.

First the beta derivative effects: In Figures 1 and 2, if $\gamma = 0$, we notice that the profile of the graphs is pressed as the value of β decreases:

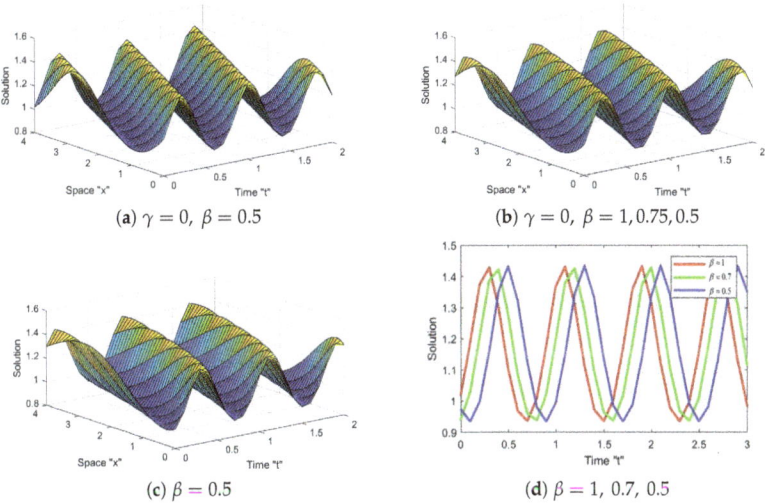

Figure 1. (a–c) Display of 3D-graph of Equation (29) with $\gamma = 0$ and several values of $\beta = 1, 0.75, 0.5$, and (d) shows 2D-graph of Equation (29) with several values of $\beta = 1, 0.75, 0.5$.

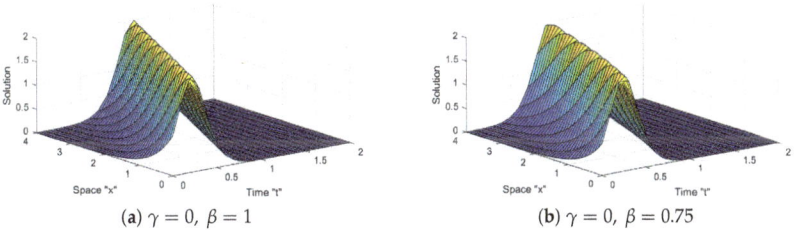

Figure 2. Cont.

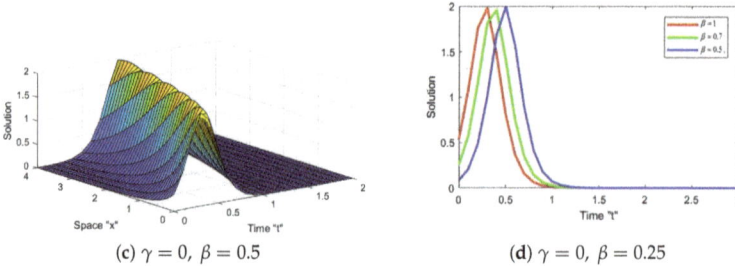

(c) $\gamma = 0$, $\beta = 0.5$ (d) $\gamma = 0$, $\beta = 0.25$

Figure 2. (a–c) Display of 3D-graph of Equation (31) with $\gamma = 0$ and several values of $\beta = 1, 0.75, 0.5$, and (d) shows 2D-graph of Equation (31) for several values of $\beta = 1, 0.75, 0.5$.

We deduced from Figures 1 and 2 that no overlap exists between the contours of the solutions. Additionally, the surface moves to the right as the order of the beta derivative decreases.

Second the noise effects:

In Figure 3, the surface is not flat and contains various imperfections when $\gamma = 0$ (i.e., there is no noise).

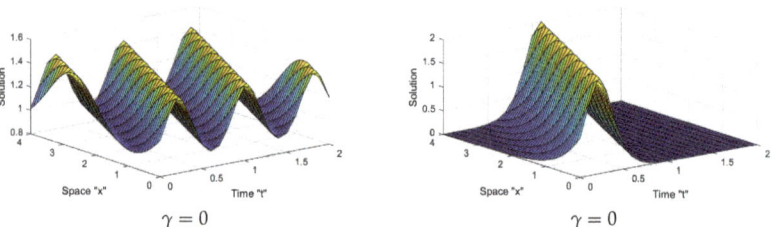

$\gamma = 0$ $\gamma = 0$

Figure 3. Diplay of 3D-profile of solution $\mathcal{R}(x, y, t)$ in Equations (29) and (31).

Meanwhile, we can see in Figures 4 and 5, after small movement patterns, the surface becomes more flat:

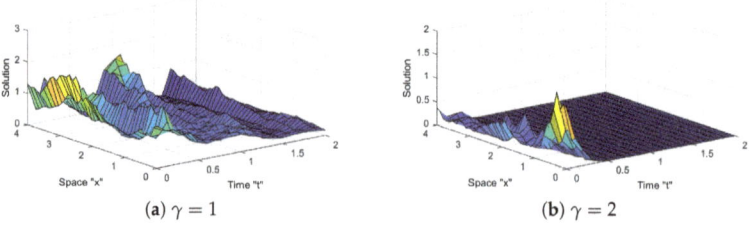

(a) $\gamma = 1$ (b) $\gamma = 2$

Figure 4. Display of 3D-profile of solution $\mathcal{R}(x, y, t)$ in Equation (29) for various $\gamma = 1, 2$.

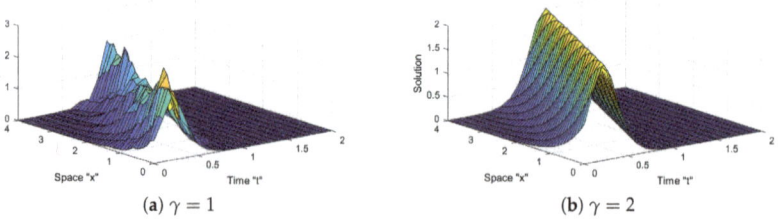

(a) $\gamma = 1$ (b) $\gamma = 2$

Figure 5. Diplay of 3D-profile of solution $\mathcal{R}(x, y, t)$ in Equation (31) for various $\gamma = 1, 2$.

In the end, we can deduce from Figures 3–5 that several solutions exist when noise is disregarded (i.e., at $\gamma = 0$), such as periodic solutions, kink solutions, and others. After minor transit patterns, the surface becomes significantly flattened when noise occurs and its intensity is increased by $\gamma = 1, 2$. This demonstrates that the multiplicative white noise has an impact on the SKPE-BD solutions and stabilizes them at zero.

5. Discussion and Physical Meaning

In this paper, we take into consideration stochastic Kadomtsev–Petviashvili equation with beta-derivative (SKPE-BD). Finding an exact stochastic solution to the KP equation is a challenging task due to its nonlinearity and complexity. Here, we applied two methods, the RE-Method and JEF-Method, to attain the exact solutions for this equation. The first method provided solutions in the form of trigonometric, hyperbolic, and rational functions, while the second method gave elliptic solutions. Additionally, the specific characteristics of the stochastic term play a crucial role in the effect it has on the solution. Overall, understanding the stochastic effects is essential for accurately modeling and analyzing systems in the presence of uncertainty. The obtained solutions provide insights into the behavior of waves in different physical systems and can aid in the development of innovative technologies. They serve as foundational tools for advancing our understanding of nonlinear wave phenomena and can lead to significant advancements in fields such as plasma physics, fluid dynamics, and engineering.

6. Conclusions

In the current study, the stochastic (2 + 1)-dimensional Kadomtsev–Petviashvili equation with beta derivative (SKPE-BD) was derived. By employing two distinct methods such as the Riccati equation and Jacobi elliptic function, we obtained the exact solutions of SKPE-BD (1). Due to the importance of KP in the field of fluid dynamics and plasma physics, the acquired solutions are important for illustrating a wide range of intriguing and complex physical phenomena. Finally, the MATLAB tool was applied to illustrate the effect of SWP and BD on the obtained solutions of the SKPE-BD (1). We deduced that the beta-derivative shifted the surface to the left when the fractional-order derivative increased and the Wiener process stabilized the solutions at zero.

Author Contributions: Data curation, F.M.A.-A. and W.W.M.; formal analysis, W.W.M., F.M.A.-A. and C.C.; funding acquisition, F.M.A.-A.; methodology, C.C.; project administration, W.W.M.; software, W.W.M.; supervision, C.C.; visualization, F.M.A.-A.; writing—original draft, F.M.A.-A.; writing—review and editing, W.W.M. and C.C. All authors have read and agreed to the published version of the manuscript.

Funding: Princess Nourah bint Abdulrahman University Researcher Supporting Project number (PNURSP2023R 273).

Data Availability Statement: Not applicable.

Acknowledgments: Princess Nourah bint Abdulrahman University Researcher Supporting Project number (PNURSP2023R 273), Princess Nourah bint Abdulrahman University, Riyadh, Saudi Arabia.

Conflicts of Interest: The authors declare no conflict of interest.

References

1. Yuste, S.B.; Acedo, L.; Lindenberg, K. Reaction front in an $A + B \to C$ reaction–subdiffusion process. *Phys. Rev. E* **2004**, *69*, 036126. [CrossRef] [PubMed]
2. Benson, D.A.; Wheatcraft, S.W.; Meerschaert, M.M. The fractional-order governing equation of Lévy motion. *Water Resour.* **2000**, *36*, 1413–1423. [CrossRef]
3. Al-Askar, F.M.; Mohammed, W.W.; Alshammari M. Impact of Brownian Motion on the Analytical Solutions of the Space-Fractional Stochastic Approximate Long Water Wave Equation. *Symmetry* **2022**, *14*, 740. [CrossRef]
4. Niazi, A.U.K.; Iqbal, N.; Mohammed, W.W. Optimal control of nonlocal fractional evolution equations in the a-norm of order (1,2). *Adv. Differ. Equ.* **2021**, *2021*, 142. [CrossRef]

5. Shah, N.A. El-Zahar, E.R. Akgul, A.; Khan, A.; Kafle, J. Analysis of fractional-order regularized long-wave models via a novel transform. *J. Funct. Spaces* **2022**, *2022*, 2754507. [CrossRef]
6. Shah, N.A.; Agarwal, P.; Chung, J.D.; El-Zahar, E.R.; Hamed, Y.S. Analysis of Optical Solitons for Nonlinear Schrodinger Equation with Detuning Term by Iterative Transform Method. *Symmetry* **2020**, *12*, 1850. [CrossRef]
7. Shah, N.A.; Ahammad, N.A.; Vieru, D.; Yook, S.J.; Alrabaiah, H. Analytical solutions for time-fractional diffusion equation with heat absorption in spherical domains. *Ain Shams Eng. J.* **2023**, *14*, 102031. [CrossRef]
8. Wang, M.L.; Li, X.Z.; Zhang, J.L. The (G'/G)-expansion method and travelling wave solutions of nonlinear evolution equations in mathematical physics. *Phys. Lett. A* **2008**, *372*, 417–423. [CrossRef]
9. Zhang, H. New application of the (G'/G)-expansion method. *Commun. Nonlinear Sci. Numer. Simul.* **2009**, *14*, 3220–3225. [CrossRef]
10. Zafar, A.; Ali, K.K.; Raheel, M.; Jafar, N.; Nisar, K.S. Soliton solutions to the DNA Peyrard-Bishop equation with beta-derivative via three distinctive approaches. *Eur. Phys. J. Plus* **2020**, *135*, 726. [CrossRef]
11. Ewees, A.A.; Abd Elaziz, M.; Al-Qaness, M.A.A.; Khalil, H.A.; Kim, S. Improved Artificial Bee Colony Using Sine-Cosine Algorithm for Multi-Level Thresholding Image Segmentation. *IEEE Access* **2020**, *8*, 26304–26315. [CrossRef]
12. Wazwaz, A.M. A sine-cosine method for handling nonlinear wave equations. *Math. Comput. Model.* **2004**, *40*, 499–508. [CrossRef]
13. Yan, C. A simple transformation for nonlinear waves. *Phys. Lett. A* **1996** *224*, 77–84. [CrossRef]
14. Khan, K.; Akbar, M.A. The $exp(-\mathcal{R}(\varsigma))$-expansion method for finding travelling wave solutions of Vakhnenko-Parkes equation. *Int. J. Dyn. Syst. Differ. Equ.* **2014**, *5*, 72–83.
15. Sadat, R.; Kassem, M.M. Lie Analysis and Novel Analytical Solutions for the Time-Fractional Coupled Whitham–Broer–Kaup Equations. *Int. J. Appl. Comput. Math.* **2019**, *5*, 28. [CrossRef]
16. Mohammed, W.W.; Iqbal, N. Impact of the same degenerate additive noise on a coupled system of fractional space diffusion equations. *Fractals* **2022**, *30*, 2240033. [CrossRef]
17. Mohammed, W.W. Stochastic amplitude equation for the stochastic generalized Swift–Hohenberg equation. *J. Egypt. Math. Soc.* **2015**, *23*, 482–489. [CrossRef]
18. Wazwaz, A.M. The tanh method: Exact solutions of the Sine–Gordon and Sinh–Gordon equations. *Appl. Math. Comput.* **2005**, *167*, 1196–1210. [CrossRef]
19. Malfliet, W.; Hereman, W. The tanh method. I. Exact solutions of nonlinear evolution and wave equations. *Phys. Scr.* **1996**, *54*, 563–568. [CrossRef]
20. Arafa, A.; Elmahdy, G. Application of residual power series method to fractional coupled physical equations arising in fluids flow. *Int. J. Differ. Equ.* **2018**, *2018*, 7692849. [CrossRef]
21. Yan, Z.L. Abundant families of Jacobi elliptic function solutions of the dimensional integrable Davey-Stewartson-type equation via a new method. *Chaos Solitons Fractals* **2003**, *18*, 299–309. [CrossRef]
22. Atangana, A.; Goufo, E.F.D. Extension of matched asymptotic method to fractional boundary layers problems. *Math. Probl. Eng.* **2014**, *2014*, 107535. [CrossRef]
23. Arnold, L. *Random Dynamical Systems*; Springer: New York, NY, USA, 1998.
24. Imkeller, P.; Monahan, A.H. Conceptual stochastic climate models. *Stoch. Dyn.* **2002**, *2*, 311–326. [CrossRef]
25. Mohammed, W.W. Fast-diffusion limit for reaction-diffusion equations with degenerate multiplicative and additive noise. *J. Dyn. Differ. Equ.* **2021**, *33*, 577–592. [CrossRef]
26. Kadomtzev, B.B.; Petviashvili, V.I. On stability of solitary waves in weakly dispersive media. *C. R. Acad. Sci. USSR* **1970**, *192*, 753.
27. Tsikis1, E.K.; Raychaudhuri, S.; Gabl, E.F.; Lonngren, K.E. On the excitation of linear and nonlinear ion-acoustic waves in a double plasma machine. *Plasma Phys. Control. Fusion* **1985**, *27*, 419. [CrossRef]
28. Wazwaz, A.M. New compactons, solitons and periodic solutions for nonlinear variants of the KdV and the KP equations. *Chaos Solitons Fractals* **2004**, *22*, 249–260. [CrossRef]
29. Wazwaz, A.M. Multiple-soliton solutions for a (3 + 1)-dimensional generalized KP equation. *Commun. Nonlinear Sci. Numer. Simul.* **2012**, *17*, 491–495. [CrossRef]
30. Hereman, W.; Nuseir, A. Symbolic methods to construct exact solutions of nonlinear partial differential equations. *Math. Comput. Simul.* **1997**, *43*, 13–27. [CrossRef]
31. Pandir, Y.; Gurefe, Y.; Misirli, E. Classification of exact solutions to the generalized Kadomtsev–Petviashvili equation. *Phys. Scr.* **2013**, *87*, 025003. [CrossRef]
32. Alam, M.N.; Tunc, C. New solitary wave structures to the (2 + 1)-dimensional KD and KP equations with spatio-temporal dispersion. *J. King Saud Univ. Sci.* **2020**, *32*, 3400–3409. [CrossRef]
33. Peng, Y.; Krishnan, E.V. Exact travelling wave solutions to the (3 + 1) D Kadomtsev-Petviashvili equation. *Acta Phys. Pol.* **2005**, *108*, 421–428. [CrossRef]
34. Seadawy, A.R.; El-Rashidy, K. Dispersive solitary wave solutions of Kadomtsev–Petviashvili and modified Kadomtsev-Petviashvili dynamical equations in unmagnetized dust plasma. *Results Phys.* **2018**, *8*, 1216–1222. [CrossRef]
35. Al-Askar, F.M.; Cesarano, C.; Mohammed, W.W. Abundant Solitary Wave Solutions for the Boiti–Leon–Manna–Pempinelli Equation with M-Truncated Derivative. *Axioms* **2023**, *12*, 466. [CrossRef]

36. Fan, E.; Zhang, J. Applications of the Jacobi elliptic function method to special-type nonlinear equations. *Phys. Lett. A* **2002**, *305*, 383–392. [CrossRef]
37. Duan, W.S.; Shi, Y.R.; Hong, X.R. Theoretical study of resonance of the Kadomtsev–Petviashvili equation. *Phys. Lett. A* **2004**, *323*, 89–94. [CrossRef]

Disclaimer/Publisher's Note: The statements, opinions and data contained in all publications are solely those of the individual author(s) and contributor(s) and not of MDPI and/or the editor(s). MDPI and/or the editor(s) disclaim responsibility for any injury to people or property resulting from any ideas, methods, instructions or products referred to in the content.

Article

Study of Time-Fractional Nonlinear Model Governing Unsteady Flow of Polytropic Gas

Brajesh K. Singh [1], Haci Mehmet Baskonus [2,*], Neetu Singh [1,3], Mukesh Gupta [1] and D. G. Prakasha [4]

1 School of Physical and Decision Sciences, Department of Mathematics, Babasaheb Bhimrao Ambedkar University Lucknow, Lucknow 226025, India
2 Department of Mathematics and Science Education, Faculty of Education, Harran University, Sanliurfa 63100, Turkey
3 Department of Applied Sciences and Humanities, Kendriya Vidyalaya NIT, Banda 210001, India
4 Department of Mathematics, Davangere University, Davangere 577007, India
* Correspondence: hmbaskonus@gmail.com

Abstract: The present study is concerned with studying the dynamical behavior of two space-dimensional nonlinear time-fractional models governing the unsteady-flow of polytropic-gas (in brief, pGas) that occurred in cosmology and astronomy. For this purpose, two efficient hybrid methods so-called optimal homotopy analysis $\mathbb{J}$-transform method ($_O$HAJTM) and $\mathbb{J}$-variational iteration transform method ($\mathbb{J}$-VITM) have been adopted. The $_O$HAJTM is the hybrid method, where optimal-homotopy analysis method ($_O$HAM) is utilized after implementing the properties of $\mathbb{J}$-transform ($\mathbb{J}$T), and in $\mathbb{J}$-VITM is the $\mathbb{J}$-transform-based variational iteration method. Banach's fixed point approach is adopted to analyze the convergence of these methods. It is demonstrated that $\mathbb{J}$-VITM is T-stable, and the evaluated dynamics of pGas are described in terms of Mittag–Leffler functions. The proposed evaluation confirms that the implemented methods perform better for the referred model equation of pGas. In addition, for a given iteration, the proposed behavior via $_O$HAJTM performs better in producing more accurate behavior in comparison to $\mathbb{J}$-VITM and the methods introduced recently.

Keywords: caputo derivative; polytropic gas; $\mathbb{J}$-transform; variational calculus; optimal homotopy analysis method

MSC: 35R11; 65F10; 26A33

Citation: Singh, B.K.; Baskonus, H.M.; Singh, N.; Gupta, M.; Prakasha, D.G. Study of Time-Fractional Nonlinear Model Governing Unsteady Flow of Polytropic Gas. *Axioms* **2023**, *12*, 285. https://doi.org/10.3390/axioms12030285

Academic Editor: Giovanni Nastasi

Received: 5 December 2022
Revised: 2 February 2023
Accepted: 20 February 2023
Published: 8 March 2023

Copyright: © 2023 by the authors. Licensee MDPI, Basel, Switzerland. This article is an open access article distributed under the terms and conditions of the Creative Commons Attribution (CC BY) license (https://creativecommons.org/licenses/by/4.0/).

1. Introduction

Fractional calculus (FC) is one of the growing/youthful branches of applied mathematics that is a generalized concept of differential equations from an integer order to positive fractional order. It is a preferred selection in modeling complicated physical realistic situations marked by hereditary/memory behaviors. It is because of the nonlocal nature of these operators [1,2]. FC is a useful tool for showcasing the transition of highly complicated nonlinear dynamics with long-term memory effects. In contrast to ordinary derivatives, identifying fractional order derivatives of a function requires its entire history [3]. This nonlocal property, referred as the memory consequence, allows it even more convenient to characterize real-world physical systems using differential equations with fractional derivatives. In recent decades, investigating the evolution of fractional order systems, such as chaos, complexity, stability, bifurcation, and synchronization has emerged as an exciting area of research in areas of research and development [4–7], and the fractional partial differential equations (FPDEs) are more appropriate for modeling numerous realistic situations such as in optics, earthquake propagation, population growth, volcanic eruption, signal processing, the process of reaction/diffusion, in electrical networking, control theory, hydrology, astrophysics, and in biological systems [8–13].

To know about the behavior of a model, one must know about its solution behaviors, and many physical phenomena can be represented by a suitable model in terms of the nonlinear fractional partial differential equations (NFPDEs), and the evaluation of the solution behaviors of such type of model is quite difficult, and so the study of these NFPDEs is of vital importance. In the last three decades, various rigorous new techniques are investigated to elucidate a system of NFPDEs. In consequence, Liao [14] developed a rigorous technique so-called homotopy analysis method for studying many types of nonlinear partial differential equations (NPDEs) like differential-integral/algebraic equations/partial differential equations/ordinary differential equations and associated coupled systems or the fractional models of the above-mentioned types equations. Differ from all the perturbation/nonperturbation approaches for nonlinear differential equations (NDEs), HAM generates an effective/easy technique to assure the convergent solutions by suitable selection of different base functions (see [9,13,15] and inside articles for more details).

In this article, the fractional order model of gas-dynamic equations administering the development of the two-space dimensional unsteady flow of an ideal gas has been studied. Write $P = K\rho^{1+(1/\kappa)}$, where $\rho = U/V \to$ energy density, $U \to$ total energy of the gas, $V \to$ container volume, $\kappa \to$ polytropic index, and $K \to$ a constant. In the sequel, degenerate electron gas and adiabatic gas are two instances of such types of gases. The investigation of polytropic gases identified an essential job in cosmology and astronomy [16], and its behavior is found dark energy-like [11], and the special case of the pGas model has been utilized in astrophysics in stellar wind and accretion problems. In recent years, the researchers generalized the model of gas-dynamic equations governing the advancement of unsteady progression of an ideal-gas of fraction order [17,18]. We need both evolution equations for ρ and P due to the energy density and ρ and polytropic index. The value of $P = K\rho^{1+(1/k)}$ in the below system (1) is due to the dynamics of a strongly nonlocal reaction–diffusion population model [19]. The fractional model of equations of a pGas [15,20] given below in (1) via two hybrid techniques, namely - $_0$HAJTM and J-VITM

$$\begin{aligned}
&_\tau\mathcal{D}_C^\alpha \wp_1 + \wp_1 \frac{\partial \wp_1}{\partial z_1} + \wp_2 \frac{\partial \wp_1}{\partial z_2} + \frac{1}{\rho}\frac{\partial P}{\partial z_1} = 0 \\
&_\tau\mathcal{D}_C^\alpha \wp_2 + \wp_1 \frac{\partial \wp_2}{\partial z_1} + \wp_2 \frac{\partial \wp_2}{\partial z_2} + \frac{1}{\rho}\frac{\partial P}{\partial z_2} = 0 \\
&_\tau\mathcal{D}_C^\alpha \rho + \wp_1 \frac{\partial \rho}{\partial z_1} + \wp_2 \frac{\partial \rho}{\partial z_2} + \rho\frac{\partial \wp_1}{\partial z_1} + \rho\frac{\partial \wp_2}{\partial z_2} = 0 \\
&_\tau\mathcal{D}_C^\alpha P + \wp_1 \frac{\partial P}{\partial z_1} + \wp_2 \frac{\partial P}{\partial z_2} + \Omega P\frac{\partial \wp_1}{\partial z_1} + \Omega P\frac{\partial \wp_2}{\partial z_2} = 0
\end{aligned} \quad (1)$$

with initial condition

$$\wp_1(z_{1,2},0) = f_1(z_{1,2}), \quad \wp_2(z_{1,2},0) = f_2(z_{1,2}), \quad \rho(z_{1,2},0) = f_3(z_{1,2}), \quad P(z_{1,2},0) = f_4(z_{1,2}), \quad z_{1,2} = (z_1, z_2),$$

where $\wp_1(z_{1,2}, \tau)$ and $\wp_2(z_{1,2}, \tau) \to$ velocity components, $\rho(z_{1,2}, \tau)$ is the density, $P(z_{1,2}, \tau) \to$ pressure and $\Omega \to$ ratio of specific heat and refers adiabatic index. $_\tau\mathcal{D}_C^\alpha(\cdot)$ is the Caputo-fractional differential operator (C-FDO) as defined below:

Definition 1 ([1,2]). *The C-FDO $_\tau\mathcal{D}_C^\alpha \varphi(z_{1,2}, \tau)$ of order $\kappa - 1 < \alpha \leq \kappa$ of a function $\varphi \in C_\mu$, $\mu \geq -1$ is defined by $_\tau\mathcal{D}_C^\kappa \varphi(z_{1,2}, \tau) := \frac{\partial^\kappa \varphi(z_{1,2},\tau)}{\partial \tau^\kappa}$ and*

$_\tau\mathcal{D}_C^\alpha \varphi(z_{1,2}, \tau) = {_\tau\mathcal{D}_C^{-(\kappa-\alpha)}} {_\tau\mathcal{D}_C^\kappa} \varphi(z_{1,2}, \tau) = \frac{1}{\Gamma(\kappa-\alpha)}\int_0^\tau (\tau-\epsilon)^{\kappa-(\alpha+1)}\frac{\partial^\kappa \varphi(z_{1,2},\epsilon)}{\partial \epsilon^\kappa} d\epsilon$, *whenever* $\kappa - 1 < \alpha < \kappa$

In addition, let $_\tau\mathcal{D}_C^{-\alpha}\varphi(z_{1,2}, \tau)$ is the αth order Riemann–Liouville fractional integral operator (RLFIO) on φ. Then

$$_\tau\mathcal{D}_C^0 \varphi(z_{1,2}, \tau) := \varphi(z_{1,2}, \tau)$$

and

$${}_\tau \mathcal{D}_C^{-\alpha} \varphi(z_{1,2}, \tau) = \frac{1}{\Gamma(\alpha)} \int_0^\tau (\tau - \epsilon)^{\alpha-1} \varphi(z_{1,2}, \epsilon) d\epsilon, \quad \alpha > 0, \quad \tau > 0.$$

The readers are referred to [1,2,21,22] for more details on fractional calculus. The researchers have beendeveloped/ implemented various rigorous methods for studying behaviors of various models occurred in terms of NFPDEs (see [22–37]). The behavior of the integer order system of the referred model equations was analyzed using distinct techniques like Adomian decomposition method (ADM) [38], variational iteration technique (VIT) [17], and HAM [18]. Recently, numerical simulation and behavior of fractional order system have been investigated by fractional natural decomposition method (NDM) [20] and q-homotopy analysis transform method (q-HATM) [15]. In the present work, the novel integral transform called $\mathbb{J}$-transform is implemented in combination with two efficient techniques, namely oHAM and VIM to investigate the nonlinear time-fractional model governing unsteady flow of polytropic. The main strategy of our work in considering the $\mathbb{J}$-transform is that it is the generalized form of the Laplace transform and the Elzaki transform. Also, in case of the $\mathbb{J}$-transform, we will get the two-dimensional frequency domain, which will give us more degree of freedom to analyze the respective solutions. The proposed fractional model interprets the most realistic behavior for considered fractional orders and which states the originality of the paper. The relative error solutions are presented in terms of logarithmic plots for different fractional orders. We have achieved the faster rate of convergence of the obtained series solution to the exact solution with the help of optimal value of the convergence control parameter.

The rest part of the work is structured as follows: Section 2 reports some basic literature to complete understanding of the work. In Section 3, we report the basic procedure for $\mathbb{J}$-VITM and its stability/convergence analysis. In Section 4, we report the basic procedure for $_O$HA$\mathbb{J}$TM and its convergence analysis. Validity/effectiveness/efficiency of the aforesaid methods is tested in Section 5 by considering test examples of the fractional model equation of pGas. At last, concluding remark is reported in Section 6.

2. Basic Concepts

Banach's fixed point approach and $\mathbb{J}$T-based basics are revisited to understand the rest part of the study. Let us denote $\Pi = (\Pi, d)$ as a metric space.

Definition 2 ([39]). *Let* T *be a contraction on metric space* Π*; this is a map that satisfies the following condition*

$$d(Ty, Ty_1) \leq \gamma d(y, y_1) \quad y, y_1 \in \Pi, \tag{2}$$

for some positive real $\gamma \in \mathbb{R}^+$ *less than unity, i.e.,* $0 < \gamma < 1$*, where* $\mathbb{R}^+$ *be set of positive reals.*

Theorem 1 (Banach's Fixed-Point Theorem [39])**.** *A contraction* T *over complete space* Π *always has a unique fixed point.*

In the sequel, if $\{y_\lambda\}_{\lambda=1}^\infty$ is a iterative sequence formulated via the iterative procedure $y_{\lambda+1} = Ty_\lambda$ with $y_0 \in \Pi$ (arbitrary) such that y_λ approaches the unique fixed point y as $\lambda \to \infty$, the error estimates are evaluated as follows

$d(y_\lambda, y) \leq \frac{\gamma^\lambda}{1-\gamma} d(y_0, y_1)$, (prior-etimate), and

and

$d(y_\lambda, y) \leq \frac{\gamma}{1-\gamma} d(y_{\lambda-1}, y_\lambda)$. (posterior-estimate).

Theorem 2 ([40,41])**.** *A self-map* T *defined over* Π *(Banach space) is termed as Picard T-stable if the condition* $d(Ty, Ty_1) \leq \kappa d(y, Ty) + \gamma d(y, y_1)$*,* $\forall y, y_1 \in \Pi$ *holds true for some non-negative real* κ*, and* γ *with* $0 \leq \gamma < 1$*.*

J-Transform and Its Properties

The transformation

$$\mathbb{J}[\psi(\tau)](s,\vartheta) = \Psi(s,\vartheta) := \vartheta \int_0^\infty e^{\left(\frac{-s\tau}{\vartheta}\right)} \psi(\tau) d\tau, \qquad (3)$$

is referred to as $\mathbb{J}$-transform of $\psi \in \mathcal{F}$ (provided it exists), s, ϑ are transformed variables, and $\mathcal{F}$ is the set functions of exponential order satisfying the following conditions

$$\mathcal{F} = \left\{ \psi : \exists m_1, m_2 > 0, 0 < \Gamma < \infty \text{ such that } |\psi(\tau)| \leq \Gamma \exp\left(\frac{|\tau|}{r_j}\right), \text{ if } \tau \in (-1)^j \times [0,\infty) \right\},$$

The properties of $\mathbb{J}T$ are listed is the following

Lemma 1 (Properties of $\mathbb{J}T$, [42]). *Let $\mathcal{G}(z,s,\vartheta)$ and $\Psi(z,s,\vartheta)$ are $\mathbb{J}T$ of $g(z,\tau), \psi(z,\tau) \in \mathcal{F}$, respectively. Then*

(a) $\mathbb{J}\left[\frac{\tau^{\kappa\alpha+\lambda}}{\Gamma(1+\lambda+\kappa\alpha)}\right](s,\vartheta) = \frac{\vartheta^{\kappa\alpha+\lambda+2}}{s^{\kappa\alpha+\lambda+1}}, \quad \lambda, \kappa = 0,1,2,\ldots$

(b) $\mathbb{J}\left[\frac{\partial^\kappa g(z,\tau)}{\partial \tau^\kappa}\right](s,\vartheta) = \frac{s^\kappa}{\vartheta^\kappa}\mathcal{G}(z,s,\vartheta) - \sum_{\ell=1}^{\kappa}\frac{s^{\kappa-\ell}}{\vartheta^{\kappa-(\ell+1)}}\frac{\partial^{\ell-1}g(z,0^+)}{\partial \tau^{\ell-1}}, \quad \kappa \geq 1;$

(c) $\mathbb{J}[A_1 g(z,\tau) + A_2 \psi(z,\tau)](s,\vartheta) = A_1 \mathcal{G}(z,s,\vartheta) + A_2 \Psi(z,s,\vartheta);$

(d) $\mathbb{J}[(g*\psi)(z,\tau)](s,\vartheta) = \frac{1}{\vartheta}\mathcal{G}(z,s,\vartheta)\Psi(z,s,\vartheta)$, where $g * \psi$ is the convolution of g and ψ.

The properties of $\mathbb{J}T$ for fractional calculus [31] that we use to study the behavior of referred model equation is mentioned below

Lemma 2. *If $\Theta(z_{1,2},s,\vartheta)$ is the $\mathbb{J}$-transform of $\psi(z_{1,2},\tau) \in \mathcal{F}$, then*

(i) $\mathbb{J}[_\tau \mathcal{D}_C^{-\alpha}\psi(z_{1,2},\tau)](s,\vartheta) = \frac{\vartheta^\alpha}{s^\alpha}\Psi(z_{1,2},s,\vartheta),$

(ii) $\mathbb{J}[_\tau \mathcal{D}_C^\alpha \psi(z_{1,2},\tau)](s,\vartheta) = \left(\frac{s}{\vartheta}\right)^\alpha \Psi(z_{1,2},s,\vartheta) - \sum_{\ell=1}^\kappa \frac{s^{\alpha-\ell}}{\vartheta^{\alpha-(\ell+1)}}\frac{\partial^{\ell-1}\psi(z,0^+)}{\partial \tau^{\ell-1}}, \kappa-1 < \alpha \leq \kappa \in \mathbb{N}.$

where $_\tau \mathcal{D}_C^\alpha \psi(z_{1,2},\tau)$, $_\tau \mathcal{D}_C^{-\alpha}\psi(z_{1,2},\tau)$ denote C-FDO and Riemann–Liouville FIO of ψ of order α.

Proof. The proof is reported in [31]. □

3. Procedure of Variational Iteration Technique (VIT)

The variational theory-based technique so-called VIT is an efficient technique introduced by He [43] for the study of various models that occurred in terms of classical differential equations. After He's seminal work, VIT and its modified forms has been introduced for studying various types of nonlinear problems of integer orders [44–47] and fractional order [47–51].

Consider time-fractional nonlinear partial differential equation (TF-NPDE).

$$_\tau \mathcal{D}_C^\alpha \psi(z_{1,2},\tau) + \mathcal{T}\psi(z_{1,2},\tau) = 0, \qquad \kappa-1 < \alpha \leq \kappa, \qquad (4)$$

where $z_{1,2} = (z_1, z_2)$ be space-variable of 2-dimensions, $_\tau \mathcal{D}_C^\alpha(\cdot)$ is Caputo FDO [23–25], $\mathcal{T}(\cdot)$ nonlinear differential operator involving linear operators and nonhomogeneous/source term as well, and $\kappa \in \mathbb{N}$.

The basic procedure of VIT for TF-NPDE, the correction functional of (4) in mVIT [47], is given via

$$\psi_{\lambda+1}(z_{1,2},\tau) = \psi_\lambda(z_{1,2},\tau) + \int_0^\tau \theta(\tau,\epsilon)[_\tau \mathcal{D}_C^\alpha \psi(z_{1,2},\epsilon) + \mathcal{T}\tilde{\psi}_\lambda(z_{1,2},\epsilon)]d\epsilon, \qquad (5)$$

where $\theta(\tau,\epsilon)$ refers to Lagrange multiplier to be determine, ψ_λ is λth-iteration solution, and $\tilde{\psi}_\lambda$ is the restricted variation [52]. The evaluation of the Lagrange multiplier is a tedious task in studying the behavior of TF-NPDE. On imposing optimality criteria to the functional as in (5), we have

$$\delta\psi_{\lambda+1}(z_{1,2},\tau) = \delta\psi_\lambda(z_{1,2},\tau) + \delta \int_0^t \theta(\tau,\epsilon) \,_\tau \mathcal{D}_C^\alpha \psi_\lambda(z_{1,2},\epsilon)d\epsilon = 0,$$

The evaluation of the Lagrange multiplier $\theta(\tau,\epsilon)$ in the above equation is tough for fraction case $(\alpha \neq \kappa)$ [51]. The implementation of the properties of an integral transform with variational theory [53,54] makes the evaluation procedure for finding the optimal value of the Lagrange multiplier easily.

3.1. Procedure of $\mathbb{J}$-VITM For NFPDEs

The $\mathbb{J}$-VITM is a hybrid method that is based on properties of $\mathbb{J}$T and variational theory (see [31]) that we implemented for studying nonlinear fractional partial differential equations (NFPDEs).

Impose $\mathbb{J}$T to NFPDEs (4) and adopt the property ${}_\tau\mathcal{D}_C^\alpha \psi(z_{1,2},\tau)$ of $\mathbb{J}$T from Theorem 2(ii), we have

$$\left(\frac{s}{\vartheta}\right)^\alpha \psi(z_{1,2},s,\vartheta) - \sum_{\ell=1}^\kappa \frac{s^{\alpha-\ell}}{\vartheta^{\alpha-(\ell+1)}} \frac{\partial^{\ell-1}\psi}{\partial \tau^{\ell-1}}\bigg|_{\tau=0} + \mathbb{J}[\mathcal{T}\tilde{\psi}_\lambda(z_{1,2},\epsilon)]\theta(s,\vartheta) = 0. \quad (6)$$

In sequel to modified variational iteration technique, correction functional for (6) constructed as

$$\psi_{\lambda+1}(z_{1,2},s,\vartheta) = \psi_\lambda(z_{1,2},s,\vartheta) + \theta(s,\vartheta)\left(\left(\frac{s}{\vartheta}\right)^\alpha \psi_\lambda(z_{1,2},s,\vartheta) - \sum_{\ell=1}^\kappa \frac{s^{\alpha-\ell}}{\vartheta^{\alpha-(\ell+1)}} \frac{\partial^{\ell-1}\psi_\lambda}{\partial \tau^{\ell-1}}\bigg|_{\tau=0}\right) \quad (7)$$
$$- \theta(s,\vartheta)\mathbb{J}[\tilde{\mathcal{T}}\psi_\lambda(z_{1,2},\tau)](s,\vartheta).$$

where $\tilde{\psi}_\lambda$ and $\tilde{\mathcal{T}}$ restricted variations, i.e., $\delta\tilde{\phi}_\lambda = 0$ and $\delta\tilde{\mathcal{T}} = 0$.

The variational operator δ to (7) with the above-mentioned property leads to

$$\delta\psi_{\lambda+1}(z_{1,2},s,\vartheta) = \delta\psi_\lambda(z_{1,2},s,\vartheta)\left(1+\theta(s,\vartheta)\left(\frac{s}{\vartheta}\right)^\alpha\right), \quad (8)$$

The optimality condition: $\delta\psi_{\lambda+1}(z_{1,2},s,\vartheta) = 0$ for (7) in (8) leads to the optimal value of the Lagrange multiplier $\theta(s,\vartheta) = -\left(\frac{\vartheta}{s}\right)^\alpha$. Thus, (7) reduces to

$$\psi_{\lambda+1}(z_{1,2},s,\vartheta) = \sum_{\ell=1}^\kappa \left(\frac{\vartheta^{\ell+1}}{s^\ell}\right) \frac{\partial^{\ell-1}\psi_\lambda}{\partial \tau^{\ell-1}}\bigg|_{\tau=0} - \left(\frac{\vartheta}{s}\right)^\alpha \mathbb{J}[\mathcal{T}\psi_\lambda(z_{1,2},\tau)](s,\vartheta). \quad (9)$$

The inverse $\mathbb{J}$T operator with (9) leads to

$$\psi_{\lambda+1}(z_{1,2},\tau) = T\psi_\lambda(z_{1,2},\tau), \quad \lambda = 0,1,2,\ldots \quad (10)$$

where

$T\psi_\lambda(z_{1,2},\tau) = \psi_\lambda^0(z_{1,2},\tau) - \mathbb{J}^{-1}\left[\left(\frac{\vartheta}{s}\right)^\alpha \mathbb{J}[\mathcal{T}\psi_\lambda(z_{1,2},\tau)](s,\vartheta)\right]$, and
$\psi_\lambda^0(z_{1,2},\tau) = \sum_{\ell=1}^\kappa \left(\frac{\tau^{\ell-1}}{\Gamma(\ell)}\right) \frac{\partial^{\ell-1}\psi_\lambda}{\partial \tau^{\ell-1}}\bigg|_{\tau=0}.$

it is the desired $(\lambda+1)$th iterative solution of NFPDEs (4), and when $\kappa=1$, the solution at $(\lambda+1)$th iteration read from (10) as

$$\psi_{\lambda+1}(z_{1,2},\tau) = T\psi_\lambda(z_{1,2},\tau) = \psi_\lambda(z_{1,2},0) - \mathbb{J}^{-1}\left[\left(\frac{\vartheta}{s}\right)^\alpha \mathbb{J}[\mathcal{T}\psi_\lambda(z_{1,2},\tau)](s,\vartheta)\right]. \quad (11)$$

3.2. Convergence and Stability Analysis of $\mathbb{J}$-VITM

The analysis of convergence and stability for the aforesaid $\mathbb{J}$-VITM is provided in the following theorem. For sake of convenience, we read ψ_n in place of $\psi_n(z_{1,2},\tau)$ throughout this section

Theorem 3 (Stability analysis). *Let a self-map* $T: \mathbf{B} \to \mathbf{B}$, *where* $(\mathbf{B}, \|\cdot\|)$ *is the Banach space; then, the iterative results via iteration formula (10) are:* $\psi_{\lambda+1}(X,\tau) = T\psi_\lambda(X,\tau)$ *is Picard T stable if* $\exists \eta_0 > 0$ *for which the following axioms hold true for every* τ.

(a) $\|\mathcal{T}(\psi_p) - \mathcal{T}(\psi_n)\| \leq \|\mathcal{T}(\psi_p - \psi_n)\| \leq \eta_0 \|\psi_p - \psi_n\|$

(b) $\theta = \eta_0 \left\|\frac{\tau^\alpha}{\Gamma(\alpha+1)}\right\| < 1.$

Proof. Let $p, n \in \mathbb{N}$. Then,

$$\begin{aligned} T\psi_p - T\psi_n &= \psi_p^0 - \psi_n^0 + \mathbb{J}^{-1}\left[\left(\frac{\vartheta}{s}\right)^\alpha \mathbb{J}[\mathcal{T}\psi_p](s,\vartheta)\right] - \mathbb{J}^{-1}\left[\left(\frac{\vartheta}{s}\right)^\alpha \mathbb{J}[\mathcal{T}\psi_n](s,\vartheta)\right], \\ &= \psi_p^0 - \psi_n^0 + \mathbb{J}^{-1}\left[\left(\frac{\vartheta}{s}\right)^\alpha \mathbb{J}[\mathcal{T}\psi_p - \mathcal{T}\psi_n](s,\vartheta)\right], \end{aligned} \quad (12)$$

as $\psi_p^0 = \psi_n^0$ at each iteration holds from the initial condition. Imposing norm to both sides of (12) with condition (a) leads to

$$\begin{aligned} \|T\psi_p - T\psi_n\| &\leq \mathbb{J}^{-1}\left[\left(\frac{\vartheta}{s}\right)^\alpha \mathbb{J}[\|\mathcal{T}\psi_p - \mathcal{T}\psi_n\|](s,\vartheta)\right] \\ &\leq \eta_0 \|\psi_p - \psi_n\| \left(\mathbb{J}^{-1}\left[\frac{\vartheta^{2+\alpha}}{s^\alpha}\right]\right) \leq \theta \|\psi_p - \psi_n\|, \end{aligned}$$

and this can be expressed in the following form

$$\|T\psi_p - T\psi_n\| \leq \beta\|\psi_p - T\psi_p\| + \theta\|\psi_p - \psi_n\|, \quad \text{for } \beta \geq 0 \quad (13)$$

which confirms that the proposed $\mathbb{J}$-VITM is Picard T stable whever $\theta < 1$ (see Theorem 2). □

Theorem 4 (Convergence analysis). *In a Banach space* $\mathbf{B} = (C[\Omega \times (0,T)], \|\cdot\|)$, *let* $\{\psi_n\}_1^\infty$ *be a sequence from the iteration procedure* (10): $\psi_{\lambda+1} = T\psi_\lambda$, *where T be associated self-map on* $\mathbf{B}$. *Then*

(a) $\{\psi_n\}_1^\infty$ *with* $\psi_0 \in \mathbf{B}$ *(initial value) is convergent.*
(b) *A unique fixed point exist for T in* $\mathbf{B}$.
(b) *In κth order iterative results, the error bounds as derived as*

$\|\psi - \psi_\kappa\| \leq \frac{\theta^\kappa}{1-\theta}\|\psi_1 - \psi_0\|$ (Prior-estimate of error),

and

$\|\psi - \psi_\kappa\| \leq \frac{1}{1-\theta}\|\psi_1 - \psi_0\|, \quad 0 \leq \theta < 1$ (posterior-error estimate)

Proof. For the complete proof please visit [31]. □

4. Basic Procedure of $_O$HA$\mathbb{J}$TM

The basic solution procedure of $_O$HA$\mathbb{J}$TM for NFPDEs (4) is derived in [31], is reported in the following. On operating $\mathbb{J}T$ to NFPDEs (4) with the help of the property of $\mathbb{J}T$ to get (6) that can be expressed as

$$\mathbb{J}[\psi(z_{1,2},\tau)](s,\vartheta) - \sum_{\ell=1}^\kappa \frac{\vartheta^{\ell+1}}{s^\ell}\frac{\partial^{\ell-1}\psi}{\partial\tau^{\ell-1}}\bigg|_{\tau=0} + \left(\frac{\vartheta}{s}\right)^\alpha \mathbb{J}[\mathcal{T}\tilde\psi_\lambda(z_{1,2},\tau)](s,\vartheta) = 0.$$

Set nonlinear operator as

$$\beth[\varphi(z_{1,2},\tau;\aleph)] = \mathbb{J}[\varphi(z_{1,2},\tau;\aleph)](s,\vartheta) - \sum_{\ell=1}^\kappa \frac{\vartheta^{\ell+1}}{s^\ell}\frac{\partial^{\ell-1}\psi}{\partial\tau^{\ell-1}}\bigg|_{\tau=0} + \left(\frac{\vartheta}{s}\right)^\alpha \mathbb{J}[\mathcal{T}\varphi(z_{1,2},\tau;\aleph)](s,\vartheta).$$

where $\varphi(z_{1,2},\tau;\aleph)$ is the real-valued map of $\aleph, z_{1,2}, \tau; \aleph \in [0,1] \to$ standard embedded-parameter.

The following zeroth-order deformation equation as in [12,14] is

$$(1-\aleph)\mathbb{J}[\varphi(z_{1,2},\tau;\aleph) - \psi_0(z_{1,2},\tau)](s,\vartheta) = \aleph\hbar H(z_{1,2},\tau)\beth[\varphi(z_{1,2},\tau;\aleph)], \quad (14)$$

where $\hbar \neq 0$, $H(z_{1,2}, \tau) \to$ is the auxiliary function/parameter, and $\psi_0(z_{1,2}, \tau) \to$ is the initial guess of $\psi(z_{1,2}, \tau)$. Remark that $_O$HAJTM have a merit in selecting auxiliary things in procedure.

For $\aleph = 01$,

$$\varphi(z_{1,2}, \tau; 0) = \psi(z_{1,2}, 0) \text{ and } \varphi(z_{1,2}, \tau; 1) = \psi(z_{1,2}, \tau),$$

and it signifies that when $\aleph$ moving from 0 to 1, the solution $\varphi(z_{1,2}, \tau; \aleph)$ moves simultaneously from initial approximation: $\psi_0(z_{1,2}, \tau)$ to the exact solution behavior: $\psi(z_{1,2}, \tau)$.

Expand $\varphi(z_{1,2}, \tau; \aleph)$ via Taylor's formula in the powers of $\aleph$ as:

$$\varphi(z_{1,2}, \tau; \aleph) = \psi_0(z_{1,2}, \tau) + \sum_{\lambda=1}^{\infty} \psi_\lambda(z_{1,2}, \tau) \aleph^\lambda, \quad (15)$$

where $\psi_\lambda(z_{1,2}, \tau) = \frac{1}{\lambda!} \frac{\partial^\lambda \varphi}{\partial \aleph^\lambda}\Big|_{\aleph=0}$, on selecting suitable value of $\hbar$ improves convergence region to the solution as in (15). Convergence of result (15) at $\aleph = 1$ can be secured via selecting appropriate values of $\hbar$, $H(z_{1,2}, \tau) \neq 0$ and the initial guess, and so

$$\psi(z_{1,2}, \tau) = \psi_0(z_{1,2}, \tau) + \sum_{\lambda=1}^{\infty} \psi_\lambda(z_{1,2}, \tau). \quad (16)$$

Set

$$\vec{\psi}_\lambda(z_{1,2}, \tau) = (\psi_0(z_{1,2}, \tau), \psi_1(z_{1,2}, \tau), \psi_2(z_{1,2}, \tau), \ldots, \psi_\lambda(z_{1,2}, \tau)).$$

In the squel, λth order deformation equation is evaluated as

$$\mathbb{J}[\psi_\lambda(z_{1,2}, \tau) - \chi_\lambda \psi_{\lambda-1}(z_{1,2}, \tau)](s, \vartheta) = \hbar \aleph H(z_{1,2}, \tau) \mathcal{P}_\lambda(\vec{\psi}_{\lambda-1}(z_{1,2}, \tau)), \quad (17)$$

where $\chi_\lambda = 0$ if $\lambda \leq 1$ and 1 otherwise.

On imposing inverse operator of $\mathbb{J}$T to (17) with $\aleph = 1$, $H(z_{1,2}, \tau) = 1$, we have

$$\psi_\lambda(z_{1,2}, \tau) = \chi_\lambda \psi_{\lambda-1}(z_{1,2}, \tau) + \hbar \mathbb{J}^{-1}\left[\mathcal{P}_\lambda(\vec{\psi}_{\lambda-1}(z_{1,2}, \tau))\right] \quad (18)$$

where

$$\mathcal{P}_\lambda\left(\vec{\psi}_{\lambda-1}(z_{1,2}, \tau)\right) = \frac{1}{(\lambda-1)!} \frac{\partial^{\lambda-1} \mathcal{T}[\varphi(z_{1,2}, \tau, \aleph)]}{\partial \aleph^{\lambda-1}}\Big|_{\aleph=0}.$$

On evaluation $\psi_\lambda(z_{1,2}, \tau)$, $\lambda \geq 1$. We can calculate Mth-order series behavior of (4) is evaluated as:

$$S_M(z_{1,2}, \tau) = \sum_{\lambda=0}^{M} \psi_\lambda(z_{1,2}, \tau), \quad (19)$$

which converges to $\psi(z_{1,2}, \tau)$, the exact behavior of the Equation (4) accurately for sufficiently large M (see the following).

Theorem 5 (Convergence & Error Estimates in $_O$HAJTM). *If $\exists \theta$ with $0 < \theta < 1$, for which the condition $\|\psi_{\ell+1}(z_{1,2}, \tau)\| \leq \theta \|\psi_\ell(z_{1,2}, \tau)\|$, $\ell \geq 1$ holds true, then*
(a) *The approximate Mth order $_O$HAJTM result $S_M(z_{1,2}, \tau)$ in (19) for NFPDEs (4) evaluated from converges (16) as $M \to \infty$.*
(b) *the maximum absolute error in $S_M(z_{1,2}, \tau)$ is*

$$\|\psi(z_{1,2}, \tau) - S_M(z_{1,2}, \tau)\| \leq \frac{\theta^{M+1}}{1-\theta} \|\psi_0(z_{1,2}, \tau)\|. \quad (20)$$

(c) *In addition, as for as the result in (16) convergent, where $\psi_\lambda(z_{1,2}, \tau)$'s are evaluated by (18). Then, the result recorded from (16) is the exact solution behavior of NFPDEs (4).*

Proof. The assumption leads to

$$\|\psi_1(z_{1,2},\tau)\| \le \theta\|\psi_0(z_{1,2},\tau)\|, \quad \|\psi_2(z_{1,2},\tau)\| \le \theta\|\psi_1(z_{1,2},\tau)\| \le \theta^2\|\psi_0(z_{1,2},\tau)\|, \quad \ldots \quad \|\psi_\ell(z_{1,2},\tau)\| \le \theta^\ell\|\psi_0(z_{1,2},\tau)\|.$$

In consequence, and so, for $M, N \in \mathbb{N}$ with $N > M$, we get

$$\|S_M(z_{1,2},\tau) - S_N(z_{1,2},\tau)\| = \left\|\sum_{j=M+1}^{N}\psi_j(z_{1,2},\tau)\right\| \le \|\psi_0(z_{1,2},\tau)\|\sum_{j=M+1}^{N}\theta^j = \|\psi_0(z_{1,2},\tau)\|\frac{(1-\theta^{N-M})\theta^{M+1}}{1-\theta}.$$

Moreover, $1 - \lambda^{N-M} < 1$ as $0 < \lambda < 1$, and so, the above inequality reduces to

$$\|S_M(z_{1,2},\tau) - S_N(z_{1,2},\tau)\| \le \|\psi_0(z_{1,2},\tau)\|\frac{\theta^{M+1}}{1-\theta} \to 0 \quad \text{as} \quad M \to \infty. \tag{21}$$

implying that $\{S_M(z_{1,2},\tau)\}_{M=1}^{\infty}$ is Cauchy sequence, and so, it is convergent. Part **(b)** is obtained direct by taking $N \to \infty$ in (21) as follows

$$\|S_M(z_{1,2},\tau) - \psi(z_{1,2},\tau)\| \le \|\psi_0(z_{1,2},\tau)\|\frac{\theta^{M+1}}{1-\theta}. \tag{22}$$

(c) In special case, when $N - 1 = M = \kappa$. Then, from Equation (21), we get

(*) $\lim_{\kappa \to \infty}\psi_\kappa(z_{1,2},\tau) = 0$.

Since

(**) $\psi_\kappa(z_{1,2},\tau) = \sum_{\lambda=1}^{\kappa}[\psi_\lambda(z_{1,2},\tau) - \chi_\lambda\psi_{\lambda-1}(z_{1,2},\tau)]$.

Use condition (*) and (**) in (18) with property $\aleph \ne 0$ to get

$\lim_{\kappa \to \infty}\sum_{\lambda=1}^{\kappa}\mathcal{P}_\lambda(\vec{\psi}_{\lambda-1}(z_{1,2},\tau)) = \sum_{\lambda=1}^{\infty}\mathcal{P}_\lambda(\vec{\psi}_{\lambda-1}(z_{1,2},\tau)) = 0$.

and so

$$\sum_{\lambda=1}^{\infty}\mathcal{P}_\lambda(\vec{\psi}_{\lambda-1}(z_{1,2},\tau)) = \sum_{\lambda=1}^{\infty}\left[\mathbb{J}[\psi_{\lambda-1}(z_{1,2},\tau)](s,\vartheta) - (1-\chi_\lambda)\sum_{\ell=1}^{\lambda}\frac{\theta^{\ell+1}}{s^\ell}\frac{\partial^{\ell-1}\psi}{\partial\tau^{\ell-1}}\bigg|_{\tau=0} + \left(\frac{\theta}{s}\right)^\alpha \mathbb{J}[\mathcal{T}\tilde\psi_{\lambda-1}(z_{1,2},\tau)](s,\vartheta)\right]$$
$$= \left(\frac{\theta}{s}\right)^\alpha \mathbb{J}[\tau \mathcal{D}_\alpha^C(\psi(z_{1,2},\tau)) + \mathcal{T}[\psi(z_{1,2},\tau)]] = 0 \Longrightarrow_\tau \mathcal{D}_\alpha^C(\psi(z_{1,2},\tau)) + \mathcal{T}[\phi(z_{1,2},\tau)] = 0,$$

which confirms that the behavior $\psi(z_{1,2},\tau)$ in (16) is the exact exact behavior to NF-PDEs (4). □

Evaluation of Optimal Value of the Convergence Control Parameter ($\hbar$)

The efficiency/validity of $_\circ$HAJTM is confirmed by measuring the L_2 or residual-errors. The square residual error [12,14] in the Mth-order solution behavior $S_M(z_{1,2},\tau)$ as in (19)

$$\Delta_M(\hbar) = \int_{a_1}^{b_1}\int_{a_2}^{b_2}\int_{a_3}^{b_3}\left(\mathcal{R}^\circ[S_M(z_1,z_2,\tau)]\right)^2 dz_1 dz_2 d\tau, \tag{23}$$

where $\mathcal{R}^\circ[S_M(z_{1,2},\tau)]$ is refer to residual error in the solution behavior of order M as $S_M(z_{1,2},\tau)$, and controlling parameter $\hbar$ appeared in solution (19) have a significant role and that receive faster convergence rate on suitable adjustment of $\hbar$. Precisely, the optimal value for $\hbar$ is values of $\hbar$ within the $\hbar$-region correspond to that $\Delta_M(\hbar)$ is minimized, and so $\hbar$ correspond for which $\frac{d\Delta_M(\hbar)}{d\hbar} = 0$. To CPU time under consideration, following formula in place of (23) is preferred.

$$\Delta_M(\hbar) = \frac{1}{c_1 c_2 c_3}\sum_{j=0}^{c_1}\sum_{k=0}^{c_2}\sum_{l=0}^{c_3}\left(\mathcal{R}^\circ[S_M(j\delta z_1, k\delta z_2, l\delta t)]^2\right). \tag{24}$$

where $\delta z_1 = \frac{b_1-a_1}{c_1}$, $\delta z_2 = \frac{b_2-a_2}{c_2}$ and $\delta\tau = \frac{b_3-a_3}{c_3}$. We set $c_1 = c_2 = c_3 = 10$.

5. Validation of Technique

To validate the efficiency and accuracy of the proposed techniques, we consider the fractional order system of equations of governing unsteady flow of a polytropic gas.

Take the fractional order system as described in Equation (1) subject to the initial conditions:

$$\psi_1(z_{1,2},0) = e^{z_1+z_2}, \quad \psi_2(z_{1,2},0) = -1 - e^{z_1+z_2}, \quad \rho(z_{1,2},0) = e^{z_1+z_2}, \quad P(z_{1,2},0) = \eta \quad (25)$$

where η is a real constant.

5.1. Validation of $\mathbb{J}$-VITM

By implementing the iteration formula Equation (10) of $\mathbb{J}$-VITM on the system of Equation (1) with ICs (25), we obtain the following recurrence relation

$$\wp_{1,\lambda+1} = \wp_{1,\lambda}(z_{1,2},0) - \mathbb{J}^{-1}\left[\left(\frac{\vartheta}{s}\right)^\alpha \mathbb{J}\left[\wp_{1,\lambda}\frac{\partial \wp_{1,\lambda}}{\partial z_1} + \wp_{2,\lambda}\frac{\partial \wp_{1,\lambda}}{\partial z_2} + \frac{1}{\rho_\lambda}\frac{\partial P_\lambda}{\partial z_1}\right](s,\vartheta)\right]$$

$$\wp_{2,\lambda+1} = \wp_{2,\lambda}(z_{1,2},0) - \mathbb{J}^{-1}\left[\left(\frac{\vartheta}{s}\right)^\alpha \mathbb{J}\left[\wp_{1,\lambda}\frac{\partial \wp_{2,\lambda}}{\partial z_1} + \wp_{2,\lambda}\frac{\partial \wp_{2,\lambda}}{\partial z_2} + \frac{1}{\rho_\lambda}\frac{\partial P_\lambda}{\partial z_2}\right](s,\vartheta)\right] \quad (26)$$

$$\rho_{\lambda+1} = \rho_\lambda(z_{1,2},0) - \mathbb{J}^{-1}\left[\left(\frac{\vartheta}{s}\right)^\alpha \mathbb{J}\left[\wp_{1,\lambda}\frac{\partial \rho_\lambda}{\partial z_1} + \wp_{2,\lambda}\frac{\partial \rho_\lambda}{\partial z_2} + \rho_\lambda\frac{\partial \wp_{1,\lambda}}{\partial z_1} + \rho_\lambda\frac{\partial \wp_{2,\lambda}}{\partial z_2}\right](s,\vartheta)\right]$$

$$P_{\lambda+1} = P_\lambda(z_{1,2},0) - \mathbb{J}^{-1}\left[\left(\frac{\vartheta}{s}\right)^\alpha \mathbb{J}\left[\wp_{1,\lambda}\frac{\partial P_\lambda}{\partial z_1} + \wp_{2,\lambda}\frac{\partial P_\lambda}{\partial z_2} + \Omega P_\lambda\frac{\partial \wp_{1,\lambda}}{\partial z_1} + \Omega P\frac{\partial \wp_{2,\lambda}}{\partial z_2}\right](s,\vartheta)\right]$$

On solving the recurrence (26), we get
At first iteration:

$$\wp_{1,1} = e^{z_1+z_2}\left(1 + \frac{\tau^\alpha}{\Gamma(\alpha+1)}\right); \quad \wp_{2,1} = -1 - e^{z_1+z_2}\left(1 + \frac{\tau^\alpha}{\Gamma(\alpha+1)}\right)$$

$$\rho_1 = e^{z_1+z_2}\left(1 + \frac{\tau^\alpha}{\Gamma(\alpha+1)}\right); \quad P_1 = \eta$$

At second iteration:

$$\wp_{1,2} = e^{z_1+z_2}\left(1 + \frac{\tau^\alpha}{\Gamma(\alpha+1)} + \frac{\tau^{2\alpha}}{\Gamma(2\alpha+1)}\right); \quad \wp_{2,2} = -1 - e^{z_1+z_2}\left(1 + \frac{\tau^\alpha}{\Gamma(\alpha+1)} + \frac{\tau^{2\alpha}}{\Gamma(2\alpha+1)}\right)$$

$$\rho_2 = e^{z_1+z_2}\left(1 + \frac{\tau^\alpha}{\Gamma(\alpha+1)} + \frac{\tau^{2\alpha}}{\Gamma(2\alpha+1)}\right); \quad P_2 = \eta$$

At third iteration:

$$\wp_{1,3} = e^{z_1+z_2}\sum_{j=0}^{3}\frac{\tau^{j\alpha}}{\Gamma(j\alpha+1)}, \quad \wp_{2,3} = -1 - e^{z_1+z_2}\sum_{j=0}^{3}\frac{\tau^{j\alpha}}{\Gamma(j\alpha+1)},$$

$$\rho_3 = e^{z_1+z_2}\sum_{j=0}^{3}\frac{\tau^{j\alpha}}{\Gamma(j\alpha+1)}, \quad P_3 = \eta$$

In similar fashion, κth order iterative results for $\kappa = 6, 10$ are given computed as

$$\wp_{1,6} = e^{z_1+z_2}\sum_{j=0}^{6}\frac{\tau^{j\alpha}}{\Gamma(j\alpha+1)}, \quad \wp_{2,6} = -1 - e^{z_1+z_2}\sum_{j=0}^{6}\frac{\tau^{j\alpha}}{\Gamma(j\alpha+1)},$$

$$\rho_6 = e^{z_1+z_2}\sum_{j=0}^{6}\frac{\tau^{j\alpha}}{\Gamma(j\alpha+1)}, \quad P_6 = \eta,$$

and

$$\wp_{1,10} = e^{z_1+z_2} \sum_{j=0}^{10} \frac{\tau^{j\alpha}}{\Gamma(j\alpha+1)}, \qquad \wp_{2,10} = -1 - e^{z_1+z_2} \sum_{j=0}^{10} \frac{\tau^{j\alpha}}{\Gamma(j\alpha+1)}$$

$$\rho_{10} = e^{z_1+z_2} \sum_{j=0}^{10} \frac{\tau^{j\alpha}}{\Gamma(j\alpha+1)}, \qquad P_{10} = \eta.$$

This concludes that general κth order iterative solutions is of the form

$$\wp_{1,\kappa} = e^{z_1+z_2} \sum_{j=0}^{\kappa} \frac{\tau^{j\alpha}}{\Gamma(j\alpha+1)}, \qquad \wp_{2,\kappa} = -1 - e^{z_1+z_2} \sum_{j=0}^{\kappa} \frac{\tau^{j\alpha}}{\Gamma(j\alpha+1)}$$

$$\rho_\kappa = e^{z_1+z_2} \sum_{j=0}^{\kappa} \frac{\tau^{j\alpha}}{\Gamma(j\alpha+1)}, \qquad P_\kappa = \eta.$$

In consequence, κth order iterative solutions converges to the exact solutions as $\kappa \to \infty$:

$$\wp_1 = e^{z_1+z_2} \sum_{j=0}^{\infty} \frac{\tau^{j\alpha}}{\Gamma(j\alpha+1)} = e^{z_1+z_2} E_{\alpha,1}(\tau^\alpha)$$

$$\wp_2 = -1 - e^{z_1+z_2} \sum_{j=0}^{\infty} \frac{\tau^{j\alpha}}{\Gamma(j\alpha+1)} = -1 - e^{z_1+z_2} E_{\alpha,1}(\tau^\alpha)$$

$$\rho = e^{z_1+z_2} \sum_{j=0}^{\infty} \frac{\tau^{j\alpha}}{\Gamma(j\alpha+1)} = e^{z_1+z_2} E_{\alpha,1}(\tau^\alpha)$$

$$P = \eta.$$

In special case, when $\alpha = 1$ the above results converges to the exact solutions:

$$\wp_1(z_{1,2},\tau) = e^{z_1+z_2+\tau}, \quad \wp_2(z_{1,2},\tau) = -1 - e^{z_1+z_2+\tau}, \quad \rho(z_{1,2},\tau) = e^{z_1+z_2+\tau}, \quad P(z_{1,2},\tau) = \eta. \tag{27}$$

5.2. Validation of $_O$HAJTM

Imposing $\mathbb{J}$-transform on system of Equation (1) with ICs (25), we get

$$\mathbb{J}[\wp_1(z_{1,2},\tau)](s,\vartheta) - \frac{\vartheta^2}{s} e^{z_1+z_2} + \left(\frac{\vartheta}{s}\right)^\alpha \mathbb{J}\left[\wp_1 \frac{\partial \wp_1}{\partial z_1} + \wp_2 \frac{\partial \wp_1}{\partial z_2} + \frac{1}{\rho}\frac{\partial P}{\partial z_1}\right](s,\vartheta) = 0.$$

$$\mathbb{J}[\wp_2(z_{1,2},\tau)](s,\vartheta) - \frac{\vartheta^2}{s}(-1 - e^{z_1+z_2}) + \left(\frac{\vartheta}{s}\right)^\alpha \mathbb{J}\left[\wp_1 \frac{\partial \wp_2}{\partial z_1} + \wp_2 \frac{\partial \wp_2}{\partial z_2} + \frac{1}{\rho}\frac{\partial P}{\partial z_2}\right](s,\vartheta) = 0. \tag{28}$$

$$\mathbb{J}[\rho(z_{1,2},\tau)](s,\vartheta) - \frac{\vartheta^2}{s} e^{z_1+z_2} + \left(\frac{\vartheta}{s}\right)^\alpha \mathbb{J}\left[\wp_1 \frac{\partial \rho}{\partial z_1} + \wp_2 \frac{\partial \rho}{\partial z_2} + \rho\frac{\partial \wp_1}{\partial z_1} + \rho\frac{\partial \wp_2}{\partial z_2}\right](s,\vartheta) = 0.$$

$$\mathbb{J}[P(z_{1,2},\tau)](s,\vartheta) - \frac{\vartheta^2}{s}\eta + \left(\frac{\vartheta}{s}\right)^\alpha \mathbb{J}\left[\wp_1 \frac{\partial P}{\partial z_1} + \wp_2 \frac{\partial P}{\partial z_2} + \mho P\frac{\partial \wp_1}{\partial z_1} + \mho P\frac{\partial \wp_2}{\partial z_2}\right](s,\vartheta) = 0.$$

Formulate nonlinear operator as follows:

$$\beth_1[\varphi_1(z_{1,2},\tau;\aleph),\varphi_2(z_{1,2},\tau;\aleph),\varphi_3(z_{1,2},\tau;\aleph),\varphi_4(z_{1,2},\tau;\aleph)] = \mathbb{J}[\varphi_1(z_{1,2},\tau;\aleph)](s,\vartheta) - \frac{\vartheta^2}{s}e^{z_1+z_2}$$

$$+\left(\frac{\vartheta}{s}\right)^\alpha \mathbb{J}\left[\varphi_1(z_{1,2},\tau;\aleph)\frac{\partial}{\partial z_1}\varphi_1(z_{1,2},\tau;\aleph) + \varphi_2(z_{1,2},\tau;\aleph)\frac{\partial}{\partial z_2}\varphi_1(z_{1,2},\tau;\aleph) + \frac{1}{\varphi_3(z_{1,2},\tau;\aleph)}\frac{\partial}{\partial z_1}\varphi_4(z_{1,2},\tau;\aleph)\right](s,\vartheta)$$

$$\beth_2[\varphi_1(z_{1,2},\tau;\aleph),\varphi_2(z_{1,2},\tau;\aleph),\varphi_3(z_{1,2},\tau;\aleph),\varphi_4(z_{1,2},\tau;\aleph)] = \mathbb{J}[\varphi_2(z_{1,2},\tau;\aleph)](s,\vartheta) - \frac{\vartheta^2}{s}\left(-1 - e^{z_1+z_2}\right) + \left(\frac{\vartheta}{s}\right)^\alpha$$

$$\mathbb{J}\left[\varphi_1(z_{1,2},\tau;\aleph)\frac{\partial}{\partial z_1}\varphi_2(z_{1,2},\tau;\aleph) + \varphi_2(z_{1,2},\tau;\aleph)\frac{\partial}{\partial z_2}\varphi_2(z_{1,2},\tau;\aleph) + \frac{1}{\varphi_3(z_{1,2},\tau;\aleph)}\frac{\partial}{\partial z_2}\varphi_4(z_{1,2},\tau;\aleph)\right](s,\vartheta)$$

$$\beth_3[\varphi_1(z_{1,2},\tau;\aleph),\varphi_2(z_{1,2},\tau;\aleph),\varphi_3(z_{1,2},\tau;\aleph),\varphi_4(z_{1,2},\tau;\aleph)] = \mathbb{J}[\varphi_2(z_{1,2},\tau;\aleph)](s,\vartheta) \quad (29)$$

$$-\frac{\vartheta^2}{s}e^{z_1+z_2} + \left(\frac{\vartheta}{s}\right)^\alpha \mathbb{J}\left[\varphi_1(z_{1,2},\tau;\aleph)\frac{\partial}{\partial z_1}\varphi_3(z_{1,2},\tau;\aleph) + \varphi_2(z_{1,2},\tau;\aleph)\frac{\partial}{\partial z_2}\varphi_3(z_{1,2},\tau;\aleph)\right.$$

$$\left.+\varphi_3(z_{1,2},\tau;\aleph)\frac{\partial}{\partial z_1}\varphi_1(z_{1,2},\tau;\aleph) + \varphi_3(z_{1,2},\tau;\aleph)\frac{\partial}{\partial z_2}\varphi_2(z_{1,2},\tau;\aleph)\right](s,\vartheta)$$

$$\beth_4[\varphi_1(z_{1,2},\tau;\aleph),\varphi_2(z_{1,2},\tau;\aleph),\varphi_3(z_{1,2},\tau;\aleph),\varphi_4(z_{1,2},\tau;\aleph)] = \mathbb{J}[\varphi_1(z_{1,2},\tau;\aleph)](s,\vartheta) - \frac{\vartheta^2}{s}\eta$$

$$+\left(\frac{\vartheta}{s}\right)^\alpha \mathbb{J}\left[\varphi_1(z_{1,2},\tau;\aleph)\frac{\partial}{\partial z_1}\varphi_4(z_{1,2},\tau;\aleph) + \varphi_2(z_{1,2},\tau;\aleph)\frac{\partial}{\partial z_2}\varphi_4(z_{1,2},\tau;\aleph)\right.$$

$$\left.+\Omega\varphi_4(z_{1,2},\tau;\aleph)\frac{\partial}{\partial z_1}\varphi_1(z_{1,2},\tau;\aleph) + \Omega\varphi_4(z_{1,2},\tau;\aleph)\frac{\partial}{\partial z_2}\varphi_2(z_{1,2},\tau;\aleph)\right](s,\vartheta).$$

Utilizing (31) in (18) to obtain the recursive formula

$$\begin{aligned}
\wp_{1,\lambda}(z_{1,2},\tau) &= \chi_\lambda \wp_{1,\lambda-1}(z_{1,2},\tau) + \hbar \mathbb{J}^{-1}\left[\mathcal{P}_\lambda^1\left[\vec{\wp}_{1,\lambda-1},\vec{\wp}_{2,\lambda-1},\vec{\rho}_{\lambda-1},\vec{P}_{\lambda-1}\right]\right] \\
\wp_{2,\lambda}(z_{1,2},\tau) &= \chi_\lambda \wp_{2,\lambda-1}(z_{1,2},\tau) + \hbar \mathbb{J}^{-1}\left[\mathcal{P}_\lambda^2\left[\vec{\wp}_{1,\lambda-1},\vec{\wp}_{2,\lambda-1},\vec{\rho}_{\lambda-1},\vec{P}_{\lambda-1}\right]\right] \\
\rho_\lambda(z_{1,2},\tau) &= \chi_\lambda \rho_{\lambda-1}(z_{1,2},\tau) + \hbar \mathbb{J}^{-1}\left[\mathcal{P}_\lambda^3\left[\vec{\wp}_{1,\lambda-1},\vec{\wp}_{2,\lambda-1},\vec{\rho}_{\lambda-1},\vec{P}_{\lambda-1}\right]\right] \\
P_\lambda(z_{1,2},\tau) &= \chi_\lambda P_{\lambda-1}(z_{1,2},\tau) + \hbar \mathbb{J}^{-1}\left[\mathcal{P}_\lambda^4\left[\vec{\wp}_{1,\lambda-1},\vec{\wp}_{2,\lambda-1},\vec{\rho}_{\lambda-1},\vec{P}_{\lambda-1}\right]\right]
\end{aligned} \quad (30)$$

where

$$\mathcal{P}_\lambda^1\left[\vec{\wp}_{1,\lambda-1},\vec{\wp}_{2,\lambda-1},\vec{\rho}_{\lambda-1},\vec{P}_{\lambda-1}\right] = \mathbb{J}[\wp_{1,\lambda-1}(z_{1,2},\tau)](s,\vartheta) - \frac{(1-\chi_\lambda)\vartheta^2}{s}e^{z_1+z_2}$$

$$+\left(\frac{\vartheta}{s}\right)^\alpha \mathbb{J}\left[\sum_{j=0}^{\lambda-1}\left[\wp_{1,\lambda-1-j}\frac{\partial \wp_{1,j}}{\partial z_1} + \wp_{2,\lambda-1-j}\frac{\partial \wp_{1,j}}{\partial z_2} + \frac{1}{\rho_j}\frac{\partial}{\partial z_1}P_{\lambda-1-j}\right]\right](s,\vartheta)$$

$$\mathcal{P}_\lambda^2(\vec{\wp}_{1,\lambda-1},\vec{\wp}_{2,\lambda-1},\vec{\rho}_{\lambda-1},\vec{P}_{\lambda-1}) = \mathbb{J}[\wp_{2,\lambda-1}(z_{1,2},\tau)](s,\vartheta) - \frac{(1-\chi_\lambda)\vartheta^2}{s}\left(-1 - e^{z_1+z_2}\right)$$

$$+\left(\frac{\vartheta}{s}\right)^\alpha \mathbb{J}\left[\sum_{j=0}^{\lambda-1}\left[\wp_{1,\lambda-1-j}\frac{\partial \wp_{2,j}}{\partial z_1} + \wp_{2,\lambda-1-j}\frac{\partial \wp_{2,j}}{\partial z_2} + \frac{1}{\rho_j}\frac{\partial}{\partial z_2}P_{\lambda-1-j}\right]\right](s,\vartheta)$$

$$\mathcal{P}_\lambda^3(\vec{\wp}_{1,\lambda-1},\vec{\wp}_{2,\lambda-1},\vec{\rho}_{\lambda-1},\vec{P}_{\lambda-1}) = \mathbb{J}[\rho_{\lambda-1}(z_{1,2},\tau)](s,\vartheta) - \frac{(1-\chi_\lambda)\vartheta^2}{s}e^{z_1+z_2} \quad (31)$$

$$+\left(\frac{\vartheta}{s}\right)^\alpha \mathbb{J}\left[\sum_{j=0}^{\lambda-1}\left[\wp_{1,\lambda-1-j}\frac{\partial \rho_j}{\partial z_1} + \wp_{2,\lambda-1-j}\frac{\partial \rho_j}{\partial z_2} + \rho_{\lambda-1-j}\frac{\partial \wp_{1,j}}{\partial z_1} + \rho_{\lambda-1-j}\frac{\partial \wp_{2,j}}{\partial z_2}\right]\right](s,\vartheta)$$

$$\mathcal{P}_\lambda^4(\vec{\wp}_{1,\lambda-1},\vec{\wp}_{2,\lambda-1},\vec{\rho}_{\lambda-1},\vec{P}_{\lambda-1}) = \mathbb{J}[P_{\lambda-1}(z_{1,2},\tau)](s,\vartheta) - \frac{(1-\chi_\lambda)\vartheta^2}{s}\eta$$

$$+\left(\frac{\vartheta}{s}\right)^\alpha \mathbb{J}\left[\sum_{j=0}^{\lambda-1}\left[\wp_{1,\lambda-j-1}\frac{\partial P_j}{\partial z_1} + \wp_{2,\lambda-j-1}\frac{\partial P_j}{\partial z_2} + \Omega P_{\lambda-j-1}\frac{\partial \wp_{1,j}}{\partial z_1} + \Omega P_{\lambda-j-1}\frac{\partial \wp_{2,j}}{\partial z_2}\right]\right](s,\vartheta).$$

with the aid of Mathematica software, solve recurrence relation (30).
At first iteration:

$$\wp_{1,1}(z_{1,2},\tau) = -\frac{\hbar\tau^{\alpha}e^{z_1+z_2}}{\Gamma(\alpha+1)}; \quad \wp_{2,1}(z_{1,2},\tau) = \frac{\hbar\tau^{\alpha}e^{z_1+z_2}}{\Gamma(\alpha+1)}; \quad \rho_1(z_{1,2},\tau) = -\frac{\hbar\tau^{\alpha}e^{z_1+z_2}}{\Gamma(\alpha+1)}; \quad P_1(z_{1,2},\tau) = 0.$$

At second iteration:

$$\wp_{1,2}(z_{1,2},\tau) = e^{z_1+z_2}\left(\frac{\hbar^2\tau^{2\alpha}}{\Gamma(2\alpha+1)} - \frac{(\hbar+\hbar^2)\tau^{\alpha}}{\Gamma(\alpha+1)}\right); \quad \wp_{2,2}(z_{1,2},\tau) = e^{z_1+z_2}\left(-\frac{\hbar^2\tau^{2\alpha}}{\Gamma(2\alpha+1)} + \frac{(\hbar+\hbar^2)\tau^{\alpha}}{\Gamma(\alpha+1)}\right)$$

$$\rho_2(z_{1,2},\tau) = e^{z_1+z_2}\left(\frac{\hbar^2\tau^{2\alpha}}{\Gamma(2\alpha+1)} - \frac{(\hbar+\hbar^2)\tau^{\alpha}}{\Gamma(\alpha+1)}\right); \quad P_2(z_{1,2},\tau) = 0.$$

At third iteration:

$$\wp_{1,3}(z_{1,2},\tau) = e^{z_1+z_2}\left(-\frac{\hbar^3\tau^{3\alpha}}{\Gamma(3\alpha+1)} - \frac{2(\hbar^2+\hbar^3)\tau^{2\alpha}}{\Gamma(2\alpha+1)} - \frac{(\hbar+\hbar^2+\hbar^3)\tau^{\alpha}}{\Gamma(\alpha+1)}\right)$$

$$\wp_{2,3}(z_{1,2},\tau) = e^{z_1+z_2}\left(\frac{\hbar^3\tau^{3\alpha}}{\Gamma(3\alpha+1)} - \frac{2(\hbar^2+\hbar^3)\tau^{2\alpha}}{\Gamma(2\alpha+1)} + \frac{(\hbar+\hbar^2+\hbar^3)\tau^{\alpha}}{\Gamma(\alpha+1)}\right)$$

$$\rho_3(z_{1,2},\tau) = e^{z_1+z_2}\left(-\frac{\hbar^3\tau^{3\alpha}}{\Gamma(3\alpha+1)} - \frac{2(\hbar^2+\hbar^3)\tau^{2\alpha}}{\Gamma(2\alpha+1)} - \frac{(\hbar+\hbar^2+\hbar^3)\tau^{\alpha}}{\Gamma(\alpha+1)}\right)$$

$$P_3(z_{1,2},\tau) = 0.$$

In sequel, the terms corresponding to $\lambda \geq 4$ for the system of equation can be computed from (30). The 6th order approximate results for the system is

$$S_6\wp_1(z_{1,2},\tau) = \sum_{\lambda=0}^{6} \wp_{1,\lambda}(z_{1,2},\tau); \quad S_6\wp_2(z_{1,2},\tau) = \sum_{\lambda=0}^{6} \wp_{2,\lambda}(z_{1,2},\tau),$$

$$S_6\rho(z_{1,2},\tau) = \sum_{\lambda=0}^{6} \rho_\lambda(z_{1,2},\tau); \quad S_6P(z_{1,2},\tau) = \sum_{\lambda=0}^{6} P_\lambda(z_{1,2},\tau).$$
(32)

This series solution (32) with $\hbar = -1$ reduced to

$$S_6\wp_1(z_{1,2},\tau) = e^{z_1+z_2}\sum_{\lambda=0}^{6}\frac{\tau^{\lambda\alpha}}{\Gamma(\lambda\alpha+1)}, \quad S_6\wp_2(z_{1,2},\tau) = -1 - e^{z_1+z_2}\sum_{\lambda=0}^{6}\frac{\tau^{\lambda\alpha}}{\Gamma(\lambda\alpha+1)}$$

$$S_6\rho(z_{1,2},\tau) = e^{z_1+z_2}\sum_{\lambda=0}^{6}\frac{\tau^{\lambda\alpha}}{\Gamma(\lambda\alpha+1)}, \quad S_6P(z_{1,2},\tau) = \eta.$$

which is the adjacent form of the exact solution (27) obtained via $\mathbb{J}$-VITM. In addition for $\alpha = 1$, it is an adjacent form of the exact solution (27).

5.3. Result and Discussion

Throughout computation fixed $z_2 = 1$. The comparison in absolute errors κth order results ($\kappa = 6, 10$) for $\wp_1/\rho$ and $\wp_2$ via $\mathbb{J}$-VITM and $_o$HA$\mathbb{J}$TM in $0 < \tau, z_1 < 1$ are reported in Table 1 and Table 2, respectively. In consequence, Table 3 reports the comparison of exact results with 10th order results for $\wp_1$ and $\wp_2$ computed via $_o$HA$\mathbb{J}$TM with optimal value of $\hbar$ for $0 < z_1 < 1, z_2 = 1$ at different time levels $0 < \tau \leq 1$. The computation is carried out by taking $\hbar = -1$ and $\hbar = -1.0692$ (optimal value). One can see that, we can achieve faster convergence rate with the help of optimal value of the convergence control parameter ($\hbar$). The obtained error solutions witness the efficacy of the projected schemes.

Table 1. Comparison of absolute errors κth order results ($\kappa = 6, 10$) for $\wp_1 / \rho$ via J-VITM and $_0$HAJTM for $0 < z_1 < 1, z_2 = 1$ at different time levels $0 < \tau \leq 1$.

(z_1, z_2, τ)	$\wp_1 6(\rho 6)$			$\wp_1 10(\rho 10)$		
		$\hbar = -1$	$\hbar = -1.0692$		$\hbar = -1$	$\hbar = -1.0349$
	J-VITM	HAJTM	$_0$HAJTM	J-VITM	HAJTM	$_0$HAJTM
(0.25,1,0.25)	4.3627×10^{-8}	4.3627×10^{-8}	2.0887×10^{-9}	2.1316×10^{-14}	3.9968×10^{-14}	2.5757×10^{-14}
(0.25,1,0.5)	5.7683×10^{-6}	5.7683×10^{-6}	1.6874×10^{-7}	4.4546×10^{-11}	4.4606×10^{-11}	1.1191×10^{-13}
(0.25,1,0.75)	1.0189×10^{-4}	1.0189×10^{-4}	3.4828×10^{-7}	3.9379×10^{-9}	3.9380×10^{-9}	3.3333×10^{-12}
(0.25,1,1)	7.8977×10^{-5}	7.8977×10^{-4}	1.5869×10^{-5}	9.5331×10^{-8}	9.5331×10^{-8}	1.7106×10^{-10}
(0.5,1,0.25)	5.6018×10^{-8}	5.6018×10^{-8}	2.6820×10^{-9}	2.7534×10^{-14}	6.0396×10^{-14}	1.7764×10^{-15}
(0.5,1,0.5)	7.4066×10^{-6}	7.4066×10^{-6}	2.1667×10^{-7}	5.7198×10^{-11}	5.7214×10^{-11}	4.0856×10^{-14}
(0.5,1,075)	1.3083×10^{-4}	1.3083×10^{-4}	4.4720×10^{-7}	5.0564×10^{-9}	5.0564×10^{-9}	4.6523×10^{-12}
(0.5,1,1)	1.0141×10^{-3}	1.0141×10^{-3}	2.0376×10^{-5}	1.2241×10^{-7}	1.2241×10^{-7}	2.1923×10^{-10}
(0.75,1,0.25)	7.1929×10^{-8}	7.1929×10^{-8}	3.4437×10^{-9}	3.4639×10^{-14}	4.1744×10^{-14}	6.3949×10^{-14}
(0.75,1,0.5)	9.5103×10^{-6}	9.5103×10^{-6}	2.7821×10^{-7}	7.3443×10^{-11}	7.3399×10^{-11}	6.5725×10^{-14}
(0.75,1,0.75)	1.6799×10^{-4}	1.6799×10^{-4}	5.7422×10^{-7}	6.4926×10^{-9}	6.4929×10^{-9}	5.4818×10^{-12}
(0.75,1,1)	1.3021×10^{-3}	1.3021×10^{-3}	2.6164×10^{-5}	1.5717×10^{-7}	1.5717×10^{-7}	2.8172×10^{-10}
(1,1,0.25)	9.2359×10^{-8}	9.2359×10^{-8}	4.4219×10^{-9}	4.4409×10^{-14}	2.6645×10^{-14}	4.7962×10^{-14}
(1,1,0.5)	1.2211×10^{-5}	1.2211×10^{-5}	3.5723×10^{-7}	9.4301×10^{-11}	9.4241×10^{-11}	3.8547×10^{-13}
(1,1,0.75)	2.1570×10^{-4}	2.1570×10^{-4}	7.3731×10^{-7}	8.3366×10^{-9}	8.3368×10^{-9}	6.9846×10^{-12}
(1,1,1)	1.6719×10^{-3}	1.6719×10^{-3}	3.3595×10^{-5}	2.0181×10^{-7}	2.0181×10^{-7}	3.6275×10^{-10}
CPU Time	1.8290	4.0150		3.2340	12.0300	

For $\wp_1$: Figure 1a,b depict 2D and 3D behavior of 10th-order computed results for different α. There is a significant variation in the obtained solutions for different fractional order α. For the accuracy of the projected schemes, we can consider plots for α = 1 where the secured solutions are in best match with the exact solutions of the problem under consideration. Figure 1c,d depicts logarithmic plots of relative errors in κth iterative results ($\kappa = 6, 8, 10$) via $_0$HAJTM for α = 0.85, 1, respectively, while Figure 1e,f depicts logarithmic plots of relative errors in κth iterative results ($\kappa = 6, 8, 10$) via J-VITM for α = 0.85, 1, respectively. The value of the relative error for the obtained solution is decreases as we increase the iterations. In the 10th-order iteration, we have achieved the better solutions as compare to the previous iterations.

For $\wp_2$: Figure 2a,b, depict 2D and 3D behavior of 10th-order computed results for different α. The velocity $\wp_2$ decreases with increase in time variable τ. α = 1 curve matches exactly with the exact solution of the considered problem. The velocity $\wp_2$ drops faster for the decreasing fractional order α. The 3D view of variation of the solution $\wp_2$ for different fractional order is presented to analyze the influence of fractional parameter α. Figure 2c,d depicts logarithmic plots of relative errors in κth iterative results ($\kappa = 6, 8, 10$) via $_0$HAJTM for α = 0.85, 1, respectively while Figure 2e,f depicts logarithmic plots of relative errors in κth iterative results ($\kappa = 6, 8, 10$) via J-VITM for α = 0.85, 1 respectively. As we increase the number of iterations, we are getting the better approximate solution for both projected algorithms. These plots gives an explaination about how large the absolute error is in comparision with the exact numerical value of the solution.

Table 2. Comparison of absolute errors κth order results ($\kappa = 6, 10$) for $\wp_2$ via $\mathbb{J}$-VITM and $_O$HA$\mathbb{J}$TM for $0 < z_1 < 1, z_2 = 1$ at different time levels $0 < \tau \leq 1$.

	$\wp_2 6$			$\wp_2 10$		
(z_1, z_2, τ)		$\hbar = -1$	$\hbar = -1.0692$		$\hbar = -1$	$\hbar = -1.0349$
	$\mathbb{J}$-VITM	HA$\mathbb{J}$TM	$_O$HA$\mathbb{J}$TM	$\mathbb{J}$-VITM	HA$\mathbb{J}$TM	$_O$HA$\mathbb{J}$TM
(0.25,1,0.25)	4.3627×10^{-8}	4.3627×10^{-8}	9.3490×10^{-12}	2.0428×10^{-14}	2.5757×10^{-14}	2.5757×10^{-14}
(0.25,1,0.5)	5.7683×10^{-6}	5.7683×10^{-6}	1.7979×10^{-7}	4.4546×10^{-11}	4.4578×10^{-11}	1.1191×10^{-13}
(0.25,1,0.75)	1.0189×10^{-4}	1.0189×10^{-4}	5.4706×10^{-7}	3.9379×10^{-9}	3.9380×10^{-9}	3.3342×10^{-12}
(0.25,1,1)	7.8977×10^{-4}	7.8977×10^{-4}	1.5031×10^{-5}	9.5331×10^{-8}	9.5331×10^{-8}	1.7106×10^{-10}
(0.5,1,0.25)	5.6018×10^{-8}	5.6018×10^{-8}	1.2006×10^{-11}	2.8422×10^{-14}	6.0396×10^{-14}	1.7764×10^{-15}
(0.5,1,0.5)	7.4066×10^{-6}	7.4066×10^{-6}	2.3086×10^{-7}	5.7197×10^{-11}	5.7213×10^{-11}	4.0856×10^{-14}
(0.5,1,075)	1.3083×10^{-4}	1.3083×10^{-4}	7.0244×10^{-7}	5.0564×10^{-9}	5.0564×10^{-9}	4.6523×10^{-12}
(0.5,1,1)	1.0141×10^{-3}	1.0141×10^{-3}	1.9301×10^{-5}	1.2241×10^{-7}	1.2241×10^{-7}	2.1923×10^{-10}
(0.75,1,0.25)	7.1929×10^{-8}	7.1929×10^{-8}	1.5415×10^{-11}	3.5527×10^{-14}	4.2633×10^{-14}	6.3949×10^{-14}
(0.75,1,0.5)	9.5103×10^{-6}	9.5103×10^{-6}	2.9643×10^{-7}	7.3443×10^{-11}	7.3399×10^{-11}	6.5725×10^{-14}
(0.75,1,0.75)	1.6799×10^{-4}	1.6799×10^{-4}	9.0195×10^{-7}	6.4926×10^{-9}	6.4929×10^{-9}	5.3682×10^{-12}
(0.75,1,1)	1.3021×10^{-3}	1.3021×10^{-3}	2.4783×10^{-5}	1.5717×10^{-7}	1.5717×10^{-7}	2.8173×10^{-10}
(1,1,0.25)	9.2359×10^{-8}	9.2359×10^{-8}	1.9796×10^{-11}	4.4409×10^{-14}	5.1514×10^{-14}	9.5923×10^{-14}
(1,1,0.5)	1.2211×10^{-5}	1.2211×10^{-5}	3.8062×10^{-7}	9.4301×10^{-11}	9.4298×10^{-11}	3.6415×10^{-13}
(1,1,0.75)	2.1570×10^{-4}	2.1570×10^{-4}	1.1581×10^{-6}	8.3366×10^{-9}	8.3369×10^{-9}	7.0415×10^{-12}
(1,1,1)	1.6719×10^{-3}	1.6719×10^{-3}	3.1822×10^{-5}	2.0181×10^{-7}	2.0181×10^{-7}	3.6265×10^{-10}

Table 3. Comparison of 10th order results for $\wp_1$ and $\wp_2$ via $_O$HA$\mathbb{J}$TM with optimal value of $\hbar$ for $0 < z_1 < 1, z_2 = 1$ at different time levels $0 < \tau \leq 1$ with exact results.

	$\wp_1$			$\wp_2$		
(z_1, z_2, τ)	$\alpha = 0.85$	$\alpha = 1$	Exact	$\alpha = 0.85$	$\alpha = 1$	Exact
(0.25,1,0.25)	4.8728202329	4.4816890703	4.4816890703	5.8728202329	5.4816890703	5.4816890703
(0.25,1,0.5)	6.4418579146	5.7546026760	5.7546026760	7.4418579146	6.7546026760	6.7546026760
(0.25,1,0.75)	8.4088209398	7.3890560989	7.3890560989	9.4088209398	8.3890560989	8.3890560989
(0.25,1,1)	10.9090468543	9.4877358365	9.4877358364	11.9090468543	10.4877358365	10.4877358364
(0.5,1,0.25)	6.2568250301	5.7546026760	5.7546026760	7.2568250301	6.7546026760	6.7546026760
(0.5,1,0.5)	8.2715092930	7.3890560989	7.3890560989	9.2715092930	8.3890560989	8.3890560989
(0.5,1,075)	10.7971398111	9.4877358364	9.4877358364	11.7971398111	10.4877358364	10.4877358364
(0.5,1,1)	14.0074934328	12.1824939609	12.1824939607	15.0074934328	13.1824939609	13.1824939607
(0.75,1,0.25)	8.0339223664	7.3890560989	7.3890560989	9.0339223664	8.3890560989	8.3890560989
(0.75,1,0.5)	10.6208281666	9.4877358364	9.4877358364	11.6208281666	10.4877358364	10.4877358364
(0.75,1,0.75)	13.8638019450	12.1824939607	12.1824939607	14.8638019450	13.1824939607	13.1824939607
(0.75,1,1)	17.9859775918	15.6426318845	15.6426318842	18.9859775918	16.6426318845	16.6426318842
(1,1,0.25)	10.3157605141	9.4877358364	9.4877358364	11.3157605141	10.4877358364	10.4877358364
(1,1,0.5)	13.6374133121	12.1824939607	12.1824939607	14.6374133121	13.1824939607	13.1824939607
(1,1,0.75)	17.8014740693	15.6426318842	15.6426318842	18.8014740693	16.6426318842	16.6426318842
(1,1,1)	23.0944523718	20.0855369235	20.0855369232	24.0944523718	21.0855369236	21.0855369232

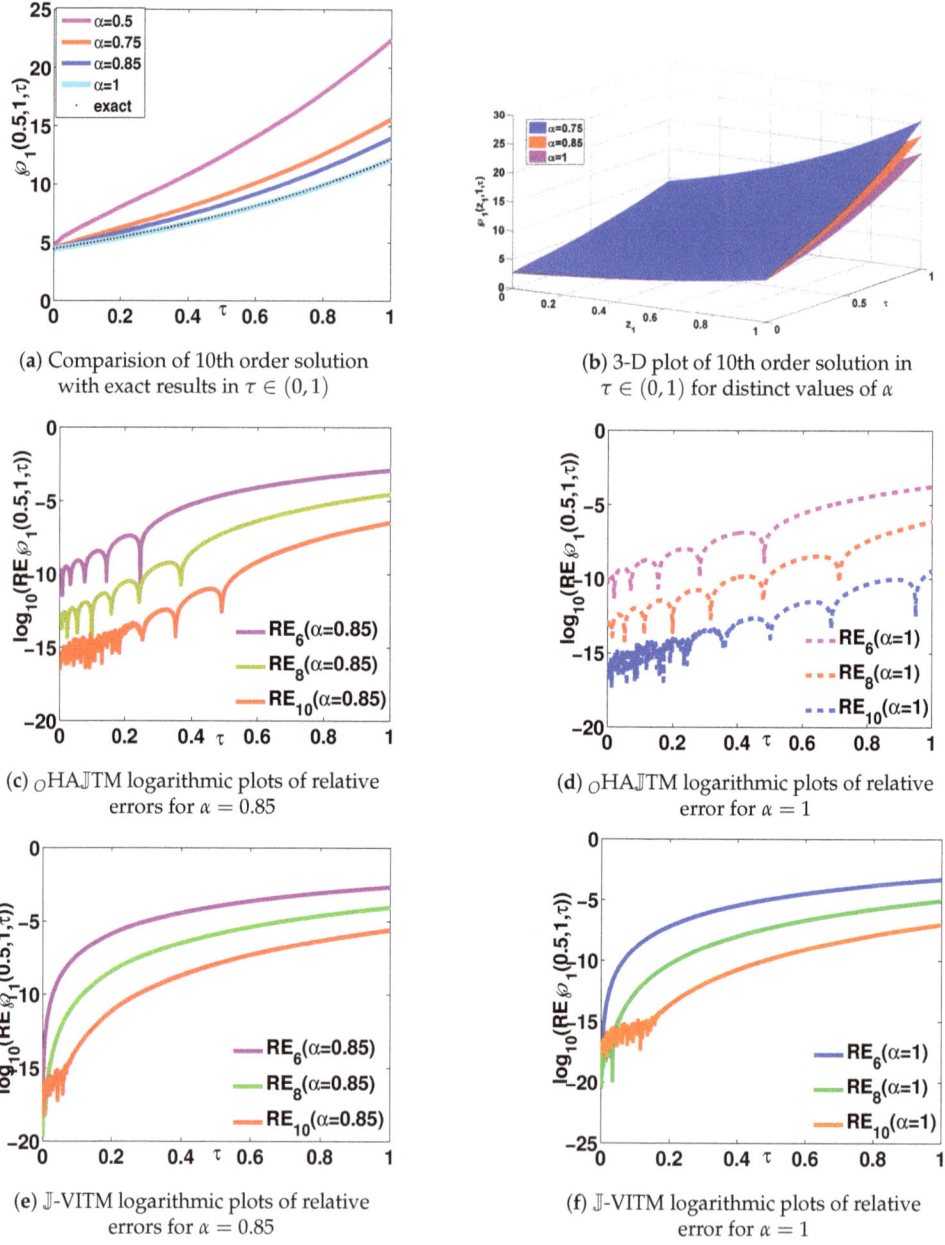

Figure 1. Solutions for $\wp_1(z_{1,2}, \tau)$. (**a**) Behavior of computed results from ${}_O$HAJTM at 10th iteration with exact results; (**b**) logarithmic plots of relative errors in κth iterative results ($\kappa = 6, 8, 10$) for (**c,e**) $\alpha = 0.85$, (**d,f**) $\alpha = 1$; at $z_1 = 0.5, z_2 = 1$ and optimal value of $\hbar$, for $\wp_1$ obtained from ${}_O$HAJTM (**c,d**), J-VITM (**e,f**) respectively.

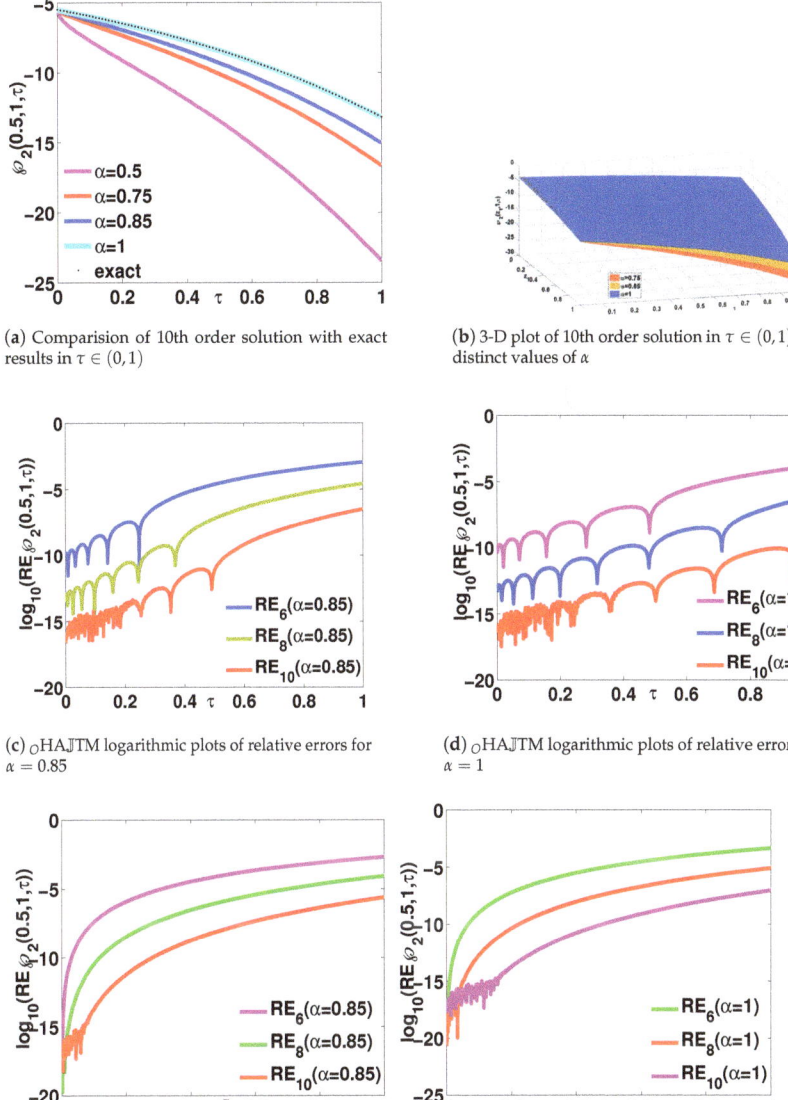

Figure 2. Solutions for $\wp_2(z_{1,2}, \tau)$. (**a**) Behavior of computed results from $_O$HAJTM at 10th iteration with exact results; (**b**) logarithmic plots of relative errors in κth iterative results ($\kappa = 6, 8, 10$) for (**c**,**e**) $\alpha = 0.85$, (**d**,**f**) $\alpha = 1$; at $z_1 = 0.5, z_2 = 1$ and optimal value of $\hbar$, for $\wp_2$ obtained from $_O$HAJTM (**c**,**d**), J-VITM (**e**,**f**) respectively.

For ρ: Figure 3a,b depict 2D and 3D behavior of 10th-order computed results for different α. We can see that the density ρ increases with increase in time τ. The density distribution over the space with coordinates (z_1, z_2, τ) is presented in Figure 3b. Figure 3c,d depicts logarithmic plots of relative errors in κth iterative results ($\kappa = 6, 8, 10$) via $_O$HAJTM for $\alpha = 0.85, 1$, respectively, while Figure 3e,f depicts logarithmic plots of relative errors in κth iterative results ($\kappa = 6, 8, 10$) via $\mathbb{J}$-VITM for $\alpha = 0.85, 1$, respectively. Table 3 cites that we have achieved the solution which is in best match with the exact solution of the considered problem. We can observe the same in Figure 3.

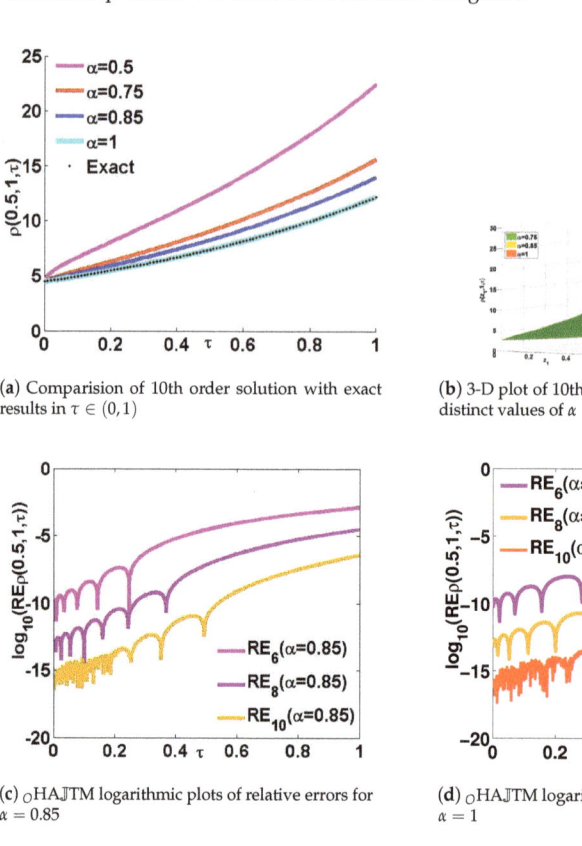

Figure 3. Solutions for $\rho(z_{1,2}, \tau)$. (a) Behavior of computed results from $_O$HA$\mathbb{J}$TM at 10th iteration with exact results; (b) logarithmic plots of relative errors in κth iterative results ($\kappa = 6, 8, 10$) for (c,e) $\alpha = 0.85$, (d,f) $\alpha = 1$; at $z_1 = 0.5$, $z_2 = 1$ and optimal value of $\hbar$, for ρ obtained from $_O$HA$\mathbb{J}$TM (c,d), $\mathbb{J}$-VITM (e,f), respectively.

It is easy to demonstrate numerically from Figures 1c–f–3c–f and Tables 1 and 2 that for a given order of approximation, $_O$HAJTM with optimal $\hbar$ are of high accuracy but requires larger CPU time as compared to J-VITM. In addition both of the proposed hybrid methods converges, that is, $_O$HAJTM with optimal $\hbar$ converges faster than J-VITM. For $\hbar = -1$, the rate of convergence of $_O$HAJTM is the same as that of J-VITM while J-VITM requires less computational timethan $_O$HAJTM.

6. Conclusions

In that present work studied, two space-dimensional time-fractional models governing the unsteady flow of pGas via two new efficient techniques so-called $_O$HAJTM and J-VITM. Both techniques are shown convergent with help of the Banach's fixed point approach, and J-VITM is shown T-stable.

For an arbitrary fractional order α, the evaluated solution behavior of the referred model equation is expressed in the form of well known Mittag–Leffler function. The effectiveness/validity of the evaluated new approximations is demonstrated via a numerical test example of a two space-dimensional time-fractional model governing the unsteady flow of a pGas by computing the absolute-errors/relative-error.

The numerical evaluation demonstrates that both of the developed techniques are convergent and perform better for the considered time-fractional model governing the unsteady flow of pGas. In addition, for given iteration new results by $_O$HAJTM with optimal convergence control parameter ($\hbar$) are of high accuracy but require larger CPU time as compared to J-VITM, that is, $_O$HAJTM with optimal $\hbar$ converges faster than J-VITM. It is remarkably mentioned that for $\hbar = -1$, both methods converge to the exact results with the same rate of convergence while J-VITM requires less computational time than $_O$HAJTM. The motivation of this work is to explore the fractional behaviour of the considered model. We have observed the significant variations in the solutions for different fractional orders, which may lead to various physical consequences for the future work.

Author Contributions: Methodology, B.K.S.; Formal analysis, N.S.; Supervision, H.M.B.; Project administration, M.G. and D.G.P. All authors have read and agreed to the published version of the manuscript.

Funding: This research received no external funding.

Conflicts of Interest: The authors want to declare that there are no competing interests.

References

1. Miller, K.S.; Ross, B. *An Introduction to the Fractional Calculus and Fractional Differential Equations*; John Wiley and Sons: New York, NY, USA, 1993.
2. Podlubny, I. *Fractional Differential Equations*; Academic Press: New York, NY, USA, 1999.
3. Srivastava, H.M.; Trujillo, J.J.; Kilbas, A.A. *Theory and Applications of Fractional Differential Equations*; Elsevier: Amsterdam, The Netherlands, 2006.
4. Atangana, A. Blind in a commutative world: Simple illustrations with functions and chaotic attractors. *Chaos Solitons Fractals* **2018**, *114*, 347–363. [CrossRef]
5. Atangana, A. Fractle-fractional differentiation and integration: Connecting fractal calculus and fractional calculus to predict complex system. *Chaos Solitons Fractals* **2017**, *102*, 396–406. [CrossRef]
6. Altizer, S.M.; Oberhauser, K.S. Effects of the protozoan parasite ophryocystis elektroscirrha on the fitness of monarch butterflies (danaus plexippus). *J. Invertebr. Pathol.* **1999**, *74*, 76–88. [CrossRef]
7. Ahmad, S.; Ullah, A.; Al-Mdallal, Q.M.; Khan, H.; Shah, K.; Khan, A. Fractional order mathematical modelling of covid-19 transmission. *Chaos Solitons Fractals* **2020**, *139*, 396–406. [CrossRef]
8. Gupta, S. Numerical simulation of time-fractional black-scholes equation using fractional variational iteration method. *J. Comput. Math. Sci.* **2019**, *9*, 1101–1110. [CrossRef]
9. Liao, S. On the homotopy analysis method for nonlinear problems. *Appl. Math. Comput.* **2004**, *147*, 499–513. [CrossRef]
10. Song, L.; Xu, S.; Yang, J. Dynamical models of happiness with fractional order. *Commun. Nonlinear Sci. Numer. Simul.* **2010**, *15*, 616–628. [CrossRef]
11. Moradpour, H.; Abri, A. Thermodynamic behavior and stability of polytropic gas. *Int. J. Mod. Phys. D* **2016**, *12*, 1650014. [CrossRef]

12. Liao, S.J. *Beyond Perturbation: Introduction to Homotopy Analysis Method*; Chapman and Hall/CRC: Boca Raton, FL, USA, 2003.
13. Liao, S. An optimal homotopy-analysis approach for strongly nonlinear differential equations. *Commun Nonlinear Sci Numer Simulat.* **2010**, *15*, 2003–2016. [CrossRef]
14. Liao, S. The Proposed Homotopy Analysis Techniques for the Solution of Nonlinear Problems. Ph.D. Thesis, Shanghai Jiao Tong University, Shanghai, China, 1992.
15. Prakasha, D.G.; Veeresha, P.; Baskonus, H.M. An efficient technique for a fractional-order system of equations describing the unsteady flow of a polytropic gas. *Pramana J. Phys.* **2019**, *93*, 75.
16. Dalsgard, J.C. *Lecture Notes on Stellar Structure and Evolution*; Aarhus University Press: Aarhus, Denmark, 2004.
17. Matinfar, M.; Nodeh, S.J. Application of he's variational iteration method for solving the equation governing the unsteady flow of a polytropic gas. *J. Math. Ext.* **2009**, *3*, 61–67.
18. Matinfar, M.; Saeidy, M. Homotopy analysis method for solving the equation governing the unsteady flow of a polytropic gas. *World Appl. Sci. J.* **2010**, *9*, 980–983.
19. Billingham, J. Dynamics of a strongly nonlocal reaction-diffusion population model. *Nonlinearity* **2003**, *17*, 313. [CrossRef]
20. Cherif, M.A.; Ziane, D.; Belghaba, K. Fractional natural decomposition method for solving fractional system of nonlinear equations of unsteady flow of a polytropic gas. *Nonlinear Std.* **2018**, *25*, 753–764.
21. Adel, W.; Srinivasa, K. A new clique polynomial approach for fractional differential equations. *Int. J. Nonlinear Sci. Numer. Simul.* **2022**. [CrossRef]
22. Yadav, L.K.; Agarwal, G.; Suthar, D.L.; Purohit, S.D. Time-fractional partial differential equations: A novel technique for analytical and numerical solutions. *Arab. J. Basic Appl. Sci.* **2022**, *29*, 86–98. [CrossRef]
23. Shah, R.; Khan, H.; Kumam, P.; Arif, M. An analytical system to solve the system of nonlinear fractional differential equations. *Mathematics* **2019**, *7*, 505. [CrossRef]
24. Srivastava, V.K.; Singh, B.K. Approximate series solution of multi-dimensional, time fractional-order (heat-like) diffusion equations using frdtm. *R. Soc. Open Sci.* **2015**, *2*, 140511.
25. Saleh, R.; Kassem, M.; Mabrauk, S.M. Exact solutions of nonlinear fractional order partial differential equations via singular manifold method. *Chin. J. Phys.* **2019**, *61*, 290–300. [CrossRef]
26. Weiguo, R. Comments on whether nonlinear fractional partila differential equations have soliton solutions. *Partial. Differ. Equ. Appl. Math.* **2022**, *5*, 100396.
27. Ali, H.M.; Ahmad, H.; Askar, S.; Ameen, I.G. Efficient apporaches for solving system of nonlinear time-fractional partial differential equations. *Fractal Fract.* **2022**, *6*, 32. [CrossRef]
28. Shakeel, M.; Shah, N.A.; Chung, J.D. Novel analytical technique to find closed form solutions of time fractional partial differential equations. *Fractal Fract.* **2022**, *6*, 24. [CrossRef]
29. Hosseini, V.R.; Zou, W. The peridynamic differential opertaor for solving time-fractional partial differential equations. *Nonlinear Dyn.* **2022**, *109*, 1823–1850. [CrossRef]
30. Malagi, N.S.; Prakasha, D.G.; Veeresha, P.; Prasannakumara, B.C. *Fractional Reaction-Diffusion Model: An Efficient Computational Technique for Nonlinear Time-Fractional Schnackenberg Model*; Springer: Singapore, 2022.
31. Joujehi, A.S.; Derakhshan, M.H.; Marasi, H.R. An efficient hybrid numerical method for multi-term time fractional partial differential equations in fluid mechanics with convergence and error analysis. *Commun. Nonlinear Sci. Numer. Simul.* **2022**, *114*, 106620. [CrossRef]
32. Alesemi, M.; Shahrani, J.S.A.; Iqbal, N.; Shah, R.; Nonlapon, K. Analysis and numerical simulation of system of fractional partial differential equations with non-singular kernel operators. *Symmetry* **2023**, *15*, 233. [CrossRef]
33. Laoubi, M.; Odibat, Z.; Maayah, B. Effective optimized decomposition algorithms for solving nonlinear fractional differential equations. *J. Comput. Nonlinear Dyn.* **2023**, *18*, 021001. [CrossRef]
34. Elshenhab, A.M.; Wang, X.T.; Mofarreh, F.; Bazighifan, O. Exact solutions and finite time stability of linear conformable fractional systems with pure delay. *Comput. Model. Eng. Sci.* **2023**, *134*, 927–940. [CrossRef]
35. Wang, S.; Luo, X.; Riaz, S.; Zaman, H.; Zhou, C.; Hao, P. A fractional order fast repetitive control paradigm ofvienna rectifier for power quality improvement. *Cmes-Comput. Model. Eng. Sci.* **2023**, *135*, 259–273.
36. Khan, H.; Kumam, P.; Nawaz, A.; Khan, Q.; Khan, S. The fractional investigation of fornberg-whitham equation using an efficient technique. *Cmes-Comput. Model. Eng. Sci.* **2023**, *134*, 1159–1176. [CrossRef]
37. Veeresha, P.; Ilhan, E.; Prakasha, D.G.; Baskonus, H.M.; Gao, W. Regarding on the fractional mathematical model of tumor invasion and metastasis. *Cmes-Comput. Model. Eng. Sci.* **2021**, *127*, 1013–1036.
38. Mohamed, M.A. Adomian decomposition method for solving the equation governing the unsteady flow of a polytropic gas. *Appl. Appl. Math.* **2009**, *4*, 52–61.
39. Kreyszig, E. *Introductory Functional Analysis with Applications*; John Wiley and Sons: New York, NY, USA, 1978.
40. Qing, Y.; Rhoades, B.E. T-Stability of Picard iteration in metric spaces. *Fixed Point Theory Appl.* **2008**, *2008*, 418971. [CrossRef]
41. Khan, H.; Khan, A.; Chen, W.; Shah, K. Stability analysis and a numerical scheme for fractional Klein-Gordon equations. *Math. Meth. Appl. Sci.* **2019**, *42*, 723–732. [CrossRef]
42. Maitama, S.; Zhao, W. Beyond sumudu transform and natural transform: *j*-transform properties and applications. *J. Appl. Anal. Comput.* **2020**, *10*, 1223–1241.

43. He, J.H. Approximate analytical solution for seepage flow with fractional derivatives in porous media. *Comput. Methods Appl. Mech. Eng.* **1998**, *167*, 57–68. [CrossRef]
44. He, J.H. Variational iteration method—A kind of non-linear analytical technique: Some examples. *Int. J. -Non-Linear Mech.* **1999**, *167*, 57–68. [CrossRef]
45. He, J.H. Variational iteration method-Some recent results and new interpretations. *J. Comput. Appl. Math.* **2007**, *207*, 3–17. [CrossRef]
46. Odibat, Z.M. A study on the convergence of variational iteration method. *Math. Comput. Model.* **2010**, *51*, 1181–1192. [CrossRef]
47. Abassy, T.A.; El-Tawil, M.A.; El-Zoheiry, H. Modified variational iteration method for Boussinesq equation. *Comput. Math. Appl.* **2007**, *54*, 955–965. [CrossRef]
48. Singh, B.K.; Kumar, P. Fractional variational iteration method for solving fractional partial differential equations with proportional delay. *Int. J. Differ. Equ.* **2017**, *88*, 1–11. [CrossRef]
49. Momani, S.; Odibat, Z.M. The variational iteration method: An efficient scheme for handling fractional partial differential equation in fluid mechanics. *Comput. Math. Appl.* **2009**, *58*, 2199–2208.
50. Jafari, H.; Alipoor, A. A new method for calculating general Lagrange multiplier in the variational iteration method. *Numer. Methods Partial. Differ. Equ.* **2011**, *27*, 996–1001. [CrossRef]
51. Goswami, P.; Alqahtani, R. Solutions of fractional differential equations by sumudu transform and variational iteration method. *J. Nonlinear Sci. Appl.* **2016**, *9*, 1944–1951. [CrossRef]
52. Finlayson, B.A. *The Method of Weighted Residuals and Variational Principles*; Academic Press: New York, NY, USA, 1972.
53. Khuri, S.A.; Sayfy, A. A laplace variational iteration strategy for the solution of differential equations. *Appl. Math. Lett.* **2012**, *25*, 2298–2305. [CrossRef]
54. Li, F.; Nadeem, H.A.M. Modified laplace variational iteration method for solving fourth-order parabolic partial differential equation with variable coefficients. *Comput. Math. Appl.* **2020**, *78*, 2052–2062.

Disclaimer/Publisher's Note: The statements, opinions and data contained in all publications are solely those of the individual author(s) and contributor(s) and not of MDPI and/or the editor(s). MDPI and/or the editor(s) disclaim responsibility for any injury to people or property resulting from any ideas, methods, instructions or products referred to in the content.

Article

Electrothermal Monte Carlo Simulation of a GaAs Resonant Tunneling Diode

Orazio Muscato

Department of Mathematics and Computer Science, University of Catania, 95125 Catania, Italy; orazio.muscato@unict.it

Abstract: This paper deals with the electron transport and heat generation in a Resonant Tunneling Diode semiconductor device. A new electrothermal Monte Carlo method is introduced. The method couples a Monte Carlo solver of the Boltzmann–Wigner transport equation with a steady-state solution of the heat diffusion equation. This methodology provides an accurate microscopic description of the spatial distribution of self-heating and its effect on the detailed nonequilibrium carrier dynamics.

Keywords: Monte Carlo methods; statistical mechanics of semiconductors; heat transfer

MSC: 65C05; 82D37; 80M31

Citation: Muscato, O. Electrothermal Monte Carlo Simulation of a GaAs Resonant Tunneling Diode. *Axioms* **2023**, *12*, 216. https://doi.org/10.3390/axioms12020216

Academic Editor: Angel Ricardo Plastino

Received: 12 January 2023
Revised: 14 February 2023
Accepted: 16 February 2023
Published: 19 February 2023

Copyright: © 2023 by the authors. Licensee MDPI, Basel, Switzerland. This article is an open access article distributed under the terms and conditions of the Creative Commons Attribution (CC BY) license (https://creativecommons.org/licenses/by/4.0/).

1. Introduction

Due to the continued miniaturization of integrated circuits and the current trend toward nanoscale electronics, power densities, heat generation, and chip temperatures will reach levels that will prevent the reliable operation of such circuits. In order to minimize self-heating effects, the development of accurate electrothermal simulators is required, which takes into account the coupling between electronic and lattice dynamics. In the active regions of such small devices, heat generation is a direct consequence of the nonequilibrium carrier transport. In high electric field regions, the electrons are accelerated and collide with the lattice in such a way that the emission of a large number of phonons contributes to heat transport in the device. In the framework of semiclassical charge transport, electrothermal simulators are based on drift–diffusion or hydrodynamic models [1,2], which are able to capture nonequilibrium transport effects. Alternatively, the direct simulation Monte Carlo (MC) can provide an accurate nonequilibrium charge transport simulation, which is free from the approximations made in the drift–diffusion or hydrodynamic model. Electrothermal Monte Carlo simulators have been developed during these years [3–5] but not in quantum regimes where the Boltzmann Transport Equation must be replaced by the Wigner Transport Equation (WTE). Since electron devices are quantum systems outside of thermodynamic equilibrium, scattering by phonons should be included in the WTE for a realistic simulation. Many proposals for the collision operator can be found in the literature [6,7], which provide an accurate description of the phenomena at the price of a high requirement of computational resources. Because of that, the use of such operators is restricted to very simple (idealized) systems. In this paper, the effects of scattering with phonons are taken into account via a semiclassical Boltzmann collision operator, which employs transition rates calculated using Fermi's golden rule, obtaining the so called Boltzmann–Wigner transport equation (BWTE). Numerical solvers of the WTE can be based on finite-difference schemes [8–13], where scattering was restricted to the relaxation time approximation and the momentum space to one dimension. The Monte Carlo method allows for scattering processes to be included on a more detailed level, assuming a three-dimensional momentum–space. In this paper, we shall use the so-called *Signed Particle Monte Carlo* method (SPMC) [14,15] in which the effect of Wigner potential is interpreted as a probabilistic generation of couples of positive and negative particles, where the quantum information is carried by their sign. The huge number of generated particles can be controlled by an annihilation process: two particles with an opposite sign entering a given phase space cell are canceled. Recently, this method has also been understood in terms of the Markov jump process theory [16], producing a class of new stochastic algorithms. Algorithms that belong to this class are a standard time-splitting algorithm and a new no-splitting algorithm that avoids errors due to time-discretization [17,18].

Taking advantage of previous Electrothermal Monte Carlo semiclassical models, in this paper, we shall study the heating effect in a Resonant Tunneling Diode (RTD), coupling the SPMC solver of the BWTE with a steady-state solution of the heat diffusion equation. To the author's knowledge, this model is the first of its kind in terms of model accuracy. The paper is organized as follows. Details of the Boltzmann–Wigner transport equation are provided in Section 2, and in Section 3 we deal with the *Signed Particle Monte Carlo* method. In Section 3, we introduce the Resonant Tunneling diode structure and in Section 5 the Electrothermal Signed Particle Monte Carlo Method. Simulation results are shown in Section 6, and conclusions are drawn in Section 7.

2. The Boltzmann–Wigner Transport Equation

The BWTE writes [19]

$$\frac{\partial}{\partial t} f_w(t,x,k) + \frac{\hbar}{m^*} k \cdot \nabla_x f_w(t,x,k) + \frac{e}{\hbar} \nabla_x \varphi \cdot \nabla_k f_w(t,x,k) = \mathcal{Q}(f_w) + \mathcal{C}(f_w). \quad (1)$$

$x \in \mathbb{R}^3$ and $\hbar k \in \mathbb{R}^3$ are the electron position and momentum, respectively, m^* is the electron effective mass, and φ the slowly-varying potential satisfying the Poisson equation

$$\nabla \cdot [\varepsilon_0 \varepsilon_r \nabla \varphi(x)] = -e(N_D - N_A - n), \quad (2)$$

where e is the elementary charge, ε_0 the absolute dielectric constant, ε_r the relative dielectric constant, N_D, N_A are the donors and acceptors' doping profiles, and n the particle density

$$n(t,x) = \int f_w(x,k,t) \, dk \quad . \quad (3)$$

$\mathcal{C}(f_w)$ is the Boltzmann scattering operator which, in the not-degenerate case, is as follows [20]:

$$\mathcal{C}(f_w) = \int \left[w_s(k',k) f_w(k') - w_s(k,k') f_w(k) \right] dk', \quad (4)$$

where $w_s(k,k')$ is the scattering rate at which electrons suffer with phonons and impurities, given by the Fermi's golden rule. The quantum evolution is taken into account by the term

$$\mathcal{Q}(f_w) = \int_{\mathbb{R}^d} V_w(x, k-k') f_w(t,x,k') \, dk', \quad (5)$$

where V_w is the Wigner potential

$$V_w(x,k) = \frac{1}{i\hbar(2\pi)^d} \int_{\mathbb{R}^d} dx' \, e^{-ik \cdot x'} \left[V\left(x + \frac{x'}{2}\right) - V\left(x - \frac{x'}{2}\right) \right], \quad (6)$$

and V is the rapidly-varying term of the potential energy.

3. The Signed Particle Monte Carlo Method

The quantum evolution term (5) can be interpreted like the *Gain* term of the collisional operator of the Boltzmann transport equation, in which the *Loss* term is missing. However, the Wigner potential (6) is not always positive and, for this reason, cannot be considered a scattering term. The main idea of the *Signed Particle Monte Carlo* method [14] consists of separating V_w into a positive and negative part V_w^+, V_w^- such that

$$V_w = V_w^+ - V_w^- \quad , \quad V_w^+, V_w^- \geq 0 \tag{7}$$

Consequently, we can define an integrated scattering probability per unit time as

$$\gamma(x) = \int dk' \, V_w^+(x, k - k') = \int dk' \, V_w^-(x, k - k') \tag{8}$$

and rewrite the quantum evolution term as the difference between *Gain* and *Loss* terms, i.e.,

$$Q(f_w) = \int dk' w(k', k) f_w(t, x, k') - \gamma(x) f_w(t, x, k) \tag{9}$$

$$w(k', k) = V_w^+(x, k - k') - V_w^-(x, k - k') + \gamma(x) \delta(k - k') \quad . \tag{10}$$

The interpretation of the scattering term $w(k', k)$ is that a particle produces, in the same position, a couple of new particles with weight u and $-u$ according to a generation rate given by the function $\gamma(x)$. The momentum of the new particles is generated with probability $V_w^+(x, k)/\gamma(x)$. Since usually γ is rapidly oscillating, an exponential growth of particle numbers is expected and, in order to control the particle number, a cancellation procedure is mandatory.

This procedure has been understood using the theory of the piecewise deterministic Markov processes [16], where the state space is

$$z_j(t) = (u_j(t), x_j(t), k_j(t)), \quad t \geq 0 \quad , \quad j = 1, \ldots, N(t), \tag{11}$$

and $u_j \in \{-1, +1\}$ is the weight. The time evolution of the particle system (11) is assigned by a deterministic motion according to the flow

$$F(t, z) = (u, x + v(k)t, k) \quad , \quad v = \frac{\hbar}{m} k \tag{12}$$

and a jump kernel $Q(z_j(t))$. The random waiting time τ until the next jump satisfies

$$\mathbb{P}(\tau \geq t) = \exp\left(-\int_0^t Q(F(s, z)) \, ds\right) \quad . \tag{13}$$

For numerical purposes, we introduce a majorant $\hat{V}_w$ such that

$$|V_w(x, k)| \leq \hat{V}_w(x, k) \quad \forall x, k \in \mathbb{R}^3 \quad . \tag{14}$$

If the j-th particle generates two new particles with

$$z'_1 = (u_j \, \text{sign} V_w(x_j, k), x_j, k_j + k) \quad , \quad z'_2 = (u_j \, \text{sign} V_w(x_j, k), x_j, k_j - k) \tag{15}$$

the jump kernel takes the form [17]

$$Q(z_j) = \frac{1}{2} \int \hat{V}_w(x_j, k) \, dk \tag{16}$$

and Equation (13) writes

$$\mathbb{P}(\tau \geq t) = \exp\left(-\int_0^t \hat{\gamma}(x_j + v(k_j)s) \, ds\right) \tag{17}$$

where

$$\hat{\gamma}(x) = \frac{1}{2} \int \hat{V}_w(x, k) \, dk \tag{18}$$

represents the generation probability. It is possible to prove that functionals of the solution of the Wigner equation are expressed in terms of the particle system using the representation [16]

$$\int\int \phi(x,k)f(t,x,k)dkdx = \frac{1}{N_{ini}} \mathbb{E}\left(\sum_{j=1}^{N(t)} u_j(t)\phi(x_j(t),k_j(t))\right) \qquad (19)$$

where ϕ is an appropriate test function, and $N_{ini} = N(0)$ is the initial particle number. In order to to separate the transport and the jump processes, usually a splitting time step Δt is used at the expense of a discretization error. This can be avoided by using a no-splitting algorithm recently introduced in [17,18]. By introducing a majorant for the generation process (8) and one for the total phonon scattering rate

$$\Gamma_s \geq \max \lambda(k) \quad , \quad \lambda(k) = \sum_\alpha \int w_\alpha(k,k')\, dk' \qquad (20)$$

The total majorant is

$$\Gamma = \Gamma_s + \hat{\gamma} \qquad (21)$$

and Equation (17), for all particles, now is as follows:

$$\mathbb{P}(\tau \geq t) = \exp\left(-\sum_{j=1}^N \int_0^t [\Gamma_s + \hat{\gamma}(x_j + v(k_j)s)]\, ds\right) . \qquad (22)$$

In the case in which $\hat{\gamma}$ does not depend on the position, we have

$$\mathbb{P}(\tau \geq t) = \exp(-\Gamma N t) \to \quad \tau = -\frac{1}{\Gamma N}\log r \qquad (23)$$

where $r \in U[0,1]$, and τ is completely determined. With respect to the splitting case, now the transport and the generation process can not be separated, and the results shall not be affected by any discretization error.

4. The Resonant Tunneling Diode

A standard Resonant Tunneling Diode structure [21] has been implemented, as shown in Figure 1. The barriers have depth $b = 3$ nm, height $a = 0.3$, and the quantum well dimension is $b_w = 5$ nm, symmetric with respect to the mid-point $L/2$ (total length $L = 150$ nm). The barrier structure is embedded in a 30 nm lightly doped region ($N_D = 10^{16}$ cm^{-3}) which is connected to 60 nm highly doped regions on either side ($N_D^+ = 10^{18}$ cm^{-3}).

In this case, the Wigner potential (6) can be easily evaluated in addition to the majorant (18) (see [18] for the details). The device considered is made by Gallium Arsenide (GaAs) (with $m^* = 0.067$), and polar optical phonons (POP) within a single Γ band [20] in the parabolic band approximation used are taken into account. The total scattering rate is written as follows [20]:

$$\lambda(k, T_L) = \lambda^-(k, T_L) + \lambda^+(k, T_L) \qquad (24)$$

where the first term represents POP absorption and the second one emission

$$\lambda^-(k, T_L) = \frac{e^2 \omega_p \left(\frac{1}{\epsilon_\infty} - \frac{1}{\epsilon_r}\right)}{2\pi\epsilon_0 \hbar \sqrt{\frac{2\epsilon(k)}{m^*}}} n_0 \sinh^{-1}\sqrt{\frac{\epsilon(k)}{\hbar\omega_p}} \qquad (25)$$

$$\lambda^+(k, T_L) = \frac{e^2 \omega_p \left(\frac{1}{\epsilon_\infty} - \frac{1}{\epsilon_r}\right)}{2\pi\epsilon_0 \hbar \sqrt{\frac{2\epsilon(k)}{m^*}}} (n_0 + 1) \sinh^{-1}\sqrt{\frac{\epsilon(k)}{\hbar\omega_p} - 1} \qquad (26)$$

The term $n_0(T_L)$ is the phonon equilibrium distribution, i.e.,

$$n_0(T_L) = \frac{1}{\exp\left(\frac{\hbar\omega_p}{k_B T_L}\right) - 1} \tag{27}$$

$\hbar\omega_p$ is the polar optical phonon energy (0.03536 eV) and T_L the lattice temperature. The initial lattice temperature is 300 K, and ohmic boundary conditions are used.

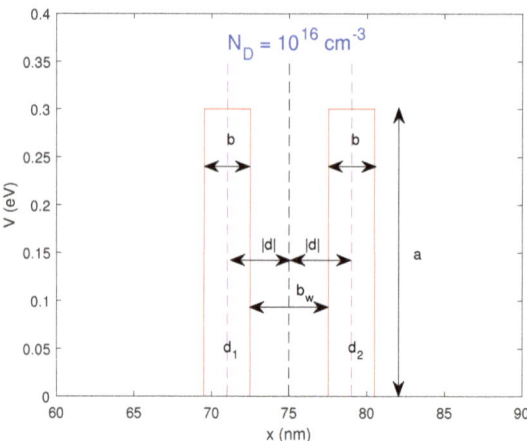

Figure 1. The quantum well region.

5. The Electrothermal Signed Particle Monte Carlo Method

An important issue that arises from the coupling of an MC electronic transport algorithm to any thermal model is the significant difference in the characteristic time scales of electronic and thermal transport. Electronic transients in GaAs systems are of the order of picoseconds, whereas thermal transients may be of the order of nanoseconds, microseconds, or even longer. Performing MC computations for the duration of thermal transients across the whole semiconductor die would not be feasible. Consequently, the method used in this paper extracts steady-state electrothermal device characteristics only. The electrothermal SPMC method of simulation is an iterative approach:

- The initial SPMC iteration is run at a room temperature of 300 K for a few ps, in order to reach a steady-state;
- As the steady state is reached, electronic parameters are sampled for typically 15 ps, in order to evaluate the heat generation rate $H(x)$;
- The lattice temperature $T_L(x)$ is obtained by solving the steady-state heat diffusion equation

$$\nabla_x(\kappa \nabla_x T_L(x)) + H(x) = 0 \tag{28}$$

κ being the thermal conductivity in GaAs;
- The SPMC solver is rerun, in the next iteration, with the new lattice temperature $T_L(x)$. We observe that the scattering rates (25) and (26) depend on the lattice temperature;
- We repeat this procedure until convergence is reached.

This model does not account for temperature changes beyond the semiconductor die. Radiation losses are neglected, as their contribution at the small die surface areas is insignificant.

The mechanism through which Joule heating occurs is that of electron scattering with phonons, and consequently only a simulation approach which deliberately incorporates all such scattering events will capture the complete microscopic, detailed picture of lattice heating. The phonon emission and absorption events during a simulation run are tallied and full heat generation statistics can be collected. We wait until the steady state has been reached at time t_0. Then, we count our events in the observation points t_i, $i = 0, \ldots, N_{obs}$. We evaluate the heat generation rate in two ways:

1. **Counting the phonon number.**
   We introduce the quantity [22]

$$H^c(t_{i-1}, t_i, x) = \frac{n(t_i, x)}{N_p(t_i, x)} \frac{\hbar \omega_p [C^+ - C^-]}{dt}, \qquad (29)$$

where $C^+(t_{i-1}, t_i, x)$, $C^-(t_{i-1}, t_i, x)$ are the numbers of the phonon emitted and absorbed in the time interval (t_{i-1}, t_i) in the x-th grid point, $n(t, x)$ the charge density, and $N_p(t, x)$ the particle number at time t in the x-th cell. Then, the heat generation rate is

$$\langle H^c(x) \rangle = \frac{1}{N_{obs}} \sum_{i=1}^{N_{obs}} H^c(t_{i-1}, t_i, x) \qquad (30)$$

2. using the **integrated probability scattering function**.
   From the integrated probability scattering (25) and (26) we can define

$$H^F(t_i, x) = \frac{n(t_i, x)}{N_{ini}} \sum_{j=1}^{N(t_i)} u_j G(\varepsilon(k_j)) \quad , \quad G(\varepsilon) = \hbar \omega_p [\lambda^+(k) - \lambda^-(k)] \qquad (31)$$

Then, the heat generation rate is

$$\left\langle H^F(x) \right\rangle = \frac{1}{N_{obs}} \sum_{i=1}^{N_{obs}} H^F(t_i, x) \quad . \qquad (32)$$

The heat generation is reduced to the usual calculation of functionals according to Equation (19). This estimator enjoys better approximation properties due to reduced statistical fluctuations [5].

6. Numerical Results

In order to have a significant lattice temperature increase with respect to the equilibrium temperature of 300 K, the applied bias voltage V_b must be greater than 0.8 V. In Figure 2, we plot the heat generation rate versus the position, evaluated by means of the counting estimator (30) and the integrated probability estimator (32), for $V_b = 0.8$ V. From this figure, we can see that the maximum heat is produced inside the quantum well region, representing a so-called *hot spot region*.

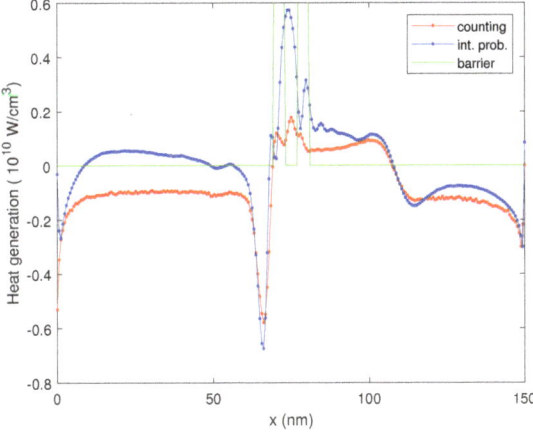

Figure 2. The heat generation rate versus the position for $V_b = 0.8$ V evaluated by means of the counting estimator (30) and the integrated probability estimator (32).

In Figure 3, we plot the corresponding standard deviation, proving the variance reduction of the integrated probability estimator (32). In Figure 4, we plot a zoom of Figure 2 with the error bar, proving that the integrated probability estimator is always inside the tolerance band of the counting estimator. Figure 5 shows the density for the first two iterations, showing no appreciable variation.

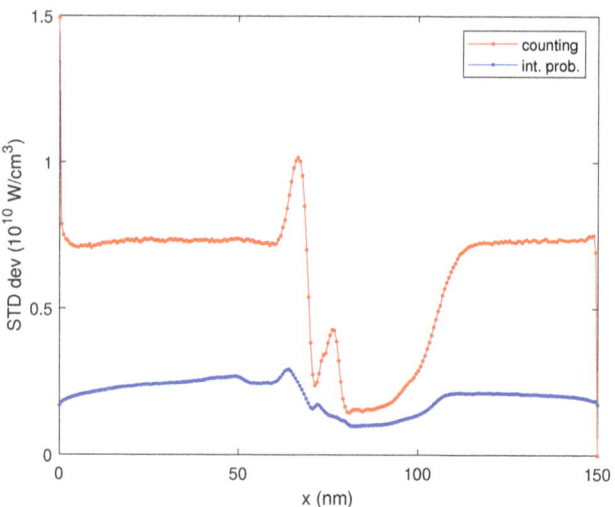

Figure 3. The standard deviation of the counting estimator (30) and the integrated probability estimator (32) versus position, for $V_b = 0.8$ V.

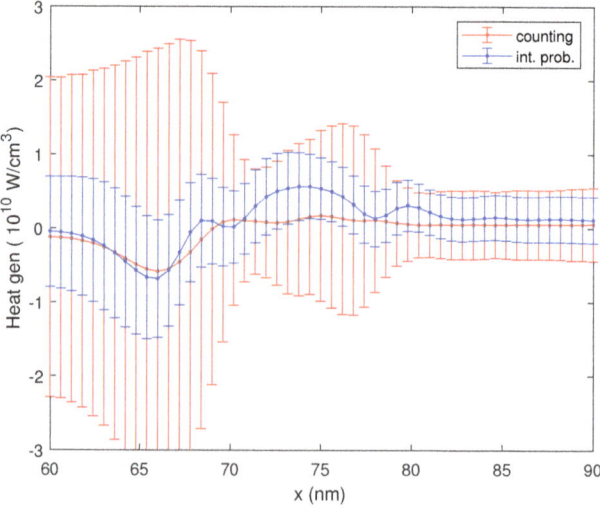

Figure 4. The heat generation rate vs. position for $V_b = 0.8$ V evaluated by means of the counting estimator (30) and the integrated probability estimator (32), with error bar.

Figure 6 shows the lattice temperature evaluated by means of the heat diffusion Equation (28) for the first two iterations, which are enough to reach the convergence. We observe that the lattice temperature is decreasing with the iteration number. To explain this behavior, one must consider the function $G(\varepsilon)$ in Equation (31). This function represents the difference between the emitted and absorbed phonon probability; if this quantity is positive, more phonons are released into the lattice and in turn the temperature increases. We plot this quantity in Figure 7 showing that, for this particular kind of scattering mechanism, it decreases with the lattice temperature. In Figure 8, we plot the current versus the iteration number, proving that this quantity is constant. If we double the applied voltage to $V_b = 1.6$ V, the increase of temperature is of a factor 5 as shown in Figure 9.

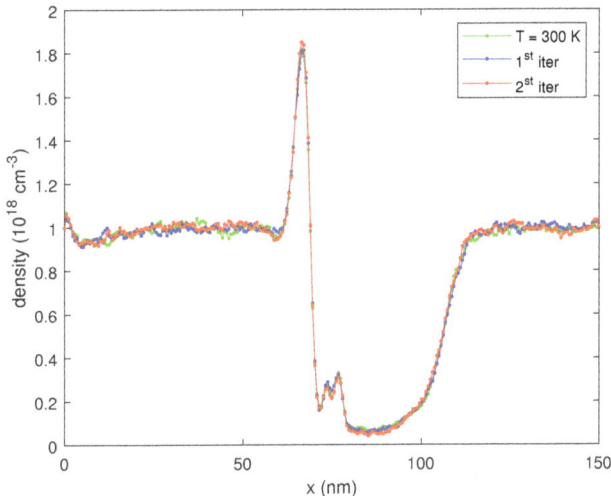

Figure 5. The density versus position for some iterations, for $V_b = 0.8$ V.

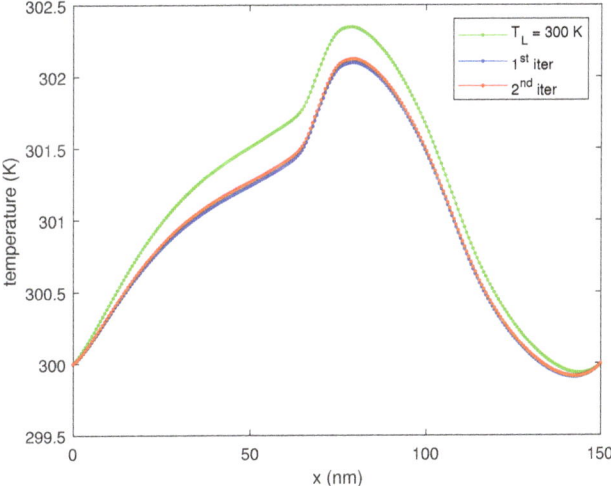

Figure 6. The lattice temperature T_L versus position for some iterations, for $V_b = 0.8$ V.

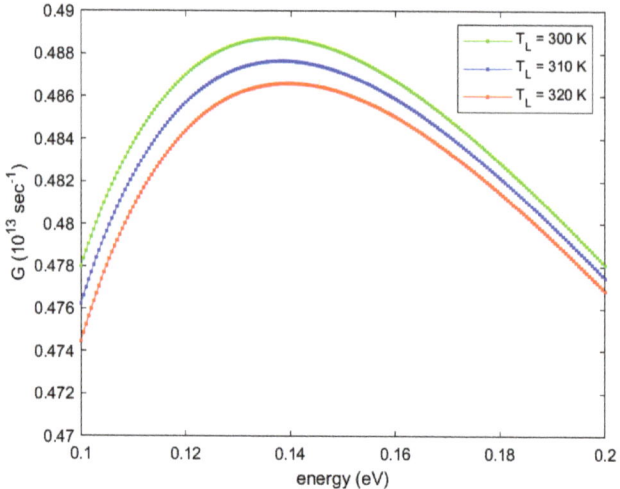

Figure 7. The function $G(\varepsilon)$ (31) versus energy for some lattice temperature.

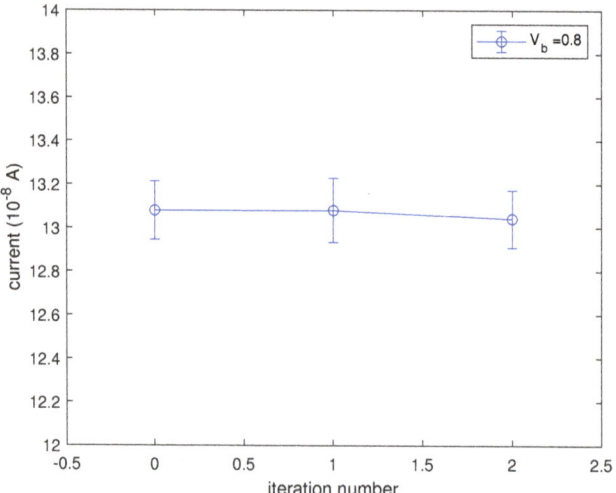

Figure 8. The current versus iteration number, for $V_b = 0.8$ V.

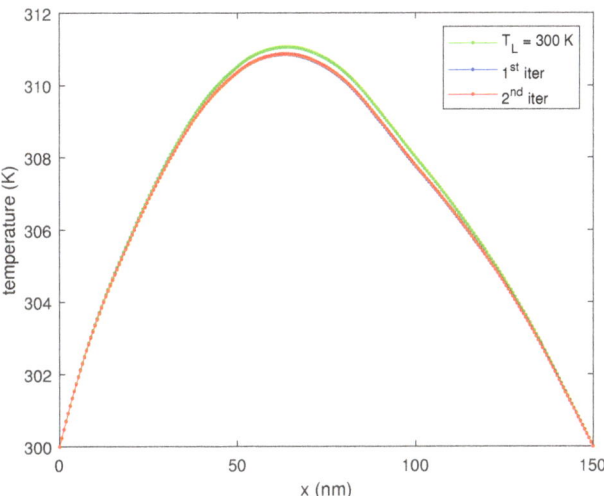

Figure 9. The lattice temperature T_L versus position for some iterations, for $V_b = 1.6$ V.

7. Conclusions

The Electrothermal Signed Particle Monte Carlo algorithm provides an accurate tool for studying heat generation and quantum effects in nanometric semiconductor devices, at the expense of huge computational effort. The coupling between the MC charge transport and the heat diffusion equation is given by a term called heat generation rate obtained, usually, by counting the number of phonons emitted/absorbed during the steady-state. Alternatively, a new estimator of the heat generation rate, based on the integrated scattering probability function (32), can be used, which enjoys reduced statistical fluctuations. Simulation results for a Resonant Tunneling Diode are shown, proving that the heat is produced almost entirely inside the quantum well and estimating the lattice temperature, which depends on the applied voltage. The localization of hot spot regions can be useful in the design of such devices, in order to optimize the heat removal.

Funding: This research received no external funding.

Data Availability Statement: Data is contained within the article.

Acknowledgments: The author acknowledges the support of the project "Developing a Computational Framework for Quantum Information and Communication Technologies", Piano di incentivi per la ricerca di Ateneo 2020/2022—linea 2, Università degli Studi di Catania, and by the National Group of Mathematical Physics (GNFM-INDAM).

Conflicts of Interest: The author declares no conflict of interest.

References

1. Muscato, O.; Di Stefano, V. Hydrodynamic modeling of the electro-thermal transport in silicon semiconductors. *J. Phys. A Math. Theor.* **2011**, *44*, 105501. [CrossRef]
2. Mascali, G. Exploitation of the Maximum Entropy Principle in the Study of Thermal Conductivity of Silicon, Germanium and Graphene. *Energies* **2022**, *15*, 4718. [CrossRef]
3. Sadi, T.; Kensal, R.; Pilgrim, N. Simulation of Electron Transport in InGaAs/AlGaAs HEMTs Using an Electrothermal Monte Carlo Method. *IEEE Trans. Electr. Dev.* **2006**, *53*, 1768–1774. [CrossRef]
4. Sadi, T.; Kensal, R.W.; Pilgrim, N.; Thobel, J.L.; Dessenne, F. Monte Carlo study of self-heating in nanoscale devices. *J. Comput. Electr.* **2012**, *11*, 118–128. [CrossRef]
5. Muscato, O.; Di Stefano, V.; Wagner, W. A variance-reduced electrothermal Monte Carlo method for semiconductor device simulation. *Comput. Math. Appl.* **2013**, *65*, 520–527. [CrossRef]
6. Zhan, Z.; Colomes, E.; Oriols, X. Unphysical features in the application of the Boltzmann collision operator in the time-dependent modeling of quantum transport. *J. Comput. Electron.* **2016**, *15*, 1206–1218. [CrossRef]

rate among COVID-19 patients is 3–4% [5]. The precautionary measures implemented by governments to limit the transmission of COVID-19 can play a role in reducing the transmission of influenza [6]. Currently, there are eleven vaccines for COVID-19 [7] and three types of influenza vaccines used worldwide [8].

One study by Zhu et al. [9] reported that 94.2% of COVID-19-infected individuals were also co-infected with many other types of microorganisms, such as viruses, fungi, and bacteria. Many co-infections of COVID-19 and influenza were reported in several studies [5,9–12] (see also the review articles [13–16]). Infection with multiple competitive respiratory viruses can cause the phenomenon of viral interference. It may happen that a certain type of virus has the ability to suppress the development and growth of another virus [17,18]. In [18,19], it was found that SARS-CoV-2 had a slower growth rate than that of IAV if the two infections started at the same time. If the influenza infection started after COVID-19, then influenza and COVID-19 co-infection could be detected. The progression and outcome of COVID-19 are highly dependent on a patient's immunity. The risk of co-infection may be increased for persons who are immunocompromised [17]. In addition, Hashemi et al. [20] conducted a study that reported that, in patients with co-infection of influenza and COVID-19, the presence of underlying diseases, such as chronic neurological pathologies, diabetes, asthma, and heart disease, may lead to an increase in mortality.

Mathematical models of mono-infection or co-infection of viruses are important for understanding in-host viral infections and for developing antiviral drugs and vaccines. Models of in-host influenza mono-infection were formulated in many works (see the review papers [21–24]). Baccam et al. [25] presented a basic target-cell-limited influenza infection model. Several extensions were made for this model by incorporating the impacts of innate immunity [25,26], adaptive immunity [27,28], both innate and adaptive immunities [3,29–32], drug therapies [33], and time delays [34].

The model presented in [25] was used to describe the in-host COVID-19 dynamics in [35]. Li et al. [36] considered the regeneration and death of susceptible ECs. A model that was limited to target cells and a model with the regeneration and death of susceptible ECs were presented, respectively, in [35,36], where they were modified and extended by taking into account the influences of immune response [37–44], drug therapies [45–47], time delays [48], and reaction diffusion [49]. In [50], a two-state mathematical model of within-host SARS-CoV-2-neutralizing antibody dynamics in response to vaccination was considered. The stability of in-host COVID-19 mono-infection models was investigated in [41–43,48,51,52].

Pinky and Dobrovolny [18] constructed a SARS-CoV-2/IAV co-infection model that was limited to target cells. The authors mentioned that some types of respiratory viruses may be able to inhibit the progression of SARS-CoV-2. In [18], the effect of the immune response was not included. Moreover, the production and death of susceptible ECs were not considered. Elaiw et al. [53,54] examined the global properties of a SARS-CoV-2/IAV co-infection model with antibody immune response. However, a time delay was not considered in these papers. Time delay is one of the key factors for studying innovative insights into viral dynamics. In the process of SARS-CoV-2 and IAV infections, it takes time for the viruses to infect susceptible ECs and then release new mature viral particles. Therefore, it is important to include a time delay in COVID-19 and influenza co-infection models. The aim of this article is to construct a system of delayed differential equations (DDEs) that describe the in-host co-dynamics of influenza and COVID-19. The model extends the model presented in [53] by incorporating four time delays: (i) a delay in the SARS-CoV-2 infection of ECs, (ii) a delay in the IAV infection of ECs, (iii) a maturation delay of newly released SARS-CoV-2 virions, and (iv) a maturation delay of newly released IAV virions. We first investigate the basic properties of the DDEs; then, we find all equilibria and examine their global stability. We illustrate the theoretical results via numerical simulations. The effects of time delays on the dynamics of COVID-19 and influenza co-infection are discussed.

2. Model Formulation

This section develops a system of DDEs that describe influenza and COVID-19 co-infection with four time delays. Let t represent the time and let $X(t)$, $Y(t)$, $I(t)$, $V(t)$, $P(t)$, $Z(t)$, and $M(t)$ represent the concentrations of susceptible ECs, SARS-CoV-2-infected ECs, IAV-infected ECs, SARS-CoV-2 particles, IAV particles, SARS-CoV-2 antibodies, and IAV antibodies. The following system of DDEs is to be studied:

$$\frac{dX(t)}{dt} = \overbrace{\delta}^{\text{ECs production}} - \overbrace{\varrho X(t)}^{\text{natural death}} - \overbrace{\xi_V X(t)V(t)}^{\text{SARS-CoV-2 infectious transmission}} - \overbrace{\xi_P X(t)P(t)}^{\text{IAV infectious transmission}}, \quad (1)$$

$$\frac{dY(t)}{dt} = \overbrace{e^{-\alpha_1 \tau_1}\xi_V X(t-\tau_1)V(t-\tau_1)}^{\text{SARS-CoV-2 infectious transmission}} - \overbrace{\beta_Y Y(t)}^{\text{natural death}}, \quad (2)$$

$$\frac{dI(t)}{dt} = \overbrace{e^{-\alpha_3 \tau_3}\xi_P X(t-\tau_3)P(t-\tau_3)}^{\text{IAV infectious transmission}} - \overbrace{\beta_I I(t)}^{\text{natural death}}, \quad (3)$$

$$\frac{dV(t)}{dt} = \overbrace{e^{-\alpha_2 \tau_2}\theta_V Y(t-\tau_2)}^{\text{SARS-CoV-2 production}} - \overbrace{\lambda_V V(t)}^{\text{natural death}} - \overbrace{\rho_V V(t)Z(t)}^{\text{SARS-CoV-2 neutralization}}, \quad (4)$$

$$\frac{dP(t)}{dt} = \overbrace{e^{-\alpha_4 \tau_4}\theta_P I(t-\tau_4)}^{\text{IAV production}} - \overbrace{\lambda_P P(t)}^{\text{natural death}} - \overbrace{\rho_P P(t)M(t)}^{\text{IAV neutralization}}, \quad (5)$$

$$\frac{dZ(t)}{dt} = \overbrace{\eta_Z V(t)Z(t)}^{\text{proliferation SARS-CoV-2 antibodies}} - \overbrace{\gamma_Z Z(t)}^{\text{natural death}}, \quad (6)$$

$$\frac{dM(t)}{dt} = \overbrace{\eta_M P(t)M(t)}^{\text{proliferation IAV antibodies}} - \overbrace{\gamma_M M(t)}^{\text{natural death}}. \quad (7)$$

Here, τ_1 and τ_3 are the delays between the entries of SARS-CoV-2 and IAV into ECs and the start of production of immature SARS-CoV-2 and IAV virions, respectively. τ_2 and τ_4 are the maturation delays of newly released SARS-CoV-2 and IAV virions, respectively. The probabilities of SARS-CoV-2-infected ECs and IAV-infected ECs surviving to the ages of τ_1 and τ_3 are represented by $e^{-\alpha_1 \tau_1}$ and $e^{-\alpha_3 \tau_3}$, respectively. The probabilities of released SARS-CoV-2 and IAV virions surviving to the ages τ_2 and τ_4 are denoted by $e^{-\alpha_2 \tau_2}$ and $e^{-\alpha_4 \tau_4}$, respectively.

The initial states (conditions) for system (1)–(7) are given as:

$$\begin{aligned} &X(u) = \psi_1(u), \quad Y(u) = \psi_2(u), \quad I(u) = \psi_3(u), \quad V(u) = \psi_4(u), \\ &P(u) = \psi_5(u), \quad Z(u) = \psi_6(u), \quad M(u) = \psi_7(u), \\ &\psi_i(u) \geq 0, \quad u \in [-\tau^*, 0], \\ &\psi_i(u) \in C([-\tau^*, 0], \mathbb{R}_{\geq 0}), \quad i = 1, 2, \ldots, 7, \end{aligned} \quad (8)$$

where $\tau^* = \max\{\tau_1, \tau_2, \tau_3, \tau_4\}$, and C is the Banach space of continuous functions mapping the interval $[-\tau^*, 0]$ into $\mathbb{R}_{\geq 0}$ with $\|\psi_i\| = \sup_{-\tau^* \leq u \leq 0} |\psi_i(u)|$ for $\psi_i \in C$. We note that system (1)–(7), with initial conditions (8), has a unique solution [55].

3. Well-Posedness of the Solutions

Here, we investigate the non-negativity and ultimate boundedness of system (1)–(7).

Lemma 1. *The solutions of system (1)–(7) with initial states (8) are non-negative and ultimately bounded.*

Proof. We have that
$$\frac{dX}{dt}\Big|_{X=0} = \delta > 0, \quad \frac{dZ}{dt}\Big|_{Z=0} = 0, \quad \frac{dM}{dt}\Big|_{M=0} = 0.$$

Hence, $X(t), Z(t), M(t) \geq 0$ for all $t \geq 0$. Moreover, for all $t \in [0, \tau^*]$, we have:

$$Y(t) = \psi_2(0)e^{-\beta_Y t} + \xi_V e^{-\alpha_1 \tau_1} \int_0^t e^{-\beta_Y(t-u)} X(u-\tau_1) V(u-\tau_1) du \geq 0,$$

$$I(t) = \psi_3(0)e^{-\beta_I t} + \xi_P e^{-\alpha_3 \tau_3} \int_0^t e^{-\beta_I(t-u)} X(u-\tau_3) P(u-\tau_3) du \geq 0,$$

$$V(t) = \psi_4(0)e^{-\int_0^t (\lambda_V + \rho_V Z(r))dr} + \theta_V e^{-\alpha_2 \tau_2} \int_0^t e^{-\int_u^t (\lambda_V + \rho_V Z(r))dr} Y(u-\tau_2) du \geq 0,$$

$$P(t) = \psi_5(0)e^{-\int_0^t (\lambda_P + \rho_P M(r))dr} + \theta_P e^{-\alpha_4 \tau_4} \int_0^t e^{-\int_u^t (\lambda_P + \rho_P M(r))dr} I(u-\tau_4) du \geq 0.$$

Hence, $Y(t), I(t), V(t), P(t) \geq 0$ for all $t \in [0, \tau^*]$. Through recursive argumentation, we get $Y(t), I(t), V(t), P(t)$ for all $t \geq 0$. Therefore, X, Y, I, V, P, Z, and M are non-negative.

The non-negativity of the system's solution implies that:

$$\frac{dX(t)}{dt} \leq \delta - \varrho X \implies \limsup_{t \to \infty} X(t) = \frac{\delta}{\varrho}.$$

Let us define
$$\Psi_1(t) = e^{-\alpha_1 \tau_1} X(t-\tau_1) + Y(t).$$

Then,
$$\frac{d\Psi_1(t)}{dt} = e^{-\alpha_1 \tau_1} \delta - e^{-\alpha_1 \tau_1} \varrho X(t-\tau_1) - e^{-\alpha_1 \tau_1} \xi_P X(t-\tau_1) P(t-\tau_1) - \beta_Y Y(t)$$
$$\leq \delta - e^{-\alpha_1 \tau_1} \varrho X(t-\tau_1) - \beta_Y Y(t)$$
$$\leq \delta - \varphi_1 \left[e^{-\alpha_1 \tau_1} X(t-\tau_1) + Y(t) \right] = \delta - \varphi_1 \Psi_1(t),$$

where $\varphi_1 = \min\{\varrho, \beta_Y\}$. This implies that

$$\limsup_{t \to \infty} \Psi_1(t) \leq \frac{\delta}{\varphi_1} = A_1 \implies \limsup_{t \to \infty} Y(t) \leq A_1.$$

Let
$$\Psi_2(t) = e^{-\alpha_3 \tau_3} X(t-\tau_3) + I(t)$$
$$\frac{d\Psi_2(t)}{dt} = e^{-\alpha_3 \tau_3} \delta - e^{-\alpha_3 \tau_3} \varrho X(t-\tau_3) - e^{-\alpha_3 \tau_3} \xi_V X(t-\tau_3) V(t-\tau_3) - \beta_I I(t)$$
$$\leq \delta - e^{-\alpha_3 \tau_3} \varrho X(t-\tau_3) - \beta_I I(t)$$
$$\leq \delta - \varphi_2 \left[e^{-\alpha_3 \tau_3} X(t-\tau_3) + I(t) \right] = \delta - \varphi_2 \Psi_2(t),$$

where $\varphi_2 = \min\{\varrho, \beta_I\}$. It follows that

$$\limsup_{t \to \infty} \Psi_2(t) \leq \frac{\delta}{\varphi_2} = A_2 \implies \limsup_{t \to \infty} I(t) \leq A_2.$$

Let us define

$$\Psi_3(t) = V(t) + P(t) + \frac{\rho_V}{\eta_Z}Z(t) + \frac{\rho_P}{\eta_M}M(t).$$

$$\frac{d\Psi_3(t)}{dt} = e^{-\alpha_2\tau_2}\theta_V Y(t-\tau_2) - \lambda_V V(t) + e^{-\alpha_4\tau_4}\theta_P I(t-\tau_4) - \lambda_P P(t) - \frac{\rho_V \gamma_Z}{\eta_Z}Z(t)$$
$$- \frac{\rho_P \gamma_M}{\eta_M}M(t).$$

Since $Y(t) \leq A_1, I(t) \leq A_2$, then

$$\frac{d\Psi_3(t)}{dt} \leq \theta_V A_1 + \theta_P A_2 - \lambda_V V(t) - \lambda_P P(t) - \frac{\rho_V \gamma_Z}{\eta_Z}Z(t) - \frac{\rho_P \gamma_M}{\eta_M}M(t)$$
$$\leq \theta_V A_1 + \theta_P A_2 - \varphi_3 \left[V(t) + P(t) + \frac{\rho_V}{\eta_Z}Z(t) + \frac{\rho_P}{\eta_M}M(t) \right]$$
$$= \theta_V A_1 + \theta_P A_2 - \varphi_3 \Psi_3(t)$$

where $\varphi_3 = \min\{\lambda_V, \lambda_P, \gamma_Z, \gamma_M\}$. Then, we get

$$\limsup_{t\to\infty} \Psi_3(t) \leq \frac{\theta_V A_1 + \theta_P A_2}{\varphi_3} = A_3.$$

Since $V(t) > 0, P(t) > 0, Z(t) > 0$ and $M(t) > 0$, then

$$\limsup_{t\to\infty} V(t) \leq A_3, \quad \limsup_{t\to\infty} P(t) \leq A_3,$$
$$\limsup_{t\to\infty} Z(t) \leq \frac{\eta_Z}{\rho_V}A_3 = A_4 \quad \text{and} \quad \limsup_{t\to\infty} M(t) \leq \frac{\eta_M}{\rho_P}A_3 = A_5.$$

□

Based on Lemma 1, we can show that the domain

$$\Phi = \{(X, Y, I, V, P, Z, M) \in C^7_{\geq 0} : \|X\|, \|Y\| \leq A_1, \|I\| \leq A_2, \|V\|, \|P\| \leq A_3, \|Z\| \leq A_4, \|M\| \leq A_5\}$$

is positively invariant for model (1)–(7).

4. Equilibria

Here, we calculate the system's equilibria and deduce the condition of their existence. Any equilibrium point $\Delta = (X, Y, I, V, P, Z, M)$ satisfies:

$$0 = \delta - \varrho X - \xi_V XV - \xi_P XP, \tag{9}$$
$$0 = e^{-\alpha_1\tau_1}\xi_V XV - \beta_Y Y, \tag{10}$$
$$0 = e^{-\alpha_3\tau_3}\xi_P XP - \beta_I I, \tag{11}$$
$$0 = e^{-\alpha_2\tau_2}\theta_V Y - \lambda_V V - \rho_V VZ, \tag{12}$$
$$0 = e^{-\alpha_4\tau_4}\theta_P I - \lambda_P P - \rho_P PM, \tag{13}$$
$$0 = \eta_Z VZ - \gamma_Z Z, \tag{14}$$
$$0 = \eta_M PM - \gamma_M M. \tag{15}$$

Solving Equations (9)–(15), we get eight equilibria.
(i) Infection-free equilibrium, $\Delta_0 = (X_0, 0, 0, 0, 0, 0, 0)$, where $X_0 = \delta/\varrho$.

(ii) COVID-19 mono-infection equilibrium with inactive antibody response $\Delta_1 = (X_1, Y_1, 0, V_1, 0, 0, 0)$, where

$$X_1 = \frac{\beta_Y \lambda_V}{e^{-\alpha_1 \tau_1 - \alpha_2 \tau_2} \theta_V \xi_V}, \quad Y_1 = \frac{\varrho \lambda_V}{e^{-\alpha_2 \tau_2} \theta_V \xi_V} \left[\frac{e^{-\alpha_1 \tau_1 - \alpha_2 \tau_2} X_0 \theta_V \xi_V}{\beta_Y \lambda_V} - 1 \right],$$

$$V_1 = \frac{\varrho}{\xi_V} \left[\frac{e^{-\alpha_1 \tau_1 - \alpha_2 \tau_2} X_0 \theta_V \xi_V}{\beta_Y \lambda_V} - 1 \right].$$

Therefore, $Y_1 > 0$ and $V_1 > 0$ when

$$\frac{e^{-\alpha_1 \tau_1 - \alpha_2 \tau_2} X_0 \theta_V \xi_V}{\beta_Y \lambda_V} > 1.$$

We define the basic COVID-19 mono-infection reproduction number as:

$$\Re_1 = \frac{e^{-\alpha_1 \tau_1 - \alpha_2 \tau_2} X_0 \theta_V \xi_V}{\beta_Y \lambda_V}.$$

Thus, we can write:

$$X_1 = \frac{X_0}{\Re_1}, \quad Y_1 = \frac{\varrho \lambda_V}{e^{-\alpha_2 \tau_2} \theta_V \xi_V}(\Re_1 - 1), \quad V_1 = \frac{\varrho}{\xi_V}(\Re_1 - 1).$$

Consequently, Δ_1 exists if $\Re_1 > 1$.

(iii) Influenza mono-infection equilibrium with inactive antibody response, $\Delta_2 = (X_2, 0, I_2, 0, P_2, 0, 0)$, where

$$X_2 = \frac{\beta_I \lambda_P}{e^{-\alpha_3 \tau_3 - \alpha_4 \tau_4} \theta_P \xi_P}, \quad I_2 = \frac{\varrho \lambda_P}{e^{-\alpha_4 \tau_4} \theta_P \xi_P} \left[\frac{e^{-\alpha_3 \tau_3 - \alpha_4 \tau_4} X_0 \theta_P \xi_P}{\beta_I \lambda_P} - 1 \right],$$

$$P_2 = \frac{\varrho}{\xi_P} \left[\frac{e^{-\alpha_3 \tau_3 - \alpha_4 \tau_4} X_0 \theta_P \xi_P}{\beta_I \lambda_P} - 1 \right].$$

Therefore, $I_2 > 0$ and $P_2 > 0$ when

$$\frac{e^{-\alpha_3 \tau_3 - \alpha_4 \tau_4} X_0 \theta_P \xi_P}{\beta_I \lambda_P} > 1.$$

We define the basic influenza mono-infection reproduction number as:

$$\Re_2 = \frac{e^{-\alpha_3 \tau_3 - \alpha_4 \tau_4} X_0 \theta_P \xi_P}{\beta_I \lambda_P}.$$

In terms of $\Re_2$, we write

$$X_2 = \frac{X_0}{\Re_2}, \quad I_2 = \frac{\varrho \lambda_P}{e^{-\alpha_4 \tau_4} \theta_P \xi_P}(\Re_2 - 1), \quad P_2 = \frac{\varrho}{\xi_P}(\Re_2 - 1).$$

Therefore, Δ_2 exists if $\Re_2 > 1$.

(iv) COVID-19 mono-infection equilibrium with activated SARS-CoV-2-specific antibody response, $\Delta_3 = (X_3, Y_3, 0, V_3, 0, Z_3, 0)$, where

$$X_3 = \frac{\delta \eta z}{\xi_V \gamma z + \varrho \eta z}, \quad Y_3 = \frac{e^{-\alpha_1 \tau_1} \delta \xi_V \gamma z}{\beta_Y (\xi_V \gamma z + \varrho \eta z)},$$

$$V_3 = \frac{\gamma z}{\eta z}, \quad Z_3 = \frac{\lambda_V}{\rho_V} \left[\frac{e^{-\alpha_1 \tau_1 - \alpha_2 \tau_2} \delta \xi_V \eta z \theta_V}{\beta_Y \lambda_V (\xi_V \gamma z + \varrho \eta z)} - 1 \right].$$

We note that Δ_3 exists when

$$\frac{e^{-\alpha_1\tau_1-\alpha_2\tau_2}\delta\xi_V\eta z\theta_V}{\beta_Y\lambda_V(\xi_V\gamma z+\varrho\eta z)} > 1.$$

Let us define the SARS-CoV-2-specific antibody response activation number for COVID-19 mono-infection as:

$$\Re_3 = \frac{e^{-\alpha_1\tau_1-\alpha_2\tau_2}\delta\xi_V\eta z\theta_V}{\beta_Y\lambda_V(\xi_V\gamma z+\varrho\eta z)}.$$

Thus, $Z_3 = \frac{\lambda_V}{\rho_V}(\Re_3 - 1)$.

(v) Influenza mono-infection equilibrium with activation of IAV-specific antibody response, $\Delta_4 = (X_4, 0, I_4, 0, P_4, 0, M_4)$, where

$$X_4 = \frac{\delta\eta_M}{\xi_P\gamma_M+\varrho\eta_M}, \quad I_4 = \frac{e^{-\alpha_3\tau_3}\delta\xi_P\gamma_M}{\beta_I(\xi_P\gamma_M+\varrho\eta_M)},$$

$$P_4 = \frac{\gamma_M}{\eta_M}, \quad M_4 = \frac{\lambda_P}{\rho_P}\left[\frac{e^{-\alpha_3\tau_3-\alpha_4\tau_4}\delta\xi_P\eta_M\theta_P}{\beta_I\lambda_P(\xi_P\gamma_M+\varrho\eta_M)} - 1\right].$$

We note that Δ_4 exists when

$$\frac{e^{-\alpha_3\tau_3-\alpha_4\tau_4}\delta\xi_P\eta_M\theta_P}{\beta_I\lambda_P(\xi_P\gamma_M+\varrho\eta_M)} > 1.$$

The IAV-specific antibody response activation number for influenza mono-infection is defined as:

$$\Re_4 = \frac{e^{-\alpha_3\tau_3-\alpha_4\tau_4}\delta\xi_P\eta_M\theta_P}{\beta_I\lambda_P(\xi_P\gamma_M+\varrho\eta_M)}.$$

Thus, $M_4 = \frac{\lambda_P}{\rho_P}(\Re_4 - 1)$.

(vi) Influenza and COVID-19 co-infection equilibrium with only the activated SARS-CoV-2-specific antibody response, $\Delta_5 = (X_5, Y_5, I_5, V_5, P_5, Z_5, 0)$, where

$$X_5 = \frac{\beta_I\lambda_P}{e^{-\alpha_3\tau_3-\alpha_4\tau_4}\theta_P\xi_P}, \quad Y_5 = \frac{e^{-\alpha_1\tau_1}\xi_V\beta_I\lambda_P\gamma z}{e^{-\alpha_3\tau_3-\alpha_4\tau_4}\theta_P\xi_P\beta_Y\eta z},$$

$$I_5 = \frac{\lambda_P(\xi_V\gamma z+\varrho\eta z)}{e^{-\alpha_4\tau_4}\theta_P\xi_P\eta z}\left[\frac{e^{-\alpha_3\tau_3-\alpha_4\tau_4}\delta\xi_P\theta_P\eta z}{\beta_I\lambda_P(\xi_V\gamma z+\varrho\eta z)} - 1\right], \quad V_5 = \frac{\gamma z}{\eta z},$$

$$P_5 = \frac{\xi_V\gamma z+\varrho\eta z}{\xi_P\eta z}\left[\frac{e^{-\alpha_3\tau_3-\alpha_4\tau_4}\delta\xi_P\theta_P\eta z}{\beta_I\lambda_P(\xi_V\gamma z+\varrho\eta z)} - 1\right],$$

$$Z_5 = \frac{\lambda_V}{\rho_V}\left[\frac{e^{-\alpha_1\tau_1-\alpha_2\tau_2}\theta_V\xi_V\beta_I\lambda_P}{e^{-\alpha_3\tau_3-\alpha_4\tau_4}\theta_P\xi_P\beta_Y\lambda_V} - 1\right] = \frac{\lambda_V}{\rho_V}(\Re_1/\Re_2 - 1).$$

Hence, Δ_5 exists when

$$\frac{\Re_1}{\Re_2} > 1 \text{ and } \frac{e^{-\alpha_3\tau_3-\alpha_4\tau_4}\delta\xi_P\theta_P\eta z}{\beta_I\lambda_P(\xi_V\gamma z+\varrho\eta z)} > 1.$$

The influenza infection reproduction number in the presence of COVID-19 infection is stated as:

$$\Re_5 = \frac{e^{-\alpha_3\tau_3-\alpha_4\tau_4}\delta\xi_P\theta_P\eta z}{\beta_I\lambda_P(\xi_V\gamma z+\varrho\eta z)}.$$

Hence,

$$I_5 = \frac{\lambda_P(\xi_V\gamma z+\varrho\eta z)}{e^{-\alpha_4\tau_4}\theta_P\xi_P\eta z}(\Re_5 - 1), \quad P_5 = \frac{\xi_V\gamma z+\varrho\eta z}{\xi_P\eta z}(\Re_5 - 1),$$

and then Δ_5 exists if $\frac{\Re_1}{\Re_2} > 1$ and $\Re_5 > 1$.

(vii) Influenza and COVID-19 co-infection equilibrium with only the activated IAV-specific antibody response, $\Delta_6 = (X_6, Y_6, I_6, V_6, P_6, 0, M_6)$, where

$$X_6 = \frac{\beta_Y \lambda_V}{e^{-\alpha_1 \tau_1 - \alpha_2 \tau_2} \theta_V \xi_V}, \quad Y_6 = \frac{\lambda_V (\xi_P \gamma_M + \varrho \eta_M)}{e^{-\alpha_2 \tau_2} \theta_V \xi_V \eta_M} \left[\frac{e^{-\alpha_1 \tau_1 - \alpha_2 \tau_2} \delta \xi_V \theta_V \eta_M}{\beta_Y \lambda_V (\xi_P \gamma_M + \varrho \eta_M)} - 1 \right],$$

$$I_6 = \frac{e^{-\alpha_3 \tau_3} \xi_P \gamma_M \beta_Y \lambda_V}{e^{-\alpha_1 \tau_1 - \alpha_2 \tau_2} \theta_V \xi_V \beta_I \eta_M}, \quad V_6 = \frac{\xi_P \gamma_M + \varrho \eta_M}{\xi_V \eta_M} \left[\frac{e^{-\alpha_1 \tau_1 - \alpha_2 \tau_2} \delta \xi_V \theta_V \eta_M}{\beta_Y \lambda_V (\xi_P \gamma_M + \varrho \eta_M)} - 1 \right],$$

$$P_6 = \frac{\gamma_M}{\eta_M}, \quad M_6 = \frac{\lambda_P}{\rho_P} \left[\frac{e^{-\alpha_3 \tau_3 - \alpha_4 \tau_4} \theta p \xi_P \beta_Y \lambda_V}{e^{-\alpha_1 \tau_1 - \alpha_2 \tau_2} \theta_V \xi_V \beta_I \lambda_P} - 1 \right] = \frac{\lambda_P}{\rho_P} (\Re_2 / \Re_1 - 1).$$

We note that Δ_6 exists when

$$\frac{\Re_2}{\Re_1} > 1 \quad \text{and} \quad \frac{e^{-\alpha_1 \tau_1 - \alpha_2 \tau_2} \delta \xi_V \theta_V \eta_M}{\beta_Y \lambda_V (\xi_P \gamma_M + \varrho \eta_M)} > 1.$$

The COVID-19 infection reproduction number in the presence of influenza infection is stated as:

$$\Re_6 = \frac{e^{-\alpha_1 \tau_1 - \alpha_2 \tau_2} \delta \xi_V \theta_V \eta_M}{\beta_Y \lambda_V (\xi_P \gamma_M + \varrho \eta_M)}.$$

Thus,

$$Y_6 = \frac{\lambda_V (\xi_P \gamma_M + \varrho \eta_M)}{e^{-\alpha_2 \tau_2} \theta_V \xi_V \eta_M} (\Re_6 - 1), \quad V_6 = \frac{\xi_P \gamma_M + \varrho \eta_M}{\xi_V \eta_M} (\Re_6 - 1).$$

(viii) Influenza and COVID-19 co-infection equilibrium with activation of both SARS-CoV-2 and IAV antibody responses $\Delta_7 = (X_7, Y_7, I_7, V_7, P_7, Z_7, M_7)$, where

$$X_7 = \frac{\delta \eta z \eta_M}{\xi_P \gamma_M \eta z + \xi_V \gamma z \eta_M + \varrho \eta z \eta_M}, \quad Y_7 = \frac{e^{-\alpha_1 \tau_1} \delta \xi_V \gamma z \eta_M}{\beta_Y (\xi_P \gamma_M \eta z + \xi_V \gamma z \eta_M + \varrho \eta z \eta_M)},$$

$$I_7 = \frac{e^{-\alpha_3 \tau_3} \delta \xi_P \gamma_M \eta z}{\beta_I (\xi_P \gamma_M \eta z + \xi_V \gamma z \eta_M + \varrho \eta z \eta_M)}, \quad V_7 = \frac{\gamma z}{\eta z}, \quad P_7 = \frac{\gamma_M}{\eta_M},$$

$$Z_7 = \frac{\lambda_V}{\rho_V} \left[\frac{e^{-\alpha_1 \tau_1 - \alpha_2 \tau_2} \delta \xi_V \theta_V \eta_M \eta z}{\beta_Y \lambda_V (\xi_P \gamma_M \eta z + \xi_V \gamma z \eta_M + \varrho \eta z \eta_M)} - 1 \right],$$

$$M_7 = \frac{\lambda_P}{\rho_P} \left[\frac{e^{-\alpha_3 \tau_3 - \alpha_4 \tau_4} \delta \xi_P \theta_P \eta_M \eta z}{\beta_I \lambda_P (\xi_P \gamma_M \eta z + \xi_V \gamma z \eta_M + \varrho \eta z \eta_M)} - 1 \right].$$

It is obvious that Δ_7 exists when

$$\frac{e^{-\alpha_1 \tau_1 - \alpha_2 \tau_2} \delta \xi_V \theta_V \eta_M \eta z}{\beta_Y \lambda_V (\xi_P \gamma_M \eta z + \xi_V \gamma z \eta_M + \varrho \eta z \eta_M)} > 1 \quad \text{and} \quad \frac{e^{-\alpha_3 \tau_3 - \alpha_4 \tau_4} \delta \xi_P \theta_P \eta_M \eta z}{\beta_I \lambda_P (\xi_P \gamma_M \eta z + \xi_V \gamma z \eta_M + \varrho \eta z \eta_M)} > 1.$$

Now, we define

$$\Re_7 = \frac{e^{-\alpha_1 \tau_1 - \alpha_2 \tau_2} \delta \xi_V \theta_V \eta_M \eta z}{\beta_Y \lambda_V (\xi_P \gamma_M \eta z + \xi_V \gamma z \eta_M + \varrho \eta z \eta_M)},$$

$$\Re_8 = \frac{e^{-\alpha_3 \tau_3 - \alpha_4 \tau_4} \delta \xi_P \theta_P \eta_M \eta z}{\beta_I \lambda_P (\xi_P \gamma_M \eta z + \xi_V \gamma z \eta_M + \varrho \eta z \eta_M)}.$$

Here, $\Re_7$ is the SARS-CoV-2-specific antibody response activation number for influenza and COVID-19 co-infection, and $\Re_8$ is the IAV-specific antibody response activation number for influenza and COVID-19 co-infection. Hence, $Z_7 = \frac{\lambda_V}{\rho_V}(\Re_7 - 1)$ and $M_7 = \frac{\lambda_P}{\rho_P}(\Re_8 - 1)$. If $\Re_7 > 1$ and $\Re_8 > 1$, then Δ_7 exists.

From what was stated above, we obtain eight threshold parameters that establish the existence of eight equilibria:

$$\Re_1 = \frac{e^{-\alpha_1\tau_1-\alpha_2\tau_2}X_0\theta_V\xi_V}{\beta_Y\lambda_V}, \qquad \Re_2 = \frac{e^{-\alpha_3\tau_3-\alpha_4\tau_4}X_0\theta_P\xi_P}{\beta_I\lambda_P}, \qquad (16)$$

$$\Re_3 = \frac{e^{-\alpha_1\tau_1-\alpha_2\tau_2}\delta\xi_V\eta_Z\theta_V}{\beta_Y\lambda_V(\xi_V\gamma_Z+\varrho\eta_Z)}, \qquad \Re_4 = \frac{e^{-\alpha_3\tau_3-\alpha_4\tau_4}\delta\xi_P\eta_M\theta_P}{\beta_I\lambda_P(\xi_P\gamma_M+\varrho\eta_M)},$$

$$\Re_5 = \frac{e^{-\alpha_3\tau_3-\alpha_4\tau_4}\delta\xi_P\theta_P\eta_Z}{\beta_I\lambda_P(\xi_V\gamma_Z+\varrho\eta_Z)}, \qquad \Re_6 = \frac{e^{-\alpha_1\tau_1-\alpha_2\tau_2}\delta\xi_V\theta_V\eta_M}{\beta_Y\lambda_V(\xi_P\gamma_M+\varrho\eta_M)},$$

$$\Re_7 = \frac{e^{-\alpha_1\tau_1-\alpha_2\tau_2}\delta\xi_V\theta_V\eta_M\eta_Z}{\beta_Y\lambda_V(\xi_P\gamma_M\eta_Z+\xi_V\gamma_Z\eta_M+\varrho\eta_Z\eta_M)}, \qquad \Re_8 = \frac{e^{-\alpha_3\tau_3-\alpha_4\tau_4}\delta\xi_P\theta_P\eta_M\eta_Z}{\beta_I\lambda_P(\xi_P\gamma_M\eta_Z+\xi_V\gamma_Z\eta_M+\varrho\eta_Z\eta_M)}.$$

5. Global Stability

This section is devoted to the study of the global asymptotic stability of all equilibria. We configure the Lyapunov functions by following the way that was outlined in [56,57].

Let $\Lambda_k(X, Y, I, V, P, Z, M)$ be a Lyapunov function and let Θ_k be the largest invariant subset of

$$\Theta_k = \left\{(X, Y, I, V, P, Z, M) : \frac{d\Lambda_k}{dt} = 0\right\}, \quad k = 0, 1, 2, \dots, 7.$$

We define a function $F : (0, \infty) \longrightarrow [0, \infty)$ as $F(u) = u - 1 - \ln u$. We denote $(X, Y, I, V, P, Z, M) = (X(t), Y(t), I(t), V(t), P(t), Z(t), M(t))$.

Theorem 1. *If $\Re_1 \leq 1$ and $\Re_2 \leq 1$, then Δ_0 is globally asymptotically stable (GAS).*

Proof. We define

$$\Lambda_0 = X_0 F\left(\frac{X}{X_0}\right) + e^{\alpha_1\tau_1}Y + e^{\alpha_3\tau_3}I + \frac{\beta_Y}{\theta_V}e^{\alpha_1\tau_1+\alpha_2\tau_2}V + \frac{\beta_I}{\theta_P}e^{\alpha_3\tau_3+\alpha_4\tau_4}P$$

$$+ \frac{\rho_V\beta_Y}{\eta_Z\theta_V}e^{\alpha_1\tau_1+\alpha_2\tau_2}Z + \frac{\rho_P\beta_I}{\eta_M\theta_P}e^{\alpha_3\tau_3+\alpha_4\tau_4}M + \xi_V\int_{t-\tau_1}^{t} X(u)V(u)du$$

$$+ \xi_P\int_{t-\tau_3}^{t} X(u)P(u)du + \beta_Y e^{\alpha_1\tau_1}\int_{t-\tau_2}^{t} Y(u)du + \beta_I e^{\alpha_3\tau_3}\int_{t-\tau_4}^{t} I(u)du.$$

Clearly, $\Lambda_0 > 0$ for all $X, Y, I, V, P, Z, M > 0$, and $\Lambda_0(X_0, 0, 0, 0, 0, 0, 0) = 0$. We calculate $\frac{d\Lambda_0}{dt}$ along the solutions of model (1)–(7) as:

$$\frac{d\Lambda_0}{dt} = \left(1 - \frac{X_0}{X}\right)\frac{dX}{dt} + e^{\alpha_1\tau_1}\frac{dY}{dt} + e^{\alpha_3\tau_3}\frac{dI}{dt} + \frac{\beta_Y}{\theta_V}e^{\alpha_1\tau_1+\alpha_2\tau_2}\frac{dV}{dt} + \frac{\beta_I}{\theta_P}e^{\alpha_3\tau_3+\alpha_4\tau_4}\frac{dP}{dt}$$

$$+ \frac{\rho_V\beta_Y}{\eta_Z\theta_V}e^{\alpha_1\tau_1+\alpha_2\tau_2}\frac{dZ}{dt} + \frac{\rho_P\beta_I}{\eta_M\theta_P}e^{\alpha_3\tau_3+\alpha_4\tau_4}\frac{dM}{dt} + \xi_V[XV - X(t-\tau_1)V(t-\tau_1)]$$

$$+ \xi_P[XP - X(t-\tau_3)P(t-\tau_3)] + \beta_Y e^{\alpha_1\tau_1}[Y - Y(t-\tau_2)] + \beta_I e^{\alpha_3\tau_3}[I - I(t-\tau_4)].$$

Substituting from Equations (1)–(7), we obtain

$$\frac{d\Lambda_0}{dt} = \left(1 - \frac{X_0}{X}\right)[\delta - \varrho X - \xi_V XV - \xi_P XP] + e^{\alpha_1\tau_1}\left[e^{-\alpha_1\tau_1}\xi_V X(t-\tau_1)V(t-\tau_1) - \beta_Y Y\right]$$

$$+ e^{\alpha_3\tau_3}\left[e^{-\alpha_3\tau_3}\xi_P X(t-\tau_3)P(t-\tau_3) - \beta_I I\right]$$

$$+ \frac{\beta_Y}{\theta_V}e^{\alpha_1\tau_1+\alpha_2\tau_2}\left[e^{-\alpha_2\tau_2}\theta_V Y(t-\tau_2) - \lambda_V V - \rho_V V Z\right]$$

$$+ \frac{\beta_I}{\theta_P}e^{\alpha_3\tau_3+\alpha_4\tau_4}\left[e^{-\alpha_4\tau_4}\theta_P I(t-\tau_4) - \lambda_P P - \rho_P PM\right] + \frac{\rho_V\beta_Y}{\eta_Z\theta_V}e^{\alpha_1\tau_1+\alpha_2\tau_2}[\eta_Z VZ - \gamma_Z Z]$$

$$+ \frac{\rho_P\beta_I}{\eta_M\theta_P}e^{\alpha_3\tau_3+\alpha_4\tau_4}[\eta_M PM - \gamma_M M] + \xi_V[XV - X(t-\tau_1)V(t-\tau_1)]$$

$$+ \xi_P[XP - X(t-\tau_3)P(t-\tau_3)] + \beta_Y e^{\alpha_1\tau_1}[Y - Y(t-\tau_2)] + \beta_I e^{\alpha_3\tau_3}[I - I(t-\tau_4)]. \tag{17}$$

Simplifying Equation (17), we get:

$$\frac{d\Lambda_0}{dt} = \left(1 - \frac{X_0}{X}\right)(\delta - \varrho X) + \left(\xi_V X_0 - \frac{\beta_Y \lambda_V}{\theta_V} e^{\alpha_1\tau_1 + \alpha_2\tau_2}\right)V$$

$$+ \left(\xi_P X_0 - \frac{\beta_I \lambda_P}{\theta_P} e^{\alpha_3\tau_3 + \alpha_4\tau_4}\right)P - \frac{\rho_V \beta_Y \gamma Z}{\eta_Z \theta_V} e^{\alpha_1\tau_1 + \alpha_2\tau_2} Z - \frac{\rho_P \beta_I \gamma M}{\eta_M \theta_P} e^{\alpha_3\tau_3 + \alpha_4\tau_4} M.$$

Using the equilibrium condition $\delta = \varrho X_0$, we obtain:

$$\frac{d\Lambda_0}{dt} = -\varrho \frac{(X - X_0)^2}{X} + \frac{\beta_Y \lambda_V}{e^{-\alpha_1\tau_1 - \alpha_2\tau_2}\theta_V}(\Re_1 - 1)V + \frac{\beta_I \lambda_P}{e^{-\alpha_3\tau_3 - \alpha_4\tau_4}\theta_P}(\Re_2 - 1)P$$

$$- \frac{\rho_V \beta_Y \gamma Z}{\eta_Z \theta_V} e^{\alpha_1\tau_1 + \alpha_2\tau_2} Z - \frac{\rho_P \beta_I \gamma M}{\eta_M \theta_P} e^{\alpha_3\tau_3 + \alpha_4\tau_4} M.$$

Since $\Re_1 \le 1$ and $\Re_2 \le 1$, then $\frac{d\Lambda_0}{dt} \le 0$ for all $X, V, P, Z, M > 0$. Further, $\frac{d\Lambda_0}{dt} = 0$ when $X = X_0$ and $V = 0, P = 0, Z = 0$, and $M = 0$. The solutions of system (1)–(7) converge to $\bar{\Theta}_0$ [55], which contains elements with $V = 0$ and $P = 0$. Hence, $\frac{dV}{dt} = 0$ and $\frac{dP}{dt} = 0$, and from Equations (4) and (5), we obtain

$$0 = \frac{dV}{dt} = e^{-\alpha_2\tau_2}\theta_V Y(t-\tau_2) \implies Y(t) = 0, \text{ for all } t,$$

$$0 = \frac{dP}{dt} = e^{-\alpha_4\tau_4}\theta_P I(t-\tau_4) \implies I(t) = 0, \text{ for all } t.$$

Consequently, $\bar{\Theta}_0 = \{\Delta_0\}$, and by applying the Lyapunov–LaSalle asymptotic stability theorem (L-LAST) [58–60], we find that Δ_0 is GAS. □

Theorem 2. *If $\Re_1 > 1$, $\Re_2/\Re_1 \le 1$, and $\Re_3 \le 1$, then Δ_1 is GAS.*

Proof. We formulate a Lyapunov function Λ_1 as:

$$\Lambda_1 = X_1 F\left(\frac{X}{X_1}\right) + e^{\alpha_1\tau_1} Y_1 F\left(\frac{Y}{Y_1}\right) + e^{\alpha_3\tau_3} I + \frac{\beta_Y}{\theta_V} e^{\alpha_1\tau_1 + \alpha_2\tau_2} V_1 F\left(\frac{V}{V_1}\right)$$

$$+ \frac{\beta_I}{\theta_P} e^{\alpha_3\tau_3 + \alpha_4\tau_4} P + \frac{\rho_V \beta_Y}{\eta_Z \theta_V} e^{\alpha_1\tau_1 + \alpha_2\tau_2} Z + \frac{\rho_P \beta_I}{\eta_M \theta_P} e^{\alpha_3\tau_3 + \alpha_4\tau_4} M$$

$$+ \xi_V X_1 V_1 \int_{t-\tau_1}^{t} F\left(\frac{X(u)V(u)}{X_1 V_1}\right) du + \xi_P \int_{t-\tau_3}^{t} X(u)P(u) du$$

$$+ \beta_Y e^{\alpha_1\tau_1} Y_1 \int_{t-\tau_2}^{t} F\left(\frac{Y(u)}{Y_1}\right) du + \beta_I e^{\alpha_3\tau_3} \int_{t-\tau_4}^{t} I(u) du.$$

We calculate $\frac{d\Lambda_1}{dt}$ as:

$$\frac{d\Lambda_1}{dt} = \left(1 - \frac{X_1}{X}\right)\frac{dX}{dt} + e^{\alpha_1\tau_1}\left(1 - \frac{Y_1}{Y}\right)\frac{dY}{dt} + e^{\alpha_3\tau_3}\frac{dI}{dt}$$

$$+ \frac{\beta_Y}{\theta_V} e^{\alpha_1\tau_1 + \alpha_2\tau_2}\left(1 - \frac{V_1}{V}\right)\frac{dV}{dt} + \frac{\beta_I}{\theta_P} e^{\alpha_3\tau_3 + \alpha_4\tau_4}\frac{dP}{dt}$$

$$+ \frac{\rho_V \beta_Y}{\eta_Z \theta_V} e^{\alpha_1\tau_1 + \alpha_2\tau_2}\frac{dZ}{dt} + \frac{\rho_P \beta_I}{\eta_M \theta_P} e^{\alpha_3\tau_3 + \alpha_4\tau_4}\frac{dM}{dt}$$

$$+ \xi_V X_1 V_1 \left[\frac{XV}{X_1 V_1} - \frac{X(t-\tau_1)V(t-\tau_1)}{X_1 V_1} + \ln\left(\frac{X(t-\tau_1)V(t-\tau_1)}{XV}\right)\right]$$

$$+ \xi_P[XP - X(t-\tau_3)P(t-\tau_3)] + \beta_Y e^{\alpha_1\tau_1}Y_1\left[\frac{Y}{Y_1} - \frac{Y(t-\tau_2)}{Y_1} + \ln\left(\frac{Y(t-\tau_2)}{Y}\right)\right]$$
$$+ \beta_I e^{\alpha_3\tau_3}[I - I(t-\tau_4)].$$

From Equations (1)–(7), we get

$$\frac{d\Lambda_1}{dt} = \left(1 - \frac{X_1}{X}\right)[\delta - \varrho X - \xi_V XV - \xi_P XP]$$
$$+ e^{\alpha_1\tau_1}\left(1 - \frac{Y_1}{Y}\right)[e^{-\alpha_1\tau_1}\xi_V X(t-\tau_1)V(t-\tau_1) - \beta_Y Y]$$
$$+ e^{\alpha_3\tau_3}[e^{-\alpha_3\tau_3}\xi_P X(t-\tau_3)P(t-\tau_3) - \beta_I I]$$
$$+ \frac{\beta_Y}{\theta_V}e^{\alpha_1\tau_1+\alpha_2\tau_2}\left(1 - \frac{V_1}{V}\right)[e^{-\alpha_2\tau_2}\theta_V Y(t-\tau_2) - \lambda_V V - \rho_V VZ]$$
$$+ \frac{\beta_I}{\theta_P}e^{\alpha_3\tau_3+\alpha_4\tau_4}[e^{-\alpha_4\tau_4}\theta_P I(t-\tau_4) - \lambda_P P - \rho_P PM]$$
$$+ \frac{\rho_V \beta_Y}{\eta_Z \theta_V}e^{\alpha_1\tau_1+\alpha_2\tau_2}[\eta_Z VZ - \gamma_Z Z] + \frac{\rho_P \beta_I}{\eta_M \theta_P}e^{\alpha_3\tau_3+\alpha_4\tau_4}[\eta_M PM - \gamma_M M]$$
$$+ \xi_V X_1 V_1\left[\frac{XV}{X_1 V_1} - \frac{X(t-\tau_1)V(t-\tau_1)}{X_1 V_1} + \ln\left(\frac{X(t-\tau_1)V(t-\tau_1)}{XV}\right)\right]$$
$$+ \xi_P[XP - X(t-\tau_3)P(t-\tau_3)] + \beta_Y e^{\alpha_1\tau_1}Y_1\left[\frac{Y}{Y_1} - \frac{Y(t-\tau_2)}{Y_1} + \ln\left(\frac{Y(t-\tau_2)}{Y}\right)\right]$$
$$+ \beta_I e^{\alpha_3\tau_3}[I - I(t-\tau_4)]. \qquad (18)$$

Simplifying Equation (18), we get

$$\frac{d\Lambda_1}{dt} = \left(1 - \frac{X_1}{X}\right)(\delta - \varrho X) + \xi_V X_1 V + \xi_P X_1 P - \xi_V X(t-\tau_1)V(t-\tau_1)\frac{Y_1}{Y}$$
$$+ e^{\alpha_1\tau_1}\beta_Y Y_1 - e^{\alpha_1\tau_1+\alpha_2\tau_2}\frac{\beta_Y \lambda_V}{\theta_V}V - e^{\alpha_1\tau_1}\beta_Y Y(t-\tau_2)\frac{V_1}{V} + e^{\alpha_1\tau_1+\alpha_2\tau_2}\frac{\beta_Y \lambda_V}{\theta_V}V_1$$
$$+ e^{\alpha_1\tau_1+\alpha_2\tau_2}\frac{\beta_Y \rho_V}{\theta_V}V_1 Z - e^{\alpha_3\tau_3+\alpha_4\tau_4}\frac{\beta_I \lambda_P}{\theta_P}P - e^{\alpha_1\tau_1+\alpha_2\tau_2}\frac{\beta_Y \rho_V \gamma_Z}{\theta_V \eta_Z}Z - e^{\alpha_3\tau_3+\alpha_4\tau_4}\frac{\beta_I \rho_P \gamma_M}{\theta_P \eta_M}M$$
$$+ \xi_V X_1 V_1 \ln\left(\frac{X(t-\tau_1)V(t-\tau_1)}{XV}\right) + e^{\alpha_1\tau_1}\beta_Y Y_1 \ln\left(\frac{Y(t-\tau_2)}{Y}\right).$$

Using the equilibrium conditions for Δ_1,

$$\delta = \varrho X_1 + \xi_V X_1 V_1, \quad \xi_V X_1 V_1 = e^{\alpha_1\tau_1}\beta_Y Y_1,$$
$$Y_1 = e^{\alpha_2\tau_2}\frac{\lambda_V}{\theta_V}V_1,$$

we obtain

$$\frac{d\Lambda_1}{dt} = \left(1 - \frac{X_1}{X}\right)(\varrho X_1 - \varrho X) + 3\xi_V X_1 V_1 - \xi_V X_1 V_1 \frac{X_1}{X} - \xi_V X_1 V_1 \frac{X(t-\tau_1)V(t-\tau_1)Y_1}{X_1 V_1 Y}$$
$$- \xi_V X_1 V_1 \frac{Y(t-\tau_2)V_1}{Y_1 V} + \xi_V X_1 V_1 \ln\left(\frac{X(t-\tau_1)V(t-\tau_1)}{XV}\right) + \xi_V X_1 V_1 \ln\left(\frac{Y(t-\tau_2)}{Y}\right)$$
$$+ e^{\alpha_3\tau_3+\alpha_4\tau_4}\frac{\beta_I \lambda_P}{\theta_P}\left[\frac{\xi_P X_1 \theta_P}{\beta_I \lambda_P}e^{-\alpha_3\tau_3-\alpha_4\tau_4} - 1\right]P + e^{\alpha_1\tau_1+\alpha_2\tau_2}\frac{\beta_Y \rho_V \gamma_Z}{\theta_V \eta_Z}\left[\frac{\eta_Z}{\gamma_Z}V_1 - 1\right]Z$$
$$- e^{\alpha_3\tau_3+\alpha_4\tau_4}\frac{\beta_I \rho_P \gamma_M}{\theta_P \eta_M}M. \qquad (19)$$

Then, collecting the terms of (19), we get

$$\frac{d\Lambda_1}{dt} = -\varrho \frac{(X-X_1)^2}{X} + 3\xi_V X_1 V_1 - \xi_V X_1 V_1 \frac{X_1}{X} - \xi_V X_1 V_1 \frac{X(t-\tau_1)V(t-\tau_1)Y_1}{X_1 V_1 Y}$$
$$- \xi_V X_1 V_1 \frac{Y(t-\tau_2)V_1}{Y_1 V} + e^{\alpha_3 \tau_3 + \alpha_4 \tau_4} \frac{\beta_I \lambda_P}{\theta_P}(\Re_2/\Re_1 - 1)P$$
$$+ \xi_V X_1 V_1 \left[\ln\left(\frac{X(t-\tau_1)V(t-\tau_1)Y_1}{X_1 V_1 Y}\right) + \ln\left(\frac{X_1}{X}\right) + \ln\left(\frac{Y(t-\tau_2)V_1}{Y_1 V}\right)\right]$$
$$+ \frac{\beta_Y \rho_V(\varrho \eta z + \xi_V \gamma z)}{e^{-\alpha_1 \tau_1 - \alpha_2 \tau_2} \eta_Z \xi_V \theta_V}(\Re_3 - 1)Z - e^{\alpha_3 \tau_3 + \alpha_4 \tau_4} \frac{\beta_I \rho_P \gamma_M}{\theta_P \eta_M} M.$$
$$= -\varrho \frac{(X-X_1)^2}{X} - \xi_V X_1 V_1 \left[F\left(\frac{X_1}{X}\right) + F\left(\frac{Y(t-\tau_2)V_1}{Y_1 V}\right) + F\left(\frac{X(t-\tau_1)V(t-\tau_1)Y_1}{X_1 V_1 Y}\right)\right]$$
$$+ \frac{\beta_I \lambda_P}{e^{-\alpha_3 \tau_3 - \alpha_4 \tau_4}\theta_P}(\Re_2/\Re_1 - 1)P + \frac{\beta_Y \rho_V(\varrho \eta z + \xi_V \gamma z)}{e^{-\alpha_1 \tau_1 - \alpha_2 \tau_2}\eta_Z \xi_V \theta_V}(\Re_3 - 1)Z - e^{\alpha_3 \tau_3 + \alpha_4 \tau_4}\frac{\beta_I \rho_P \gamma_M}{\theta_P \eta_M} M.$$

Since $\Re_2/\Re_1 \leq 1$ and $\Re_3 \leq 1$, then $\frac{d\Lambda_1}{dt} \leq 0$ for all $X, Y, V, P, Z, M > 0$. Moreover, $\frac{d\Lambda_1}{dt} = 0$ when $X = X_1$, $Y = Y_1$, $V = V_1$, $P = 0$, $Z = 0$, and $M = 0$. The trajectories of system (1)–(7) converge to $\bar{\Theta}_1$, where $P = 0$. Thus, $\frac{dP}{dt} = 0$, and Equation (5) yields

$$0 = \frac{dP}{dt} = e^{-\alpha_4 \tau_4} \theta_P I(t-\tau_4) \Longrightarrow I(t) = 0, \text{ fot all } t.$$

Then, $\bar{\Theta}_1 = \{\Delta_1\}$ and Δ_1 is GAS by utilizing the L-LAST. □

Theorem 3. *Let $\Re_2 > 1$, $\Re_1/\Re_2 \leq 1$ and $\Re_4 \leq 1$; then, Δ_2 is GAS.*

Proof. Consider

$$\Lambda_2 = X_2 F\left(\frac{X}{X_2}\right) + e^{\alpha_1 \tau_1} Y + e^{\alpha_3 \tau_3} I_2 F\left(\frac{I}{I_2}\right) + \frac{\beta_Y}{\theta_V} e^{\alpha_1 \tau_1 + \alpha_2 \tau_2} V$$
$$+ \frac{\beta_I}{\theta_P} e^{\alpha_3 \tau_3 + \alpha_4 \tau_4} P_2 F\left(\frac{P}{P_2}\right) + \frac{\rho_V \beta_Y}{\eta_Z \theta_V} e^{\alpha_1 \tau_1 + \alpha_2 \tau_2} Z + \frac{\rho_P \beta_I}{\eta_M \theta_P} e^{\alpha_3 \tau_3 + \alpha_4 \tau_4} M$$
$$+ \xi_V \int_{t-\tau_1}^{t} X(u)V(u)du + \xi_P X_2 P_2 \int_{t-\tau_3}^{t} F\left(\frac{X(u)P(u)}{X_2 P_2}\right) du$$
$$+ e^{\alpha_1 \tau_1} \beta_Y \int_{t-\tau_2}^{t} Y(u)du + e^{\alpha_3 \tau_3} \beta_I I_2 \int_{t-\tau_4}^{t} F\left(\frac{I(u)}{I_2}\right) du.$$

We calculate $\frac{d\Lambda_2}{dt}$ as:

$$\frac{d\Lambda_2}{dt} = \left(1 - \frac{X_2}{X}\right)\frac{dX}{dt} + e^{\alpha_1 \tau_1}\frac{dY}{dt} + e^{\alpha_3 \tau_3}\left(1 - \frac{I_2}{I}\right)\frac{dI}{dt} + \frac{\beta_Y}{\theta_V} e^{\alpha_1 \tau_1 + \alpha_2 \tau_2}\frac{dV}{dt}$$
$$+ \frac{\beta_I}{\theta_P} e^{\alpha_3 \tau_3 + \alpha_4 \tau_4}\left(1 - \frac{P_2}{P}\right)\frac{dP}{dt} + \frac{\rho_V \beta_Y}{\eta_Z \theta_V} e^{\alpha_1 \tau_1 + \alpha_2 \tau_2}\frac{dZ}{dt} + \frac{\rho_P \beta_I}{\eta_M \theta_P} e^{\alpha_3 \tau_3 + \alpha_4 \tau_4}\frac{dM}{dt}$$
$$+ \xi_V[XV - X(t-\tau_1)V(t-\tau_1)]$$
$$+ \xi_P X_2 P_2 \left[\frac{XP}{X_2 P_2} - \frac{X(t-\tau_3)P(t-\tau_3)}{X_2 P_2} + \ln\left(\frac{X(t-\tau_3)P(t-\tau_3)}{XP}\right)\right]$$
$$+ \beta_Y e^{\alpha_1 \tau_1}[Y - Y(t-\tau_2)] + \beta_I e^{\alpha_3 \tau_3} I_2 \left[\frac{I}{I_2} - \frac{I(t-\tau_4)}{I_2} + \ln\left(\frac{I(t-\tau_4)}{I}\right)\right].$$

From Equations (1)–(7), we have

$$\frac{d\Lambda_2}{dt} = \left(1 - \frac{X_2}{X}\right)[\delta - \varrho X - \xi_V XV - \xi_P XP] + e^{\alpha_1 \tau_1}\left[e^{-\alpha_1 \tau_1}\xi_V X(t-\tau_1)V(t-\tau_1) - \beta_Y Y\right]$$
$$+ e^{\alpha_3 \tau_3}\left(1 - \frac{I_2}{I}\right)\left[e^{-\alpha_3 \tau_3}\xi_P X(t-\tau_3)P(t-\tau_3) - \beta_I I\right]$$
$$+ \frac{\beta_Y}{\theta_V}e^{\alpha_1 \tau_1 + \alpha_2 \tau_2}\left[e^{-\alpha_2 \tau_2}\theta_V Y(t-\tau_2) - \lambda_V V - \rho_V VZ\right]$$
$$+ \frac{\beta_I}{\theta_P}e^{\alpha_3 \tau_3 + \alpha_4 \tau_4}\left(1 - \frac{P_2}{P}\right)\left[e^{-\alpha_4 \tau_4}\theta_P I(t-\tau_4) - \lambda_P P - \rho_P PM\right]$$
$$+ \frac{\rho_V \beta_Y}{\eta_Z \theta_V}e^{\alpha_1 \tau_1 + \alpha_2 \tau_2}[\eta_Z VZ - \gamma_Z Z] + \frac{\rho_P \beta_I}{\eta_M \theta_P}e^{\alpha_3 \tau_3 + \alpha_4 \tau_4}[\eta_M PM - \gamma_M M]$$
$$+ \xi_V[XV - X(t-\tau_1)V(t-\tau_1)]$$
$$+ \xi_P X_2 P_2 \left[\frac{XP}{X_2 P_2} - \frac{X(t-\tau_3)P(t-\tau_3)}{X_2 P_2} + \ln\left(\frac{X(t-\tau_3)P(t-\tau_3)}{XP}\right)\right]$$
$$+ \beta_Y e^{\alpha_1 \tau_1}[Y - Y(t-\tau_2)] + \beta_I e^{\alpha_3 \tau_3} I_2 \left[\frac{I}{I_2} - \frac{I(t-\tau_4)}{I_2} + \ln\left(\frac{I(t-\tau_4)}{I}\right)\right]. \tag{20}$$

Then, simplifying Equation (20), we get

$$\frac{d\Lambda_2}{dt} = \left(1 - \frac{X_2}{X}\right)(\delta - \varrho X) + \xi_P X_2 P - \xi_P X(t-\tau_3)P(t-\tau_3)\frac{I_2}{I} + e^{\alpha_3 \tau_3}\beta_I I_2$$
$$- e^{\alpha_3 \tau_3 + \alpha_4 \tau_4}\frac{\beta_I \lambda_P}{\theta_P}P - e^{\alpha_3 \tau_3}\beta_I I(t-\tau_4)\frac{P_2}{P} + e^{\alpha_3 \tau_3 + \alpha_4 \tau_4}\frac{\beta_I \lambda_P}{\theta_P}P_2$$
$$+ \xi_P X_2 P_2 \ln\left(\frac{X(t-\tau_3)P(t-\tau_3)}{XP}\right) + e^{\alpha_3 \tau_3}\beta_I I_2 \ln\left(\frac{I(t-\tau_4)}{I}\right)$$
$$+ \frac{\beta_Y \lambda_V}{e^{-\alpha_1 \tau_1 - \alpha_2 \tau_2}\theta_V}\left(\frac{\xi_V X_2 \theta_V e^{-\alpha_1 \tau_1 - \alpha_2 \tau_2}}{\beta_Y \lambda_V} - 1\right)V + \frac{\beta_I \rho_P \gamma_M}{e^{-\alpha_3 \tau_3 - \alpha_4 \tau_4}\theta_P \eta_M}\left(\frac{\eta_M}{\gamma_M}P_2 - 1\right)M$$
$$- e^{\alpha_1 \tau_1 + \alpha_2 \tau_2}\frac{\rho_V \beta_Y \gamma_Z}{\eta_Z \theta_V}Z.$$

Using the equilibrium conditions for Δ_2,

$$\delta = \varrho X_2 + \xi_P X_2 P_2, \quad \xi_P X_2 P_2 = e^{\alpha_3 \tau_3}\beta_I I_2,$$
$$I_2 = e^{\alpha_4 \tau_4}\frac{\lambda_P}{\theta_P}P_2,$$

we obtain

$$\frac{d\Lambda_2}{dt} = \left(1 - \frac{X_2}{X}\right)(\varrho X_2 - \varrho X) + 3\xi_P X_2 P_2 - \xi_P X_2 P_2\frac{X_2}{X} - \xi_P X_2 P_2\frac{X(t-\tau_3)P(t-\tau_3)I_2}{X_2 P_2 I}$$
$$- \xi_P X_2 P_2\frac{I(t-\tau_4)P_2}{I_2 P} + \xi_P X_2 P_2 \ln\left(\frac{X(t-\tau_3)P(t-\tau_3)}{XP}\right) + \xi_P X_2 P_2 \ln\left(\frac{I(t-\tau_4)}{I}\right)$$
$$+ \frac{\beta_Y \lambda_V}{e^{-\alpha_1 \tau_1 - \alpha_2 \tau_2}\theta_V}\left(\frac{\Re_1}{\Re_2} - 1\right)V + \frac{\beta_I \rho_P(\varrho\eta_M + \gamma_M \xi_P)}{e^{-\alpha_3 \tau_3 - \alpha_4 \tau_4}\xi_P \eta_M \theta_P}(\Re_4 - 1)M - e^{\alpha_1 \tau_1 + \alpha_2 \tau_2}\frac{\rho_V \beta_Y \gamma_Z}{\eta_Z \theta_V}Z. \tag{21}$$

Then, simplifying Equation (21), we get:

$$\frac{d\Lambda_2}{dt} = -\varrho\frac{(X-X_2)^2}{X} + 3\xi_P X_2 P_2 - \xi_P X_2 P_2\frac{X_2}{X} - \xi_P X_2 P_2\frac{I(t-\tau_4)P_2}{I_2 P}$$
$$- \xi_P X_2 P_2\frac{X(t-\tau_3)P(t-\tau_3)I_2}{X_2 P_2 I} + \frac{\beta_Y \lambda_V}{e^{-\alpha_1 \tau_1 - \alpha_2 \tau_2}\theta_V}(\Re_1/\Re_2 - 1)V$$

$$+ \frac{\beta_I \rho_P (\varrho \eta_M + \gamma_M \xi_P)}{e^{-\alpha_3 \tau_3 - \alpha_4 \tau_4} \xi_P \eta_M \theta_P} (\Re_4 - 1) M - e^{\alpha_1 \tau_1 + \alpha_2 \tau_2} \frac{\rho_V \beta_Y \gamma_Z}{\eta_Z \theta_V} Z$$

$$+ \xi_P X_2 P_2 \left[\ln\left(\frac{X_2}{X}\right) + \ln\left(\frac{I(t-\tau_4) P_2}{I_2 P}\right) + \ln\left(\frac{X(t-\tau_3) P(t-\tau_3) I_2}{X_2 P_2 I}\right) \right]$$

$$= -\varrho \frac{(X - X_2)^2}{X} - \xi_P X_2 P_2 \left[F\left(\frac{X_2}{X}\right) + F\left(\frac{I(t-\tau_4) P_2}{I_2 P}\right) + F\left(\frac{X(t-\tau_3) P(t-\tau_3) I_2}{X_2 P_2 I}\right) \right]$$

$$+ \frac{\beta_Y \lambda_V}{e^{-\alpha_1 \tau_1 - \alpha_2 \tau_2} \theta_V} (\Re_1 / \Re_2 - 1) V + \frac{\beta_I \rho_P (\varrho \eta_M + \gamma_M \xi_P)}{e^{-\alpha_3 \tau_3 - \alpha_4 \tau_4} \xi_P \eta_M \theta_P} (\Re_4 - 1) M$$

$$- e^{\alpha_1 \tau_1 + \alpha_2 \tau_2} \frac{\rho_V \beta_Y \gamma_Z}{\eta_Z \theta_V} Z.$$

If $\Re_1 / \Re_2 \leq 1$ and $\Re_4 \leq 1$, then $\frac{d\Lambda_2}{dt} \leq 0$ for all $X, I, V, P, Z, M > 0$. In addition, $\frac{d\Lambda_2}{dt} = 0$ when $X = X_2$, $I = I_2$, $P = P_2$, $V = 0$, $M = 0$, and $Z = 0$. The trajectories of system (1)–(7) converge to $\tilde{\Theta}_2$, which includes solutions with $V = 0$, and thus, $\frac{dV}{dt} = 0$. Equation (4) implies that

$$0 = \frac{dV}{dt} = e^{-\alpha_2 \tau_2} \theta_V Y(t - \tau_2) \implies Y(t) = 0, \text{ for all } t.$$

Hence, $\tilde{\Theta}_2 = \{\Delta_2\}$, and the global stability of Δ_2 follows from applying the L-LAST. □

Theorem 4. *Let $\Re_3 > 1$ and $\Re_5 \leq 1$; then, Δ_3 is GAS.*

Proof. We define

$$\Lambda_3 = X_3 F\left(\frac{X}{X_3}\right) + e^{\alpha_1 \tau_1} Y_3 F\left(\frac{Y}{Y_3}\right) + e^{\alpha_3 \tau_3} I + \frac{\beta_Y}{\theta_V} e^{\alpha_1 \tau_1 + \alpha_2 \tau_2} V_3 F\left(\frac{V}{V_3}\right)$$

$$+ \frac{\beta_I}{\theta_P} e^{\alpha_3 \tau_3 + \alpha_4 \tau_4} P + \frac{\rho_V \beta_Y}{\eta_Z \theta_V} e^{\alpha_1 \tau_1 + \alpha_2 \tau_2} Z_3 F\left(\frac{Z}{Z_3}\right) + \frac{\rho_P \beta_I}{\eta_M \theta_P} e^{\alpha_3 \tau_3 + \alpha_4 \tau_4} M$$

$$+ \xi_V X_3 V_3 \int_{t-\tau_1}^{t} F\left(\frac{X(u) V(u)}{X_3 V_3}\right) du + \xi_P \int_{t-\tau_3}^{t} X(u) P(u) du$$

$$+ e^{\alpha_1 \tau_1} \beta_Y Y_3 \int_{t-\tau_2}^{t} F\left(\frac{Y(u)}{Y_3}\right) du + e^{\alpha_3 \tau_3} \beta_I \int_{t-\tau_4}^{t} I(u) du.$$

We calculate $\frac{d\Lambda_3}{dt}$ as:

$$\frac{d\Lambda_3}{dt} = \left(1 - \frac{X_3}{X}\right) \frac{dX}{dt} + e^{\alpha_1 \tau_1} \left(1 - \frac{Y_3}{Y}\right) \frac{dY}{dt} + e^{\alpha_3 \tau_3} \frac{dI}{dt}$$

$$+ \frac{\beta_Y}{\theta_V} e^{\alpha_1 \tau_1 + \alpha_2 \tau_2} \left(1 - \frac{V_3}{V}\right) \frac{dV}{dt} + \frac{\beta_I}{\theta_P} e^{\alpha_3 \tau_3 + \alpha_4 \tau_4} \frac{dP}{dt}$$

$$+ \frac{\rho_V \beta_Y}{\eta_Z \theta_V} e^{\alpha_1 \tau_1 + \alpha_2 \tau_2} \left(1 - \frac{Z_3}{Z}\right) \frac{dZ}{dt} + \frac{\rho_P \beta_I}{\eta_M \theta_P} e^{\alpha_3 \tau_3 + \alpha_4 \tau_4} \frac{dM}{dt}$$

$$+ \xi_V X_3 V_3 \left[\frac{XV}{X_3 V_3} - \frac{X(t-\tau_1) V(t-\tau_1)}{X_3 V_3} + \ln\left(\frac{X(t-\tau_1) V(t-\tau_1)}{XV}\right) \right]$$

$$+ \xi_P [XP - X(t-\tau_3) P(t-\tau_3)]$$

$$+ e^{\alpha_1 \tau_1} \beta_Y Y_3 \left[\frac{Y}{Y_3} - \frac{Y(t-\tau_2)}{Y_3} + \ln\left(\frac{Y(t-\tau_2)}{Y}\right) \right] + e^{\alpha_3 \tau_3} \beta_I [I - I(t-\tau_4)].$$

From Equations (1)–(7), we get

$$\frac{d\Lambda_3}{dt} = \left(1 - \frac{X_3}{X}\right)[\delta - \varrho X - \xi_V XV - \xi_P XP]$$

$$+ e^{\alpha_1 \tau_1}\left(1 - \frac{Y_3}{Y}\right)[e^{-\alpha_1 \tau_1}\xi_V X(t-\tau_1)V(t-\tau_1) - \beta_Y Y]$$

$$+ e^{\alpha_3 \tau_3}[e^{-\alpha_3 \tau_3}\xi_P X(t-\tau_3)P(t-\tau_3) - \beta_I I]$$

$$+ \frac{\beta_Y}{\theta_V}e^{\alpha_1 \tau_1 + \alpha_2 \tau_2}\left(1 - \frac{V_3}{V}\right)[e^{-\alpha_2 \tau_2}\theta_V Y(t-\tau_2) - \lambda_V V - \rho_V VZ]$$

$$+ \frac{\beta_I}{\theta_P}e^{\alpha_3 \tau_3 + \alpha_4 \tau_4}[e^{-\alpha_4 \tau_4}\theta_P I(t-\tau_4) - \lambda_P P - \rho_P PM]$$

$$+ \frac{\rho_V \beta_Y}{\eta_Z \theta_V}e^{\alpha_1 \tau_1 + \alpha_2 \tau_2}\left(1 - \frac{Z_3}{Z}\right)[\eta_Z VZ - \gamma_Z Z] + \frac{\rho_P \beta_I}{\eta_M \theta_P}e^{\alpha_3 \tau_3 + \alpha_4 \tau_4}[\eta_M PM - \gamma_M M]$$

$$+ \xi_V X_3 V_3 \left[\frac{XV}{X_3 V_3} - \frac{X(t-\tau_1)V(t-\tau_1)}{X_3 V_3} + \ln\left(\frac{X(t-\tau_1)V(t-\tau_1)}{XV}\right)\right]$$

$$+ \xi_P[XP - X(t-\tau_3)P(t-\tau_3)]$$

$$+ e^{\alpha_1 \tau_1}\beta_Y Y_3 \left[\frac{Y}{Y_3} - \frac{Y(t-\tau_2)}{Y_3} + \ln\left(\frac{Y(t-\tau_2)}{Y}\right)\right] + e^{\alpha_3 \tau_3}\beta_I[I - I(t-\tau_4)]. \quad (22)$$

Then, simplifying Equation (22), we get:

$$\frac{d\Lambda_3}{dt} = \left(1 - \frac{X_3}{X}\right)(\delta - \varrho X) + \xi_V X_3 V - \xi_V X(t-\tau_1)V(t-\tau_1)\frac{Y_3}{Y}$$

$$+ e^{\alpha_1 \tau_1}\beta_Y Y_3 - e^{\alpha_1 \tau_1 + \alpha_2 \tau_2}\frac{\beta_Y \lambda_V}{\theta_V}V - e^{\alpha_1 \tau_1}\beta_Y Y(t-\tau_2)\frac{V_3}{V} + e^{\alpha_1 \tau_1 + \alpha_2 \tau_2}\frac{\beta_Y \lambda_V}{\theta_V}V_3$$

$$+ e^{\alpha_1 \tau_1 + \alpha_2 \tau_2}\frac{\beta_Y \rho_V}{\theta_V}V_3 Z - e^{\alpha_1 \tau_1 + \alpha_2 \tau_2}\frac{\beta_Y \rho_V \gamma_Z}{\theta_V \eta_Z}Z - e^{\alpha_1 \tau_1 + \alpha_2 \tau_2}\frac{\beta_Y \rho_V}{\theta_V}Z_3 V$$

$$+ e^{\alpha_1 \tau_1 + \alpha_2 \tau_2}\frac{\beta_Y \rho_V \gamma_Z}{\theta_V \eta_Z}Z_3 - e^{\alpha_3 \tau_3 + \alpha_4 \tau_4}\frac{\beta_I \rho_P \gamma_M}{\theta_P \eta_M}M$$

$$+ e^{\alpha_3 \tau_3 + \alpha_4 \tau_4}\frac{\beta_I \lambda_P}{\theta_P}\left[\frac{\xi_P X_3 \theta_P}{\beta_I \lambda_P}e^{-\alpha_3 \tau_3 - \alpha_4 \tau_4} - 1\right]P + \xi_V X_3 V_3 \ln\left(\frac{X(t-\tau_1)V(t-\tau_1)}{XV}\right)$$

$$+ e^{\alpha_1 \tau_1}\beta_Y Y_3 \ln\left(\frac{Y(t-\tau_2)}{Y}\right).$$

Using the equilibrium conditions for Δ_3,

$$\delta = \varrho X_3 + \xi_V X_3 V_3, \quad \xi_V X_3 V_3 = e^{\alpha_1 \tau_1}\beta_Y Y_3,$$

$$Y_3 = e^{\alpha_2 \tau_2}\frac{\lambda_V}{\theta_V}V_3 + e^{\alpha_2 \tau_2}\frac{\rho_V}{\theta_V}Z_3 V_3,$$

$$V_3 = \frac{\gamma_Z}{\eta_Z},$$

we obtain

$$\frac{d\Lambda_3}{dt} = \left(1 - \frac{X_3}{X}\right)(\varrho X_3 - \varrho X) + 3\xi_V X_3 V_3 - \xi_V X_3 V_3 \frac{X_3}{X}$$

$$- \xi_V X_3 V_3 \frac{X(t-\tau_1)V(t-\tau_1)Y_3}{X_3 V_3 Y} - \xi_V X_3 V_3 \frac{Y(t-\tau_2)V_3}{Y_3 V}$$

$$+ \xi_V X_3 V_3 \ln\left(\frac{X(t-\tau_1)V(t-\tau_1)}{XV}\right) + \xi_V X_3 V_3 \ln\left(\frac{Y(t-\tau_2)}{Y}\right)$$

$$+ e^{\alpha_3 \tau_3 + \alpha_4 \tau_4}\frac{\beta_I \lambda_P}{\theta_P}(\Re_5 - 1)P - e^{\alpha_3 \tau_3 + \alpha_4 \tau_4}\frac{\beta_I \rho_P \gamma_M}{\theta_P \eta_M}M. \quad (23)$$

Equation (23) can be written as:

$$\frac{d\Lambda_3}{dt} = -\varrho\frac{(X-X_3)^2}{X} + 3\xi_V X_3 V_3 - \xi_V X_3 V_3\frac{X_3}{X} - \xi_V X_3 V_3\frac{Y(t-\tau_2)V_3}{Y_3 V}$$
$$-\xi_V X_3 V_3\frac{X(t-\tau_1)V(t-\tau_1)Y_3}{X_3 V_3 Y} + e^{\alpha_3\tau_3+\alpha_4\tau_4}\frac{\beta_I\lambda_P}{\theta_P}(\Re_5-1)P - e^{\alpha_3\tau_3+\alpha_4\tau_4}\frac{\beta_I\rho_P\gamma_M}{\theta_P\eta_M}M$$
$$+\xi_V X_3 V_3\left[\ln\left(\frac{X_3}{X}\right) + \ln\left(\frac{Y(t-\tau_2)V_3}{Y_3 V}\right) + \ln\left(\frac{X(t-\tau_1)V(t-\tau_1)Y_3}{X_3 V_3 Y}\right)\right]$$
$$= -\varrho\frac{(X-X_3)^2}{X}$$
$$-\xi_V X_3 V_3\left[F\left(\frac{X_3}{X}\right) + F\left(\frac{X(t-\tau_1)V(t-\tau_1)Y_3}{X_3 V_3 Y}\right) + F\left(\frac{Y(t-\tau_2)V_3}{Y_3 V}\right)\right]$$
$$+ e^{\alpha_3\tau_3+\alpha_4\tau_4}\frac{\beta_I\lambda_P}{\theta_P}(\Re_5-1)P - e^{\alpha_3\tau_3+\alpha_4\tau_4}\frac{\beta_I\rho_P\gamma_M}{\theta_P\eta_M}M.$$

Obviously, $\frac{d\Lambda_3}{dt} \leq 0$ for all $X, Y, V, P, M > 0$ when $\Re_5 \leq 1$. Further, $\frac{d\Lambda_3}{dt} = 0$ when $X = X_3$, $Y = Y_3$, $V = V_3$, $P = 0$, and $M = 0$. Similarly to the proofs of the previous theorems, one can complete the proof. □

Theorem 5. *If $\Re_4 > 1$ and $\Re_6 \leq 1$, then Δ_4 is GAS.*

Proof. We define a function Λ_4 as:

$$\Lambda_4 = X_4 F\left(\frac{X}{X_4}\right) + e^{\alpha_1\tau_1}Y + e^{\alpha_3\tau_3}I_4 F\left(\frac{I}{I_4}\right) + \frac{\beta_Y}{\theta_V}e^{\alpha_1\tau_1+\alpha_2\tau_2}V$$
$$+ \frac{\beta_I}{\theta_P}e^{\alpha_3\tau_3+\alpha_4\tau_4}P_4 F\left(\frac{P}{P_4}\right) + \frac{\rho_V\beta_Y}{\eta_Z\theta_V}e^{\alpha_1\tau_1+\alpha_2\tau_2}Z + \frac{\rho_P\beta_I}{\eta_M\theta_P}e^{\alpha_3\tau_3+\alpha_4\tau_4}M_4 F\left(\frac{M}{M_4}\right)$$
$$+ \xi_V \int_{t-\tau_1}^{t} X(u)V(u)du + \xi_P X_4 P_4 \int_{t-\tau_3}^{t} F\left(\frac{X(u)P(u)}{X_4 P_4}\right)du$$
$$+ e^{\alpha_1\tau_1}\beta_Y \int_{t-\tau_2}^{t} Y(u)du + e^{\alpha_3\tau_3}\beta_I I_4 \int_{t-\tau_4}^{t} F\left(\frac{I(u)}{I_4}\right)du.$$

We calculate $\frac{d\Lambda_4}{dt}$ as:

$$\frac{d\Lambda_4}{dt} = \left(1 - \frac{X_4}{X}\right)\frac{dX}{dt} + e^{\alpha_1\tau_1}\frac{dY}{dt} + e^{\alpha_3\tau_3}\left(1 - \frac{I_4}{I}\right)\frac{dI}{dt} + \frac{\beta_Y}{\theta_V}e^{\alpha_1\tau_1+\alpha_2\tau_2}\frac{dV}{dt}$$
$$+ \frac{\beta_I}{\theta_P}e^{\alpha_3\tau_3+\alpha_4\tau_4}\left(1 - \frac{P_4}{P}\right)\frac{dP}{dt} + \frac{\rho_V\beta_Y}{\eta_Z\theta_V}e^{\alpha_1\tau_1+\alpha_2\tau_2}\frac{dZ}{dt}$$
$$+ \frac{\rho_P\beta_I}{\eta_M\theta_P}e^{\alpha_3\tau_3+\alpha_4\tau_4}\left(1 - \frac{M_4}{M}\right)\frac{dM}{dt} + \xi_V[XV - X(t-\tau_1)V(t-\tau_1)]$$
$$+ \xi_P X_4 P_4\left[\frac{XP}{X_4 P_4} - \frac{X(t-\tau_3)P(t-\tau_3)}{X_4 P_4} + \ln\left(\frac{X(t-\tau_3)P(t-\tau_3)}{XP}\right)\right]$$
$$+ e^{\alpha_1\tau_1}\beta_Y[Y - Y(t-\tau_2)] + e^{\alpha_3\tau_3}\beta_I I_4\left[\frac{I}{I_4} - \frac{I(t-\tau_4)}{I_4} + \ln\left(\frac{I(t-\tau_4)}{I}\right)\right].$$

Substituting from Equations (1)–(7), we obtain

$$\frac{d\Lambda_4}{dt} = \left(1 - \frac{X_4}{X}\right)[\delta - \varrho X - \xi_V XV - \xi_P XP] + e^{\alpha_1\tau_1}\left[e^{-\alpha_1\tau_1}\xi_V X(t-\tau_1)V(t-\tau_1) - \beta_Y Y\right]$$

$$+ e^{\alpha_3\tau_3}\left(1 - \frac{I_4}{I}\right)\left[e^{-\alpha_3\tau_3}\xi_P X(t-\tau_3)P(t-\tau_3) - \beta_I I\right]$$

$$+ \frac{\beta_Y}{\theta_V} e^{\alpha_1\tau_1+\alpha_2\tau_2}\left[e^{-\alpha_2\tau_2}\theta_V Y(t-\tau_2) - \lambda_V V - \rho_V VZ\right]$$

$$+ \frac{\beta_I}{\theta_P} e^{\alpha_3\tau_3+\alpha_4\tau_4}\left(1 - \frac{P_4}{P}\right)\left[e^{-\alpha_4\tau_4}\theta_P I(t-\tau_4) - \lambda_P P - \rho_P PM\right]$$

$$+ \frac{\rho_V \beta_Y}{\eta_Z \theta_V} e^{\alpha_1\tau_1+\alpha_2\tau_2}[\eta_Z VZ - \gamma_Z Z] + \frac{\rho_P \beta_I}{\eta_M \theta_P} e^{\alpha_3\tau_3+\alpha_4\tau_4}\left(1 - \frac{M_4}{M}\right)[\eta_M PM - \gamma_M M]$$

$$+ \xi_V[XV - X(t-\tau_1)V(t-\tau_1)]$$

$$+ \xi_P X_4 P_4\left[\frac{XP}{X_4 P_4} - \frac{X(t-\tau_3)P(t-\tau_3)}{X_4 P_4} + \ln\left(\frac{X(t-\tau_3)P(t-\tau_3)}{XP}\right)\right]$$

$$+ e^{\alpha_1\tau_1}\beta_Y[Y - Y(t-\tau_2)] + e^{\alpha_3\tau_3}\beta_I I_4\left[\frac{I}{I_4} - \frac{I(t-\tau_4)}{I_4} + \ln\left(\frac{I(t-\tau_4)}{I}\right)\right]. \tag{24}$$

Collecting the terms of Equation (24), we get:

$$\frac{d\Lambda_4}{dt} = \left(1 - \frac{X_4}{X}\right)(\delta - \varrho X) + \xi_P X_4 P - \xi_P X(t-\tau_3)P(t-\tau_3)\frac{I_4}{I} + e^{\alpha_3\tau_3}\beta_I I_4$$

$$- e^{\alpha_3\tau_3+\alpha_4\tau_4}\frac{\beta_I \lambda_P}{\theta_P}P - e^{\alpha_3\tau_3}\beta_I I(t-\tau_4)\frac{P_4}{P} + e^{\alpha_3\tau_3+\alpha_4\tau_4}\frac{\beta_I \lambda_P}{\theta_P}P_4$$

$$+ e^{\alpha_3\tau_3+\alpha_4\tau_4}\frac{\beta_I \rho_P}{\theta_P}P_4 M - e^{\alpha_1\tau_1+\alpha_2\tau_2}\frac{\beta_Y \rho_V \gamma_Z}{\theta_V \eta_Z}Z - e^{\alpha_3\tau_3+\alpha_4\tau_4}\frac{\beta_I \rho_P \gamma_M}{\theta_P \eta_M}M$$

$$- e^{\alpha_3\tau_3+\alpha_4\tau_4}\frac{\beta_I \rho_P}{\theta_P}M_4 P + e^{\alpha_3\tau_3+\alpha_4\tau_4}\frac{\beta_I \rho_P \gamma_M}{\theta_P \eta_M}M_4$$

$$+ e^{\alpha_1\tau_1+\alpha_2\tau_2}\frac{\beta_Y \lambda_V}{\theta_V}\left[\frac{\xi_V X_4 \theta_V}{\beta_Y \lambda_V}e^{-\alpha_1\tau_1-\alpha_2\tau_2} - 1\right]V + \xi_P X_4 P_4 \ln\left(\frac{X(t-\tau_3)P(t-\tau_3)}{XP}\right)$$

$$+ e^{\alpha_3\tau_3}\beta_I I_4 \ln\left(\frac{I(t-\tau_4)}{I}\right).$$

Using the equilibrium conditions for Δ_4,

$$\delta = \varrho X_4 + \xi_P X_4 P_4, \quad \xi_P X_4 P_4 = e^{\alpha_3\tau_3}\beta_I I_4,$$

$$I_4 = e^{\alpha_4\tau_4}\frac{\lambda_P}{\theta_P}P_4 + e^{\alpha_4\tau_4}\frac{\rho_P}{\theta_P}P_4 M_4, \quad P_4 = \frac{\gamma_M}{\eta_M},$$

we obtain

$$\frac{d\Lambda_4}{dt} = \left(1 - \frac{X_4}{X}\right)(\varrho X_4 - \varrho X) + 3\xi_P X_4 P_4 - \xi_P X_4 P_4 \frac{X_4}{X} - \xi_P X_4 P_4 \frac{X(t-\tau_3)P(t-\tau_3)I_4}{X_4 P_4 I}$$

$$- \xi_P X_4 P_4 \frac{I(t-\tau_4)P_4}{I_4 P} + \xi_P X_4 P_4 \ln\left(\frac{X(t-\tau_3)P(t-\tau_3)}{XP}\right) + \xi_P X_4 P_4 \ln\left(\frac{I(t-\tau_4)}{I}\right)$$

$$+ e^{\alpha_1\tau_1+\alpha_2\tau_2}\frac{\beta_Y \lambda_V}{\theta_V}(\Re_6 - 1)V - e^{\alpha_1\tau_1+\alpha_2\tau_2}\frac{\beta_Y \rho_V \gamma_Z}{\theta_V \eta_Z}Z. \tag{25}$$

Then, simplifying Equation (25), we get:

$$\frac{d\Lambda_4}{dt} = -\varrho\frac{(X-X_4)^2}{X} + 3\xi_P X_4 P_4 - \xi_P X_4 P_4 \frac{X_4}{X} - \xi_P X_4 P_4 \frac{I(t-\tau_4)P_4}{I_4 P}$$

$$- \xi_P X_4 P_4 \frac{X(t-\tau_3)P(t-\tau_3)I_4}{X_4 P_4 I} + e^{\alpha_1\tau_1+\alpha_2\tau_2}\frac{\beta_Y \lambda_V}{\theta_V}(\Re_6 - 1)V - e^{\alpha_1\tau_1+\alpha_2\tau_2}\frac{\beta_Y \rho_V \gamma_Z}{\theta_V \eta_Z}Z$$

$$+ \xi_P X_4 P_4 \left[\ln\left(\frac{X_4}{X}\right) + \ln\left(\frac{X(t-\tau_3)P(t-\tau_3)I_4}{X_4 P_4 I}\right) + \ln\left(\frac{I(t-\tau_4)P_4}{I_4 P}\right)\right]$$

$$= -\varrho \frac{(X - X_4)^2}{X} - \xi_P X_4 P_4 \left[F\left(\frac{X_4}{X}\right) + F\left(\frac{X(t-\tau_3)P(t-\tau_3)I_4}{X_4 P_4 I}\right) + F\left(\frac{I(t-\tau_4)P_4}{I_4 P}\right) \right]$$
$$+ e^{\alpha_1 \tau_1 + \alpha_2 \tau_2} \frac{\beta_Y \lambda_V}{\theta_V} (\Re_6 - 1) V - e^{\alpha_1 \tau_1 + \alpha_2 \tau_2} \frac{\beta_Y \rho_V \gamma Z}{\theta_V \eta_Z} Z.$$

Since $\Re_6 \leq 1$, then $\frac{d\Lambda_4}{dt} \leq 0$ for all $X, I, V, P, Z > 0$. In addition, $\frac{d\Lambda_4}{dt} = 0$ when $X = X_4$, $I = I_4$, $P = P_4$, $V = 0$, and $Z = 0$. The proof can be completed similarly to the previous theorems. □

Theorem 6. *If $\Re_5 > 1$, $\Re_8 \leq 1$, and $\Re_1/\Re_2 > 1$, then Δ_5 is GAS.*

Proof. We define

$$\Lambda_5 = X_5 F\left(\frac{X}{X_5}\right) + e^{\alpha_1 \tau_1} Y_5 F\left(\frac{Y}{Y_5}\right) + e^{\alpha_3 \tau_3} I_5 F\left(\frac{I}{I_5}\right) + \frac{\beta_Y}{\theta_V} e^{\alpha_1 \tau_1 + \alpha_2 \tau_2} V_5 F\left(\frac{V}{V_5}\right)$$
$$+ \frac{\beta_I}{\theta_P} e^{\alpha_3 \tau_3 + \alpha_4 \tau_4} P_5 F\left(\frac{P}{P_5}\right) + \frac{\rho_V \beta_Y}{\eta_Z \theta_V} e^{\alpha_1 \tau_1 + \alpha_2 \tau_2} Z_5 F\left(\frac{Z}{Z_5}\right) + \frac{\rho_P \beta_I}{\eta_M \theta_P} e^{\alpha_3 \tau_3 + \alpha_4 \tau_4} M$$
$$+ \xi_V X_5 V_5 \int_{t-\tau_1}^{t} F\left(\frac{X(u)V(u)}{X_5 V_5}\right) du + \xi_P X_5 P_5 \int_{t-\tau_3}^{t} F\left(\frac{X(u)P(u)}{X_5 P_5}\right) du$$
$$+ e^{\alpha_1 \tau_1} \beta_Y Y_5 \int_{t-\tau_2}^{t} F\left(\frac{Y(u)}{Y_5}\right) du + e^{\alpha_3 \tau_3} \beta_I I_5 \int_{t-\tau_4}^{t} F\left(\frac{I(u)}{I_5}\right) du.$$

We calculate $\frac{d\Lambda_5}{dt}$ as:

$$\frac{d\Lambda_5}{dt} = \left(1 - \frac{X_5}{X}\right)\frac{dX}{dt} + e^{\alpha_1 \tau_1}\left(1 - \frac{Y_5}{Y}\right)\frac{dY}{dt} + e^{\alpha_3 \tau_3}\left(1 - \frac{I_5}{I}\right)\frac{dI}{dt}$$
$$+ \frac{\beta_Y}{\theta_V} e^{\alpha_1 \tau_1 + \alpha_2 \tau_2}\left(1 - \frac{V_5}{V}\right)\frac{dV}{dt} + \frac{\beta_I}{\theta_P} e^{\alpha_3 \tau_3 + \alpha_4 \tau_4}\left(1 - \frac{P_5}{P}\right)\frac{dP}{dt}$$
$$+ \frac{\rho_V \beta_Y}{\eta_Z \theta_V} e^{\alpha_1 \tau_1 + \alpha_2 \tau_2}\left(1 - \frac{Z_5}{Z}\right)\frac{dZ}{dt} + \frac{\rho_P \beta_I}{\eta_M \theta_P} e^{\alpha_3 \tau_3 + \alpha_4 \tau_4}\frac{dM}{dt}$$
$$+ \xi_V X_5 V_5 \left[\frac{XV}{X_5 V_5} - \frac{X(t-\tau_1)V(t-\tau_1)}{X_5 V_5} + \ln\left(\frac{X(t-\tau_1)V(t-\tau_1)}{XV}\right)\right]$$
$$+ \xi_P X_5 P_5 \left[\frac{XP}{X_5 P_5} - \frac{X(t-\tau_3)P(t-\tau_3)}{X_5 P_5} + \ln\left(\frac{X(t-\tau_3)P(t-\tau_3)}{XP}\right)\right]$$
$$+ e^{\alpha_1 \tau_1} \beta_Y Y_5 \left[\frac{Y}{Y_5} - \frac{Y(t-\tau_2)}{Y_5} + \ln\left(\frac{Y(t-\tau_2)}{Y}\right)\right]$$
$$+ e^{\alpha_3 \tau_3} \beta_I I_5 \left[\frac{I}{I_5} - \frac{I(t-\tau_4)}{I_5} + \ln\left(\frac{I(t-\tau_4)}{I}\right)\right].$$

It follows from Equations (1)–(7) that

$$\frac{d\Lambda_5}{dt} = \left(1 - \frac{X_5}{X}\right)[\delta - \varrho X - \xi_V XV - \xi_P XP]$$
$$+ e^{\alpha_1 \tau_1}\left(1 - \frac{Y_5}{Y}\right)\left[e^{-\alpha_1 \tau_1} \xi_V X(t-\tau_1)V(t-\tau_1) - \beta_Y Y\right]$$
$$+ e^{\alpha_3 \tau_3}\left(1 - \frac{I_5}{I}\right)\left[e^{-\alpha_3 \tau_3} \xi_P X(t-\tau_3)P(t-\tau_3) - \beta_I I\right]$$
$$+ \frac{\beta_Y}{\theta_V} e^{\alpha_1 \tau_1 + \alpha_2 \tau_2}\left(1 - \frac{V_5}{V}\right)\left[e^{-\alpha_2 \tau_2} \theta_V Y(t-\tau_2) - \lambda_V V - \rho_V VZ\right]$$

$$
\begin{aligned}
&+ \frac{\beta_I}{\theta_P} e^{\alpha_3 \tau_3 + \alpha_4 \tau_4} \left(1 - \frac{P_5}{P}\right) \left[e^{-\alpha_4 \tau_4} \theta_P I(t - \tau_4) - \lambda_P P - \rho_P P M\right] \\
&+ \frac{\rho_V \beta_Y}{\eta_Z \theta_V} e^{\alpha_1 \tau_1 + \alpha_2 \tau_2} \left(1 - \frac{Z_5}{Z}\right) [\eta_Z V Z - \gamma_Z Z] + \frac{\rho_P \beta_I}{\eta_M \theta_P} e^{\alpha_3 \tau_3 + \alpha_4 \tau_4} [\eta_M P M - \gamma_M M] \\
&+ \xi_V X_5 V_5 \left[\frac{XV}{X_5 V_5} - \frac{X(t - \tau_1) V(t - \tau_1)}{X_5 V_5} + \ln\left(\frac{X(t - \tau_1) V(t - \tau_1)}{XV}\right)\right] \\
&+ \xi_P X_5 P_5 \left[\frac{XP}{X_5 P_5} - \frac{X(t - \tau_3) P(t - \tau_3)}{X_5 P_5} + \ln\left(\frac{X(t - \tau_3) P(t - \tau_3)}{XP}\right)\right] \\
&+ e^{\alpha_1 \tau_1} \beta_Y Y_5 \left[\frac{Y}{Y_5} - \frac{Y(t - \tau_2)}{Y_5} + \ln\left(\frac{Y(t - \tau_2)}{Y}\right)\right] \\
&+ e^{\alpha_3 \tau_3} \beta_I I_5 \left[\frac{I}{I_5} - \frac{I(t - \tau_4)}{I_5} + \ln\left(\frac{I(t - \tau_4)}{I}\right)\right]. \quad (26)
\end{aligned}
$$

Equation (26) can be simplified as:

$$
\begin{aligned}
\frac{d\Lambda_5}{dt} &= \left(1 - \frac{X_5}{X}\right)(\delta - \varrho X) + \xi_V X_5 V + \xi_P X_5 P - \xi_V X(t - \tau_1) V(t - \tau_1) \frac{Y_5}{Y} \\
&+ e^{\alpha_1 \tau_1} \beta_Y Y_5 - \xi_P X(t - \tau_3) P(t - \tau_3) \frac{I_5}{I} + e^{\alpha_3 \tau_3} \beta_I I_5 - e^{\alpha_1 \tau_1 + \alpha_2 \tau_2} \frac{\beta_Y \lambda_V}{\theta_V} V \\
&- e^{\alpha_1 \tau_1} \beta_Y Y(t - \tau_2) \frac{V_5}{V} + e^{\alpha_1 \tau_1 + \alpha_2 \tau_2} \frac{\beta_Y \lambda_V}{\theta_V} V_5 + e^{\alpha_1 \tau_1 + \alpha_2 \tau_2} \frac{\beta_Y \rho_V}{\theta_V} Z V_5 \\
&- e^{\alpha_3 \tau_3 + \alpha_4 \tau_4} \frac{\beta_I \lambda_P}{\theta_P} P - e^{\alpha_3 \tau_3} \beta_I I(t - \tau_4) \frac{P_5}{P} + e^{\alpha_3 \tau_3 + \alpha_4 \tau_4} \frac{\beta_I \lambda_P}{\theta_P} P_5 \\
&- e^{\alpha_1 \tau_1 + \alpha_2 \tau_2} \frac{\beta_Y \rho_V \gamma_Z}{\theta_V \eta_Z} Z - e^{\alpha_1 \tau_1 + \alpha_2 \tau_2} \frac{\beta_Y \rho_V}{\theta_V} Z_5 V + e^{\alpha_1 \tau_1 + \alpha_2 \tau_2} \frac{\beta_Y \rho_V \gamma_Z}{\theta_V \eta_Z} Z_5 \\
&+ \xi_V X_5 V_5 \ln\left(\frac{X(t - \tau_1) V(t - \tau_1)}{XV}\right) + \xi_P X_5 P_5 \ln\left(\frac{X(t - \tau_3) P(t - \tau_3)}{XP}\right) \\
&+ e^{\alpha_1 \tau_1} \beta_Y Y_5 \ln\left(\frac{Y(t - \tau_2)}{Y}\right) + e^{\alpha_3 \tau_3} \beta_I I_5 \ln\left(\frac{I(t - \tau_4)}{I}\right) \\
&+ e^{\alpha_3 \tau_3 + \alpha_4 \tau_4} \frac{\beta_I \rho_P \gamma_M}{\theta_P \eta_M} \left[\frac{\eta_M}{\gamma_M} P_5 - 1\right] M.
\end{aligned}
$$

Using the equilibrium conditions for Δ_5,

$$
\delta = \varrho X_5 + \xi_V X_5 V_5 + \xi_P X_5 P_5, \quad \xi_V X_5 V_5 = e^{\alpha_1 \tau_1} \beta_Y Y_5,
$$

$$
\xi_P X_5 P_5 = e^{\alpha_3 \tau_3} \beta_I I_5, \quad Y_5 = e^{\alpha_2 \tau_2} \frac{\lambda_V}{\theta_V} V_5 + e^{\alpha_2 \tau_2} \frac{\rho_V}{\theta_V} V_5 Z_5,
$$

$$
I_5 = e^{\alpha_4 \tau_4} \frac{\lambda_P}{\theta_P} P_5, \quad V_5 = \frac{\gamma_Z}{\eta_Z},
$$

we obtain

$$
\begin{aligned}
\frac{d\Lambda_5}{dt} &= \left(1 - \frac{X_5}{X}\right)(\varrho X_5 - \varrho X) + 3\xi_V X_5 V_5 + 3\xi_P X_5 P_5 - \xi_V X_5 V_5 \frac{X_5}{X} - \xi_P X_5 P_5 \frac{X_5}{X} \\
&- \xi_V X_5 V_5 \frac{X(t - \tau_1) V(t - \tau_1) Y_5}{X_5 V_5 Y} - \xi_P X_5 P_5 \frac{X(t - \tau_3) P(t - \tau_3) I_5}{X_5 P_5 I} \\
&- \xi_V X_5 V_5 \frac{Y(t - \tau_2) V_5}{Y_5 V} - \xi_P X_5 P_5 \frac{I(t - \tau_4) P_5}{I_5 P} + \xi_V X_5 V_5 \ln\left(\frac{X(t - \tau_1) V(t - \tau_1)}{XV}\right) \\
&+ \xi_P X_5 P_5 \ln\left(\frac{X(t - \tau_3) P(t - \tau_3)}{XP}\right) + \xi_V X_5 V_5 \ln\left(\frac{Y(t - \tau_2)}{Y}\right) \\
&+ \xi_P X_5 P_5 \ln\left(\frac{I(t - \tau_4)}{I}\right) + e^{\alpha_3 \tau_3 + \alpha_4 \tau_4} \frac{\beta_I \rho_P (\xi_P \gamma_M \eta_Z + \xi_V \gamma_Z \eta_M + \varrho \eta_Z \eta_M)}{\xi_P \theta_P \eta_M \eta_Z} (\Re_8 - 1) M. \quad (27)
\end{aligned}
$$

Then, simplifying Equation (27), we get:

$$\begin{aligned}
\frac{d\Lambda_5}{dt} &= -\varrho\frac{(X-X_5)^2}{X} + 3\xi_V X_5 V_5 + 3\xi_P X_5 P_5 - \xi_V X_5 V_5 \frac{X_5}{X} - \xi_V X_5 V_5 \frac{Y(t-\tau_2)V_5}{Y_5 V} \\
&\quad - \xi_V X_5 V_5 \frac{X(t-\tau_1)V(t-\tau_1)Y_5}{X_5 V_5 Y} - \xi_P X_5 P_5 \frac{X(t-\tau_3)P(t-\tau_3)I_5}{X_5 P_5 I} - \xi_P X_5 P_5 \frac{I(t-\tau_4)P_5}{I_5 P} \\
&\quad + \xi_V X_5 V_5\left[\ln\left(\frac{X_5}{X}\right) + \ln\left(\frac{Y(t-\tau_2)V_5}{Y_5 V}\right) + \ln\left(\frac{X(t-\tau_1)V(t-\tau_1)Y_5}{X_5 V_5 Y}\right)\right] \\
&\quad - \xi_P X_5 P_5 \frac{X_5}{X} + \xi_P X_5 P_5 \left[\ln\left(\frac{X_5}{X}\right) + \ln\left(\frac{X(t-\tau_3)P(t-\tau_3)I_5}{X_5 P_5 I}\right) + \ln\left(\frac{I(t-\tau_4)P_5}{I_5 P}\right)\right] \\
&\quad + e^{\alpha_3\tau_3+\alpha_4\tau_4}\frac{\beta_I \rho_P (\xi_P \gamma_M \eta_Z + \xi_V \gamma_Z \eta_M + \varrho \eta_Z \eta_M)}{\xi_P \theta_P \eta_M \eta_Z}(\Re_8 - 1)M \\
&= -\varrho\frac{(X-X_5)^2}{X} \\
&\quad - \xi_V X_5 V_5\left[F\left(\frac{X_5}{X}\right) + F\left(\frac{X(t-\tau_1)V(t-\tau_1)Y_5}{X_5 V_5 Y}\right) + F\left(\frac{Y(t-\tau_2)V_5}{Y_5 V}\right)\right] \\
&\quad - \xi_P X_5 P_5\left[F\left(\frac{X_5}{X}\right) + F\left(\frac{X(t-\tau_3)P(t-\tau_3)I_5}{X_5 P_5 I}\right) + F\left(\frac{I(t-\tau_4)P_5}{I_5 P}\right)\right] \\
&\quad + e^{\alpha_3\tau_3+\alpha_4\tau_4}\frac{\beta_I \rho_P (\xi_P \gamma_M \eta_Z + \xi_V \gamma_Z \eta_M + \varrho \eta_Z \eta_M)}{\xi_P \theta_P \eta_M \eta_Z}(\Re_8 - 1)M.
\end{aligned}$$

If $\Re_8 \leq 1$, then $\frac{d\Lambda_5}{dt} \leq 0$ for all $X, Y, I, V, P, M > 0$. Moreover, we have $\frac{d\Lambda_5}{dt} = 0$ when $X = X_5, Y = Y_5, V = V_5, I = I_5, P = P_5$, and $M = 0$. One can show that $\bar{\Theta}_5 = \{\Delta_5\}$, and then Δ_5 is GAS. □

Theorem 7. *Let $\Re_6 > 1$, $\Re_7 \leq 1$ and $\Re_2/\Re_1 > 1$; then, Δ_6 is GAS.*

Proof. Consider

$$\begin{aligned}
\Lambda_6 &= X_6 F\left(\frac{X}{X_6}\right) + e^{\alpha_1\tau_1}Y_6 F\left(\frac{Y}{Y_6}\right) + e^{\alpha_3\tau_3}I_6 F\left(\frac{I}{I_6}\right) + \frac{\beta_Y}{\theta_V}e^{\alpha_1\tau_1+\alpha_2\tau_2}V_6 F\left(\frac{V}{V_6}\right) \\
&\quad + \frac{\beta_I}{\theta_P}e^{\alpha_3\tau_3+\alpha_4\tau_4}P_6 F\left(\frac{P}{P_6}\right) + \frac{\rho v \beta_Y}{\eta_Z \theta_V}e^{\alpha_1\tau_1+\alpha_2\tau_2}Z + \frac{\rho_P \beta_I}{\eta_M \theta_P}e^{\alpha_3\tau_3+\alpha_4\tau_4}M_6 F\left(\frac{M}{M_6}\right) \\
&\quad + \xi_V X_6 V_6 \int_{t-\tau_1}^{t} F\left(\frac{X(u)V(u)}{X_6 V_6}\right)du + \xi_P X_6 P_6 \int_{t-\tau_3}^{t} F\left(\frac{X(u)P(u)}{X_6 P_6}\right)du \\
&\quad + e^{\alpha_1\tau_1}\beta_Y Y_6 \int_{t-\tau_2}^{t} F\left(\frac{Y(u)}{Y_6}\right)du + e^{\alpha_3\tau_3}\beta_I I_6 \int_{t-\tau_4}^{t} F\left(\frac{I(u)}{I_6}\right)du.
\end{aligned}$$

We calculate $\frac{d\Lambda_6}{dt}$ as:

$$\begin{aligned}
\frac{d\Lambda_6}{dt} &= \left(1 - \frac{X_6}{X}\right)\frac{dX}{dt} + e^{\alpha_1\tau_1}\left(1 - \frac{Y_6}{Y}\right)\frac{dY}{dt} + e^{\alpha_3\tau_3}\left(1 - \frac{I_6}{I}\right)\frac{dI}{dt} \\
&\quad + \frac{\beta_Y}{\theta_V}e^{\alpha_1\tau_1+\alpha_2\tau_2}\left(1 - \frac{V_6}{V}\right)\frac{dV}{dt} + \frac{\beta_I}{\theta_P}e^{\alpha_3\tau_3+\alpha_4\tau_4}\left(1 - \frac{P_6}{P}\right)\frac{dP}{dt} \\
&\quad + \frac{\rho v \beta_Y}{\eta_Z \theta_V}e^{\alpha_1\tau_1+\alpha_2\tau_2}\frac{dZ}{dt} + \frac{\rho_P \beta_I}{\eta_M \theta_P}e^{\alpha_3\tau_3+\alpha_4\tau_4}\left(1 - \frac{M_6}{M}\right)\frac{dM}{dt} \\
&\quad + \xi_V X_6 V_6\left[\frac{XV}{X_6 V_6} - \frac{X(t-\tau_1)V(t-\tau_1)}{X_6 V_6} + \ln\left(\frac{X(t-\tau_1)V(t-\tau_1)}{XV}\right)\right]
\end{aligned}$$

$$+ \xi_P X_6 P_6 \left[\frac{XP}{X_6 P_6} - \frac{X(t-\tau_3)P(t-\tau_3)}{X_6 P_6} + \ln\left(\frac{X(t-\tau_3)P(t-\tau_3)}{XP}\right) \right]$$
$$+ e^{\alpha_1 \tau_1} \beta_Y Y_6 \left[\frac{Y}{Y_6} - \frac{Y(t-\tau_2)}{Y_6} + \ln\left(\frac{Y(t-\tau_2)}{Y}\right) \right]$$
$$+ e^{\alpha_3 \tau_3} \beta_I I_6 \left[\frac{I}{I_6} - \frac{I(t-\tau_4)}{I_6} + \ln\left(\frac{I(t-\tau_4)}{I}\right) \right].$$

It follows from Equation (1)–(7) that

$$\frac{d\Lambda_6}{dt} = \left(1 - \frac{X_6}{X}\right)[\delta - \varrho X - \xi_V XV - \xi_P XP]$$
$$+ e^{\alpha_1 \tau_1}\left(1 - \frac{Y_6}{Y}\right)[e^{-\alpha_1 \tau_1}\xi_V X(t-\tau_1)V(t-\tau_1) - \beta_Y Y]$$
$$+ e^{\alpha_3 \tau_3}\left(1 - \frac{I_6}{I}\right)[e^{-\alpha_3 \tau_3}\xi_P X(t-\tau_3)P(t-\tau_3) - \beta_I I]$$
$$+ \frac{\beta_Y}{\theta_V} e^{\alpha_1 \tau_1 + \alpha_2 \tau_2}\left(1 - \frac{V_6}{V}\right)[e^{-\alpha_2 \tau_2}\theta_V Y(t-\tau_2) - \lambda_V V - \rho_V VZ]$$
$$+ \frac{\beta_I}{\theta_P} e^{\alpha_3 \tau_3 + \alpha_4 \tau_4}\left(1 - \frac{P_6}{P}\right)[e^{-\alpha_4 \tau_4}\theta_P I(t-\tau_4) - \lambda_P P - \rho_P PM]$$
$$+ \frac{\rho_V \beta_Y}{\eta_Z \theta_V} e^{\alpha_1 \tau_1 + \alpha_2 \tau_2}[\eta_Z VZ - \gamma_Z Z] + \frac{\rho_P \beta_I}{\eta_M \theta_P} e^{\alpha_3 \tau_3 + \alpha_4 \tau_4}\left(1 - \frac{M_6}{M}\right)[\eta_M PM - \gamma_M M]$$
$$+ \xi_V X_6 V_6 \left[\frac{XV}{X_6 V_6} - \frac{X(t-\tau_1)V(t-\tau_1)}{X_6 V_6} + \ln\left(\frac{X(t-\tau_1)V(t-\tau_1)}{XV}\right)\right]$$
$$+ \xi_P X_6 P_6 \left[\frac{XP}{X_6 P_6} - \frac{X(t-\tau_3)P(t-\tau_3)}{X_6 P_6} + \ln\left(\frac{X(t-\tau_3)P(t-\tau_3)}{XP}\right)\right]$$
$$+ e^{\alpha_1 \tau_1} \beta_Y Y_6 \left[\frac{Y}{Y_6} - \frac{Y(t-\tau_2)}{Y_6} + \ln\left(\frac{Y(t-\tau_2)}{Y}\right)\right]$$
$$+ e^{\alpha_3 \tau_3} \beta_I I_6 \left[\frac{I}{I_6} - \frac{I(t-\tau_4)}{I_6} + \ln\left(\frac{I(t-\tau_4)}{I}\right)\right]. \tag{28}$$

We collect the terms of Equation (28) as follows:

$$\frac{d\Lambda_6}{dt} = \left(1 - \frac{X_6}{X}\right)(\delta - \varrho X) + \xi_V X_6 V + \xi_P X_6 P - \xi_V X(t-\tau_1)V(t-\tau_1)\frac{Y_6}{Y}$$
$$+ e^{\alpha_1 \tau_1}\beta_Y Y_6 - \xi_P X(t-\tau_3)P(t-\tau_3)\frac{I_6}{I} + e^{\alpha_3 \tau_3}\beta_I I_6 - e^{\alpha_1 \tau_1 + \alpha_2 \tau_2}\frac{\beta_Y \lambda_V}{\theta_V}V$$
$$- e^{\alpha_1 \tau_1}\beta_Y Y(t-\tau_2)\frac{V_6}{V} + e^{\alpha_1 \tau_1 + \alpha_2 \tau_2}\frac{\beta_Y \lambda_V}{\theta_V}V_6 - e^{\alpha_3 \tau_3 + \alpha_4 \tau_4}\frac{\beta_I \lambda_P}{\theta_P}P$$
$$- e^{\alpha_3 \tau_3}\beta_I I(t-\tau_4)\frac{P_6}{P} + e^{\alpha_3 \tau_3 + \alpha_4 \tau_4}\frac{\beta_I \lambda_P}{\theta_P}P_6 + e^{\alpha_3 \tau_3 + \alpha_4 \tau_4}\frac{\beta_I \rho_P}{\theta_P}P_6 M$$
$$- e^{\alpha_3 \tau_3 + \alpha_4 \tau_4}\frac{\beta_I \rho_P \gamma_M}{\theta_P \eta_M}M - e^{\alpha_3 \tau_3 + \alpha_4 \tau_4}\frac{\beta_I \rho_P}{\theta_P}M_6 P + e^{\alpha_3 \tau_3 + \alpha_4 \tau_4}\frac{\beta_I \rho_P \gamma_M}{\theta_P \eta_M}M_6$$
$$+ e^{\alpha_1 \tau_1 + \alpha_2 \tau_2}\frac{\beta_Y \rho_V \gamma_Z}{\theta_V \eta_Z}\left[\frac{\eta_Z}{\gamma_Z}V_6 - 1\right]Z + \xi_V X_6 V_6 \ln\left(\frac{X(t-\tau_1)V(t-\tau_1)}{XV}\right)$$
$$+ \xi_P X_6 P_6 \ln\left(\frac{X(t-\tau_3)P(t-\tau_3)}{XP}\right) + e^{\alpha_1 \tau_1}\beta_Y Y_6 \ln\left(\frac{Y(t-\tau_2)}{Y}\right)$$
$$+ e^{\alpha_3 \tau_3}\beta_I I_6 \ln\left(\frac{I(t-\tau_4)}{I}\right).$$

Using the equilibrium conditions for Δ_6,

$$\delta = \varrho X_6 + \xi_V X_6 V_6 + \xi_P X_6 P_6, \quad \xi_V X_6 V_6 = e^{\alpha_1 \tau_1} \beta_Y Y_6, \quad \xi_P X_6 P_6 = e^{\alpha_3 \tau_3} \beta_I I_6,$$

$$Y_6 = e^{\alpha_2 \tau_2} \frac{\lambda_V}{\theta_V} V_6, \quad I_6 = e^{\alpha_4 \tau_4} \frac{\lambda_P}{\theta_P} P_6 + e^{\alpha_4 \tau_4} \frac{\rho_P}{\theta_P} P_6 M_6, \quad P_6 = \frac{\gamma_M}{\eta_M},$$

we obtain

$$\begin{aligned}\frac{d\Lambda_6}{dt} &= \left(1 - \frac{X_6}{X}\right)(\varrho X_6 - \varrho X) + 3\xi_V X_6 V_6 + 3\xi_P X_6 P_6 - \xi_V X_6 V_6 \frac{X_6}{X} \\
&- \xi_P X_6 P_6 \frac{X_6}{X} - \xi_V X_6 V_6 \frac{X(t-\tau_1)V(t-\tau_1)Y_6}{X_6 V_6 Y} \\
&- \xi_P X_6 P_6 \frac{X(t-\tau_3)P(t-\tau_3)I_6}{X_6 P_6 I} - \xi_V X_6 V_6 \frac{Y(t-\tau_2)V_6}{Y_6 V} \\
&- \xi_P X_6 P_6 \frac{I(t-\tau_4)P_6}{I_6 P} + \xi_V X_6 V_6 \ln\left(\frac{X(t-\tau_1)V(t-\tau_1)}{XV}\right) \\
&+ \xi_P X_6 P_6 \ln\left(\frac{X(t-\tau_3)P(t-\tau_3)}{XP}\right) + \xi_V X_6 V_6 \ln\left(\frac{Y(t-\tau_2)}{Y}\right) \\
&+ \xi_P X_6 P_6 \ln\left(\frac{I(t-\tau_4)}{I}\right) + e^{\alpha_1 \tau_1 + \alpha_2 \tau_2} \frac{\beta_Y \rho_V (\xi_P \gamma_M \eta_Z + \xi_V \gamma_Z \eta_M + \varrho \eta_Z \eta_M)}{\xi_V \theta_V \eta_M \eta_Z}(\Re_7 - 1)Z.\end{aligned} \quad (29)$$

Then, simplifying Equation (29), we get:

$$\begin{aligned}\frac{d\Lambda_6}{dt} &= -\varrho \frac{(X-X_6)^2}{X} \\
&- \xi_V X_6 V_6 \left[F\left(\frac{X_6}{X}\right) + F\left(\frac{X(t-\tau_1)V(t-\tau_1)Y_6}{X_6 V_6 Y}\right) + F\left(\frac{Y(t-\tau_2)V_6}{Y_6 V}\right)\right] \\
&- \xi_P X_6 P_6 \left[F\left(\frac{X_6}{X}\right) + F\left(\frac{X(t-\tau_3)P(t-\tau_3)I_6}{X_6 P_6 I}\right) + F\left(\frac{I(t-\tau_4)P_6}{I_6 P}\right)\right] \\
&+ e^{\alpha_1 \tau_1 + \alpha_2 \tau_2} \frac{\beta_Y \rho_V (\xi_P \gamma_M \eta_Z + \xi_V \gamma_Z \eta_M + \varrho \eta_Z \eta_M)}{\xi_V \theta_V \eta_M \eta_Z}(\Re_7 - 1)Z.\end{aligned}$$

If $\Re_7 \leq 1$, then $\frac{d\Lambda_6}{dt} \leq 0$ for all $X, Y, I, V, P, Z > 0$. In addition, $\frac{d\Lambda_6}{dt} = 0$ occurs at $X = X_6$, $Y = Y_6, I = I_6, V = V_6, P = P_6$, and $Z = 0$. The proof can be completed similarly to the previous theorems. □

Theorem 8. *If $\Re_7 > 1$ and $\Re_8 > 1$, then Δ_7 is GAS.*

Proof. We define a function Λ_7 as:

$$\begin{aligned}\Lambda_7 &= X_7 F\left(\frac{X}{X_7}\right) + e^{\alpha_1 \tau_1} Y_7 F\left(\frac{Y}{Y_7}\right) + e^{\alpha_3 \tau_3} I_7 F\left(\frac{I}{I_7}\right) + \frac{\beta_Y}{\theta_V} e^{\alpha_1 \tau_1 + \alpha_2 \tau_2} V_7 F\left(\frac{V}{V_7}\right) \\
&+ \frac{\beta_I}{\theta_P} e^{\alpha_3 \tau_3 + \alpha_4 \tau_4} P_7 F\left(\frac{P}{P_7}\right) + \frac{\rho_V \beta_Y}{\eta_Z \theta_V} e^{\alpha_1 \tau_1 + \alpha_2 \tau_2} Z_7 F\left(\frac{Z}{Z_7}\right) + \frac{\rho_P \beta_I}{\eta_M \theta_P} e^{\alpha_3 \tau_3 + \alpha_4 \tau_4} M_7 F\left(\frac{M}{M_7}\right) \\
&+ \xi_V X_7 V_7 \int_{t-\tau_1}^{t} F\left(\frac{X(u)V(u)}{X_7 V_7}\right) du + \xi_P X_7 P_7 \int_{t-\tau_3}^{t} F\left(\frac{X(u)P(u)}{X_7 P_7}\right) du \\
&+ e^{\alpha_1 \tau_1} \beta_Y Y_7 \int_{t-\tau_2}^{t} F\left(\frac{Y(u)}{Y_7}\right) du + e^{\alpha_3 \tau_3} \beta_I I_7 \int_{t-\tau_4}^{t} F\left(\frac{I(u)}{I_7}\right) du.\end{aligned}$$

We calculate $\frac{d\Lambda_7}{dt}$ as:

$$\frac{d\Lambda_7}{dt} = \left(1 - \frac{X_7}{X}\right)\frac{dX}{dt} + e^{\alpha_1\tau_1}\left(1 - \frac{Y_7}{Y}\right)\frac{dY}{dt} + e^{\alpha_3\tau_3}\left(1 - \frac{I_7}{I}\right)\frac{dI}{dt}$$
$$+ \frac{\beta_Y}{\theta_V}e^{\alpha_1\tau_1+\alpha_2\tau_2}\left(1 - \frac{V_7}{V}\right)\frac{dV}{dt} + \frac{\beta_I}{\theta_P}e^{\alpha_3\tau_3+\alpha_4\tau_4}\left(1 - \frac{P_7}{P}\right)\frac{dP}{dt}$$
$$+ \frac{\rho_V\beta_Y}{\eta_Z\theta_V}e^{\alpha_1\tau_1+\alpha_2\tau_2}\left(1 - \frac{Z_7}{Z}\right)\frac{dZ}{dt} + \frac{\rho_P\beta_I}{\eta_M\theta_P}e^{\alpha_3\tau_3+\alpha_4\tau_4}\left(1 - \frac{M_7}{M}\right)\frac{dM}{dt}$$
$$+ \xi_V X_7 V_7 \left[\frac{XV}{X_7 V_7} - \frac{X(t-\tau_1)V(t-\tau_1)}{X_7 V_7} + \ln\left(\frac{X(t-\tau_1)V(t-\tau_1)}{XV}\right)\right]$$
$$+ \xi_P X_7 P_7 \left[\frac{XP}{X_7 P_7} - \frac{X(t-\tau_3)P(t-\tau_3)}{X_7 P_7} + \ln\left(\frac{X(t-\tau_3)P(t-\tau_3)}{XP}\right)\right]$$
$$+ e^{\alpha_1\tau_1}\beta_Y Y_7 \left[\frac{Y}{Y_7} - \frac{Y(t-\tau_2)}{Y_7} + \ln\left(\frac{Y(t-\tau_2)}{Y}\right)\right]$$
$$+ e^{\alpha_3\tau_3}\beta_I I_7 \left[\frac{I}{I_7} - \frac{I(t-\tau_4)}{I_7} + \ln\left(\frac{I(t-\tau_4)}{I}\right)\right].$$

It follows from Equations (1)–(7) that

$$\frac{d\Lambda_7}{dt} = \left(1 - \frac{X_7}{X}\right)[\delta - \varrho X - \xi_V XV - \xi_P XP]$$
$$+ e^{\alpha_1\tau_1}\left(1 - \frac{Y_7}{Y}\right)\left[e^{-\alpha_1\tau_1}\xi_V X(t-\tau_1)V(t-\tau_1) - \beta_Y Y\right]$$
$$+ e^{\alpha_3\tau_3}\left(1 - \frac{I_7}{I}\right)\left[e^{-\alpha_3\tau_3}\xi_P X(t-\tau_3)P(t-\tau_3) - \beta_I I\right]$$
$$+ \frac{\beta_Y}{\theta_V}e^{\alpha_1\tau_1+\alpha_2\tau_2}\left(1 - \frac{V_7}{V}\right)\left[e^{-\alpha_2\tau_2}\theta_V Y(t-\tau_2) - \lambda_V V - \rho_V VZ\right]$$
$$+ \frac{\beta_I}{\theta_P}e^{\alpha_3\tau_3+\alpha_4\tau_4}\left(1 - \frac{P_7}{P}\right)\left[e^{-\alpha_4\tau_4}\theta_P I(t-\tau_4) - \lambda_P P - \rho_P PM\right]$$
$$+ \frac{\rho_V\beta_Y}{\eta_Z\theta_V}e^{\alpha_1\tau_1+\alpha_2\tau_2}\left(1 - \frac{Z_7}{Z}\right)[\eta_Z VZ - \gamma_Z Z]$$
$$+ \frac{\rho_P\beta_I}{\eta_M\theta_P}e^{\alpha_3\tau_3+\alpha_4\tau_4}\left(1 - \frac{M_7}{M}\right)[\eta_M PM - \gamma_M M]$$
$$+ \xi_V X_7 V_7 \left[\frac{XV}{X_7 V_7} - \frac{X(t-\tau_1)V(t-\tau_1)}{X_7 V_7} + \ln\left(\frac{X(t-\tau_1)V(t-\tau_1)}{XV}\right)\right]$$
$$+ \xi_P X_7 P_7 \left[\frac{XP}{X_7 P_7} - \frac{X(t-\tau_3)P(t-\tau_3)}{X_7 P_7} + \ln\left(\frac{X(t-\tau_3)P(t-\tau_3)}{XP}\right)\right]$$
$$+ e^{\alpha_1\tau_1}\beta_Y Y_7 \left[\frac{Y}{Y_7} - \frac{Y(t-\tau_2)}{Y_7} + \ln\left(\frac{Y(t-\tau_2)}{Y}\right)\right]$$
$$+ e^{\alpha_3\tau_3}\beta_I I_7 \left[\frac{I}{I_7} - \frac{I(t-\tau_4)}{I_7} + \ln\left(\frac{I(t-\tau_4)}{I}\right)\right]. \tag{30}$$

We collect the terms of Equation (30) as follows:

$$\frac{d\Lambda_7}{dt} = \left(1 - \frac{X_7}{X}\right)(\delta - \varrho X) + \xi_V X_7 V + \xi_P X_7 P - \xi_V X(t-\tau_1)V(t-\tau_1)\frac{Y_7}{Y}$$
$$+ e^{\alpha_1\tau_1}\beta_Y Y_7 - \xi_P X(t-\tau_3)P(t-\tau_3)\frac{I_7}{I} + e^{\alpha_3\tau_3}\beta_I I_7 - e^{\alpha_1\tau_1+\alpha_2\tau_2}\frac{\beta_Y\lambda_V}{\theta_V}V$$
$$- e^{\alpha_1\tau_1}\beta_Y Y(t-\tau_2)\frac{V_7}{V} + e^{\alpha_1\tau_1+\alpha_2\tau_2}\frac{\beta_Y\lambda_V}{\theta_V}V_7 + e^{\alpha_1\tau_1+\alpha_2\tau_2}\frac{\beta_Y\rho_V}{\theta_V}ZV_7$$
$$- e^{\alpha_3\tau_3+\alpha_4\tau_4}\frac{\beta_I\lambda_P}{\theta_P}P - e^{\alpha_3\tau_3}\beta_I I(t-\tau_4)\frac{P_7}{P} + e^{\alpha_3\tau_3+\alpha_4\tau_4}\frac{\beta_I\lambda_P}{\theta_P}P_7$$

$$
\begin{aligned}
&+ e^{\alpha_3\tau_3+\alpha_4\tau_4}\frac{\beta_I\rho_P}{\theta_P}P_7M - e^{\alpha_1\tau_1+\alpha_2\tau_2}\frac{\beta_Y\rho_V\gamma Z}{\theta_V\eta_Z}Z - e^{\alpha_1\tau_1+\alpha_2\tau_2}\frac{\beta_Y\rho_V}{\theta_V}VZ_7\\
&+ e^{\alpha_1\tau_1+\alpha_2\tau_2}\frac{\beta_Y\rho_V\gamma Z}{\theta_V\eta_Z}Z_7 - e^{\alpha_3\tau_3+\alpha_4\tau_4}\frac{\beta_I\rho_P\gamma M}{\theta_P\eta_M}M - e^{\alpha_3\tau_3+\alpha_4\tau_4}\frac{\beta_I\rho_P}{\theta_P}M_7P\\
&+ e^{\alpha_3\tau_3+\alpha_4\tau_4}\frac{\beta_I\rho_P\gamma M}{\theta_P\eta_M}M_7 + \xi_V X_7 V_7 \ln\left(\frac{X(t-\tau_1)V(t-\tau_1)}{XV}\right)\\
&+ \xi_P X_7 P_7 \ln\left(\frac{X(t-\tau_3)P(t-\tau_3)}{XP}\right) + e^{\alpha_1\tau_1}\beta_Y Y_7 \ln\left(\frac{Y(t-\tau_2)}{Y}\right)\\
&+ e^{\alpha_3\tau_3}\beta_I I_7 \ln\left(\frac{I(t-\tau_4)}{I}\right).
\end{aligned}
$$

Using the equilibrium conditions for Δ_7,

$$
\begin{aligned}
&\delta = \varrho X_7 + \xi_V X_7 V_7 + \xi_P X_7 P_7,\\
&\xi_V X_7 V_7 = e^{\alpha_1\tau_1}\beta_Y Y_7, \quad \xi_P X_7 P_7 = e^{\alpha_3\tau_3}\beta_I I_7,\\
&Y_7 = e^{\alpha_2\tau_2}\frac{\lambda_V}{\theta_V}V_7 + e^{\alpha_2\tau_2}\frac{\rho_V}{\theta_V}V_7 Z_7, \quad I_7 = e^{\alpha_4\tau_4}\frac{\lambda_P}{\theta_P}P_7 + e^{\alpha_4\tau_4}\frac{\rho_P}{\theta_P}P_7 M_7,\\
&V_7 = \frac{\gamma Z}{\eta_Z}, \quad P_7 = \frac{\gamma M}{\eta_M},
\end{aligned}
$$

we obtain

$$
\begin{aligned}
\frac{d\Lambda_7}{dt} &= \left(1 - \frac{X_7}{X}\right)(\varrho X_7 - \varrho X) + 3\xi_V X_7 V_7 + 3\xi_P X_7 P_7 - \xi_V X_7 V_7 \frac{X_7}{X} - \xi_P X_7 P_7 \frac{X_7}{X}\\
&- \xi_V X_7 V_7 \frac{X(t-\tau_1)V(t-\tau_1)Y_7}{X_7 V_7 Y} - \xi_P X_7 P_7 \frac{X(t-\tau_3)P(t-\tau_3)I_7}{X_7 P_7 I}\\
&- \xi_V X_7 V_7 \frac{Y(t-\tau_2)V_7}{Y_7 V} - \xi_P X_7 P_7 \frac{I(t-\tau_4)P_7}{I_7 P} + \xi_V X_7 V_7 \ln\left(\frac{X(t-\tau_1)V(t-\tau_1)}{XV}\right)\\
&+ \xi_P X_7 P_7 \ln\left(\frac{X(t-\tau_3)P(t-\tau_3)}{XP}\right) + \xi_V X_7 V_7 \ln\left(\frac{Y(t-\tau_2)}{Y}\right)\\
&+ \xi_P X_7 P_7 \ln\left(\frac{I(t-\tau_4)}{I}\right).
\end{aligned}
\tag{31}
$$

Then, simplifying Equation (31), we get:

$$
\begin{aligned}
\frac{d\Lambda_7}{dt} &= -\varrho\frac{(X-X_7)^2}{X}\\
&- \xi_V X_7 V_7\left[F\left(\frac{X_7}{X}\right) + F\left(\frac{X(t-\tau_1)V(t-\tau_1)Y_7}{X_7 V_7 Y}\right) + F\left(\frac{Y(t-\tau_2)V_7}{Y_7 V}\right)\right]\\
&- \xi_P X_7 P_7\left[F\left(\frac{X_7}{X}\right) + F\left(\frac{X(t-\tau_3)P(t-\tau_3)I_7}{X_7 P_7 I}\right) + F\left(\frac{I(t-\tau_4)P_7}{I_7 P}\right)\right].
\end{aligned}
$$

Clearly, $\frac{d\Lambda_7}{dt} \leq 0$ for all $X, Y, I, V, P > 0$, where $\frac{d\Lambda_7}{dt} = 0$ when $X = X_7$, $Y = Y_7$, $V = V_7$, $I = I_7$, and $P = P_7$. One can show that $\bar{\Theta}_7 = \{\Delta_7\}$, and by using the L-LAST, we find that Δ_7 is GAS. □

The existence and global stability conditions of the equilibria are summarized in Table 1.

Table 1. Existence and stability conditions of the equilibria.

Equilibrium Point	Existence Conditions	Global Stability Conditions
$\Delta_0 = (X_0, 0, 0, 0, 0, 0, 0)$	None	$\Re_1 \leq 1$ and $\Re_2 \leq 1$
$\Delta_1 = (X_1, Y_1, 0, V_1, 0, 0, 0)$	$\Re_1 > 1$	$\Re_1 > 1, \Re_2/\Re_1 \leq 1$ and $\Re_3 \leq 1$
$\Delta_2 = (X_2, 0, I_2, 0, P_2, 0, 0)$	$\Re_2 > 1$	$\Re_2 > 1, \Re_1/\Re_2 \leq 1$ and $\Re_4 \leq 1$
$\Delta_3 = (X_3, Y_3, 0, V_3, 0, Z_3, 0)$	$\Re_3 > 1$	$\Re_3 > 1$ and $\Re_5 \leq 1$
$\Delta_4 = (X_4, 0, I_4, 0, P_4, 0, M_4)$	$\Re_4 > 1$	$\Re_4 > 1$ and $\Re_6 \leq 1$
$\Delta_5 = (X_5, Y_5, I_5, V_5, P_5, Z_5, 0)$	$\Re_5 > 1$ and $\Re_1/\Re_2 > 1$	$\Re_5 > 1, \Re_8 \leq 1$ and $\Re_1/\Re_2 > 1$
$\Delta_6 = (X_6, Y_6, I_6, V_6, P_6, 0, M_6)$	$\Re_6 > 1$ and $\Re_2/\Re_1 > 1$	$\Re_6 > 1, \Re_7 \leq 1$ and $\Re_2/\Re_1 > 1$
$\Delta_7 = (X_7, Y_7, I_7, V_7, P_7, Z_7, M_7)$	$\Re_7 > 1$ and $\Re_8 > 1$	$\Re_7 > 1$ and $\Re_8 > 1$

6. Numerical Simulations

We illustrate the global stability of the model's equilibria via numerical simulations. We use the values of the parameters presented in Table 2. In addition, we discuss the effects of antiviral treatments and time delays on the co-infection dynamics.

Table 2. Model parameters.

Parameter	Description	Value
δ	Production rate of susceptible ECs	0.5
ϱ	Death rate constant of susceptible ECs	0.05
β_Y	Death rate constant of SARS-CoV-2-infected ECs	0.11
β_I	Death rate constant of IAV-infected ECs	0.2
θ_V	Virus–cell incidence rate constant between SARS-CoV-2 particles and susceptible ECs	0.2
λ_V	Death rate constant of SARS-CoV-2 particles	0.2
ρ_V	Neutralization rate constant of SARS-CoV-2 by SARS-CoV-2-specific antibodies	0.05
θ_P	Virus–cell incidence rate constant between IAV particles and susceptible ECs	0.4
λ_P	Death rate constant of IAV particles	0.1
ρ_P	Neutralization rate constant of IAV by IAV-specific antibodies	0.04
γ_Z	Death rate constant of SARS-CoV-2-specific antibodies	0.05
γ_M	Death rate constant of IAV-specific antibodies	0.04
α_1	Constant	1
α_2	Constant	1
α_3	Constant	0.1
α_4	Constant	0.1

6.1. Stability of the Equilibria

Here, we fix the delay parameters as $\tau_1 = 0.1$, $\tau_2 = 0.1$, $\tau_3 = 0.2$, and $\tau_4 = 0.2$. In addition, we solve system (1)–(7) with the following initial states:

$$\text{IS(I)} : (X(u), Y(u), I(u), V(u), P(u), Z(u), M(u)) = (5, 1, 0.5, 0.03, 0.5, 1, 4),$$
$$\text{IS(II)} : (X(u), Y(u), I(u), V(u), P(u), Z(u), M(u)) = (4, 1.5, 0.7, 0.06, 0.8, 2, 6),$$
$$\text{IS(III)} : (X(u), Y(u), I(u), V(u), P(u), Z(u), M(u)) = (3, 2, 1, 0.3, 1.4, 3, 8),$$

where $u \in [-0.2, 0]$.

We use the values given in Table 2 and select eight sets of values of $(\tilde{\varsigma}_V, \tilde{\varsigma}_P, \eta_Z, \eta_M)$ for the following strategies.

First strategy (Stability of Δ_0): $(\xi_V, \xi_P, \eta_Z, \eta_M) = (0.001, 0.001, 0.01, 0.02)$. These values gives $\Re_1 = 0.0744 < 1$ and $\Re_2 = 0.1922 < 1$. It is shown in Figure 1 that the trajectories starting with initials IS(I)-IS(III) tend to the equilibrium, $\Delta_0 = (10, 0, 0, 0, 0, 0, 0)$. This supports the global stability results given in Theorem 1. In this strategy, both influenza and COVID-19 will be cleared. In fact, making $\Re_1 \leq 1$ and $\Re_2 \leq 1$ can be achieved in one or more of the following ways: (i) applying two antiviral drugs for blocking SARS-CoV-2 and IAV infections with drug efficacies of ϵ_V and ϵ_P, respectively, where $0 \leq \epsilon_V \leq 1$ and $0 \leq \epsilon_P \leq 1$; then, the parameters ξ_V and ξ_P will be reduced to $(1 - \epsilon_V)\xi_V$ and $(1 - \epsilon_P)\xi_P$, respectively; (ii) applying two antiviral drugs for blocking the replication of SARS-CoV-2 and IAV with drug efficacies of ε_V and ε_P, respectively, where $0 \leq \varepsilon_V \leq 1$ and $0 \leq \varepsilon_P \leq 1$. Then, the parameters θ_V and θ_P will be reduced to $(1 - \varepsilon_V)\theta_V$ and $(1 - \varepsilon_P)\theta_P$, respectively.

Second strategy (Stability of Δ_1): $(\xi_V, \xi_P, \eta_Z, \eta_M) = (0.05, 0.001, 0.002, 0.02)$. This selection provides $\Re_1 = 3.7215 > 1$, $\Re_3 = 0.1431 < 1$, and $\Re_2/\Re_1 = 0.0516 < 1$. The equilibrium Δ_1 exists with $\Delta_1 = (2.69, 3.008, 0, 2.72, 0, 0, 0)$. Figure 2 shows that the trajectories initiated with IS(I)-IS(III) converge to Δ_1, and this result agrees with Theorem 2. This strategy suggests that a COVID-19 mono-infection with an inactive antibody response will be established.

Third strategy (Stability of Δ_2): $(\xi_V, \xi_P, \eta_Z, \eta_M) = (0.005, 0.03, 0.01, 0.001)$. This gives $\Re_2 = 5.7647 > 1$, $\Re_4 = 0.2306 < 1$, and $\Re_1/\Re_2 = 0.0646 < 1$. The numerical solution confirms that $\Delta_2 = (1.73, 0, 2.03, 0, 7.94, 0, 0)$ exists. It can be observed from Figure 3 that the solutions initiated with IS(I)-IS(III) converge to Δ_2, and this result agrees with Theorem 3. This strategy suggests that an influenza mono-infection with an inactive antibody response will be established.

Fourth strategy (Stability of Δ_3): $(\xi_V, \xi_P, \eta_Z, \eta_M) = (0.09, 0.002, 0.05, 0.05)$. This yields $\Re_3 = 2.3924 > 1$ and $\Re_5 = 0.1373 < 1$. Figure 4 illustrates that the solutions tend to $\Delta_3 = (3.57, 2.64, 0, 1, 0, 5.57, 0)$ regardless of the initial states. This result supports the global stability result given in Theorem 4. This strategy shows that a COVID-19 mono-infection with an activated SARS-CoV-2-specific antibody response will be attained.

Fifth strategy (Stability of Δ_4): $(\xi_V, \xi_P, \eta_Z, \eta_M) = (0.01, 0.1, 0.01, 0.02)$. The values of $\Re_4$ and $\Re_6$ are computed as $\Re_4 = 3.8432 > 1$ and $\Re_6 = 0.1489 < 1$. Thus, Δ_4 exists with $\Delta_4 = (2, 0, 1.96, 0, 2, 0, 7.11)$. The numerical solutions with initials IS(I)-IS(III) tend to Δ_4 (see Figure 5). This shows the global stability of Δ_4 given in Theorem 5. In this strategy, an influenza mono-infection with a stimulated IAV-specific antibody response will be achieved.

Sixth strategy (Stability of Δ_5): $(\xi_V, \xi_P, \eta_Z, \eta_M) = (0.09, 0.01, 0.9, 0.001)$. Then, we calculate $\Re_5 = 1.7469 > 1$, $\Re_8 = 0.2112 < 1$, and $\Re_1/\Re_2 = 3.486 > 1$. The numerical results displayed in Figure 6 establish that $\Delta_5 = (5.2, 0.21, 1.05, 0.06, 4.11, 9.94, 0)$ exists and that it is GAS; this agrees with the result of Theorem 6. This result suggests that a co-infection with influenza and COVID-19 with only an active SARS-CoV-2-specific antibody response will be attained.

Seventh strategy (Stability of Δ_6): $(\xi_V, \xi_P, \eta_Z, \eta_M) = (0.04, 0.05, 0.01, 0.05)$. We compute $\Re_6 = 1.654 > 1$, $\Re_7 = 0.5133 < 1$, and $\Re_2/\Re_1 = 3.2272 > 1$. We find that the equilibrium $\Delta_6 = (3.36, 1.63, 0.66, 1.47, 0.8, 0, 5.57)$ exists. Figure 7 draws the numerical solutions of the DDEs with initials IS(I)-IS(III). It is shown that Δ_6 is GAS, and this supports the result of Theorem 7. This strategy leads to a co-infection with influenza and COVID-19 with only an active IAV-specific antibody response.

Eighth strategy 8 (Stability of Δ_7): $(\xi_V, \xi_P, \eta_Z, \eta_M) = (0.09, 0.09, 0.5, 0.5)$. This selection gives $\Re_7 = 5.0594 > 1$ and $\Re_8 = 13.0621 > 1$. Figure 8 shows that $\Delta_7 = (7.55, 0.56, 0.27, 0.1, 0.08, 16.24, 30.16)$ exists and that it is GAS according to Theorem 8. This strategy leads to the case of co-infection with influenza and COVID-19 in which both types of antibody responses are active.

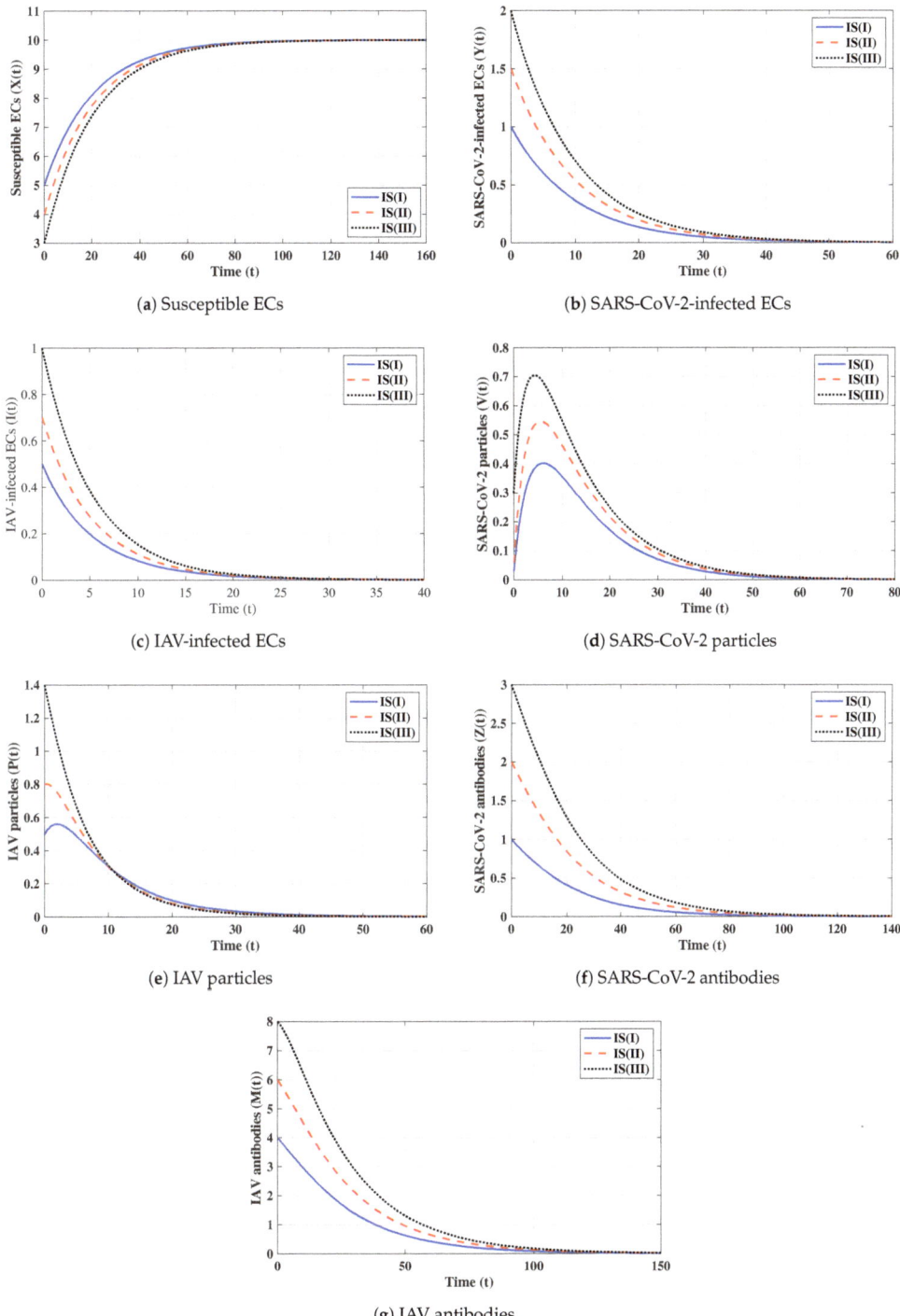

Figure 1. Solutions of system (1)–(7) when $\Re_1 \leq 1$ and $\Re_2 \leq 1$ (first strategy).

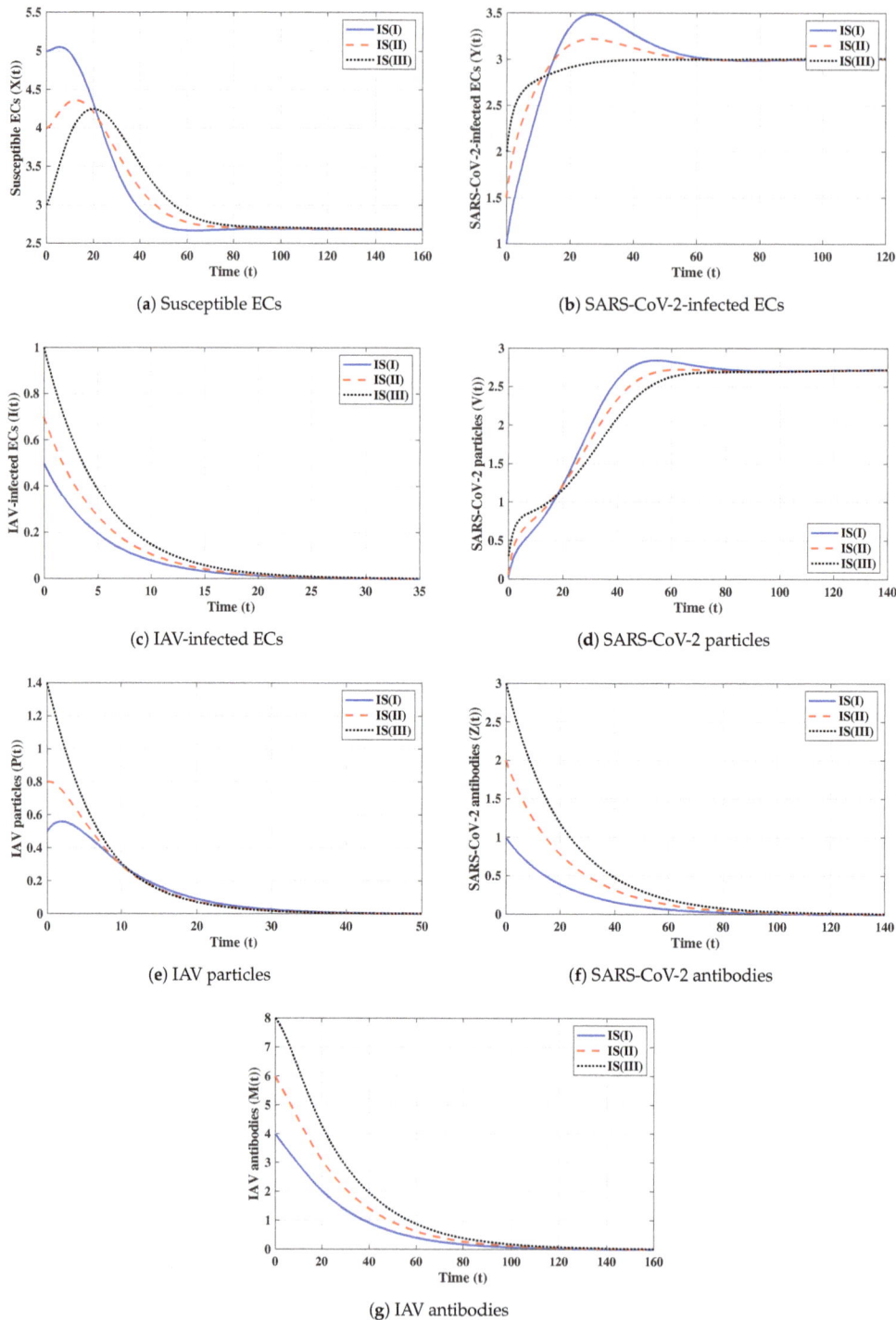

Figure 2. Solutions of system (1)–(7) when $\Re_1 > 1$, $\Re_2/\Re_1 \leq 1$, and $\Re_3 \leq 1$ (second strategy).

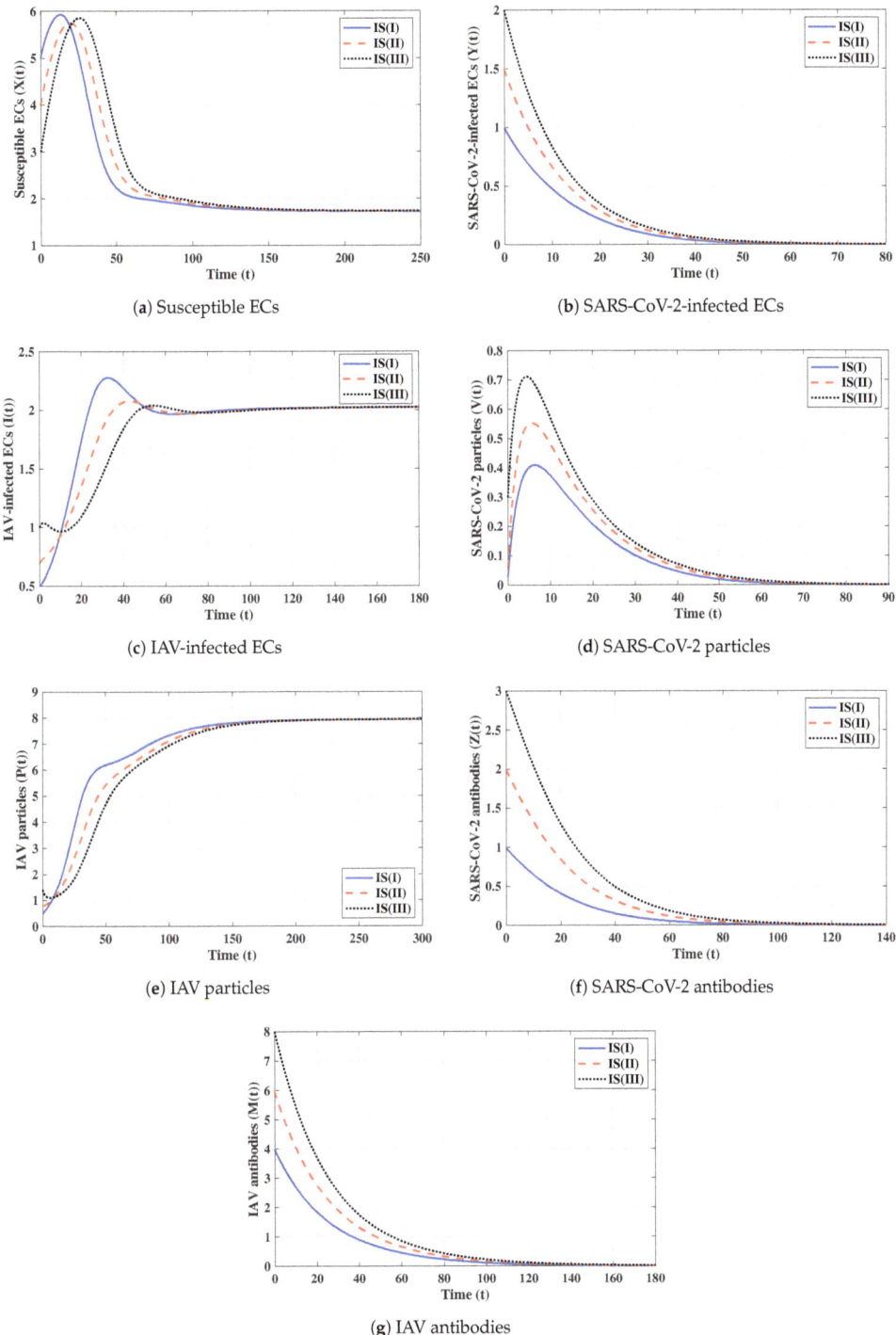

Figure 3. Solutions of system (1)–(7) when $\Re_2 > 1$, $\Re_1/\Re_2 \leq 1$, and $\Re_4 \leq 1$ (third strategy).

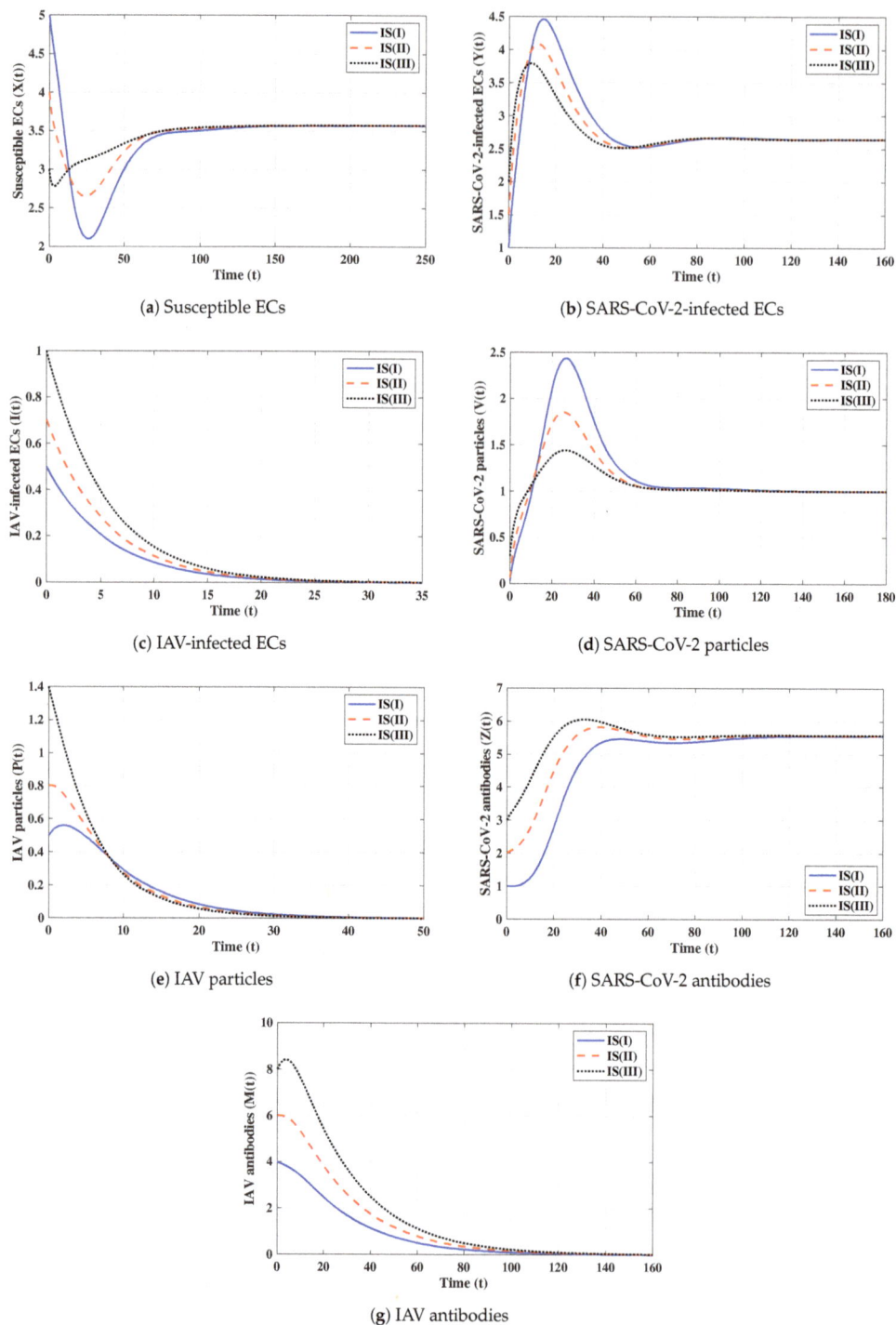

(a) Susceptible ECs
(b) SARS-CoV-2-infected ECs
(c) IAV-infected ECs
(d) SARS-CoV-2 particles
(e) IAV particles
(f) SARS-CoV-2 antibodies
(g) IAV antibodies

Figure 4. Solutions of system (1)–(7) when $\Re_3 > 1$ and $\Re_5 \leq 1$ (fourth strategy).

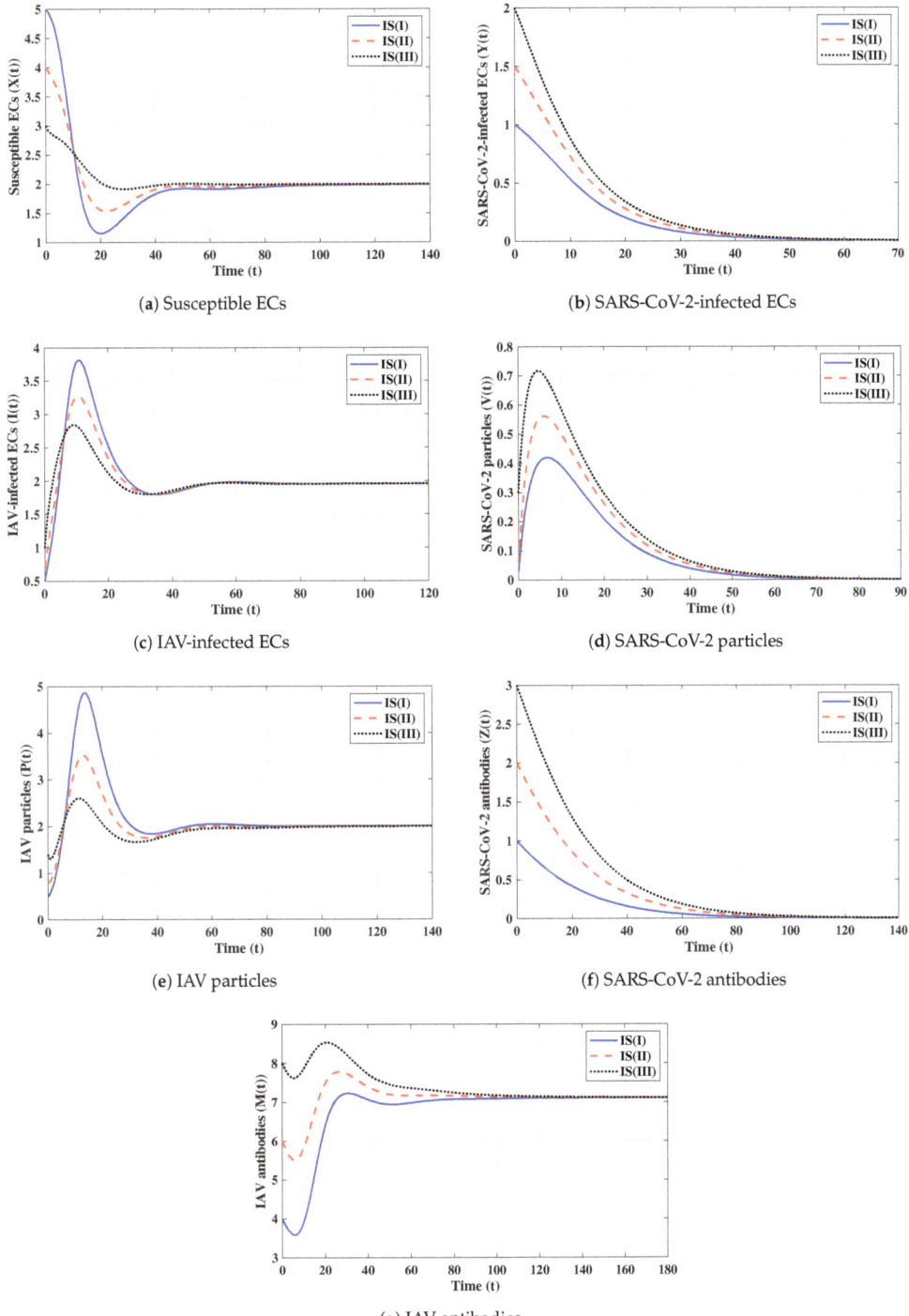

Figure 5. Solutions of system (1)–(7) when $\Re_4 > 1$ and $\Re_6 \leq 1$ (fifth strategy).

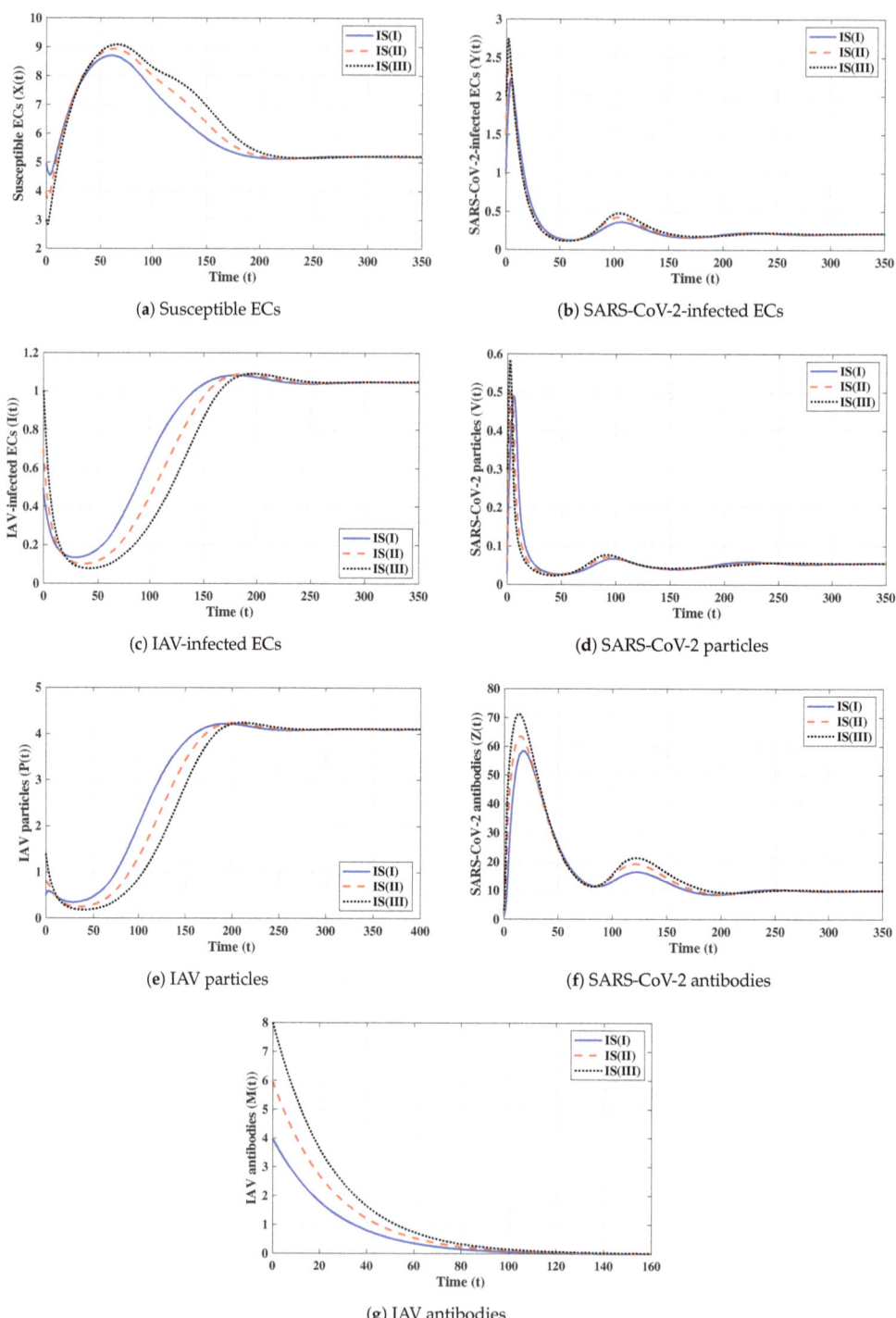

Figure 6. Solutions of system (1)–(7) when $\Re_5 > 1$, $\Re_1/\Re_2 > 1$, and $\Re_8 \leq 1$ (sixth strategy).

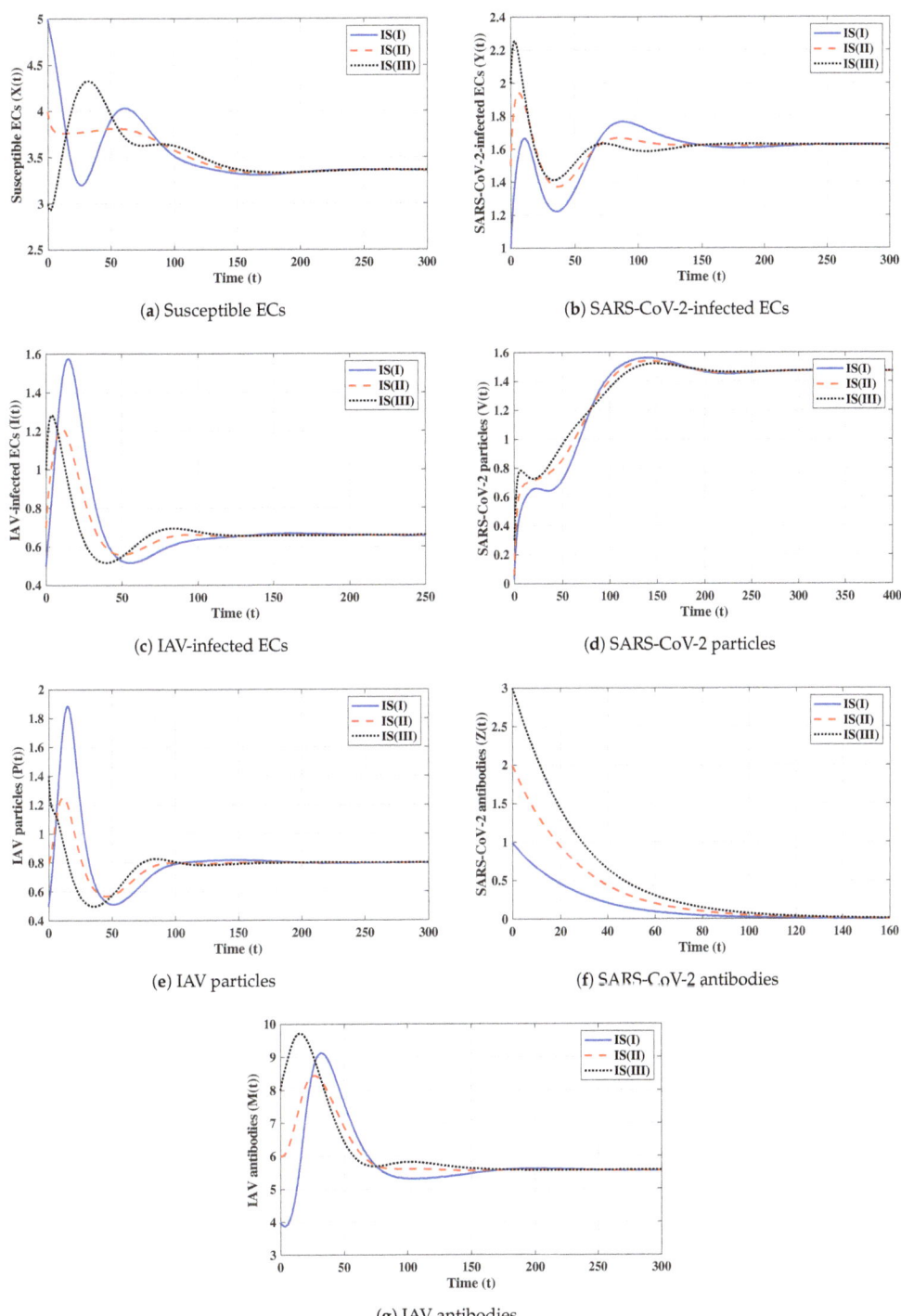

Figure 7. Solutions of system (1)–(7) when $\Re_6 > 1$, $\Re_2/\Re_1 > 1$, and $\Re_7 \leq 1$ (seventh strategy).

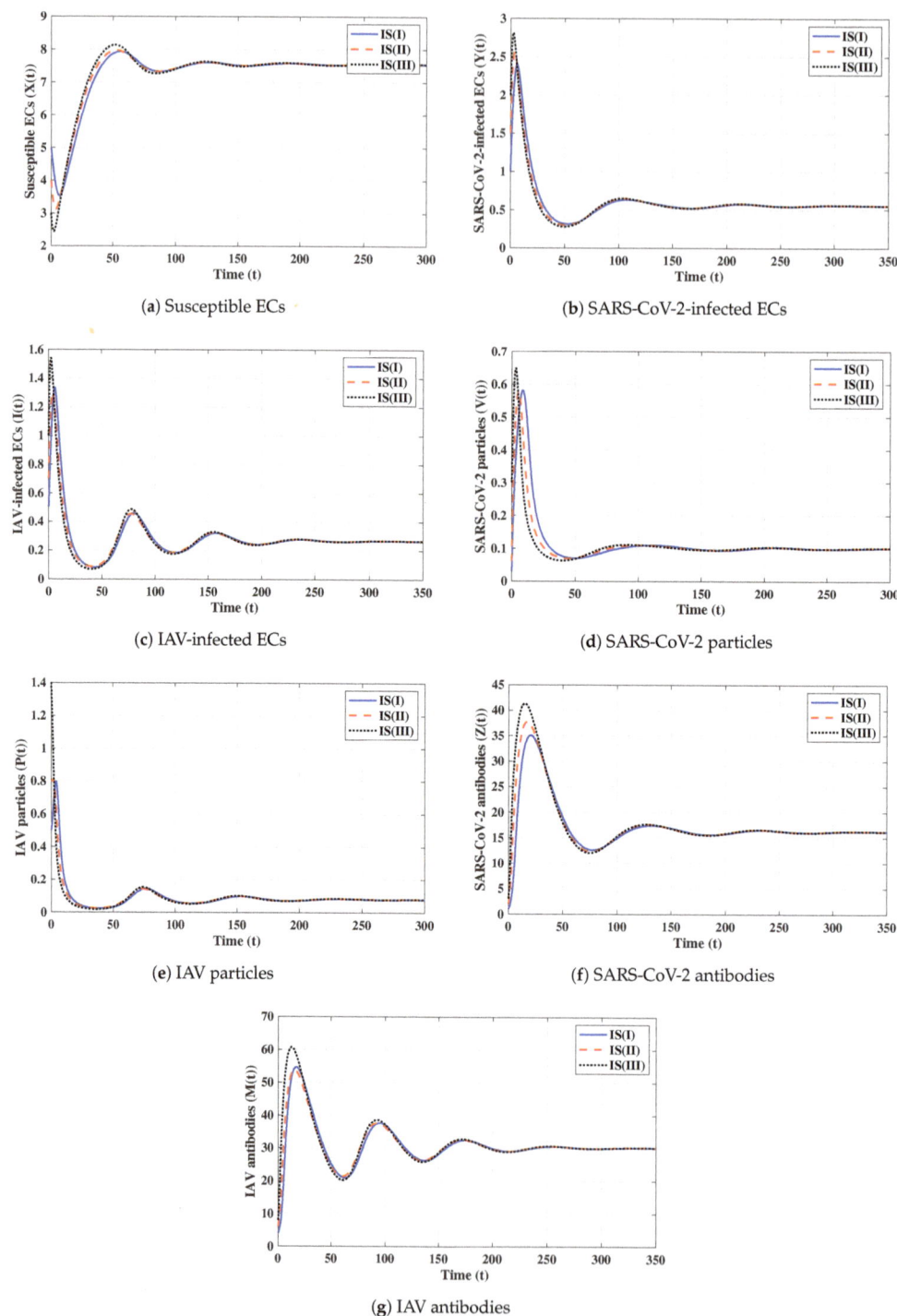

Figure 8. Solutions of system (1)–(7) when $\Re_7 > 1$ and $\Re_8 > 1$ (eighth strategy).

6.2. Effect of Antiviral Treatment on the Dynamics of Influenza and COVID-19 Co-Infection

We consider two antiviral drugs for SARS-CoV-2 and IAV with drug efficacies of ϵ_V and ϵ_P, respectively, where $0 \leq \epsilon_V \leq 1$ and $0 \leq \epsilon_P \leq 1$. Then, the parameters ζ_V and ζ_P will be changed to $(1 - \epsilon_V)\zeta_V$ and $(1 - \epsilon_P)\zeta_P$, respectively. Moreover, $\Re_1$ and $\Re_2$ become functions of ϵ_V and ϵ_P, respectively, when all other parameters are fixed:

$$\Re_1(\epsilon_V) = \frac{(1-\epsilon_V)e^{-\alpha_1\tau_1 - \alpha_2\tau_2} X_0 \theta_V \zeta_V}{\lambda_V \beta_Y}, \quad \Re_2(\epsilon_P) = \frac{(1-\epsilon_P)e^{-\alpha_3\tau_3 - \alpha_4\tau_4} X_0 \theta_P \zeta_P}{\lambda_P \beta_I}.$$

To make $\Re_1 \leq 1$ and $\Re_2 \leq 1$, the effectiveness of ϵ_V and ϵ_P has to satisfy

$$\epsilon_V^{\min} \leq \epsilon_V \leq 1, \quad \epsilon_V^{\min} = \max\left\{0, 1 - \frac{e^{\alpha_1\tau_1 + \alpha_2\tau_2}\lambda_V\beta_Y}{X_0\theta_V\zeta_V}\right\},$$

$$\epsilon_P^{\min} \leq \epsilon_P \leq 1, \quad \epsilon_P^{\min} = \max\left\{0, 1 - \frac{e^{\alpha_3\tau_3 + \alpha_4\tau_4}\lambda_P\beta_I}{X_0\theta_P\zeta_P}\right\}.$$

It follows that, if $\epsilon_V^{\min} \leq \epsilon_V \leq 1$ and $\epsilon_P^{\min} \leq \epsilon_P \leq 1$, then Δ_0 is GAS, and both influenza and COVID-19 are cleared. Therefore, if real data from patients co-infected with influenza and COVID-19 are used, the model's parameters can be estimated and the model can be used to determine the minimum drug efficacies required to eliminate both SARS-CoV-2 and IAV from the body.

6.3. Effects of Time Delays on the Dynamics of Influenza and COVID-19 Co-Infection

In this subsection, we analyze the impacts of time delays with various delay parameters τ_i, $i = 1, 2, 3, 4$. We fix the parameters $\zeta_V = 0.13$, $\zeta_P = 0.1$, $\eta_Z = 0.3$, and $\eta_M = 0.5$. Let us consider the following scenarios:

S1: $\tau_1 = 0.1$, $\tau_2 = 0.3$, $\tau_3 = 0.5$, $\tau_4 = 0.8$,
S2: $\tau_1 = 1$, $\tau_2 = 0.9$, $\tau_3 = 13$, $\tau_4 = 14$,
S3: $\tau_1 = 1.2348$, $\tau_2 = 1.2348$, $\tau_3 = 14.9787$, $\tau_4 = 14.9787$,
S4: $\tau_1 = 3$, $\tau_2 = 4$, $\tau_3 = 20$, $\tau_4 = 25$.

From the above values, we solve the system (1)–(7) under the following initial condition:

IS(IV) : $(X(u), Y(u), I(u), V(u), P(u), Z(u), M(u)) = (7, 0.6, 0.5, 0.05, 0.05, 7, 8)$,
$u \in [-\tau^*, 0]$.

The numerical results are displayed in Figure 9. We note that time delays can significantly increase the concentration of susceptible ECs and reduce the concentrations of other factors. Since $\Re_1$ and $\Re_2$ are given in (16), they depend on τ_i, $i = 1, 2, 3, 4$ when all other parameters are fixed. We observe from Table 3 that $\Re_1$ and $\Re_2$ decrease if τ_i increases; hence, the stability of Δ_0 will be changed.

Now, we need to calculate the critical value of the time delays that makes the system stable around the equilibrium point Δ_0. Let $\tau_{12} = \tau_1 = \tau_2$ and $\tau_{34} = \tau_3 = \tau_4$, and we write $\Re_1(\tau_{12})$ and $\Re_2(\tau_{34})$ as:

$$\Re_1(\tau_{12}) = \frac{e^{-(\alpha_1+\alpha_2)\tau_{12}} X_0 \theta_V \zeta_V}{\beta_Y \lambda_V}, \quad \Re_2(\tau_{34}) = \frac{e^{-(\alpha_3+\alpha_4)\tau_{34}} X_0 \theta_P \zeta_P}{\beta_I \lambda_P}.$$

Clearly, when all other parameters are fixed, $\Re_1$ and $\Re_2$ are decreasing functions of τ_{12} and τ_{34}, respectively. Let us calculate $\tau_{12}^{\min}$ and $\tau_{34}^{\min}$ such that $\Re_1(\tau_{12}^{\min}) = 1$ and $\Re_2(\tau_{34}^{\min}) = 1$ as:

$$\tau_{12}^{\min} = \max\left\{0, \frac{1}{\alpha_1 + \alpha_2} \ln\left(\frac{X_0 \theta_V \zeta_V}{\beta_Y \lambda_V}\right)\right\},$$

$$\tau_{34}^{\min} = \max\left\{0, \frac{1}{\alpha_3 + \alpha_4} \ln\left(\frac{X_0 \theta_P \zeta_P}{\beta_I \lambda_P}\right)\right\}.$$

Consequently,

$$\Re_1(\tau_{12}) \leq 1, \text{ for all } \tau_{12} \geq \tau_{12}^{\min},$$

$$\Re_2(\tau_{34}) \leq 1, \text{ for all } \tau_{34} \geq \tau_{34}^{\min}.$$

Therefore, Δ_0 is GAS when $\tau_{12} \geq \tau_{12}^{\min}$ and $\tau_{34} \geq \tau_{34}^{\min}$. Using the values of the parameters, we get $\tau_{12} = 1.2348$ and $\tau_{34} = 14.9787$. It follows that:

(i) If $\tau_{12} \geq 1.2348$ and $\tau_{34} \geq 14.9787$, then $\Re_1(\tau_{12}) \leq 1$, $\Re_2(\tau_{34}) \leq 1$, and Δ_0 is GAS.

(ii) If $\tau_{12} < 1.2348$ or $\tau_{34} < 14.9787$, then $\Re_1(\tau_{12}) > 1$ or $\Re_2(\tau_{34}) > 1$, and Δ_0 will lose its stability.

We note that time delays can play a similar role to that of antiviral drugs. This can guide researchers to create new treatments for influenza and COVID-19 co-infection that work to prolong time delays.

Table 3. The variation in $\Re_1$ and $\Re_2$ with respect to the delay parameters.

Delay Parameters	$\Re_1$	$\Re_2$
$\tau_1 = 0.1$, $\tau_2 = 0.3$, $\tau_3 = 0.5$ and $\tau_4 = 0.8$	7.92	17.56
$\tau_1 = 0.5$, $\tau_2 = 0.6$, $\tau_3 = 10$ and $\tau_4 = 11$	3.93	2.45
$\tau_1 = 1$, $\tau_2 = 0.9$, $\tau_3 = 13$ and $\tau_4 = 14$,	1.77	1.34
$\tau_1 = \tau_2 = 1.2348$ and $\tau_3 = \tau_4 = 14.9787$,	1.0	1.0
$\tau_1 = 2$, $\tau_2 = 3$, $\tau_3 = 15$ and $\tau_4 = 16$	0.08	0.9
$\tau_1 = 3$, $\tau_2 = 4$, $\tau_3 = 20$ and $\tau_4 = 25$.	0.011	0.22

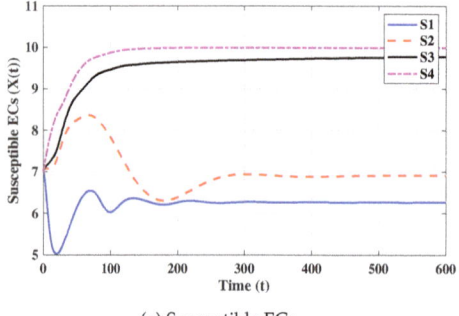
(a) Susceptible ECs

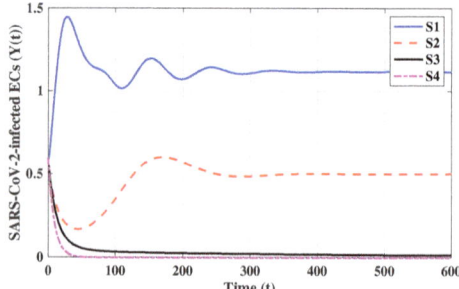
(b) SARS-CoV-2-infected ECs.

Figure 9. Cont.

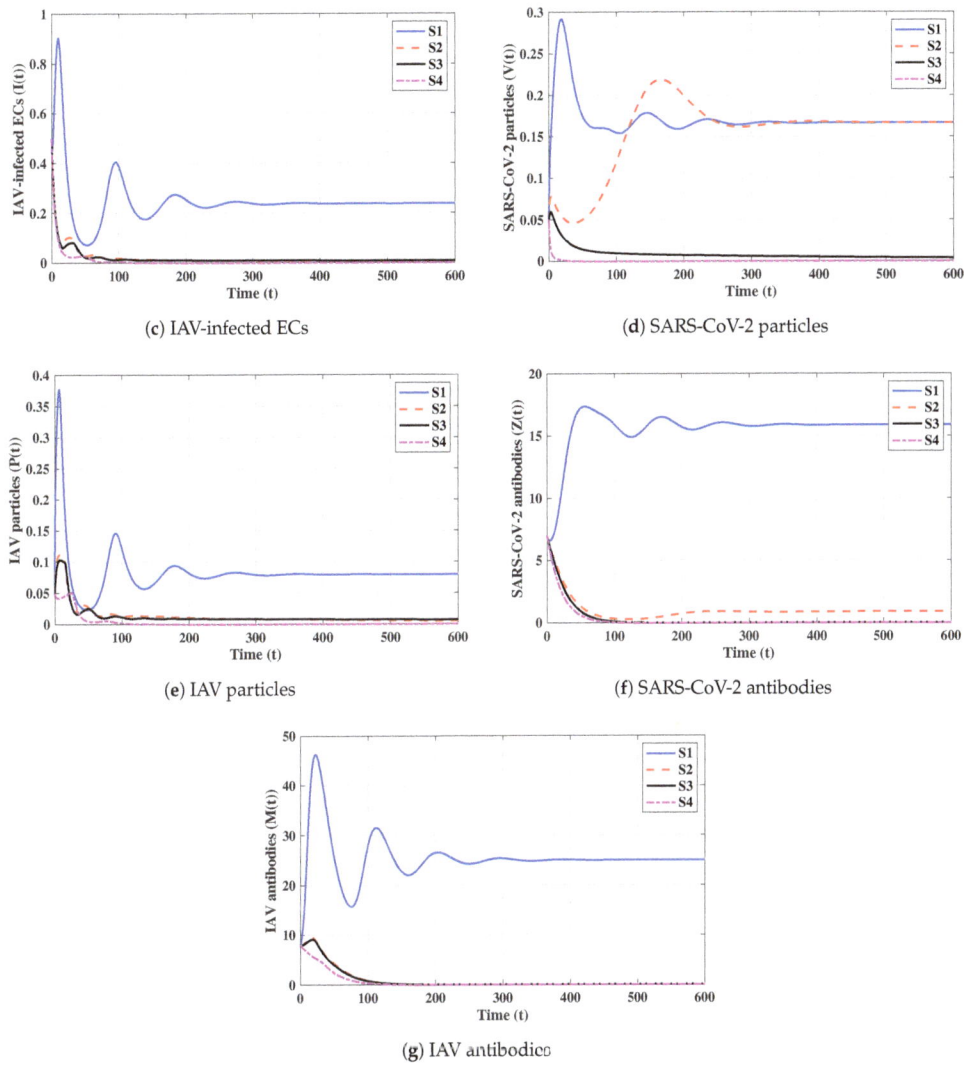

Figure 9. Effects of delay parameters τ_i, $i = 1,2,3,4$, on the trajectories of system (1)–(7).

7. Conclusions

Influenza and COVID-19 co-infection cases were reported in recent works (see, e.g., [5,9–11]). Mathematical models can be helpful for understanding the dynamics of influenza and COVID-19 co-infection within a host. In this paper, we developed and examined a system of DDEs to describe the in-host dynamics of influenza and COVID-19 co-infection under the effects of humoral immunity. The model considered the interactions among susceptible ECs, SARS-CoV-2-infected ECs, IAV-infected ECs, SARS-CoV-2 particles, IAV particles, SARS-CoV-2 antibodies, and IAV antibodies. The model included four time delays: τ_1 and τ_3 for the delays between the entries of SARS-CoV-2 and IAV into ECs and the start of production of immature SARS-CoV-2 and IAV virions, respectively, and τ_2 and τ_4 for the maturation delays of newly released SARS-CoV-2 and IAV virions, respectively. We showed the non-negativity and ultimate boundedness of the solutions. We deduced that the system had eight equilibria, and their existence and stability were governed by eight threshold parameters ($\Re_i$, $i = 1, 2, \ldots, 8$). We used the Lyapunov method to prove the global stability of the equilibria. We carried out some numerical simulations and showed that they agreed with the theoretical results. We addressed the effects of antiviral drugs and time delays on the co-infection dynamics. We showed that both antiviral drugs and time delays had the same effect in eradicating co-infection from the body. This can guide scientists and pharmaceutical companies in synthesizing new drugs that prolong time delays. Our proposed model can be useful for determining the minimum drug doses that are required to eliminate both SARS-CoV-2 and IAV infections from the body. Moreover, the model can be used to describe the in-host dynamics of co-infection with two or more viral strains or co-infections with SARS-CoV-2 (or IAV) and other respiratory viruses.

The model presented in this article can be extended to include several biological aspects, such as viral mutation [61], stochastic interactions [62], and reaction diffusion [63].

Author Contributions: Conceptualization, A.M.E. and R.S.A.; Formal analysis, A.M.E., R.S.A. and A.D.H.; Investigation, A.M.E. and R.S.A.; Methodology, A.M.E. and A.D.H.; Writing—original draft, R.S.A.; Writing—review & editing, A.M.E. and R.S.A. All authors have read and agreed to the published version of the manuscript.

Funding: This research work was funded by Institutional Fund Projects under grant no. (IFPIP: 69-130-1443) provided by the Ministry of Education and King Abdulaziz University, DSR, Jeddah, Saudi Arabia.

Data Availability Statement: Not applicable.

Acknowledgments: This research work was funded by Institutional Fund Projects under grant no. (IFPIP: 69-130-1443). The authors gratefully acknowledge technical and financial support provided by the Ministry of Education and King Abdulaziz University, DSR, Jeddah, Saudi Arabia.

Conflicts of Interest: The authors declare no conflict of interest.

References

1. World Health Organization (WHO). Coronavirus Disease (COVID-19), Weekly Epidemiological Update (18 December 2022). 2022. Available online: https://www.who.int/publications/m/item/covid-19-weekly-epidemiological-update (accessed on 21 December 2022).
2. Iuliano, A.D.; Roguski, K.M.; Chang, H.H.; Muscatello, D.J.; Palekar, R.; Tempia, S.; Cohen, C.; Gran, J.M.; Schanzer, D.; Cowling, N.J.; et al. Estimates of global seasonal influenza-associated respiratory mortality: A modelling study. *Lancet* **2018**, *391*, 1285–1300. [CrossRef] [PubMed]
3. Hancioglu, B.; Swigon, D.; Clermont, G. A dynamical model of human immune response to influenza A virus infection. *J. Theor. Biol.* **2007**, *246*, 70–86. [CrossRef] [PubMed]
4. Varga, Z.; Flammer, A.J.; Steiger, P.; Haberecker, M.; Andermatt, R.; Zinkernagel, A.S.; Mehra, M.P.; Schuepbach, R.A.; Ruschitzka, F.; Moch, H.; et al. Endothelial cell infection and endotheliitis in COVID-19. *Lancet* **2020**, 395, 1417–1418. [CrossRef] [PubMed]
5. Ozaras, R. Influenza and COVID-19 coinfection: Report of six cases and review of the literature. *J. Med. Virol.* **2020**, *92*, 2657–2665. [CrossRef]
6. World Health Organization (WHO). Influenza Update No. 428, (19 September 2022). 2022. Available online: https://www.who.int/publications/m/item/influenza-update-n-428 (accessed on 21 December 2022).
7. World Health Organization (WHO). Coronavirus Disease (COVID-19), Vaccine Tracker, 2022. Available online: https://covid19.trackvaccines.org/agency/who/ (accessed on 21 December 2022).
8. Nuwarda, R.F.; Alharbi, A.A.; Kayser, V. An overview of influenza viruses and vaccines. *Vaccines* **2021**, *9*, 1032. [CrossRef]
9. Zhu, X.; Ge, Y.; Wu, T.; Zhao, K.; Chen, Y.; Wu, B.; Zhu, F.; Zhu, B.; Cui, L. Co-infection with respiratory pathogens among COVID-2019 cases. *Virus Res.* **2020**, *285*, 198005. [CrossRef]
10. Ding, Q.; Lu, P.; Fan, Y.; Xia, Y.; Liu, M. The clinical characteristics of pneumonia patients coinfected with 2019 novel coronavirus and influenza virus in Wuhan, China. *J. Med. Virol.* **2020**, *92*, 1549–1555. [CrossRef]
11. Wang, G.; Xie, M.; Ma, J.; Guan, J.; Song, Y.; Wen, Y.; Fang, D.; Wang, M.; Tian, D.-a.; Li, P.; et al. Is Co-Infection with Influenza Virus a Protective Factor of COVID-19? 2020. Available online: https://papers.ssrn.com/sol3/papers.cfm?abstract_id=3576904 (accessed on 21 December 2022).
12. Wang, M.; Wu, Q.; Xu, W.; Qiao, B.; Wang, J.; Zheng, H.; Jiang, S.; Mei, J.; Wu, Z.; Deng, Y.; et al. Clinical diagnosis of 8274 samples with 2019-novel coronavirus in Wuhan. *MedRxiv* **2020**. [CrossRef]
13. Lansbury, L.; Lim, B.; Baskaran, V.; Lim, W.S. Co-infections in people with COVID-19: A systematic review and meta-analysis. *J. Infect.* **2020**, *81*, 266–275. [CrossRef]

14. Ghaznavi, H.; Shirvaliloo, M.; Sargazi, S.; Mohammadghasemipour, Z.; Shams, Z.; Hesari, Z.; Shahraki, O.; Nazarlou, Z.; Sheervalilou, R.; Shirvaliloo, S. SARS-CoV-2 and influenza viruses: Strategies to cope with coinfection and bioinformatics perspective. *Cell Biol. Int.* **2022**, *46*, 1009–1020. [CrossRef]
15. Khorramdelazad, H.; Kazemi, M.H.; Najafi, A.; Keykhaee, M.; Emameh, R.Z.; Falak, R. Immunopathological similarities between COVID-19 and influenza: Investigating the consequences of co-infection. *Microb. Pathog.* **2021**, *152*, 104554. [CrossRef] [PubMed]
16. Xiang, X.; Wang, Z.H.; Ye, L.L.; He, X.L.; Wei, X.S.; Ma, Y.L.; Li, H.; Chen, L.; Wang, X.-r.; Zhou, Q. Co-infection of SARS-COV-2 and influenza A virus: A case series and fast review. *Curr. Med. Sci.* **2021**, *41*, 51–57. [CrossRef]
17. Nowak, M.D.; Sordillo, E.M.; Gitman, M.R.; Mondolfi, A.E.P. Coinfection in SARS-CoV-2 infected patients: Where are influenza virus and rhinovirus/enterovirus? *J. Med. Virol.* **2020**, *92*, 1699. [CrossRef]
18. Pinky, L.; Dobrovolny, H.M. SARS-CoV-2 coinfections: Could influenza and the common cold be beneficial? *J. Med. Virol.* **2020**, *92*, 2623–2630. [CrossRef]
19. Pinky, L.; Dobrovolny, H.M. Coinfections of the respiratory tract: Viral competition for resources. *PLoS ONE* **2016**, *11*, e0155589. [CrossRef] [PubMed]
20. Hashemi, S.A.; Safamanesh, S.; Ghasemzadeh-moghaddam, H.; Ghafouri, M.; Azimian, A. High prevalence of SARS-CoV-2 and influenza A virus (H1N1) coinfection in dead patients in Northeastern Iran. *J. Med. Virol.* **2021**, *93*, 1008–1012. [CrossRef]
21. Smith, A.M.; Ribeiro, R.M. Modeling the viral dynamics of influenza A virus infection. *Crit. Rev. Immunol.* **2010**, *30*, 291–298. [CrossRef] [PubMed]
22. Beauchemin, C.A.; Handel, A. A review of mathematical models of influenza A infections within a host or cell culture: Lessons learned and challenges ahead. *BMC Public Health* **2011**, *11*, S7. [CrossRef] [PubMed]
23. Canini, L.; Perelson, A.S. Viral kinetic modeling: State of the art. *J. Pharmacokinet. Pharmacodyn.* **2014**, *41*, 431–443. [CrossRef] [PubMed]
24. Handel, A.; Liao, L.E.; Beauchemin, C.A. Progress and trends in mathematical modelling of influenza A virus infections. *Curr. Opin. Syst. Biol.* **2018**, *12*, 30–36. [CrossRef]
25. Baccam, P.; Beauchemin, C.; Macken, C.A.; Hayden, F.G.; Perelson, A. Kinetics of influenza A virus infection in humans. *J. Virol.* **2006**, *80*, 7590–7599. [CrossRef]
26. Saenz, R.A.; Quinlivan, M.; Elton, D.; MacRae, S.; Blunden, A.S.; Mumford, J.A.; Daly, J.M.; Digard, P.; Cullinane, A.; Grenfell, B.T.; et al. Dynamics of influenza virus infection and pathology. *J. Virol.* **2010**, *84*, 3974–3983. [CrossRef] [PubMed]
27. Lee, H.Y.; Topham, D.J.; Park, S.Y.; Hollenbaugh, J.; Treanor, J.; Mosmann, T.R.; Jin, X.; Ward, B.M.; Miao, H.; Holden-Wiltse, J.; et al. Simulation and prediction of the adaptive immune response to influenza A virus infection. *J. Virol.* **2009**, *83*, 7151–7165. [CrossRef]
28. Tridane, A.; Kuang, Y. Modeling the interaction of cytotoxic T lymphocytes and influenza virus infected epithelial cells. *MBE* **2010**, *7*, 171–185. [PubMed]
29. Hernandez-Vargas, E.A.; Wilk, E.; Canini, L.; Toapanta, F.R.; Binder, S.C.; Uvarovskii, A.; Ross, T.M.; Guzmán, C.A.; Perelson, A.S.; Meyer-Hermann, M. Effects of aging on influenza virus infection dynamics. *J. Virol.* **2014**, *88*, 4123–4131. [CrossRef] [PubMed]
30. Li, K.; McCaw, J.M.; Cao, P. Modelling within-host macrophage dynamics in influenza virus infection. *J. Theor. Biol.* **2021**, *508*, 110492. [CrossRef] [PubMed]
31. Chang, D.B.; Young, C.S. Simple scaling laws for influenza A rise time, duration, and severity. *J. Theor. Biol.* **2007**, *246*, 621–635. [CrossRef]
32. Handel, A.; Longini, I.M., Jr.; Antia, R. Towards a quantitative understanding of the within-host dynamics of influenza A infections. *J. R. Soc. Interface* **2010**, *7*, 35–47. [CrossRef]
33. Handel, A.; Longini, I.M., Jr.; Antia, R. Neuraminidase inhibitor resistance in influenza: Assessing the danger of its generation and spread. *PLoS Comput.* **2007**, *3*, e240. [CrossRef]
34. Beauchemin, C.A.; McSharry, J.J.; Drusano, G.L.; Nguyen, J.T.; Went, G.T.; Ribeiro, R.M.; Perelson, A.S. Modeling amantadine treatment of influenza A virus in vitro. *J. Theor. Biol.* **2008**, *254*, 439–451. [CrossRef]
35. Hernandez-Vargas, E.A.; Velasco-Hernandez, J.X. In-host mathematical modelling of COVID-19 in humans. *Annu. Rev. Control* **2020**, *50*, 448–456. [CrossRef] [PubMed]
36. Li, C.; Xu, J.; Liu, J.; Zhou, Y. The within-host viral kinetics of SARS-CoV-2. *MBE* **2020**, *17*, 2853–2861. [CrossRef]
37. Ke, R.; Zitzmann, C.; Ho, D.D.; Ribeiro, R.M.; Perelson, A.S. In vivo kinetics of SARS-CoV-2 infection and its relationship with a person's infectiousness. *Proc. Natl. Acad. Sci. USA* **2021**, *118*, e2111477118. [CrossRef] [PubMed]
38. Sadria, M.; Layton, A.T. Modeling within-host SARS-CoV-2 infection dynamics and potential treatments. *Viruses* **2021**, *13*, 1141. [CrossRef] [PubMed]
39. Ghosh, I. Within host dynamics of SARS-CoV-2 in humans: Modeling immune responses and antiviral treatments. *SN Comput. Sci.* **2021**, *2*, 482. [CrossRef] [PubMed]
40. Du, S.Q.; Yuan, W. Mathematical modeling of interaction between innate and adaptive immune responses in COVID-19 and implications for viral pathogenesis. *J. Med. Virol.* **2020**, *92*, 1615–1628. [CrossRef] [PubMed]
41. Hattaf, K.; Yousfi, N. Dynamics of SARS-CoV-2 infection model with two modes of transmission and immune response. *MBE* **2020**, *17*, 5326–5340. [CrossRef]
42. Mondal, J.; Samui, P.; Chatterjee, A.N. Dynamical demeanour of SARS-CoV-2 virus undergoing immune response mechanism in COVID-19 pandemic. *Eur. Phys. J. Spec. Top.* **2022**, *231*, 3357–3370. [CrossRef]

43. Almoceraa, A.E.S.; Quiroz, G.; Hernandez-Vargas, E.A. Stability analysis in COVID-19 within-host model with immune response. *CNSNS* **2021**, *95*, 105584. [CrossRef]
44. Leon, C.; Tokarev, A.; Bouchnita, A.; Volpert, V. Modelling of the innate and adaptive immune response to SARS viral infection, cytokine storm and vaccination. *Vaccines* **2023**, *11*, 127. [CrossRef]
45. Gonçalves, A.; Bertr, J.; Ke, R.; Comets, E.; De Lamballerie, X.; Malvy, D.; Pizzorno, A.; Terrier, O.; Calatrava, M.R.; Mentré, F.; et al. Timing of antiviral treatment initiation is critical to reduce SARS-CoV-2 viral load. *CPT Pharmacomet. Syst. Pharmacol.* **2020**, *9*, 509–514. [CrossRef] [PubMed]
46. Abuin, P.; Anderson, A.; Ferramosca, A.; Hernandez-Vargas, E.A.; Gonzalez, A.H. Characterization of SARS-CoV-2 dynamics in the host. *Annu. Rev. Control* **2020**, *50*, 457–468. [CrossRef] [PubMed]
47. Chhetri, B.; Bhagat, V.M.; Vamsi, D.K.K.; Ananth, V.S.; Prakash, D.B.; Mandale, R.; Muthusamy, S.; Sanjeevi, C.B. Within-host mathematical modeling on crucial inflammatory mediators and drug interventions in COVID-19 identifies combination therapy to be most effective and optimal. *Alex. Eng. J.* **2021**, *60*, 2491–2512. [CrossRef]
48. Elaiw, A.M.; Alsaedi, A.J.; Agha, A.D.A.; Hobiny, A.D. Global stability of a humoral immunity COVID-19 model with logistic growth and delays. *Mathematics* **2022**, *10*, 1857. [CrossRef]
49. Mahiout, L.A.; Bessonov, N.; Kazmierczak, B.; Volpert, V. Mathematical modeling of respiratory viral infection and applications to SARS-CoV-2 progression. *Math. Methods Appl. Sci.* **2023**, *46*, 1740–1751. [CrossRef]
50. dePillis, L.; Caffrey, R.; Chen, G.; Dela, M.D.; Eldevik, L.; McConnell, J.; Shabahang, S.; Varvel, S.A. A mathematical model of the within-host kinetics of SARS-CoV-2 neutralizing antibodies following COVID-19 vaccination. *J. Theor. Biol.* **2023**, *556*, 111280. [CrossRef]
51. Nath, B.J.; Dehingia, K.; Mishra, V.N.; Chu, Y.-M.; Sarmah, H.K. Mathematical analysis of a within-host model of SARS-CoV-2. *Adv. Differ. Equ.* **2021**, *2021*, 113. [CrossRef]
52. Hattaf, K.; Karimi, E.; Ismail, M.; Mohsen, A.A.; Hajhouji, Z.; El Younoussi, M.; Yousfi, N. Mathematical modeling and analysis of the dynamics of RNA viruses in presence of immunity and treatment: A case study of SARS-CoV-2. *Vaccines* **2023**, *11*, 201. [CrossRef]
53. Elaiw, A.M.; Alsulami, R.S.; Hobiny, A.D. Modeling and stability analysis of within-host IAV/SARS-CoV-2 coinfection with antibody immunity. *Mathematics* **2022**, *10*, 4382. [CrossRef]
54. Elaiw, A.M.; Alsulami, R.S.; Hobiny, A.D. Global dynamics of IAV/SARS-CoV-2 coinfection model with eclipse phase and antibody immunity. *Math. Biosci. Eng.* **2023**, *20*, 3873–3917. [CrossRef]
55. Hale, J.K.; Lunel, S.V. *Introduction to Functional Differential Equations*; Springer Science & Business Media: New York, NY, USA, 1993.
56. Korobeinikov, A. Global properties of basic virus dynamics models. *Bull. Math. Biol.* **2004**, *66*, 879–883. [CrossRef] [PubMed]
57. Korobeinikov, A. Global properties of infectious disease models with nonlinear incidence. *Bull. Math. Biol.* **2007**, *69*, 1871–1886. [CrossRef] [PubMed]
58. Barbashin, E.A. *Introduction to the Theory of Stability*; Wolters-Noordhoff: Groningen, The Netherlands, 1970.
59. LaSalle, J.P. *The Stability of Dynamical Systems*; SIAM: Philadelphia, PA, USA, 1976.
60. Lyapunov, A.M. *The General Problem of the Stability of Motion*; Taylor & Francis Ltd.: London, UK, 1992.
61. Bellomo, N.; Burini, D.; Outada, N. Pandemics of mutating virus and society: A multi-scale active particles approach. *Philos. Trans. A Math. Phys. Eng. Sci.* **2022**, *380*, 20210161. [CrossRef] [PubMed]
62. Gibelli, L.; Elaiw, A.M.; Alghamdi, M.A.; Althiabi, A.M. Heterogeneous population dynamics of active particles: Progression, mutations, and selection dynamics. *Math. Model. Methods Appl. Sci.* **2017**, *27*, 617–640. [CrossRef]
63. Bellomo, N.; Outada, N.; Soler, J.; Tao, Y.; Winkler, M. Chemotaxis and cross diffusion models in complex environments: Modeling towards a multiscale vision. *Math. Model. Methods Appl. Sci.* **2022**, *32*, 713–792. [CrossRef]

Disclaimer/Publisher's Note: The statements, opinions and data contained in all publications are solely those of the individual author(s) and contributor(s) and not of MDPI and/or the editor(s). MDPI and/or the editor(s) disclaim responsibility for any injury to people or property resulting from any ideas, methods, instructions or products referred to in the content.

Article

Analysis of Finite Solution Spaces of Second-Order ODE with Dirac Delta Periodic Forcing

Susmit Bagchi

Department of Aerospace and Software Engineering (Informatics), Gyeongsang National University, Jinju 660-701, Republic of Korea; profsbagchi@gmail.com

Abstract: Second-order Ordinary Differential Equations (ODEs) with discontinuous forcing have numerous applications in engineering and computational sciences. The analysis of the solution spaces of non-homogeneous ODEs is difficult due to the complexities in multidimensional systems, with multiple discontinuous variables present in forcing functions. Numerical solutions are often prone to failures in the presence of discontinuities. Algebraic decompositions are employed for analysis in such cases, assuming that regularities exist, operators are present in Banach (solution) spaces, and there is finite measurability. This paper proposes a generalized, finite-dimensional algebraic analysis of the solution spaces of second-order ODEs equipped with periodic Dirac delta forcing. The proposed algebraic analysis establishes the conditions for the convergence of responses within the solution spaces without requiring relative smoothness of the forcing functions. The Lipschitz regularizations and Lebesgue measurability are not considered as preconditions maintaining generality. The analysis shows that smooth and locally finite responses can be admitted in an exponentially stable solution space. The numerical analysis of the solution spaces is computed based on combinatorial changes in coefficients. It exhibits a set of locally uniform responses in the solution spaces. In contrast, the global response profiles show localized as well as oriented instabilities at specific neighborhoods in the solution spaces. Furthermore, the bands of the expansions–contractions of the stable response profiles are observable within the solution spaces depending upon the values of the coefficients and time intervals. The application aspects and distinguishing properties of the proposed approaches are outlined in brief.

Keywords: ODE; convergence; sequence; algebraic decomposition; numerical solution

MSC: 34B37; 34D20; 34D23; 34G10

Citation: Bagchi, S. Analysis of Finite Solution Spaces of Second-Order ODE with Dirac Delta Periodic Forcing. *Axioms* **2023**, *12*, 85. https://doi.org/10.3390/axioms12010085

Academic Editor: Zacharias A. Anastassi

Received: 11 December 2022
Revised: 11 January 2023
Accepted: 12 January 2023
Published: 13 January 2023

Copyright: © 2023 by the author. Licensee MDPI, Basel, Switzerland. This article is an open access article distributed under the terms and conditions of the Creative Commons Attribution (CC BY) license (https://creativecommons.org/licenses/by/4.0/).

1. Introduction

Ordinary differential equations (ODEs) have a wide array of applications with respect to modeling engineering systems and performing numerical (computational) analyses of data. The systems of differential equations often contain discontinuous forcing functions (or forcing factors) with applications in physics, engineering, data science, biology, and geology [1–3]. The comprehensive treatments concerning the solving of differential equations with discontinuous and periodic forcing functions stem from Filippov [4]. The generalized form of such equations (termed feedback equations) with single-variable discontinuity can be represented as $\dot{x} = Ax - BF(x)$, where $F(x)$ is a discontinuous forcing function and A, B are the constant matrices of finite dimensions [5]. However, if a differential equation contains multi-variable discontinuous forcing, then the corresponding two-variable forcing can be represented as $F_2(x, t)$, which has numerous applications in physical systems modeling [1]. It has been noted that the determination of classical solutions to such an equation is both difficult and insufficient [5,6]. Furthermore, the numerical solution techniques using software solvers are often prone to failures due to the presence of discontinuous forcing functions [7]. In order to simplify the equation for the determination of an analytical solution, it is often assumed that the single-variable discontinuous function $F(x)$ is finitely Lebesgue-measurable and linear. Similar problems arise regarding differential equations in the four-dimensional numerical analysis of meteorological data, which are equipped with the discontinuous forcing function given in the form $G(u(x,t), x, t)$, where (x, t) is a pair of space-time variables and the first variable is a function represented as $u = f(x,t)|_c$ at a critical state c representing the state of discontinuity [8]. In this particular case, the analytic evaluation of the term $\partial G/\partial u$ is not straightforward; as a consequence, a different functional form is formulated, which is given as $F_2(x,t) = G(u(x,t), x, t)$. However, such a function does not greatly reduce analytical complexity. Thus, the discontinuous forcing function $F_2(x,t)$ is further algebraically decomposed as $F_2(x,t) = S(x)D(t)$, where $S(x) \in C^\infty$ and the function $D(t)$ constitutes a discontinuous function [8].

1.1. Motivations

The presence of (discontinuous) Dirac delta functions in the forcing factor is often considered as multiplicative variety. These types of differential equations with Dirac delta discontinuity have numerous applications in non-smooth mechanics [9–12]. In general, the multiplicative variety of a differential equation with Dirac delta forcing is given as $dy/dt = u(t,y) + v(y)\delta(t)$, where $\delta(t)$ is the Dirac function. In general, the solution is formulated by incorporating regularizations, wherein the continuous function $u(.,.)$ should be locally Lipschitz with respect to y and it should be compact in terms of its time interval within the solution space [12]. Moreover, the additionally required condition is that the function $v(.)$ should have the following property: $v \in C^1(R)$, where R is the set of real numbers. It is known that if $u(.,.)$ and $v(.)$ are globally Lipschitz, then the solution is a convergent (limiting) function [12]. In this case, the restriction is that regularization is mandatory to find a solution if the singularity is superimposed at the initial condition. This motivated us to ask a general question: How do we algebraically analyze a second-order differential equation with periodic Dirac delta forcing given in general form? Moreover, our corollary question is as follows: what are the behaviors of such equations under additive as well as discontinuous and impulsive forcing factors? We address these questions comprehensively in this paper.

1.2. Contributions

The contributions made in this paper can be summarized as follows: We present the generalized algebraic analysis and numerical simulations of the behavior of solution spaces of non-homogeneous ODEs endowed with Dirac delta periodic forcing (refer to Equation (1)). Our algebraic analysis considers the combinatorial changes in the set of coefficients of the ODE. The algebraic analysis of the convergence of solution within an exponentially stable solution space is presented by employing the polynomial expansions of functions. The proposed algebraic analysis of the solution space does not employ any external function decomposition or Lipschitz regularizations as preconditions. It is shown that discontinuous periodic forcing can be regularized within a smooth, exponential solution space admitting locally finite responses. This results in the formation of sharp boundaries of stable responses and occasional appearances of instabilities at specific neighborhoods within the solution spaces, mostly at sharp boundaries. We present the numerical analysis of local and global response profiles in-detail under varying coefficients and time intervals within the solution spaces, while considering different algebraic relations between the constant factors of the governing equation. The results of the numerical analysis are presented as a set of surface maps exposing the interrelationships between the ranges of constant factors, the algebraic relations between them, and the degree of non-linearity covering negative and positive domains. In this paper, DD stands for Dirac Delta, which generates a periodic forcing factor of the non-homogeneous ODE. The sets of real numbers and integers are denoted by R, Z respectively, where $R = (-\infty, +\infty)$.

The rest of the paper is organized as follows. The algebraic analysis is presented in Section 2. Section 3 presents the numerical simulations in detail. Section 4 presents the application aspects of the proposed analysis. Finally, Section 5 concludes the paper.

2. Analysis of ODE with Periodic DD Forcing

The general form of a second-order non-homogeneous ODE with a periodic DD forcing factor can be represented as given in the following equation (note that D is a differentiation operator and the product $f(t)\delta(t)$ constitutes forcing):

$$D^2 x + k x^n = \sum_{t=0}^{t=+\infty} f(t)\delta(t), \qquad (1)$$
$$k \in R \setminus \{0\}.$$

Note that the forcing factor is of the discrete (discontinuous) variety, controlling the dynamic behavior of the equation in the solution space. Moreover, it is considered that the sequence generated by the periodic DD forcing factor must be convergent for the solution to exist. Note that in almost all practical application cases, the finite subsequences are considered due to computational limitations (i.e., practical cases consider the presence of convergence within bounded solution spaces). The corresponding finite form of the general equation for the terms $N \in Z^+$ can be formulated as:

$$D^2 x + k x^n = \sum_{t=0}^{t=N} f(t)\delta(t), \qquad (2)$$
$$1 \le N < +\infty.$$

Let us consider the corresponding homogeneous equation with an exponentially smooth variety of solutions in the solution spaces for the ODE under investigation. Let $x = ae^{bt}, \{a, b\} \subset R$ be a solution of a homogenized form of Equation (2). This leads to the following algebraic conditions to be satisfied:

$$\begin{aligned} ab^2 + k a^n e^{(n-1)bt} &= 0, \\ \text{and,} & \\ x &= -(k a^n / b^2) e^{nbt}. \end{aligned} \qquad (3)$$

It is important to note that the solution of x given in Equation (3) is applicable only for the homogenized form of Equation (2). However, as Equation (2) is not in a homogeneous form, we need to resolve the degree of discrete forcing by using the corresponding series within the solution spaces. Let us consider that there is a sequence in time $\langle s_t \rangle_{t=0}^{t=+\infty}$ at a finite interval such that $s_t \in [-\alpha_1, +\alpha_2]$, where $\alpha_i \in R, i \in \{1,2\}$ are the boundaries. As a subsequence of a bounded sequence is convergent following the Cauchy criteria, the periodic DD forcing factor can be represented as:

$$\langle v_t \rangle_{t=0}^{t=N} \subset \langle s_t \rangle_{t=0}^{t=+\infty},$$
$$\sum_{t=0}^{t=N} f(t)\delta(t) = \sum_{t=0}^{t=N} v_t. \qquad (4)$$

This leads to the following result in view of the algebraic expansion of Equation (3), while considering the preservation of the conditions given in Equation (4):

$$ab^2 + k a^n + (n-1) k a^n bt + ((n-1)^2/2!) k a^n (bt)^2 + \ldots = \sum_{t=0}^{t=N} v_t. \qquad (5)$$

In order to resolve the finite series at multiple time instants, we need a set of varying sums of sequences satisfying Equation (5). Let us consider a discrete and convergent sequence space; then, we construct a set of series at different time instants, as given below:

$$[t = 0] \Rightarrow [\varepsilon_t = 0],$$
$$[t = 1] \Rightarrow [\varepsilon_t = (n-1)b + ((n-1)^2/2)b^2 + ((n-1)^3/3!)b^3 + \ldots\ldots],$$
$$[t = 2] \Rightarrow [\varepsilon_t = 2(n-1)b + 2(n-1)^2 b^2 + (4/3)(n-1)^3 b^3 + \ldots\ldots], \qquad (6)$$
$$\ldots\ldots$$
$$[t = N] \Rightarrow [\varepsilon_t = bN((n-1) + (1/2)(n-1)^2 bN + (1/3!)(n-1)^3 (bN)^2 + \ldots\ldots)].$$

Note that Equation (5) is of a discrete variety, and it needs to satisfy the following algebraic conditions by considering Equation (6):

$$v_t = ab^2 + ka^n(1 + \varepsilon_t),$$
$$\varepsilon_t < \varepsilon_{t+1}. \qquad (7)$$

This immediately leads to the following set of results, which are presented as a set of theorems that consider the degree of non-linearity (n) as a constant, while the other set of constants $\{a, b, k\}$ is considered to constitute finite-valued elements. We present the first result in the following theorem considering Equation (7).

Theorem 1. *If $\langle \varepsilon_t \rangle_{t=1}^{+\infty}$ is a Cauchy sequence with $b > 0$, then $L_v = \lim_{t \to +\infty} \left(\sum_t v_t \right)$ is not convergent if $ka \neq 0$.*

Proof. Let us consider a Cauchy sequence $\langle \varepsilon_t \rangle_{t=1}^{+\infty}$ such that $b > 0$. Note that in this case the condition of $\forall t \in (0, +\infty]$, $\varepsilon_t > 0$ is preserved, and the sequence $\langle \varepsilon_t \rangle_{t=1}^{+\infty}$ is not considered to be bounded as a precondition. Thus, if the corresponding sum of the series is computed as $l = \sum_t (1 + \varepsilon_t)$, then we can conclude that $l \to +\infty$ as $t \to +\infty$. As a consequence, the sum of the limiting value, computed as $L_v = \lim_{t \to +\infty} \left(\sum_t v_t \right)$, is not convergent if $ka \neq 0$. □

This leads to the following lemma representing the strict boundedness condition of $L_{v(N)} = \lim_{t \to N} \left(\sum_t v_t \right)$ within the local space of responses.

Lemma 1. *If $b \in [0, 1)$ and $N < +\infty$, then $L_{v(N)}$ is strictly convergent.*

Proof. If we consider that $b \in [0, 1)$, we obtain the condition given as $b^m > b^{m+1}$. As a result, we can conclude that $\varepsilon_t \in (0, M)$, where $M < +\infty$ and $t \in (0, N]$. Hence, if we consider an exponentially stable and finite solution space with $N < +\infty$, then $-\infty < K_l \leq L_{v(N)} \leq K_h < +\infty$, depending on the values of the set of constants $\{a, n\}$, and as a result $L_{v(N)}$ is strictly convergent. Note that the finite boundaries K_l, K_h are real numbers. □

On the other hand, if we impose an additional condition on Equation (7) such that $b < 0, \varepsilon_t < 0$, we obtain the corresponding convergence criteria presented in the following theorem as a result.

Theorem 2. *If the sequence $\langle \varepsilon_t \rangle_{t=1}^{+\infty}$ maintains the conditions that $b < 0$, $\varepsilon_t < \varepsilon_{t+1} < 0$ and $\varepsilon_t \to -1$, then $\lim_{t \to +\infty} v_t$ is convergent.*

Proof. The proof is relatively straightforward. In this case, the sequence $\langle \varepsilon_t \rangle_{t=1}^{+\infty}$ is a monotone sequence if we consider that $\varepsilon_t < \varepsilon_{t+1}$; moreover, it is possible that $\varepsilon_t \to -1$ if we impose the following restriction: $\varepsilon_t \in (-\infty, -1]$. As a result, the limit $(\lim_{t \to +\infty} v_t) \to ab^2$ is convergent, wherein the set of constants $\{a, b\}$ is finite-valued. □

Remark 1. *It is important to note in Theorem 2 that $\lim_{t \to +\infty} v_t$ is finite even if $k \neq 0$. In other words, in this case, the convergence of v_t is independent of the vanishing k. Moreover, we can generalize the observation by the condition as $\forall t \in [0, +\infty]$, $\varepsilon_t \in R$ indicating that ε_t is finite at every time instant if the sequence $\langle \varepsilon_t \rangle_{t=1}^{+\infty}$ is a finitely bounded Cauchy sequence.*

Note that we have mentioned earlier that the complete solution of a non-homogeneous ODE with periodic DD forcing needs to be convergent within the solution spaces. The representation of Equation (7) and the aforesaid theorems illustrate that convergence analysis is necessary within the solution space to maintain the finiteness of the responses of the ODE under periodic DD forcing at different time instants. The detailed algebraic analyses of the sequential convergence of the terms within the solution space are presented in the following subsection.

Convergence Analysis

These algebraic convergence analyses consider the complete solution of a generalized non-homogeneous ODE along with the incorporated periodic DD forcing factor. The following identity must be satisfied by the complete solution space of the non-homogeneous ODE with discontinuities:

$$ab^2 + ka^n e^{(n-1)bt} = ab^2 N + ka^n \sum_{t=0}^{t=N} (1 + \varepsilon_t). \quad (8)$$

This leads to the following conclusion considering the condition that $ka^n \in R \setminus \{0\}$, where an exponential function is strictly convergent (because the solution space is finite):

$$-\infty < \sum_{t=0}^{t=N} (1 + \varepsilon_t) < +\infty,$$
$$\sum_{t=0}^{t=N} (1 + \varepsilon_t) = e^{(n-1)bt} + \left(\frac{1-N}{ka^n}\right) ab^2. \quad (9)$$

The above algebraic condition controlling the proposed exponential type of response is of a smooth variety and is convergent, thereby resolving the non-homogeneities generated by the periodic DD forcing factor. The solution space is termed a *locally stable space* if we consider a finite time interval $[0, N]$, where the responses are also finite. We can derive an interesting observation, as presented in the following theorem, before proceeding to the numerical simulations.

Theorem 3. *If the solution space is locally stable in the finite time interval $[0, N]$, then it preserves the condition $-\infty < \varepsilon_t < +\infty$ and $ka \neq 0$.*

Proof. Let us consider Equation (9) such that $\sum_{t=0}^{t=N} (1 + \varepsilon_t) - e^{(n-1)bt} = a^{(1-n)} k^{-1} b^2 (1 - N)$. Note that the right side of the expression is a constant and finite if $ka \neq 0$. Hence, the expression $\sum_{t=0}^{t=N} (1 + \varepsilon_t) - e^{(n-1)bt}$ is convergent at the time interval $[0, N]$, indicating that $-\infty < \varepsilon_t < +\infty$ at the local responses within the locally stable solution space. □

It can be observed from Theorem 3 that the finiteness of ε_t can be admitted under the convergence conditions. The local and global behaviors of the response profiles of the ODE within the solution space are numerically analyzed in-detail in the following section.

3. Numerical Analysis

The simulations are performed through numerical computation, where time (t) is varied in the two different half-open intervals. In one set of simulations, the time interval is kept very short within the solution space to evaluate the local response profiles. In another set of simulations, the time interval is comparatively larger (the supremum is more than 10 times larger) to evaluate the global response profiles of the ODE under consideration. As a result, if the time, t, is fixed in the interval $(0, 11)$, then the generated responses are called local responses of the ODE. On the other hand, if time t is varied in the interval $(0, 400)$, then the generated responses of the ODE are called global responses. The simulations are performed in three categories based on the values of the constant factor $k \in \{1, h, w\}$, where $h \in R \backslash [0, +\infty)$ and $w \in (1, +\infty)$. The other constants, such as a, b, are varied as a relationally ordered pair $(a \Delta b)$ considering various ordering relations, such as $\Delta \in \{\neq, <, >, =\}$. In all the cases, the degree of non-linearity (n) of variable x is varied in the interval $[-100, 100]$, covering a wide range in both positive and negative domains. The response profiles of $x(t)$ are presented for various numerical values of the constants and the mutual algebraic relations between them considering the homogeneous form, where the response of ODE at $t = 0$ is trivially computable and is not emphasized in the corresponding response profiles. The response profiles are presented as 3D surface maps, where the X-axis represents time, the Y-axis represents the degree of non-linearity, and the variations in the responses of $x(t)$ are given by the Z-axis. The computable regions are presented as surface maps, where the instabilities or singularities in responses are visible at specific neighborhoods within the solution spaces at boundary regions.

3.1. Response Profiles for $k = 1$ and $a \neq b$

In the first set of simulations, we consider that $k = 1$, while the other constant factors are kept finite but unequal within the solution space. The generated 3D response profile is presented in Figure 1 as a surface map for the varying degrees of non-linearity.

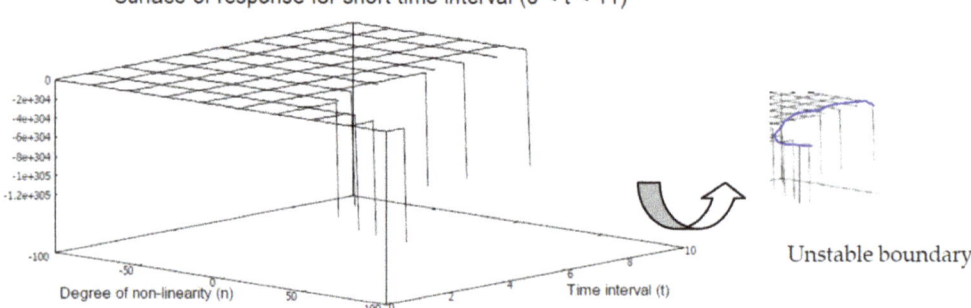

Figure 1. Surface map of local response for $k = 1$, $a = 1$, $b = 10$.

The surface map illustrates that the local response is uniformly flat in the interior of the solution space, thus signifying extreme smoothness for the negative values of non-linearity. However, there are several neighborhoods wherein the local responses attain instabilities in the solution space when the degree of non-linearity is increased more towards the positive domain. The corresponding global response profile is presented in Figure 2.

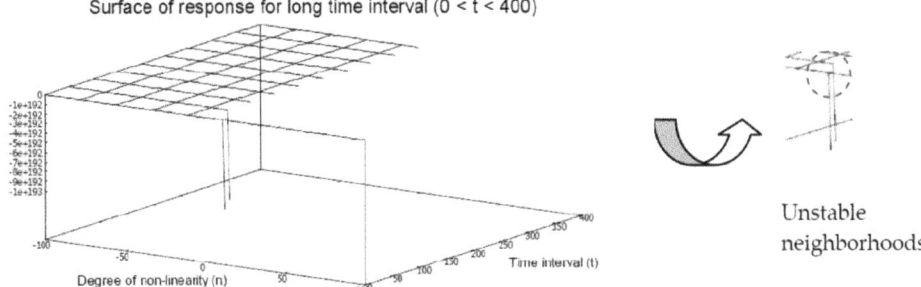

Figure 2. Surface map of global response for $k = 1$, $a = 1$, $b = 10$.

It is observable that the global response profile preserves the local response due to the fixed values of the constants and their mutual algebraic relation (an inequality relation in this case). Note that the simulations in these cases consider $a = k$, and the algebraic ordering is $b > a$. If we relax the restriction on one of the constants such that $a > 1$ while enhancing the values of another constant 10 times compared to the earlier case, then the generated local response profile retains smoothness, as presented in Figure 3. Interestingly, in this case, the local response profile is comparable to the global response with constrained values of the constants, as given in Figure 2.

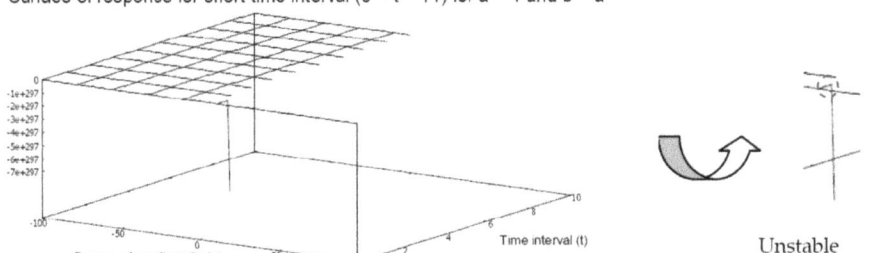

Figure 3. Surface map of local response for $k = 1$, $a = 7$, $b = 100$.

The surface map of the global response profile with $a > 1$ and $b > a$ is illustrated in Figure 4. The global response profile retains local smoothness, and the boundary of the solution space is sharp near the origin, which contrasts with the earlier 3D surface maps.

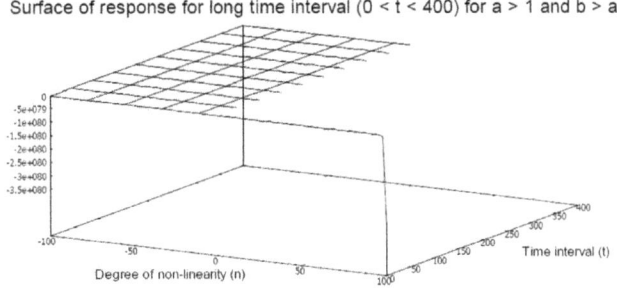

Figure 4. Surface map of global response for $k = 1$, $a = 7$, $b = 100$.

Interestingly, if we reverse the combinatorial selection of the constants such that $k = 1$, $a = 10$, $b = 1$, then the 3D surface map of local response profile is extended into the positive domain of non-linearity, as presented in Figure 5. Note that in this case, the smoothness is preserved for an extended interval within the solution space and the neighborhood of instability is confined within a narrow zone at a comparatively higher time interval.

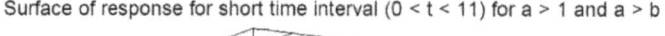

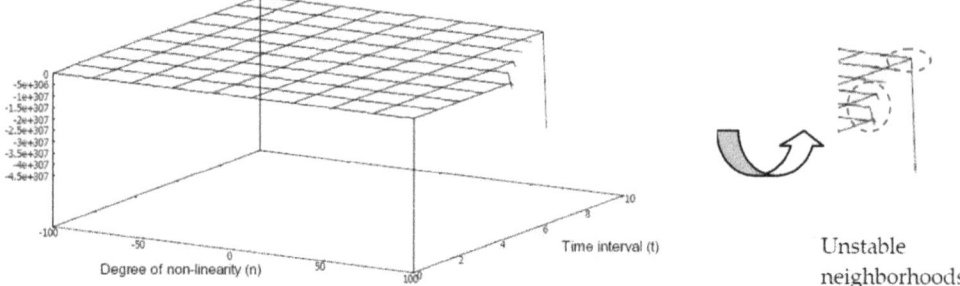

Figure 5. Surface map of local response for $k = 1$, $a = 10$, $b = 1$.

The corresponding global response profile is illustrated as the surface map given in Figure 6. The pronounced effect of non-linearity is observable in the global response profile as compared to the local response profile, wherein the values of the constants remain unaltered. The location of the neighborhood of instability is also shifted closer to the origin, where the boundary of the solution space is sharp.

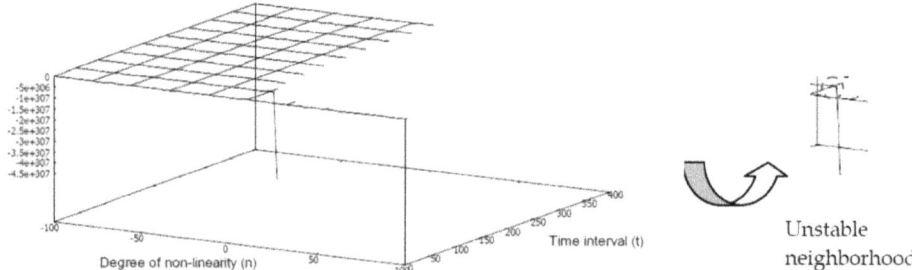

Figure 6. Surface map of global response for $k = 1$, $a = 10$, $b = 1$.

However, the local response profile of the ODE is moderately altered if we increase one of the constants as $b > 1$ while keeping $k = 1$. The corresponding 3D surface map is shown in Figure 7. It is relatively clear to see that smoothness is retained mostly in the negative index of non-linearity and that there are instabilities at the boundary region for the increased degree of non-linearity in the positive domain.

On the contrary, the global response profile exhibits a retraction mode if we increase the time interval while keeping all other parameters unaltered. This observation is depicted in Figure 8. The neighborhood of instability is present in the surface map very close to origin.

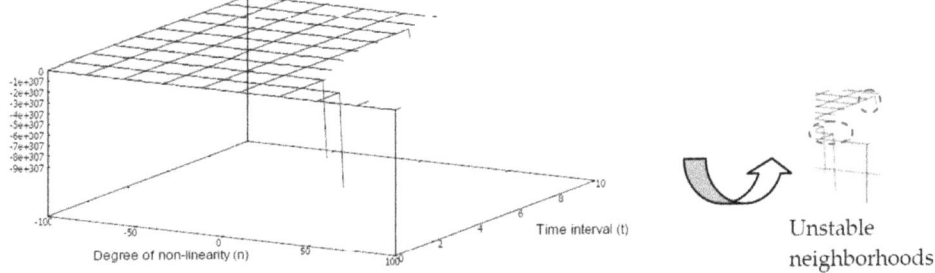

Figure 7. Surface map of local response for $k = 1$, $a = 100$, $b = 7$.

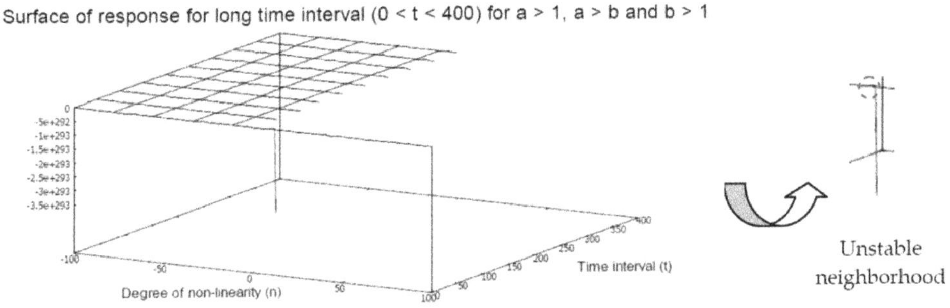

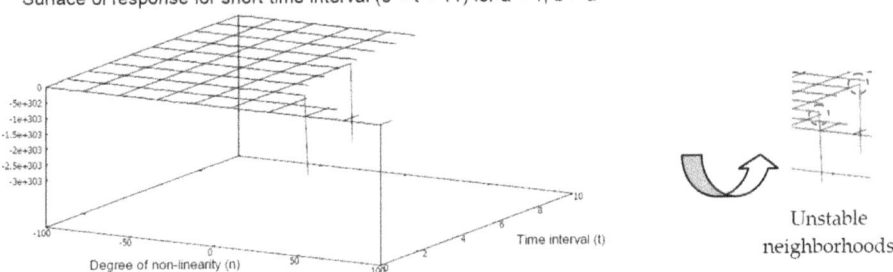

Figure 8. Surface map of global response for $k = 1$, $a = 100$, $b = 7$.

The comparisons of the surface maps illustrate that the response profiles of the ODE in Figure 3, Figure 6, and Figure 8 are nearly comparable. This indicates that the effects of the combinatorial choices of the constants a, b determine the dynamics of the local and global responses for the fixed value of $k = 1$ (i.e., in the positive domain closer to the origin).

3.2. Response Profiles for $k > 1$ and $a \neq b$

The simulation results presented in this section illustrate the effects of increasing the value of k in the positive domain away from origin. The 3D surface map of the local response profile for $k = 40$, $a = 1$, $b = 10$ is given in Figure 9. The comparisons of the response profiles given in Figures 1 and 9 show that the increasing value of k reduces the neighborhoods of instabilities within the solution space.

Figure 9. Surface map of local response for $k = 40$, $a = 1$, $b = 10$.

Interestingly, the comparisons of the global response profiles given in Figures 2 and 10 show that the surface maps are nearly similar in both cases. This indicates that at longer time intervals, the effect of the moderately increased value of k is negligible.

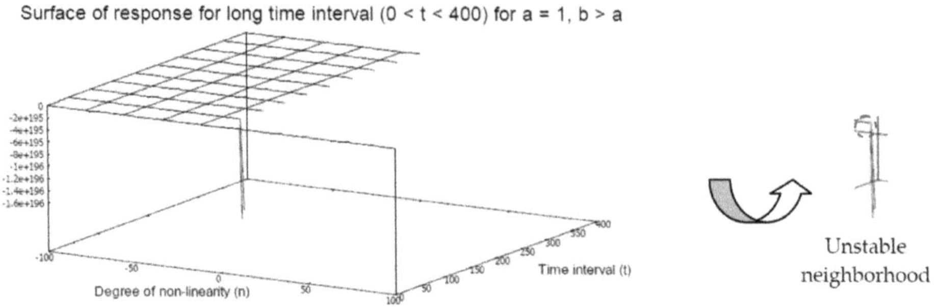

Figure 10. Surface map of global response for $k = 40$, $a = 1$, $b = 10$.

Likewise, if the values of constants a, b are increased while maintaining the algebraic ordering relation $b > a$, then the surface map of the local response profile, represented in Figure 11, remains nearly identical to that of Figure 10. This indicates that the values of the respective constants do not heavily influence the response when the corresponding algebraic ordering relation is maintained.

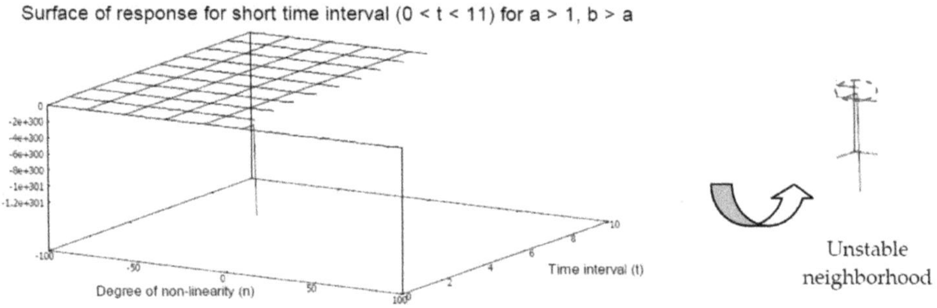

Figure 11. Surface map of local response for $k = 40$, $a = 7$, $b = 100$.

The global response profile of the ODE under consideration is largely similar to those of Figures 10 and 11, except for the elimination of instabilities at the boundary regions, as shown in Figure 12.

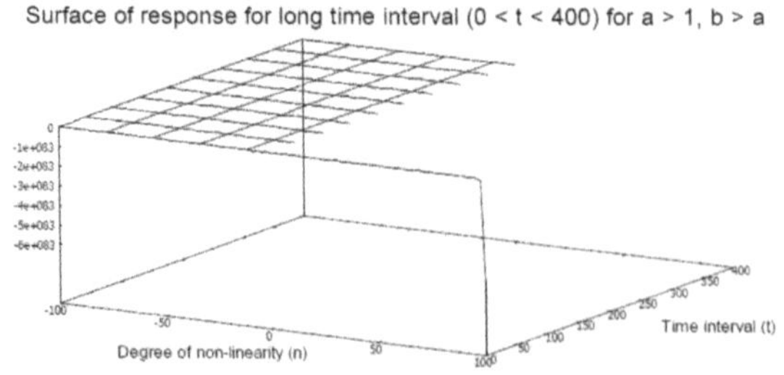

Figure 12. Surface map of global response for $k = 40$, $a = 7$, $b = 100$.

The similarity between Figures 4 and 12 suggests that the global response of the ODE is stable under the corresponding choices of the constants a, b and the algebraic ordering $b > a$ and that it is not sensitive to the values of k.

The noticeable shift in the local response profile of the ODE is observable if the algebraic ordering relation between constants is changed to $a > b$. The corresponding 3D surface map of the response profile is shown in Figure 13. Note that the response surface largely covers both positive and negative domains of varying degrees of non-linearity (i.e., an expansion of a uniformly stable solution space emerges). The neighborhood of instability is locally restricted at the sharp boundary region.

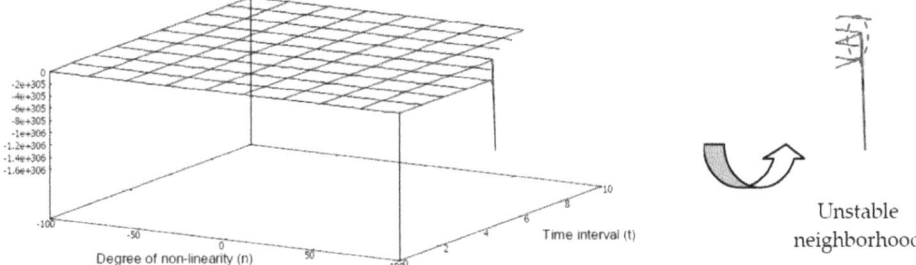

Figure 13. Surface map of local response for $k = 40$, $a = 10$, $b = 1$.

The global response profile of the ODE with an algebraic ordering of constants of $a > b$ and a value of $k = 40$ is given in Figure 14. Interestingly, it is nearly identical to the responses shown in Figure 3, Figure 6, Figure 8, and Figure 11. This observation illustrates that both the local and global dynamics of the ODE under consideration are highly stable irrespective of the combinatorial effects exerted by the set of constants $\{a, b, k\}$.

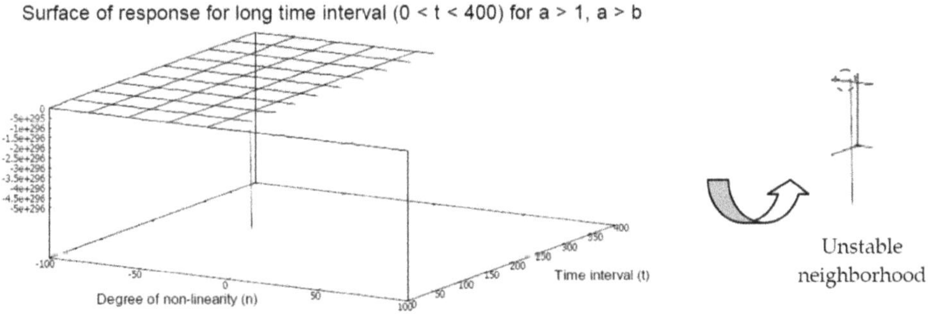

Figure 14. Surface map of global response for $k = 40$, $a = 100$, $b = 7$.

3.3. Response Profiles for $k > 1$ and $a = b$

The results of the numerical simulation presented in this section compute the global and local response profiles of the ODE under periodic DD forcing, while the parameters are set as $a, b, k \in (1, +\infty)$ and the algebraic restriction is enforced as $a = b$. The corresponding local response profile is presented in Figure 15.

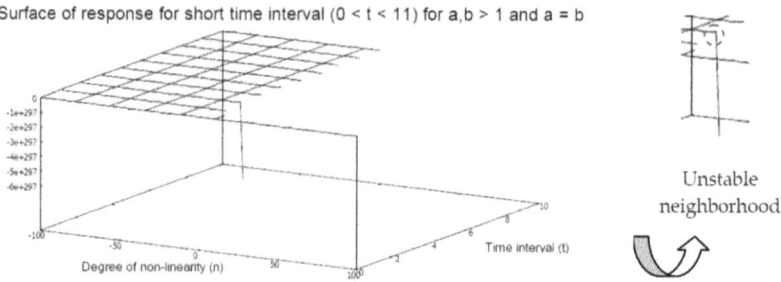

Figure 15. Surface map of local response for $k = 40$, $a = b = 100$.

The surface map of the local response of the ODE appears to be fairly smooth and uniform with a varying degree of non-linearity. However, the neighborhood of instability is observable within the solution space. Interestingly, if we compute the global response of the ODE in a relatively longer time interval, then the uniformity and smoothness of the surfaces are retained within the sharp boundary, as presented in Figure 16.

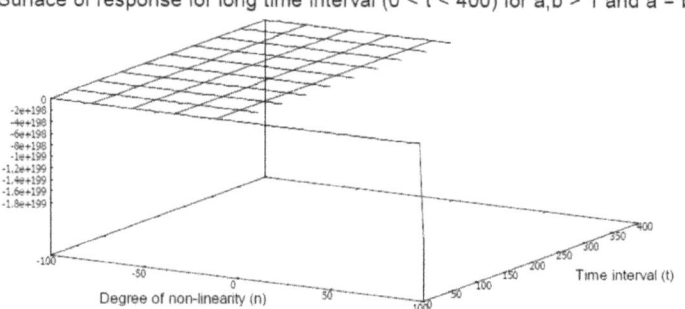

Figure 16. Surface map of global response for $k = 40$, $a = b = 100$.

Notably, the response surfaces are not computable when covering the entire region of the varying degree of non-linearity. In other words, the global and local response profiles appear to be incompletely identical across the large solution space under the parameters applied in this case.

However, if we reverse the sign of k into the negative domain, then the influence of the degree of varying non-linearity is reduced and the response surfaces are extended, as presented in the following section.

3.4. Local Response Profiles for $k < 0$

In this section, we present the local response profiles of the ODE, while reversing the sign of k into the negative domain away from the origin and fixing the constant $b = 1$. However, the other constant is changed to $a \in (1, +\infty)$. The corresponding local response profile is presented in Figure 17, where $a = 10$. It is easily observable that the uniform solution space free of instability is expanded. The oriented instabilities appear in multiple local neighborhoods at sharp boundary regions.

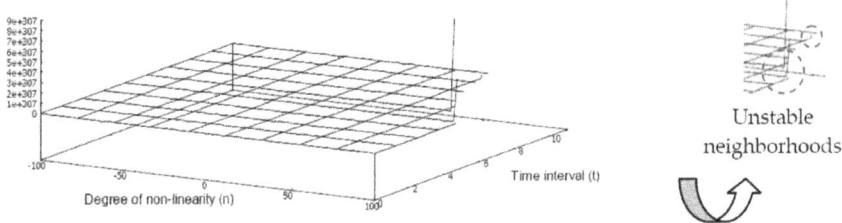

Figure 17. Surface map of local response for $k = -40$, $a = 10$.

Next, we increase the value of constant b such that $b = 30$ (i.e., three times greater than the earlier value of constant a), and we reduce the value of constant a such that an algebraic relation wherein $a < b$ is enforced. As a result, the effect of the varying degree of non-linearity is observable in the local response profile, as presented in Figure 18. Note that the space of uniformity and smoothness of the surface has contracted. This indicates that the choices of the values of the constants and the algebraic ordering have effects on the local response of the ODE under periodic DD forcing.

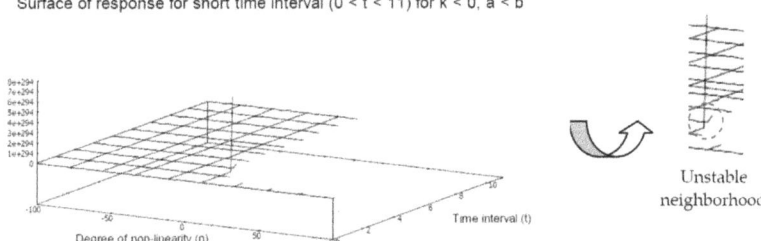

Figure 18. Surface map of local response for $k = -40$, $a = 4$, $b = 30$.

Finally, we reverse the algebraic ordering relation of constants $\{a, b\}$ again and we keep the value of constant k unaltered in the negative domain. The corresponding local response profile is presented in Figure 19.

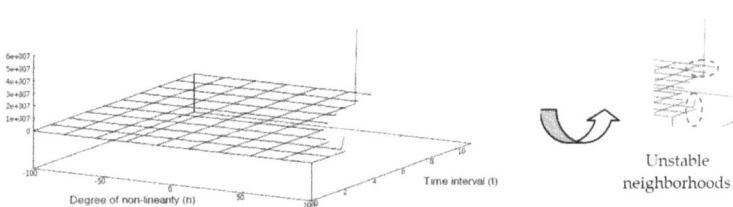

Figure 19. Surface map of local response for $k = -40$, $a = 10$, $b = 2$.

Observe that the space with a stable response is expanded, covering widely varying degrees of non-linearity unlike the earlier case. However, the neighborhoods of instabilities at the boundary within the solution space are observable in the response profile.

3.5. Evaluations of Variations of Sum of Series

In this section, we present the variations of the sum of series $\sum_t (1 + \varepsilon_t)$ as given in Equation (9) with respect to the variations of t, N and the degree of non-linearity (n). The variations of the sum of series are presented on the Z-axis. First, we show that the sum of series is bounded for the second degree of non-linearity, the short range of series $N = [0, 100]$, and the positive values of the elements of the set $\{a = 10, b = 1, k = 100\}$. The resulting response profile is given in Figure 20.

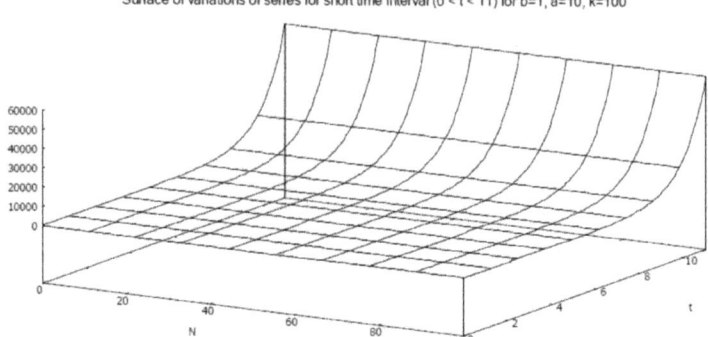

Figure 20. Surface map of local variations of $\sum_t (1 + \varepsilon_t)$ (on Z-axis) for $n = 2$.

Next, we increase the range of series to a relatively large value such that $N = [0, 1000]$ while keeping the other parameters unchanged. The resulting response profile is presented in Figure 21. It is interesting to note that the enhancement of the range of series does not have any large influence on the response profile.

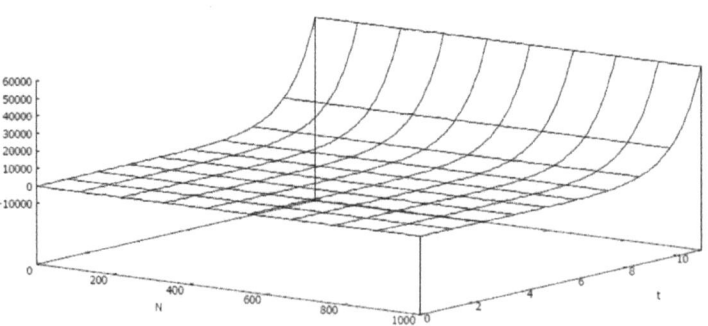

Figure 21. Surface map of local variations of $\sum_t (1 + \varepsilon_t)$ (on Z-axis) for $N = [0, 1000]$.

In the next experiment, we reduced the range of the series and computed the global response profile, and the results are given in Figure 22. The rapid increase in the values of the sum of the series is observable at the sharp boundary.

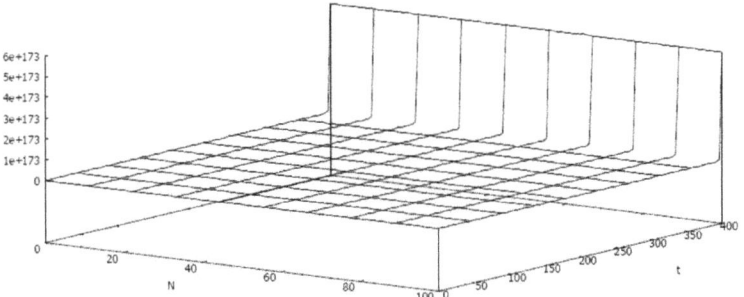

Figure 22. Surface map of global variations of $\sum_t (1+\varepsilon_t)$ for $N = [0, 100]$, $n = 2$.

A similar effect is sustained in the global response profile if we enhance the range of the series by ten-fold, as presented in Figure 23.

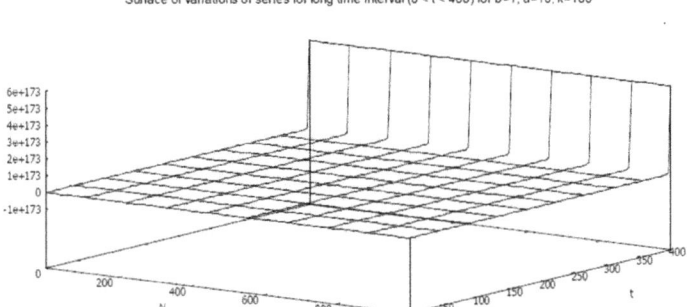

Figure 23. Surface map of global variations of $\sum_t (1+\varepsilon_t)$ for $N = [0, 1000]$, $n = 2$.

However, the increase in the values of the sum of the series becomes relatively gradual if we rearrange the combinatorial values of constants such that $\{a = 1, b = 10, k = 100\}$. The resulting response profile is given in Figure 24.

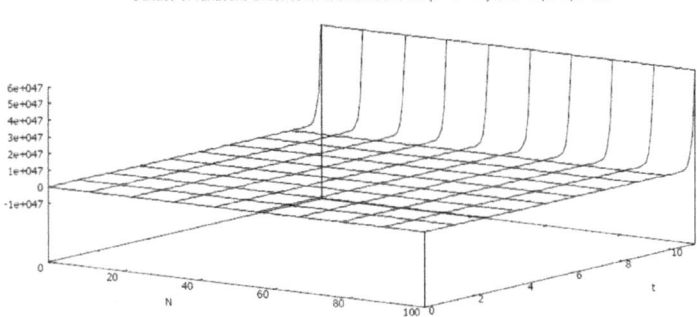

Figure 24. Surface map of local variations of $\sum_t (1+\varepsilon_t)$ for $N = [0, 100]$ and $n = 2$.

An observable shift in the variations in the sum of the series appears if the global response profile is computed for a relatively short range of the series, i.e., $N = [0, 100]$. The resulting response profile is presented in Figure 25.

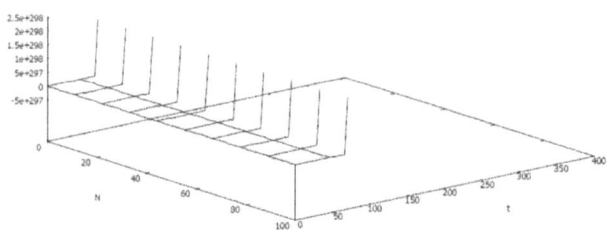

Figure 25. Surface map of global variations of $\sum_t (1 + \varepsilon_t)$ for $N = [0, 100]$ and $n = 2$.

Interestingly, the aforesaid shift in the response is retained, as presented in Figure 26., even if we increase the range of the series to ten times that of the earlier experiment. Note that the degree of non-linearity remains unchanged.

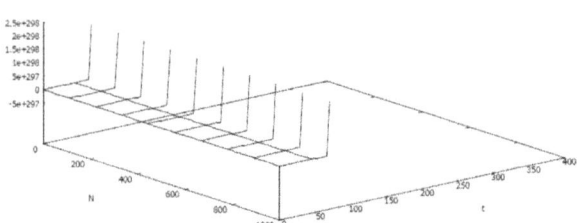

Figure 26. Surface map of global variations of $\sum_t (1 + \varepsilon_t)$ for $N = [0, 1000]$ and $n = 2$.

In the next experiment, we make combinatorial changes to the set of constants such that $\{a = -10, b = -1, k = -100\}$. This reverses the domain of the set of constants from positive to negative. The resulting response profile is presented in Figure 27. Interestingly, the influence of the domain of the set of constants is visible in the response profile, where the sum of series shows a gradual decline to a stable surface.

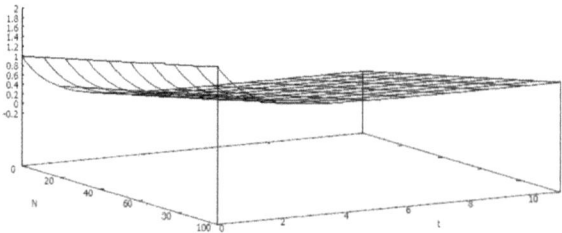

Figure 27. Surface map of local variations of $\sum_t (1 + \varepsilon_t)$ (on Z-axis) for $N = [0, 100]$, $n = 2$.

The slope of the reduction in the values of the sum of series becomes steeper than that of the previous response if we increase the degree of non-linearity five times in the positive domain. The resulting response profile is shown in Figure 28.

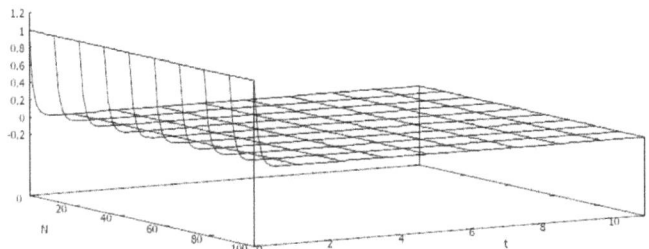

Figure 28. Surface map of local variations of $\sum_t (1 + \varepsilon_t)$ for $N = [0, 100]$ and $n = 10$.

The effect of the degree of non-linearity on the series is observable (Figure 29) when we change the degree of non-linearity from the positive domain to the negative domain.

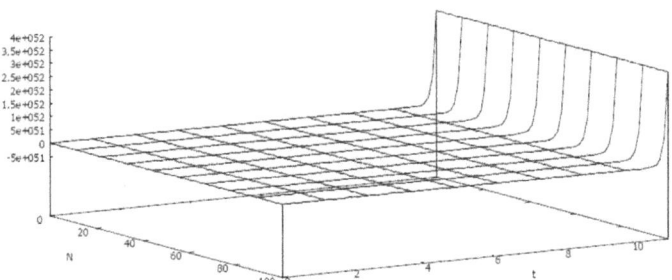

Figure 29. Surface map of local variations of $\sum_t (1 + \varepsilon_t)$ for $N = [0, 100]$ and $n = -10$.

On the other hand, the response profile of the sum of series shows sensitivity with respect to the range of the series. This effect is visible in Figure 30.

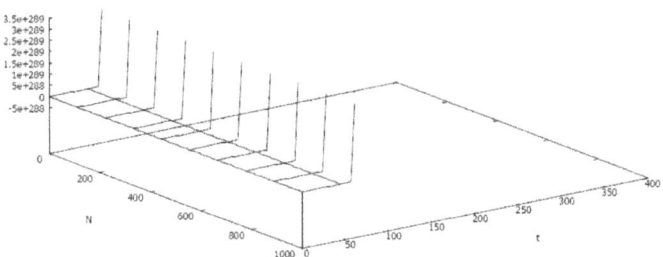

Figure 30. Surface map of global variations of $\sum_t (1 + \varepsilon_t)$ for $N = [0, 1000]$ and $n = -10$.

Evidently, the overall effects of the domain of non-linearity and the domains of the constants on the variations of the sum of series are significantly different. However, in all cases, the variations are finite. Moreover, the mutual variations of the domain of non-linearity and the range of the series have greater effects on the response profiles.

4. Applicational Prospects

In this section, the applicational prospects of the differential equations with discontinuous forcing are presented, and the distinguishing properties of the proposed approach are outlined comprehensively. In general, the ODEs involving sporadic disturbances have applications in fluid-flow modeling, wherein the uncertainties are considered to be the governing factors of the respective dynamics [13]. ODEs and PDEs (Partial Differential Equations) with Dirac delta forcing have a wide array of applications in physical sciences and engineering [14]. For example, the one-dimensional and two-dimensional differential equations equipped with Dirac-type discrete forcing are given as $-u_{xx} = \delta(x-a)$, $a \in R$ and $-\nabla^2 u_{xy} = \delta(x,y)$, respectively, with applications in geology and hydrology [14,15]. On the other hand, the non-homogeneous ODE in the form given in Equation (1) has potential applications in the jitter modeling of networked systems [16–18]. Specifically, in computer network modeling involving sporadic jitters, the constant factor is considered to be positive (i.e., $k > 0$). The main focus of the analysis of such differential equations with discontinuous forcing is to ascertain the convergence in the solution spaces and the rapidity of such convergence [19]. In general, the ODEs of perturbed systems consider uniform convergence of solutions within $[a,b]$, where the solution intervals are finite in the set of reals R. Let us consider that the forcing factor $f(.)$ is restricted to relative smoothness (i.e., the forcing $f \in C^3([a,b])$ for a singularly perturbed system [19]. This indicates that the governing equations of such systems do not consider discontinuities in the forcing factors. As a distinction, the analyses presented in this paper consider periodic discontinuities in the forcing function $f(.)$. Furthermore, the positions of the roots of characteristic equations do not play any significant role with respect to maintaining generality, as proposed in this paper. The modeling of systems with input disturbances considers cascaded PDE-ODE formulation given by $DX = AX(t) + Bu(0,t)$ with the condition $u_x(1,t) = U(t) + \omega(t)$, where $U(t)$ is the control input, $\omega(t)$ is the disturbance within input, A is an $n \times n$ constant matrix, and B is an $n \times 1$ constant matrix [20]. It is important to note that the elements of constant matrices A, B are real numbers such that the ordered pair (A, B) is stabilizable. The formulation depends on the precondition that $\omega(t)$ can be resolved as $\omega(t) = \sum_i f_i(t)$, where every $f_i(t)$ is periodic and $i \in [1,m]$, $m < +\infty$. Furthermore, it is required that $|f_i(t)| < +\infty$ in the system under consideration. The distinctive property of the algebraic analyses proposed in this paper is that the forcing factor is periodic as well as discontinuous and does not specially distinguish any control input $U(t)$ separately. Moreover, the resolution of periodic forcing does not require the convergent finite sum of other periodic functions within a finite interval (i.e., we are not decomposing Dirac forcing into external function forms). In other words, our proposed algebraic analyses consider a generalized analytical formulation. Note that numerical solution approaches are frequently employed rather than complete analytical methods in order to avoid complexities. It has been observed that numerical solution approaches are prone to the effects of varying dimensionalities [14,19]. In such cases, the convergence analyses deal with the limiting value property $\delta_\varepsilon \to \delta, \varepsilon > 0$ through the regularization of the discrete delta function δ_ε towards the Dirac delta forcing. However, the algebraic and numerical analyses presented in this paper are in a general form that does not require any specific regularization.

5. Conclusions

Second-order, non-homogeneous ODEs with both discontinuous and periodic forcing have numerous applications in engineering sciences as well as computational sciences. Second-order ODEs equipped with Dirac delta forcing comprise a variety of this class of equations. Analyses of such equations are difficult in multi-dimensional cases and the complexities are increased if the number of variables with discontinuities is increased. In order to analyze such equations, Lipschitz regularizations and Lebesgue measurability conditions are often employed. The generalized analytical approach presented in this paper was conducted with two directions: conducting algebraic analyses of convergence in lower-dimensional cases in simple forms under Dirac delta forcing and determining the corresponding numerical simulations of the behaviors of the solution spaces. The algebraic analyses proposed in this paper do not assume any specific preconditions or pre-regularizations. It has been shown that locally finite and smooth responses are admissible within exponential solution spaces and that discontinuous forcing can be resolved. Numerical simulations exhibit a set of consistent local uniformities in solution spaces. However, the global response profiles show occasional appearances of oriented discontinuities at specific local neighborhoods in the solution spaces with sharp boundaries. The expansion–contraction of smooth and uniformly stable response profiles is observable depending on the chosen sets of parameters and time intervals influencing the governing equation. The analyses proposed in this paper consider the sequential convergence property within the solution spaces, without requiring any relative smoothness of the forcing function.

Funding: This research (Article Processing Charge (APC)) is funded by Gyeongsang National University, Jinju, Korea (ROK).

Data Availability Statement: Not applicable.

Acknowledgments: The author would like to thank the reviewers and editors for their valuable comments and suggestions during the peer-review process.

Conflicts of Interest: The author declares no conflict of interest.

References

1. Precup, R.; Rodríguez-López, J. Positive solutions for ϕ-Laplace equations with discontinuous state-dependent forcing terms. *Nonlinear Anal. Model. Control* **2019**, *24*, 447–461. [CrossRef]
2. Brauer, F. Nonlinear Differential Equations with Forcing Terms. *Proc. Am. Math. Soc.* **1964**, *15*, 758–765. [CrossRef]
3. Walsh, J.; Widiasih, E. A discontinuous ODE model of the glacial cycles with diffusive heat transport. *Mathematics* **2020**, *8*, 316. [CrossRef]
4. Filippov, A.F. *Differential Equations with Discontinuous Righthand Sides*; Kluwer Academic Publishers: Dordrecht, The Netherlands, 1988.
5. Hajek, O. Discontinuous differential equations. *J. Diff. Eqn.* **1979**, *32*, 149–170. [CrossRef]
6. Eich-Soellner, E.; Führer, C. Integration of ODEs with Discontinuities. In *Numerical Methods in Multibody Dynamics*; Chapter 6; Springer Fachmedien Wiesbaden: Wiesbaden, Germany, 1998.
7. Gear, C.W.; Osterby, O. Solving Ordinary Differential Equations with Discontinuities. *ACM Trans. Math. Softw.* **1984**, *10*, 23–44. [CrossRef]
8. Lu, C.; Browning, G. Discontinuous forcing generating rough initial conditions in 4DVAR data assimilation. *J. Atmos. Sci.* **2000**, *57*, 1646–1656. [CrossRef]
9. Moreau, J.J.; Panagiotopoulos, P.D.; Strang, G. (Eds.) *Topics in Nonsmooth Mechanics*; Birkhäuser Verlag: Basel, Switzerland, 1988.
10. Brogliato, B. Nonsmooth Impact Mechanics. In *Models, Dynamics and Control*; Springer: London, UK, 1996.
11. Akhmet, M. *Principles of Discontinuous Dynamical Systems*; Springer: New York, NY, USA, 2010.
12. Nedeljkov, M.; Oberguggenberger, M. Ordinary differential equations with delta function terms. *Publ. de L'institut Mathématique* **2012**, *91*, 125–135. [CrossRef]
13. Kumar, V.; Singh, S.K.; Kumar, V.; Jamshed, W.; Nisar, K.S. Thermal and thermo-hydraulic behaviour of alumina-graphene hybrid nanofluid in minichannel heat-sink: An experimental study. *Int. J. Energy Res.* **2021**, *45*, 20700–20714. [CrossRef]
14. Cola, V.S.D.; Cuomo, S.; Severino, G. Remarks on the approximation of Dirac delta functions. *Results Appl. Math.* **2021**, *12*, 100200. [CrossRef]
15. Indelman, P. Steady-state source flow in heterogeneous porous media. *Trans. Porous Media* **2001**, *45*, 105–127. [CrossRef]
16. Cveticanin, L. *Strongly Nonlinear Oscillators, 233 Undergraduate Lecture Notes in Physics/L. Cveticanin*; Springer International Publishing: Cham, Switzerland, 2016.
17. Taqqu, M.; Willinger, W.; Sherman, R. Proof of a fundamental result in self-similar traffic modelling. *Comput. Commun. Rev.* **1997**, *27*, 5–23. [CrossRef]
18. Medykovsky, M.; Droniuk, I.; Nazarkevich, M.; Fedevych, O. Modelling the perturbation of traffic based on Ateb-functions. In *International Conference on Computer Networks*; Springer: Lwowek Slaski, Poland, 2013; pp. 38–44.

19. Vrabel, R. Non-resonant non-hyperbolic singularly perturbed Neumann problem. *Axioms* **2022**, *11*, 394. [CrossRef]
20. Li, J.; Liu, Y.; Xu, Z. *Adaptive Stabilization for Cascaded PDE-ODE Systems with a Wide Class of Input Disturbances*; IEEE: Piscataway, NJ, USA, 2019; Volume 7, pp. 29563–29574.

Disclaimer/Publisher's Note: The statements, opinions and data contained in all publications are solely those of the individual author(s) and contributor(s) and not of MDPI and/or the editor(s). MDPI and/or the editor(s) disclaim responsibility for any injury to people or property resulting from any ideas, methods, instructions or products referred to in the content.

Article

Boundary-Value Problem for Nonlinear Fractional Differential Equations of Variable Order with Finite Delay via Kuratowski Measure of Noncompactness

Benoumran Telli [1,†], Mohammed Said Souid [2,†] and Ivanka Stamova [3,*,†]

1. Department of Mathematics, University of Tiaret, Tiaret 14035, Algeria
2. Department of Economic Sciences, University of Tiaret, Tiaret 14035, Algeria
3. Department of Mathematics, University of Texas at San Antonio, San Antonio, TX 78249, USA
* Correspondence: ivanka.stamova@utsa.edu
† These authors contributed equally to this work.

Abstract: This paper is devoted to boundary-value problems for Riemann–Liouville-type fractional differential equations of variable order involving finite delays. The existence of solutions is first studied using a Darbo's fixed-point theorem and the Kuratowski measure of noncompactness. Secondly, the Ulam–Hyers stability criteria are examined. All of the results in this study are established with the help of generalized intervals and piecewise constant functions. We convert the Riemann–Liouville fractional variable-order problem to equivalent standard Riemann–Liouville problems of fractional-constant orders. Finally, two examples are constructed to illustrate the validity of the observed results.

Keywords: fractional differential equations of variable order; finite delay; boundary-value problem; fixed-point theorem; green function; Ulam–Hyers stability

MSC: 26A33; 34A37

1. Introduction and Motivations

The concept of fractional calculus, whose origin goes back to 1695, is considered as one of the most important branches in mathematics. It has been shown that models with fractional derivatives may more accurately represent complex phenomena than integer-order models. Fractional integrals and derivatives have attracted the attention of the researchers due to their essential features such as long-term dependence properties and more degrees of freedom. As a result, in the last few decades we have witnessed the application of fractional calculus methods in modeling processes studied in computer sciences, physics, neuroscience, biology, medicine, engineering, etc. [1–7]. In view of their advantages, the Riemann–Liouville and Caputo types are the most applied fractional derivatives [3,5].

Additionally, various techniques have been introduced and applied to establish existence criteria for analytical, semi-analytical, and numerical solutions of fractional-order boundary-value problems. Different researchers applied fixed-point theorems [3], nondifferentiable traveling-wave techniques [8], the homotopy perturbation transform method and the Yang transform decomposition method [9], iteration transformation techniques [10], the natural transform method [11], measures of noncompactmess [12], almost sectorial operators [13], and some others.

On the other hand, the extended class of variable-order fractional derivatives have also been recently developed [14–17]. In fact, the generalizations performed by the fractional derivatives of a variable order offered great opportunities for applications and mathematical modeling approaches [18–20].

The main idea of variable-order fractional calculus is to substitute the constant fractional order μ with a function $\mu(.)$. Although this difference seems simple, a variable-order operator can explain and model several physical and natural phenomena [21,22]. The recent publications in the field confirm our understanding of the importance of this consideration [23–27].

Despite the proven potential in applications to describe the complicated behavior of real-world problems, the theory of variable-order delayed fractional differential equations is not well developed. Some numerical approaches to solve such differential equations have been developed in several articles. For example, in [28] a collocation numerical approach is applied with the aid of shifted Chebyshev polynomials to solve a multiterm variable-order fractional delay differential equation. The existence, uniqueness criteria, and stability results have been presented in [29] for linear systems with distributed delays and distributed-order fractional derivatives based on Caputo type single fractional derivatives with respect to a nonnegative density function. In [30], a numerical method based on the Lagrangian piece-wise interpolation is proposed to solve variable-order fractal-fractional time delay equations with power law, exponential decay, and Mittag–Leffler memories. The paper [31] applied a method based on the fundamental theorem of fractional calculus and the Lagrange polynomial interpolation to numerically solve a type of variable-order fractional delay differential equation.

However, as stated in [28], analytical solutions for variable-order delayed fractional differential equations are difficult to obtain since the kernel of the variable-order operators has a variable exponent. This explains the limited number of results related to the fundamental and qualitative results for the solutions of such equations. To the best of the authors' knowledge, the existence results are established only for a damped fractional subdiffusion equation with time delay with a variable-order fractional Caputo operator in a very resent publication [32] where the authors applied shifted Chebyshev polynomials to solve the presented problem by a matrix discretization technique. Similar results for delayed variable-order fractional differential equations involving Riemann–Liouville derivatives have not yet been reported in the existing literature. This is the main aim of our research.

In [33], the authors studied the existence of solutions for the following nonlinear fractional differential equations of constant order:

$$\begin{cases} D_{0+}^{\mu} \xi(s) = \varphi(s, \xi_s), & s \in \mathcal{N} := [0, N], \ \mu \in]0,1], \\ \xi(s) = \chi(s), & s \in (-\infty, 0], \end{cases}$$

where D_{0+}^{μ} is the standard Riemann–Liouville fractional derivative, $0 < N < +\infty$, φ and χ are well defined functions, and ξ_s is an element of $C((-\infty, 0], \mathbb{R})$ defined by

$$\xi_s(\tau) := \xi(s + \tau), \ \tau \in (-\infty, 0]$$

for any function ξ defined on $(-\infty, N]$ and any $s \in \mathcal{N}$, $C((-\infty, 0], \mathbb{R})$ is the class of all continuous functions from $(-\infty, 0]$ to $\mathbb{R}$.

Since the paper [33] considers an infinite delay, the obtained existence results can be examined as a generalization of several existence results for delayed fractional differential equations with fractional constant-order derivatives. In fact, there have been some important existence results for such equations where different techniques have been applied [34–38]. However, as stated above, the corresponding results for delayed fractional variable-order boundary-value problems are very few.

Motivated by [15,23–27,33], in this paper we study the existence of solutions for the boundary-value problem of the nonlinear fractional differential equation of variable order with finite delay in the format

$$\begin{cases} D_{0+}^{\mu(s)} \xi(s) = \varphi(s, \xi_s), & s \in \mathcal{N} := [0, N], \\ \xi(s) = \chi(s), & s \in [-\gamma, 0], \gamma > 0, \end{cases} \quad (1)$$

where $1 < \mu(s) \le 2$, $D_{0+}^{\mu(s)}$ is the Riemann–Liouville fractional derivative of the variable-order $\mu(.)$, $\varphi : \mathcal{N} \times C([-\gamma, 0], \mathbb{R}) \to \mathbb{R}$. The initial function $\chi \in C([-\gamma, 0], \mathbb{R})$ and $\chi(0) = 0$, ξ_s in $C([-\gamma, 0], \mathbb{R})$ is given by

$$\xi_s(\tau) := \xi(s + \tau), \ \tau \in [-\gamma, 0],$$

for any function ξ defined on $[-\gamma, N]$ and any $s \in \mathcal{N}$.

Such problems have a great potential to model numerous real-world phenomena studied in science and engineering.

The main novelty of the paper is in the following five points: (1) a fractional boundary-value problem for delay differential equations in the variable-order Riemann–Liouville settings is introduced, which generalizes the fractional constant-order concepts; (2) new existence specifications of solutions are established; (3) we consider generalized subintervals by combining the existing notions in relation to the Kuratowski measure of noncompactness in the context of Darbo's fixed-point theorem; (4) we apply piecewise constant functions to convert the Riemann–Liouville fractional boundary-value problem of variable order (1) to standard Riemann–Liouville fractional constant-order boundary-value problems, which allows for the more accurate estimation of the solution operator and leads to a better exploration of the effect of the variable fractional order; and (5) the Ulam–Hyers stability behavior of the fractional variable-order problem is analyzed, and new stability criteria are proved.

The organization of the paper is as follows. Some definitions and preliminary results are presented in Section 2. In Section 3, the main existence criteria for solutions of the boundary-value problem of variable order (1) are established using Darbo's fixed-point theorem. Section 4 presents our main Ulam–Hyers stability results. Two illustrative examples are presented in Section 5 to complete the consistency of our findings. Finally, some conclusion notes and the future scope of this paper are given in Section 6.

2. Preliminaries

In this section, we introduce notations, definitions, and preliminary facts, which are used throughout this paper.

We denote by $C(\mathcal{N}, \mathbb{R})$ the space of real-valued continuous functions on $\mathcal{N}$ equipped with the supremum norm

$$\|\xi\|_{\mathcal{N}} = \sup\{|\xi(s)| : s \in \mathcal{N}\},$$

for any $\xi \in C(\mathcal{N}, \mathbb{R})$.

Definition 1 ([39,40]). *The left Riemann–Liouville fractional integral of variable-order $\mu(.)$, $\mu : [c, d] \to (0, +\infty)$, $-\infty < c < d < +\infty$, for a function $\xi(.)$, is defined by*

$$I_{c+}^{\mu(s)} \xi(s) = \int_c^s \frac{(s-\tau)^{\mu(\tau)-1}}{\Gamma(\mu(\tau))} \xi(\tau) d\tau, \ s > c, \tag{2}$$

where the standard Gamma function is denoted by $\Gamma(.)$.

Definition 2 ([39,40]). *For $-\infty < c < d < +\infty$, we consider the mapping $\mu : [c, d] \to (m-1, m)$, $m \in \mathbb{N}$. Then, the left Riemann–Liouville fractional derivative of variable-order $\mu(.)$ for a function ξ is defined by*

$$D_{c+}^{\mu(s)} \xi(s) = \left(\frac{d}{ds}\right)^m I_{c+}^{m-\mu(s)} \xi(s) = \left(\frac{d}{ds}\right)^m \int_c^s \frac{(s-\tau)^{m-\mu(\tau)-1}}{\Gamma(m-\mu(\tau))} \xi(\tau) d\tau, \ s > c. \tag{3}$$

Obviously, if the order $\mu(.)$ is a constant function, then the Riemann–Liouville fractional variable order derivative (3) and Riemann–Liouville fractional integral of variable-order (2) are reduced to the classical Riemann–Liouville fractional derivative and Riemann–Liouville fractional integral, respectively; see [3,5,14,39].

The following properties are some of the main ones of the fractional derivatives and integrals that we will use in our analysis.

Lemma 1 ([3]). *Let $\varrho > 0, c \geq 0, \xi \in L^1(c,d), D_{c+}^{\varrho}\xi \in L^1(c,d)$. Then, the differential equation*

$$D_{c+}^{\varrho}\xi = 0$$

has a solution

$$\xi(s) = \eta_1(s-c)^{\varrho-1} + \eta_2(s-c)^{\varrho-2} + \cdots + \eta_\ell(s-c)^{\varrho-\ell} + \cdots + \eta_m(s-c)^{\varrho-m},$$

where $m = [\varrho] + 1, \eta_\ell \in \mathbb{R}, \ell = 1, 2, \ldots, m$.

Lemma 2 ([3]). *Let $\varrho > 0, c \geq 0, \xi \in L^1(c,d), D_{c+}^{\varrho}\xi \in L^1(c,d)$. Then,*

$$I_{c+}^{\varrho} D_{c+}^{\varrho} \xi(s) = \xi(s) + \eta_1(s-c)^{\varrho-1} + \eta_2(s-c)^{\varrho-2} + \cdots + \eta_\ell(s-c)^{\varrho-\ell} + \cdots + \eta_m(s-c)^{\varrho-m}, \quad (4)$$

where $m = [\varrho] + 1, \eta_\ell \in \mathbb{R}, \ell = 1, 2, \ldots, m$.

Lemma 3 ([3]). *Let $\varrho > 0, c \geq 0, \xi \in L^1(c,d), D_{c+}^{\varrho}\xi \in L^1(c,d)$. Then,*

$$D_{c+}^{\varrho} I_{c+}^{\varrho} \xi(s) = \xi(s).$$

Lemma 4 ([3]). *Let $\varrho, \rho > 0, c \geq 0, \xi \in L^1(c,d)$. Then,*

$$I_{c+}^{\varrho} I_{c+}^{\rho} \xi(s) = I_{c+}^{\rho} I_{c+}^{\varrho} \xi(s) = I_{c+}^{\varrho+\rho} \xi(s).$$

Remark 1 ([41,42]). *Generally, for two functions $\mu_1(s)$ and $\mu_2(s)$, the semigroup property does not hold, i.e.,*

$$I_{c+}^{\mu_1(s)} I_{c+}^{\mu_2(s)} \xi(s) \neq I_{c+}^{\mu_1(s)+\mu_2(s)} \xi(s).$$

Definition 3 ([43]). *Let E be a Banach space and $\mathcal{P}_b(E)$ the family of bounded subsets of E. Then, $\zeta : \mathcal{P}_b(E) \to [0, +\infty[$ defined by*

$$\zeta(U) = \inf\{\lambda > 0 : U \subseteq \cup_{k=1}^n B_k \text{ and } diam(B_k) < \lambda\}.$$

for every $U \in \mathcal{P}_b(E)$ is called the Kuratowski measure of noncompactness.

The Kuratowski measure of noncompactness satisfies the following properties:

Proposition 1 ([44,45]). *Let E be a Banach space. Then, for all bounded subsets U, V of E, the following assertions hold:*

1. $\zeta(U) = 0 \iff \overline{U}$ is compact;
2. $\zeta(\phi) = 0$;
3. $\zeta(U) = \zeta(\overline{U}) = \zeta(convU)$;
4. $(U \subset V) \implies \zeta(U) \leq \zeta(V)$;
5. $\zeta(U + V) \leq \zeta(U) + \zeta(V)$;
6. $\zeta(\lambda U) = |\lambda|\zeta(U), \lambda \in \mathbb{R}$;
7. $\zeta(U \cup V) = max\{\zeta(U), \zeta(V)\}$;
8. $\zeta(U \cap V) \leq min\{\zeta(U), \zeta(V)\}$;
9. $\zeta(U + x_0) = \zeta(U)$ for any $x_0 \in E$.

Lemma 5 ([45]). *If the bounded set $U \subset C(\mathcal{N}, E)$ is equicontinuous, then*

(i) the function $\zeta(U(s))$ is continuous for $s \in \mathcal{N}$, and

$$\zeta_{\mathcal{N}}(U) = \sup_{s \in \mathcal{N}} \zeta(U(s)).$$

(ii) $\zeta\left(\int_0^N \xi(s)ds : \xi \in U\right) \leq \int_0^N \zeta(U(s))ds$,

where

$$U(s) = \{\xi(s) : \xi \in U\}, \, s \in \mathcal{N}.$$

Remark 2. *For the definition and properties of equicontinuous sets, we refer to [45].*

Remark 3. *In the following, we shall use ζ and $\zeta_{\mathcal{N}}$ to denote the Kuratowski measures of noncompactness of sets in space $\mathbb{R}$ and space $C(\mathcal{N}, \mathbb{R})$ respectively.*

The following theorem will be needed.

Theorem 1 (Darbo's fixed-point theorem [43]). *Let M be a nonempty, bounded, convex, and closed subset of a Banach space E and $T: M \longrightarrow M$ is a continuous operator satisfying $\zeta(TA) \leq L\zeta(A)$ for any nonempty subset A of M and for some constant $L \in [0, 1)$. Then, T has at least one fixed point in M.*

Definition 4 ([46,47]). *Equation (1) is Ulam–Hyers is stable if there exists a real number $c_\varphi > 0$ such that for each $\epsilon > 0$ and any solution $y \in C([-\gamma, N], \mathbb{R})$ of the inequality*

$$\begin{cases} |D_{0+}^{\mu(s)} y(s) - \varphi(s, y_s)| \leq \epsilon, & s \in \mathcal{N} := [0, N], \\ y(s) = \chi(s), & s \in [-\gamma, 0], \end{cases} \quad (5)$$

there exists a solution $\xi \in C([-\gamma, N], \mathbb{R})$ of Equation (1) with

$$|y(s) - \xi(s)| \leq c_\varphi \epsilon, \, s \in [-\gamma, N].$$

Remark 4. *A function $y \in C([-\gamma, N], \mathbb{R})$ is a solution of the inequality (5) if and only if a function $h \in C([-\gamma, N], \mathbb{R})$ (which depends on solution y) exists such that*

(i) $|h(s)| \leq \epsilon$, for all $s \in [-\gamma, N]$.

(ii) $D_{0+}^{\mu(s)} y(s) = \varphi(s, y_s) + h(s)$ for all $s \in \mathcal{N}$.

Definition 5 ([15,48]). *Let $I \subset \mathbb{R}$.*

(a) *The interval I is called a generalized interval if it is either an interval or $\{\rho_1\}$ or $\emptyset$.*
(b) *A partition of I is a finite set $\mathcal{P}$ such that each x in I lies in exactly one of the generalized intervals E in $\mathcal{P}$.*
(c) *A function $g: I \to \mathbb{R}$ is called piecewise constant with respect to the partition $\mathcal{P}$ of I if for any $E \in \mathcal{P}$, g is constant on E.*

3. Existence Criteria

We will begin with the introduction of some main hypotheses:

(Hyp1) For an integer $n \in \mathbb{N}$, let the finite sequence of points $\{N_k\}_{k=0}^n$ be given such that $0 = N_0 < N_{k-1} < N_k < N_n = N$, $k = 2, \ldots, n-1$. Denote $\mathcal{N}_k := (N_{k-1}, N_k]$, $k = 1, 2, \ldots, n$ and consider the partition $\mathcal{P} = \{\mathcal{N}_k : 1 = 1, 2, \ldots, n\}$ of the interval $\mathcal{N}$. Let $\mu : \mathcal{N} \to (1, 2]$ be a piecewise constant function with respect to $\mathcal{P}$, represented as follows:

$$\mu(s) = \sum_{k=1}^{n} \mu_k I_k(s) = \begin{cases} \mu_1, & \text{if } s \in \mathcal{N}_1, \\ \mu_2, & \text{if } s \in \mathcal{N}_2, \\ \vdots \\ \mu_n, & \text{if } s \in \mathcal{N}_n, \end{cases}$$

where $1 < \mu_k \leq 2$ are constants and I_k is an indicator of the interval $\mathcal{N}_k, k = 1, 2, \ldots, n$ defined by

$$I_k(s) = \begin{cases} 1, & \text{for } s \in \mathcal{N}_k, \\ 0, & \text{elsewhere}. \end{cases}$$

(Hyp2) Let $s^\sigma \varphi : \mathcal{N} \times C([-\gamma, 0], \mathbb{R}) \to \mathbb{R}$ be continuous $(0 < \sigma < 1)$. $K > 0$ exists, such that $s^\sigma |\varphi(s, y_s) - \varphi(s, z_s)| \leq K \|y_s - z_s\|_{[-\gamma, 0]}$, for any $y, z \in C([-\gamma, N], \mathbb{R})$ and $s \in \mathcal{N}$.

The next definition of a solution of the problem (1) will be essential in this paper.

Definition 6. Problem (1) has a solution, if there are functions $\xi_k, k = 1, 2, \ldots, n$, so that $\xi_k \in C([-\gamma, N_k], \mathbb{R})$ satisfying Equation (7) for $s \in [0, N_k]$, $\xi_k(s) = \chi(s)$ for $s \in [-\gamma, 0]$ and $\xi_k(0) = \xi_k(N_k) = 0$.

In order to apply Darbo's fixed-point theorem and the Kuratowski measure of non-compactness, we will perform an essential analysis to the problem (1).

Using (3), we represent the equation of the problem (1) in the following form:

$$\frac{d^2}{ds^2} \int_0^s \frac{(s-\tau)^{1-\mu(\tau)}}{\Gamma(2-\mu(\tau))} \xi(\tau) d\tau = \varphi(s, \xi_s), \quad s \in \mathcal{N}. \tag{6}$$

According to **(Hyp1)**, we can represent Equation (6) on the interval $\mathcal{N}_k, k = 1, 2, \ldots, n$ as

$$\frac{d^2}{ds^2} \left(\int_0^{N_1} \frac{(s-\tau)^{1-\mu_1}}{\Gamma(2-\mu_1)} \xi(\tau) d\tau + \ldots + \int_{N_{k-1}}^{s} \frac{(s-\tau)^{1-\mu_k}}{\Gamma(2-\mu_k)} \xi(\tau) d\tau \right) = \varphi(s, \xi_s) \tag{7}$$

for $s \in \mathcal{N}_k$.

For $0 \leq s \leq N_{k-1}$, by taking $\xi(s) \equiv 0$, Equation (7) is reduced to

$$D_{N_{k-1}^+}^{\mu_k} \xi(s) = \varphi(s, \xi_s), \quad s \in \mathcal{N}_k.$$

Let us consider the following problem:

$$\begin{cases} D_{N_{k-1}^+}^{\mu_k} \xi(s) = \varphi(s, \xi_s), \quad s \in \mathcal{N}_k, \\ \xi(N_{k-1}) = 0, \quad \xi(N_k) = 0, \\ \xi(s) = \chi_k(s), \quad s \in [N_{k-1} - \gamma', N_{k-1}], \end{cases} \tag{8}$$

where $\gamma' = N_{k-1} + \gamma$ and

$$\chi_k(s) = \begin{cases} 0, & \text{if } s \in [0, N_{k-1}] \\ \chi(s), & \text{if } s \in [-\gamma, 0]. \end{cases}$$

The following auxiliary lemma will offer existence criteria for solutions for the problem (8).

Lemma 6. The function $\xi \in C([-\gamma, N_k], \mathbb{R})$ is a solution of problem (8) if and only if ξ satisfies the integral equation

$$\xi(s) = \begin{cases} -\int_{N_{k-1}}^{N_k} G_k(s, \tau) \varphi(\tau, \xi_\tau) d\tau, & \text{if } s \in \mathcal{N}_k, \\ \chi_k(s), & \text{if } s \in [-\gamma, N_{k-1}], \end{cases} \tag{9}$$

where $G_k(s,\tau)$ is a Green's function defined by

$$G_k(s,\tau) = \begin{cases} \frac{1}{\Gamma(\mu_k)}\left[(N_k - N_{k-1})^{1-\mu_k}(s - N_{k-1})^{\mu_k-1}(N_k - \tau)^{\mu_k-1} - (s-\tau)^{\mu_k-1}\right], \\ \qquad N_{k-1} \leq \tau \leq s \leq N_k, \\ \frac{1}{\Gamma(\mu_k)}(N_k - N_{k-1})^{1-\mu_k}(s - N_{k-1})^{\mu_k-1}(N_k - \tau)^{\mu_k-1}, \\ \qquad N_{k-1} \leq s \leq \tau \leq N_k, \end{cases}$$

$k = 1, 2, \ldots, n$.

Proof. Let $\zeta \in C([-\gamma, N_k], \mathbb{R})$ be a solution of the problem (8). From (4), we have

$$\zeta(s) = \eta_1(s - N_{k-1})^{\mu_k-1} + \eta_2(s - N_{k-1})^{\mu_k-2} + I^{\mu_k}_{N^+_{k-1}}\varphi(s,\zeta_s), \quad s \in \mathcal{N}_k,\ k \in \{1,2,\ldots,n\}. \tag{10}$$

Using $\zeta(N_{k-1}) = \zeta(N_k) = 0$, we find that $\eta_2 = 0$ and

$$\eta_1 = -(N_k - N_{k-1})^{1-\mu_k} I^{\mu_k}_{N^+_{k-1}} \varphi(N_k, \zeta_{N_k}).$$

By substituting the values of η_1 and η_2 in (10), we obtain

$$\zeta(s) = -(N_k - N_{k-1})^{1-\mu_k}(s - N_{k-1})^{\mu_k-1} I^{\mu_k}_{N^+_{k-1}}\varphi(N_k, \zeta_{N_k}) + I^{\mu_k}_{N^+_{k-1}}\varphi(s, \zeta_s),\quad s \in \mathcal{N}_k.$$

Then, the solution of the problem (8) is given by

$$\begin{aligned}\zeta(s) &= -(N_k - N_{k-1})^{1-\mu_k}(s - N_{k-1})^{\mu_k-1}\frac{1}{\Gamma(\mu_k)}\int_{N_{k-1}}^{N_k}(N_k - \tau)^{\mu_k-1}\varphi(\tau,\zeta_\tau)d\tau \\ &\quad + \frac{1}{\Gamma(\mu_k)}\int_{N_{k-1}}^{s}(s - \tau)^{\mu_k-1}\varphi(\tau,\zeta_\tau)d\tau \\ &= -\frac{1}{\Gamma(\mu_k)}\Big[\int_{N_{k-1}}^{s}\left[(N_k - N_{k-1})^{1-\mu_k}(s - N_{k-1})^{\mu_k-1}(N_k - \tau)^{\mu_k-1} - (s-\tau)^{\mu_k-1}\right]\varphi(\tau,\zeta_\tau)d\tau \\ &\quad + \int_s^{N_k}(N_k - N_{k-1})^{1-\mu_k}(s - N_{k-1})^{\mu_k-1}(N_k - \tau)^{\mu_k-1}\varphi(\tau,\zeta_\tau)d\tau\Big] \\ &= -\Big[\int_{N_{k-1}}^{s}G_k(s,\tau)\varphi(\tau,\zeta_\tau)d\tau + \int_s^{N_k}G_k(s,\tau)\varphi(\tau,\zeta_\tau)d\tau\Big]\end{aligned}$$

and the continuity of the Green function gives

$$\zeta(s) = -\int_{N_{k-1}}^{N_k}G_k(s,\tau)\varphi(\tau,\zeta_\tau)d\tau,\quad s \in \mathcal{N}_k.$$

Conversely, let $\zeta \in C([-\gamma, N_k], \mathbb{R})$ be a solution of integral Equation (9); then, by the continuity of function $S^\sigma\varphi$ and Lemma 3, we can easily obtain that ζ is the solution of the problem (8). □

Proposition 2 ([16]). *Let $0 < \sigma < 1$ and assume that $s^\sigma\varphi : \mathcal{N}_k \times C([-\gamma, 0], \mathbb{R}) \to \mathbb{R}$ is continuous, and $\mu : \mathcal{N}_k \to (1,2]$ satisfies* **(Hyp1)**. *Then, the Green's function of problem (8) satisfies the following properties:*

(1) $G_k(s,\tau) \geq 0$ for all $N_{k-1} \leq s, \tau \leq N_k$,
(2) $\max_{s \in \mathcal{N}_k} G_k(s,\tau) = G_k(\tau,\tau),\ \tau \in \mathcal{N}_k$,

(3) $G_i(s,s)$ has a unique maximum given by

$$\max_{\tau \in \mathcal{N}_k} G_k(\tau, \tau) = \frac{1}{\Gamma(\mu_k)} \left(\frac{N_k - N_{k-1}}{4}\right)^{\mu_k - 1},$$

where $k = 1, 2, \ldots, n$.

We will now establish the existence results for the Riemann–Liouville constant-order fractional problem (8). Our first result is based on Darbo's fixed-point theorem.

Theorem 2. *Suppose that both (**Hyp1**) and (**Hyp2**) hold, and*

$$\frac{K\left(N_k^{1-\sigma} - N_{k-1}^{1-\sigma}\right)\left(N_k - N_{k-1}\right)^{\mu_k - 1}}{4^{\mu_k - 1}(1-\sigma)\Gamma(\mu_k)} < 1. \qquad (11)$$

Then, the Riemann–Liouville constant-order fractional problem (8) possesses at least one solution on $C([-\gamma, N_k], \mathbb{R})$.

Proof. Consider the operator

$$\mathcal{L} : C([-\gamma, N_k], \mathbb{R}) \to C([-\gamma, N_k], \mathbb{R}),$$

defined by

$$(\mathcal{L}\xi)(s) = \begin{cases} \chi_k(s), \ s \in [-\gamma, N_{k-1}], \\ -\int_{N_{k-1}}^{N_k} G_k(s, \tau) \varphi(\tau, \xi_\tau) d\tau, \ s \in \mathcal{N}_k. \end{cases}$$

Let $v(.) : [-\gamma, N_k] \to \mathbb{R}$ be a function defined by

$$v(s) = \begin{cases} 0, \ if \ s \in \mathcal{N}_k, \\ \chi_k(s), \ if \ s \in [-\gamma, N_{k-1}]. \end{cases}$$

For each $z \in C([N_{k-1}, N_k], \mathbb{R})$, with $z(N_{k-1}) = 0$, we denote by $\bar{z}$ the function defined by

$$\bar{z}(s) = \begin{cases} z(s), \ if \ s \in \mathcal{N}_k, \\ 0, \ if \ s \in [-\gamma, N_{k-1}]. \end{cases}$$

If $\xi(.)$ satisfies the integral equation

$$\xi(s) = -\int_{N_{k-1}}^{N_k} G_k(s, \tau) \varphi(\tau, \xi_\tau) d\tau,$$

then we can decompose $\xi(.)$ as $\xi(s) = z(s) + v(s)$, $N_{k-1} \le s \le N_k$, which implies $\xi_s = \bar{z}_s + v_s$ for every $N_{k-1} \le s \le N_k$, and the function $z(.)$ satisfies

$$z(s) = -\int_{N_{k-1}}^{N_k} G_k(s, \tau) \varphi(\tau, z_\tau + v_\tau) d\tau.$$

Set

$$C_{N_{k-1}} = \{z \in C([N_{k-1}, N_k], \mathbb{R}) : z(N_{k-1}) = 0\}$$

and let $\|.\|_{N_k}$ be the norm in $C_{N_{k-1}}$ defined by

$$\|z\|_{N_k} = \sup_{s \in \mathcal{N}_k} |z(s)|, \ z \in C_{N_{k-1}}.$$

Thus, $C_{N_{k-1}}$ is a Banach space with the norm $\|.\|_{N_k}$. Let the operator $\mathcal{P}: C_{N_{k-1}} \to C_{N_{k-1}}$ be defined by

$$(\mathcal{P}z)(s) = -\int_{N_{k-1}}^{N_k} G_k(s,\tau)\varphi(\tau, \bar{z}_\tau + v_\tau)d\tau, \ s \in \mathcal{N}_k. \tag{12}$$

It follows from the properties of fractional integrals and from the continuity of function $s^\sigma \varphi$ that the operator $\mathcal{P}: C_{N_{k-1}} \to C_{N_{k-1}}$ in (12) is well defined.

Then, it is enough to show that the operator $\mathcal{P}$ has a fixed point z that will guarantee that the operator $\mathcal{L}$ has a fixed point $\xi = \bar{z} + v$, and in consequence, this fixed point will correspond to a solution of the problem (8). Indeed,

$$\begin{aligned}
\xi(s) &= \bar{z}(s) + v(s) \\
&= \begin{cases} z(s), & \text{if } s \in \mathcal{N}_k, \\ \chi_k(s), & \text{if } s \in [-\gamma, N_{k-1}] \end{cases} \\
&= \begin{cases} -\int_{N_{k-1}}^{N_k} G_k(s,\tau)\varphi(\tau, \bar{z}_\tau + v_\tau)d\tau, & \text{if } s \in \mathcal{N}_k, \\ \chi_k(s), & \text{if } s \in [-\gamma, N_{k-1}] \end{cases} \\
&= \begin{cases} -\int_{N_{k-1}}^{N_k} G_k(s,\tau)\varphi(\tau, \xi_\tau)d\tau, & \text{if } s \in \mathcal{N}_k, \\ \chi_k(s), & \text{if } s \in [-\gamma, N_{k-1}] \end{cases} \\
&= (\mathcal{L}\xi)(s).
\end{aligned}$$

Let

$$R_k \geq \frac{\frac{(K\|\chi\|_{[-\gamma,0]} + \varphi^\star)(N_k - N_{k-1})^{\mu_k - 1}\left(N_k^{1-\sigma} - N_{k-1}^{1-\sigma}\right)}{4^{\mu_k - 1}\Gamma(\mu_k)(1-\sigma)}}{1 - \frac{K\left(N_k^{1-\sigma} - N_{k-1}^{1-\sigma}\right)(N_k - N_{k-1})^{\mu_k - 1}}{4^{\mu_k - 1}(1-\sigma)\Gamma(\mu_k)}}$$

with $\varphi^\star = \sup_{s \in \mathcal{N}} s^\sigma |\varphi(s,0)|$, and consider the following set:

$$B_{R_k} = \{z \in C_{N_{k-1}}, \|z\|_{N_k} \leq R_k\}.$$

Clearly, B_{R_k} is nonempty, convex, bounded, and closed.

For $z \in B_{R_k}$ and $s \in \mathcal{N}_k$, we have

$$\begin{aligned}
\|\bar{z}_s\|_{[-\gamma',0]} &= \sup_{-N_{k-1}-\gamma \leq \theta \leq 0} |\bar{z}_s(\theta)| \\
&= \sup_{-N_{k-1}-\gamma \leq \theta \leq 0} |\bar{z}(s+\theta)| \\
&\leq \sup_{-\gamma \leq \tau \leq N_k} |\bar{z}(\tau)| \\
&= \sup_{\tau \in \mathcal{N}_k} |z(\tau)| = \|z\|_{N_k}
\end{aligned}$$

and

$$\begin{aligned}
\|v_s\|_{[-\gamma',0]} &= \sup_{-N_{k-1}-\gamma \leq \theta \leq 0} |v_s(\theta)| \\
&= \sup_{-N_{k-1}-\gamma \leq \theta \leq 0} |v(s+\theta)| \\
&\leq \sup_{-\gamma \leq \tau \leq N_k} |v(\tau)| \\
&= \sup_{-\gamma \leq \tau \leq 0} |v(\tau)| = \sup_{-\gamma \leq \tau \leq 0} |\chi(\tau)| = \|\chi\|_{[-\gamma,0]}.
\end{aligned}$$

We shall show that $\mathcal{P}$ satisfies Theorem 1 in five steps.

Step 1: $P(B_{R_k}) \subseteq (B_{R_k})$.

For $z \in B_{R_k}$, by Proposition 2 and **(Hyp2)**, we obtain

$$
\begin{aligned}
|\mathcal{P}z(s)| &= \left|\int_{N_{k-1}}^{N_k} G_k(s,\tau)\varphi(\tau,\overline{z}_\tau + v_\tau)d\tau\right| \\
&\leq \int_{N_{k-1}}^{N_k} G_k(s,\tau)|\varphi(\tau,\overline{z}_\tau + v_\tau)|d\tau \\
&\leq \frac{1}{\Gamma(\mu_k)}\left(\frac{N_k - N_{k-1}}{4}\right)^{\mu_k-1}\int_{N_{k-1}}^{N_k}|\varphi(\tau,\overline{z}_\tau + v_\tau)|d\tau \\
&\leq \frac{1}{\Gamma(\mu_k)}\left(\frac{N_k - N_{k-1}}{4}\right)^{\mu_k-1}\int_{N_{k-1}}^{N_k}\tau^{-\sigma}\tau^{\sigma}\left|\varphi(\tau,\overline{z}_\tau + v_\tau) - f(\tau,0)\right|d\tau \\
&+ \frac{1}{\Gamma(\mu_k)}\left(\frac{N_k - N_{k-1}}{4}\right)^{\mu_k-1}\int_{N_{k-1}}^{N_k}\tau^{-\sigma}\tau^{\sigma}|\varphi(\tau,0)|d\tau \\
&\leq \frac{1}{\Gamma(\mu_k)}\left(\frac{N_k - N_{k-1}}{4}\right)^{\mu_k-1}\int_{N_{k-1}}^{N_k}\tau^{-\sigma}(K\|\overline{z}_\tau + v_\tau\|_{[-\gamma',0]})d\tau \\
&+ \frac{\varphi^\star (N_k - N_{k-1})^{\mu_k-1}}{\Gamma(\mu_k)4^{\mu_k-1}}\int_{N_{k-1}}^{N_k}\tau^{-\sigma}d\tau \\
&\leq \frac{K}{\Gamma(\mu_k)}\left(\frac{N_k - N_{k-1}}{4}\right)^{\mu_k-1}\int_{N_{k-1}}^{N_k}(\|\overline{z}_\tau\|_{[-\gamma',0]} + \|v_\tau\|_{[-\gamma',0]})\tau^{-\sigma}d\tau \\
&+ \frac{\varphi^\star\left(N_k - N_{k-1}\right)^{\mu_k-1}\left(N_k^{1-\sigma} - N_{k-1}^{1-\sigma}\right)}{4^{\mu_k-1}\Gamma(\mu_k)(1-\sigma)} \\
&\leq \frac{K}{\Gamma(\mu_k)}\left(\frac{N_k - N_{k-1}}{4}\right)^{\mu_k-1}(\|z\|_{N_k} + \|\chi\|_{[-\gamma,0]})\int_{N_{k-1}}^{N_k}\tau^{-\sigma}d\tau \\
&+ \frac{\varphi^\star\left(N_k - N_{k-1}\right)^{\mu_k-1}\left(N_k^{1-\sigma} - N_{k-1}^{1-\sigma}\right)}{4^{\mu_k-1}\Gamma(\mu_k)(1-\sigma)} \\
&\leq \frac{K}{\Gamma(\mu_k)}\left(\frac{N_k - N_{k-1}}{4}\right)^{\mu_k-1}R_k\left(\frac{N_k^{1-\sigma} - N_{k-1}^{1-\sigma}}{1-\sigma}\right) \\
&+ \frac{K}{\Gamma(\mu_k)}\left(\frac{N_k - N_{k-1}}{4}\right)^{\mu_k-1}\|\chi\|_{[-\gamma,0]}\left(\frac{N_k^{1-\sigma} - N_{k-1}^{1-\sigma}}{1-\sigma}\right)
\end{aligned}
$$

$$
\begin{aligned}
&+ \frac{\varphi^\star\left(N_k - N_{k-1}\right)^{\mu_k-1}\left(N_k^{1-\sigma} - N_{k-1}^{1-\sigma}\right)}{4^{\mu_k-1}\Gamma(\mu_k)(1-\sigma)} \\
&\leq \frac{K\left(N_k^{1-\sigma} - N_{k-1}^{1-\sigma}\right)\left(N_k - N_{k-1}\right)^{\mu_k-1}}{4^{\mu_k-1}(1-\sigma)\Gamma(\mu_k)}R_k \\
&+ \frac{\left(N_k - N_{k-1}\right)^{\mu_k-1}\left(N_k^{1-\sigma} - N_{k-1}^{1-\sigma}\right)}{4^{\mu_k-1}\Gamma(\mu_k)(1-\sigma)}\left(K\|\chi\|_{[-\gamma,0]} + \varphi^\star\right) \\
&\leq R_k,
\end{aligned}
$$

which means that $\mathcal{P}(B_{R_k}) \subseteq B_{R_k}$.

Step 2: $\mathcal{P}$ is continuous.

We presume that the sequence (z_n) converges to z in $C_{N_{k-1}}$ and $s \in \mathcal{N}_k$. Then,

$$|\mathcal{P}(z_n)(s) - (\mathcal{P}z)(s)| \leq \int_{N_{k-1}}^{N_k} G_k(s,\tau)\left|\varphi(\tau,\overline{z_n}_\tau + v_\tau) - \varphi(\tau,\overline{z}_\tau + v_\tau)\right|d\tau$$

$$\leq \frac{1}{\Gamma(\mu_k)}\left(\frac{N_k - N_{k-1}}{4}\right)^{\mu_k-1}\int_{N_{k-1}}^{N_k}\left|\varphi(\tau,\overline{z_n}_\tau + v_\tau) - \varphi(\tau,\overline{z}_\tau + v_\tau)\right|d\tau$$

$$\leq \frac{1}{\Gamma(\mu_k)}\left(\frac{N_k - N_{k-1}}{4}\right)^{\mu_k-1}\int_{N_{k-1}}^{N_k}\tau^{-\sigma}K\|\overline{z_n}_\tau - \overline{z}_\tau\|_{[-\gamma',0]}d\tau$$

$$\leq \frac{1}{\Gamma(\mu_k)}\left(\frac{N_k - N_{k-1}}{4}\right)^{\mu_k-1}(K\|z_n - z\|_{N_k})\int_{N_{k-1}}^{N_k}\tau^{-\sigma}d\tau$$

$$\leq \frac{K\left(N_k^{1-\sigma} - T_{k-1}^{1-\sigma}\right)\left(N_k - N_{k-1}\right)^{\mu_k-1}}{4^{\mu_k-1}(1-\sigma)\Gamma(\mu_k)}\|z_n - z\|_{N_k}.$$

Hence, we obtain
$$\|(\mathcal{P}z_n) - (\mathcal{P}z)\|_{N_k} \to 0 \text{ as } n \to \infty.$$

Then, the operator $\mathcal{P}$ is a continuous on $C_{N_{k-1}}$.

Step 3: $\mathcal{P}(B_{R_k})$ is bounded set in $C_{N_{k-1}}$.

As in Step 1, we have $\mathcal{P}(B_{R_k}) \subset B_{R_k}$. This implies that $\mathcal{P}(B_{R_i})$ is bounded set in $C_{T_{i-1}}$.

Step 4: $\mathcal{P}(B_{R_k})$ is equicontinuous set in $C_{N_{k-1}}$.

For arbitrary $s_1, s_2 \in \mathcal{N}_k$, with $s_1 < s_2$, let $z \in B_{R_k}$. Estimate

$$|\mathcal{P}(z)(t_2) - (\mathcal{P}z)(t_1)| = \left|\int_{N_{k-1}}^{N_k} G_k(s_2,\tau)\varphi(\tau,\overline{z}_\tau + v_\tau)d\tau - \int_{N_{k-1}}^{N_k} G_k(s_1,\tau)\varphi(\tau,\overline{z}_\tau + v_\tau)d\tau\right|$$

$$\leq \int_{N_{k-1}}^{N_k}\left|\left(G_k(s_2,\tau) - G_k(s_1,\tau)\right)\varphi(\tau,\overline{z}_\tau + v_\tau)\right|d\tau$$

$$\leq \int_{N_{k-1}}^{N_k}\left|G_k(s_2,\tau) - G_k(s_1,\tau)\right||\varphi(\tau,\overline{z}_\tau + v_\tau)|d\tau$$

$$\leq \int_{N_{k-1}}^{N_k}\left|G_k(s_2,\tau) - G_k(s_1,\tau)\right|\tau^{-\sigma}\left(\tau^\sigma\left|\varphi(\tau,\overline{z}_\tau + v_\tau) - \varphi(\tau,0)\right| + \tau^\sigma|\varphi(\tau,0)|\right)d\tau$$

$$\leq \int_{N_{k-1}}^{N_k}\left|G_k(s_2,\tau) - G_k(s_1,\tau)\right|\left[\tau^{-\sigma}(K\|\overline{z}_\tau + v_\tau\|_{[-\gamma',0]}) + \tau^{-\sigma}\varphi^\star\right]ds$$

$$\leq \int_{N_{k-1}}^{N_k}\left|G_k(s_2,\tau) - G_k(s_1,\tau)\right|\left[\tau^{-\sigma}K(\|\overline{z}_\tau\|_{[-\gamma',0]} + \|v_\tau\|_{[-\gamma',0]}) + \tau^{-\sigma}\varphi^\star\right]d\tau$$

$$\leq \int_{N_{k-1}}^{N_k} \left|G_k(s_2,\tau) - G_k(s_1,\tau)\right| \left[\tau^{-\sigma} K(\|z\|_{N_k} + \|\chi\|_{[-\gamma,0]}) + \varphi^\star\right] d\tau$$

$$\leq K N_{k-1}^{-\sigma}(R + \|\chi\|_{[-\gamma,0]}) \int_{N_{k-1}}^{N_k} \left|G_k(s_2,\tau) - G_k(s_1,\tau)\right| d\tau$$

$$+ \varphi^\star N_{k-1}^{-\sigma} \int_{N_{k-1}}^{N_k} \left|G_k(s_2,\tau) - G_k(s_1,\tau)\right| d\tau.$$

Hence, $|\mathcal{P}(z)(s_2) - (\mathcal{P}z)(s_1)| \to 0$ as $|s_2 - s_1| \to 0$. This implies that $\mathcal{P}(B_{R_k})$ is equicontinuous.

Note that [49] the inequality

$$\zeta\left(s^\delta \varphi(s, B_1)\right) \leq K\zeta_{[-\gamma,0]}(B_1)$$

is equivalent to **(Hyp2)** for each $B_1 \subset C([-\gamma,0], \mathbb{R})$ and $s \in \mathcal{N}$, where B_1 is bounded.

Step 5: $\mathcal{P}$ is L-set contraction.

For $U \subset B_{R_k}, s \in \mathcal{N}_k$, we obtain

$$\begin{aligned}
\zeta(\mathcal{P}(U)(s)) &= \zeta(\{(\mathcal{P}z)(s), z \in U\}) \\
&= \zeta(\{-\int_{N_{k-1}}^{N_k} G_k(s,\tau)\varphi(\tau, \bar{z}_\tau + v_\tau)d\tau, z \in U\}) \\
&\leq \int_{N_{k-1}}^{N_k} G_k(s,\tau)\zeta(\{\varphi(\tau, \bar{z}_\tau + v_\tau), z \in U\}) \\
&\leq \int_{N_{k-1}}^{N_k} G_k(s,\tau)\tau^{-\sigma}\zeta(\{\tau^\sigma \varphi(\tau, \bar{z}_\tau + v_\tau), z \in U\}).
\end{aligned}$$

Remark 3 indicates that

$$\begin{aligned}
\zeta(\mathcal{P}(U)(s)) &\leq \int_{N_{k-1}}^{N_k} G_k(s,\tau)\tau^{-\sigma}[K(\zeta_{[-\gamma',0]}\{\bar{z}_\tau + v_\tau, z \in U\})]d\tau \\
&\leq \int_{N_{k-1}}^{N_k} G_k(s,\tau)\tau^{-\sigma}[K\zeta_{[-\gamma',0]}(\{\bar{z}_\tau, z \in U\} + v_\tau)]d\tau \\
&\leq \int_{N_{k-1}}^{N_k} G_k(s,\tau)\tau^{-\sigma}K[\zeta_{[-\gamma',0]}(\{\bar{z}_\tau, z \in U\})]d\tau \\
&\leq \int_{N_{k-1}}^{N_k} G_k(s,\tau)\tau^{-\sigma}K \sup_{-\gamma' \leq \theta \leq 0} \zeta(\{\bar{z}_\tau(\theta), z \in U\}d\tau \\
&\leq \int_{N_{k-1}}^{N_k} G_k(s,\tau)\tau^{-\sigma}K \sup_{-\gamma' \leq \theta \leq 0} \zeta(\{\bar{z}(\tau+\theta), z \in U\})d\tau \\
&\leq \int_{N_{k-1}}^{N_k} G_k(s,\tau)\tau^{-\sigma}K \sup_{-r \leq t \leq N_k} \zeta(\{\bar{z}(t), z \in U\})d\tau \\
&= \int_{N_{k-1}}^{N_k} G_k(s,\tau)\tau^{-\sigma}K \sup_{N_{k-1} \leq t \leq N_k} \zeta(\{\bar{z}(t), z \in U\} \cup \{0\})d\tau
\end{aligned}$$

$$\leq \int_{N_{k-1}}^{N_k} G_i(s,\tau)\tau^{-\sigma} K \sup_{N_{k-1}\leq t\leq N_k} \zeta(\{\overline{z}(t), z\in U\})d\tau$$

$$\leq \int_{N_{k-1}}^{N_k} G_k(s,\tau)\tau^{-\sigma} K \sup_{N_{k-1}\leq t\leq N_k} \zeta(\{z(t), z\in U\})d\tau$$

$$\leq \int_{N_{k-1}}^{N_k} G_k(s,\tau)\tau^{-\sigma} K \sup_{t\in\mathcal{N}_k} \zeta(U(t))d\tau$$

$$\leq \frac{1}{\Gamma(\mu_k)}\left(\frac{N_k - N_{k-1}}{4}\right)^{\mu_k-1}\left[K\zeta_{\mathcal{N}_k}(U)\int_{\mathcal{N}_{k-1}}^{N_k}\tau^{-\sigma}ds\right],$$

$$\leq \frac{K\left(N_k^{1-\delta} - N_{k-1}^{1-\delta}\right)\left(N_k - N_{k-1}\right)^{\mu_k-1}}{4^{\mu_k-1}(1-\sigma)\Gamma(\mu_k)}\zeta_{\mathcal{N}_k}(U).$$

Therefore,

$$\zeta_{\mathcal{N}_k}(\mathcal{P}U) \leq \frac{K\left(N_k^{1-\sigma} - N_{k-1}^{1-\sigma}\right)\left(N_k - N_{k-1}\right)^{\mu_k-1}}{4^{\mu_k-1}(1-\sigma)\Gamma(\mu_k)}\zeta_{\mathcal{N}_k}(U).$$

Consequently by (11), we deduce that $\mathcal{P}$ is a $\mathcal{L}$-set contraction, where

$$L := \frac{K\left(N_k^{1-\sigma} - N_{k-1}^{1-\sigma}\right)\left(N_k - N_{k-1}\right)^{\mu_k-1}}{4^{\mu_k-1}(1-\sigma)\Gamma(\mu_k)}.$$

Therefore, since all conditions of Theorem 1 are fulfilled we deduce that $\mathcal{P}$ has a fixed point $z_k \in B_{R_k}$.

Then, $\mathcal{L}$ has a fixed point; thus, the Riemann–Liouville constant-order fractional boundary-value problem (8) has at least one solution $\xi_k = \overline{z_k} + v \in C([-\gamma, N_k], \mathbb{R})$. □

Now, we will prove the existence result for the Riemann–Liouville fractional problem of variable order (1).

Theorem 3. *Let the hypotheses (Hyp1), (Hyp2) and inequality (11) be satisfied for all $k \in \{1, 2, \ldots, n\}$. Then, the Riemann–Liouville fractional problem of variable order (1) possesses at least one solution in $C([-\gamma, N], \mathbb{R})$.*

Proof. For all $k \in \{1, 2, \ldots, n\}$ according to Theorem 2, the Riemann–Liouville constant-order fractional boundary-value problem (8) possesses at least one solution $\xi_k \in C([-\gamma, N_k], \mathbb{R})$. For any $k \in \{1, 2, \ldots, n\}$, we have

$$\xi_1(s) = \overline{z_1}(s) + v(s) = \begin{cases} \chi(s), & s \in [-\gamma, 0], \\ z_1(s), & s \in \mathcal{N}_1 \end{cases}$$

and for any $k \in \{2, \ldots, n\}$

$$\xi_k(s) = \overline{z_k}(s) + v(s) = \begin{cases} \chi(s), & s \in [-\gamma, 0], \\ 0, & s \in [0, N_{k-1}], \\ z_k(s), & s \in \mathcal{N}_k. \end{cases}$$

Thus, the function $\xi_k \in C([-\gamma, N_k], \mathbb{R})$ satisfies the integral Equation (7) for $s \in \mathcal{N}_k$ with $\xi_k(0) = 0$, $\xi_k(N_k) = z_k(N_k) = 0$ and $\xi_k(s) = \chi(s)$ for $s \in [-\gamma, 0]$.

Then, the function

$$\zeta(s) = \begin{cases} \zeta_1(s) = \begin{cases} \chi(s), & s \in [-\gamma, 0], \\ z_1(s), & s \in \mathcal{N}_1, \end{cases} \\ \zeta_2(s) = \begin{cases} \chi(s), & s \in [-\gamma, 0], \\ 0, & s \in \mathcal{N}_1, \\ z_2(s), & s \in \mathcal{N}_2, \end{cases} \\ \vdots \\ \zeta_n(s) = \begin{cases} \chi(s), & s \in [-\gamma, 0], \\ 0, & s \in [0, N_{n-1}], \\ z_n(s), & s \in \mathcal{N}_n, \end{cases} \end{cases}.$$

gives the solution for the Riemann–Liouville fractional problem of variable order (1). □

Remark 5. *The existence results for fractional delay differential equations of constant order are well established [33–38], but very little research has been done on delay fractional variable-order systems because of the complex features of fractional variable-order derivatives [32]. Theorems 2 and 3 extend the existent results to boundary-value problems for variable-order fractional delay differential equations. The offered results are established by converting the Riemann–Liouville fractional boundary-value problem of variable order (1) to a standard Riemann–Liouville fractional boundary-value problem with constant-order fractional derivatives (8), and using piecewise constant functions, the Kuratowski measure of noncompactness in the context of Darbo's fixed-point theorem.*

Remark 6. *Our results also extend and generalize some recently published existence results on boundary-value problems for fractional variable-order differential equations without delays [15,23,24,26,27,50] to the delay case, considering that the delay terms in the models are more general and more relevant to the real-world applied problems.*

Remark 7. *Unlike the existing results in [32] for the delay fractional variable-order problem, in this study we consider the Riemann–Liouville variable-order fractional derivatives of order $\mu : \mathcal{N} \to (1,2]$ and apply Darbo's fixed-point theorem together with the Kuratowski measure of noncompactness. In fact, due to the superiority of this strategy, it is intensively applied to fractional variable-order problems [23,27]. In the further investigations of the proposed boundary-value problem, different approaches may be applied, and the corresponding comparisons can be made.*

We expect that the proposed results will motivate the researchers regarding further development of the topic.

4. Ulam–Hyers Stability

Existence criteria are necessary when we study the qualitative behavior of the solutions. In order to demonstrate the applicability of the proposed in Section 2 criteria, we will provide Ulam–Hyers stability results.

Theorem 4. *Assume that conditions **(Hyp1)**, **(Hyp2)** and (11) hold. Then, the Equation (1) is Ulam–Hyers stable.*

Proof. Let $\epsilon > 0$ be arbitrary, and the function $y \in C([-\gamma, N], \mathbb{R})$ satisfies the following inequality:

$$\begin{cases} |D_{0^+}^{\mu(s)} y(s) - \varphi(s, y_s)| \leq \epsilon, & s \in \mathcal{N} := [0, N], \\ y(s) = \chi(s), & s \in [-\gamma, 0]. \end{cases} \quad (13)$$

We define the functions

$$y_1(s) = \begin{cases} y(s), & s \in [0, N_1], \\ \chi(s), & s \in [-\gamma, 0] \end{cases} \quad (14)$$

and for $k = 2, 3, \ldots, n$:

$$y_k(s) = \begin{cases} \chi(s), & s \in [-\gamma, 0], \\ 0, & s \in [0, N_{k-1}], \\ y(s), & s \in \mathcal{N}_k. \end{cases} \quad (15)$$

For any $k \in \{1, 2, \ldots, n\}$ according to equality (7) for $s \in \mathcal{N}_k$, we obtain

$$D_{0+}^{\mu(s)} y_k(s) = \frac{1}{\Gamma(2-\mu_k)} \left(\frac{d}{ds}\right)^2 \int_{N_{k-1}}^{s} (s-\tau)^{1-\mu_k} y(\tau) d\tau.$$

Taking $I_{N_{k-1}^+}^{\mu_k}$ on both sides of (13), we obtain

$$\left| y(s) + \int_{N_{k-1}}^{N_k} G_k(s,\tau) \varphi(\tau, y_\tau) d\tau \right| \leq \frac{\epsilon}{\Gamma(\mu_k)} \int_{N_{k-1}}^{s} (s-\tau)^{\mu_k - 1} d\tau$$

$$\leq \epsilon \frac{(N_k - N_{k-1})^{\mu_k}}{\Gamma(\mu_k + 1)}.$$

According to Theorem 3, the Riemann–Liouville fractional problem (1) of variable order has a solution $\xi \in C([-\gamma, N], \mathbb{R})$ defined by $\xi(s) = \xi_k(s)$ for $s \in [0, N_k]$, $k = 1, 2, \ldots, n$, where

$$\xi_1(s) = \begin{cases} \chi(s), & s \in [-\gamma, 0] \\ z_1(s), & s \in \mathcal{N}_1, \end{cases} \quad (16)$$

and for any $k \in \{2, \ldots, n\}$

$$\xi_k(s) = \begin{cases} \chi(s), & s \in [-\gamma, 0], \\ 0, & s \in [0, N_{k-1}], \\ z_k(s), & s \in \mathcal{N}_k \end{cases} \quad (17)$$

and $\xi_k \in C([-\gamma, N_k], \mathbb{R})$ is a solution of the Riemann–Liouville constant-order fractional problem (8). According to Lemma 6, we have

$$\xi_k(s) = -\int_{N_{k-1}}^{N_k} G_k(s,\tau) \varphi(\tau, (\xi_k)_\tau) d\tau. \quad (18)$$

Let $s \in \mathcal{N}_k$, $k \in \{1, 2, \ldots, n\}$. Then, by (15), (16), (17), and (18), we obtain

$$\begin{aligned}
|y(s) - \xi(s)| &= |y(s) - \xi_k(s)| = |y_k(s) - \xi_k(s)| \\
&= \left| y_k(s) + \int_{N_{k-1}}^{N_k} G_k(s,\tau) \varphi(\tau, (\xi_k)_\tau) d\tau \right| \\
&\leq \left| y_k(s) + \int_{N_{k-1}}^{N_k} G_k(s,\tau) \varphi(\tau, (y_k)_\tau) d\tau \right| + \int_{N_{k-1}}^{N_k} G_k(s,\tau) \left| \varphi(\tau, (y_k)_\tau) - \varphi(\tau, (\xi_k)_\tau) \right| d\tau \\
&\leq \epsilon \frac{(N_k - N_{k-1})^{\mu_k}}{\Gamma(\mu_k + 1)} \\
&\quad + K \frac{1}{\Gamma(\mu_k)} \left(\frac{N_k - N_{k-1}}{4}\right)^{\mu_k - 1} \int_{N_{k-1}}^{N_k} \tau^{-\sigma} \|(y_k)_\tau - (\xi_k)_\tau\|_{[-\gamma', 0]} d\tau
\end{aligned}$$

$$\leq \epsilon \frac{(N_k - N_{k-1})^{\mu_k}}{\Gamma(\mu_k + 1)}$$
$$+ K \frac{1}{\Gamma(\mu_k)} \left(\frac{N_k - N_{k-1}}{4}\right)^{\mu_k - 1} \int_{N_{k-1}}^{N_k} \tau^{-\sigma} \sup_{-N_{k-1} - \gamma \leq \theta \leq 0} |(y_k)_\tau(\theta) - (\xi_k)_\tau(\theta)| d\tau$$

$$\leq \epsilon \frac{(N_k - N_{k-1})^{\mu_k}}{\Gamma(\mu_k + 1)}$$
$$+ K \frac{1}{\Gamma(\mu_k)} \left(\frac{N_k - N_{k-1}}{4}\right)^{\mu_k - 1} \int_{N_{k-1}}^{N_k} \tau^{-\sigma} \sup_{-N_{k-1} - \gamma \leq \theta \leq 0} |y_k(\tau + \theta) - \xi_k(\tau + \theta)| d\tau$$

$$\leq \epsilon \frac{(N_k - N_{k-1})^{\mu_k}}{\Gamma(\mu_k + 1)}$$
$$+ K \frac{1}{\Gamma(\mu_k)} \left(\frac{N_k - N_{k-1}}{4}\right)^{\mu_k - 1} \int_{N_{k-1}}^{N_k} \tau^{-\sigma} \sup_{-\gamma \leq t \leq T_k} |y_k(t) - x_k(t)| d\tau$$

$$\leq \epsilon \frac{(N_k - N_{k-1})^{\mu_k}}{\Gamma(\mu_k + 1)}$$
$$+ K \frac{1}{\Gamma(\mu_k)} \left(\frac{N_k - N_{k-1}}{4}\right)^{\mu_k - 1} \int_{N_{k-1}}^{N_k} \tau^{-\sigma} \|y_k - \xi_k\|_{[-\gamma, N_k]} d\tau$$

$$\leq \epsilon \frac{(N_k - N_{k-1})^{\mu_k}}{\Gamma(\mu_k + 1)}$$
$$+ K \frac{1}{\Gamma(\mu_k)} \left(\frac{N_k - N_{k-1}}{4}\right)^{\mu_k - 1} \|y_k - \xi_k\|_{[-\gamma, N_k]} \int_{N_{k-1}}^{N_k} \tau^{-\sigma} d\tau$$

$$\leq \epsilon \frac{(N_k - N_{k-1})^{\mu_k}}{\Gamma(\mu_k + 1)} + \frac{K \left(N_k^{1-\sigma} - N_{k-1}^{1-\sigma}\right) \left(N_k - N_{k-1}\right)^{\mu_k - 1}}{4^{\mu_k - 1}(1 - \sigma)\Gamma(\mu_k)} \|y_k - \xi_k\|_{[-\gamma, N_k]}$$

$$\leq \epsilon \frac{(N_k - N_{k-1})^{\mu_k}}{\Gamma(\mu_k + 1)} + \nu \|y_k - \xi_k\|_{[-\gamma, N_k]},$$

where
$$\nu = \max_{k=1,2,\ldots,n} \frac{K \left(N_k^{1-\sigma} - N_{k-1}^{1-\sigma}\right) \left(N_k - N_{k-1}\right)^{\mu_k - 1}}{4^{\mu_k - 1}(1 - \sigma)\Gamma(\mu_k)}.$$

Then,
$$\|y - \xi\|_{[-\gamma, N_k]}(1 - \nu) \leq \epsilon \frac{(N_k - N_{k-1})^{\mu_k}}{\Gamma(\mu_k + 1)},$$

and so for $c_\varphi := \frac{(N_k - N_{k-1})^{\mu_k}}{(1-\nu)\Gamma(\mu_k + 1)}$,

$$\|y - \xi\|_{[-\gamma, N_k]} \leq c_\varphi \epsilon,$$

i.e.,
$$|y(s) - \xi(s)| \leq c_\varphi \epsilon, \ s \in [-\gamma, N_k].$$

Then, by Definition 4, the Riemann–Liouville fractional problem (1) of variable order is Ulam–Hyers stable. □

Remark 8. *With the established result in this section, we contribute to the development of the Ulam–Hyers stability theory for fractional variable-order models. In fact, due to the great opportunities for applications, this stability notion has been studied by numerous authors [24,46,47,50]. In addition,* the qualitative results offered by Theorem 4 demonstrate the opportunities for applications of the existence criteria proved in Theorems 2 and 3.

5. Illustrative Examples

Example 1. Let $\gamma > 0$,

$$\mu(s) = \begin{cases} \frac{7}{5}, & s \in \mathcal{N}_1 := [0,1], \\ \frac{3}{2}, & s \in \mathcal{N}_2 :=]1,2] \end{cases} \tag{19}$$

and consider the following Riemann–Liouville fractional variable-order boundary-value problem:

$$\begin{cases} D_{0^+}^{\mu(s)} \xi(s) = \frac{s^{-\frac{1}{2}}}{4e^s(1+\|\xi_s\|_{[-\gamma,0]})}, & s \in \mathcal{N} :=]0,2], \\ \xi(s) = \chi(s), & s \in [-\gamma, 0]. \end{cases} \tag{20}$$

The choice of $\mu(s)$ guarantee that **(Hyp1)** holds. Let

$$\varphi(s, y_s) = \frac{s^{-\frac{1}{2}}}{4e^s(1+\|y_s\|_{[-\gamma,0]})}, \quad (s, y_s) \in [0,2] \times C([-\gamma, 0], \mathbb{R}).$$

For $y, z \in C([-\gamma, 2], \mathbb{R})$ and $s \in \mathcal{N}$, we have

$$\begin{aligned}
s^{\frac{1}{2}}|\varphi(s, y_s) - \varphi(s, z_s)| &= \left| \frac{1}{4e^s} \left(\frac{1}{1+\|y_s\|_{[-\gamma,0]}} - \frac{1}{1+\|z_s\|_{[-\gamma,0]}} \right) \right| \\
&\leq \frac{|\|y_s\|_{[-\gamma,0]} - \|z_s\|_{[-\gamma,0]}|}{4e^s(1+\|y_s\|_{[-\gamma,0]})(1+\|y_s\|_{[-\gamma,0]})} \\
&\leq \frac{1}{4e^s}(\|y_s - z_s\|_{[-\gamma,0]}) \\
&\leq \frac{1}{4}\|y_s - z_s\|_{[-\gamma,0]}.
\end{aligned}$$

Hence, **(Hyp2)** holds for $\sigma = \frac{1}{2}$ and $K = \frac{1}{4}$.

By (19), according to (8) we consider the following two auxiliary problems for Riemann–Liouville fractional differential equations of constant orders:

$$\begin{cases} D_{0^+}^{\frac{7}{5}} \xi(s) = \frac{s^{-\frac{1}{2}}}{4e^s(1+\|\xi_s\|_{[-\gamma,0]})}, & s \in \mathcal{N}_1, \\ \xi(0) = 0, \ \xi(1) = 0, \\ \xi(s) = \chi_1(s), & s \in [-\gamma, 0] \end{cases} \tag{21}$$

and

$$\begin{cases} D_{0^+}^{\frac{3}{2}} \xi(s) = \frac{s^{-\frac{1}{2}}}{4e^s(1+\|\xi_s\|_{[-\gamma,0]})}, & s \in \mathcal{N}_2, \\ \xi(1) = 0, \ \xi(2) = 0, \\ \xi(s) = \chi_2(s), & s \in [-\gamma, 1], \end{cases} \tag{22}$$

where $\chi_1 = \chi$ and

$$\chi_2(s) = \begin{cases} 0, & \text{if } s \in [0,1], \\ \chi(s), & \text{if } s \in [-\gamma, 0]. \end{cases}$$

We will show also that condition (11) is satisfied for $k = 1$. Indeed,

$$\frac{K\left(N_1^{1-\sigma} - N_0^{1-\sigma}\right)(N_1 - N_0)^{\mu_1 - 1}}{4^{\mu_1 - 1}(1-\sigma)\Gamma(\mu_1)} = \frac{\frac{1}{4}\left(1^{1-\frac{1}{2}} - 0^{1-\frac{1}{2}}\right)(1-0)^{\frac{7}{5}-1}}{4^{\frac{7}{5}-1}(1-\frac{1}{2})\Gamma(\frac{7}{5})} \simeq 0.323663 < 1.$$

By Theorem 2, the problem (21) has a solution $\xi_1 \in C([-\gamma, 1], \mathbb{R})$, where

$$\xi_1(s) = \begin{cases} \chi(s), & s \in [-\gamma, 0], \\ z_1(s), & s \in \mathcal{N}_1. \end{cases}$$

We also have that

$$\frac{K\left(N_2^{1-\sigma} - N_1^{1-\sigma}\right)(N_2 - N_1)^{\mu_2 - 1}}{4^{\mu_2 - 1}(1-\sigma)\Gamma(\mu_2)} = \frac{\frac{1}{4}\left(2^{1-\frac{1}{2}} - 1^{1-\frac{1}{2}}\right)(2-1)^{\frac{3}{2}-1}}{4^{\frac{3}{2}-1}(1-\frac{1}{2})\Gamma(\frac{3}{2})}$$

$$\simeq 0.11684748 < 1.$$

Thus, (11) is fulfilled for $k = 2$. According to Theorem 2, the problem (22) possesses a solution $\xi_2 \in C([-\gamma, 2], \mathbb{R})$, where

$$\xi_2(s) = \begin{cases} \chi(s), & s \in [-\gamma, 0], \\ 0, & s \in [0, 1], \\ z_2(s), & t \in \mathcal{N}_2. \end{cases}$$

Then, by Theorem 3, the problem (20) has a solution

$$\xi(s) = \begin{cases} \xi_1(s) = \begin{cases} \chi(s), & s \in [-\gamma, 0], \\ z_1(s), & s \in \mathcal{N}_1, \end{cases} \\ \xi_2(s) = \begin{cases} \chi(s), & s \in [-\gamma, 0], \\ 0, & s \in \mathcal{N}_1, \\ z_2(s), & s \in \mathcal{N}_2, \end{cases} \end{cases}$$

In addition, according to Theorem 4, problem (20) is Ulam–Hyers-stable.

Example 2. Let $\gamma > 0$,

$$\mu(s) = \begin{cases} \frac{7}{5}, & s \in \mathcal{N}_1 := [0, 1], \\ \frac{8}{5}, & s \in \mathcal{N}_2 :=]1, \frac{3}{2}], \\ \frac{3}{2}, & s \in \mathcal{N}_3 :=]\frac{3}{2}, 2]. \end{cases} \quad (23)$$

and consider the following Riemann–Liouville fractional variable-order boundary-value problem:

$$\begin{cases} D_{0^+}^{\mu(s)}\xi(s) = \dfrac{s^{-\frac{1}{3}}}{(e^{e^{\frac{s^3}{1+s}}} + 6)(1 + \|x_s\|_{[-\gamma, 0]})}, & s \in \mathcal{N} :=]0, 2], \\ \xi(s) = \chi(s), & s \in [-\gamma, 0], \end{cases} \quad (24)$$

The choice of $\mu(s)$ guarantees that **(Hyp1)** holds. Let

$$\varphi(s, y_s) = \frac{s^{-\frac{1}{3}}}{(e^{e^{\frac{s^3}{1+s}}} + 6)(1 + \|y_s\|_{[-\gamma, 0]})}, \quad (s, y_s) \in [0, 2] \times C([-\gamma, 0], \mathbb{R}).$$

For $y, z \in C([-\gamma, 2], \mathbb{R})$ and $s \in \mathcal{N}$, we have

$$s^{\frac{1}{3}}|\varphi(s, y_s) - \varphi(s, z_s)| = \left|\frac{1}{(e^{e^{\frac{s^3}{1+s}}} + 6)}\left(\frac{1}{1 + \|y_s\|_{[-\gamma, 0]}} - \frac{1}{1 + \|z_s\|_{[-\gamma, 0]}}\right)\right|$$

$$\leq \frac{|\|y_s\|_{[-\gamma, 0]} - \|z_s\|_{[-\gamma, 0]}|}{(e^{e^{\frac{s^3}{1+s}}} + 6)(1 + \|y_s\|_{[-\gamma, 0]})(1 + \|y_s\|_{[-\gamma, 0]})}$$

$$\leq \frac{1}{(ee^{\frac{s^3}{1+s}}+6)}\|y_t - z_s\|_{[-\gamma,0]}$$

$$\leq \frac{1}{e+6}\|y_s - z_s\|_{[-\gamma,0]}.$$

Hence, **(Hyp2)** holds for $\sigma = \frac{1}{3}$ and $K = \frac{1}{e+6}$.

By (23), according to (8) we consider three auxiliary problems for Riemann–Liouville fractional differential equations of constant order

$$\begin{cases} D_{0^+}^{\frac{7}{5}}\zeta(s) = \frac{s^{-\frac{1}{3}}}{(ee^{\frac{s^3}{1+s}}+6)(1+\|x_s\|_{[-\gamma,0]})}, & s \in \mathcal{N}_1, \\ \zeta(0) = 0, \ \zeta(1) = 0, \\ \zeta(s) = \chi_1(s), & s \in [-\gamma, 0], \end{cases} \quad (25)$$

$$\begin{cases} D_{0^+}^{\frac{6}{5}}\zeta(s) = \frac{s^{-\frac{1}{3}}}{(ee^{\frac{s^3}{1+s}}+6)(1+\|x_s\|_{[-\gamma,0]})}, & s \in \mathcal{N}_2, \\ \zeta(1) = 0, \ \zeta(\frac{3}{2}) = 0, \\ \zeta(s) = \chi_2(s), & s \in [-\gamma, 1], \end{cases} \quad (26)$$

and

$$\begin{cases} D_{0^+}^{\frac{3}{2}} = \frac{s^{-\frac{1}{3}}}{(ee^{\frac{s^3}{1+s}}+6)(1+\|x_s\|_{[-\gamma,0]})}, & s \in \mathcal{N}_3, \\ \zeta(\frac{3}{2}) = 0, \ x(2) = 0, \\ \zeta(s) = \chi_2(s), & s \in [-\gamma, \frac{3}{2}], \end{cases} \quad (27)$$

where $\chi_1 = \chi$,

$$\chi_2(s) = \begin{cases} 0, & \text{if } s \in [0,1], \\ \chi(s), & \text{if } s \in [-\gamma, 0] \end{cases}$$

and

$$\chi_3(s) = \begin{cases} 0, & \text{if } s \in [0, \frac{3}{2}], \\ \chi(s), & \text{if } s \in [-\gamma, 0]. \end{cases}$$

We will also show that condition (11) is satisfied for $k = 1$. Indeed,

$$\frac{K\left(N_1^{1-\sigma} - N_0^{1-\sigma}\right)\left(N_1 - N_0\right)^{\mu_1 - 1}}{4^{\mu_1 - 1}(1-\sigma)\Gamma(\mu_1)} = \frac{\frac{1}{e+6}\left(1^{1-\frac{1}{3}} - 0^{1-\frac{1}{3}}\right)(1-0)^{\frac{7}{5}-1}}{4^{\frac{7}{5}-1}(1-\frac{1}{3})\Gamma(\frac{7}{5})} \simeq 0.11137 < 1.$$

By Theorem 2, the problem (25) has a solution $\zeta_1 \in C([-\gamma, 1], \mathbb{R})$, where

$$\zeta_1(s) = \begin{cases} \chi(s), & s \in [-\gamma, 0] \\ z_1(s), & s \in \mathcal{N}_1. \end{cases}$$

We also have that

$$\frac{K\left(N_2^{1-\sigma} - N_1^{1-\sigma}\right)\left(N_2 - N_1\right)^{\mu_2 - 1}}{4^{\mu_2 - 1}(1-\sigma)\Gamma(\mu_2)} = \frac{\frac{1}{e+6}\left(\frac{3}{2}^{1-\frac{1}{3}} - 1^{1-\frac{1}{3}}\right)\left(\frac{3}{2}-1\right)^{\frac{6}{5}-1}}{4^{\frac{6}{5}-1}(1-\frac{1}{3})\Gamma(\frac{6}{5})}$$

$$\simeq 0.03837 < 1.$$

Thus, (11) is fulfilled for $k = 2$. According to Theorem 2, the BVP (26) possesses a solution $\zeta_2 \in C([-\gamma, \frac{3}{2}], \mathbb{R})$, where

$$\zeta_2(s) = \begin{cases} \chi(s), & s \in [-\gamma, 0], \\ 0, & s \in [0, 1], \\ z_2(s), & s \in \mathcal{N}_2. \end{cases}$$

We also have that

$$\frac{K\left(N_3^{1-\sigma} - N_2^{1-\sigma}\right)(N_3 - N_2)^{\mu_3 - 1}}{4^{\mu_3 - 1}(1-\sigma)\Gamma(\mu_3)} = \frac{\frac{1}{e+6}\left(2^{1-\frac{1}{3}} - \frac{3}{2}^{1-\frac{1}{3}}\right)\left(2 - \frac{3}{2}\right)^{\frac{3}{2}-1}}{4^{\frac{3}{2}-1}(1-\frac{1}{3})\Gamma(\frac{3}{2})}$$

$$\simeq 0.01901 < 1.$$

Thus, (11) is fulfilled for $k = 3$. According to Theorem 2, the BVP (27) possesses a solution $\zeta_3 \in C([-\gamma, 2], \mathbb{R})$, where

$$\zeta_3(s) = \begin{cases} \chi(s), & s \in [-\gamma, 0], \\ 0, & s \in [0, \frac{3}{2}], \\ z_3(s), & s \in \mathcal{N}_3. \end{cases}$$

Then, by Theorem 3, problem (24) has a solution

$$\zeta(s) = \begin{cases} \zeta_1(s) = \begin{cases} \chi(s), & s \in [-\gamma, 0], \\ z_1(s), & s \in \mathcal{N}_1, \end{cases} \\ \zeta_2(s) = \begin{cases} \chi(s), & s \in [-\gamma, 0], \\ 0, & s \in]0, N_1], \\ z_2(s), & s \in \mathcal{N}_2, \end{cases} \\ \zeta_3(s) = \begin{cases} \chi(s), & s \in [-\gamma, 0], \\ 0, & s \in]0, N_2], \\ z_3(s), & s \in \mathcal{N}_3. \end{cases} \end{cases}$$

In addition, according to Theorem 4, problem (24) is Ulam–Hyers stable.

Remark 9. *The constructed examples show the capability of the elaborated existence and stability results.*

6. Conclusions

This research introduces a boundary-value problem for a Riemann–Liouville nonlinear fractional differential equation of variable order with finite delay. The analytical solutions have been successfully investigated via three strategies: the Kuratowski measure of noncompactness, Darbo's fixed-point theorem, and the Ulam–Hyers stability concept. We established existence and stability criteria for the solutions of the problem under consideration. The presented new results generalize some existing results for the Riemann–Liouville delayed fractional differential equation of constant order considering the variable order of fractional derivatives. Two examples are given at the end to support and validate the potentiality of the obtained results. We expect that the proposed results will motivate the researchers in the further development of the topic. The established existence results are essential in the qualitative investigation of the introduced problem. Additionally, since the Riemann–Liouville delayed fractional differential equations of variable order are intensively applied in the mathematical modeling, our research is practically important. Hence, the application of our results to some Riemann–Liouville fractional-neural-network models of variable order with finite delay is an interesting topic for a future research. The obtained results can also be applied in the investigation of numerous qualitative properties of the solutions. In addition, it is possible to extend the proposed results to the impulsive case and study the effect of some impulsive controllers on the fundamental and qualitative behavior of the solutions.

Author Contributions: Conceptualization, B.T. and M.S.S.; methodology, B.T., M.S.S. and I.S.; formal analysis, B.T., M.S.S. and I.S.; investigation, B.T., M.S.S. and I.S.; and writing—original draft preparation, I.S. All authors have read and agreed to the published version of the manuscript.

Funding: This research received no external funding.

Institutional Review Board Statement: Not applicable.

Informed Consent Statement: Not applicable.

Data Availability Statement: Not applicable.

Conflicts of Interest: The authors declare no conflict of interest.

References

1. Baleanu, D.; Diethelm, K.; Scalas, E.; Trujillo, J.J. *Fractional Calculus: Models and Numerical Methods*, 1st ed.; World Scientific: Singapore, 2012; ISBN 978-981-4355-20-9.
2. Magin, R. *Fractional Calculus in Bioengineering*, 1st ed.; Begell House: Redding, CA, USA, 2006; ISBN 978-1567002157.
3. Kilbas, A.; Srivastava, H.M.; Trujillo, J.J. *Theory and Applications of Fractional Differential Equations*, 1st ed.; Elsevier: New York, NY, USA, 2006; ISBN 9780444518323.
4. Petráš, I. *Fractional-Order Nonlinear Systems*, 1st ed.; Springer: Heidelberg, Germany; Dordrecht, The Netherlands; London, UK; New York, NY, USA, 2011; ISBN 978-3-642-18101-6.
5. Samko, S.G.; Kilbas, A.A.; Marichev, O.I. *Fractional Integrals and Derivatives: Theory and Applications*, 1st ed.; Gordon and Breach: Yverdon, Switzerland, 1993; ISBN 9782881248641.
6. Stamova, I.M.; Stamov, G.T. *Functional and Impulsive Differential Equations of Fractional Order: Qualitative Analysis and Applications*, 1st ed.; Taylor & Francis Group: Boca Raton, FL, USA, 2017; ISBN 9781498764834.
7. Tarasov, V.E. *Fractional Dynamics: Application of Fractional Calculus to Dynamics of Particles, Fields and Media*, 1st ed.; Springer: Beijing, China, 2015; ISBN 978-3-642-14003-7.
8. Abdelhadi, M.; Alhazmi, S.E.; Al-Omari, S. On a class of partial differential equations and their solution via local factional integrals and derivatives. *Fractal Fract.* **2022**, *6*, 210. [CrossRef]
9. Al-Sawalha, M.M.; Shah, R.; Nonlaopon, K.; Ababneh, O.Y. Numerical investigation of fractional-order wave-like equation. *AIMS Mathem.* **2023**, *8*, 5281–5302. [CrossRef]
10. Al-Sawalha, M.M.; Shah, R.; Nonlaopon, K.; Khan, I.; Ababneh, O.Y. Fractional evaluation of Kaup–Kupershmidt equation with the exponential-decay kernel. *AIMS Mathem.* **2022**, *8*, 3730–3746. [CrossRef]
11. Al-Sawalha, M.M.; Ababneh, O.Y.; Shah, R.; Khan, I.; Nonlaopon, K. Numerical analysis of fractional-order Whitham–Broer–Kaup equations with non-singular kernel operators. *AIMS Mathem.* **2022**, *8*, 2308–2336. [CrossRef]
12. Qin, H.; Liu, J.; Zuo, X. Controllability problem for fractional integrodifferential evolution systems of mixed type with the measure of noncompactness. *J. Inequal. Appl.* **2014**, *2014*, 292. [CrossRef]
13. Sivasankar, S.; Udhayakumar, R.; Subramanian, V.; AlNemer, G.; Elshenhab, A.M. Existence of Hilfer fractional stochastic differential equations with nonlocal conditions and delay via almost sectorial operators. *Mathematics* **2022**, *10*, 4392. [CrossRef]
14. Almeida, R.; Tavares, D.; Torres, D.F.M. *The Variable-Order Fractional Calculus of Variations*, 1st ed.; Springer: Cham, Switzerland, 2019; ISBN 978-3-319-94005-2.
15. Benkerrouche, A.; Souid, M.S.; Stamov, G.; Stamova, I. On the solutions of a quadratic integral equation of the Urysohn type of fractional variable order. *Entropy* **2022**, *24*, 886. [CrossRef]
16. Zhang, S.; Hu, L. The existence of solutions and generalized Lyapunov-type inequalities to boundary-value problems of differential equations of variable order. *AIMS Math.* **2020**, *5*, 2923–2943. [CrossRef]
17. Zhang, S.; Sun, S.; Hu, L. Approximate solutions to initial value problem for differential equation of variable order. *J. Fract. Calc. Appl.* **2018**, *9*, 93–112.
18. Odzijewicz, T.; Malinowska, A.B.; Torres, D.F.M. Fractional variational calculus of variable order. In *Advances in Harmonic Analysis and Operator Theory. Operator Theory: Advances and Applications*, 1st ed.; Almeida, A., Castro, L., Speck, F.O., Eds.; Birkhäuser: Basel, Switzerland, 2013; Volume 229, pp. 291–301.
19. Patnaik, S.; Hollkamp, J.P.; Semperlotti, F. Applications of variable-order fractional operators: A review. *Proc. R. Soc. A* **2020**, *476*, 20190498. [CrossRef]
20. Sun, H.G.; Chen, W.; Chen, Y.Q. Variable-order fractional differential operators in anomalous diffusion modeling. *Physica A* **2009**, *388*, 4586–4592. [CrossRef]
21. Lu, X.; Li, H.; Chen, N. An indicator for the electrode aging of lithium-ion batteries using a fractional variable order model. *Electrochim. Acta* **2019**, *299*, 378–387. [CrossRef]

22. Sweilam, N.H.; AL-Mekhlafi, S.M.; Alshomrani, A.S.; Baleanu, D. Comparative study for optimal control nonlinear variable-order fractional tumor model. *Chaos Solitons Fract.* **2020**, *136*, 1–10. [CrossRef]
23. Benkerrouche, A.; Baleanu, D.; Souid, M.S.; Hakem, A.; Inc, M. Boundary-value problem for nonlinear fractional differential equations of variable order via Kuratowski MNC technique. *Adv. Differ. Equ.* **2021**, *365*, 1–19. [CrossRef]
24. Benkerrouche, A.; Souid, M.S.; Etemad, S.; Hakem, A.; Agarwal, P.; Rezapour, S.; Ntouyas, S.K.; Tariboon, J. Qualitative study on solutions of a Hadamard variable order boundary problem via the Ulam–Hyers-Rassias stability. *Fractal Fract.* **2021**, *5*, 108. [CrossRef]
25. Benkerrouche, A.; Souid, M.S.; Karapinar, E.; Hakem, A. On the boundary-value problems of Hadamard fractional differential equations of variable order. *Math. Meth. Appl. Sci.* **2022**. [CrossRef]
26. Benkerrouche, A.; Souid, M.S.; Sitthithakerngkiet, K.; Hakem, A. Implicit nonlinear fractional differential equations of variable order. *Bound. Value Probl.* **2021**, *2021*, 64. [CrossRef]
27. Refice, A.; Souid, M.S.; Stamova, I. On the boundary-value problems of Hadamard fractional differential equations of variable order via Kuratowski MNC technique. *Mathematics* **2021**, *9*, 1134. [CrossRef]
28. Ali, K.K.; Mohamed, E.M.H.; El-Salam, M.A.A.; Nisar, K.S.; Khashan, M.M.; Zakarya, M. A collocation approach for multiterm variable-order fractional delay-differential equations using shifted Chebyshev polynomials. *Alex. Eng. J.* **2022**, *61*, 3511–3526. [CrossRef]
29. Boyadzhiev, D.; Kiskinov, H.; Veselinova, M.; Zahariev, A. Stability analysis of linear distributed order fractional systems with distributed delays. *Fract. Calc. Appl. Anal.* **2017**, *20*, 914–935. [CrossRef]
30. Solís–Pérez, J.E.; Gómez-Aguilar, J.F. Variable-order fractal-fractional time delay equations with power, exponential and Mittag–Leffler laws and their numerical solutions. *Eng. Comput.* **2022**, *38*, 555–577. [CrossRef]
31. Zúñiga–Aguilar, C.J.; Gómez-Aguilar, J.F.; Escobar-Jiménez, R.F.; Romero-Ugalde, H.M. A novel method to solve variable-order fractional delay differential equations based in lagrange interpolations. *Chaos Solitons Fract.* **2019**, *126*, 266–282. [CrossRef]
32. Bockstal, K.; Zaky, M.A.; Hendy, A.S. On the existence and uniqueness of solutions to a nonlinear variable order time-fractional reaction–diffusion equation with delay. *Commun. Nonlinear Sci. Numer. Simul.* **2022**, *115*, 106755. [CrossRef]
33. Benchohra, M.; Henderson, J.; Ntouyas, S.K.; Ouahab, A. Existence results for fractional order functional differential equations with infinite delay. *J. Math. Anal. Appl.* **2008**, *338*, 1340–1350. [CrossRef]
34. Abbas, S. Existence of solutions to fractional order ordinary and delay differential equations and applications. *Electron. J. Differ. Equ.* **2011**, *2011*, 1–11.
35. Borisut, P.; Auipa-arch, C. Fractional-order delay differential equation with separated conditions. *Thai J. Math.* **2021**, *19*, 842–853.
36. Jalilian, Y.; Jalilian, R. Existence of solution for delay fractional differential equations. *Mediterr. J. Math.* **2013**, *10*, 1731–1747. [CrossRef]
37. Jiang, D.; Bai, C. Existence results for coupled implicit ψ-Riemann–Liouville fractional differential equations with nonlocal conditions. *Axioms* **2022**, *11*, 103. [CrossRef]
38. Li, M.; Wang, J.R. Representation of solution of a Riemann–Liouville fractional differential equation with pure delay. *Appl. Math. Lett.* **2018**, *85*, 118–124. [CrossRef]
39. Samko, S. Fractional integration and differentiation of variable order: An overview. *Nonlinear Dyn.* **2013**, *71*, 653–662. [CrossRef]
40. Valerio, D.; Costa, J.S. Variable-order fractional derivatives and their numerical approximations. *Signal Process.* **2011**, *91*, 470–483. [CrossRef]
41. Zhang, H.; Li, S.; Hu, L. The existence and uniqueness result of solutions to initial value problems of nonlinear diffusion equations involving with the conformable variable derivative. *Rev. Real Acad. Cienc. Exactas Fis. Nat. Ser. A Mat.* **2019**, *113*, 1601–1623. [CrossRef]
42. Zhang, S. Existence of solutions for two-point boundary-value problems with singular differential equations of variable order. *Electron. J. Differ. Equ.* **2013**, *2013*, 1–16.
43. Banas, J. On measures of noncompactness in Banach spaces. *Comment. Math. Univ. Carol.* **1980**, *21*, 131–143.
44. Akhmerov, R.R.; Kamenskii, M.I.; Patapov, A.S.; Rodkina, A.E.; Sadovskii, B.N. *Measures of Noncompactness and Condensing Operators*, 1st ed.; Birkhauser: Basel, Switzerland, 1992; ISBN 978-3-0348-5727-7.
45. Guo, D.; Lakshmikantham, V.; Liu, X. *Nonlinear Integral Equations in Abstract Spaces*, 1st ed.; Springer: New York, NY, USA, 1996; ISBN 978-1-4613-1281-9.
46. Benchohra, M.; Lazreg, J.E. Existence and Ulam stability for nonlinear implicit fractional differential equations with Hadamard derivative. *Stud. Univ. Babes-Bolyai Math.* **2017**, *62*, 27–38. [CrossRef]
47. Rus, I.A. Ulam stabilities of ordinary differential equations in a Banach space. *Carpathian J. Math.* **2010**, *26*, 103–107.
48. An, J.; Chen, P. Uniqueness of solutions to initial value problem of fractional differential equations of variable-order. *Dyn. Syst. Appl.* **2019**, *28*, 607–623.

49. Benchohra, M.; Bouriah, S.; Lazreg, J.E.; Nieto, J.J. Nonlinear implicit Hadamard's fractional differential equations with delay in Banach space. *Acta Univ. Palack. Olomuc. Fac. Rerum Natur. Math.* **2016**, *55*, 15–26.
50. Benkerrouche, A.; Souid, M.S.; Stamov, G.; Stamova, I. Multiterm impulsive Caputo–Hadamard type differential equations of fractional variable order. *Axioms* **2022**, *11*, 634. [CrossRef]

Disclaimer/Publisher's Note: The statements, opinions and data contained in all publications are solely those of the individual author(s) and contributor(s) and not of MDPI and/or the editor(s). MDPI and/or the editor(s) disclaim responsibility for any injury to people or property resulting from any ideas, methods, instructions or products referred to in the content.

Article

Analytical and Numerical Simulations of a Delay Model: The Pantograph Delay Equation

Essam Roshdy El-Zahar [1,2,*] and Abdelhalim Ebaid [3]

[1] Department of Mathematics, Faculty of Sciences and Humanities, Prince Sattam bin Abdulaziz University, Alkharj 11942, Saudi Arabia
[2] Department of Basic Engineering Science, Faculty of Engineering, Menofia University, Shebin El-Kom 32511, Egypt
[3] Department of Mathematics, Faculty of Science, University of Tabuk, P.O. Box 741, Tabuk 71491, Saudi Arabia
* Correspondence: er.elzahar@psau.edu.sa

Abstract: In this paper, the pantograph delay differential equation $y'(t) = ay(t) + by(ct)$ subject to the condition $y(0) = \lambda$ is reanalyzed for the real constants a, b, and c. In the literature, it has been shown that the pantograph delay differential equation, for $\lambda = 1$, is well-posed if $c < 1$, but not if $c > 1$. In addition, the solution is available in the form of a standard power series when $\lambda = 1$. In the present research, we are able to determine the solution of the pantograph delay differential equation in a closed series form in terms of exponential functions. The convergence of such a series is analysed. It is found that the solution converges for $c \in (-1,1)$ such that $\left|\frac{b}{a}\right| < 1$ and it also converges for $c > 1$ when $a < 0$. For $c = -1$, the exact solution is obtained in terms of trigonometric functions, i.e., a periodic solution with periodicity $\frac{2\pi}{\sqrt{b^2-a^2}}$ when $b > a$. The current results are introduced for the first time and have not been reported in the relevant literature.

Keywords: delay differential equation; ordinary differential equation; pantograph; analytic solution; exact solution

MSC: 34k06

Citation: El-Zahar, E.R.; Ebaidd, A. Analytical and Numerical Simulations of a Delay Model: The Pantograph Delay Equation. *Axioms* **2022**, *11*, 741. https://doi.org/10.3390/axioms11120741

Academic Editor: Giovanni Nastasi

Received: 2 November 2022
Accepted: 13 December 2022
Published: 17 December 2022

Copyright: © 2022 by the authors. Licensee MDPI, Basel, Switzerland. This article is an open access article distributed under the terms and conditions of the Creative Commons Attribution (CC BY) license (https://creativecommons.org/licenses/by/4.0/).

1. Introduction

The dynamics of an overhead current collection system for an electric locomotive has been discussed earlier by Fox et al. [1]. Such analysis gives rise to linear first-order ordinary differential equations (1st-ODEs) in which the argument of one of the dependent variables is multiplied by a factor, e.g., c. This kind of 1st-ODEs is well-known as the pantograph delay differential equations (PDDEs) in the form:

$$y'(t) = ay(t) + by(ct), \quad y(0) = \lambda, \tag{1}$$

where $a, b, c,$ and λ are real constants. The PDDE in (1) was extensively studied by numerous researchers in the literature [2–5] because of its wide applications including the modelling of tumour cells growth [6]. Moreover, the function y represents a probability density function (pdf) as described in other applications such as the cell growth model of Hall and Wake [7,8] and the absorption probability problem originating in the waiting line theory [9] and light absorption in the Milky Way [10].

Two direct solutions for the PDDE in (1) are obvious at specific values of c, mainly $c = 1$ and $c = 0$. For $c = 1$, it converts to the ODE $y'(t) = (a+b)y(t)$ and the corresponding solution is clearly given as $y(t) = \lambda e^{(a+b)t}$. Moreover, at $c = 0$, the PDDE in (1) converts to $y'(t) - ay(t) = b\lambda$ which is a first-order linear ODE and its solution is $y(t) = -\lambda b/a + \lambda(1 + b/a)e^{at}$. For other values of $c \in \mathbb{R} - \{0,1\}$, the solution of Equation (1) is still a challenge. Thus, we focus in this paper on obtaining analytic solutions for the PDDE in (1) at the real values of c such that $c \notin \{0,1\}$.

As a special case, if $a = -1$ and $b = c = \frac{1}{q}$ ($q > 1$), then the PDDE in (1) transforms to the Ambartsumian delay differential equation (ADDE) [11]:

$$y'(t) = -y(t) + \frac{1}{q}y\left(\frac{t}{q}\right), \quad y(0) = \lambda. \tag{2}$$

The solutions of the standard ADDE have been obtained by numerous approaches in the literature [11–13]. Moreover, possible generalizations of the ADDE have been introduced and discussed by the authors in Refs. [14,15]. Searching for a simple analytical solution for the PDDE in (1) is still of manifest practical interest. In order to contribute to an improved solution of this problem, two different cases are to be analysed separately, mainly, $c \in \mathbb{R} - \{\pm 1\}$ and $c = -1$. For $c \in \mathbb{R} - \{\pm 1\}$, the solution is determined in a closed series form and the convergence issue is addressed in detail. In addition, the solution in the case $c = -1$ is provided in exact form in terms of trigonometric functions, which is a periodic solution. Moreover, it is shown in this paper that the solution obtained by Aharbi and Ebaid [12] for the ADDE in (2) can be recovered as a special case of the current solution of the PDDE in (1).

2. Analytic Solution at $c \in \mathbb{R}$, $c \neq \pm 1$

In this section, we search for a solution of Equation (1) in the following form

$$y(t) = \sum_{n=0}^{\infty} d_n e^{\alpha c^n t}, \tag{3}$$

where α is a constant to be determined. Substituting Equation (3) into Equation (1), we obtain

$$(\alpha - a)d_0 e^{\alpha t} + \sum_{n=0}^{\infty} \left(\left(\alpha c^{n+1} - a\right)d_{n+1} - bd_n\right)e^{\alpha c^{n+1} t} = 0, \tag{4}$$

which gives $\alpha = a$ where $d_0 \neq 0$, and

$$d_{n+1} = \frac{(b/a)d_n}{c^{n+1} - 1}, \quad n \geq 0. \tag{5}$$

Accordingly,

$$d_m = d_0 \left(\frac{(b/a)^m}{\prod_{k=1}^{m}(c^k - 1)}\right), \quad m \geq 1. \tag{6}$$

Hence,

$$y(t) = d_0 e^{at} + \sum_{n=1}^{\infty} d_n e^{ac^n t} = d_0 \left(e^{at} + \sum_{n=1}^{\infty} \frac{(b/a)^n e^{ac^n t}}{\prod_{k=1}^{n}(c^k - 1)}\right). \tag{7}$$

Applying the initial condition $y(0) = \lambda$, d_0 is obtained as $d_0 = \frac{\lambda}{1 + \sum_{n=1}^{\infty} \frac{(b/a)^n}{\prod_{k=1}^{n}(c^k - 1)}}$.

Therefore, the closed-form solution is obtained by inserting d_0 into Equation (7) as

$$y(t) = \lambda \left(\frac{e^{at} + \sum_{n=1}^{\infty} \frac{(b/a)^n e^{ac^n t}}{\prod_{k=1}^{n}(c^k - 1)}}{1 + \sum_{n=1}^{\infty} \frac{(b/a)^n}{\prod_{k=1}^{n}(c^k - 1)}}\right). \tag{8}$$

Using the property $\prod_{k=1}^{n}\left(c^k - 1\right) = (-1)^n \prod_{k=1}^{n}\left(1 - c^k\right)$, then

$$y(t) = \lambda \left(\frac{e^{at} + \sum_{n=1}^{\infty} \frac{(-b/a)^n e^{ac^n t}}{\prod_{k=1}^{n}(1-c^k)}}{1 + \sum_{n=1}^{\infty} \frac{(-b/a)^n}{\prod_{k=1}^{n}(1-c^k)}} \right), \quad a \neq 0, \quad c \neq \pm 1. \tag{9}$$

The Solution in Simplest Form

In this section, we aim to derive a simpler form for the solution given by Equation (9). This is achieved by implementing some well-known properties in q-calculus (quantum calculus) [16] such as the product $(p:q)_n = \prod_{k=0}^{n-1}(1-pq^k)$, where $(p:q)_n$ denotes the Pochhammer symbol. For $p = q = c$, we have $(c:c)_n = \prod_{k=0}^{n-1}(1-c^{k+1}) = \prod_{k=1}^{n}(1-c^k)$. Thus,

$$y(t) = \lambda \left(\frac{e^{at} + \sum_{n=1}^{\infty} \frac{(-b/a)^n}{(c:c)_n} e^{ac^n t}}{1 + \sum_{n=1}^{\infty} \frac{(-b/a)^n}{(c:c)_n}} \right) = \lambda \left(\frac{\sum_{n=0}^{\infty} \frac{(-b/a)^n}{(c:c)_n} e^{ac^n t}}{\sum_{n=0}^{\infty} \frac{(-b/a)^n}{(c:c)_n}} \right), \tag{10}$$

where $(c:c)_n = 1$ for $n = 0$, hence

$$y(t) = \lambda \left(\frac{\sum_{n=0}^{\infty} \beta_n e^{ac^n t}}{\sum_{n=0}^{\infty} \beta_n} \right), \quad \beta_n = \frac{(-b/a)^n}{(c:c)_n}, \quad a \neq 0, \quad c \neq \pm 1, \tag{11}$$

or

$$y(t) = \frac{\lambda}{S} \sum_{n=0}^{\infty} \beta_n e^{ac^n t}, \quad S = \sum_{n=0}^{\infty} \beta_n. \tag{12}$$

3. Convergence Analysis

Theorem 1. *The series*

$$\sum_{n=0}^{\infty} \beta_n = \sum_{n=0}^{\infty} \frac{(-b/a)^n}{(c:c)_n}, \quad a \neq 0, \tag{13}$$

is convergent for $|c| < 1$ provided $\left|\frac{b}{a}\right| < 1$, and the sum S in (12) becomes

$$S = \sum_{n=0}^{\infty} \frac{(-b/a)^n}{(c:c)_n} = \frac{1}{(-b/a:c)_\infty}. \tag{14}$$

If $|c| > 1$, the series in (13) is convergent $\forall a \in \mathbb{R} - \{0\}$ and $\forall b \in \mathbb{R}$.

Proof. Applying the ratio test, we have

$$\lim_{n\to\infty} \left|\frac{\beta_{n+1}}{\beta_n}\right| = \left|\frac{b}{a}\right| \lim_{n\to\infty} \left|\frac{\prod_{k=1}^{n}(1-c^k)}{\prod_{k=1}^{n+1}(1-c^k)}\right| = \left|\frac{b}{a}\right| \lim_{n\to\infty} \left|\frac{1}{1-c^{n+1}}\right| = \begin{cases} \left|\frac{b}{a}\right| & \text{if } |c| < 1, \\ 0 & \text{if } |c| > 1. \end{cases} \tag{15}$$

It is obvious that $\sum \beta_n$ is convergent for the two cases (i) $\left|\frac{b}{a}\right|$ ($|c| < 1$), (ii) $a \in \mathbb{R} - \{0\}$, $b \in \mathbb{R}$ ($|c| > 1$). However, for $\left|\frac{b}{a}\right|$ and $|c| < 1$, we have

$$\sum_{n=0}^{\infty} \frac{(-b/a)^n}{(c:c)_n} = \frac{1}{(-b/a:c)_\infty}, \tag{16}$$

where the identity [16]:

$$\sum_{n=0}^{\infty} \frac{x^n}{(c:c)_n} = \frac{1}{(x:c)_\infty}, \quad |x| < 1, \quad |c| < 1, \tag{17}$$

is applied for $x = -b/a$. Moreover, it follows from Equation (15), for $|c| > 1$, that the series in (13) is convergent $\forall\, a \in \mathbb{R} - \{0\}$ and $\forall\, b \in \mathbb{R}$, which completes the proof. □

Theorem 2. *For all $t > 0$, the series*

$$\sum_{n=0}^{\infty} \beta_n e^{ac^n t} = \sum_{n=0}^{\infty} \frac{(-b/a)^n}{(c:c)_n} e^{ac^n t}, \qquad (18)$$

converges for $|c| < 1$ provided that $\left|\frac{b}{a}\right| < 1$. If $c > 1$, the series in (18) is convergent $\forall\, a < 0$ and $\forall\, b \in \mathbb{R}$.

Proof. Assuming that

$$\sigma_n(t) = \beta_n e^{ac^n t}, \quad t > 0, \qquad (19)$$

and applying the ratio test yields

$$\lim_{n \to \infty} \left|\frac{\sigma_{n+1}(t)}{\sigma_n(t)}\right| = \lim_{n \to \infty} \left|\frac{\beta_{n+1}}{\beta_n} e^{ac^n(c-1)}\right| = \lim_{n \to \infty} \left|\frac{\beta_{n+1}}{\beta_n}\right| \cdot \lim_{n \to \infty} e^{ac^n(c-1)}. \qquad (20)$$

The two limits in the last equation are

$$\lim_{n \to \infty} \left|\frac{\beta_{n+1}}{\beta_n}\right| = \begin{cases} \left|\frac{b}{a}\right| & \text{if } |c| < 1, \\ 0 & \text{if } |c| > 1, \end{cases} \quad \lim_{n \to \infty} e^{ac^n(c-1)} = \begin{cases} 1 & \text{if } |c| < 1, \\ L & \text{if } |c| > 1, \end{cases} \qquad (21)$$

where L is either zero, ∞, or undetermined according to the signs of a and c^n in the domains $c > 1$ and $c < -1$ (i.e., $|c| > 1$), as detailed below.

$$L = \begin{cases} 0 & \text{if } c > 1,\ a < 0, \\ \infty & \text{if } c > 1,\ a > 0, \\ \text{undetermined} & \text{if } c < -1,\ a \in \mathbb{R} - \{0\}. \end{cases} \qquad (22)$$

However, by combining Equations (20)–(22), we get

$$\lim_{n \to \infty} \left|\frac{\sigma_{n+1}(t)}{\sigma_n(t)}\right| = \begin{cases} \left|\frac{b}{a}\right| & \text{if } |c| < 1, \\ 0 & \text{if } c > 1,\ a < 0, \end{cases} \qquad (23)$$

which completes the proof. □

Lemma 1. *For $t > 0$, the solution given by Equation (12) converges for $|c| < 1$ provided that $\left|\frac{b}{a}\right| < 1$ and this yields*

$$y(t) = \lambda (-b/a : c)_\infty \sum_{n=0}^{\infty} \frac{(-b/a)^n e^{ac^n t}}{(c:c)_n}. \qquad (24)$$

Moreover, the solution in (12) converges for $c > 1\ \forall\, a < 0,\ \forall\, b \in \mathbb{R}$ such that the sum $S \not\to 0$.

Proof. The proof follows immediately from Theorems 1 and 2. Moreover, for $|c| < 1$ and $\left|\frac{b}{a}\right| < 1$, we have from Theorem 1 that

$$S = \sum_{n=0}^{\infty} \beta_n = \sum_{n=0}^{\infty} \frac{(-b/a)^n}{(c:c)_n} = \frac{1}{(-b/a:c)_\infty}. \qquad (25)$$

Substituting (25) into (12) gives (24), which completes the proof. □

Remark 1. *The above analysis gives the solution and convergence of the PDDE in (1) for the cases $|c| < 1$ and $|c| > 1$. However, such an analysis does not include the solution at $c = \pm 1$. This is because the coefficients $\beta_n = \frac{(-b/a)^n}{(c:c)_n}$ are not defined at such values, where $(1:1)_n = 0$ for all $n \geq 1$ and $(-1:-1)_n = 0$ for all $n > 1$; hence, these cases lead to $\beta_n = \pm\infty$. As mentioned in the introduction, the exact solution is available when $c = 1$ and given by $y(t) = \lambda e^{(a+b)t}$, but the solution at the special case $c = -1$ is to be determined through a separate analysis in the next section.*

4. Exact Solution at $c = -1$

In this section, we aim to derive the exact solution of the PDDE in (1) when $c = -1$. In this case, Equation (1) becomes

$$y'(t) = ay(t) + by(-t), \quad y(0) = \lambda. \tag{26}$$

In view of the assumption in (3), the solution takes the form:

$$y(t) = \sum_{n=0}^{\infty} h_n e^{\gamma(-1)^n t} = (h_0 + h_2 + h_4 + \ldots)e^{\gamma t} + (h_1 + h_3 + h_5 + \ldots)e^{-\gamma t} = \mu e^{\gamma t} + \nu e^{-\gamma t}, \tag{27}$$

where μ, ν, and γ are constants to be determined. Applying the initial condition $y(0) = \lambda$ leads to $\mu + \nu = \lambda$. Substituting (27) into (26) yields

$$\mu\gamma e^{\gamma t} - \nu\gamma e^{-\gamma t} = (\mu a + \nu b)e^{\gamma t} + (\nu a + \mu b)\gamma e^{-\gamma t}. \tag{28}$$

Comparing both sides, we obtain the algebraic system:

$$(\gamma - a)\mu = \nu b, \qquad (\gamma + a)\nu = -\mu b, \tag{29}$$

which gives γ as

$$\gamma = \pm\sqrt{a^2 - b^2}. \tag{30}$$

Note that γ is real if $a > b$. Hence, we obtain μ and ν in terms of γ as $\mu = \frac{\lambda b}{\gamma - a + b}$ and $\nu = \frac{\lambda(\gamma - a)}{\gamma - a + b}$, thus

$$y(t) = \frac{\lambda}{\gamma - a + b}\left(be^{\gamma t} + (\gamma - a)e^{-\gamma t}\right), \tag{31}$$

or equivalently

$$y(t) = \lambda\left[\cosh(\gamma t) - \left(\frac{\gamma - a - b}{\gamma - a + b}\right)\sinh(\gamma t)\right]. \tag{32}$$

Although the form (32) is simple, it can be further simplified as follows. The magnitude $\left(\frac{\gamma - a - b}{\gamma - a + b}\right)$ can be calculated explicitly in terms of a and b as

$$\frac{\gamma - a - b}{\gamma - a + b} = \frac{\gamma - (a + b)}{\gamma - (a - b)} \times \frac{\gamma + (a - b)}{\gamma + (a - b)} = -\frac{\gamma}{a - b} = \mp\sqrt{\frac{a + b}{a - b}}. \tag{33}$$

Therefore, Equation (32) becomes

$$y(t) = \lambda\left[\cosh(\pm\sqrt{a^2 - b^2}\,t) \pm \sqrt{\frac{a + b}{a - b}}\sinh(\pm\sqrt{a^2 - b^2}\,t)\right], \tag{34}$$

which finally gives

$$y(t) = \lambda\left[\cosh(\sqrt{a^2 - b^2}\,t) + \sqrt{\frac{a + b}{a - b}}\sinh(\sqrt{a^2 - b^2}\,t)\right], \quad a > b. \tag{35}$$

This solution transforms to the following trigonometric functions if $b > a$:

$$y(t) = \lambda\left[\cos(\sqrt{b^2 - a^2}\,t) + \sqrt{\frac{b+a}{b-a}}\sin(\sqrt{b^2 - a^2}\,t)\right]. \tag{36}$$

It is clear from (36) that the solution is periodic with a period $\frac{2\pi}{\sqrt{b^2-a^2}}$, which is in full agreement with the obtained results in Ref. [17].

5. Results

In this section, numerical results are obtained about the behaviours/properties and convergence of the obtained solutions in previous sections. In addition, the convergence introduced by previous theorems and lemma is numerically confirmed here. Three different cases are analysed which depend on the values/intervals of c, a, and b.

5.1. $c \in (-1, 1)$, $\left|\frac{b}{a}\right| < 1$, $a \in \mathbb{R} - \{0\}$

In this case, it was indicated and proved by Lemma 1 that the solution of Equation (1) takes the form:

$$y(t) = \lambda(-b/a : c)_\infty \sum_{n=0}^{\infty} \frac{(-b/a)^n e^{ac^n t}}{(c : c)_n}. \tag{37}$$

This closed-form solution can be approximated by taking m-terms, $m \geq 1$ from the right-hand side. Consequently, the approximate solution $\phi_m(t)$ is

$$\phi_m(t) = \lambda(-b/a : c)_\infty \sum_{n=0}^{m-1} \frac{(-b/a)^n e^{ac^n t}}{(c : c)_n}, \quad m \geq 1. \tag{38}$$

In Figures 1–4, the approximations $\phi_3(t)$, $\phi_5(t)$, $\phi_7(t)$, and $\phi_9(t)$ are plotted versus t at $\lambda = 1$ and different four sets of values of c, a, and b. In these figures, the values of the inputs c, a, and b were chosen so that the convergence conditions are satisfied, i.e., $c \in (-1, 1)$, $\left|\frac{b}{a}\right| < 1$. It is observed from these figures that the approximate solutions $\phi_3(t)$, $\phi_5(t)$, $\phi_7(t)$, and $\phi_9(t)$ converge rapidly to a certain function which validates Lemma 1 for the convergence of solution (38).

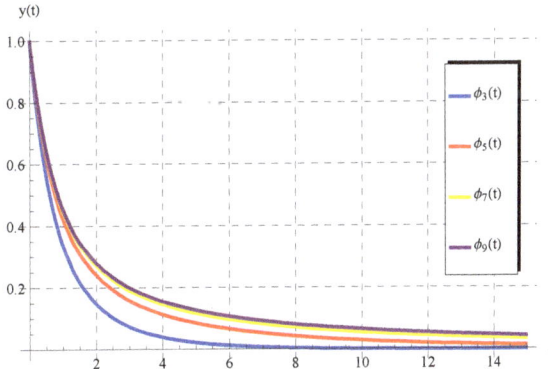

Figure 1. Plots of the approximate solutions $\phi_m(t)$, $m = 3, 5, 7, 9$ in Equation (38) vs. t at $\lambda = 1$, $c = \frac{1}{2}$, $b = 1$, and $a = -2$.

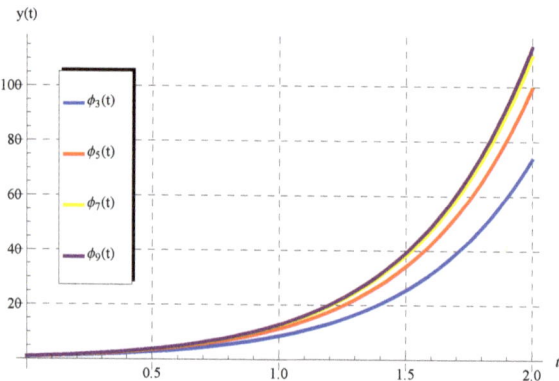

Figure 2. Plots of the approximate solutions $\phi_m(t)$, $m = 3, 5, 7, 9$ in Equation (38) vs. t at $\lambda = 1$, $c = \frac{1}{2}$, $b = 1$, and $a = 2$.

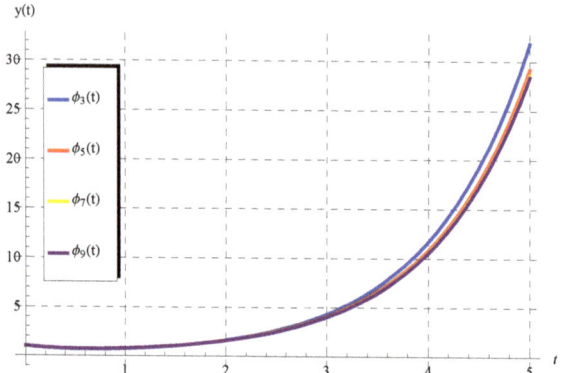

Figure 3. Plots of the approximate solutions $\phi_m(t)$, $m = 3, 5, 7, 9$ in Equation (38) vs. t at $\lambda = 1$, $c = -\frac{1}{2}$, $b = 1$, and $a = -2$.

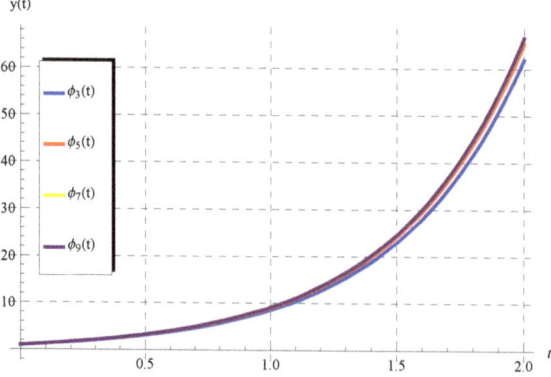

Figure 4. Plots of the approximate solutions $\phi_m(t)$, $m = 3, 5, 7, 9$ in Equation (38) vs. t at $\lambda = 1$, $c = -\frac{1}{2}$, $b = 1$, and $a = 2$.

5.2. $c > 1$, $a < 0$, $b \in \mathbb{R}$

The solution provided by Equation (12) is valid for $c > 1$ and $a < 0$, which can be approximated by the following m-term approximate solution $\phi_m(t)$:

$$\phi_m(t) = \frac{\lambda}{S_m} \sum_{n=0}^{m-1} \beta_n e^{ac^n t}, \quad S_m = \sum_{n=0}^{m-1} \beta_n = \sum_{n=0}^{m-1} \frac{(-b/a)^n e^{ac^n t}}{(c:c)_n}, \quad m \geq 1. \tag{39}$$

The second part of Lemma 1 teaches us that the sequence of approximate solutions $\{\phi_m(t)\}$ converges for all $c > 1$ such that $a < 0$ and $S_m \neq 0$. For a validation, different sets of approximations are depicted in Figures 5–8 at various values of the inputs $a < 0$, b, and $c > 1$. Rapid convergence is detected from these figures, especially when c is increased as can be shown in Figure 8 ($c = 5$). In this case, a few terms of the series solution in (39) is sufficient to achieve the convergence, where the $\phi_1(t)$, $\phi_2(t)$, $\phi_3(t)$ and $\phi_4(t)$ in Figure 8 are nearly identical.

5.3. $c = -1$, $a, b \in \mathbb{R}$

Really, this is an interesting case because it allows us to obtain the exact solutions given by Equation (35) and Equation (36) for $a > b$ and $b > a$, respectively. Two types of solutions are obtained for this case, the first is given in terms of hyperbolic functions when $a > b$, while the second is expressed is terms of trigonometric functions if $b > a$. The first solution is plotted in Figure 9 and the hyperbolic curves of the solution in (35) are observed when $a > b$. Moreover, the second solution is plotted in Figure 10 and the periodic curves of the solution in (36) can be seen when $b > a$.

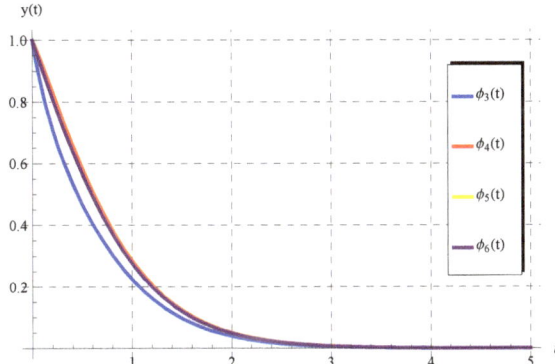

Figure 5. Plots of the approximate solutions $\phi_m(t)$, $m = 3, 4, 5, 6$ in Equation (39) vs. t at $\lambda = 1, c = \frac{3}{2}$, $b = 1$, and $a = -2$.

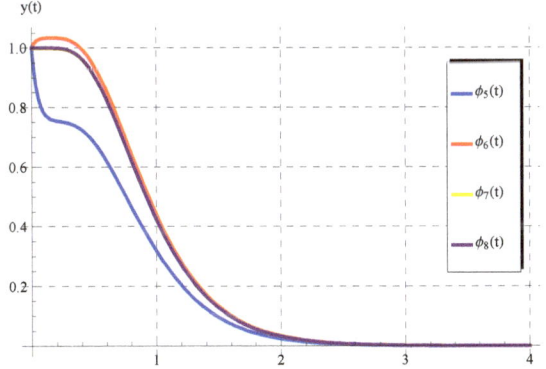

Figure 6. Plots of the approximate solutions $\phi_m(t)$, $m = 5, 6, 7, 8$ in Equation (39) vs. t at $\lambda = 1, c = \frac{3}{2}$, $b = 3$, and $a = -3$.

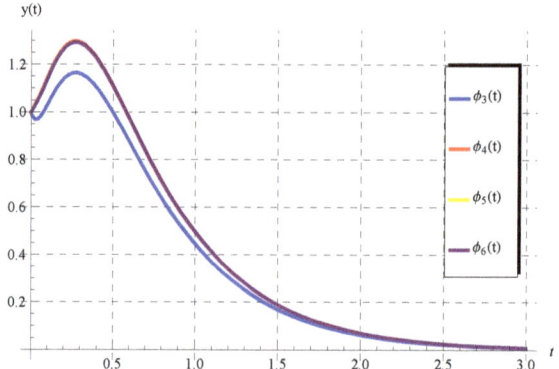

Figure 7. Plots of the approximate solutions $\phi_m(t)$, $m = 3, 4, 5, 6$ in Equation (39) vs. t at $\lambda = 1$, $c = \frac{5}{2}$, $b = 3$, and $a = -2$.

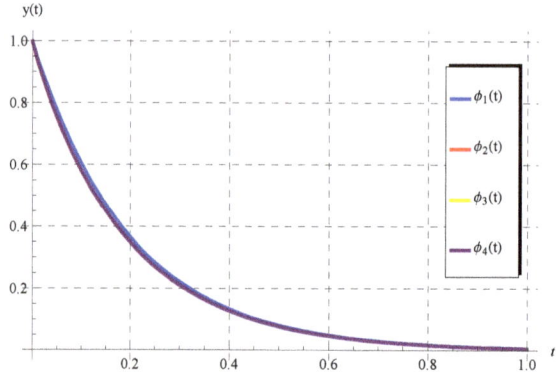

Figure 8. Plots of the approximate solutions $\phi_m(t)$, $m = 1, 2, 3, 4$ in Equation (39) vs. t at $\lambda = 1$, $c = 5$, $b = -1$, and $a = -5$.

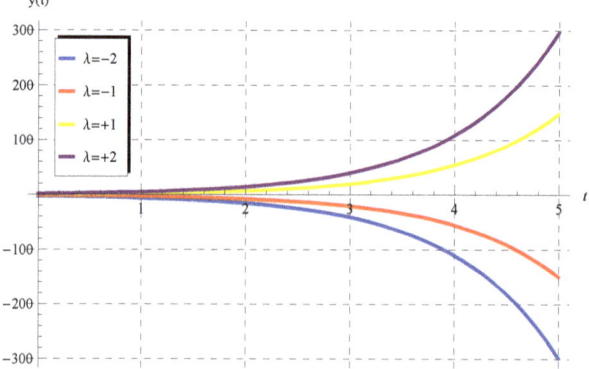

Figure 9. Plots of the exact solution in Equation (35) vs. t at different values of λ when $a = 1$ and $b = 0$.

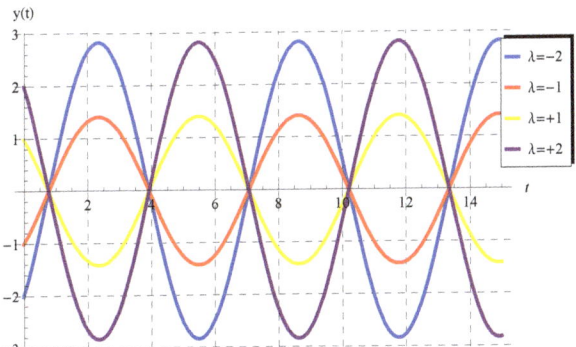

Figure 10. Plots of the exact solution in Equation (36) vs. t at different values of λ when $a = 0$ and $b = 1$.

5.4. $a = -1$, $b = c = \frac{1}{q}$, $q > 1$

Let $a = -1$ and $b = c = \frac{1}{q}$ ($q > 1$), then Equation (1) becomes

$$y'(t) = -y(t) + \frac{1}{q} y\left(\frac{t}{q}\right), \quad y(0) = \lambda, \tag{40}$$

which is well-known as the Ambartsumian equation [12]. The following closed-form solution for Equation (40) was obtained by Alharbi and Ebaid [12]:

$$y(t) = \lambda \left(\frac{e^{-t} + \sum_{n=1}^{\infty} \frac{\alpha^n e^{-\alpha^n t}}{\prod_{k=1}^{n}(1-\alpha^k)}}{1 + \sum_{n=1}^{\infty} \frac{\alpha^n}{\prod_{k=1}^{n}(1-\alpha^k)}} \right), \quad \alpha = \frac{1}{q}. \tag{41}$$

In fact, this solution can be directly determined by substituting $a = -1$ and $b = c = \frac{1}{q}$ into Equation (8). Hence, the solution obtained in Ref. [12] is a special case of the present results.

6. Conclusions

The analytic solution for the PDDE model $y'(t) = ay(t) + by(ct)$, $y(0) = \lambda$ was obtained in this paper. In the literature [1], the solution was obtained in the form of a standard power series when $\lambda = 1$. However, the present research determined the solution in a closed series form in terms of exponential functions. The convergence of the obtained series was theoretically proved and then confirmed through numerical calculations and plots. It was demonstrated that the solution converged for $c \in (-1, 1)$ such that $\left|\frac{b}{a}\right| < 1$ and also converged for $c > 1$ when $a < 0$. Furthermore, the exact solution was obtained when $c = -1$. This solution was expressed in terms of trigonometric functions and was periodic if $b > a$. It was also shown that this solution was periodic with periodicity $\frac{2\pi}{\sqrt{b^2-a^2}}$, which was in full agreement with the corresponding results in Ref. [17]. Moreover, the solution was determined in terms of hyperbolic functions when $b < a$. Finally, numerical results were conducted to describe the behaviours/properties and convergence of the obtained solutions. The present analysis can be further extended to include other mathematical models [18–20].

Author Contributions: The authors contributed equally in this manuscript. All authors have read and agreed to the published version of the manuscript.

Funding: The authors extend their appreciation to the Deputyship for Research & Innovation, Ministry of Education in Saudi Arabia for funding this research work through the project number (IF2/PSAU/2022/01/21495).

Data Availability Statement: Not applicable.

Acknowledgments: The authors extend their appreciation to the Deputyship for Research & Innovation, Ministry of Education in Saudi Arabia for funding this research work through the project number (IF2/PSAU/2022/01/21495).

Conflicts of Interest: The authors declare no conflict of interest.

References

1. Fox, L.; Mayers, D.F.; Ockendon, J.R.; Tayler, A.B. On a Functional Differential Equation. *IMA J. Appl. Math.* **1971**, *8*, 271–307. [CrossRef]
2. Kato, T.; McLeod, J.B. The functional-differential equation $y'(x) = ay(\lambda x) + by(x)$. *Bull. Am. Math. Soc.* **1971**, *77*, 891–935.
3. Derfel, G.; Iserles, A. The pantograph equation in the complex plane. *J. Math. Anal. Appl.* **1997**, *213*, 117–132. [CrossRef]
4. Iserles, A. On the generalized pantograph functional differential equation. *Eur. J. Appl. Math.* **1993**, *4*, 1–38. [CrossRef]
5. Marshall, J.; van-Brunt, B.; Wake, G. Natural boundaries for solutions to a certain class of functional differential equations. *J. Math. Anal. Appl.* **2002**, *268*, 157–170. [CrossRef]
6. Basse, B.; Baguley, B.; Marshall, E.; Joseph, W.; van Brunt, B.; Wake, G.; Wall, D. Modelling cell death in human tumour cell lines exposed to the anticancer drug paclitaxel. *J. Math. Biol.* **2004**, *49*, 329–357. [CrossRef]
7. Hall, A.J.; Wake, G.C. A functional differential equation arising in the modelling of cell-growth. *J. Aust. Math. Soc. Ser. B* **1989**, *30*, 424–435. [CrossRef]
8. Hall, A.J.; Wake, G.C. A functional differential equation determining steady size distributions for populations of cells growing exponentially. *J. Aust. Math. Soc. Ser. B* **1990**, *31*, 344–353. [CrossRef]
9. Gaver, D.P. An absorption probability problem. *J. Math. Anal. Appl.* **1964**, *9*, 384–393. [CrossRef]
10. Ambartsumian, V.A. On the fluctuation of the brightness of the milky way. *Doklady Akad Nauk USSR* **1994**, *44*, 223–226.
11. Patade, J.; Bhalekar, S. On Analytical Solution of Ambartsumian Equation. *Natl. Acad. Sci. Lett.* **2017**, *40*, 291–293. [CrossRef]
12. Alharbi, F.M.; Ebaid, A. New Analytic Solution for Ambartsumian Equation. *J. Math. Syst. Sci.* **2018**, *8*, 182–186. [CrossRef]
13. Bakodah, H.O.; Ebaid, A. Exact solution of Ambartsumian delay differential equation and comparison with Daftardar-Gejji and Jafari approximate method. *Mathematics* **2018**, *6*, 331. [CrossRef]
14. Khaled, S.M.; El-Zahar, E.R.; Ebaid, A. Solution of Ambartsumian delay differential equation with conformable derivative. *Mathematics* **2019**, *7*, 425. [CrossRef]
15. Kumar, D.; Singh, J.; Baleanu, D.; Rathore, S. Analysis of a fractional model of the Ambartsumian equation. *Eur. Phys. J. Plus.* **2018**, *133*, 133–259. [CrossRef]
16. Kac, V.G.; Cheung, P. *Quantum Calculus*; Springer: New York, NY, USA, 2002.
17. Ebaid, A.; Al-Jeaid, H.K. On the exact solution of the functional differential equation $y'(t) = ay(t) + by(-t)$. *Adv. Differ. Equ. Control Process.* **2022**, *26*, 39–49. [CrossRef]
18. Ruan, S. Delay Differential Equations In Single Species Dynamics. In *Delay Differential Equations and Applications*; NATO Science Series; Arino, O., Hbid, M., Dads, E.A., Eds.; Springer: Dordrecht, The Netherlands, 2006; Volume 205. [CrossRef]
19. Yousef, F.; Alkam, O.; Saker, I. The dynamics of new motion styles in the time-dependent four-body problem: Weaving periodic solutions. *Eur. Phys. J. Plus.* **2020**, *135*, 742. [CrossRef]
20. Folly-Gbetoula, M.; Nyirenda, D. A generalised two-dimensional system of higher order recursive sequences. *J. Differ. Equ. Appl.* **2020**, *26*, 244–260. [CrossRef]

MDPI
St. Alban-Anlage 66
4052 Basel
Switzerland
www.mdpi.com

Axioms Editorial Office
E-mail: axioms@mdpi.com
www.mdpi.com/journal/axioms

Disclaimer/Publisher's Note: The statements, opinions and data contained in all publications are solely those of the individual author(s) and contributor(s) and not of MDPI and/or the editor(s). MDPI and/or the editor(s) disclaim responsibility for any injury to people or property resulting from any ideas, methods, instructions or products referred to in the content.

www.ingramcontent.com/pod-product-compliance
Lightning Source LLC
LaVergne TN
LVHW070500100526
838202LV00014B/1759